LORDS OF THE
SCROLLS

PETER LANG
New York • Washington, D.C./Baltimore • Bern
Frankfurt am Main • Berlin • Brussels • Vienna • Oxford

Donald K. Sharpes

LORDS OF THE SCROLLS

Literary Traditions in the Bible and Gospels

PETER LANG
New York • Washington, D.C./Baltimore • Bern
Frankfurt am Main • Berlin • Brussels • Vienna • Oxford

Library of Congress Cataloging-in-Publication Data
Sharpes, Donald K.
Lords of the scrolls: literary traditions
in the Bible and Gospels / Donald K. Sharpes.
p. cm.
Includes bibliographical references and index.
1. Bible as literature. 2. Bible—Sources. I. Title.
BS535.S49   220.6'6—dc22   2004027914
ISBN 978-0-8204-7849-4

Bibliographic information published by **Die Deutsche Bibliothek**.
Die Deutsche Bibliothek lists this publication in the "Deutsche
Nationalbibliografie"; detailed bibliographic data is available
on the Internet at http://dnb.ddb.de/.

Cover image: cuneiform tablet, reprinted courtesy
of Loyola Marymount University; photograph by Mac James.
Cover design by Joni Holst

The paper in this book meets the guidelines for permanence and durability
of the Committee on Production Guidelines for Book Longevity
of the Council of Library Resources.

© 2005, 2007 Peter Lang Publishing, Inc., New York
29 Broadway, 18th Floor, New York, NY 10006
www.peterlang.com

All rights reserved.
Reprint or reproduction, even partially, in all forms such as microfilm,
xerography, microfiche, microcard, and offset strictly prohibited.

Printed in Germany

To the Mike Sharpes and Mary Peramas families

TABLE OF CONTENTS

A Partial Chronology	xi
Preface	xiii
Acknowledgments	xvii
List of Abbreviations	xix
Introduction	1

PART I VINTAGE SCRIPTURES

1. The Narrative Tradition — 11
   - The Magic of Writing — 20
   - Myths as Origins of the Narrative Tradition — 23
   - Lords of the Scrolls: Scribes of God — 31

2. Words of God, Words of Men — 37
   - The Biblical Tradition — 37
   - The Septuagint and Vulgate — 41
   - The Names of God in the Bible — 42
   - Ethnocentrism: Fear of the Gentile — 45

3. Middle Eastern Divinities and Prophets — 53
   - Babylonian Deities — 55
   - Canaanite Deities: Destiny, El and Baal — 57
   - Selected Middle Eastern Divinities — 61
   - Zoroaster (628 BCE–551 BCE) — 64

4. Creation and *Genesis* — 73
   - *Enuma Elish*: The Babylonian Creation Myth — 75
   - Male and Female: The Birth of Humans — 76
   - The Garden: Trees and Knowledge — 79
   - The Serpent and the Maiden — 83
   - Parallels between Gilgamesh and *Genesis* — 89

5. Cain and Abel — 93
   - Gilgamesh and Endiku — 93
   - Osiris and Seth — 94
   - Catal Huyuk — 95
   - Farmers and Shepherds: The Allegorical Interpretation — 101

6.	The Flood	105
	Noah and His Sons	107
	Flood Stories	115
	The Naming of Ancestors	117
	The Tower of Babel	118
7.	Abraham, First of the Patriarchs	121
	Name Calling	122
	Covenants and Sacrifice	123
	Rebecca and Jacob	127
	Sumerians and Semites	129
	Sodom and Early Bronze Age Cities	131
	Land and Foreskin	134
8.	Esau, Jacob and Joseph	137
	Isaac and the Blessing	139
	Dream On: Jacob and Herodotus	140
	Jacob's Return	143
	Egypt: The Legacy of Civilization	145
	Juda: An Interruption in *Genesis*	148
	Joseph in Egypt	149
	Conclusions to *Genesis*	151
9.	*Exodus* and Egyptian Biblical Themes	155
	Sinai	157
	Law and Order: Hammurabi and Solon	159
	Akhenaten, Founder of Monotheism	164
	Moses	167
	The Golden Calf	172

PART II: CHRISTIAN LITERARY ORIGINS

10.	The Manufactured Jesus: Evidence and Mystery	181
	Stoicism	182
	Parallel Stoic and Gospel Sayings	183
	The Essenes	190
	Names and Designations	191
	Birth, Ministry and Mission	195
	The Halo Effect	200
	Death and Resurrection	202

11. Greek Influence on Scripture	211
Pythagoras, Orpheus, & the Eleusian Mysteries	215
Ulysses and Jesus	219
Socrates and Plato	223
Epictetus (50–138 CE)	225
Philo of Alexandria (c.20 BCE–50 CE)	226
Justin Martyr (c.100–165 CE)	230
Clement of Alexandria (c.150–215 CE)	231
Plotinus (205–270 CE)	234
12. Cyrus, Mithras and Jesus	237
Parallels between Cyrus and Jesus	237
Mithras, The Bull-Slayer	239
Parallels between Mithras and Jesus	244
13. Gnosticism	247
Hindu Roots	254
Modern Gnostic Movements	255
14. Christianity and First Century Ideologies	259
Paul and the Invention of Christianity	261
The First Century: Political Turmoil	265
The Gospels: Origins and Themes	273
15. Christianity in the Second and Third Centuries	281
Acts of the Apostles	281
Irenaeus (c.140-200 CE)	284
Literary Fragments from Canaan and Egypt	285
The 2nd Century CE: Celsus and Origen (c.185-254 CE)	288
The 3rd Century: Constantine and Christianity	291
Mani and Manichaeism	299
16. Arius, Athanasius, and Augustine	303
Arius (c.256–336 CE) and Arianism	304
Athanasius (297–373)	308
Augustine (354–430): The Christian Neo-Platonist	312
Epilogue	319
Endnotes	327
Glossary of Selected Terms	363
References	365
Index	385

A PARTIAL CHRONOLOGY

Before the Common Era (BCE)

c. 2000	Sumerian civilization, *Epic of Gilgamesh*
c. 1792—1750	*The Code of Hammurabi*
c. 1200?	Abraham (?), Akkadian creation myth, *Enuma Elish*
c. 1250	Moses and the *Exodus* (?)
c. 1250—1200	Joshua and the Conquest of Canaan (?)
c. 1020—1000	Samuel and Saul
c. 1000—960	David's Reign
c. 960—920	Solomon
c. 950—900	The Book of J (Yahwist), the first biblical scribe
c. 850—800	E's (Elohist) revision of J's writings
c. 750	Homer flourished, *Iliad* and *Odyssey* composed
c. 700	Hesiod flourished, *Theogony* and *Works and Days*,
c. 650—600	*Deuteronomy* composed
c. 636—546	Thales, first philosopher to propose physical reality as origin of world & matter
c. 587—538	Fall of Jerusalem; Babylonian Exile
c. 550—500	The P (priestly author) text of the Bible
c. 400	The Redactor, Editor of J, E, and P, (the Torah as it exists now)
c. 250—100	The Septuagint, the 70+ editors of the Scriptures

GREEK ANGELS
From a 5th Century BCE Vase

PREFACE
Veritas filia temporis

I was reared in a devout Catholic family. A great, great aunt on my maternal side, Esther Blondin, foundress of the Sisters of St. Anne in Quebec, was beatified by the Pope in 2001. On my paternal side, Kate Golden was my Jewish grandmother. In a Catholic parochial school I accepted without understanding abstruse images the nuns described, such as that a mortal sin was like a great inky blot on the soul. I memorized the catechism, unhesitatingly accepted conduct that was required of me, avoided arenas of temptation, and formed my view of the world through religious eyes.

At the end of high school in 1953 I joined the Jesuits, whose incubation would give me an academic and monastic environment in which to commit a life of prayer, study, teaching and preaching. I took vows of poverty, chastity and obedience after two years of novitiate in a program that would take 13 years to become a priest. I felt comfortable and uncomplicated in absorbing devotional readings, the classics, science, philosophy and theology in seven years of full-time study. For three years I taught English, French and history at a Jesuit high school.

In 1963 during theological studies in California I had a yearly oral examination of conscience with the Rector. During that informal confession, I told him about my one-time evening dinner and tryst with a woman and her mother at their home the previous summer. He replied that it would be better if I left the Jesuits. I was dumbfounded. I would not have revealed my indiscretion, which did not result in intercourse, had I known its repercussions, and that it was a prerequisite for exclusion. I was indiscreet but I was still a virgin. But since I had taken a vow of obedience, wasn't this God's will speaking to me through my superior? After talking to other priests and friends over the next month, I decided to leave the Society of Jesus.

I had been a Jesuit seminarian for 10 years, and knew little about how to navigate in ordinary affairs. I didn't know what a W-2 form was or why insurance was necessary. Having bonded with men of like mind, I certainly knew nothing of the subtle and intricate world of social relationships with women for which I had received no training nor gathered any experience beyond fumbling adolescent experiments. After nearly a half century, I don't think I'm any better equipped. All other major decisions, what courses to take, where to teach, when and where to vacation, even what to eat, had been made for me. It was less the vagaries of the job market than the psychological adjustment that presented me with the greatest dilemma. Nevertheless, the next year I married, completed my doctorate soon afterwards, and over the next 40 years raised two children, and entered years of government service and academia.

I had learned to take scriptural stories with a grain of salt and to assume that most of them were allegories about God's revealed truths. But on a visit to the British Museum in 1979, I had purchased R. D. Barnett's 1977 second edition of *Illustrations of Old Testament History* a book which opened my eyes, like the scales which dropped from Paul's eyes, to the archaeological evidence to, among other things, the Babylonian flood narratives, the papyrus text of *The Wisdom of Amenemope* containing proverbs which parallel the *Book of Proverbs* but which was written hundreds of year earlier. Edmond Solberger's 1971 British Museum book, *The Babylonian Legend of the Flood* confirmed that the Bible was literature, and George Mendenhall's excellent explanations in *The Tenth Generation, The Origins of the Biblical Tradition* (1973) shed further light. I found Dame Kathleen Kenyon's analysis from her 1978 book, *The Bible and Recent Archaeology*, to be the scientific evidence refuting textual inconsistencies in the Bible. I was stunned at my ignorance, wondered why such knowledge had never been a part of my education. I vowed to pursue further reading and studies at the pace work and family obligations allowed.

My skepticism was shunted in favor of interpreting the Bible as a source of a rich literary tradition percolating from the earliest written sources in the Middle East. This was especially true after I read Van Seters' 1983 book, *In Search of History, Historiography in the Ancient World and the Origins of Biblical History* and *Jesus, The Evidence* by the British writer Ian Wilson in 1984, a provocative book that accumulated all the missing historical evidence about the life of Jesus and synopsized the critical reviews of serious scholars of the gospels. I read Herodotus, the celebrated father of history, and Xenophon to glean stories that pre-dated biblical sources and formed a part of the heroic tradition of legendary figures.

I was taught that the Bible was divinely inspired, that these were words from prophets and inspired men which came directly from God to instruct humankind in how God works. This view was reaffirmed by Catholic church councils and by papal directives: Leo XIII in *Providentissimus Deus* (1893); by Benedict XV in *Spiritus Paraclitus* (1920); and by Pius XII in *Divino Afflante Spiritu* (1943). "For all the books which the Church receives as sacred and canonical are written wholly and entirely, with all their parts, at the direction of the Holy Spirit; and so far is it from being possible that any error can coexist with inspiration, that inspiration not only is essentially incompatible with error, but excludes and rejects it as absolutely and necessarily as it is impossible that God Himself, the Supreme Truth, can utter that which is not true."

I began first to question the authenticity of the creation story since so much about Christianity hung on the assumption that a divine redeemer would come to rectify original disobedience. Believing, as scripture proclaimed, that the sins of the fathers are not visited on the sons ("The Lord commanded: "Fathers shall not be put to death for their children, nor children put to death for their fathers; each is to die for his own sins") I questioned why original sin should visit all humanity which had no choice in the dilemma, and contrary to God's commandment in 2 *Chronicles*, nor any option for having such a hard ethical choice as permanent banishment unless rescued by blessed water conducted in a baptismal ceremony in which the infant still had no choice. Where free will and choice were absolutely crucial in deciding acceptance into heaven, original sin presented contrary evidence for any choice at all in the first step in attaining heavenly status. If it were possible to proclaim that the creation story was not to be taken literally, because it seemed so improbable, then why wasn't it similarly acceptable to question in whole or part any of the implausible biblical stories?

Adam and Eve represented an allegory of God's plan for human origins. But if Adam and Eve were not real, since there were similar creation stories in Sumerian and Mesopotamian literature, and if Adam and Eve's judgment about good and evil were also allegorical depictions, then why was there a need for a Messiah to rescue anyone from condemnation? The role of Jesus as Redeemer rested on the premise that the Adam and Eve story was absolutely true when its mythical truth as literature was more compelling. If Adam and Eve were just literary inventions there was no need for a Messiah.

Surprisingly, in my youthful contemplations I had never asked myself this fundamental question nor had anyone posed it to me. Now the burden of proof justifying the religious edifice of belief fell on the rationale for the creation myth when its literalness, stolen ribs and talking serpents, was laughable. And if the Adam and Eve story was intellectually untenable, the rest of the biblical events, like the flood narrative, were also just parallel myths about the Hebrews coming to grips with Babylonian creation and flood stories, the multiple gods of the Canaanites, a monotheism spawned in Egypt, and a rising Jewish nationalism. The entire edifice of my belief system imploded like an unsafe building.

A Hindu Swami I met by accident in Los Angeles had told me that I should go to Rishikesh in northwest India saying it would change my life. Rishikesh was a Hindu holy site of pilgrimage located at the headwaters of the Ganges where it begins its descent from the Himalayas plunging 1,500 miles across the broad plains of India and Bangladesh before emptying into the Bay of Bengal. This is the place, Hindus believe, where the sacred water begins to flow from Shiva's head. As one of a handful of foreigners one night, I watched 40,000 devotees, standing knee deep in shallow pools in the Ganges, light candles and place them on lotus leaves to float down the river. How could so many people be errant in the faith of my fathers and why had not God revealed himself to them if he truly wanted them saved? Could it be that all who accepted the dictates of their own consciences were saved anyway? If true, then that meant that faith in any one particular religion was not necessary and perhaps even deviant if it meant going against personal conscience.

I now felt a strong affinity with Hindu believers, though I was both curious and incredulous about their beliefs. But this experience of deep sensibility with other believers, combined with questioning the basis of the Judaic-Christian religious tenets as I learned more about the writings of Sumerian, Babylonian, Greek and Egyptian stories similar to the Bible's but written centuries earlier, was enough to convince me that my personal religious beliefs had been misinformed and misguided. Whether one believes in the scriptures of the Moslems or Mormons, Jews or Catholics, one is born and educated into a religious environment and a specific culture that has a religious preference.

Like Descartes who employed doubt as methodology for gaining understanding, I tried to disown my previous convictions after devouring devotional works for years and decided to bring fresh vision and objectivity to this study. In intuitive and spiritual deconstruction beginning in 1984, I sought to examine biblical content free of dogmatism and subjectivity, not to demythologize but rather to show mythic and literary origins, drawing together scripture, literature, history, social science and critical examination to the place of scripture in literary scholarship.

ACKNOWLEDGMENTS

For timely financial support in pursuit of this inquiry, grateful thanks to Charles Scarborough, Chuck Summers, and Richard Peak. Special thanks to Prof. Hans Kung for correspondence on his struggles with Catholic Church authority in 1980; to Dr. Jacques Barzun, Mike Morrison and Dan Quarnstrom for encouragement and understanding. For knowledgeable commentary and critique: Dr. Gloria London (Middle East Center, University of Washington and Burke Museum, Seattle), Rev. William Fulco, S.J., (Chair, Ancient Mediterranean Studies, Loyola Marymount University), Dr. Karlheinz Rebel (Professor Emeritus, University of Tubingen), Prof. Lotte Schou (Danish University of Education for information on Scandanavian creation myths), Dr. Lisa George (Dept. of Languages & Literature, Arizona State University), Dr. Robert Willis (formerly of Rider College), Dr. Roger Desmarais (formerly of Seattle University), Tracey Schuster (Getty Library and Research Institute), and Dr. Gary Greif (retired Chair of Philosophy, University of Wisconsin, Green Bay). For invaluable photo assistance of cuneiform tablets, Mac E. James, Associate Curator, Archaeology Center, Loyola Marymount University. For computer assistance, Anders Friberg at Arizona State University. For editorial and production assistance, Phyllis Korper and Sophie Appel at Peter Lang Publishing.

The following museums and libraries provided me with inspiration and insights into this study: Damascus and Aleppo Museums (Syria), the Anthropological and Tokapi Museums (Istanbul), the Ashmolean Museum and Bodleian Library (Oxford), Arizona State University Library, British Library and British Museum, Coptic and National Museums (Cairo), Archaeological Museum (Nicosia), Getty Research Institute (Santa Monica), Israel Museum (Jerusalem), London Museum, The Louvre, Loyola Marymount University Museum and Library of Archaeology, Metropolitan Museum (New York), and Roman Museum (Amman).

For the authors cited in the references, I owe inestimable thanks.

The author gratefully acknowledges kind permission to reprint from *Akhenaten, King of Egypt* by Cyril Aldred. ©1988 Thames & Hudson Ltd, London.

LIST OF ABBREVIATIONS

AKE	*Akhenaten, King of Egypt*
ART	*An Anthology of Religion Texts from Ugarit*
BADB	*Biblical Archaeology, Documents from the British Museum*
BANE	*The Bible and the Ancient Near East*
BAR	*Biblical Archaeology Review*
BASOR	*Bulletin of the American Schools of Oriental Research*
BG	*Bhagavad Gita*
BH	*The Bible as History*
BWSA	*Basic Writings of St. Augustine*
CE	*Clementis Alexandrini opera quae extant omnia.*
CH	*Corpus Hermeticum*
DF	*The Decline and Fall of the Roman Empire*
EBD	*Egyptian Book of the Dead*
EG	*Epic of Gilgamesh*
FFF	*Fragments of a Faith Forgotten*
FFGP	*Four Famous Greek Plays*
GGIG	*Gods, Goddesses, and Images of God in Ancient Israel*
HCCC	*History of the Church from Christ to Constantine*
HH	*Herodotus, The Histories*
HZ	*Hymns of Zarathustra*
JBL	*Journal of Biblical literature*
JECS	*Journal of Early Christian Studies*
JEH	*Journal of Ecclesiastical History*
JHS	*Journal of Hellenic Studies*
JRS	*Journal of Roman Studies*
JHI	*Journal of the History of Ideas*
LEP	*Lives of Eminent Philosophers*
LRE	*The Late Roman Empire*
LFS	*Letters from a Stoic*
LS	*Lost Scriptures, Books not included in the New Tesatment*
MLBA	*Myths and Legends of Babylonia and Assyria*
NH	*Nag Hammadi Texts*
NTG	*Novum Testamentum Graece*
OCC	*Contra Celsum*
OHBW	*Oxford History of the Biblical World*
TG	*The Tenth Generation, The Origins of the Biblical Tradition*
TM	*The Teachings of the Magi*
WWNT	*Who Wrote the New Testament*
WP	*The Works of Plato*

INTRODUCTION

I would advise none to read this work unless such as are able and willing to meditate with me in earnest, to detach their minds from commerce with the senses, and likewise to deliver themselves from all prejudice.
                    (Rene Descartes, Meditations on the First Philosophy, 1641)

The traditional view of western civilization is that it is the confluence of the twin cultures of Hellenism and Judaism, the rich aesthetic, literary life of ancient Greece and the religious and prophetic visions of the Bible. These linked civilizations, so different in their worldviews and perspectives on life and nature, laid the foundations for the intellectual pursuits of the western mind and merged when Christianity forged a new identity combined of Hebrew apocalyptic and the Greek Neo-platonic ideals. What is not so well accepted is that both Greek and Hebrew writings are blends of literature inherited from more ancient civilizations and have more thematically in common than the differences in language might suggest. It is the common and selective literary traits I explore in this book because the impact of literary study, neglected in history of religion research, has yet to be synthesized into Israelite religion. Based on the evidence I conclude that the Bible and gospels are folk narratives in part derivative of previous literary motifs.

The traditional approach to biblical studies has been to try to locate events, figures and trends that match the biblical stories. But this approach is flawed. It is more instructive to read previous literature to see how biblical scribes liberally borrowed from these sources to compose the Bible and gospels. The mythical pattern in the comparison is relatively easy to discern once texts are compared and key elements and passages identified.

The Bible is the perpetuation of the ancient myths about the creation of the world, of humans, of the destruction of humans and their survival. Even science has not yet yielded complete answers to such portentous issues, but has proposed new theories like the Big Bang and the bifurcation of bipedal hominids from other primates. Indeed, if one were to interchange the concepts, that *Genesis* is a theory, that science is a myth, that text Y is sacred but not text X, the playfulness demonstrates how cultural accretions have overlaid our terminology to help explain the world and our presence in it. Myth is the whole set of values supporting the cultural life of a people, but narrative and pictorial evidence is our principal form for examining it.

Primary sources for biblical writings are the Sumerian *Epic of Gilgamesh*, the Akkadian *Atrahasis*, the Babylonian *Enuma Elish*, the Ebla and Ugarit texts from Canaanite culture, the extensive writings of Egypt, including *The Book of the Dead* and the *Pyramid texts*, Greek myths, Homeric epics, and the histories of Herodotus. Biblical scribes and gospel narrators copied and adapted stories and wove them into a series of books that today constitute the canon of Judaic and Christian religions. Numerous scholars have concluded that the Bible is a continuation of ancient literary traditions and an amalgam of myths and stories from ancient Near Eastern literature. (1)

Historiography assumed a less important role in post-biblical literature beginning in the Second Temple period (c. 538 BCE–70 CE) and left no trace in rabbinic literature from the 1st to the 3rd centuries CE. By the Second Temple period the rabbis had transformed temple worship with sacrifices to the Torah as the central element in religious worship. The Law became the main platform and history was considered inconsequential, a conclusion that was to shape the subsequent thinking of all Judaic writers and editors.

Borrowing existing literary themes and episodes was common among ancient scribes and the Bible and gospels are rife with examples of similar motifs. In the centuries when story telling was ubiquitous, writing was a prized skill, literary analogies were prevalent, and scribes were merely showing familiarity with neighboring cultures by repeating stories in their native languages. Even Shakespeare lifted wholesale the plot of an Italian story about a Jewish usurer by Giovanni Fiorentino called *Il Pecorone* and renamed it *The Merchant of Venice*. The themes of creation, relationships to deities, the cosmos, brothers, inheritances, litigations, vengeance and justice, sacrifice, the prerogatives of royalty, all these are in the Bible and *The Iliad*. Biblical scribes copied, imitated, extrapolated, and paraphrased existing narratives, themes and allegories to make a mosaic of new books that helped define the Hebrew identity.

About 2,700 hundred years ago writing consisted of extensive recordings of business and trade transactions, formulae for religious services, recordings of harvests and land transactions, manuals for sacrificial rituals, but, except for the Greeks, only minimal fiction. Since most people were illiterate those anxious to have imaginations enlivened listened to storytellers. They memorized sagas and repeated them over several evenings in the town square, taverns or amphitheaters. In later centuries once stories were written, only the literate few were privileged to read these chronicles. Subsequent generations forgot or never learned these older myths, many buried under the silt and sands of time, the debris of lost civilizations, and thus assumed the Hebrew testament was without literary precedents. The Bible thus became a government book, a collection of documents sponsored by and for the Davidic and successive monarchies. At the opening are the first books in a mythical continuum of heroes like Adam, Abraham and Moses, and at the other end are the prophets, selected history, and adherents of the Law.

Biblical archaeology, essentially a theological orientation, has now been discredited since its presence was to locate artifacts that confirmed the biblical narratives and not for evidence that might contradict them. Archaeological discoveries have furnished new textual parallels with the Bible and evidence of its literary antecedents. Gospel narrators in later centuries liberally borrowed from histories, epics, religious and ideological writings to describe a heroic legend and create a new religion blended with prophetic remnants of Judaism and trendy intellectual movements of the day like Stoicism and Gnosticism. Later theological commentators accorded the Bible a sanctified status the original editors neither sought nor claimed. We may never know the actual extent of overall literary pilfering because so many classical writings have been lost or destroyed. For example, the world has only seven of Aeschylus's 80 plays; seven of Sophocles 120 plays; and 19 of more than the 90 known plays of Euripedes.

The worlds of myth, religion and science are not at odds with each other but are colliding cultural developments of the use of symbol and metaphor to understand the world, tools to find meaning. In the ancient world, mathematics was more certain than myth, but its deductive logic was more practical in building pyramids than it was powerful as a source of belief. Today, myth, religion and science are explanations of how we view the world. Because science is the more recent method for understanding does not necessarily mean it is superior. Myth is the record of human history and perceptions of events and is vulnerable to misinterpretation when translated. Myth evolved into religion, the imagination's answer to the mind's questions.

Consider a few ideas, symbols and myths we assume are biblical. Angels like Seraphim and Cherubim were a part of the cosmos as envisioned by the Sumerians in the 3rd millennium BCE. The British Museum contains an example of a winged lion with a woman's head and a similar design likely used for the cherubim noted in *Exodus* 25:20. The concept of angels, as evidenced by archaeological artifacts and literature, originated with the Sumerians, became a part of Akkadian mythology and was adopted into Hebrew lore. The concept of soul came from the Egyptians and Greeks. By the time of Augustus there was widespread belief among Romans who were not Christians of the existence of soul and the afterlife. Episodes of notable men found in Herodotus and in *The Epic of Gilgamesh* and the *Iliad* were attributed to biblical heroes. Jewish beliefs of the 3rd century BCE, certainly by the writer of the *Book of Proverbs*, were infused with Platonism and Gnosticism.

Scholars know that the Babylonian Creation myth, *Enuma Elish*, and *Genesis* have nearly exact motifs of creation and that the Sumerian epic *Gilgamesh* and *Genesis* have parallel stories of the Deluge. Canaanite and Egyptian poetry contain passages later enveloped in the *Psalms* and other prophetic sayings. The *Code of Hammarabi* and the Torah have comparable rules of justice. (2) Canaanite literature was copied by biblical scribes. Even the word that describes biblical interpretation, hermeneutics, originates from the same root word for Hermes, the Greek messenger god.

Biblical books appear to form a single narrative from the creation to the Babylonian exile and the restoration of the temple. But the separate compositions frequently overlap and were later edited to portray the unity of belief in Yahweh. But it is clear that scribes did not share that conviction as they were situated in a polytheistic Canaanite culture. More literary eminence is accorded this textual coherence than the individual stories deserve, and indeed most scholarly analyses, while dissecting the narratives internally, do not acknowledge the obvious attribution to non-biblical writings, failing to look beyond the context of the Bible. In several locations the biblical narrator, for example, appears to know God's feelings and thoughts (*Gen.* 6:6 and 6:8 and *Exod.* 4:14) and the emotions of principal characters like Moses (*Exod.* 32:19) and Jacob (*Gen.* 31:32), a rare intuition, but a common literary practice among Homeric epics and Greek tragedians. (3)

The cultural history of the Bible is not just the history of the Hebrew nation. It is the collected social history of Middle Eastern people, a peek into the history of civilization, and of writing as its most precious invention. The stories selected for re-telling, their interpretation of events through heroic figure is a mythical distortion of reality to appeal to the imagination. (4) As the anonymity of the biblical scribes makes clear, the work of the individual author, editor or redactor is secondary to the recording of national and ethnic collective remembrances. Having absorbed the literature from so many cultural sources, the Hebrew canon may be the first literary adventure not only to define a national identity but to encapsulate a multi-cultural literary blend. It's inevitable that a century hence that the discovery of more parchments and tablets will yield new insights about the sources of biblical narratives.

Ancient civilizations unquestioningly contained many of the written sources for biblical scribes, who, like movie technicians, created a literature of special effects, painting scenes of events and figures that only simulated reality. Like Achilles, Hector, Paris, Odysseus, we might have assumed that biblical heroes, like Abraham, Moses and Samson and their heroic feats were equally true. Like the Greeks, Jewish and Christian theologians invested ordinary written concepts with divine significance. (5) Besides the obvious purloining of literary conventions, the Bible's editors even in the era of the judges reconstructed stories from historical periods in Hebrew history and superimposed or rearranged them to conform to Israel's cause on behalf of Yahweh and religious supremacy. As a result, the chronology of events and the positioning of some figures, like Joshua and Samson, are artificial, edited to conform to a theological formula of deliverance. (6)

The beginning chapters of *Genesis* describing the creation story have been hallowed by long tradition, enshrined by popular veneration, making claims to its historical legitimacy though not its authenticity as literature, difficult to accept. Interpretation through allegory, commentary, and etymological extrapolation sought to find new meanings in the obvious contradictions and inconsistencies in the tale. Few have been bold enough to challenge the fact that the story itself might be a recounting of more ancient stories. Greek myths and fables were manifestations of truths about the relationships between man and God elaborated by the slow process of reasoning which for Hebrews were moral and authoritative declarations of truth that permitted no alternative explanations.

There is general scholarly agreement that the earliest part of the Bible was composed in Jerusalem in the 8th century BCE, and the later writings like the psalms, prophecies and histories, were written from the mid-5th century to the end of the 2nd century BCE. The present collection of books dates from roughly the time of the return from the Babylonian exile during the reign of King Josiah, 639–609 BCE. If we return to that era from the 8th to the 4th century BCE we find an extraordinary effervescence of intellectual activity in Greece, India and China. In China, Lao Tzu composed the *Tao Te Ching* and Confucius *The Analects*. In India, the philosophy bred by the *Upanishads* and *Bhagavad Gita* led to a revolt by the Buddha and Mahavira, the founder of Jainism, against the established, Brahmin religious order. Meanwhile in Greece, Thales, Anaximander and Heraclitus were giving birth to western philosophy and stimulus to Pythagoras, Socrates, Plato and Aristotle. Additionally, there must have been writings irretrievably lost in earthquakes, fires, pillages, floods, and the destruction associated with invading armies who looted and burned entire cities, and with the zeal of the orthodox intent on destroying what was not their beliefs.

Although it is commonly believed that the state of Israel was formed by the time of David and Solomon, no extensive literary tradition existed until about 250 years later, or toward the end of the 8th century BCE. The collection of documents known as the Torah was not written until a sufficient body of literate scribes began recording national and religious history with literary legends to support the unification of two diverse sources, Judah in the south with its capitol at Jerusalem and Israel in the north.

The recurrent theme of the books of the Bible, besides the poetry of *Psalms* and *Proverbs* and the artful prose of the stories of *Ruth, Daniel, Job*, David, Solomon and the histories, is the validity of the establishment of the Hebrew prerogative: Israel's unwavering national and religious sovereignty and dedication to its monotheistic heritage. To tell this story and implant these national and religious ideals, Hebrew scribes created heroic deeds around ancient heroes, principally the founders of the dynasty, Abraham, Isaac,

Jacob, Moses, and Joshua. In an inventive way, these scribes managed to turn cultural hegemony and national destruction into religious advantage. According to them it was not the military prowess of the Arameans in 720 BCE or the Babylonians in 586 BCE that defeated the Israelites, but the unfaithfulness of the people to God's commandments that subdued their proud hearts.

The time span described for this inquiry is about 2,300 years, from the early Bronze Age to the first Iron Age, a period which, if we look backward in time from the present places us in the classical period of Greece. If we were lucky enough to be in Athens, our gods would be Pallas Athena, Zeus, Dionysius and a multitude of lesser deities. It's unlikely that any of these deities are worshipped today. In other parts of the Middle East, Baal was worshipped, Zoroastrians were bowing before fire, and the Romans were favoring Etruscan deities. This time warp analogy illustrates how cultures rearrange and assimilate deities over the centuries and how supposedly new sources of revelation change the religious landscape. The culture of worship is preferably understood in its situated context, its unique culture-bound milieu. Once the Bible became canonized as God's revelation in the first century CE by Philo of Alexandria and others, and validated by Christian dogma by the Council of Nicaea in 325 CE, no new interpretation, much less criticism, could change its content from the ecclesiastically defined text. Biblical and gospel language became sanctified.

Words and phrases acquired new meanings over the centuries. But until recently a psychological mindset kept biblical scholars from seriously analyzing the textual and linguistic similarities between Canaanite and Hebrew literature. Despite this scholarship gap there is ample evidence of the preservation of an extended cultural continuity and of borrowed religious beliefs. Texts found in the archives of Ebla originating about 2,500 BCE, and therefore contemporary with the age of the pyramids in Egypt, reveal similar meanings in the *Book of Job,* composed centuries later. (7) The Ebla texts lend currency to the acceptance that refined and highly cultured writing is not only much older than biblical texts but also richer in artistic merit. Comparing more than 3,000 vocabulary words from the Ebla archive with the 8,000 words in the Hebrew Bible (about 1,700 appearing only once), it is possible to translate the Bible more accurately and in the process raise new questions about its derivative meanings. The Ebla texts are to the Hebrew Bible what modern English is to Latin: a source of derived word roots spanning two millennia.

There are several scholarly layers of the methodology of biblical criticism. Form criticism examines formats used in the transmission of a tradition, such as a speech or dialogue. Source criticism tries to determine who is copying from whom. Redaction criticism seeks to establish why something was added or omitted from a later text. Tradition criticism seeks to determine the different layers of development. For this study I have combined aspects of each in analyzing a more global approach to biblical development by primarily focusing on extra-biblical sources to find commonalities. In the end, like a jury, one draws reasonable conclusions based on analysis of all the evidence.

It is just as arduous to resurrect the cultural context of a particular time since we bring our own view of the world and tend to read into words or artifacts meanings that might have been foreign to the people of a particular era. Until archaeological or textual evidence is forthcoming, hypothetical reconstructions or conjectures, using comparable techniques with their obvious limitations, is the most useful methodology. I apply the same methodology to an examination of canonical documents of the gospels. This method is associative, meant to show the connections between non-biblical literature and what emerged as canon. The associations can be found in:

quotations that are similar;
allusions to people or objects, such as an emperors' image on a coin;
imitation of the content, sequence or episode of an activity or event such as superhero passing through a crowd without anyone noticing. (8)

MacDonald has demonstrated that every student in the 1st century learned Greek through Homer. Mark imitates Homeric narratives from the *Iliad* and *Odyssey*, an ordinary student compositional assignment, and places them in the narrative of the life of Jesus. (9) MacDonald has identified at least 18 episodes in the *Iliad* and *Odyssey* that have parallels in Mark's gospel highlighting the imitative narrative of Odysseus, Achilles and Hector, both figures favored by the gods, with events Mark uses in the life of Jesus. Mark created the heroic life of Jesus modeled after epic heroes and characters in Greek poetic literature. (10) Goodman observes in his study of ancient Rome that those who spoke and wrote Greek, and this includes the gospel narrators, would have understandably been schooled in the cultural history of Greece. (11) Exhaustive studies of ancient texts reveal similar forms including myths and epic tales, funerary texts, history, legal texts, prayers, hymns, and didactic and wisdom literature. This is as true of Egyptian, Sumerian, Hittite, and Akkadian texts as it is the composition of the Bible.

The earliest Hebrew literature beginning in the 10th century BCE was poetic and imaginative, borrowed from Mesopotamian sources and paralleled a Canaanite style of writing. Over time editors transformed them into prose narratives during Solomon's reign perhaps in conformity with Egyptian characteristics. But soon Israelite writing became more historical and formalistic, and records of battles, victories, king lists and accomplishments replaced epic adventures and storytelling. (12) Likewise, Gospel narrators used existing literary devices and themes, just as biblical scribes did, to tell a mystical, transcendent story about Jesus. Few biblical commentators cite relevant non-biblical texts. Yet it is abundantly clear that biblical and gospel scribes borrowed from non-canonical sources, not just themes, phrases and allusions but narrative styles and events.

I was wary in this study of making facile similarities between myths from different cultures. Not that there aren't similarities, but that it is too easy to presume that one mythical theme, a struggle, a hero, a heroine, a monster, a devil, is simply transported into another cultural setting without modification. Does Marduk become Baal who becomes Zeus? Who named the individual angels, and why do they have names at all? Is the devil who offered Jesus a territorial kingdom the same as the serpent in the garden? We look backwards through the centuries with eyes clouded with contemporary contextual overlays.

This inquiry, completed over several decades in bits and pieces, began a half-century ago in a scholarly investigation of the literary origins of biblical literature. I seek to enlighten the origins of the Bible with intellectual ardor and not denigrate pagan gods and non-biblical literature with moral righteousness, but to enter a mythical world far from the present cultural landscape where religion is adherence to dogma. I suggest that this is true for the gospels as well, which did indeed draw upon rabbinic literature, but also upon Hellenic heroic epics. I make no claim that the results will be absolutely definitive, only that the cumulative evidence that biblical scribes borrowed from existing literature will be more compelling than that these same scribes had divine revelations limited to one set of collected documents as a test of divine authenticity.

PART I: VINTAGE SCRIPTURES

CHAPTER ONE
THE NARRATIVE TRADITION

Creation and flood stories, the intervention of gods in human activities, patriarchs and journeys, are all themes found in mythical literature. (1) The Bible is a Hebrew national narrative derived from oral and written stories thousands of years old.

Ancient peoples recorded their thoughts and transactions on discarded potsherds, stone, clay tablets, and only much later on parchment and papyrus. Ancient documents were not meant to be read by strangers but to service the needs of professional storytellers, scribes and accountants. The difficulty of recapturing the past is that history leaves only clues, not certitude. Because most religious texts are of extreme antiquity and have undergone transmission errors as manuscripts were copied, the opportunity for exactitude fades. Religious texts, like all ancient manuscripts where multiple copies of the same document exist, are fragile in form and content.

Ancient scribes did not have the tools of modern scholarship. They made no distinction between primary and secondary sources, cited no references, had no footnotes and did not acknowledge where or how they obtained inspiration. The scholarly mode of writing, a product of the Enlightenment and scientific accuracy, is a relatively modern development in intellectual history. Scholarship is meant to be objective and to separate fact from myth, error, fantasy, and superstition. If the source of a document is unknown, is it possible to say whether passages from the *Psalms, Epistles of Paul, the Upanishads*, the *Rig Veda*, the *Epic of Gilgamish*, the *Avesta*, the *Dead Sea Scrolls*, the *Song of Songs* or the *Koran* is or is not a sacred text? Texts become embroidered with sanctity when devotees believe that God revealed himself through writings and not, as for example Gnostics, Hindus or Buddhists believe, through personal enlightenment.

Take the accumulated record of five hundred years of one country's literary output, place it all in one book and compare it to the first five hundred years of its native literature. Whichever country you choose, you will find legends, myths, allegories, prose, speculation, poetry and history. The same time span of Hebrew literature from approximately 900 to 500 BCE with all its forms of literature, is contained in the Bible. Comparative textual analysis offers only a glancing peek from 2,500 to 2,000 years ago into this Hebrew scribal society, an elite group whom I call the Lords of the Scrolls. It was this anonymous group who composed the texts that eventually were chosen as the Hebrew national identity, a collection permanently engraved in the cultural mindset of western civilization. Unlike conversation and oral discourse, no text can answer questions about its meaning. If we could question any of the original scribes we would discover, and they would undoubtedly admit, that they altered earlier stories from more ancient civilizations and continuously made modifications to them as the times warranted.

The Bible is like a multi-generational novel written when writing was in infancy, a book composed by multiple scribes describing real, imagined and imitated events and figures in Hebrew history, a way of keeping religious memory alive. Scribes sought to establish a literary heritage in a tribal society struggling for intellectual distinction. Joshua's pillaging and warrior exploits are but one example of such fiction, as no confirmatory evidence has ever been found to verify his exploits. (2) *The Book of Daniel*, reputedly written at the time of the prophet, was more realistically composed in the middle of the 2nd century BCE and is a blizzard of historical inaccuracies. Like Homeric legends, the initial stories in *Genesis* are about conflicts between the God of the Hebrews and so-called false gods. Later, just as the Greeks settled on Zeus as the chief divinity, biblical scribes settled on one God, Yahweh, the divine national patron.

Myth best describes most biblical books, certainly *Genesis* and *Exodus*, because myth implies a truth coloring a story. Fiction, however, is always entertainment and does not imply any allegorical content, although meaning and literary satisfaction can be derived from a story or character. Zoroaster's *Avesta*, for example, a sacred set of texts and hymns dating from about the 6th century BCE, is a compilation of stories, hymns and writings from different sources collected over a long period and attributed to Zoroaster.

But if fiction is entertainment so is literary fabrication. When Hellenic culture was sweeping the Mediterranean by the 3rd century BCE carried by Alexander's troops, Judaism was not immune from its pervasive incursions. Jewish Hellenic authors like Artapanus and Aristobulus in the 2nd century BCE wrote that the Bible was the source of Greek artistic invention and that, astonishingly, Moses was the true stimulus for Greek philosophers and poets. Such falsifications endeared the writers to the biases of a Jewish audience but corrupted the concept of cultural accommodation and the achievements of a few geniuses in an enlightened era. Jewish compilers compounded these forgeries by manufacturing passages from the Greeks to prove their point, and thus confirmed that the preservation of Jewish nationalistic purity was paramount even if the result was literary desecration.

The use of metaphor or figurative language, and allegory or symbolic language, to convey truths is common to all literature. Hindus, Muslims, and Jews not only believe they have sacred texts but sacred languages and thus reading holy books is a spiritual exercise. (3) Sacred writings all acquired such a status in different cultures, the *Popul Vuh*, the *Bhagavad Gita*, the *Upanishads*, the Buddhist canon, Egyptian and Tibetan books of the dead, the *Koran*, the *Book of Mormon*. Each in its own way has inspired millions to more productive and virtuous lives, devotional, spiritual and religious enlightenment, while secondarily promoting literacy. The ultimate confirmation of the use of metaphor, as Thomas Aquinas noted, is that the Bible itself is a metaphor for faith: "It is appropriate to sacred scripture to treat divine and spiritual matters under the similitude of bodily things." (4) But more importantly, once faith is assumed, again quoting Aquinas, the literature which generated it cannot be allowed to have error otherwise faith is compromised. "Falsity cannot form the basis of divine scripture which has been handed down by the Holy Spirit; nor can there be an falsity in the faith that is taught therein." (5) Such authoritative statements only solidified that faith followed from scripture. Whether faith also devolved if scripture followed myth was unresolved.

Scholars are unable to verify historically any of the characters or conditions from the 2nd millennium BCE because *Genesis* provides no corroborating evidence and appears uninterested in the cultural context of nearby civilizations, like the demise of Egypt's Old Kingdom c. 2,100 BCE whose rulers built the pyramids for their immortality if not their solvency. Pharaohs are not mentioned by name. No dates are provided for any of the principal characters. No events or figures from other nations are described within the time frame. Chapters 12-50 of *Genesis* appear to be in geographically specific locations but within a nationalistic time warp.

Biblical narratives are thus the soap operas of ancient Hebrews, short stories containing all the attention-getting ingredients, sex, deceit, alienation, alliances, journeys, broken promises, heirs, foreign spirits, prophecies about the future, war, destruction and religious imperatives. The narratives were translated, written in Hebrew, codified with a pervasive cloak of Judaism, categorized in books and sanctified. Once accepted as holy and inviolate, there was no returning to viewing such stories as just narratives. They had to be accepted as sacred, their assumptions inspired with puffs of divinity, even though, taken at face value, like the fables of Adam and Eve, Noah and the flood, Jonah and the whale, they are risible and substitute as children's bedtime stories. (6)

On the other hand, consider this passage among many others from the *Song of Songs* or *The Book of Solomon*: "Oh may your breasts be like clusters of the vine, and the scent of your breath like apples, and your mouth like the best wine." (7: 6-9) Such amorous love poetry is unique in the Bible, and nonexistent in the gospels, and for the purist can only be interpreted allegorically. Reputedly written by Solomon, the scribe compares his love's navel to a bowl filled with wine, her belly to a heap of wheat, and her nose to a "tower of Lebanon," (is this a grain silo?) apparently a thing of beauty now lost in translation from the other agricultural comparisons. It is highly probable that the story came from the Babylonia myth of the love adventures of Enki and

Ianna (Ishtar) who has to fulfill her destiny as goddess of fertility and love. The songs found in this more ancient myth are more erotically explicit but not unlike biblical canticles.

Consider all the biblical themes: journeys (Abraham, Moses), a fulfillment of the past (prophecies), fantastic creatures (angels, talking serpents, gate-guarding Cherubim, Balaam's talking ass in *Numbers* 22), unusual places (Eden), the presence of evil (Satan), the securing of a land (Israel), fellowship, the sense of loss, redemption, returning home. All of these themes are in epics from *Gilgamesh* to the *Iliad* to *Beowulf*, to Tolkien's *The Lord of the Rings*. In Tolkien's epic peaceful people (the Hobbits) are threatened in their shire and must find a remedy (the ring/God) to release them from destruction. To accomplish this, they must seek the assistance of unusual colleagues, dwarfs (Gollum), wizards (Gandalf), elves, to confront the impersonalized enemy, (dark Lord of Mordor, Sauron (sounds like Satan) and the Orcs (Canaanites, Egyptians). A great battle (Middle Earth/Armageddon) with warrior heroes (Aragorn/ Joshua) will decide the fate of the people. The mission accomplished, whether Frodo, Abraham or Moses, the heroes return to the land of their fathers. Myth captivates imagination because it includes similar haunting and evocative themes.

The picaresque Latin novel, Lucius Apuleius' *The Golden Ass*, reads like the *Thousand and One Nights* of Scheherazade, full of laughable stories to entertain evening guests. Written in the second century CE it clearly influenced Boccaccio, Cervantes and Shakespeare's rendition of an ass in *A Midsummer Night's Dream*. Instead of a god becoming a mortal, Lucius in *The Golden Ass*, probably the world's first novel, is unwittingly transformed into a jackass and forced to spend time with disreputable bandits and a variety of owners who abuse him mercilessly. The theft of themes from older authors is and always has been a literary propensity.

For the 1st century apologist Origen, scripture held an historical, moral and mystical understanding and contained divine expressions of God's spirit. Scriptural writers did not deceive so much as to adopt other myths as if they were their own. Except for *Kings* and *Chronicles* where the history stands the simplest tests of validation, myth is the source of biblical inspiration. The Hebrew Bible is a literary tradition which began in ancient Sumer and extended forward to the Ebla culture in the 3rd millennium BCE, the Ugarit or Canaanite in the 2nd millennium, the Greek in the 1st millennium BCE, to the Hebrew when, according to the concurrence of scholars, the author known simply as J wrote the oldest part of the Pentateuch about 950 BCE. (7)

Consider a modest comparison between one of the earliest Greek poets, Hesiod who lived about 700 BCE and the use of similar biblical motifs.

HESIOD (*The Theogony*)	BIBLICAL SCRIBES
Zeus' war with the Titans	God's war with a band of Destroying angels (*Job* 1:6, *Job* 2:1)
No one escapes all-seeing Zeus	God sees and knows all
Zeus, the son of Kronos, was hidden in a cave as an infant	Jesus, the son of God, was born in a cave
Zeus has goddesses hidden in his belly and retrieves them	God extracts a woman from Adam's rib
Echidna is a half-nymph and half-snake creature who never dies nor grows old	The serpent in the garden has unusual powers like those of a goddess
The deceit of women	Eve's deceit
Zeus punished mortals	God punishes mortals
Titans are walled in on all sides and gates of bronze are guarded	Adam & Eve are banished and angels guard the entrance with flaming swords

These mythical themes are not precise and exact, but there are enough likenesses to conclude that Hesiod, the classical Greek poet, was known to biblical scribes and that key elements of *Genesis* parallel Hesiod's narrative of the creation of the gods in *The Theogony*. (8) The recurrent themes in both narratives are: the deceit of the gods (the Titans/the deceit and disobedience of the fallen angels and mankind); the disguise of lesser divinities (Echidna/the serpent); the hidden face of God (Zeus from his father/God from Adam); God hides beings in his middle anatomy (Metis in Zeus' belly/Eve in Adam's rib); God clothes mortals (Pallas Athene the woman/God clothes Adam & Eve); fallen lesser divinities are excluded (Titans walled in/Adam & Eve walled out); God overcome by his own son (Kronos by Zeus/Yahweh by Jesus). By highlighting such non-biblical sources, even a casual observer can make comparative analyses that conclude that biblical scribes pirated myths and heroic episodes. (More similarities between *Genesis* and the *Epic of Gilgamesh* are explored in Chapter Four).

As is true in archaeology, context in literature determines significance. It seems bizarre to think that surrounding dirt and rock strata can help identify whether a pot, vessel, figurine, or household god can have its age and use known depending on where it is found. But a temple sanctuary will command a different meaning than a bedroom, granary or trash heap and at a sedimentary level indicating its antiquity. Every civilization is composed, like geological strata visible in hillsides from layers of sediment, of folds of its past. Likewise, each emerging religion is composed of elements of past religions, despite claims by prophets that its religion is a profession of new divine utterances. Similarly, the cultural context of scripture exists in events, wars, kings, assassinations, philosophies and the whole intellectual milieu of an era. Reading the Bible as if its content were devoid of a thriving context of the time of composition minimizes its literary power. The Bible is the embodiment of the literature of the whole Middle East from 5,000 to 2,000 years ago, drawing on sources created since writing began and even earlier oral traditions.

To understand and appreciate what Biblical scribes knew we must transport ourselves conceptually back to the Bronze and Iron ages (see the chart below) with all the imprecision that speculative journey implies, to view the world through eyes unaccustomed to keen observation, careful analysis, deductive logic and science and enter a world filled with invisible beings, principalities and powers of astrological speculation, of a cycle of seasons bounded by creation myths, archaic figures, a concept of paradise, of leave-taking and journeys, of covenants with tribes, clans and gods, of entry into new lands and blessed experiences in the neighborhood temple and the temple of heaven. To achieve any one of these mysterious stages of life, one accesses dreams, magic spells, oracles, astrologers, apocalyptic visions, angels and prophets who have special powers to ease the journey and point the way. This is far from the world of science.

We have become so enraptured by the explanations of natural science to enlighten us about everything that we cannot imagine an age when natural science, as a way of discovering truth, did not exist. In such times, feelings of awe and mystery, of temples erected to unknown gods, and what appear to be absurd rituals, were the legitimized knowledge base, and woe to the one, like Anaxagoras or Socrates, who resisted or violated the established civil code for behavior to the gods.

The literate language of the 1st century CE was imbued with philosophical terms, some on loan from heroic literature, others from Aristotle, the Greek mysteries, and the Gnostics. The world was differentiated into substance and accidents (like color and texture), essence and existence, being and non-being, and spirit and matter, terms designating elemental conditions of existence absent a physics delineating the world of micro-organisms, inert particles like neutrinos and biologically active cells like neurons. Spirit and breath, thought of as a distinct form of existence not associated with matter, is known to be air-borne particles of organic life. Yet spirit remains as a term designating non-material reality even though biblical angels who speak appear to violate immateriality.

The Bible is filled with Hebrew heroes who struggle with God, Adam, Abraham, Isaac Moses, Job, whose rage, unlike other epic heroes such as Achilles, is restrained. All the heroes are confused about their heroism, knowing they have been specially chosen but unsure of their destiny and what their legacy is supposed to mean to others. Biblical heroes occur because of divine choice and not from a self-imposed moral identity. Heroes personalize the myths and socialize the culture, but do not typify answers to the mysteries of the universe or human agonies.

The Bible is a book of memories and a book to remember because its purpose is to instill institutional and social memory in the Chosen People. In fact, the Hebrew verb *zakhar*, "remember," occurs 169 times in the Bible, one of the most frequent words, more than the counsel to pray (140 times), and it is nearly always associated with God or Israel. (9) "Remember the days of old, consider the years of many generations." (10) Jewish feasts like Passover are ritual reminders of special commemorative importance and the Christian liturgy serves the same purpose: "Do this in remembrance of me." (*Luke* 22:19) The memory is of the Law, the Torah, and the Tabernacle, or in Christianity the presence of Jesus in the Eucharist.

The Hebrews, living at the crossroads of great civilizations, Mesopotamian to the east, Hittite and Canaanite to the north, Greek to the west and Egyptian to the southwest, assimilated cultural traits and sought to create their own separate nationality by accentuating two main principles: justifiable right to the land and monotheism. Hebrew writings contain borrowed creation, flood, and brother stories, descriptions of the wanderings of nomadic Patriarchs, the reputed exodus of an oppressed people, and archaic laws and rituals of a tribal society, some history and exalted poetry all blended with an unusual mix of apocalyptic visions and rabbinic ideas of submission to Yahweh. Syncretism, a term first coined by Plutarch to describe the union of cultic deities like the incorporation of the rituals of Isis from Egypt into Greek and Roman beliefs, is the merging of cultic and religious beliefs and practices. This process of blending deities and the practices associated with them occurred with regularity as cultures came into frequent contact through trade.

The Hebrews came under the influence, if not the suzerainty, of neighboring powers whose literary and cultural stature was richer. Tiglath-Pileser II came to the Assyrian throne in 745 BCE and within a decade had subjugated northern Israel and incorporated into in a vassal province. The southern kingdom of Judah too fell under Assyrian domination until the empire itself was overthrown by a coalition of Babylonians under Nebuchadnezzar in 597 BCE who occupied Jerusalem and deported all skilled inhabitants to Babylon. A revolt in Jerusalem in 586 BCE was brutally crushed and Solomon's temple burned and the Davidic monarchy eliminated. Assyrian and Babylonian cultural accoutrements became absorbed into Hebrew society. The royal successors (romanticized by Hebrew scribes as glorious kings but in reality never more than tribal chieftains) made Yahweh the center of the new religion and adorned its literature with Canaanite gods and hymns, Akkadian legends, Babylonian myths and Egyptian cosmology, folklore and theology

Appropriating ancient myths for native literature was not just a Hebrew trait. The Greeks, making slight alterations in the names, usurped the stories of the Babylonians. The Akkadian Ishtar becomes the Phoenician Astarte, who in turn becomes the Greek Aphrodite, who plays a role in the Adonis story similar to roles played by Ishtar in the Tammuz legend. Tammuz is the Akkadian vegetation and shepherd god, the symbol of death and rebirth in nature. He dies in the summer months (tammus = June/July) and his soul is taken by demons to the underworld. Ishtar descends to the underworld world and brings him back so that fertility can return to the earth. The Akkadian legend is identical to the Greek myth of Adonis and Persephone, or Ceres among the Romans, after whom we have the name cereal. The earliest myths and divinities revolve around the earth's fertility, a tale woven around the earth goddess and the sky god, essential to the sustenance of life. The first humans in *Genesis* were not in a jungle or a desert but a garden, which presumes agricultural cultivation. The Jewish feast of Purim, celebrated in March and derived from *The Book of Esther* (Ishtar?), the only book in the Bible that does not mention God or divine intervention, is considered an allegory for the ancient Persian spring festival of the earth's replenishment.

The story of Jonah and the whale is quoted because gospel narrators used it as a metaphor for Jesus' death and resurrection. "A wicked and adulterous generation looks for a miraculous sign, but none will be given it except the sign of Jonah." (11) But if evangelists were more truthful they would have to acknowledge that "the sign of Jonah" is also a sign of Tiawah, Hercules, Vishnu Purana and, to a lesser degree, Andromeda, all of whom spent three days in a large fish. Jonah was summoned by God to go to Nineveh to prophesy against the city but ran away from this obligation and found a ship bound for Joppa. After paying the fare, he went aboard and sailed. When a storm emerged the sailors were afraid and each cried out to his god, while throwing the cargo into the sea to lighten the ship. But Jonah had gone below deck, where he lay down and fell into a deep sleep. Then the sailors said to each other, "Come, let us cast lots to find out who is responsible for this calamity." They cast lots and the lot fell on Jonah. (When on a cruise where the ship is sinking, always attend the meeting where lots are cast to get into a lifeboat). Then they took Jonah and threw him overboard, and the raging sea grew calm. But the Lord provided a great fish to swallow Jonah, and Jonah was inside the fish three days and three nights. Jonah prayed to the Lord from inside the fish, and, relenting, God commanded the fish and it vomited Jonah onto dry land.

The marine form of Tiawah, the Assyrian god, is a large fish, and the three days in which she is interred in Assyrian cosmology are the winter months when nothing is harvested. The divinity of ancient gods is associated closely with the stars, sun, weather and crops. Hercules descended into the belly of a fish and came out after three days. The love god in the Hindu *Vishnu Purana* is thrown into the sea and swallowed by a fish. Poseidon, because he was told that Andromeda was more beautiful than the nereids, sent a sea monster to prey upon the local country. Andromeda was sacrificed by being chained to a rock by the sea but was rescued by Perseus who slew the monster off the coast of Joppa (where Jonah was sailing to) and then married her. None of the fish in any of these myths eats anyone: the heroes or heroines are swallowed whole and this implies the myth arose from a single source. The whole of the *Book of Jonah* is a re-telling of a very old myth salted with a prophecy about God sparing repentant Nineveh, the probable city in which the myth originated.

Symbolism is one literary method, prophecy another. Biblical prophets are supposed to enlighten the devotees of what the deity has planned for them. But throughout the Mediterranean world oracles like those at Delphi and Cumae, and fortune-tellers like the blind seer Tereisias in Homer's *Odyssey* and Sophocles' *Oedipus Rex*, astrologers and Magi are all predictors of the future. In that sense, theatrical audiences were knowledgeable since they too knew in advance, like the three witches in *MacBeth*, of the protagonist's impending downfall and tragedy. The playwright's artifice of prior knowledge created for live audiences, known since the days of Aristophanes and Plautus, is translated into scripture for divine action.

If we find it hard to think of the sun or fire as a god, or to sacrifice a bull or a sheep to propitiate an unknown god, then we are limited in understanding religious beliefs that preceded monotheism. The purpose of ancient peoples was to find meaning in life without either religious absolutism or science, and answers to why the cosmos and biology act the way they do. Questioning the meaning of life and the universe presumes on the ability to be awed by nature and existence. Polytheism existed from an indeterminate time in early civilization until roughly 1,000 BCE in Hebrew history, or about the time of David, let's round the figure to a minimum of at least 4,000 years of polytheistic practices, a fourth older than Hebrew monotheism, twice as old as

Christianity, and three-fourths older than Islam. Monotheism is a relative newcomer in human history.

The fortuitous discoveries in Ebla of Canaanite documents, and in Egypt of the discarded or hidden manuscripts of Gnostic writings in gospel and epistle form, and the *Dead Sea Scrolls* has confirmed the abundant literature extant during the expansion of early Christianity. Gnostic writings reveal the search for the mystical aspects of Christianity. Whatever intellectual energy and enrichment heresies poured into the ferment of early Christianity has been irretrievably lost in a maelstrom of purging, ridding the world of unorthodoxy but also dissipating a lively intellectual environment, a rich discourse that might have softened and tempered the abstract definitions of faith. Orthodoxy, or the right way, has the disadvantage of limiting a broad appeal and creating the conditions for intolerance.

Let's enter the world of the early Bronze Age about 5,000 years ago, or about two millennia before the composition of the first Bible documents, when writing first became a form of communication and a way to disseminate stories, to understand why we believe revelation has to ber written at all.

The Magic of Writing

Narrative began with speech but, until the 20th century, the only preservation of speech was in writing, the technological innovation transforming the oral message from listeners within earshot to audiences at a distance. Storytellers reached far beyond their locales. The myths they recited and the hymns they sang became permanent when writing was invented and did not have to rely upon memorization to be retold. When invented first in China and then in Europe in 1453, the printing press would distribute the message to anyone capable of reading.

Other technologies have changed the way we view the world: sculpture and painting, the telescope and microscope, photography and the cinema. But of all communicative innovations, writing allows us to peer backwards in time and partially reconstruct the cultural context of a people. Translating ancient languages is difficult enough but pales in comparison to attempting to understand word usage, subtleties and nuances in a social context that no longer exist. For example, the Phaistos Disk, a round disk of clay containing 61 words with a script called Linear A and dating from 1,700 BCE, has eluded decipherment. Separating whether or not several hands have composed or amended the texts, which is assuredly true in the case of the ancient scrolls that have become the Bible, compounds the problem. Writers inscribed the deeds of kings on obelisks, stone monuments, terra cotta, ostraca (bone) and cuneiform tablets until Egypt invented a use for the papyrus reed and used reed pens to write on wax tablets.

At Uruk in present day Iraq (the biblical Erech), hundreds of clay tablets were first discovered in the 1930s, the oldest inscribed before 3,000 BCE, some were as old as 8,000 BCE. Besides stone tools, they are some of the oldest human artifacts of ancient civilizations, the first objects baked in ovens for commercial purposes, tokens which predate writing, presumed to be business transactions, like a record of a village's contributions to grain or livestock. The first numerals on clay were invented about 3,100 BCE, and these incised tokens had the origins of a numerical system for counting. (12) A scribe's life would have consisted of recording census and taxation data, military logistics, construction details, business documents, registering harvests, transcribing court decisions and royal degrees, international treaties, in addition to documenting and copying sacred writings. (13)

The Greek word *cuneus* means wedge or nail. Cuneiform script has come to represent the writing first introduced into the world by the Sumerians, the creators of civilization about 5,000 years ago. Cuneiform was then borrowed by the Akkadians who ruled the upper Mesopotamian valley, and by the Babylonians, Canaanites and Hittites. Some version of cuneiform writing was the *lingua franca* of the whole known world until about 2,500 years ago when Chinese and Egyptians developed their own symbols. Ancient scribes used a stylus that ended its point with a triangle with which scribes incised on soft, wet clay that was then baked or dried. It lasted for over 3,000 years. (14) Unless stored in encased earthen jars and hidden in caves like the Dead Sea Scrolls, ink will quickly wash off clay and papyrus will eventually disintegrate. Cuneiform tablets, on the other hand, like those discovered in Mari, Ebla and Amarna, survive and are not easily biodegradable. Over time, several cuneiform languages, some of which have still not been translated, were developed by peoples like the Elamites and Hittites. Such languages were both alike and distinct, as, for example, Hebrew, Aramaic and Arabic are today. (15)

The most numerous of cuneiform tablets are Assyrian texts from Nineveh dating from the 8th and 7th centuries BCE. Both the history of Israel regarding Babylonia recorded in the Bible, and the cuneiform tablets found in Babylonia, are a cross-reference to actual historical events. The unearthing of this great library of Assurbanipal (c.669–629 BCE) includes fragments of cuneiform tablets of the flood story of Gilgamesh. A scholar named George Smith (1840-1876), piecing together broken tablets for the British Museum, found in 1872 that the 11th tablet of the Gilgamesh tablets contained a flood story very similar to that in *Genesis*. It was his conclusion that the biblical flood story was based on the earlier Babylonian narrative and perhaps the Babylonian story on an even earlier version. The British Museum houses human-headed winged lions that once guarded the palace at Nimrud during the time of Ashurnasirpal (883–859 BCE) that are similar to descriptions of composite beasts found in the books of *Ezekiel, Daniel, Zechariah* and *Revelations*.

How cuneiform came to be translated in the middle of the 19th century is a detective story of some suspense. An Irish scholar named Edward Hincks (1792–1866) correctly understood that the cuneiform signs in Babylonian writing represented a whole syllable including a vowel and not just a consonant, or even an ideogram or a determinative, that like for a god or a country. The translation of this writing was not only complicated by the multiple uses in different civilizations but also by its long use. It would be similar to a translator suddenly finding that he could read modern English, and then discover an earlier version of Anglo-Saxon writing, the written English of a 1,000 years ago.

The Phoenicians were Canaanites, the same people with whom the Hebrews had quarrels, and were conquered by the Persians in the 6th century BCE, and later by Alexander the Great in the 3rd century BCE. Thereafter, Phoenicians absorbed all the cultured elements of their military conquerors, the Babylonians, Persians, Greeks and Romans. (16)

Writing took a giant leap to recognizable modern form in Phoenicia when its ancient city of Ugarit about 1,500 BCE a cuneiform script was developed with 30 consonants and three vowels. The phonetic language was a pronounceable language because vowels gave written language sound. The Phoenicians developed the alphabet out of symbols that represented sounds, and this recognition of the consonant symbols of both cuneiform and hieroglyphics was a major accomplishment. About the same time in the Middle Bronze Age the Minoans at Knossos on Crete had Linear A that was not Greek. Its successor, Linear B survived as a script from 1,500 to 1,200 BCE, is likely a combination of Linear A and Linear B, or archaic Greek. About 800 BCE the Greeks modified the Phoenician alphabet, and the Greek first and second symbols of that language, alpha and beta, became the name for the whole list of symbols, the alphabet.

In the latest leap to uncover ancient writings, scroll fragments from a library in the buried town of Herculaneum engulfed in a thick layer of ash and volcanic detritus, are beginning to be deciphered. The Villa of Papyri was Herculaneum's library facing the sea in 79 CE when Vesuvius lifted plumes of ash and smoldering debris 20 miles high and buried Pompei and the seaside town of Herculaneum in minutes. The papyrus scrolls were carbonized and when first unearthed by amateur archaeologists in the 18th century were thought to be logs but were thankfully stored in a Naples library for safekeeping. Today, thanks to digital photography, preservation techniques and computer imaging, these scrolls are being painstakingly peeled back in tiny fragments, reassembled, read and translated. The language of the papyri is Greek even though Herculaneum was a Roman town because Greek was the intellectual and educated language of the Mediterranean even as late as the late first century, about the same time as the gospel compositions.

Myths as Origins of the Narrative Tradition

Myths are metaphors for the human condition, imaginative and poetic impressions that illuminate dreams or delusions, making the indefinable expressible. We find a prince, the symbol of economic security, by losing a slipper. We weave a loom to demonstrate domestic skill and faithfulness to duty. We undertake arduous journeys to reveal our resourcefulness and enterprise. We face down dragons and dangers to show persistence and courage. Whether the myth originates in Sumer, Babylon, Athens, Thebes or Jerusalem, and whether or not which scribe copied it from which archive, the result is the existential encounter with the paragons of our inner natures and unconscious impulses and desires. Myths embedded in all ancient writings have become the essence of the language of religion.

Mythologies of the divine, whether as religious dogma or a wider part of cultural identity, are a natural human groping for an understanding of individual actions and the world. Myths are essential for defining who we are and who we want to be by providing guidance from other people's adventures. Myth is humankind's first intellectual experiment with categorizing the world into formulas based on human encounters. Among a long list of written traditions, the Bible, although it also contains histories, poetry, some drama, is one large mythological collection. Ancient poets and writers were circumscribed by the prevailing mythologies of the day, much as we are confined by the realities of science, to view the world from a particular perspective. Myths, according to Joseph Campbell, are public dreams that shape a society, the organization of images and ideas that move and define a culture. (17) Folk tales entertain us but myth instructs in psychological ways by recreating life experiences and providing clues to discover potential in our lives, the songs of the imagination and thresholds to other dimensions of experience.

Storytelling is a part of human communication involving creative license. Touches of human pathos and drama embellish an otherwise dry account of a major occurrence, details that are un-interesting are omitted, and divine intervention often invited if not demanded to show the significance of the occasion. These literary artifices are applied even if the writer has limited creative gifts. The biblical scribe's story is not necessarily invalidated by his tendency to appear to be an eyewitness to events described. But mixing memory and emotion about an event tends to dilute both the event and reconstructed memory. The description takes on a dramatically different context from the historical reality. Writing vividly does not necessarily mean writing truthfully.

The popularity of science fiction, *Alice in Wonderland*, Tolkien's *Lord of the Rings*, the Harry Potter books, *The Lion King*, spy novels, mysteries, fairy tales are all indicative of the power of the imagination to entertain. The number of Greek legends showing humankind's exploits and strained relationships with the gods and goddesses shows the widespread literacy of the ancient Greek world and the pervasiveness of mythology. There are truths hidden in children's stories and myths that, like Aesop's fables, are moral lessons for all time. Myths evoke all grand themes already in nature and their primordial symbols are older than history, assembled, as Jung notes, in the collective unconscious. (18) It is wise to return to them frequently, and music, opera, drama, poetry, dance and religion help us to do so.

The Hindu cosmology expressed in the *Upanishads* has some of the same mythology as the Bible, but is interpreted differently. Deities exist but they are also projections of inner psychological powers. Chinese and Indian modes of participation were through the individual, not the culture, and the ultimate, fulfilling reach was through self-realization and transcendence.

One potent myth of the Bible is that human lives are in perpetual exile, exiled from a garden and threatened with eternal banishment to an uncomfortable abode with demons. In the Christian perspective, everyone is exiled throughout life from the real abode of happiness only attainable based upon the good graces of a savior and proper human actions defined by negative behaviors. Yet exile and the journey to complete an adventure is true of all epic heroes: Gilgamesh, Achilles, Ulysses, Agamemnon, Osiris, Abraham, Moses and military men like Sargon, Cyrus and Alexander.

In many cultures, an interpreter was essential in getting the mythical and religious experiences right, the shamans or medicine men, the guardians of all mythological lore; the priests who alone can perform the rites and ceremonies; the prophets who are designated to interpret the messages of God. Then it became necessary to build the chambers where divinities were worshipped, rites where myths were re-enacted and performed and the faithful gathered: the caves of Cro-Magnon men who drew symbols of the hunt, the ziggurats of Sumer, the hills of sanctuary and sacrifice, the cave of the oracles, the Mithraeums, the Temple at Karnak, the Temple of Diana at Ephesus, the synagogues of the towns and the temples of the cities, the pilgrimage to the Kaaba in Mecca, the Gothic cathedrals.

Borrowing narrative themes from myths appears to be universal among scribes of antiquity. Dumezil, recounting a Nordic myth used as background for the Saga of Hadingus, a 9th century BCE Danish king who raided France, reports that "the saga writer has taken the episode from the myth and twisted it to make it fit...has reworked the scene as presented in the myth in order to make it conform with a narrative motif." (19) Saga writers, epic poets and Hebrew scribes indisputably made use of ancient myths in narrative motifs.

Cultural coincidences were a part of civilized life at least 3,000 years ago and certainly occurred when ancient Greeks adopted traditions from India. Plato's *Republic* asks questions about the highest good, as does Arjuna to Krisna in the *Bhagavad Gita*. Both Plato and ancient Indian philosophers and moralizers proposed a vigorous course for moral education, warning about the corrupting influence good things in life can have on the soul. Both employ the dialogue technique to generate ideas. *The Laws of Manu* and *The Republic* have classic definitions of justice, making future speculators wonder how such culturally similar ideas could be separated by such a wide geography. The concept of merit as the basis for selection to office is as much Confucian as it is Indian in the caste system, as it is in Plato's idea of philosopher kings. The progress of the soul towards salvation is the theme in the *Upanishads* and *The Republic* (20) If the weight of evidence points to ideological similarities in the ancient world, facilitated by trade and travel routes and the spread of literacy, mythological similarities would accrue in Hebrew religious stories as well. (21)

Let's assume that it is possible to create something from nothing, that there is a tree of miraculous fruit visited by a woman and the possibility of dying from eating this fruit, that certain people have powers beyond the natural, and assume further that arrogance and brotherly abuse leads to a murder and that there is a place for punishment for misdeeds. What text for such stories comes to mind? Clearly, it is the stories in *Genesis*. But the theme is also true of the *Popul Vuh*, the great mythological book of the ancient Mayan peoples. (22)

Allegory is finding submerged meaning or symbolic representation in a story, uncovering the layers of meaning in a text such as that the Hebrews wandering in the Sinai desert were eating manna and drinking water from the rock constituted, as Paul noted in *I Cor.* 10:3-4, that this implied spiritual meat and drink. Hence, creation, the creation of man and woman, the loss of innocence, the ancestry of generations, the flood, the patriarchs, exodus, revelation, finding the promised land, all are examples of the personal experiences of an individual life and not just an historical recounting of a people.

Moreover, metaphor cannot be a rationale for adhering to interpretations which directly contradict scripture, for example *The Book of Mormon*, the scripture of Mormonism (The Church of Jesus Christ of Latter Day Saints) first made public in 1830. At the time, hieroglyphics, in which the divine plates given to Joseph Smith by the angel Moroni was supposedly written, had not yet been deciphered. One of its teachings is that American Indians are descendants of ancient Israelites who came to America about 600 CE. (23)

Superstitions are other peoples' religious beliefs. What might appear to be unintelligible in one religion might be devoutly held in another and practiced with fanatical zeal. Whether we believe that our characters are established by the order of the stars at birth, or we wear amulets to ward off evil, or think some days unlucky, or that God speaks to us in dreams, or that dreams predict our future, the collective superstitions of all peoples, together with a host of myths and legends, becomes a part of our cultural baggage. Often the deepest hatred is specifically reserved for those of other beliefs.

The life questions are more or less the same in all cultures. Why did something happen? Why did it happen to me? What's an appropriate response? Who should I turn to? What will happen in the future? Whether the questions or the answers fall under a certain category of understanding, philosophy, religion, myth, psychotherapy, the response has changed from conferring with oracles, divinations, and magicians and placing votive offerings, to consulting priests, rabbis, imans and psychiatrists and leaving a check for the synagogue, church, mosque or physician. Rituals of mystery religions did not fully satisfy those who sought the succor of revelation either from prophets, astrological charts, or chicken entrails.

I have emphasized myth as the dominant theme for ancient narration and not history because the Bible is mostly narrative prose and not history. But two thousand years ago there were historians abounding. Hecataeus (c. 550–490 BCE) assembled some of the existing stories from oral traditions. Herodotus, who composed his works for public readings, combined stories from everywhere he traveled, and his great detail and sobriety make him characteristically Greek. Thucydides had unusual insights and an absence of bias, but intended his history to be a book to read and keep, a truthful rendition of the Peloponnesian War. Polybius was accurate. Tacitus was the finest stylistic writer of history prior to Edward Gibbon and Thomas Jefferson's favorite author. Suetonius was workmanlike but detailed. Caesar himself was original and very readable which is why his *Gallic Wars* were used as textbooks well into the 20th century. Plutarch was extremely descriptive and his biographies filled with characterizations. And Ammianus Marcellinus, the last of the Roman historians, gave both the strengths and weaknesses of his chosen figures.

But the Hebrews, with the exception of Josephus and the *Book of Kings*, had no historians or written traditions that weren't borrowed from other cultures. What the Hebrews had was an oral tradition which, when it came to be anonymously written, was incorporated with literature from pre-existing civilizations mingled with national tendencies of a people set apart who belonged in a determined geographic space. Herodotus tells us in the first sentence of his monumental histories who he is and that he is writing "to rescue from oblivion the memory of former incidents." There is no anonymity here. This is a personal address, direct, incisive in its ambition, available in the Bible only with Nehemiah who personalizes his narrative. Most of the Bible is written in the third person.

Biblical dates are used not for precision in time and measurement but as an approximation, an after-thought for the effect of accuracy. Biblical scribes were closeted culturally and intellectually 2,500 years ago, dominated by tribal, clan and clerical imperatives that distorted their view of history thus discrediting the integrity of the texts. Even though there were various means of calculation, lunar cycles, dynastic reigns, the rule of kings, jubilee years, historians like Herodotus and Thucydides never wrote about dates without some degree of accuracy. (24) "Egypt has certainly communicated to Greece the names of nearly all of the gods," writes Herodotus, and the Egyptians had a calendar of 365 days in a year. (25) The intent of subsequent biblical editors was to weave narrative threads to make the stories appear as an historical sequence. (26)

The warrior qualities of Achilles and Hector are likely exemplars of Joshua's exploits. Homer's Odysseus wandered for ten years through the Mediterranean and this too could have inspired the peregrinations of Abraham and the supposed forty-year desert journey of Moses. Like Moses carrying the Ark of the Covenant, Jason carried a precious cargo, the Golden Fleece that he had to protect from Medea, dangerous Nereids and other potential purloiners of precious goods. These heroic narratives may or may not tell stories of real individuals.

The Hebrews did not invent any comprehensive philosophy of life, dramatic plays, mathematics, aesthetic works that inspired other civilizations, and, with the exception of Solomon's Temple built according to prototypes of Egyptian temples, no architectural wonders worthy of emulation. Apart from tribal conquests in the hill villages of Canaan, the Hebrews were always the ones conquered: by Assyrians, Babylonians, Persians, Egyptians, Greeks and Romans. Their culture and religious ideas were borrowed wholly or in part from the great civilizations surrounding them. This cultural melting pot was then transferred to Christianity as a base from which was erected a more detailed doctrinal set of beliefs.

Creation stories and Hebrew literature, with a few exceptions like the story of David, derive largely from Sumerian and Babylonian civilizations. Many of the rules in *Deuteronomy* originated in Babylonian legal codes, like the *Code of Hammurabi*, Solon's laws and Egyptian laws. Circumcision was originally Egyptian. There is no external corroborating evidence of the existence of Abraham, the age of the patriarchs, Israel's entry into Egypt or the long stay of the Hebrews there, Moses, the Exodus, the Hebrews conquest of Canaan, or the confederacy of the twelve tribes.

Biblical literature was edited in the course of its development. What was essential was the re-telling of similar stories of old heroes applied to the new heroes so that their stature could be considered royal and kingly, and the founders of new political and religious systems. (27) Sargon was reputedly born in concealment and sent adrift in an ark of bulrushes on the river. Cyrus the Great, king of the Medes and Persians, was of kingly birth, and his identity concealed, only to be revealed by augurs and messengers sent to announce the birth. Jesus' birth was similarly described and revealed by angelic messengers and his wisdom praised by the learned rabbis in the Temple in Jerusalem when he was taken there at twelve years of age.

The anonymous scribes also composed the books of the major and minor prophets. (28) Scholars agree that many hands composed and edited *Isaiah*. Hence, the Lords of the Scrolls helped build a Hebrew heritage even in the prophetic books through edited additions. (29) What is relevant is not that the prophets may not be the actual writers of the texts ascribed to them but that all the scribes and editors are anonymous, professional writers whose only interest was in telling the story, amending it, adding new episodes, or enriching the text poetically. There is little agreement on the actual chronological order of the prophets (did Amos come first?) since the scribes are only interested in projecting a prophetic vision.

The dates of particular historical events are difficult to know precisely unless confirmed by reliable supplemental evidence, such as archaeological evidence, dated stone carvings or cylinder seals associated with the life of a known king's rule. Hence, scholars often ascribe trends, migration movements, or social transformations over a protracted period, to major epochs such as the early or middle Bronze Age. These archaeological periods are separated into century groupings from one hundred to several hundred years, with earlier periods grouped into larger time zones. The Iron Age can be more precisely dated and the final period of this age is dated from 586 to 332 BCE, a crucial period in the Hebrew history. Here are the major archaeological periods before the Common Era (BCE).

Early Bronze Age
- I   3100—2850
- II   2850—2650
- III   2650—2350
- IV   2350—2200

Middle Bronze Age
- I   2200—2000
- IIA   2000—1750
- IIB   1750—1550

Late Bronze Age
	I	1550—1400
	IIA	1400—1300
	IIB	1300—1150

Iron Age
	IA	1150—1050
	IB	1050—1000
	IIA	1000—900
	IIB	900—800
	IIC	800—586
	III	586—332 (30)

Primary historical texts, as exemplified by Herodotus and texts from cylinder seals and stele are often paired with biblical history. Modern scholarship has fused these textual studies with continuously emerging archaeological evidence and iconographic studies to convey new humanistic interpretations into the charged atmosphere of biblical scholarship. (31)

After the destruction of Jerusalem in 70 CE, many Christian communities, differing greatly among themselves over the preferred system of belief, rushed gospels, letters, pronouncements, manuals of moral instruction into circulation. The high incidence of human error in the process of copying Christian manuscripts heightened the probability of textual inaccuracies and created variant interpretations. No two copies agree in all particulars and it is conceivable that scribes actually changed the phraseology to conform to their own views. There is evidence that during the first three centuries texts were altered to conform to orthodox doctrinal beliefs. (32)

An educated author writing in the first part of the second century CE would have been familiar with the art of rhetoric from Quintilian (35-95 CE), the construction of artificial speeches from epic heroes in Homer, Herodotus, Thucydides and Xenophon, pithy sayings from Martial and stoic authors, how to arrange anecdotes and plot a story line from Homer and Virgil, showing the pleasure of the gods by having them and their designates perform miracles for their chosen favorites, and developing history from a chosen social perspective, like the fact that Jesus meant to appeal to the Gentiles not just the Jews. Such an anonymous author's use of methodological tricks of erudite composition reveal familiarity with standard literary conventions. Such literary devices were the ways in which historians regulated stories to conform to a style, to epic adventures and preferred ideology. Many were outright fictions. (33)

For example, the *Acts of the Apostles* presumed to be the work of Luke but more likely an anonymous author writing about 120 CE has 1,004 verses in its 28 chapters and 274 verses are speeches, mostly by Paul but also by Peter, Stephen, James, the Jewish elder Gamaliel, one town clerk and silversmiths. In other words, 27 percent of the content of the *Acts* is manufactured speeches similar to those in histories and epic poets in the days before stenography or recorders. The result is less to portray history than to deliver a message. The message of the *Acts* is that Paul's Hellenistic interpretation is the right one for Christians, that the Jews are antagonistic to Christ's message, that the Gentiles are the real intended converts, and that the Holy Spirit, the new Christian God, will come through Christian baptism. "But they said to him we have not even heard that there is a Holy Spirit." (*Acts* 19:2)

Another literary contrivance found 98 times in the Bible is the use of dreams often used by angels for the transmission of God's messages to selected mortals. We know that dreams are the phantasmagoria of fleeting images generated while the brain is deprived of sensory experiences. Freud's theory that dreams are the mental activities of the unconscious mind has been superceded by advanced studies in the neurosciences. The dream is a form of literary genre, thought of as a kind of window into the spirit world and as a possible connection to the future, a common theme throughout ancient literature. The ancients viewed dreams as visions of other-worldly experiences, as the conveyers of messages from the future, or at least really important messages from deities. Biblical scribes, however, also warned believers to beware of false dreams where duplicitous demons might bring false messages and even false religions.

The hero or protagonist is often portrayed with superhuman powers. Paul, the hero of the *Acts* and not Peter, in Chapter 14 of *Acts* is stoned by Jews from Antioch and Iconium so thoroughly that he is dragged outside the city and left for dead but rescued by companions. "But the disciples gathered round him and he got up and re-entered the city." (*Acts* 14:19) Without hospitalization and to demonstrate his resiliency, he immediately rises as if nothing life-threatening had occurred and leaves the next day. The hero is shown to be beyond powers of ordinary recuperation, and of course blessed by the gods whose spirit he carries with him. All these are implied but decidedly epic traits.

By the 5th century BCE naturalism, a radically new approach to viewing the world, posed an alternative to myth. Centuries earlier, Homer's epics had illustrated the arbitrary and intrusive interference of jealous and capricious gods in human life where conflicts in the world came to be seen as disharmony among the multitude of the gods. Naturalism was born of Greek intellectual curiosity, a radical perspective that omitted mythical divinities from human deliberations and destinies. (34)

The first naturalist was Thales (c.625–545 BCE) who proposed the physical nature of the universe, that observation and reason should be the guiding principle of investigation. Anaximander (c.611–547), Thales' pupil, suggested that humans came from fish-like creatures and, anticipating Darwin, that humans adapted to the environment, thus offering the first detailed study of nature. Heraclitus (c.535–475 BCE) unequivocally stated that neither god nor man created the universe and that the only reality was change. Democritus (c.460–360 BCE) explained that the universe was composed of atoms underlying all matter constantly re-arranging itself so that even human actions are the movements of atoms. Herodotus studied the culture of peoples to explain conflicts between them and in the process appealed to general laws in nature, transforming his writing from epics with gods guiding behavior to the analysis of men governing their own actions. Thucydides, a general in the Peloponnesian War, made it clear that his history is "quite clear of fable" and that he seeks to provide a sincere account of historical transactions. (35) He interprets war based on the nature of mankind and not as the result of outside forces or fates. Hippocrates (c.470–400 BCE) dismissed divine intervention in the body, that diseases have their own natural causes, and so medicine should drift away from magic, spells and charms and seek remedies in nature.

But naturalism is not without problems of logical consistency. If naturalism is grounded in observation then conflicting appearances brought about by inconsistencies in sensory perceptions lead to skepticism and relativity in judgment. As a method of intellectual inquiry and rational view of the world, naturalism never penetrated Hebrew consciousness whose moral code remained rooted in mythical literature and a Babylonian version of the law.

It is repeatedly claimed that Israel's history is more than a chronicle of transactions of the Hebrew people but a history of faith. (36) But this observation is theologically biased and is no less true of Egyptians, Persians, Greeks or Romans whose piety and faith in their gods was as intense and devout. Theological commentators dismiss sensitivity to non-Judaic and non-Christian faiths. Retelling the biblical narrative as history has proved counter-productive in understanding Israel's history because the Bible is simply not an objective and reliable account of that history. It is literature posing as history, myths masquerading as chronicles of actual events.

Lords of the Scrolls: Scribes of God

No political state can survive without a committed bureaucracy dedicated to recording its activities. A coterie of knowledgeable scribes, armed with writing tables, palettes or papyrus rolls, quills and ink wells, or wedges and wet clay, is essential to transcribing court decisions, royal decrees, harvests, trade, international alliances, even architectural plans as the Egyptian *Rhind Mathematical Papyrus* (c.1,600 BCE) illustrates. Sumerian, Akkadian, Babylonian, Canaanite and Egyptian civilizations had extensive staffs of scribes that left a legacy of accomplishments. More than a dozen inscriptions have turned up in Palestine from about 1,700–1,200 BCE written in Canaanite letters, the predecessor language of Phoenician and therefore of early Hebrew. Israelites not only adopted the language of their northern neighbors but the style and substance of their literature and all its forms of proverbs, cult and love songs and laws.

Hebrew scribes had neither clay tablets nor papyrus and relied on parchment but must have journeyed to Egypt since everyone from Abraham on "went down to Egypt." The education of an Egyptian scribe occupied twelve years and led to honorific positions in the military, courts, among the bureaucracy of the priests, treasury and temple. What the Hebrew scribes saw and learned in Egypt must have widened their intellectual and literary horizons. How are you going to keep them in the hills of Canaan after they've seen Thebes? Scholars acknowledge that the sophistication of Egyptian scribes in the New Kingdom in the epoch when the Bible was composed and the variety of kinds of literature they wrote "directly influenced some of the writings of the Old Testament." (37)

Recognition as a scribe was one of the ancient world's noblest attainments. According to the Egyptians, if your birthday is between April 1-19 or November 8-17 you were born under the astrological sign of Thoth, the Ibis-headed god who provides devotees with enthusiasm, enterprise, inventiveness, and a desire to know and create. One ancient Egyptian scribe wrote: "And when my brother Na.nefer.ka.ptah went to the cemetery of Memphis, he did nothing on earth but read the writings that are in the catacombs of the kings, and the tablets of the 'House of Life,' and the inscriptions that are seen on the monuments, and he worked hard on his writings." Likewise, Shulgi, the founder of the 3rd Dynasty at Ur, one of the more renowned kings of Sumer who reigned for almost half a century, had legendary achievements in all fields: military commander, temple builder, athlete promoter of the arts, and scribe. He could be a prototype for Solomon, a wise and passionate priest-king and beloved by the gods and by his people. (38)

Biblical scribes were members of the priestly caste whereas Greek authors, though they used deities in their plays and poems, were not composing to preserve a religious institution or promote a religious message. Hence, keepers of the Greek manuscripts were able to assemble an oeuvre much more imaginative and exploratory and to leave a richer, and more subtle set of artistic nuances. Biblical scribes were technically not forgers nor were they acting in bad faith. (39) Today, we have a different awareness of plagiarism as theft of intellectual property. Writing in the context of their age scribes simply extended the literary folklore. There was no distinction between fiction and non-fiction.

Scholars agree generally that there were at least four principal scribes to the Torah, the first five books of the Hebrew Bible, identified by the initials J, E, D, and P, although Friedman lists nine different editors, including three Deuteronomy editors and a J and E editor. (40)

J = the source of the Yahweh theme, dating from c. 970–930 BCE and written in Jerusalem

E = the Elohist (the gods known as El and Ehohim) source during Israel's independence, dating from 930–720 BCE and containing Sumerian, Babylonian and Canaanite sources

D = Deuteronomy scribes

P = a priestly source with editing throughout E, J and D.

J and E were written in the 10th to the 8th century BCE, D was written in the late 7th century, and P in the 6th or 5th century BCE. J may be the work of one author, probably from the south of Palestine, and may have been a member of the royal household during the reign of Solomon in the middle of the 10th century BCE. To locate the actual text of J or E, before alteration by the later editors, would make it the most valuable book in the history of religion. Bloom believes that J was a woman scribe because of the delicacy of the stories told as if from a feminine perspective. (41) It may be that the writings of the E source represents scribes who lived in the north of Palestine, and the date presumed here is about the 8th century BCE, or after the separation of Israel from Judah.

The priestly tradition, known as P, was added centuries later and is probably the work of a priest or priests at the temple in Jerusalem after the return from the Babylonian exile, about 530 BCE. The canon that exists today does not date much earlier than 300 BCE but covers a period of over 700 years, although the actual sources of the stories cover thousands of years of literary sagas. Friedman develops his unified text from the writings of J *ex nihilo*, as if there were no literary predecessors to biblical writings and the Hebrews were the first to write creation stories, myths of lineage and divine intervention. (42) In addition to court scribes and chroniclers promoting the Yahweh royal commitment in Judah there were other schools and scribal circles likely supported by wealthy and influential patrons operating in northern Israel. Their goal was to keep alive anti-royalist tendencies and to encourage the cults of the countryside. These were the scribes favoring the rites and cult sagas of the plural deities of antiquity.

The collapse of the Northern Kingdom followed by the Babylonian exile and the wars of liberation confirmed Yahweh's status as a war god and as the preferred deity. The establishment of the Code of Deuteronomy with Yahweh as its central god concretized the Israeli state and religion. The two schools of literature, the Elohist and the Yahwehist, were blended together by P as if they had been one extended, harmonious literary conception. In effect, the P editors combined the Canaanite and Mesopotamian cultural influences in the north with the Egyptian literary traditions in the south to create Hebrew national literature. Because of edits we may never know for certain if the twin traditions of literature contained other mythical pearls that were expurgated if they could not be integrated into the Yahweh epiphany. (43)

There are ancient Jewish writings not a part of the canon. The *Book of Esther* was the last to be added to the official text, but the *Book of Judith*, an inspiring tale of feminine deception and patriotism, the *Book of Jubilees* a revision of *Genesis* by a scribe who adds new epigrammatic details and invents narrative and dialogue, and the two books of Maccabees show a tradition of writings unincorporated into the Bible, though *Judith* and *Maccabees* were included in the Christian canon. *Nehemiah* and *Ezra* are likely eyewitness narratives. The so-called Temple Scroll found in Qumran re-writes the covenant from Mount Sinai and removes Moses as the intermediary and inserts the direct voice of Yahweh on the architecture of the Temple together with new rules for behavior. It is not an exegesis of the Mosaic Law but an audacious replacement, unlike *Exodus* containing no cumbersome geography or fake historic events to create ambiguities. (44)

The Egyptian *Wisdom of Amenemope* (c.1,360 BCE) has much in common with all wisdom literature and parts of *Proverbs* parallel it. *Proverbs* and *Habakkuk* are a compilation of sayings from a variety of sources. (45)

The following chart provides a global context to the time span when figures and events in the biblical narrative supposedly dovetail with other events in neighboring cultures.

Events and Literature Contributing to the Bible

c. 2,800 BCE Sargon the Great unifies Sumerian civilization. *The Epic of Gilgamesh* inspires *Genesis* scribes

c. 2,000 BCE Hammurabi establishes Babylonian Empire and institutes code of laws forming the basis of the 10 Commandments and part of *Deuteronomy* and *Numbers*

c. 1,350 BCE the approximate time of Akhenaten's proclamation of monotheism throughout Egypt

c. 900 BCE the approximate time of Homer's *Iliad* and *Odyssey* which influenced the gospels of *Mark, Luke* and *Acts*

c. 800 BCE Tilath-Pileser III, King of Assyria, conquers Samaria, capitol of Israel; dominates Canaanite literature

c. 600 Nebuchadnezzar conquers Judah deporting Jews to Babylon ending Semitic culture

c. 500 Cyrus the Great conquers Babylon and releases Jews to homeland; legends about Cyrus (birth, childhood, knowledge, triumphal entry into city, leaders of his people) become a part of the legend about Jesus extracted from Herodotus.

c. 400 Cambyses, King of Persia and grandson of Cyrus defeats Egyptians and allows Jews under Ezra to return to Palestine.

c. 330 Alexander conquers Middle East, enters Jerusalem which falls under Greek influences and writings; stoicism, asceticism, mystery rites, Platonism and Gnosticism become embedded in Jewish and Christian theology

The Bible is the literary treasure of the Hebrew people and the nation of Israel, but possesses an amalgamation of the literature of previous civilizations, colored by changing cultural situations and historical occurrences. For example, when the Persian Cyrus came to Babylon in 539 BCE and conquered the region, the decay of the thousand-year old tradition of the religion of the Sumerians, Akkadians and Babylonians began. By the time Alexander defeated Darius in 331 BCE, the old religion dragged on imperceptibly until it vanished under the skepticism of the Greeks, attacks by the Christians and the caprices of other religions and their variations. What remains of these ancient religions, and of writings about them once irretrievably lost, is partially embedded in the Bible.

Cyrus Gordon, the renowned scholar of the ancient Near East who pointed out in the early 1960s the clear relationship between Greek, Ugaritic and Hebrew narratives, noted: "Meanwhile, I had been noting literary resemblances between Ugaritic and Greek epic...In gathering the Homeric parallels to Ugaritic literature and collating them with the biblical parallels a striking fact impressed itself upon me: there was a notable overlap that could not be accidental. The two-way parallels unmistakably linked Homer and the Bible." (46)

The narrative tradition of the Bible constitutes the evolution of a literary history that encompasses oral traditions, the invention and development of writing, the use of existing mythical but not naturalistic literature as a source of inspiration in a new context (and perhaps another language), the portrayal of the scribe as a person of learning and imagination, and the blending of intellectual ideas like mysticism into religious beliefs. The Bible is the history of civilization from the Hebrew or Jewish nationalistic perspective and an exaltation of surviving literature that defines western culture.

CHAPTER TWO
WORDS OF GOD, WORDS OF MEN

His happy state what blessings crown
To whom the mysteries of the gods are known!
By these his life he sanctifies;
And, deep imbided their chaste and cleaning lore,
Hallows his soul for converse with the skies
Enraptured ranging the wild mountains o'er. (Euripdes, The Bacchae)

How many great works of literature have been composed in prison or in exile? Exiles, desiring that their children should remember the country of their birth and inheritance, preserve their ethnic and religious memory as the words of *Psalm* 137 do. "By the streams of Babylon we sat and wept when we remembered Sion. How could we sing a song of the Lord in a foreign land? If I forget you, Jerusalem, may my right hand be forgotten! May my tongue cleave to my palate if I remember you not, if I place not Jerusalem ahead of my joy."

This sad remembrance triggered scribes not only to record their poetic emotions and desperate sense of exile but implied a sense of urgent national identity that might be permanently lost unless an account was recorded. Scholars believe that the first stories of that national and religious identity are the books of the Bible written during the Babylonian captivity (596–539 BCE) or shortly thereafter as exiles absorbed the rich Mesopotamian culture. Because exiled Hebrews spent more than two generations in Babylon, they were able to learn Mesopotamian stories and sagas that became incorporated into scripture. The biblical tradition begins, as does civilization, in the drainage of the Tigris and Euphrates rivers.

The Biblical Tradition

The word Bible derives from the Greek word for book. According to Herodotus, *biblos* is a Greek word for a plant whose dried leaves were probably used as paper. Because of its storage of these plants used for writing, the name of the Bible has been derived from the name of the city, Byblos, the ancient town on the coast of Lebanon near modern day Beirut, a thriving trade seaport in the 2nd millennium BCE.

Genesis the first book of the Bible comes from a Greek word that means beginning. The biblical account of the occupation of the land of Israel is a condensed version of a complicated and lengthy process that actually lasted for hundreds of years that the Bible represents as only lasting during the lifetime of Joshua. This literary artifice is but one example of the how the scribes pursued national imperatives under the pretext of history. (1)

A coalition of small tribes living in the hills of Judea about the middle of the Iron Age banded together to resist the incursions of the Philistines who had once invaded Egypt and were now permanently camped along the Mediterranean seacoast. Israelites were a cultural if not an ethnic offshoot of Canaanites seeking mutual defense for protection, a new country and a new god to protect them. Some of the first Hebrew documents were written after the return from exile in Babylon. We can read that "Hilkiah said to Shaphan the secretary, "I have found the Book of the Law in the temple of the Lord," indicating that some documents had not been destroyed in the destruction of Jerusalem in 586 BCE. (2)

The oldest known biblical text was discovered in 1979 in a burial chamber at Ketef Hinnon outside the old walls of Jerusalem. The textual etching was on a silver scroll thought to be an amulet necklace. The writing was not adequately translated until 2003 when computer digital imaging and fiber optic technology enhanced the old Hebrew lettering, a script that disappeared after the Babylonian destruction of Jerusalem. Later Hebrew writings used the Aramaic alphabet. The translation reads: "May the Lord bless you and keep you; may the Lord cause his face to shine upon you and be gracious to you; may the Lord lift up his countenance upon you and grant you peace." This benediction comes from *Numbers* 6:24-26 and is evidence that the Torah dates from at least the 6th to 7th centuries BCE. The Leningrad Codex is the oldest complete manuscript of the Hebrew Bible, dating from 1008–1009 CE. The Aleppo Codex is older but has been damaged and is not complete.

Reconstructing history from archaeological evidence is helpful and to do this we turn to the history of one known city Israelites occupied: Jericho. Jericho, like Aleppo in northern Syria, is known as the oldest city in the world, geological and archaeological time charts of human settlement. Looking to the southeast from Jericho in the hazy distance you can see Mount Nebo where Moses is said to have died. To the west are the arid central mountains from which streams bring water, fill cisterns, and wash alluvial and fertile soil in the plains. Four miles to the east the Jordan River flows south to the Dead Sea. Jericho was a Canaanite town from the Middle to the late Bronze Age. This ancient town reveals the strata of civilization as we know it, the stone, bronze and iron ages. (3) But Jericho is only an oasis in a desert. In the summer the land is hot and dry and drought makes the atmosphere unbearable, especially since it is below sea level at about 230 meters. Only the slow moving Jordan and spring make the location tolerable and create the palm trees and the fertile ground nearby. The spring water is evaporated before it reaches the Dead Sea or diverted into irrigation canals for local agriculture.

The domestication of plants and the beginnings of agriculture took place in Jericho. The wild grasses the habitants ate, einkorn and emmer, are the genetically engineering ancestor grains of today's wheat and barley. (4) Modern Jericho is a city of about 25,000 in a region producing tomatoes, melons, cucumbers, bananas and a variety of citrus fruits. The most prominent feature of the old city is the round stone tower standing 8 meters tall with a diameter of 8 meters, excavated by Kathleen Kenyon in 1952-58. It resides at the base of a huge pit known as Trench I, the oldest part dated by radiocarbon testing from c. 9,250 years old and the oldest Neolithic stone building in the world. (5) Like tree rings revealing its age, the walls of Jericho provide evidence, not only of human habitation, but periods of successive settlement, decline, invasion and occupation. Joshua is said to have conquered the city about 1,250 BCE, a town at the time whose importance the Bible over-estimates as it was unoccupied at that time. The break in occupation began at the end of the Late Bronze Age and continued until Iron Age II.

Circling the city carrying the Ark on six successive days, seven times on the seventh day, blaring trumpets, people shouting, Joshua writes that the walls simply fell down. The archaeological wall thought to have collapsed in an earthquake and seeming to fit Joshua's description actually belongs to the Early Bronze Age. (6) The site was followed by a camp settlement and then an un-walled village when the semi-nomadic Amorites visited. There were similar occurrences of town destructions about 1,230–1,200 BCE but these can also be attributed to the Sea Peoples, from whom the Philistines emerged, or from Egyptian forays into trading routes, or rivalries between warring tribal factions. (7) No archaeological evidence supports the biblical account in *Joshua* 6 occurring in the 13th century BCE. But Joshua and the trumpets notwithstanding, Jericho could always be easily conquered and frequently was by invaders like the Israelites from Samaria, Egyptians like Ptolemy 1 (312 BCE), and the Romans Pompey and Vespasian. Its citizens were farmers and would not want under any circumstances to wear body armor in the enervating heat.

Since the *Book of Joshua* includes the history covering the Kingdom of Judah that ended in 587 BCE, what were scribal sources in compiling a history of Jericho's conquest already seven hundred years old? The story contains a deference to the Lord who has given the land to the newcomers and who appears to direct the war with the presence of the Ark and ritual trumpet blasts in a marching festival with the spoils "going into the treasury of the Lord." The treasury of the Lord in the temple of Jerusalem, however, did not exist for another few hundred years, thus betraying the scribe's anachronism.

Jericho's account of Joshua's conquest symbolizes a transition of a nomadic into an agricultural people. I have sipped tea in Bedouin tents and know the hospitality and independence of this proud and ancient people, shepherds not farmers, constantly moving to find new grazing fields. This shift in a way of life is the real message of Joshua: changing a lifestyle is harder than merely knocking down walls because it requires people to learn new skills. What the Hebrews knocked down were the habits of the past as they began a new existence in a new country with a new God. That was cause enough for celebration.

Historical confirmation of the existence of the Hebrews, whom the Egyptians called the Habiru, comes from the Egyptians. In the Cairo Museum is the victory stele of Merenptah, 4th king of Egypt of the 19th dynasty, 13th son of the great Rameses II. It was written c.1,207 BCE and records a rare event: the defeat of Israel, the oldest non-biblical reference to that country and its people.

The princes are prostrate saying: "Shalom!"
Not one of the Nine Bows lifts his head:
Tjehenu is vanquished, Khatti at peace,
Canaan is captive with all woe.
Ashkelon is conquered, Gezer seized,
Yanoam made nonexistent;
Israel is wasted, bare of seed,
Khor is become a widow for Egypt.
All who roamed have been subdued. (8)

Archaeological evidence contravenes biblical writings and strengthens the perception that the biblical scribes were recording a fictionalized version of their national identity. The anonymous scribes of the various books of the Bible may have had ulterior motives in writing a national script that would unify the people and give them heroic status, but subsequent editors consolidated the books together to give them the semblance of a national character.

Though the earliest Hebrew artifacts were contained in the Ark of the Covenant, the collected books of the Torah, the Mishnah and the Talmud were the Hebrew equivalent of sacred statutes and icons of the polytheistic gods of other nations, the embodiment of the divine. Hebrews placed the highest value on the written word and therefore on the repeated copying of collected texts, although later unacknowledged documents like the apocrypha, non-canonical texts like the *Book of Maccabees* and *pseudepigrapha*, false doctrinal texts, complicated the agreements of what was legitimate, inspired, or acceptable for the recognized canon. Until archaeology discovered ancient writings, it was not known that the earliest writings were themselves copies of non-Hebrew texts.

The Septuagint and Vulgate

The terms Old Testament and New Testament are Christian terms, since Jews refer to the first five books of the Bible (*Genesis, Exodus, Leviticus, Numbers* and *Deuteronomy*) as the Torah or Pentateuch, or book of the five scrolls. Scholars agree that the Pentateuch only acquired its present form after many modifications from oral and written traditions over several centuries. (9)

The earliest complete biblical writing known as the Septuagint comes from 72 Jewish scholars in Alexandria who translated the Hebrew bible into Greek about 250 BCE. This was the version used by Hellenistic Jews, like Philo of Alexandria, and Greek-speaking Christians like Paul, and is still the official text in the Greek Orthodox Church. Obviously it is a work of many hands and sections were translated at different times, but it is not a faithful representation of the original. (10)

Prior to the discovery of the *Dead Sea Scrolls* in 1948, the first complete biblical text was the *Codex Vaticanus*, a manuscript discovered by the theologian Tischendorf on Mount Sinai in Egypt and now in the Vatican museum, and the *Codex Sinaiticus*, both Greek scripts from the 4th century CE now in the British Library, the latter also the oldest complete manuscript of the New Testament.

Also in the 4th century CE, Jerome (347–c.420 CE) translated the Greek Septuagint version of the Bible into Latin, known as the Vulgate edition, from the Latin, *editio vulgata*, or "edition in general circulation," and from manuscripts Jerome had access to but we do not at the present time possess. The Vulgate translation has been used ever since as the main source of Catholic and Protestant bibles. In an age when the opportunities for imitation were widespread, Jerome is known to have copied Origen and the works of Didymus the Blind. (11)

The first major translations into English were by John Wycliff (1328–1384) who proposed the use of English, rather than Latin, for the books of the Bible in England. Wycliff proclaimed that the Bible was the supreme authority, but he also argued vigorously that the Church was not necessary to obtain grace, and for this he was condemned in 1380. The Wycliff Bible is the first English translation from the Vulgate.

William Tyndale (1494–1536) translated the complete Bible from Hebrew and Greek. Tyndale's version was the first complete English translation of the Bible, although because he criticized the Church and especially Henry VIII's divorce, he ran afoul both of the clerical and civil authorities and had to spend most of his abbreviated life in exile in Germany as a Protestant before he was caught in Belgium and mercifully strangled, as was customary, before his body was burned. However, the excellence of his translation, and the beauty of the language, became the basis for the King James translation in 1611.

One modification in translation is in the concept of God. A passage in *Leviticus* will serve as an example of disjointed logic, a failure of translation or a misrepresentation. "Tell the Israelites," God says to Moses, "anyone who curses his God shall bear the penalty of his sin; whoever blasphemes the name of the Lord shall be put to death." (12) Can it really be implied that God means to say that it is a greater evil to name God in frustration than it is to curse him? Philo's explanation is that the Greek word for God, *theon*, must refer to one of the gods of the Gentiles, since the Greeks entertained the philosophical doctrine of the Nameless One. But how is it possible to curse someone without a name? It is such contextual criticism that implies that sources now lost may also have been used to supply transferred meanings from texts even in other languages than Hebrew or Greek, a context in which gods other than Yahweh were intended.

The Names of God in the Bible

The plurality of gods in *Genesis* can be explained by means of the syntax itself, the language of the J scribe. The Babylonian god was *EL*, the supreme god, a name found in all Semitic languages. The English word for God in *Genesis* is taken from the Hebrew *ELOHIM* in one place, and *HA ELOHIM* in another. The Hebrew word *ELOHIM* is itself a plural form of *EL* and means "the gods." The root meaning of *EL* in Sumerian, Akkadian and Old Babylonian is "brightness" or "shining." The Babylonian god Marduk was the god of light. There are many references to "the shining ones" in the *Egyptian Book of the Dead.* (13)

EL for God occurs elsewhere in *Genesis*, where Jacob is said to have erected a memorial pillar and named it "El, God of Israel," (14) the new name the angel had given Jacob who had just resided 20 years in upper Babylonia, and therefore it seems reasonable that he should use the name of the chief god of the Babylonians. Bethel, is a combination of "beth" and "el" or "the place of god." Eventually, the Bible borrowed a Greek word, *Adonai*, or "Lord," to represent God's name. From a crude English translation of *Adonai*, we get a misleading name of God: Jehovah.

Yahweh, (YHWH) the Hebrew God whose name is the "Unpronounceable One," the ineffable one, is often piqued and irritated by human misgivings, just like the Greek gods. The YAH part of the name, however, appears in other names, like that of Elijah. Pieces of Bronze Age Canaanite pottery bear the name Yah or Yahu, a god who became, after adoption by the Hebrews, Yahweh, a god who regretted creating Adam, allowed Saul to slay all his enemies to become king, who approved deceit when Jacob avenged himself upon Laban, who is a "man of war," according to Moses, who somehow needs the praise of people to feel honored, and who will commit or command brutalities upon whole nations in disagreement with his policies. (15) This is someone you would quickly elect to your neighborhood watch committee.

At the height of the Ugarit civilization in the 14th to 13th centuries BCE, there were at least four and possibly seven distinct languages scribes used and that were taught in the scribal schools: Canaanite, Sumerian, Babylonian, and one non-deciphered language. Among the clay tablets are Egyptian hieroglyphics, Hittite seals and Cypriot inscribed on a silver vessel. Like the origin of humanity itself, the presence of the Ras Shamra texts push back the origin of writing well beyond the 2nd millennium BCE. Apropos the relationship between Canaanite and biblical writing, scholars know that Canaanite religious poems adhere to a strict meter and exhibit parallelism, exactly the form biblical poetry assumes centuries later. Biblical scribes sought to break free from their reliance on Canaanite literature and impugned the motives, piety and contributions of these northerly neighbors to Hebrew identity.

The literary device of borrowing sagas about gods and then having later editors attempt to blend them as if they were always meant to refer to one god, Yahweh, is revealed in the texts. For example, which God is speaking in *Exodus* and in *Genesis*? "Meanwhile Moses was tending the flock of his father-in-law Jethro, the priest of Madian. Leading the flock across the desert, he came to Horeb, the mountain of God. There an angel of the Lord appeared to him in fire flaming out of a bush." (16) Note that it is an angel not God who appears in the bush. A few stanzas later it is "the God of your father, the God of Abraham, the God of Isaac, the God of Jacob" who speaks from the bush, and not the angel. Is this *ELOHIM*, the plural form of god translated as singular? The problem is not resolved when the term YAHWEH, the common translation of which is "God," is combined with the older form *ELOHIM*, which is a plural form, to become *YAHWEH ELOHIM*. (17)

"According to the Old Testament, worship of Yahweh that included the use of one or more bull calf images was the most distinctive element of the state cult in northern Israel." (18) But in the Canaanite religious tradition, the god Ilu was depicted as a bull, and his son was known as Yammu, suspiciously close etymologically to Yahweh. The bull cult in which both the king and the principal deity were symbolized by the virility of the bull, is extremely old and representations of the birth of the bull god have been found at Catal Huyuk dating from c.6,000 BCE, and continued among Canaanites where the bull god was known as Baal.

I once stood in the center of the great Temple of Baal, dating from the 19th century BCE in Palmyra (ancient Tadmor) in the desert about 150 miles east of Damascus. There is an immense courtyard, about a mile square, surrounded by remains of walls. The temple itself is in the center of this courtyard, amazingly intact except for the roof. Within the temple is the *cella*, the holy of holies, the great sacrificial altar where the rituals of the worship of Baal occurred. Nearby stands the ritual basin ("the sea of bronze") where priests performed their ablutions and where the vessels were washed. The ruins of another temple to Baal are in Baalbek in northern Lebanon. About 4,000 years ago, Baal was the chef god everywhere in the Levant.

The following quote from the Ugarit text chants about other names for the bull deity, the precursor of Yahweh.

Ilu should appoint his son as his deputy,
the Bull Ilu should appoint Yawwu as his deputy!
And the Benevolent, Ilu the good-natured answered:
'My son (shall not be called) by the name of Yawwu, O goddess,
(but Yammu shall be his name)!
So he proclaimed the name of Yammu. (19)

By the end of Iron Age images of bulls play no significant role in the specialty crafts of the age in Israel. The Egyptian Amun (from which "Amen" for concluding prayers is derived) and finally the bull cult figure had both been supplanted in favor of Yahweh. Israel and Judah both believed that other deities besides Yahweh existed but were subordinate to him and not in competition. (20)

The Bible even contains inconsistencies regarding the name of Yahweh. For example in *Genesis* 4:26 we find: "At that time men began to call upon the name of Yahweh." The name of the principle deity is ascribed to the beginning of the peopling of the earth. But in *Exodus* 3:14 we are told that God tells Moses that he is to be called Yahweh, as if we didn't already know this from *Genesis*, and further that Yahweh had not revealed his name to Abraham, Isaac or Jacob. "But my name, Yahweh, I did not make known to them." (21) Should we pretend that the writer of *Genesis* is in error and that God's revelation to Moses is the more accurate? Or should we agree that two different careless editors were referring to two different versions of the same god but writing in different eras? The name of Yahweh is central to Hebrew and Jewish belief, but the origin of how Yahweh becomes the central deity is at best confusing. There is growing scholarly belief that the name of YA is derivative of a Canaanite deity. (22)

In *Leviticus* 24:11 we read: "and the son of the Israelite woman blasphemed the Name," where the word "Name" represents the pronunciation of the ineffable Yahweh. The use of the term "Name" occurs frequently in the books of *Ezra* and *Daniel* as a substitute for Yahweh. But terms from the Ebla tablets now indicate that the word "sem," as in "sem-Yahweh," or "The name of Yahweh," occurs as a divine element much earlier in time, and not, as some claim, a later attribution among scriptural authors. For example:

The Name is to be preferred to great riches,
to silver and gold the favor of the Good One. (23)

For ancient Israelites, Yahweh was not the only god. Archaeological, textual and linguistic evidence exists depicting various other gods and figurines among domestic and household goods even during the time of Solomon. (24) The cult of Yahweh was a folk religion of ancient Israel even as late as the Assyrian period in 721 BCE. Once Israel officially rejected polytheism as a state-sponsored religion, its scribes purged the writings of references to earlier deities, though editors were compelled to maintain the same names used for multiple gods in the texts. To further demarcate their national identity, the Hebrews made ethnic and religious distinctions that sought to set them apart from others. They became ethnocentric.

Ethnocentrism: Fear of the Gentile
The geography of lands washed by the eastern Mediterranean is more constant than the categories of peoples who have lived and traversed its boundaries. Ethnic differences among such people, like the Canaanites or Phoenicians, is not as clearly demarcated as the understandings by which the Bible categorizes them. The urban or lowland in contrast to rural or highland form of life is more relevant than an ethnic distinction. (25) The idea of one people and one land, given by God's express will is one of the biggest myths about the Israelites. The *Genesis* account of the founding of what we would understand today as a nation is one of the earliest examples of the use of divine determinism in the affairs of men, a constant theme in Greek literature, in what was obviously a series of deliberate actions chosen by men bent on occupation and granted convenient authenticity by scribes creating a national identity.

By the Iron Age the hill country of Judea, until then loosely organized in small tribal hill villages, became a national state with a king and evolved into concentrated power center with a capitol city and temple. Then the monarchy and its clerics imposed religious ideas on the nation, and its ideology, amalgamated from earlier civilization's myths and legends, has ever since become a cornerstone of western civilization. (26) The editor, probably DH, for Deuteronomic History editor, added interpretive additions to sketches of history to put a spin on the theology of the temple and city of Jerusalem, on David's dynasty, and on the active role of Yahweh in the preservation of these identities. Having established a national identity through the promulgation of its orthodoxy, scribes then set about excluding those who did not follow national or ethnic prescriptions. (27)

Semite comes from Shem, the son of Noah, on the belief that he is the ancestor of all the Semitic peoples. The truth or falsity of this claim only serves to highlight that the migration, intermarriage, enslavement and absorption of peoples over centuries from and into adjoining civilizations blurs distinctions between peoples. The concept of a Chosen People presumes cultural and geographical isolation. But Jews presumably lived for hundreds of years in Egypt, were held in bondage in Assyria and Babylon, married Canaanites, wandered in deserts and repeatedly, like Abraham, Joseph and Jesus, "went down to Egypt," whether for wives, jobs or culture is never stated.

The Bible promotes ethnocentrism, the elevation of a people, and nationalism, the elevation of a nation-state. Ethnocentrism begins with the first stirrings of nationhood. Nationalism presumes social roots, social organization, modest economic growth, and literacy. But most importantly, scriptures extol, glorify, and romanticize the extended sense of family, the social roots of the Hebrews. The long list of ancestors, of who "begat" whom, and who started the whole family tree, is consequential for a foundation of nationalism.

The entry of various tribal groups, the Moabites, Amorites, Babylonian refugees, and those who have taken flight from Egypt, into a nation and its exclusivity over other nations is the dominant theme of the Bible. One of the great truths expressed in *Genesis* is that people must be loyal to their founding families and the ancestors who created the nation, who gave them the land they now inhabit (even if taken by force and deceit), and who had divine covenants based on literary antecedents to bolster such claims.

Scribes who wrote the *Book of Kings* manufactured fables of the glory and architecture of David and Solomon when in fact these were petty chieftains from rural backwaters compared to Israel's agricultural and majestic kingdom to the north, which is why the Assyrians coveted and then conquered the north. (28) The difference in the Greek version of history and the unknown biblical scribes is that Herodotus (c.480–429 BCE), though his histories contain obvious absurdities, is a reliable eyewitness when he records events or scenes. Herodotus writes about the Persians, the Greeks, the Egyptians, the Scythians, about great military heroes like Xerxes, Darius, Cyrus and Cambyses. He even describes the circumnavigation of Africa. He does not write about the Hebrews as they performed no great role in the cultural drama of the Iron Age.

Thucydides is an even more distinguished in his historical accounts and rises to dramatic stylistic heights and more precisely chronicles the personages he encounters. Thucydides is the inventor of the scientific method in history, his geography has been verified, yet he never makes moral pronouncements. Biblical scribes, by contrast, fabricate dates and events to demonstrate a religious superiority they feel over rival neighbors and make constant moral judgments, using God to add authenticity to their denunciations. Conversely, prophets like Ezekiel, influenced by the tragedians Aeschylus and Euripedes, attempted to write tragedies in a similar style with Hebrew themes.

The *Genesis* scribes cite God incessantly as the origin of this land claim and make it clear that God has commanded Hebrews to begin migrations and settlements. Early in *Genesis*, God instructs mankind to multiply. But by the time of Abraham God is selective among peoples and decides to choose a particular group over all others: God himself becomes ethnocentric and partial to the Israelites. Is this divine inconsistency? Or is it more likely a merger of differing literary traditions, one from mythology and the other from Hebrew religious, ethnic and nationalistic prerogatives?

Israel only emerged because a severe drought occurred at the end of the 13th and beginning of the 12th century BCE causing social disruptions and massive migrations, such as that of the Sea Peoples in northern Egypt and the Philistines along the coast, which hastened the economic collapse of the dominant military powers in the region, the Egyptians and Hittites. This collapse of Late Bronze Age culture also led to the fall of Assyria and Babylonia and the decline of Canaanite civilization. (29) The branch of the family tree known as the Hebrews, who were extremely isolated in the mountains and saw an uncertain future, found it opportune to mold a nation that in hindsight for them caused even greater social and religious alienation from the civilized world.

The Hebrews supplanted the previous occupants of the land, the Canaanites, militarily and with probable violence, and gradually assimilated their culture. A new civil and religious order began, and then, as is true of the re-writing of a people's past, justified the god-given claim of Abraham and all his descendants to residency in Palestine. This was the same god who brought them out of the land of Mesopotamia, with all its mythical baggage, and the land of Egypt with its cultural refinements, and who chose sides with one people against another who were migratory, tribal, unrefined, and desperately needing some justification for their presence in a country not originally theirs.

God in *Genesis* has no biography, nor does any other ancient deity. He speaks but is not spoken to, is heard but not seen, has a presence only in voice, as simply one who is ("I am who am," *Exodus* 3:14), a spirit breath that is not really breath and beyond spirit. Even his name is not to be uttered. But in one of those ironic moments when religion changes the shape of a nation's history and not history that determines a people's belief, the

Hebrews convinced themselves that the gods of the conquering armies of Tiglath-Pileser and Nebuchadnezzar were not the most powerful but that their own God, Yahweh, was miffed at the people and allowed them to be conquered because they had been unfaithful to him. Yahweh used Hebrew enemies to punish them for the malefaction of polytheism. The age of the prophets asserts this religious righteousness and explicitly extols Yahweh's power over all other gods. "You shall have no other gods before me...for I, Yahweh your God, am a jealous god, visiting the iniquity of the fathers upon the children." (*Deut*.7). About seven centuries of Israelite history (*Joshua, Judges, Samuel* I and II, *Kings* I and II) are interpreted as the failure of the people to live up to the terms of the covenant. (30)

There are at least three major traumas in the life of the Hebrew people that are historically documented. The first is the destruction of Jerusalem under Persian rule and the exile to Babylon. The second is the return by Ezra and Nehemiah to restore the temple complements of Artaxerxes and Cyrus the Great. In 538 Cyrus allowed subject Babylonian captives to return to their homelands and to develop their own cultural and religious policies. The majority, however, elected to remain in Babylon and not return to the provincial, economically and politically marginalized backwater that was Judah. The symbolic restoration of the covenant, and the installation of Yahweh as the God of the laws, is the re-building of the walls of the city and temple under Nehemiah in 445 BCE.

Though other prophets had acknowledged the existence of other gods among the Hebrews, by the time of the editor of the *Isaiah* I during the period 547–538 BCE, Yahweh is proclaimed as the sole God. A kindler, gentler conqueror would come in 331 when Alexander established his rule over Palestine with Ptolemy at Alexandria.

The third national trauma is the second destruction of the temple and Jerusalem by the Romans in 70 CE. It was not until after the fall of Jerusalem and the temple that Christianity found that it would have to co-exist with the Romans and adopt Hellenic ways, and that it would have to distance itself from the scattered Jews. Then, according to Paul, participation in the religious community would be defined by a shared social vision and not social or ethnic status. "There is no longer Jew or Greek, there is no longer slave or free, there is no longer male and female, for all of you are one in Christ Jesus." (31) At least in principle, ethnocentrism, though not adherence to orthodoxy in belief, fell from favor.

The Bible extols warriors, bloody kings, lugubrious and unhappy prophets, the consciences of a particular age who rail against inequality, moral lawlessness and apostasy. Some are rare poets whose themes are borrowed from extant literature. But biblical scribes do not extend the veneration of the written word to their predecessors as they do their own composers. The Bible does not laud mathematicians, musicians, architects, physicians, philosophers and scientists or those who advance the cause of civilization as did the authors at Ur, Thebes, Nineveh, Babylon, or Athens.

Because of the time distance it is difficult for us to imagine a cultural context in which organized and doctrinal religion did not exist, which is why it is essential to transport ourselves into an era when mythic literature and poetic expression were the principal classifications of writing. There were no separate categories of knowledge and most of the subjects we consider elementary to our cultural existence did not exist.

We have only fragments of the works of early authors and thinkers. The fragments we do possess were likely retained like post-it notes for inspiration by unknown owners and they yield little about a consistent program of thought. But because they are fragmentary does not mean they are trifling. They reveal observations and insights into the nature of reality, humans and divinities that foretell the dawn of the age of speculation. Philosophy, and asking such abstract questions, would in time become the pursuit of countless geniuses. One man's ideas stimulated another's, one challenges and disagrees with the proposals of a predecessor, another makes radical interpretations, and soon a genius arrives to synthesize all existing knowledge and elevate the disposition of the quest itself into a divine pursuit or a pursuit for the divine.

With tape recordings, videotapes, CDs and instant messaging we have access to what people say and think and can know more or less simultaneously whether it is agreeable, controversial or explosive. Without these modern devices we can only speculate from fragmentary writings what ancient writers believed and the degree of dissention their ideas generated. But even fragmentary writing remnants reveal minds that coped with the universe's most perplexing issues.

Greek literature and the Bible and gospels, for example, have parallel themes, stories and allegories that are traceable to Mesopotamian legends. There are countless affinities and similarities between Sumerian, Babylonian and Akkadian epics and Homer, just as there are between the Bible and gospels and Homer, as we shall encounter in this text. Apsu and Tiamat in the *Enuma Elish* recur in the *Iliad* as Oceanus and Tethys. Gilgamesh's voyage to find Utnapishtim is paralleled in Ulysses' voyage in *The Odyssey*. Endiku's ghost appearing to Gilgamesh is similar to the psyche of Patroklos appearing to Achilles. The female deity Ishtar becomes enraged in *The Epic of Gilgamesh* as does Aphrodite in the *Iliad*. Homer imitates the patient Ninsun in *Gilgamesh* with Penelope in *The Odyssey*. The gods are immortal in *Gilgamesh* as they are in the *Iliad*. Hera takes an oath by "heaven and earth" in the *Iliad* (15.36) as does Yahweh in *Deuteronomy* (4:26). These parallel themes, allusions and allegories may seem trivial in individual instances, but taken together they constitute a compelling argument for scribal imitation.

Had it not been for Ashurbanipal's library preserving the tablets of astronomy, medicine and science we might never have known of the ancient's world's prior intellectual treasures. Yet we know that copying and editing of literary works began at least six centuries prior to Ashurbanipal's library collection, so that 1,200 BCE is a reasonable estimate of the expansion and cultural transference of literature.

No culture exists in isolation; each adds another layer upon an artistic foundation by building on existing literary and mythical knowledge. Humans proliferate; the earth is oppressed; the gods are angry; mankind needs to be eliminated; the gods repent and allow one man to regain their trust. This theme resounds in the *Epic of Gilgamesh*, in the *Atrahasis* (c.1,800 BCE) the Akkadian epic, in the Greek story of Prometheus, and in *Genesis*. It would be unsound to dismiss these multiple thematic similarities as mere coincidences. Greeks borrowed literary themes from the Babylonians and Akkadians, and biblical scribes borrowed from Greeks, Babylonians and Akkadians. It was only when religious orthodoxy reigned, among the Greeks prior to and during the lifetime of Socrates, among Jews after Philo, or among Christians after Constantine adopted Christianity as the state religion, that those dissenting from the accepted religious persuasion became the subjects of opprobrium, exile and in some cases like Socrates, death.

By the time the Greeks layered philosophy on top of mythology, many Pre-Socratic philosophers were impelled by dissatisfaction with mythical explanations of the universe and the origin of life, or by over-powering intellectual curiosity, or both, to begin to speculate on how the natural world began and how and why it continues to exist, an intellectual pursuit still ongoing. Although Anaxagoras and Heraclitus had purely speculative ideas about cosmology and the nature of matter, men like Pythagoras in southern Italy and Empedocles in Sicily, combined ethical philosophies with mystery and religious cultic beliefs. The paucity of surviving writings from these early thinkers complicates a full appreciation of their ideas. All that remain are fragments of documents and references, many imaginative and apocryphal, where sources are suspect and often colored by questionable legends. Pythagoras, for example, wrote nothing we know of and so we have a limited understanding of his theories and practices. But his intellectual descendants commented on these theories widely giving him legendary status.

The creative spirit necessary to embark on speculative ventures about the composition of matter, the nature of stellar existences and humankind was inevitable and its evolution has marked the progress of civilizations of which we are the heirs. The fact that one or more particular views have become entrenched in our consciousness as specifically religious and not just theoretical is regrettable because the canonical designations of truths has stultified further creativity and encouraged religious interpretations of reality.

Beliefs about gods during these early Greek centuries are not based on revelatory truths but on minds projecting the presence of omniscience, claiming that someone out there must be a know-it-all. The divinity of the gods arose, not just because the inherited mythical literary traditions from the Babylonians, but because of epistemological quests for knowledge. If men could know so much there must be someone who knows not only knows what men know but how and why everything fits together.

Athens in this between the 6th and 3rd centuries BCE had numerous deities and the legislative assembly sometimes passed laws prohibiting "wrong-doing" against the gods. One of the first decrees was promoted in 432 BC by Diopeithes. The law allowed for prosecution of offenders who did not acknowledge the gods, or anyone who taught that the heavens were not their habitations. This would include most philosophers, an unpaid occupation that suddenly became more dangerous than an infantryman in war. Among those accused, Euripedes was acquitted. Anaxagoras, who wrote that the heavens were like rocks, fled to exile. Socrates fell ultimate victim. Athens about this time was on a war footing and would eventually engage Sparta for supremacy the following year after this decree, in 433. It's possible that the legislature felt that any anti-patriot movement would dampen military enthusiasm and overturn divine favors.

With Plato we have a well-rounded theology of the gods, and the rituals of necessary piety humans must show deities. By the 3rd century BCE in Athens it was commonly understood that men were the possessions if not the playthings of the gods, and that after death humans would receive divine judgment for their actions during life. Plato's dialogues of *Phaedo, Timaeus, Theaetetus* and the *Laws*, which contain a section on how religion should be treated in an ideal state, would become incorporated into Christianity. After that, mere speculative dissenters would be classified as heretics and all hell, literally in the minds of persecutors, would be available for their fate.

But let's return in the next chapter to how divinities arose in the first place.

HERMES HOLDING UP THE HEAVENS
Aided by Angel Wings and Propitious Snakes

CHAPTER THREE
MIDDLE EASTERN DIVINITIES AND PROPHETS

I will reveal to you a mystery,
I will tell you a secret of the gods.
   (Epic of Gilgamesh)

Who has not wondered, while staring on a clear night at the endless display of stars, at the mystery of stellar origins, the sources of energy, and marveled at the infinity of space and the seeming insignificance of human life? Looking backward at the rapid period of human expansion and development in the early Bronze Age about 5,000 years ago offers the same kind of mystery. The natural forces that confronted Bronze Age peoples are the same that face humanity today, the power and destructiveness of floods and earthquakes, hurricanes, thunder and lightning, the unpredictable variety and changeableness of the weather, the threat from predatory animals, the rejuvenation of vegetative growth, and, among so many other imponderables, the mystery of human life.

One can comfortably classify ancient deities into creator gods, celestial (sun, sky, moon), weather (thunder and lightning, rain and wind), terrestrial and life cycle gods. The first divinities in literature were associated with stars and planets, waters, the earth and its fruitfulness. The sustenance of life depended on natural elements, rain, water, wind, animals, all indispensable to maintaining the agricultural food supply and animal husbandry. How rains came, rivers flowed, migrations occurred, plants thrived, diseases spread were mysterious activities, and so, according to ancient peoples, they must be controlled by numinous forces which had extraordinary powers regulating life and death. Over time unseen powers became the deities and personifications of governors of rain, thunder, the sun and moon. An Akkadian cylinder seal from 2,220–2,159 BCE shows a storm god in a chariot pulled by a lion-griffin. The most common god was symbolized as light and darkness in the Zoroastrianism and, continuing this tradition in Christianity, the Nicene Creed makes reference to "God of God, light of light." (1)

Additionally, there were humans who were part divine or who had divine patrons who protected them. This is all very convenient for the anthropologist but not for the seeker of truth, for it isn't as if a questioner could simply try to interview one of the gods to see what their function is and whether its power is still applicable today. We cannot gauge the degree of belief in divinities among ancient peoples but we can extrapolate the role deities played in human activities from the narrative myths they perpetuated.

Like circulating coins, the gods traveled easily from society to society, from the Sumerian to the Akkadian, Babylonian and Assyrian to the Egyptian, Greek and eventually Hebrew, occasionally changing divine names, becoming gods of war, but keeping the myths about divine powers and symbols relatively intact. Looking back over the millennia we might think that the plethora of gods suggests that ancient peoples could not agree, not just on the names of deities, but on the incomprehensible powers of nature.

> *The one who is first and possessed of wisdom when born; the god who strove to protect the gods with strength; the one before whose force the two worlds were afraid because of the greatness of his virility: he, O people, is Indra. (The Rig Veda, c. 1,500 BCE)*

In this chapter I propose biblical narrative precedents for prophets and divinities from among the Sumerians, Babylonians, Canaanites, Pythagoras, the Phrygian orgies of Cybele, the Orphic mysteries, the Egyptian rites of Isis and Osiris, secret mysteries of the Eleusis, the Persian Zoroaster, the Greek legends of mythology and the Gnostic movement which contributed to songs, myths, and legends. Stories about gods thousands of years ago were essentially uniform. This does not mean that there weren't skeptics about the gods even among the Greeks, like Xenophanes who spurned the gods of Hesiod and Homer, and Thucydides who left them out of his histories. Sophisticated Greeks did not take Homer's gods literally but only as a way of understanding how humans must work out their personal destinies. Poseidon told Ulysses that mankind is nothing without the gods. The Zeus of Aeschylus in *Prometheus Bound* is borrowed from Hesiod's *Theogony*, but in Aeschylus's later plays Zeus has an expanded role. The Greeks had no established religion, no priesthood, no dogmas, only exposure to human frailties and the gods as symbols of unknown, invulnerable powers that appeared from nowhere to upset human ambitions.

The world's great myths have been preserved by the shamans, sages, prophets and priests who had intuitive and ineffable experiences giving them credentials for maintaining religious totems. But in mythology the residence for such experiences is usually hidden in caves: the cave of Mithras, Bethlehem, at Cumae, Delphi, the Hindu holy cave of Batu in Malaysia, at the Catholic shrine in Lourdes. Such is not the case among the Hebrews for whom Yahweh and his one temple became the centerpiece of national belief, where mythic literature became religion, and belief and sacrifice a necessity of ethnic identification. Inscribed ostraca, written in Aramaic and dating from the 4th century BCE, names temples to Yaho (Yahweh), Uzza (a north Arabian deity), and Nabu, son of the Babylonian god Marduk, indicating that the cult of Yahweh had not been fully consolidated in the minds of the people nor yet centralized at the temple in Jerusalem. (2)

If only enough animal sacrifices are made and entreaties offered perhaps the divinities will share power or at least offer relief and remedies to soften the hardships. Gods were assigned to select life problems, marriage, birth, death, crops, the weather, or against enemies. The victories of warriors like Joshua were all attributed to Yahweh. Over time, some gods assumed the power of other gods, either through struggles or perceived superiority, and in many cases couplings with other deities and mortals. They were worshipped more enthusiastically and sacrificed to with greater frequency. The main god of one religion changed names when incorporated into a new culture, acquired different attributes, then faded into obscurity over a few centuries as another god emerged. Syncretism, as I noted earlier, a term first coined by Plutarch to describe the union of cultic deities like the incorporation of the rituals of Isis from Egypt into Greek and Roman beliefs, is the merging of cultic and religious beliefs and practices. This process of blending deities and the practices associated with them occurred with regularity as cultures came into frequent contact usually through trade.

The earliest literature portrays communion between mortals and deities, and over time intimacy and coupling results. For the deities this is an assertion of power and control, and for the mortal, usually a woman, the desire to enter into divine status. Greek mythology elevated this amorous relationship to a high art form, with sons and daughters sharing mortality and divinity. The literary love relationship between deities and mortals ceased in the West after the ascension of Christianity but lingered in Hindu mythology. Krishna excelled in loving and was said to have married 16,108 wives, exceeding that of all patriarchs combined. But his chief love in the Sanskrit epic poem *Gita Govinda* dating from the 12th century CE extols his special love for Radha. We might think this a series of fairy tales until we recognize that the coupling between gods and a mortal, as described in *Luke*, is the central belief of the nature of Jesus and the underpinning of all tenets in Christianity.

Babylonian Deities

Babylonian libraries contained writings on a variety of topics not always classified by the categories we would assemble them today. Among these would be narrative poetry and epics and myths, like the *Enuma Elish*, folk poetry like hymns and prayers, so-called wisdom literature like proverbs, rituals for the king, medicine (difficult to keep distinct from magic), lexical lists and omens. Although for the purpose of this study the narrative epics and myths are paramount, we do an injustice to these ancient writings if we limit them only to narrative. The *Book of Kings* is a form of king list and chronicle literature originating in Mesopotamia. Biblical scribes even borrowed from each other as *Isaiah* 2:2-4 and *Micah* 1:3-4 are virtually identical.

There were as many ancient Babylonian and Assyrian gods as there was imagination to create them. Every village had its protector god while the heavens provided as many deities as there were stars to illuminate their presence. There were household gods, protective gods for each person (guardian angels), fertility deities and spirits for all the natural forces, thunder and lightning topping the list. (3) Evil demons lurked in dark corners and at night and could bring sickness and madness, which is why household gods and images of favored deities carried on one's person were so valued. (4) Incantations for the removal of demons constitute the greatest number of the 22,000 literary documents in the library of Ashurbanipal (c.669–633 BCE) at Nineveh. The Babylonians seemed to have invented superstition. (5) Because of the excessive number of deities, reason soon reduced their number by giving some gods lesser status through the creation of a divine hierarchy. (6) Under Hebrew consolidation, most deities would be categorized as cherubim and seraphim, thus losing their divinity but not their spiritual and angelic nature, especially as messengers of the supreme divine will. These delivery angels, like Fed Ex or UPS curriers, occur throughout the Bible and gospels which never clarify why designates appear and not the deity himself.

All religions honor a creative principle often combined, as with Shiva in Hindu mythology, with a destructive principle. Istar in Babylonian mythology is such a goddess who becomes a prototype for Isis in Egypt, Aphrodite in Greece and Venus in Rome. (7) Istar is the goddess of love and war, the two main passions. Babylonians called her "light of the world, light of heaven," and where she gazed "the dead came to life, and the sick rose and walked," descriptions that would be applied to Jesus. (8)

Inspired prophecy probably had its origin in Assyria and was linked to the cult of Ishtar, an ecstatic, mystery cult that promised its devotees eternal life. The language and symbolism would survive in cults like that of Ianna in Sumer, Asherah in Canaan, Cybele in Phrygia, and Isis in Egypt where the symbolism, a kind of language within a language, had images like a bull, a star, the sun disk, a rainbow, all of which gave pictorial imagery to the doctrines of belief. Likewise, the symbolism of a god seated on his throne, with regal and divine symbols, and attended to by courtiers, popular in Assyrian court culture by the 7th century BCE, resonates in biblical literature and occurs regularly right through to Byzantine Christianity.

Greek, Hebrew and Christian myths are Babylonian myths with new names. Depending on the version, Tammuz is Istar's younger brother, her lover or son, but he is a shepherd that is gored by a wild boar, dies and is sent to the subterranean regions (Babylonian Aralu, or Greek Hades) where Istar goes to rescue him. In Homer's *Odyssey* Ulysses is gored by a wild boar and it is by his scar that his housekeeper recognized him, just as Thomas accepts Jesus when he sees the wound in his side. In Greek myth Adonis, who symbolizes death and resurrection, is also a shepherd and is gored by a wild boar sent against by Artemis. (9) While Istar is gone the earth does not fructify nor people procreate. Persephone would perform a similar service in Greek lore. Demeter, mother of Persephone, will not allow corn to grow during her daughter's absence. With Istar's assistance, Tammuz is resurrected and is thereafter known as "The Anointed," in Greek *Christos* or Christ. (10) "And Peter answered him, You are the Christ." (11)

The story of Istar and Tammuz symbolizes a society highly dependent on the seasons and agriculture. Birth, degeneration and revival are not just religious but agricultural symbols where floods, pestilence and destructive storms provided famine to villages and economies. The decay and fructification of vegetation, the food of a community, was obviously crucial to its sustained existence. Gods of the earth, sky and water were not just pleasant literary pastimes but powerful stories of how deities must be placated so that the community might survive.

Tammuz dwells in a great world tree, possibly a cedar, whose roots extend to the underworld and whose branches reach the heavens. Adonis is associated with the myrrh tree from whose trunk he was born. Osiris was embedded in a tamarisk tree associated with his cult. Apollo chased Daphne until she was changed into a laurel tree. Attis after his death became a pine tree. Symbols for the tree of knowledge carved in stone and as metaphors in literature, like the cross or tree of Christ, are not difficult to find in pre-biblical literature. It would be surprising had they not found their way into scripture.

MESPOTAMIAN DEITIES
AS METAPHORS FOR AGRICULTURE AND FERTILITY

AN (ANU. ANUM): SKY, HEAVEN, BULL
URUS (KI): EARTH
ENLIL: STORM, FERTILITY, AIR, WIND
ENKI (EA): SOIL, EARTH
IANNA (ISHTAR): "COW OF HEAVEN," MARRIAGE
ERESHKIGAL, SISTER OF ISHTAR, GODDESS OF UNDERWORLD
MARDUK: URBAN KING GOD, BULL SYMBOL
SHAMASH: SUN GOD

Canaanite Deities: Destiny, El and Baal

Tell Arad in the Negev desert sits atop a mound on the strategic location of an east trade route, carrying bitumen from the Dead Sea, and at a southeast trade route, carrying copper for making bronze from the Sinai. It was intermittently occupied from the early Bronze Age, c.3,000–2,300 BCE and into the Iron Age. The archaeological remains today lie about 20 miles south of Hebron and encompasses about 30 acres. Biblical references to it can be found in *Numbers* 21:1, where the king of Arad is noted as a Canaanite, and in *Joshua* 12:7-14.

A fortress was erected during the Iron Age on the summit to protect Arad's south side. Inside the fortress are the remains of a temple with a sacrificial altar for holocaust offerings in the outer courtyard, even though such temples outside of Jerusalem were forbidden (*Deut.* 12). The high stone structure, the presence of an outer courtyard, the large water basin where priests washed before entering to the sanctuary or holy of holies where two large erect stones stand, the placement of basins for incense, even the sacrificial altar that was exactly 5 cubits long, are exact replicas of the Canaanite temple at Megiddo which the Bible calls Armageddon. Israelites were under the influence of Canaanite culture and religious practices and worshipped the same gods.

Two of the more significant ancient Canaanite texts dating from about the 14th century BCE are the *Legend of Kret*, which tells the story of a man just like Abraham who was promised by the gods as many children as there are stars, and the *Legend of Aqhat*, in which a hero is rewarded with a son through divine favor, and is referred to in *Ezekiel*. In Ugarit texts Baal is restrained by two goddesses from killing the insulting messengers. Achilles draws his sword to kill Agamemnon but is held back by two goddesses. Jesus restrains Peter in the garden of Gethsemane from using his sword further against those who came to arrest him.

The god Mani, translated as "Destiny" in most biblical references, and roundly condemned by Hebrew prophets, was a god worshipped at the Canaanite kingdom of Ebla in the 3rd millennium BCE. (12) But repeatedly in the *Psalms*, the prophets invoke his name. Destiny appears in *Psalms* in 61:3, 61:8, 65:4 and 74:22. Here is one passage:

From the brink of the nether world
I call to you,
as my heart grows faint.
Upon the lofty mountain
O Destiny give me rest. (*Psalm* 61:3)

Some translations, like the Roman Catholic Confraternity text (1963), understandably eliminate these various interpretations of divine names, even in footnotes, so as not to leave the impression that multiple names of divinities occur throughout the Bible, preferring to use pronouns, such as "you," "Lord" or "God" without reference to the differences in word usage. But the words *el, elohim, lohim,* or *mani* meaning "The Light," as in "the Light of the World," or the word "sem," "name" as a surrogate for the name of a divinity, refer to Canaanite and Babylonian deities. Translating them as simply "god" in the Bible is a literary deceit and artifice designed to obfuscate the original literary inheritance. God's epithets in the early books of the Bible have Canaanite antecedents. (13)

In Canaanite mythology, El and Baal exist prior to the time of the Hebrew patriarchs. El, the original father of all the Canaanite gods, is the creator of the heavens and earth in *Genesis*. The so-called "sons of El" are known as *Elohim* and stand in the assembly of gods with El. (14) Old Akkadian literature points to the earliest Semites in Mesopotamia commonly referring to IL as the chief divinity, later to become El in the Canaanite religion (15), and in Islam the AL in Allah. (The Israeli airline, EL AL, includes both terms).

We find in *Job* (38:7): "The morning stars sang together, even all the sons of Elohim shouted for joy." The morning stars, according to scholars, are the celestial sons of El, who occurs in all Semitic languages, Hebrew, Ugaritic, Phoenician and Arabic, where it becomes AL. The name probably means "strength." (16) Baal, depicted as the storm god, is the son of El, and a rival god to Yahweh by the time of the writing of *Genesis*. Baal is seen as Yahweh's greatest adversary and appears as the main god in Canaanite mythology about 1,400 BCE and by this time seems to have usurped El's divine authority. "Cappadocian cylinder seal impressions show the Storm god with his lightning and his animal attribute, the bull." (17)

What is common among these ancient creator beings and their accompanyimg cosmologies with royal as well as cosmic significance is that the divinities resemble a male and female union and a son who emerges as a challenger, most often a usurper, to the power of the father. The question is: was Yahweh another name for El, or was El identified with Yahweh for the ancient Hebrews? Was Yahweh a substitute for El? (18)

A second common denominator is that one ethnic group of tribal affiliation chooses one god, Marduk, Dagan, El, Zeus, Baal, Ptah, or a select pantheon to worship. Broad cultural contact, the Egyptians with the Hittites, or the Canaanites with the Hebrews, caused new gods to appear. Rivalry among gods ensued creating a more assimilated pantheon whose names are slightly altered to resemble older gods, or with sons who rose up to oust the old man, as Zeus did against Kronos, the creator god. The gods of one culture, like the Amorites from the upper Euphrates river valley who entered Syria about 2,000 BCE, are mingled with the gods of an adjoining or conquering culture, like the Hurrians or the Canaanites.

Household gods are another example of this ubiquitous practice. Teraphim are the earthly gods and stand opposed to the seraphim, the angelic creatures standing in the celestial presence of the sky god in Sumerian mythology. These Sumerian labels are related to the angelic sentry cherubim in *Genesis*: "After he drove the man out, he placed on the east side of the Garden of Eden cherubim and a flaming sword flashing back and forth to guard the way to the tree of life." (*Gen.* 3:23-25) The Teraphim are usually stele, small and private, that is, not to be displayed in temples, placed in a small niche in the household wall with a table of offerings in front. (19) So, for example, Rachel steals the Teraphim, the household gods of Laban. Jacob buries the strange gods under the terebinth at Shechem. Jacob then builds an altar at Shechem and calls it "El, the god of Israel." (20)

Newer gods are accorded wider powers and often associated with military strength as the tribal groups become permanently settled in a region. The older, creator god is pushed into the background by the more virile, powerful son god often described as a bull, who becomes the god of violence and bloodshed and the propagator of endless progeny, a pattern typical in Greek myths. Such gods, like Marduk from the Babylonian, or Zeus from the Greek pantheon, exhibit human tendencies towards fertile reproduction and aggression against rivals. The names of the gods and semi-divine heroes may change but the themes do not. Marduk slays the she-monster Tiamat, goddess of the sea, and Perseus flies through the air and kills Pegasus's mother, the Gorgon Medusa, she of the head full of snakes.

When the Amorites descended into the area of Syria from the middle Euphrates region about 2,000 BCE, they brought with them the united cult of Hadad, Dagan and the sun god, introducing them into the Canaanite religion. (21) Subsequently, El was displaced from his supreme divinity and Baal replaced El by the time the Hebrews entered the region about 500 years later. Baal was the supreme deity, according to the *Book of Judges* and from the Tell Amarna letters found in Akenaten's ancient capitol city in Egypt. Temples of Baal were founded at Ugarit prior to 1,900 BCE, evidence of his very early significance. (22) The cult of Baal and his consort Asherah penetrated deep into the culture of the early Hebrews and was even introduced into the temple compound of Yahweh in Jerusalem where altars were built for them.

Drought, floods, war, famine, pestilence and the plagues that visit every nation from time to time compelled people to leave ancestral communities in search of a better life. Spurred on by a more sustaining existence elsewhere, by preferred trade, or more fertile fields for their herds, nomads roamed the well-traveled trade routes with their camels, goats and sheep bringing new stories, inventions, and household gods, symbols of their beliefs. These were the gods worshipped by the people of Mecca before their conversion to Islam about the time of Mohammed as late as 600 CE. An indispensable rain god in the desert of Arabia was not needed if a clan group settled in the fertile Bekaa valley of Phoenicia and be easily replaced by a visible storm god, like the Amorites from Syria over the Phoenicians along the Mediterranean coast, more by conquest than by peaceful assimilation.

Selected Middle Eastern Divinities

We to the gods submit, whatever they are. (23)

The south of Iraq is an inhospitable and isolated stretch of sand dunes home only to uninviting desert animals and a few scattered nomadic shepherds. Yet here in the middle of the 4th millennium urban civilization originated at a city called Ur with an estimated 40,000 residents by 3,300 BCE. In this epoch and this place were born the myths of the deities that, with the transforming invention of writing, evolved into the literary prototypes biblical scribes used in *Genesis*. Like the origin of the calculation of the calendar itself, imaginative examples of the gods in creation and human life are extremely old.

According to Sumerian mythology, the primeval sea created the cosmic mountain that consists of heaven (Anu) and his wife (Ki). From their union, the god Enlil was born creating the first trinity of gods. Enlil became Ada under the Akkadians and under the Canaanites Hadad-Baal, or Baal-Hadad. He is frequently shown brandishing lightning bolts and standing on his cult animal, the bull, as portrayed on an Assyrian relief in the Louvre in Paris. In the National Museum in Damascus stands a sculpture of Baal-Hadad with the head of a bull and a dagger at his belt, with earrings dangling from his bull ears. Here, for the first time in recorded history that we know, the bull becomes a part of religious motif and remains thus through all later civilizations, symbolized today in the entertainment rituals of bull riding and bull fighting.

The endorsement of Yahweh conquering of hill villages during the time of the patriarchs is a Sumerian religious theme. With Enlil as the chief god, various subordinate gods held sway like tribal chieftains over individual cities. If a power struggle ensued between cities, then the conquest of one city over another was seen as the rightful prerogative of the local god's dominance. Since it was the duty of citizens to serve the local gods faithfully and keep them from turning wrathful and keeping the city peaceful and stable, inhabitants assumed that a conquered city had been unfaithful in their obligations and that the deity had abandoned them. This theme is echoed repeatedly in Greek tragedies, as Aphrodite says in Euripedes *Hippolytus*, first performed in 428 BCE: "But for his sins against me, I shall punish Hippolytus this day." (24) Here is a Sumerian theme adopted by Greek tragedians and used by biblical scribes for Yahweh to take his vengeance even on his chosen people.

Another divine trinity would occur in Egypt with Osiris, Isis and their son Horus. A third trinity would develop in Christianity with the Father, Son and Holy Spirit. In Hesiod, Uranos, heaven, bows over Gaea, the earth and is castrated by a sickle by Kronos, their son. Subsequently, Zeus, Hades and

Poseidon would drive their father Kronos from the throne and divide the governance of the world between them. The castration complex occurs in other myths such as Indian (the castration of the good god, Varuna), Uranos in the Greek, and Iranian divine genealogy. Partial castration, circumcision, would become a feature of Egyptian life that the Hebrews made a permanent condition for male membership, and the Jerusalem contingent of the first Christian believers after the death of Jesus (but not Paul) thought essential for baptism into the new faith.

In an attempt to render translations according to theological beliefs rather than the evidence rendered by the instances of linguistic polytheism, some translators have simply wanted to bury the multiple distinctions of divine references by translating all divine references as God or Lord. A text in *Psalms* 54:8-9 will serve as just one example. One literal translation by a Jesuit scholar goes as follows:

For your generosity I will sacrifice to you,
I will thank your Name, Yahweh, truly good,
Because from all my adversaries He (Name) rescued me,
and my eye feasted on my foes. (25)

The subject of the verb "rescued" in verse 9 (*hissilani* in Hebrew) is unclear. Is Yahweh the rescuer, or the Name, another deity? Yahweh is addressed in the second person, whereas the third person is assumed for the person who "rescued" me. Is the subject of the verb "your name," the personification of another deity? That is the apparent assumption of a translation in a Jewish text that reads:

I will acknowledge that Your Name, Lord,
is good, for it has rescued me from your foes,
and let me gaze triumphant
upon my enemies. (26)

The translation of "Your Name" here appears to achieve an independent divine existence quite apart from the divine status of "Lord." A Catholic translation is completely different and obscures the literary difficulties by assuming that "Yahweh" and "Your Name" are one and the same reference even though two separate words are used in the original text.

Freely I will offer your sacrifice;
I will praise your name, O Lord for its goodness,
Because from all distress you have rescued me,
and my eyes look down upon my enemies. (27)

Hebrews, like all other Middle Eastern peoples, were polytheistic until they adopted monotheism but did not correct earlier transcriptions of ancient texts and left plural forms of divinity intact where they remain to confound those who believe that the scribes were simply making copying errors. Like the later Hebrews, the Israelites seem unwilling to admit that Hebrews were polytheistic worshippers and only slowly and reluctantly modified their beliefs to monotheism. Believing in one God who assumed all the forces of nature governed in polytheistic belief by multiple divinities meant for the Hebrews repudiating the beliefs of ancestors who routinely accepted belief in several divinities and a chief deity. The central theme of the Pentateuch is the forceful conversion to belief in one God, the proscription of idolatry and adherence to the codes of observance given to Moses. Eventually, one God became inexorably linked with the land and people of Israel by binding covenant. Observance of this agreement by the faithful held the nation in unity, a symbiosis of a people, a nation and a religion that was also characteristic of all civilizations preceding the rise of Israel.

Hebrews broadly worshipped the same gods as the Canaanites for a large part of their history (*Judges* 18). For example, in *Deuteronomy* 32:8 we find the expression of multiple deities in the song of Moses. "When the Most High assigned the nations their heritage, when he parceled out the descendants of Adam, he set up the boundaries of the peoples after the numbers of the sons of God." Who are the "sons of God" if not the lesser deities in the pantheon of gods current among the Canaanite, Egyptian or Babylonian deities where there is one, supreme deity, the "Most High" deity? (28) Expressions in *Psalm* 82:1 refer to multiple gods: "God arises in the divine assembly; he judges in the midst of the gods." And in *Psalm* 82:6: "I said, You are gods: all of you sons of the Most High." In *Psalm* 89 there is reference to a supreme god among lesser gods: "The heavens proclaim your wonders, O Lord, and your faithfulness, in the assembly of the holy ones. For who in the skies can rank with the Lord? Who is like the Lord among the sons of God." The psalmist conveys the impression that multiple deities, "the divine assembly," "gods," "the sons of the Most High," are expressions and sentiments compiled from early sources.

> *Chorus: With various hand the gods dispense our fates;*
> *Now showering various blessings, which our hopes*
> *Dared not aspire to; now controlling ills*
> *We deemed inevitable: thus the god*
> *To these has given an end exceeding thought.*
>   Euripedes, *The Bacchae* (29)

Zoroaster (628 BCE–551 BCE)

A major Eastern influence on scripture is a religion that originated in Persia with Zoroaster about the same time as Buddhism began in northern India. The name derives from the Greek Zarathustra, or "old camel." Several of the dominant themes associated with Judaism and Christian doctrine about monotheism, light and darkness, good and evil, angels and devils, magic and the occult, rewards and punishments in the afterlife for deeds done in this life, rituals in religion, are found in Zoroastrianism. (30) Zoroastrian ideology became embedded in biblical and gospel scripture and religious practices.

Zoroaster's writings originated in Persia about 1,700–1,400 BCE according to linguistic comparisons thus making him the oldest known prophet, though some scholars believe the writings are of later origin, about 628–551 BCE. (31) He was certainly known to the ancient Greeks and Plato in the 4th century BCE. Zoroaster was likely born in Rhages (modern Rhyy), a suburb of Tehran, a country then known as that of the Medes. He lived in what today would be eastern Iran at a time when that country had not yet been unified, as it eventually was under Cyrus, a practicing Zoroastrian. (32) Cyrus' successors Darius I and Xerxes were also followers. Zoroastrianism became extremely influential as the Persian Empire extended its boundaries through conquest.

The story of how Zoroaster came to the attention of the western word is intriguing. Abraham Anquetil-Duperron (1731–1805) gave up studying for the priesthood to pursue his interest in Eastern languages and traveled to India (1755–61) where he learned Persian, Sanskrit, Zend, Avestan, and Pahlavi. Forced to return to France as a result of the British conquests in India, he took with him 180 manuscripts, which he gave to the Royal Library. His three-volume translation of the *Zend-Avesta* (1771) introduced Zoroastrian texts to Europe. He also translated the *Upanishads* into Latin (1804) and wrote several works on India. Consequently, prior to the 18th century, the western world knew nothing of Zoroaster and hence there are no commentaries on him, his works, or influence.

Zoroastrian belief, a modified form of monotheism, is based on dualism, that the world is composed of two forces, Good, symbolized by Ahura Mazda, the God of Light, and Evil, symbolized by Angra Mainyu or Ahriman, the devil, also a pure spirit, called in the texts as "The Lie." And who was Ahura Mazda? He was the creator of heaven and earth, a source of light and darkness, the supreme giver of law, the originator of the moral order, and judge of the world. Ahura Mazda is surrounded by immortal beings (angels) known as the "beneficent immortals." All good qualities are embodied and symbolized by these immortal creatures, and these virtues just happen to be the ones desired in the followers. Both gods and men are bound to observe the same ethical principles.

The universe is portrayed as a battlefield of good and evil. Ahura Mazda, the Wise Spirit, or the spirit favoring the advance of civilization and culture, struggles to overcome Ahura Mainhu, the Evil Spirit, the Demon of the Lie, Satan. Man must choose sides in this titanic struggle. The patient cultivator of the earth is a follower of Ahura Mazda, the good god. After Ahura Mazda first expels Ahura Mainhu into darkness (note the similarity with God's expulsion of the bad angels after their rebellion and opposition to him), Ahura Mazda then created the material world, the sky, water, earth, plants, the Primeval Ox and Primeval Man.

Zoroastrians believe that a savior, Saoshyant, will appear at which time the dead will rise and be judged for their reward or punishment. Zoroastrian priests were known as Magi, specialists in the rite of purification. The Magi were similar to the three kings, according to Luke, who came to visit Jesus at his birth in Bethlehem. If we examine closely the principal beliefs of this ancient religion we will find religious threads that are common to Judaism and Christianity. The most significant religious development was monotheism. Older Persian religions, like those of the Mesopotamian river valley, had been polytheistic. The followers of Zoroastrianism today are the Parsees of India. For example, we find in the Apostles' Creed the phrase, "God of God, light of light." "Light of light" implies an association of Zoroastrian belief in Ahura Mazda, the centerpiece of belief that promises immortality, the creator of the material and immaterial worlds, the source of alternating light and darkness.

Zoroastrian religious practices were in the hands of the Magi, who Herodotus describes as a tribal group with special customs such as interpreting dreams, a common symbol of scriptural revelation. The first revelation of Muhammad came to him while he was sleeping in the cave outside Mecca. The older Iranian or Persian religions, including Zoroastrianism, were suppressed with the conquest of successive kings, like Xerxes, and even more suppressed by the Greeks after the conquests of Alexander the Great. Eventually, Zoroastrian forces were conquered by Islam in 635 CE. Pockets of religious followers survived, but only as a persecuted minority throughout Persia. Many Zoroastrian believers migrated to Gujarat province in India where they are known as Parsees (Persians) where they found asylum and still reside.

Zoroaster spoke of himself as a messenger of god, a prophet, sent to destroy idolatry (animistic polytheism) and promote the blessings of civilization, which meant settled agricultural living and not nomadic raiding. There were miraculous signs at his birth, notes about his precocious wisdom since he confounded the Magi as a youth, as Luke tells us Jesus did with the elders in the temple. The good god, Ahura Mazda, gave Zoroaster a vision, of the kind we would find common in the Bible given to the prophets, in which Zoroaster was supposed to teach the truth. The central theme was the immortality and bliss in an afterlife. The principal civil and religious authorities of his day opposed him in these teachings, just as the Pharisees did the teaching of Jesus. Zoroaster was known as the "shepherd of the poor" to his followers after his death. (33)

Zoroaster retired from active life until he was about thirty years of age when he began his teaching, as did Jesus about the same time in his life. Zoroaster's teaching about his revelations were not accepted in his home country. When Jesus returned to his home town of Nazareth to preach, he was nearly stoned and had to disappear from the midst of the hometown folks to save himself. Zoroaster ascended into heaven where he is said to receive the word of life from the Deity, and has revealed to him all the secrets of the future. The major events in his life, like ascension into heaven, conform nearly identically with those of Jesus. Zoroaster claimed repeatedly that he had been sent by Ahura Mazda himself and was merely reiterating the doctrine of the god. And thus it is with Jesus and Muhammad.

The teachings of Zoroastrianism are contained in the *Avesta*, from a Persian word meaning law, and the oldest section is known as the *Gathas*, or "songs," probably written by Zoroaster himself that contain the core of the sacred canon. One hymn describes the fate of the soul after death. The good spirits, called devas, and known as the "shining ones" in the *Rig-Veda*, became *deus* in Latin among the Romans, and comes down to us linguistically as deity and divine. They describe existence, and the drama of the relationship of men to the gods, and the role of ethics in human life. Parts are also prophetic, and parts read like prayers for enlightenment, as in the following verse:

O Ahura Mazda, I ask thee concerning the present and the future,
How shall the righteous man be dealt with,
And how the wicked
At the time of Final Judgment?

The god, Ahura Mazda replies:

The righteous alone shall be saved
From destruction and eternal darkness...
But ye wicked ones, beware,
For to these ye be delivered
Because of your evil spirit.

He who serves Ahura Mazda in mind and deed,
To him shall be granted the bliss of divine fellowship
and fullness of Health,
Immortality,
Justice and Power,
And the Good Disposition. (34)

There are many parallels of the *Gathas* and verses in *Isaiah*. *Genesis*, in describing Adam and Eve's fall from grace, contains these elements of Zoroastrianism:

1) the imperative of the good god to follow the command;
2) the temptation by the Evil One, in this case symbolized by the serpent who is the direct cause of their departure from truth, and who causes them to divert from the true god's righteous path by a lie, the hallmark of Ahura Mainhu;
3) the consequence of their choice of the Evil One through banishment. These evil spirits have always tried to corrupt man's choices. Indeed, Jesus is said to have been tempted by Satan, taken to the top of the temple where he was offered all the lands he could see. He had to choose between the good and evil gods, the deceitful ones.

Zoroastrianism is evident too in the story of Cain and Abel. Abel is the righteous, the settled herdsman, the farmer. Cain is the non-righteous, the thieving nomad, banished to wander and not produce for civilization. If one reads the *Book of Job* and attempts to describe what kind of God is toying with Job, one is more inclined to think it is the god of Zoroaster, the testing god, rather than the vengeful or benevolent god so often portrayed in other Jewish or Christian scriptures. (35)

Jews in the 6th century BCE made contact with Zoroastrians during the Babylonia captivity. As a result, many Jews felt that they had compromised their Jewish beliefs with so-called heathen practices and not upheld the purity of monotheism and the Law given by Moses. This contact with another mystic religion made them conscious and critical of what they had lost and eager to identify again with the spiritual side of Judaism. Ezra and Nehemiah were leaders who clung fast to the Mosaic loyalties.

If the Magi, wise men from the East and just as clearly priests of Zoroastrianism, brought any gifts they were the gifts of Zoroastrianism itself. The story of the Magi in *Luke* symbolizes the return of the "savior," a concept developed after the death of Zoroaster. The Magi are acknowledging that this new-born child is the new savior of the Zoroastrian religion, an idea which had since been incorporated in Judaism. In fact, the chief Magi in later times was known as the shahanshah, the "king of kings," a term also ascribed to Jesus. (36)

There are several rituals associated with Zoroastrianism with parallels in the gospels and the life of Jesus. There are three kinds of purification for the initiated into the rites of the religion. First, the ablution or bath. This is baptism, and Jesus is said to have to have submitted to it even when John, known as the Baptist, demurs and is reluctant to perform the ceremony. A second rite is purification, a confession of sins, and a resolve not to sin again. The third ceremonial rite is sacrifice, and the death of Jesus for Christians is the ultimate sacrifice.

The priests of Zoroastrianism all tend the sacred fire, the centerpiece of the place where the god is worshipped. The fire itself was not the god, but the symbol of the god through which men could recognize his influence and presence. In the *Acts of the Apostles* we have this passage: "And when the days of Pentecost were drawing to a close, they were all together in one place. And suddenly there came a sound from heaven, as of a violent wind blowing, and it filled the whole house where they were sitting. And there appeared to them parted tongues as of fire, which settled upon each of them. And they were all filled with the Holy Spirit." (37) The tongue of fire is a continuation of the tradition of fire from Zoroastrianism and reveals that the presence of the god is now resident. Ahura Mazda (the Holy Spirit) had thus, in the Zoroastrian scheme of things, judged the Apostles worthy of being righteous ones.

When a believer in Zoroastrianism dies, fire is brought into the room where the corpse is in state and the fire is kept burning for three days until the corpse is moved to the Tower of Silence. It is only after the third day that the soul reaches the next world and appears before the deities to pass judgment over its actions and deeds. Jesus is said to have been in the tomb for three days before he is said to have reappeared. For Zoroastrians the Tomb of Silence was the place where the corpse was laid out on stone, as Jesus was, lest the body contaminate other life. The corpse was the source of the greatest defilement and therefore could not be buried in the earth or the water, but was most often encased in caves, or left on slabs of stone to be eaten by birds of prey. Jesus' burial in a cave and not in the earth would be in keeping with Zoroastrian beliefs.

Parallels between Zoroastrianism and the life of Jesus extend throughout the gospels. There are the unusual events surrounding the birth of the prophet, like the host of angels at the birth of Jesus in Bethlehem, and the visions of Simeon, the old man of the temple narrated in *Luke* (2:25-31), and the fact that other kings, the Magi, come to make their obeisance. There is the defeat of the demons, both Jesus' personal rebuke to the tempting Satan and in his casting out of devils. There is the assembly of men, the disciples, chosen to help carry out a judgment; the raising of the dead to life, and the personal day of judgment after death. All are Zoroastrian themes, which have become central to Christianity.

But although Zoroastrian themes run throughout Christianity, this is not necessarily true of Jewish doctrine. The Sadducees, a sect of wealthy, conservative Jews living in the time of Jesus, accepted only the Hebrew scriptures and not oral traditions. They did not believe in immortality, the resurrection of the dead, or the existence of devils or angels. Because their religious life centered on the temple, their influence declined markedly after the destruction of the temple by the Romans in 70 CE.

The Pharisees, on the other hand, who had several running verbal battles with Jesus according to gospel narrators, did believe in immortality and life after death, as did Zoroastrians. The Pharisees insisted on the strict observance of the Law as established by Moses and the Torah and without which they claimed there could be no other authority for religious customs. They also believed in a Day of Judgment after death, and in the coming of a Messiah. Their principal opposition to Jesus was in the manner of his observances, especially regarding the Sabbath, and how he seemed to place himself above the law, and to interpret it in his own way. The corollary is with Zoroaster who also stood in opposition with the leading religious figures of his day. Jesus, in his opposition with the Pharisees, thus becomes a symbol of Zoroaster and his return.

Zoroaster, the prophet through whom Ahura Mazda speaks, separates the world into those of Good Mind and the Evildoers, the enemies of God. He has a personal relationship with God as would all succeeding prophets in all monotheistic religions, who would also receive visions and dialogue from their God. The essential act of every person was to choose between good and evil. In another world, after one crosses the "Bridge of the Separator," Ahura Mazda will divide the righteous who go to heaven from the wicked with a judgment by fire who go to hell. The chosen will pass into the abode of light, the other into darkness.

The sacrament of Confirmation is the initiation of the faithful into acceptance of the Christian set of beliefs and mission. Like Jesus, Zarathustra offers his own life as an offering: "Then will Zarathustra bring his own life to the Wise one as an offering; To Righteousness, the first choice of his Good Mind, his deeds and words, Discipline and Dominion." (38)

The parallel with Jesus as the sacrificial Lamb of God, the redeemer, is not just a Jewish or Christian theme but was enunciated at least by the 6th century BCE and probably much earlier. Even the idea of the Good Shepherd is Zoroastrian: "I have no shepherd other than you: then obtain good pastures for me." (36) Examine the oft-repeated Psalm "The Lord is my shepherd" and ask where such a poetic inspiration might have arisen. One who comes as savior is not just an Old Testament theme but a concept Zoroaster promulgated hundreds of years earlier in the text Yasma 48:9.

When I shall know you have power, O Wise One, and Righteousness
Over those who threaten me with destruction,
Let the prayer of the Good Mind be rightly spoken by me!
May the future Savior know what his destiny will be! (39)

This is the first annunciation of a savior who will save the world. This savior, according to Zoroaster, holds the power of the better life:

Shall they have their fill of the rewards who have desired them?
For this man, the holy one through Righteousness,
Holds in his spirit the force which heals existence,
Beneficent unto all, as a sworn friend, O Wise One. (40)

Zoroastrianism has had a dynamic influence on the Essenes, the monastic sect living by the Dead Sea about 2,000 years ago, and passages in the *Dead Sea Scrolls* seem to be directly borrowed from Zoroastrian sources. These texts describe the spirit of truth in conflict with the spirit of error, and a battle of the sons of light against the sons of darkness, a struggle that became a part of Christian mythology in the *Book of Revelations*.

A code of ethics, regardless of how simple, does not constitute a religion. But systematized ritual emphasizing the key points in a person's life does. Zoroastrian sacraments parallel Catholic sacraments in all major life stages, in communion with the Godhead through consecrated food and in contrition and penance for sins committed.

Catholic Sacraments	**Zoroastrian Rituals**
Baptism	birth ceremony
Confirmation	puberty ceremony
Penance	penance and contrition
Holy Communion	the consecrated Haoma
Marriage	marriage ceremony
Holy Orders	
Extreme Unction	death ceremony

The Holy Communion of Zoroastrians is the Hom or Haoma, a liquid derived from the fat of the bull, Hadhayans, who has been slain by Soshyans, the hero and Savior of his people, but not a god. This consecrated liquid is the elixir of eternal life and insures bodily immortality and is performed during the raising of the dead. (41)

Zoroastrianism has become nominally extinct as a practicing religion, it has been unknown even to the scholarly community until the last couple of centuries. But its rituals and religious themes are similar to those in Judaism and Christianity and this appears to be no comparative accident. While Hebrew scribes were commandeering literary texts from ancient sources, it was equally easy to adopt existing religious practices into an emerging monotheism. (42)

The latest monotheistic belief is Sikhism, today claiming 22 million followers, a religious community founded in the Punjab of northwest India by a Hindu ascetic named Nanak (1469–1539), roughly a contemporary of Henry VIII in England. Nanak attempted to reconcile Hinduisn and Islam by promoting a realization of God through meditation and meditative religious exercises. He opposed the caste system, prescribed rituals, a priesthood and idolatry and preached a universal equality.

Like Moslems Sikhs accept only one god. In many ways Sikhs imitate the soft, meditative side of Islam, the Sufis. Like Hindus, Sikhs believe in samsara, the repetitive cycle of birth, life and death, and in karma, sum of one's deeds, and in reincarnation, or a rebirth following death. The stricter men not only wear their hair long, they never cut it. They carry a comb, a ceremonial dagger, and a metal bracelet. Their holy book is the *Guru Granth Sahib*, a collection of prayers, devotional hymns, sagacious sayings and hymns that proclaim God, provide prescriptions for exercises on meditation, and moral and ethical rules for development of the soul, spiritual salvation and unity with God. Because of Sikhism's relative newness as a world religion, and the devotional nature of its writings, it is not a topic for our inquiry. But it is instructive in this inquiry in this sense, that it is a combination of Hinduism and Islam, a blend of religions that I believe did occur between Zoroastrianism, Judaism, Greek Gnosticism and mystery religions to form Christianity. (43)

ARTEMIS, THE "DIANA OF THE EPHESIANS" IN *ACTS*
Her Statue in Ephesus Was One of the Seven Wonders of the Ancient World

CHAPTER FOUR
CREATION AND *GENESIS*

Creation, Revelation and Redemption are linked together in a theologically causal connection that gives meaning and credibility to monotheism. The concept of God, revealing himself to a select few, showing his anger, killing those who incur his wrath, is akin to Joseph in Egypt toying with his brothers who don't recognize him, just as the unrecognized Ulysses toys with the aristocratic sons who have invaded his house during his absence. (1) While Solomon collects 700 wives and 300 concubines and kills all rival claimants to the throne, God is undisturbed and promises him untold wisdom, a disturbing theme to religious purists but consistent with Zeus' approval of his chosen mortals and to a king chosen to lead the people to achieve national prominence.

Texts appearing on the walls of the tombs of Seti I, Rameses II and Rameses III at Thebes dating from the 14th to 12th centuries BCE outline the themes of the sin of mankind, the disappointment of the creator gods and mankind's deliverance from total annihilation. The idea of human rebelliousness and the punishment of the gods was a prevalent myth prior to biblical composition in the Akkadian *Atrahasis* and in Egypt.

According to *Genesis* God created the world for the benefit of mankind and when the plan went awry because of man's disobedience, the Bible ascribes this weakness to evil perpetrated by creatures also created by God. Biblical scribes tell us that the same kind of mistake occurred when God created angels, disobedient semi-deities who rebelled and were cast into hell, though some were able to wander around earth and cause mischief and lure people away from God to their unforgiving abode. This is like Erishkigal, goddess of the Babylonian underworld holding sway, or Zeus crushing the Titans.

Did God, who cannot be all-powerful if he relinquishes some control over the fate of created beings to supernatural beings, not realize that another order of creation, of corporeal beings with volition, might also, like adolescents seeking independence, choose not to do what the father wishes? How much power and free will does Satan supposedly have in the universe? The most common answers are theological, whereas the most likely reason is that biblical scribes took Zoroastrian, Babylonian and Canaanite themes on permanent loan. Before theology there was myth that became encased in biblical literature.

Plato in the *Timaeus* describes his vision of creation and links it to the astronomy of the 4th century BCE, the world of mathematical speculation, and to his theory of the Ideal in which this world of appearances as merely a copy of the Ideal world. Plato's creation theory is colored with the intellectual pursuits of his time: mathematics and astronomical concepts. (2)

As a modern example, the Hubble space telescope has opened the heavens and revealed points of light 13 billion years old. The main reactions have been awe among most who have seen these remarkable photos. Inquiry into how the world was born and how humans originated reaches beyond theology, philosophy, myth and all the academic categories. Perhaps awe and astonishment, and myth its literary narrative form, are the only poetic and justifiable responses to the universe's mysteries.

Canaanite documents from the 3rd millennium BCE yield clues about early Hebrew myths. When ancient Ebla was first discovered in 1974 in northern Syria, over 15,000 cuneiform clay tablets were found revealing a rich urban kingdom. These tablets date from about the time, 4,300 years ago, when the Amesbury Archer lived, a Bronze Age man believed to have been the leader of the community who built Stonehenge in England. To date, the Ebla find has been the largest cache of Canaanite archival material uncovered. Ebla was a bustling trade center of foodstuffs, textiles, metals and wood products. The rich documentation contains domestic and international political conditions, dynastic rulers in the past and present, military campaigns and business transactions. (3) About 20% record literary and religious traditions. The words from one of these texts, echoing the words of *Genesis* but written centuries earlier, designate a divine creator being who created heaven, earth and the light of day, and describes the origin of the cosmos.

The citizens of Ebla incorporated Sumerian and Hurrian gods into their pantheons. (4) Ebla's king, whose chief purpose appears to have been as an administrator, was elected by an oligarchy of elders and not a religious or priestly caste. Ebla was a secular state that had a religious base. It was not, as Egypt was about the same time, a dynasty whose king was the divine head of a priestly order.

There was a tradition among the Phoenicians that a superior god used lesser gods to help clean up the mess of chaos, which they called the *shotereh*, the so-called nothingness or chaos from which everything was created. Hesiod in the *Theogony* notes: "At the first Chaos came to be," thus identifying chaos as an existence prior to creation. (5) According to *Genesis*, the spirit of the god had to move over chaos in order to bring some order to it. Yet movement implies materiality. The ancients believed that matter was eternal. Nowhere in the Bible is there any reference to something being created from nothing. Order was created from chaos, a previously existing state. The world was temporal, but matter for the ancients was eternal. In the *Rig Veda* the poet envisions a time when there is no world, only a watery chaos and a cosmic breath that gives an origin of life.

There is no geology here. The Ebla text does not pretend to be a description of the nature of matter, as the Greeks might have done, or even a philosophical inquiry into how chaos existed prior to God's acting on it. We thus are reading a rather prosaic description of how the world began, since no one, not even a Creator-God, seems to have been present when chaos was created.

Enuma Elish: *The Babylonian Creation Myth*

The *Enuma Elish* is the Mesopotamian epic creation myth drawing on earlier stories from Sumer featuring the god Enlil. These stories are told on seven tablets of about 150 lines each and were probably meant to be chanted at festival times. The *Enuma Elish* was discovered in 1876 in the palace of Assurbanipal at Nineveh and dates from about 1,200 BCE. It begins with a description of chaos as a body of water.

When in the height heaven was not named,
And the earth beneath did not yet bear a name,
And the primeval Apsu, who begat them,
And chaos, Tiamut, the mother of them both
Their waters were mingled together. (6)

In this Akkadian myth a great darkness broods over the primal waters, a vast and bottomless abyss and the gods arise from the waters. Three divinities, Tiawath, Apsu and Mummu soon had quarrels with the higher gods, and what began as a domestic dispute became an all-out war in the heavens and on earth, similar to the revolt of the angels pre-figuring the battle of light and darkness. Tiamat, god of chaos, tries to destroy other gods but is defeated.

The *Enuma Elish* consists of seven tablets similar to the seven days of creation in *Genesis*. Chaos is present, a parting of the waters, quarrelling among the gods (or angels), the creation of man and the defeat of a female goddess. The Babylonian creator god finished his work in the first 6 tablets and in the last and 7th tablet he marveled at his accomplishments, sort of like resting on the 7th day. The first tablet tells of war among the gods, just like the war among the good and bad angels in paradise prior to creation of the material world in *Genesis*. The sixth tablet describes the creation of man by Marduk, patron deity of Babylon, just like God's creation of man on the sixth day of creation in *Genesis*.

In *Genesis* before the creation when the earth was described as "waste and void, the spirit of God was stirring above the waters." The symbol of water occurs even before there is a creation. Was water such a universally shared civilized experience that no one could imagine what a real world would be like without it? The Sumerians even had a god for canals. Such literature would not come from a nomadic people who were principally shepherds, like the Semites of Canaan, who lived in the highlands far from the sea and major river routes. The literary symbol of water was Sumerian in origin because the birth of literature was Sumerian.

One of God's first acts in *Genesis* is to create light. (7) Light was the single most significant symbol, according to the scribes, of the power of creation. By the time of John's gospel, light has become more symbolic. Judas leaves the upper chamber room and "it was night." The traitor of darkness leaves at night to betray the Light of the World.

Male and Female: The Birth of Humans
Whether humans emerged from creation with a divine spark while talking to their creator or grew into a multi-cellular organism from primordial pond scum will always be controversial and subject to faith or the accumulation of evidence which informs conviction. "We are dim shapes, no more, and weightless shadow," says Odysseus in Sophocles' *Ajax*. Besides the creation stories in the *Enuma Elish*, other myths comes from the *Epic of Gilgamesh*, the Greek story of Prometheus, Hesiod's *Theogony* or the creation of the gods, and possibly Plato's account in *Timaeus*. Phoroneus was said in Greek myth to be the first man, one born of divine ancestors. Reading these pre-existing accounts and then re-reading *Genesis* creates a déjà vu impression.

Biblical scholars admit that there are two creation stories, *Genesis I* and *Genesis II*. In *Genesis I* God creates in six days sequentially, and on the last day creates humans, "male and female he created them." In *Genesis II*, God creates the earth and the heavens, then creates man, then the plants and the animals, and finally woman from man, a totally different order of organic and human creation than the earlier version. Did God then create humans together, as in *Genesis I*, or separately and at different times, as in *Genesis* II? The merger of two creation myths or the carelessness of editors says as much about editing the language of creation as it is confusing about creation itself. The irony is that belief in creationism has its own biblical ambiguities about the priority of human origins. (9)

Biblical scribes are no different from any other ancient mythical collector like Hesiod who had access to multiple versions of the same story and rather than sort out the differences in *Theogony* or *Works and Days* simply preferred to combine them into one text. What was created was confusion. God on the sixth day creates man in his image and "Male and female he created them." On Tablet VI of the *Enuma Elish*, the Akkadian epic, the counsel of deities identifies Kingu as the contriver of the uprising of the Tiamat rebellion. The gods bound him and his blood vessels severed. Out of his blood they fashioned mankind. Thus, one interpretation is that the image of god is literally the blood of gods and not a spirit copy.

But we get a more detailed story of female creation, the first woman's creation, and how a woman was actually formed from the rib of Adam hundreds of years prior to the Bible. "Frame a woman for Bata, that he may not remain alive alone," writes the Egyptian scribe from *The Tale of Two Brothers* dating c.1225 BCE. "And the rib which the Lord God took from the man, he made into a woman." She is not named until *Gen.* 3:20 where she is called Eve, or the mother of all the living. Before the fall, she is simply known as Adam's "helper."

Among early Christian theologians and Gnostic followers, however, humans were created prior to creation and thus contrary to *Genesis*. Clement of Alexandria writes: "But we were before the foundation of the world, we who, because we were destined to be in Him, were begotten beforehand by God. We are the rational images formed by God's Word, or Reason, and we date from the beginning on account of our connection with Him because 'the Word was in the beginning." (10) Although this view adds the flavor of a mystical beginning, like the Mormons' view of souls inhabiting a distant planet and waiting to be born anew on earth, this Gnostic interpretation, once a popular Hellenic idea, is a disavowed Christian perception as well as a contradiction of scripture.

The fifth day witnessed the creation of the animals and living creatures, and God told them to "Be fruitful, and multiply." Barring astral catastrophes such as destroyed the dinosaurs 165 million years ago, human fecundity was a natural, not a divine, entitlement. Animal multiplication could only have come about if animals were, in the normal course of things, already male and female. The only other possible explanation is that all vegetative and animal beings were hermaphrodites, capable of reproducing themselves at will. Indeed, it is difficult to provide a complete account of the origin of any complex organism because of the extinction of intermediate forms, incompleteness in the fossil record, and imperfections in the knowledge of genetic and developmental mechanisms that produce such features. (11)

Recent evidence has concluded that the genomes of two randomly selected members of the human species, *homo sapiens sapiens*, have 99.9% nucleotide identity but only if one compares two males or two females. If one compares a female with a male, the second X chromosome is replaced by the largely dissimilar Y chromosome and the percentage is greatly reduced to about 98%, or about the same as chimpanzees. Men and women are more different than previously presumed. (12)

The "be fruitful and multiply" command has certainly been successful. Despite insurrections, wars, natural disasters, plagues and epidemics, the world's population, at 1.6 billion in 1900, 2.5 billion in 1950, had 6 billion plus in 2005 (with China having the equivalent of the earth's population a century earlier), with projections going to 8.9 billion in 2050 and 10-12 billion in 2099. (13) The surge in population growth, however, is occurring in the least developed countries of Africa, Asia and South America, even though females in these continents were giving birth to an average of three children, down from six in the 1950s. Hence, even with half the world under 27 years of age new growth will continue even if people have small families. But with 7,500 new HIV infections in sub-Saharan Africa daily, and the curse of invasions by known and unknown killer micro-organisms, populations could become stable through natural elimination. Additionally, there is evidence that gender inequities are manifested in poor reproductive and mental health outcomes, unwanted pregnancies, unsafe abortions, an increase in maternal mortality rates, sexually transmitted infections and a few psychosomatic symptoms that can also lead to a slow population growth. Simply being female can be dangerous in some parts of the world. (14)

Chapter Two of *Genesis* closes with three comments about the male/female relationship that have forever dominated our cultural thinking about how we perceive gender relationships. First, we find in 2:24 the phrase "For this reason, a man leaves his father and mother and clings to his wife, and the two become one flesh." Suddenly, in the aftermath of all the wonders of creation, and the beginnings of human consciousness upon the earth, and the un-natural order of creation which defies known physical laws, the scribe needs to make a value statement about the importance of leaving one's parents in order to get married. This can only happen if the young groom leaves his parent's tent for his own tent. This must have been a young writer and a possible newly-wed. Can't the young groom cleave to his wife while living with his parents? Or is he somehow bound to his parents as their offspring? The young woman presumably also has to leave her parents. One mustn't ask what the parents think of this. If they said no, you can't leave, we want you here to help shepherd the sheep, fetch water and help clean out the tent, and we will later in scriptures be told to "honor the Father and the Mother," will this newly married groom honor the *Genesis* prescription or the *Exodus* law given to Moses?

Second, the scribe of *Genesis* tells us "Both the man and his wife were naked, but they felt no shame." She is no longer the woman but the wife. She was only created to be a "helper," which does not necessarily imply a sexual partner, and to dispel Adam's loneliness. Let's return to the nakedness theme later, because after the Fall, they now are ashamed of what they have done. Adam's first sight of woman is an exclamation, a poetic and flowering rendition, like that of Ariel in Shakespeare's *The Tempest* when she sees a man for the first time: "What is it? A spirit?" Their love will prevail over all opposition, family, parents, even the demands of the Almighty. (15)

Like Adam prior to the Fall, the story of a semi-human, semi-divine being punished for daring to challenge the might of the Almighty is dramatized in

Aeschylus's *Prometheus Chained*. Prometheus, according to one legend, was the creator of humankind out of clay and water. Zeus is said to have mistreated humans prompting Prometheus to steal fire form the gods to give to humans. Sympathy for humans roused Zeus to punish Prometheus for his misdeeds by chaining him to a mountain peak in the Caucasus. Zeus's commands, like God's in *Genesis*, always require a prompt observance. Prometheus, a prototype for the indomitable Job, declares: "I will bear my present fate till Jove's harsh wrath relents." (16) Prometheus even hints that "some power" will arise to rescue him and subdue Zeus's strong hand.

Prometheus is the archetype hero Adam is modeled after. Both are part human and part divine. Both seek knowledge. Both disobey God's commands, but for good reasons: Prometheus to help mankind and Adam on behalf of his new helpmate. Prometheus and Adam share a comeuppance in a confrontation with the deity and both are punished, and thereafter humanity carries around feelings of guilt, misery and isolation, crucial elements of self-definition. Mythic literature is rife with the conflict between humans and the gods and none is more compelling, or as old as Prometheus.

The Garden: Trees and Knowledge

A garden presumes an agricultural existence not a wilderness, and settled agricultural communities did not arise until the Neolithic age, c.7,000 BCE. The delights of Eden are the delights of the agricultural life, not the hunting of Stone Age people, nor the frugal existence of nomads and cave-dwellers. Adam is the first biblical farmer, a more advanced human than science has recorded, and this presumes a settled not a nomadic civilization. It also reveals the cultural context of the scribe.

Shortly after his creation, Adam receives a nice piece of real estate, the first garden located in Eden, "to the east," which likely means to the east of where the writer resides. Cities excavated in the lower Indus valley in Pakistan reveal an urban civilization equal to the Sumerians, perhaps even exceeding it architecturally. At its height the Indus Valley included 400 city sites and towns. This was known as the Harappan culture, a people conquered by the Aryans and responsible for the earliest writings, the *Rig Veda*, a series of mantras and hymns. You can take a dhow down the Persian Gulf from today's Kuwait near the ancient Sumerian cities, hug the coastline of southern Iran and southern Pakistan until you reach the area of present-day Karachi in Pakistan, and then journey north up the Indus river about 250 miles until you reach the ruins of Mohenjo-Dero near the city of Sukkur. That is the land "east of Eden," the great civilization of the Indus river valley about 5,000 years ago that rivalled the great civilizations of Sumer and Mesopotamia.

Kot Diji appears to be a large pile of stone rubble from even a short distance, the remains of a civilization that dates from 3,200–2,000 BCE, pre-dating sites in the region by several hundred years. Kot Diji is as old as the Huang Ho culture in China and the earliest civilizations in Mesopotamia and Egypt. It was a city of 50,000 inhabitants at its height, and had wide streets, two-story buildings, large civic and religious structures and an elaborate sewer system. Carnelian beads manufactured there have been found in Mesopotamia.

However, the script found on clay tablets, usually accompanied with animal drawings, has not been translated and it is not clear if the language is basically Indo-European, or even Dravidian, the language group of the Indian subcontinent.

There is an ambiguous geographical reference in *Genesis* where Abraham gives "presents to his children by his concubines: and sends them "away eastward, to the land of the East, apart from Isaac." Now Isaac was then in Mesopotamia so this reference seems to refer to a land east of the Fertile Crescent, the Indus valley, and it would thus appear that there was also contact, even in early Canaan with this urban culture with an undecipherable script.

"Paradise" is a Persian word meaning "fenced orchard." The Babylonian word for plateau or steppe is *edinnu*, close enough to Eden. Eden is not God's orchard but one he provided for man, not a place of perpetual bliss but a land to be cultivated, "to till and keep it." Work is therefore an essential part of this life, not a new burden imposed because of a felony. This garden was planted by God himself. We are next given a sort of geography lesson with the names of the rivers that separate from the river that flows through the garden. We are not given the name of the river in the garden, only the branching creeks.

On a warm, moist mid-August morning I walked pensively through a 40+ acre orchard (*Al-Bustan* in Arabic) of ripening pears to absorb the sensations of a garden of fruit. A summer squall the previous night of tempestuous rain and wind had scattered pears underneath most trees and these detached fruit were now food for birds and insects, those tiny, useful organisms that can transform anything into compost thus enriching the soil for the production of more consumables. The rain made the ground soft where I trudged down the leafy corridors. These pears would be harvested in less than a month and their pulp and sweet delicacies soon displayed in the produce sections of supermarkets everywhere. But this morning they were on display for any observer of the combination of nature's bounty and mankind's cultivation, a kind of pear garden of Eden. I sensed how gratifying a farmer feels from labors while marveling at the productivity of chemical nature if its resources are properly tamed and nurtured. Something like Adam must have felt prior to his unexpected, unwanted and unlucky moral test.

That Eve and all humans are attracted to fruit is not just because of the blandishments pouring from the serpent's tongue but because of the fruit itself, its promise of sweet desire, delicious and sugary taste and, if its juices mature properly, chemically changing to alcohol, a different kind of temptation. Even if we concede that Eden's fruit was an apple, letting the juice of the apple settle for a few weeks after pressing out the pulp yields a distillation of about seven percent alcohol. (17) The cult of Bacchus and Dionysius celebrating the fruit of the grape would have cause to be envious of the fruit from the biblical garden. Indeed, if the fermented apple juice is frozen, the unfrozen residue is applejack, at 66 proof powerful enough to go beyond temptation.

An ancient Greek vase depicts the Hesperids picking forbidden fruit for Hercules, while nearby a serpent guards Hera's sacred tree in the garden.

There are all kinds of trees growing in this garden, we are told, and all of them have food growing on them, so Adam has no problem finding his sustenance. But there are also two special kinds of trees growing there: a tree of life, and a tree of knowledge. The tree of knowledge is the tree of knowledge of good and evil. We are not told much about the tree of life and what it does or what its purpose is. We know that it was a powerful symbol of fertility found throughout Middle Eastern cultures over 3,000 years ago. The British Museum has several bas-reliefs showing a winged disk, the god of the sun with wings, flying over fruit-bearing trees of life and dating from the 9th century BCE. (18)

The symbol of the Tree of Life, first mentioned in *Genesis* 2:9 is found throughout Mesopotamian literature and art and in Canaan and Israel with variations. Here are some known artifacts featuring the tree of life.

- On a seal discovered from Warka, ancient Uruk, which is the home of Gilgamesh, the hero of the first known literary epic, of Assyrian origin and dating from the 9th century BCE, the fertility goddess Ishtar sits on a throne, and behind her a tree of life flanked by two guardian winged griffins.

- In a stone-carved mural from the British Museum, the Assyrian king Ashurnasirpal (883–859 BCE) stands by a stylized tree of life, flanked by two genii or demi-gods with the sign of the cone, a fertility symbol. These genii, winged-like sphinx creatures are called *Kariban*, strikingly similar to the winged angels Cherubim, the Hebrew equivalent.

- Tree of life depictions have been found on columns in the palaces of Jerusalem, Samaria, Hazor, and Ras Shamra. An unusual mural painting from the Amorite palace of Mari on the Euphrates illustrates the investiture of the king with the tree of life motif, and four rivers issuing from one wellspring. (Four rivers are described in *Genesis* 2:10-14).

* A stele of Urammu king of Ur (2,022–2,004 BCE) commemorates the watering of the tree of life before Shamash, the sun god.

The tree of knowledge we discover later does have a special purpose. If Adam had simply cut it down in one of his perambulations, the human race would supposedly have been spared a lot of pain and suffering. But maybe he didn't have the knowledge of what tree was the tree of knowledge until someone told him. Or possibly he confused the tree of knowledge with the tree of life. (19) Perhaps Eve herself is the dark entrance to the secret garden of knowledge.

In Buddhist tradition, the Bodi Tree, under which the Gautama Buddha sat in a lotus position of meditation, is the Tree of Wisdom and Enlightenment. The original tree is a fig tree, which figures in the gospels. Adonis in Greece is associated with the myrrh tree, Osiris in Egypt with the tamarisk, and Phrygian Attis with a pine tree. (20)

Adam, having been literally planted in this garden, but without understanding its implications, only that there was a forbidden tree, and having had one of his ribs stolen and a female formed shaped from it, is now prepared for his first lesson in character development, for which he had not received any prior instruction or advice. He has always been portrayed as rather young, after all, there are no children yet, and no age is given.

At this stage of the story, God has sympathetic feelings for Adam. This will not be true later when all hell, literally, breaks loose and God is insensitive to all human feelings and becomes vengeful, sending hurricanes, volcanoes and floods. Adam could have found other ways not to feel lonely, like giving names to the plants he found as he had done for all the animals. This would have saved botanists a lot of time, and kept all students from trying to remember the Latin names of vegetative life.

Before his rib was taken, Adam got to name "all the cattle, all the birds of the air and all the beasts of the field." God brought all of these animals into the garden for Adam to name. Naming bulls and cows cattle presumes that they are already domesticated, unlike, say, wildebeests or rhinos, and with this little slip the scribe reveals that he (or she) is way ahead of the story. Perhaps the animals were lured there by God with the promise of food in the garden. It might have been simpler for God to take Adam to where the animals were, rather than for him to bring them all to Adam. But this is yet another example of how considerate God was before the incident. Adam shouldn't have had to go round up his animals to name them. That would come later after the Fall when he didn't have such a ready supply of fruit handy, and had to go in search of animal food. Noah, on the other hand, did have to round up his animals.

There is another, more disturbing puzzle. If God created all organic species prior to the Fall, why did he create those noxious, and in many cases lethal, critters like anthrax, salmonella, smallpox and other bacterial and viral infections when he knew they could kill people? If He made them after the Fall, then he didn't complete the work of creation culminating in humans. Micro-organisms are more dangerous than myths. Besides light, animals, a snake and two humans, other nasty creatures must have been created during this period.

New viruses have been appearing and threatening stricken individuals with death. The SARS epidemic (Severe Acute Respiratory Syndrome), a highly infectious disease spread by coughing and possibly originating in animals, survives for days on surfaces. The Ebola virus, transmitted through blood and body fluids, produces a high human death rate and its symptoms are not evident until the person is highly infected and dies soon thereafter. AIDS (Acquired Immune Deficiency Syndrome) is a lethal virus in almost all cases when it enters a person's body through blood or body fluids and resists treatment and vaccines because the virus mutates within the host cells. Anthrax pores are very stable and survive indefinitely in the ground. Adam could not have named them because they are invisible.

Older known viruses like influenza, also found in animals, have a high death rate when contracted and new strains mutate into stronger descendants. The flu virus destroys the lung lining so the patient usually dies of pneumonia. Smallpox, not found in animals, spreads from person to person and one in three die after catching it. If viruses did not originate at the creation they must have been created without being named and hidden in animals and humans, implanted there to emerge at undisclosed times in order to assassinate the hosted victims. The Greeks sensibly did not overlook these organisms and mythologized them when Pandora opened the box releasing noxious insects.

The Serpent and the Maiden

Serpent and serpent images have a very old history. There are several examples pre-dating the biblical account in *Genesis*. A strange goddess appears to represent mysterious forces in nature dating from the 17th century BCE from Knossos. The representation shows a bare-breasted female with an owl atop her headdress holding in extended arms two different kinds of snakes, symbols associated with magic. (21) About 3,700 years ago women and snakes, like Medusa's hair, were associated with magical powers. Also.

- The fourth king in the Archaic period of Egypt (c.3050–2813 BCE), named Djet, had his tomb at Abydos built with two stele framed with two of his titular names, one was "serpent" (*djet*) topped with the falcon of Horus, as he was the reincarnation of the son of god.
- King Djoser (2654-2635 BCE) built the first pyramid, the Step Pyramid in Saqqara. On a paneled wall of a chapel next to the South Tomb I saw a cornice decorated with a frieze of cobras, the first time these creatures appear in stone.
- A shipwrecked sailor, in the Egyptian tale of the same name that dates from 2,134–1,785 BCE, speaks extensively with a talking serpent.
- The Uraeus is the divine cobra snake linked to Buto the goddess from Lower Egypt and appears on the white crown of the pharaoh.
- Apollo slays the huge female serpent, Pytho, names his new shrine Delphi and his new priestess Pythia.
- The Gorgon Medusa had snakes in her hair, a symbol of the sovereign snake goddess and the female mysteries, thought to represent immortality as it shed its skin annually. Anyone who looked at her met death. Perseus had to kill her by holding a shield so that she saw her own image and thus perished.
- Serpents in Egyptian mythology were protectors of the gods. The serpent in *Genesis* is protective of the secret knowledge God seeks to retain, less a representation of temptation and more of a symbol of secret understandings gods don't want revealed.

Like the serpent in the ancient Egyptian tale, the serpent in *Genesis* talks. Adam had named the beasts of the field, but it is nowhere noted that he gave them the power of speech. Herodotus writes a story about Hercules who in his travels searching for his mares wandered into a cave and "discovered a female of most unnatural appearance, resembling a woman as far as the thighs, but whose lower parts were like a serpent." (22) Serpents appear extensively in the literature of the ancient world, like Pytho in the Apollo story and Medusa. The biological linkage of woman and serpent implies cunning, possibly deceit as it does in *Genesis*, and possibly fertility as it does in Chinese mythology.

The Zoroastrian text known as the *Bundahishn* means "Creation," and is one of the great Pahlavi texts probably compiled in the 8th to 9th centuries BCE. The *Bundahishn* describes the struggle between the God of Light and Goodness (Ohrmazd) and the God of the Void and Darkness (Ahiriman).

And when these two spirits came together,
In the beginning they established life and non-life,
And that at the last the worst existence should be for the wicked,
But for the Righteous one the Best Mind. (Zoroaster, The Hymns) (23)

Placing of the serpent in the garden squares with the biblical scribe's understanding of Zoroastrian cosmology and the existence of an evil power in the world. Otherwise, it is impossible to reconcile how amid God's creation there appears from nowhere an evil power in the form of a serpent, something God apparently did not create, nor did Adam get a chance to name. In the *Bundahishn*, "The appearance of the body of the Destructive Spirit was in the form of a frog." But then shortly thereafter the Destructive Spirit, Ahiriman, "leapt forth in the form of a serpent and trampled on as much of the sky as was beneath the earth and tore it." (24)

The serpent's power of speech is the perceptible part of its cunning, because the serpent has some knowledge of good and evil that Adam and the helper woman do not have, a theme with a long mythic history. The serpent knows more about the important things in Eden than its principal gardeners do. How it came to have this knowledge, why it has this knowledge, and why it was allowed or chosen to communicate it to humans is again unknown. What we mustn't forget is that the serpent wasn't such a cunning smarty pants after all because he also experienced a fall of sorts for all his deceitful ways. The serpent got to be "cursed among all animals," and this state must have pleased the other beasts since God had decided for them all who was to be last in the pecking order of no-good animals. God made the serpent crawl around on his belly "all the days of your life." This makes one wonder how the serpent got around before his fall. Slithering seems to be the only way serpents are to travel, and it is hard to imagine any other form of transportation for them. The serpent, one long alimentary canal, didn't have a helper like Adam did.

What we do know is that the serpent coiled on the brow of every Egyptian ruler, a female cobra-, as it was the symbol of supreme royal power in ancient Egypt, found ubiquitously on wall paintings. Only after the rule of Akhenaten, who suppressed all polytheistic religious cults and founded monotheism, was the serpent symbol interrupted. (25) *The Testament of Truth*, a Gnostic document found in the Nag Hammadi discoveries in Egypt and dating from 50–100 CE, tells the story of the Garden of Eden from the viewpoint of the serpent, a principle of divine wisdom and not an evil symbol. These Ophites believed that the serpent was the glyph of the Divine Mind and Will and found satisfaction in the serpent-rod of Moses and his uplifting of the brazen serpent in the desert. Ophites borrowed from the Greek mysteries the caduceus, the rod of Mercury, and believed that the serpent who tried to give Adam and Eve the secret of knowledge was the true divinity.

An incantation exists in the Ugarit texts, found in the private library of a priest, and appears to be addressed to various deities who can neutralize the power of a snake's venom. The repetitive phrase is:

A poisonous snake has bitten,
a serpent which has sloughed its skin!
Is there someone to charm for its destructive venom?
Is there someone to expel its poison? (26)

Myths involving the serpent date from roughly the second part of the Stone Age or about 7,500 BCE. The serpents in these stories illustrate the symbolism of fertility, planting, and even eternal life. (27)

Inside the Forbidden City in Beijing, the residence of Chinese emperors, one can still view two flanking tortoises outside the entrance, the Chinese representation of harmony and balance, ying and yang. You can also see a serpent or snake climbing on the tortoise shell from the tortoise's feet. For the Chinese, the tortoise is a symbol of longevity and the serpent a symbol of luck and good fortune. Similarly, outside the imperial residence of the Dowager Queen, Ci Xi (the grandmother of Pu Li, the last Chinese emperor) at the Summer Palace in Beijing, stand two flanking deer. The symbol of the proud animal kingdom, the stag, and yet also a benign food source, is holding in its mouth the serpent snake, symbol of good luck. These serpent figures are a reminder of China's Buddhist past, for the serpent king, Mucalinda, in Buddhist tradition is a kindly protector. The Buddha, often portrayed seated on the coils of a serpent, represents an acceptance of nature and its laws, but also a triumph of mankind over nature. (28)

The symbol of serpent fertility lingered long in the West as well. A fresco painting beside a stove in the home of Julius Polibus in Pompeii depicts how the household gods were worshipped as guardians of the house and family. (29) At the bottom of the painting, below the level of the painted floor, is the snake known as the *agathodemon* who protects the hearth and provides fertility. It has wrapped itself around the round altar while the man, woman and children offer incense.

Hermes, the Greek god, has always represented an Olympian messenger of the gods guiding souls to the underworld and who has the power to be the generator of new souls and new life. Hermes' staff is a caduceus, two entwined serpents around the staff, the medical and pharmaceutical symbol for health and long life. The insignia of a serpent, entwined around a naked staff that represents the life-giving goddess, is a multiple symbol for life: the generative life of nature, the mysterious life force of the woman, and the physician who protects human life.

Serpent worship still persists in parts of rural India. When the Hindu god Vishnu sleeps, he reclines on a kind of cosmic serpent called Anata. (30) According to one story, after Siddhartha, the Gautama Buddha, had finished a meal the villagers had brought him, he placed the empty rice bowl in the river where it floated upstream to the serpent king, which, according to Buddhist mythology is the personification of nature's knowledge and wisdom. At the death of Gilgamesh, attendants weighed out the offerings and one was "bread of Ningizzida the god of the serpent, the Lord of the Tree of Life." (31)

Everyone assumes Eve ate an apple. But *Genesis* is quite un-specific in this regard, and we have always under-estimated the influence of literature, especially poetry, on the re-telling of this story. *Genesis* only says that they ate a "fruit." But Milton, in his epic poem *Paradise Lost* quite emphatically tells us it was an apple. But what magical things must have been in that fruit? After eating the fruit their eyes were opened and they realized they were naked. We were forewarned at the end of *Gen.* 2 that they were naked but felt no shame. Now they know they are naked, and this is a new revelation, because for the rest of history clothes will be needed, which pleased future tailors. Adam and the woman immediately invent sewing, for which they have not been given adequate credit.

Gods and goddesses clothing their protégés or offspring is not new. In *The Epic of Gilgamesh*, Ninsun, the goddess mother of Gilgamesh clothes him: "She divided her clothing in two and with one half she clothed him and with the other herself." (32) One of the nice little acts God did when he was finishing giving all the curses on everyone was to go into the tailoring business himself. "The Lord God made garments of skin for Adam and his wife and clothed them." (33) The skin garments must have come from some animal that would have had to have been sacrificed for this momentous occasion, and the clothes certainly would have been more fashionable.

Adam may have been confused at this point anyway, in spite of his eating of the forbidden fruit, having had a rib taken, and he may have been unsure about what was to happen to other parts of his anatomy. He says something stupid in response to God's questioning, like he was afraid because he was naked. This was questionable thinking because there wasn't anyone else around to make fun of his nakedness, unless Eve was laughing. Not to be outdone by this foolish line of reasoning, God tested Adam by asking him who told him he was naked, as if Adam couldn't tell by himself. Adam sensibly didn't respond to this inquiry because God didn't let him answer. Instead, God began his series of curses, first on the serpent, who couldn't have been that far away, especially since we don't know until after the serpent curse of slithering how he moved or how fast.

The standard religious conclusion to this synopsis of garden events is that it is highly important to obey God's instructions, even if you are unsure about what it all means and why it is necessary to go against nature when observing these prohibitions. (34) But there are other conclusions to be drawn as well. One is that not all fruit is good for you, even if it looks good, and this is especially true of smelly durian. Another conclusion is that you never know who might be lying to you, or telling you what they think is the truth. This is especially true when considering entering the stock market. And lastly, when in a luscious garden that looks too good to be true, never go near the tree in the middle of the garden, no matter what it is called.

The result of the transgression is like a court drama: the presence of the offenders, a confrontation of what they had done, a confession of guilt, and a sentencing. "O Adam, what have you done," cries the prophet Esdras, "for though it was you who sinned, the fall was not yours alone, but ours also who are your descendants." (35) God's reaction to his disobedient creations sounds like those of a militant god, specifically like Ashur, the war god without gentle qualities after whom Assyria was named. "Sing, O goddess, the anger of Achilles," writes Homer in the opening line of *The Iliad*. How the vengeful, angry, petty god of *Genesis* becomes the God of love in later scriptures is unfathomable unless we subscribe to the borrowed myths of former gods.

The little sarcastic remarks that God makes in his parting salute to the first humans prior to their expulsion from the garden of Eden is unworthy of comment here, but everyone has right to get testy from time to time when things are tough. It's unclear whether it and the tree of knowledge are one and the same tree; perhaps the scribe didn't know either. Anyway, the tree of life gets several Cherubim guards with flaming swords. Adam and Eve are ejected from the garden and join the ranks of the unemployed. But at least they have some new clothes. Why these angelic guards were assigned to protect the entrances of the garden after Adam and Eve were evicted is very unclear. Who was around to try to enter? Maybe if the guards had been there to begin with, Adam might have had a clue that God was serious about keeping him from that particular tree. He might never have discovered he was naked, and clothes would never have been invented.

Cherubim are cited 63 times in the Bible as guards, golden and carved wooden idols and images for tabernacles, with wings spread enthroned between the Ark of the Covenant, and even as a flying mount for God. (36) The use of winged creatures, angels of various dimensions and hierarchies, is frequent in ancient literature. For example, Garuda is the king of birds, with a body half man and half eagle, an ancient Indian mythological creature thought to be a devourer of serpents, often shown flying across the sky with the supreme god Vishnu and his wife Lakshmi on his back. God rides on the back of a cherub in *Psalm* 18. The sun, because it was perceived to fly across the sky daily, appears with wings in numerous stele and carvings throughout the Near East and Egypt. The head of Christ was sometimes carved in the center of a winged sun disk, though how and why the ancient motif after a thousand years should appear suddenly in the Byzantine era is unknown. (37) In Zoroastrian belief, the god of light Ahura Mazda is attended by archangels and angels, and the god of darkness Anra Mainyu by arch-demons and demons.

Parallels Between Gilgamesh and Genesis

The Epic of Gilgamesh predates Homer by about 1,500 years making it the oldest literature from any civilization. There are a minimum of twelve similarities between it and the *Genesis* story of creation. Gilgamesh actually reigned in Uruk about 4,500 years ago and archaeology has provided inscribed cuneiform tablets in several languages of legendary tales that grew up around the possible exploits of this king. The earliest were found in the library of Ashurbanipal who ruled ancient Babylon in the middle of the 7th century BCE, and are in the Akkadian language. The tradition of the epic dates back another 2,000 years. Copies of fragments found in Palestine date from about 1,200 BCE. Since his mother was a goddess, Gilgamesh is described as one-third man and two-thirds god, a common characteristic of mythical heroes. A poem in twelve songs or cantos, the epic is a universe filled with gods and mortals and has not enjoyed wide popularity because it has only been uncovered in the early 20th century.

There is no escape from the decrees of the gods in the Gilgamesh epic. When the gods created humans they gave them death and kept immortal life to themselves. Ishtar, the goddess of love in the epic, (woman in Hebrew is *ishhah*) descends to the realm of the dead, and this story, similar to the descent of the fallen angels into hell, is also found in both Sumerian and Babylonian literature. Gilgamesh searched for immortality, even then acknowledged as a fruitless quest.

The second similarity is the creation of a god-like creature or creatures with extra-human characteristics in the heroic tradition of men whose abilities exceed that of mere mortals. (38) Enkidu was created by the god Aruru, the goddess of creation, when another god Anu intercedes for the goddess to create an equal to Gilgamesh. "You made him, O Aruru, now create his equal; let it be as like him as his own reflection, his second self...So the goddess conceived an image in her mind...She dipped her hands in water and pinched off clay...and noble Enkidu was created." (39) Enkidu and Adam were created similarly and biblical scribes unblushingly borrowed whole cloth from this epic.

A third similarity is the creation in both stories of a helper or helpmate who will ease the burden of loneliness.

God says in *Genesis*: "Dust you are and unto dust you shall return." But nowhere in the previous passages has Adam been referred to as dust. God makes him dust because of his disobedience, but he was not originally created from dust as Endiku was, even though his name means dust. On the contrary, he was made in the image and likeness of God. Even in word roots there is a progression of meaning from the earth to humanity. *Adamha* is the Hebrew word for earth as Adam is for man. The Latin equivalent is *humus* from which are derived the English words human and humility. The meaning of humankind's existence has been entrenched in a metaphor composed by scripture. It is a huge leap from dust to DNA.

Genesis scribes imitate the myth of Enkidu, a god-like person, who was formed of clay. How is it that a person originally created to be god-like, like Adam, can return to a dust-like condition that he never had, unless the author is consciously or unconsciously borrowing Enkidu's creation molded from clay? Hence, a fourth similarity is that dust or clay becomes the substance from which the gods derive a higher form of life. Dust and earth symbolizes the loss of a divine origin and a return to something less, more primitive than even a biological beginning. In the *Book of Job*, Eliu says to Job: "Behold I, like yourself, have been taken from the same clay by God." (40)

The relationship with the animals is a fifth similarity. Enkidu has dominion over the wild beasts of the forests."God said...let them have dominion over...all the wild animals and every creature that crawls on the earth." (41) But Enkidu loses his dominion over the animals and beasts when he succumbs to a woman's power, a harlot who has been brought from Uruk to tame the wild beast in him. Similarly, in *Genesis*, Adam and Eve lose their power and the serpent is cursed among all the animals, created without any special powers except cunning. (42)

The description of the garden is the sixth similarity and the description of precious metals (gold) and stones is the seventh.

After the death of his friend, Enkidu, Gilgamesh goes off in search of the answer to everlasting life. When he arrives on the other side of the long darkness, he encounters "the garden of the gods." But the description then turns to the precious metals and stones: "And the gold of that land is good; bdellium and onyx are there." (43) Bdellium is a gum resin from trees. Why this sudden description of precious stones? In Gilgamesh: "There was a garden of the gods: all round him stood bushes bearing gems...fruit of carnelian with the vine hanging from it, beautiful to look at; lapis lazuli leaves hung thick with fruit, sweet to see...rare stones, agate, and pearls from out the sea." (44) This is a rich man's garden. And in *Genesis* we read: "The Lord God made to grow out of the ground all kinds of trees pleasant to the sight and good for food, the tree of life also in the garden." (45)

In Gilgamesh the serpent is the sign of the entry into death. The "serpent prow of the boat" adorns Gilgamesh's boat through the long darkness in search of an answer to everlasting life. On his return journey, Gilgamesh finds a "marvelous plant," which he believes by eating will give him back the strength of his youth. But when Gilgamesh sees a well of cool water and begins to bathe, a serpent appears, and seeing the beauty of the plant and its flower, steals it away from Gilgamesh. He has lost the plant forever.

The serpent is the thief of the fruit of everlasting life, in both the Gilgamesh epic myth and *Genesis*. The serpent parallel in both *Genesis* and Gilgamesh, as the symbol of the loss of everlasting life and of death, is the eighth similarity. Utnapishtim said to Gilgamesh, "I will reveal to you a mystery, I will tell you a secret of the gods." (46) Utnapishtim's name is translated as "He Who Saw Life." He is supposed to live where the sun rises, and is a survivor of the great deluge. The gods have a secret, and humans are not supposed to know what it is. Does the serpent in *Genesis* really know the secret, or does the serpent know that the gods will never part with their secret? Utnapishtim knows, and wants to reveal it to Gilgamesh, but never does. The secret of life is the ninth similarity. (47)

When the gods are enraged, they can be cross with their curses. Enlil says in the epic: "Why did you do this thing? From henceforth may the fire be on your faces, may it eat the bread that you eat, may it drink where you drink." God says to Adam: "Cursed be the ground because of you; in toil shall you eat of it all the days of your life." (48) The gods cursing man is the 10th similarity. "The life of man entire is misery," writes Euripedes in *Hippolytus*, "he finds no resting place, no haven from calamity."

After the disobedience of Adam and Eve, the gate to the garden is closed with a flaming sword. In Gilgamesh, the goddess Siduri sits at the edge of the garden, and when Gilgamesh approaches says: "Surely this is some felon, where is he going now? And she barred her gate against him with the crossbar and shot home the bolt." (49) The gate, and the barring of an entrance way with fire by a supernatural being, is the 11th parallel.

The story of Cain and Abel is a reflection of the brotherhood of Gilgamesh and Enkidu. Gilgamesh was a hero of the urban life, a king of Uruk. Enkidu is a rough, rural person who lives among animals. They test their strength when both fight, and although Gilgamesh wins, they accept each other as brothers. This is the 12th similarity if one accepts the Cain and Abel brotherhood.

Both epic stories re-create the analogy of the loss of innocence, the finding of a partner to live a fulfilling life, and the search for everlasting life. Gilgamesh goes literally to the ends of the earth to find an answer but is disappointed because the gods will not reveal their secret. In *Genesis*, man disobeys, and thus loses the ability to re-gain the semi-divine status and reaps death for this one act.

Gilgamesh goes out in search of a cure for death when his helpmate, Enkidu, dies in a long death-bed scene, seeking the plant of everlasting life. The consequences of death for Adam and Eve do not result from their biological condition, but from an act contrary to God. The goddess Siduri says to Gilgamesh: "When the gods created man they allotted to him death, but life they retained for their own keeping." (50) Mesopotamians were not afraid to oppose the gods, but the gods often retaliated, determining what happened to mankind who were never masters of their own destinies. All creation stories somehow seem fantastical but that is because creation itself is one of the deepest biological and human mysteries and those who spin the tales of how it first occurred make it appear as naturally unbelievable as possible. (51)

Here is the account written by the scribes of the *Epic of Atrahasis* c.1,700 BCE.

Nintu shall mix clay
With his flesh and his blood.
Then a god and a man
Will be mixed together in clay.
Let us hear the drumbeat forever after,
Let a ghost come into existence from the god's flesh,
Let her proclaim it as his living sign,
And let the ghost exist so as not to forget (the slain god). (52)

Here hundreds of years prior to *Genesis* we have the myth of a god mixing his own flesh and blood with clay to make a man and breathing a spirit into it to give it life. One of the gods in this epic is named Adad, close enough to Adam.

A Mesopotamian cylinder seal was once thought to be related to the temptation of Eve in the garden because it depicts two fully clothed, seated figures facing what appears to be a date tree. Behind each is an elongated serpent. The male figure has the headdress of a divinity and female appears to be a female worshipper. This seal dates from the 23rd century BCE, a minimum of 1,500 years prior to *Genesis*. (53)

Genesis is imitated literature from at least three mythical traditions, the Sumerian, Mesopotamian and Greek. *Genesis* conveys the caprice and conniving God imposes on humankind. It is the opposite of Greek justice (*dike*) that portrays the randomness of the fortunes of destiny and the irrational actions of humans. In this portraiture the less poetic and imaginative scribes of the Bible are in the tradition of Hesiod and Homer whose gods, the human projections of arbitrariness in life, squabble among themselves and routinely and outrageously visit their slings and arrows on less fortunate humans. From the viewpoint of the gods, as Puck says in *A Midsummer Night's Dream* (Act III. Scene II), "Lord, what fools these mortals be," humans are the play toys of the divinities. From a human perspective and among ancient peoples, gods, granted the passions of humans but with extraordinary powers, were the poetic explanations of unanswerable issues. (54)

CHAPTER FIVE
CAIN AND ABEL

This is a tale of five sets of brothers, Cain and Abel, and the literary predecessors upon whom they were modeled: Gilgamesh and Endiku, Osiris and Seth, Cambysis and Smerdis, and Castor and Pollux. The descriptions in each fable are less significant than that the moral of offending God, even if one is unsure why, is calamitous. Cain and Abel, like Adam and Eve, are copied characters in a literary tradition.

Cain is the first-born son of Adam and Eve in the chronicle, and therefore in an honored position. Eve rejoices in his birth, "with the help of the Lord." We are not told in what way the Lord helped since birth in the biological order, with a little help from Adam, is a natural occurrence. We shall learn, however, in an episode involving Mary, that the Lord can help a lot when the Holy Spirit actually contributes to conception. Later, brother Abel was born but the Lord is not said to have helped in his birth at all. (1)

The rest of this story of Cain and Abel is even stranger than the creation story that precedes it. Cain makes an offering, and these are the very first sacrifices recorded in scripture, of the "fruit of the ground." Presumably these are vegetables because Cain, the first person supposedly born in the natural way, was a tiller of the soil, which is precisely what the Lord had banished humans to be: "Cursed by the ground because of you; in toil shall you eat of it all the days of your life." (2) Earlier in *Genesis*, however, we are told that there should be farmers ("There was no man to till the ground") so why should working in agriculture be a punishment?

Gilgamesh and Endiku

As we saw in the last chapter, Gilgamesh was King of Uruk and a wise man who supposedly knew everything, especially secrets. He had a perfect body, was good-looking, had courage and strength, was two-thirds god and one-third man, a better combination than the reverse. Because of his unusual powers and abilities, he naturally had no equal, was expected to rise in political office, so the scribe has to call to the gods to find a helpmate. The gods located Endiku, made from clay by the creator god Aruru, who had been reared by wild animals, eating grass with the gazelles, whose speed and strength were legendary. After seduction by a city harlot, the righteous animals disowned him and through successive stages he became civilized in the ways of men, a symbolic journey of mankind evolving from barbarism to civilization, still an on-going process in large parts of the planet. Endiku found work among the shepherds because he chased and kept at bay lions, wolves and all wild animals. (3)

Meanwhile, Gilgamesh had a dream about a meteor falling from heaven and he lifted the stone with difficulty and brought it to Ninsun, his goddess mother, who interpreted the dream as the strength of the one he would soon meet, Endiku, whom he should welcome as a brother. (4) The harlot persuaded him to go with her to Uruk to meet Gilgamesh, the strongest, boldest man alive. He and the woman strode into Uruk and when Gilgamesh saw Endiku blocking his path they struggled like bulls and Gilgamesh heaved Endiku like a toy, and then Endiku's courage fled. They embraced as brothers and their friendship was sealed. Such tussles can lead to stronger bonds.

They then embarked on a journey to the north to fell cedars for Gilgamesh's ambitious building program. The journey is understandably long and arduous but at the end they encounter the guardian of the forest, the giant Humbala. After the usual posturing, speeches, dreams and entreaties to favored deities, both Gilgamesh and Endiku strike mortal blows killing Humbala. Since Humbala is a favorite son of Enlil, a major Sumerian god, Enlil is enraged and questions where our heroes have murdered his protégé. But Enlil is persuaded by Shamash that it was foreordained for this to happen.

If the *Genesis* scribe had set out to copy this part of the Gilgamesh epic more closely, it's possible that if Humbala and Gilgamesh were brothers because of divine connections, then the story of Cain and Abel dovetails very nicely with one brother killing another. In any case, there are enough similarities between Gilgamesh and *Genesis*, such as always seeking favor from the gods, having divinities speak through or in dreams, following the divine plan for one's destiny, berated by a god for killing, Cain and Gilgamesh are both said to have built cities, to give any careful reader pause as to biblical originality.

But there is another myth, equally intriguing as literary precedent to the Cain and Abel story, in which no speculation is required: one brother really does kill another.

Osiris and Seth

The other mythical counterpart of Cain and Abel is the Egyptian story of Osiris and Seth. Osiris and Isis were twins, born of the sky goddess, Nut. One night by mistake, Osiris slept with Nephthys, his sister-in-law and the wife of his brother Seth, and from this union Anubis, jackal-headed god associated with the dead because the jackal prowled about tombs, was conceived. Angered by his brother's deception, Seth vowed revenge. He secretly measured Osiris in order to fit him in a sarcophagus, then had one carved that would exactly fit him. At a party he arranged, Seth offered a new sarcophagus to anyone in the room who would fit into it and when Osiris got in, Seth's accomplices rushed in and clamped the lid down, strapped it together and tossed it in the Nile. Osiris becomes the first mythical mummy.

Osiris floated down the Nile into the sea and washed ashore along the beach in Lebanon. A beautiful tree sprouted where the sarcophagus landed and a wonderful fragrance filled the air. A local king delighted in the fragrance of the tree, had it cut down and used as the central pillar in his new palace. Isis, meanwhile had gone in search of her brother and consort, found her way to Lebanon and learned of the aromatic pillar. She became a nurse for the king's new son. Isis learned the pillar was her bother/husband, and convinced the king and queen to let her have the solid block of wood. He gave Isis a royal barge to transport her and the column back to Egypt. By this time back in Egypt, Seth had usurped the throne rightly belonging to Osiris. Enroute to Egypt, Isis lies on the body of her husband in the sarcophagus and conceived Horus. (5)

One night, while hunting by the light of the moon, Seth tripped over a finely decorated box, in fact the sarcophagus of Osiris with Osiris still inside. Furious, he rips Osiris into 14 bits and scatters them everywhere in Egypt. Isis learned of this new crime and again embarked to find her consort's remains. She used a papyrus boat believing that a crocodile would never attack it fearing that it might be bearing her. Wherever she found a body part of Osiris, she buried it, and built a shrine in that place. Throughout Egyptian history, but especially at the principal shrine at Abydos, Osiris, Isis and Horus constitute the holy trinity, the triad of the principal gods. Horus, the son of Osiris, fights Seth in the classic battle of good over evil and the struggle is indecisive but continuing.

Seth becomes the god of chaos, hostility and evil by murdering his brother. Seth was depicted in human form with a head said to resemble that of an aardvark with a curved snout, erect square-tipped ears and a long forked tail. Seth, like Cain in the Hebrew version, has a mark so everyone knows him.

Catal Huyuk

There are other peculiar elements of the Cain and Abel saga that deserve comment. *Genesis* notes that "Cain built a city," so he moves from the status of a farmer to that of urban designer, architect, and contractor. Founding a city is not the same as actually building one, and why would the scribe fail to name the city? But, considering that Gilgamesh was a builder and planned and executed the design and construction of Uruk it is not surprising that, since Cain is modeled on Gilgamesh, that Cain too should be a builder. Augustine allegorically assumed that Cain's city was the City of Man as opposed to Abel's City of God. No one prohibited hyperbole in allegorical interpretation of scripture even when derived from myth.

What kind of urban site was Cain supposed to have established, a farming community or a trading post, and what were his qualifications for developing and maintaining such a location? And since he and Abel were the only people around, who were the inhabitants? Answers are not logical because biblical scribes were busy extrapolating literary threads from existing epic sources and obviously did not have plot or story line editors.

The excavations of the Neolithic city of Catal Huyuk in today's Turkey covers 32 acres inhabited over 21 centuries, one of the first and largest urban centers in the Middle East, the apex of a great prehistoric civilization and extensive trading network. Catal Huyuk is unusual because as many as 10,000 people lived there at its height. The inhabitants were not farmers but traders, toolmakers and artisans. Results of radiocarbon produced dates from the period c.7,300–7,150 BCE for the earliest activity. Archaeologists estimate that the site was occupied for between 950 and 1,150 years and that individual buildings were typically occupied between fifty and eighty years, though some for a longer duration. (6)

Objects of daily life were uncovered together with paintings and murals. Some were exceptional finds, such as flint daggers with decorative bone handles and clay or stone figurines depicting human figures and animals. Other objects include obsidian, flint, pottery, carved bone and clay balls. Homes were entered through ladders from the roof, eliminating the need for doors. Inhabitants buried their dead under the floors of their platforms. An international team of excavators has been conducting digs since 1993, but has uncovered little evidence for urbanized divisions of labor. Nor have archaeologists uncovered public architecture such as temples and other public buildings that later cities like Ur and Uruk had in abundance.

What is the difference between a village, town and city? The difference lies in the social and economic relationships within a population. Uruk for example, originated because of agricultural surpluses allowing some people to quit farming and become artisans, priests, or members of other trades. Meanwhile, the farmers who provided food for these cities lived in outlying villages. A key feature of a city is that farmers don't usually live in them.

Where did Cain and Abel actually learn the ritual of giving offerings to the Lord? Adam and Eve never offered anything, nor did the Lord give them any instruction on offerings. And they had a lot of fruits to offer in the garden if they had known about this custom. But surprisingly, considering what happened to Cain and the Lord's reaction to his offerings, the custom persisted, although we're uncertain about how it got started, and why Cain and Abel sacrifices began at all. But at least we can understand why vegetables were quickly replaced with animal parts, like Abel's "fat portions" from his firstling flocks, which became a bigger hit in the Lord's eyes.

Animal sacrifice continues still on Mount Gerizim, a mountain holy to Samaritans, who offer sheep on the eve of the feast of Passover. (7) The Samaritans, numbering about 600 and living a tenuous existence perched between the Israeli and Palestinian communities, have a literal reading of the Mosaic law and hence separated themselves from mainstream Judaism. So why was God unhappy with Cain's "offering of the fruit of the ground?" Cain had not been unproductive; he had obviously labored to cultivate the earth. Was his misfortune to have offended God in some other way? Did he offer to God only those vegetables, like rutabagas and nasty turnips that he didn't like to eat? Here is the first person born of humans, offering the first sacrifices ever recorded to God, and what is the ungrateful response: "But for Cain and his offerings he had no regard." (8)

Gilgamesh offered sacrifices to his gods. Thus ritual offerings became a major motif in the Bible. When Gilgamesh rejected the goddess Istar as a lover, she sought her revenge and petitioned her divine father Anu to give her the Bull of Heaven to destroy Gilgamesh and threatened famine, grain shortages, and resurrection of the dead to eat the living. Anu gave Istar the Bull of Heaven who began by killing a few hundred men in Uruk. Both Gilgamesh and Endiku seized the bulls by their horns and thrust a sword between the nape of their necks and horns and killed them. Istar was furious and all the gods took counsel and agreed that because of this one of the brothers must die for killing Humbala and the Bull of Heaven. Endiku took sick and died and Gilgamesh grieved mightily. Anger of the gods at sacrifice that doesn't compensate for past infractions is a literary technique biblical scribes took from Sumerians that would reappear in Greek mythology. Absent this understanding from preceding mythology, we are confronted with the absurdities of the biblical record.

As if to throw salt in the wounds, the Lord says to Cain, "Why are you angry and why are your downcast? If you do well, will you not be accepted; but if you do not do well, will not sin crouch at the door! Its desire is for you, but you must master it." (9) This is the first recorded instance in which God seeks to understand human emotions when he asks about Cain's feelings. Cain probably felt that he had done well, and now must have been puzzled because maybe it wasn't just the offerings but him the Lord was displeased with. But emotions are common in *The Epic of Gilgamesh*. Gilgamesh himself grieves over Endiku's death. Enlil and Shamash quarrel. The gods seek lovers. Lamentations, wailings, repentances, disagreements, curses and the whole panoply of human emotions are in this epic. What God asks in *Genesis* is timid compared to the range of feelings in other epics, emotions that Greek tragedians would immortalize.

So Cain has to be wondering what he has to do to get a fair shake in pleasing God. His father and mother bungled their first major encounter, and we must wonder if they all sat around the evening fire and told their kids about what it must have been like in the days before they knew they were naked, and how lovely it was in the garden that no one will ever see again.

Now the four of them have to sew clothes and work in vegetable patches. Like Seth, Cain still has his mark on him, but Adam, Eve and Abel already know who he is.

There must have been a lot of experimentation to see what would grow in what soil conditions and what exactly they would find palatable enough to eat. As if to make matters worse, there is no female yet in the family so the boys can have a helper and carry on the family name, such as it was with two banished parents and a murderer.

Of course Abel went off to make a living with the sheep. The market for sheep must have been thin because to whom was Abel selling them? It could be that this is why offerings were invented because Abel had too many sheep for the first nuclear first family to eat, and decided to give some back to the Lord.

God also mentions something called sin crouching at Cain's door. It's enough that Cain has to cope with weeds, birds eating his seed crop, irrigation and fertilizer problems, but now something called sin may also be giving him a hard time. And as the first born human, he is trying to set a good example, be a hard worker, and all this without a helper like his dad who had it easier, in some respects, in the old days.

Now sin is mentioned before Cain kills Abel so it must have already been something special in the eyes of the Lord, even though nobody yet had been to catechism. Theologians will tell us that it was created, not by the Lord, but by Adam and Eve acting in consort, when they disobeyed and ate from the forbidden tree. Somehow this sin, an original sin, got passed on through the generations. This original sin of disobedience was even worse than killing a family member, because Cain, said to be the first-born human, was the first murderer in the human family. So in the final analysis, according to theologians, we all got our original sin either from Cain or Seth. For this original sin there must be a cleansing baptism. Gilgamesh too sinned by killing the guardian of the forest, Humbala and the Bull of Heaven sent by Istar. For this injustice, the gods decreed that his brother was to be executed bringing about Gilgamesh's grief. Sin was original with Gilgamesh.

Seth was born, according to Eve, as a replacement son for Abel. (9) But of course we must not forget that Seth is an Egyptian name, not Hebrew, and a part of the older myth of Osiris. This is the first instance in the Bible where not only the story but the same name is copied. The biblical Seth is said to have had a son whom he called Enos. However, if you are following the story closely, there aren't any females except Eve. So where Seth finds a wife to have a son is another unresolved mystery. There is no record of Adam and Eve having had any daughters, and there wouldn't be anyone around to invite to a wedding party anyway, so it is anyone's guess how wives suddenly appear. Hebrew sensitivity about gods and mortals copulating with gods conspired to omit the sexual unions older literatures described without pretense, hesitancy or Puritanism, though that word for that attitude hadn't been invented yet.

Where does Cain's wife come from? Must Adam yield another rib? Abel is dead, and we are not told about any other births from the mother of all the living. This is a clear indication that there has a lot of poetic license with the collapsing of narrative. But assuming that female births went unrecorded, Cain and Seth are still marrying their sisters in order to keep the human species going. Such incestuous relationships can, as we know now in modern times, produce some unwanted mental instability. So it shouldn't be surprising if we find some very odd things happening later in scriptures.

But at the conclusion of this very odd chapter of the events of the first humans, there is this sentence: "At this time men began to call on the name of the Lord." What men? Abel is dead, Adam is old but still sexually potent, Cain is already a marked man wandering someplace, and Seth is just a youngster. Moreover, Adam and Cain have had very unpleasant experiences in the early days of dealing with the Lord because the rules of human conduct haven't been published because writing hasn't been invented. Cain is now living in the land of Nod, presumably alone but anything is possible in this story, off to the east somewhere. Has the scribe here lost sight of the chronology? Adam and Seth, and Seth's son Enos if you count him, are the only men around.

Additionally, there are no women except Eve, but wives are magically produced. In some cases, like that of Enos, there is no mention of marriage or wives at all, only that Seth had a son. The *Genesis* scribe tells us that there was a big deal made of making life into genders, male and female. But this far into the story, there are only lists of male births. Descriptions of a couple of marriages might have been more interesting reading for the general public. Did the bride wear white in those days? Did she wear clothes sewn by Eve? Did she bring a dowry? Did the boys have to propose first and buy a ring? Perhaps the scribe was ashamed of offending people with a description of brothers marrying sisters just to get the species started.

A cleverer man than Cain might have offered to swap the vegetable plot for Abel's sheep business, even temporarily and for the purpose of learning another trade, knowing that the fat portions of the yearling lambs were hot commodities. Or Cain could have gone into a new line of work altogether, like the cattle business. We were told that cattle were around in *Genesis* 2:20. Cattle would have been a terrific gift offering. They were big, they already had been named by Cain's dad, and there would have been more fat portions than there were from lambs.

Cain reacted like a snippy adolescent when God questioned him about where Abel was. Like his dad, Cain didn't think carefully when it came to responding to God. Cain couldn't have expected just to murder the second human being ever born and go back to tending his veggies without some comeuppance. After all, he couldn't have known yet that if he had been Abraham it might have been OK to kill a family member like a son because God was always testing people without telling them why. Readers of the *Epic of Gilgamesh*, however, know that mortals and semi-divinities often question godly decrees and argue with them.

Normally, Cain would have been apprehended, tried and probably convicted, though witnesses would have been impossible to find. However, before there were any other people except the first family, the Lord had to perform all these functions by himself. The Lord found Cain, who apparently wasn't really hiding like his dad did, judged him, and then cursed him in his special way. And Cain got off lightly, if we judge by what cold-blooded killers get as a sentence today. There weren't enough people available yet to form a political action committee to debate the merits of capital punishment or form a jury. Not only that, there weren't any executioners available either. Of course, we don't know what was in the land of Nod where Cain wandered.

The story of a brother killing a brother is common folklore by the Middle Bronze Age, as Gilgamesh and Endiku and Seth and Osiris indicate, and certainly by the 5th century BCE when Herodotus is writing: "I am the son of Gordius, who was the son of Midas. My name is Adrastus: unwillingly I have killed my brother, for which I am banished by my father, and rendered entirely destitute." (11)

Cambyses, the son of Cyrus, has a warning dream about his brother Smerdis, whom he has murdered. (12) Cambyses set out to conquer Egypt, which he did, but distrusting his younger brother, Smerdis, of plotting a revolt, had him imprisoned and then secretly killed.

The fifth set of brothers is the fable of Castor and Pollux, the inseparable Greek mythical brothers who were born half human and half divine, an appropriate mix of heroic stature for a mythical tale. Castor and Pollux, brothers of the famous Helen of Troy, were the sons of Zeus. Zeus had posed as a Swan to seduce Leda who gave birth to an egg from which the twins were born. When Theseus and his friend abducted Helen, Castor and Pollux pursued and successfully recovered her.

Castor was famous with horses and Pollux known for boxing. During a voyage with the expedition of Jason and his Argonauts a storm arose. Orpheus prayed to the gods, played on his harp, and the storm ceased and stars appeared on the heads of the brothers. Castor and Pollux afterwards were considered the patron deities of seamen and voyagers, and the flames, also known as St. Elmo's fire, which dance around the sails and masts of ships.

Castor was slain in a war and Pollux was inconsolable and beseeched Jupiter to give his own life as a ransom. Jupiter consented to allow the two brothers to enjoy life alternately (as he had Persephone) passing one in the day and the next at night in the heavens. Known among the Romans as Dioscuri or sons of Jupiter, they appear among the stars as Gemini the Twins. Though there is only modest similarity between this fable and Cain and Abel, one of the brothers does die, so I have included it here to illustrate the relationship between brothers in fables from other literary traditions.

Farmers and Shepherds: The Allegorical Interpretation

The literary consignment of Gilgamesh into *Genesis* is as obvious as when movies create stories from popular books, although in these days of copyright infringement there is usually source acknowledgement. Cain and Abel can be metaphors for the two principal kinds of agricultural life: the settled farmer's life of the Mesopotamian basin, symbolized by Cain, and the nomadic Bedouin existence of the Semitic shepherds, represented by Abel. In this view, Cain the farmer kills the Semitic shepherd Abel, who becomes a martyr for his way of life. It is a story that would play well in Canaan, but not be enthusiastically received in Mesopotamia where farming, especially orchard work of the kind found in gardens, sustained all human existence and allowed for a cultured and artistic way of life to flourish. As I noted earlier, the gods routinely sacrificed to and worshipped were the favored divinities of the environment that supported agricultural communities, water, the sun and fertility.

If the Semites prevailed, the nomadic life overcomes the life of the flood plain of the Mesopotamia, then we have an allegory of the triumph of one kind of people with a special way of life over an urbanized life style. We know that this actually happened, as the literature of the early Middle East at the dawn of recorded human events supports the common myths between the two occupational life styles.

Here we have two sons, and fathers will understand this, who choose not to follow as apprentices in their father's occupational footsteps. Adam, having been a gentleman farmer, certainly knew something about raising fruit crops, if not wheat or sheep. However, since he got to name sheep, he must also have had some intuition about what sheep were and how valuable to a protein existence they were apart from a garden. But the boys did decide to do something different than what dad did because he got in such trouble in a garden.

Cain kills Abel, and this could be representative of a military victory of Semitic peoples, and thereafter Cain, the urbanized tiller of the soil, becomes a wanderer of the earth, in effect a nomadic Bedouin. This is the ultimate role reversal. Cain is banished because of his way of life and has incurred God's displeasure, even though God snubbed him from the very beginning by not liking any of his vegetables. The incursion of a nomadic people into settled urban life squares with the archaeological evidence according to Kenyon, (13) who locates this disruption of urban life to a migration of Amorites or Amurru peoples into the region about the presumed time of the Patriarchs, between 1,900–1,600 BCE, at least a thousand years prior to the writing of the Pentateuch. Kenyon notes that all the archaeological evidence from this period shows a break in civilized life.

God does not offer any prior advice to Adam before his presumably evil deed, as he does to Cain. Yet Cain is entitled to a better explanation than that if he does well he will be accepted. Cain has done well by bringing offerings at all. So what is the cause of God's displeasure here? Can it be that in Cain we have a prototype of a man who, under any circumstance, would incur God's displeasure? Is the real envy for the way of life a people who have a settled farming existence? Envy begets violence, the killing of Abel, and the bad faith of Cain has become a characteristic of a man who has forfeited God's grace, an example of a fallen man who is always under God's control.

Such is the allegorical interpretation. In the Cain and Abel story we have the prime example of man's violent nature, and the results of man's attempt to reach a more divine status. Man's real evil, and this is clear from the Mesopotamian myths, is impious aspiration to become more god-like. But the more persuasive reason is that the scribe is simply using the themes already established from Gilgamesh of the god's displeasure at his killing of Humbala and the Bull of Heaven and the other myths about brothers.

"Then the Lord gave Cain a token so that no one finding him should kill him." One translation is that "Yahweh touched Cain with a mark." (14) Its purpose was to prevent anyone from killing Cain and thus exacting retribution or revenge for Abel's murder. This courtesy was not extended to everyone, because later everyone would be able to exact an eye for an eye, or a life for a life. Seth in the Egyptian myth was similarly marked so everyone would know his guilt.

Cain's curse is that he becomes like Abel, a nomad, perhaps a shepherd, but, in Cain's own words, "a fugitive and a wanderer." God's curse for him is that the soil will become unproductive and God's face will be hidden from him. "And Cain went out from the presence of the Lord." Cain, the former farmer, has become Cain the nomad, an immigrant, residing to "the east of Eden." Human alienation from divine presence is complete. The real alienation is the failure to see this story in the richness of the mythology that preceded it.

The idea of retribution is picked up again in the sons of Cain, in Lamech named five generations later, who says to his plural wives: "I kill a man for wounding me, a youth for bruising me. If Cain shall be avenged sevenfold, Lamech seventy times sevenfold." (15) Is this self-defense of a particular man, or a particular way of life, that a man should consider killing 490 other men if his life is threatened? We come across this 70 times 7 again when Jesus asks all to forgive to that degree. Is Lamech, in the mind of the scribe, merely a biological extension of God's displeasure with all of Cain's succession? Does Lamech symbolize the way of life of a people who have become a menace?

Divine retribution is established in the biblical narrative as a theme for many of the collected stories and myths, a precedent that originated about a thousand years earlier. He who sins against the godhead will experience punishment, and this form of divine justice is the basis for stories included in the chronicle. A human may do well only if he pleases God. Consequently, it is man's sole responsibility to remain in God's favor. It seems that Cain symbolizes a time when men turned from worship of the gods, and that Lamech is an example of the depths of depravity a man might go without knowing the gods and their benefits. We can draw this same conclusion from the *Epic of Gilgamesh*.

After Cain moves to Nod a very strange thing happens. Cain "knows" his wife and she bears Henoch. Where does this wife come from? If you are following the story so far, a rib has become a woman, the mother of all the living. Then Cain and Abel appear in the course of events. But thus far, nobody else is supposed to be on the earth, even though Cain founds a city. Then the scribe proceeds to list the family tree of Cain, the murdering survivor, as if his ancestry should be worth remembering. Since Abel is dead, and has no surviving lineage, all of us, the scribe would have us believe, are the descendants of the world's first murderer. At the end of Cain's lone line of descendants, we are told that "Adam knew his wife again and she bore a son and called him Seth."(*Gen.* 4:25) First we have to assume that this is still Adam's first wife, and not one of Adam's un-named daughters. But since Cain found a wife that was unrecorded, we can't be absolutely sure that the scribe might not have discovered the world's first wine and sampled it while writing this saga.

At the beginning of *Genesis* 5 we get a little summary of the story thus far, including Adam's advanced age, 130 years old. Adam was 130 when Seth was born, so a lot of history could have taken place when no one was around to record it since writing hadn't yet been invented, and probably not fire or the wheel either. But the scribe then records that Adam lived for 800 years after the birth of Seth, which places him at 930 years of age. And the scribe even does this bit of simple arithmetic for us: "The whole lifetime of Adam was nine hundred and thirty years; and then he died," possibly from exhaustion since we are told he had other sons and daughters. There is no record of how long Eve lived, and if she continued to bear children into her multiple centuries. We knew Adam would die because the Lord had predicted it. (16)

The case of Henoch, the son of Jared, is extraordinary, because at the age of 365 years, he did not die, thereby avoiding the general curse of mankind and the normal laws of biology. We're told, "Henoch walked with God; and he was seen no more because God took him." (*Gen.* 5:24). Now anyone who has been to the desert in any part of the Middle East knows that it is easy to get lost. Anyone walking around, even with God, could get disoriented. But let's assume God really did take him. Where did he take him? Later, Elias was said to have been taken too. (17) Perhaps both are in the same place.

The puzzling chronology, genealogy, complicated births and deaths, complex relationship with God in *Genesis* become surprisingly unraveled if Sumerian, Mesopotamian, Greek and Egyptian myths are compared. Suddenly, the Bible's absurdities become clear since they are so obviously copied. Hebrew national literature, clumsily adapted from Sumerian and Egyptian mythology, became codified, standardized and sanctified. Further narrative research will only deepen knowledge of how scriptural text has been purloined from previous narratives.

CHAPTER SIX
THE FLOOD

George Smith had been a member of a small team of excavators working on behalf of the British Museum near Nineveh, and had read with utter astonishment an account of a flood story on excavated tablets. The earliest tablets containing flood narratives date to about 1,702–1,682 BCE. His revelations created unprecedented excitement at the Society of Biblical Archaeology meeting in London in 1872. This was evidence that a similar flood story existed prior to the Bible's, implying that other stories might have been current in other cultures prior to biblical composition.

Besides *Genesis*, three older stories of the creation of humankind combined with a flood narrative are known to exist: 1) the Sumerian Flood Story, 2) the ninth tablet of the *Epic of Gilgamesh* where the flood story is a secondary telling in the narrative, and 3) the *Atrahasis Epic* from Babylonia dating from c.1,700 BCE. Building a boat to specifications, placing animals in an ark and landing it on a mountain, sending birds to see whether the waters had receded, are the same details in all four narratives and reveal that they have a similar literary source.

If there is one narrative that arrives almost intact except for name changes from the *Epic of Gilgamesh* into *Genesis* it is the flood story. "You know the city of Shurrupak," writes the scribe of Gilgamesh, "it stands on the banks of Euphrates? That city grew old and the gods that were in it were old. There was Anu, lord of the firmament, their father, and warrior Enlil their counselor Ninurta the helper, and Ennugi watcher over canals; and with them also was Ea. In those days the world teemed, the people multiplied, the world bellowed like a wild bull, and the great god was aroused by the clamor. Enlil heard the clamor and he said to the gods in council, "The uproar of mankind is intolerable and sleep is no longer possible by reason of the babel." So the gods agreed to exterminate mankind." (1) With this introduction Sumerian scribes introduced the world of epic literature to mankind and simultaneously wrote about its extermination at least a thousand years prior to *Genesis*.

The goddess Ea apparently had a fondness for Gilgamesh and whispered to him to abandon his possessions and immediately begin the construction of a boat and told him the exact measurements, one acre of deck with seven decks, divided into nine sections with separating bulkheads. He completed it in seven days and "loaded into her all that I had of gold and living things, my family, my kin, the beast of the field both wild and tame, and all the craftsmen." (2)

Not to be outdone, Greeks borrowed the same flood narrative story. Zeus was angered by man's irreverence and flooded the earth, but Deucalion was warned in advance by his father Prometheus, and took his wife Pyrrha into refuge in an ark and after many days and nights landed on Mount Parnassus. Gilgamesh had been similarly warned in advance by Ea. The imitated narrative of the biblical Deluge is in the *Epic of Gilgamesh* epic as told to Gilgamesh by Utnapishtim, an Akkadian wise king and priest and main character of the story in the eleventh table of the epic. (3)

Utnapishtim's name is translated as "He Who Saw Life," and is a protégé of the god EA who helps him survive the flood with his family and with "the seed of all living creatures." Noah takes the actual animals; Utnapishtim takes the seeds, less weighty and cumbersome on a boat and not needing feed or waste disposal. It took him a week to build a boat and its dimensions are recorded. At the end he gave a great feast where great quantities of wine were provided. After the storm passed all mankind was turned back into clay Utnapishtim sent out a dove but it found no resting place. Then he sent out a swallow that also returned. Then he sent out a raven that returned and croaked but did no land on the boat. Then Utnapishtim offered sacrifice to the gods and the fragrant odor pacified the gods. Hebrew scribes lifted the story of Noah and the flood almost verbatim from *The Epic of Gilgamesh* and the *Epic of Atrahasis* as a dishonest student searching the Internet for an essay to submit.

Here is a partial description from Tablet III of the *Epic of Atrahasis*.

Atrahasis made his voice heard
And spoke to his master,
'Indicate to me the meaning of the dream,
I let me find out its portent (?)'
Enki made his voice heard
And spoke to his servant,'
You say, "I should find out in bed (?)
Make sure you attend to the message I shall tell you!
Wall, listen constantly to me!
Reed hut, make sure you attend to all my words!
Dismantle the house, build a boat,
Reject possessions, and save living things.
The boat that you build
Roof it like the Apsu
So that the Sun cannot see inside it!
Make upper decks and lower decks.
The tackle must be very strong,
The bitumen strong, to give strength.
I shall make rain fall on you here,
A wealth of birds, a hamper (?) of fish."...
the Flood was
Seven nights' worth.

The hero has a dream seeks to know its meaning. God hears the request and responds to the prayer, and proceeds to tell how to build a boat prior to the flood coming. Subsequently, he selects the animals to place on board and as he finishes the flood begins. Soon, the flood subsides and the epic concludes:

> *(missing lines)*
> *How we sent the Flood.*
> *But a man survived the catastrophe.*
> *You are the counsellor of the gods;*
> *On your orders I created conflict.*
> *Let the Igigi listen to this song*
> *In order to praise you,*
> *And let them record (?) your greatness.*
> *I shall sing of the Flood to all people:*
> *Listen!* (4)

Noah and His Sons

According to *Genesis*, Noah was born 1,056 years after Adam appeared on the earth. The trick in this arithmetic is to count the age of the fathers in Chapter 5 when they had sons, and not their actual age when they died. It wasn't until Noah himself was five hundred years old that he became the father of Sem, Ham, and Japheth. Whether they were all born in his 500th year as triplets, or as sons from different wives remains a mystery. (5) Fables have their logical faults although they do appeal to the imagination if one discounts reason and accountability.

Genesis 6 begins by describing the problem of multiple wives. This is before the Ten Commandments, so nobody knew what the proper number of wives was. Adam and Eve weren't supposed to taste from the tree of knowledge of good and evil, so how were they supposed to know the difference and what acts were, or were not, wicked, especially regarding women. Anyway, about the time of Noah men were taking multiple wives, "as many as they wished," (6) as some tribal chieftains in Africa and polygamous Mormons still do. The Lord was not pleased with this arrangement, but nobody asked the women whether they approved or not. The Lord decided immediately to limit men's lifetimes to 120 years, and this definitely lowered the sperm count. But as everyone knows, even with Medicare and other medical benefits and scientific knowledge and certain drugs, it is hard to reach even that personal best in advanced age as insurers and actuaries already know.

As with Adam and Cain, the Lord is very upset with the wickedness of men, usually over their relations with women, although occasionally a brother causes jealousy. Men are still not sure what wickedness is since no one, including the Lord, has told them. But the Lord saw that "man's every thought and all the inclination of his heart were only evil, he regretted that he had made man on the earth and was grieved to the heart." (7) If the Lord regrets that he even created man, this was a very bad situation. Just when man's longevity had been substantially reduced to 120 years now he faces extinction.

The biblical Lord, like Ea and Gilgamesh, had a conversation with Noah and commanded him to build a large boat. The Lord even had an architectural model. You will remember that there was much water on the earth before creation, when God divided the waters below and above the firmament, and when God said, "Let the waters below the heavens be gathered into one place and let the dry land disappear." (8) The animals didn't have any part of this wickedness but they were to suffer the consequences anyway. During those days there was no Society for the Preservation of Endangered Animals, nor any organizations like Human Rights Watch for endangered humans.

Now the narrative neglects to mention fish as one of the animals to be saved. It would appear that fish were not brought on board the Ark because there wasn't enough room for their aquariums (glass hadn't been invented yet), which could tip over and break during the storm. So the Lord and Noah must have agreed that fish could stay, they couldn't have been that wicked anyway, and there would be plenty of water for them to survive in and truly increase and multiply. On the other hand, the time when the waters receded is when they could have been most exposed and most thereby eliminated.

The approximate equivalent dimensions of this boat were to be: 450 feet long, 75 feet wide, and 45 feet high. On the face of it, this appears to be a huge boat. But once you get a couple of elephants, rhinos, hippos, buffalos, and moose on board, full capacity can be reached quickly. Furthermore, not all animals would have wanted to remain in the lower decks very long. But the big animals, except for the giraffes, would be needed as stabilizing ballast in the lower decks. There were no conveniences like an exercise room.

If Noah got any other neighborly men to help him build this boat, he would have hard pressed to tell them why he needed it. And if he did tell them the truth, he would have felt guilty afterwards for allowing perfectly good helpers to lend their valuable time being wicked to build a boat that only he and his family could use as an escape vehicle. This was not a good position for a patriarch to be in. The boat building would have attracted a lot of local attention and discussion, so maybe Noah told them he just need to go on a long cruise, or to collect supplies for the community. If he did, then he would have been lying, and that is not a good thing for a man who is said to have been blameless.

Noah and his sons must have been careful to keep certain predatory animals separate from their normal prey. There wouldn't be much room for experimentation with accommodation requests from the animals, like, say, that the lions lay down close to the lambs, or the crocodiles next to the cats. If some predatory animals supplemented the diet Noah gave them during the journey by eating a few chosen companion animals in the boat, this would have been how the first species became extinct, like dinosaurs, brought about by man's ignorance of the laws of nature, much like today. Maybe the Lord helped in the correct separation between animals. After all, he designed the boat. It would have been negligent of him not to help in assigning the various compartments for proper safety and preservation of certain species.

Noah and his sons were probably not vegetarians during this time and likely took on a few extra animals for their own consumption. This would have reduced stall space. But they still would have had to be careful not to upset the delicate gender balance when they slaughtered an animal for the evening meal. And of course chickens could always be relied upon to produce eggs.

Noah and his sons should be congratulated for the excellent roundup of these twosomes, for some of the animals would have been far from their home and not too anxious to leave their own little Edens, which took them centuries of grazing just to find, even after the coming flood was explained to them but not understood. A journey to Africa for animal collection, for example, is probably as difficult today than it was then, even if one discounts the lack of travel agents and lost luggage. Since most of the animals were wild and undomesticated, their capture was tricky and time-consuming. The animals weren't too keen either about having to walk a long distance for a boat journey they were even less enthusiastic. Noah and his sons forgot to separate some of the males and females on the trip home so a few extra young of some species arrived safely as well.

Noah and his boys must have traveled everywhere, and their wives would not have let them go alone without them along to cook and wash and keep the men themselves from falling into wickedness. Without the Lord's help how would anyone know when you had in fact collected all the world's species, unless thoughtful Adam had provided them with a list of everything he had named? And they must have collected several twosomes for fear that some, or even one male or female of each species, might not actually make it back to the place where the Ark was being built because of difficulties, like dysentery and lack of a proper visa, along the long journey.

One of Noah's sons reminded Noah that they also had to bring male and female serpents. The Lord, after all, had said all living creatures. They drew straws to decide who would actually collect the serpents, because the serpents still possessed all their cunning and might have found a way to escape capture, or, even worse, to cause the men to do something against the Lord's laws, which weren't even known at the time. We don't actually know how Noah and his sons accomplished this, but they must have got serpents on board since we still have them around today, except in Ireland, although they have certainly lost almost all of their cunning.

Just finding which animals were indeed male and female must have been a chore in several roundups. Indeed, it must have been difficult to decide which pair would best preserve that species, as there probably were not a lot of volunteers for the long and precarious mission back to the Ark, or easy choices about giving up a desired piece of grazing land even for a cruise of uncertain length. You can just imagine what it must have taken to lure, capture and convince a rhinoceros of the dangers of not coming. As always, Noah and his sons had under-estimated the travel time for the collection of animals back to the boat. So the Lord delayed the deluge until everyone arrived. By this time, even the wives were tired of traveling in the caravan and preparing meals, and would have welcomed a vacation on any boat.

Luckily, Adam had named all animals so Noah could call them what men called them, even if the animals might not have recognized their names since no one had told them what Adam called them, with the real possibility that several living things, perhaps even hybrids, would be born during the flotation period, thereby adding to the boat's overall weight and the more rapid depletion of the food supply.

This flood couldn't last forever. There could not have been much privacy. Noah's sons must have constantly been on toilet brigade throughout the entire trip, shoveling over-board the deposits of every twosome of the animal world. They could have had plenty of time for this job. No one needed to have navigation skills because no one knew where they were going. There wasn't any sail or rudder as there might be in a normal boat designed to try and get somewhere. The whole of the existing human race was literally adrift. Much like today.

The rains continued for forty days and nights, although the waters rose for 150 days. But only after another 40 days does Noah dare to open a window. After this, Noah sends a raven, which apparently does not return: "It flew to and fro until the waters had dried off the earth." (9) Noah and his family must have been excited when the rains stopped because food was low and the animals were agitated from being cooped in such tiny quarters. Only a couple of birds got to fly around looking for land.

Then Noah sent a dove, which did return with an olive branch, the symbol that the Lord had made peace with humans by exterminating them. Noah then sent the same dove again which this time did not return. Now this made life exceedingly difficult for the remaining male dove and raven since both had to find their mates later when the ark landed. We know they did find them because they have not become extinct. It's not clear where the female dove found this olive branch, because olives don't grow on mountain tops. But it is exciting to know that olives must be the hardiest of trees to grow up again so quickly after everything has been destroyed.

After seven months, and seventeen days of the eighth month, the ark came to rest on the top of Mount Ararat. Some claim parts of the ark are still up there. (10) And because everyone knows that Mount Arafat is in eastern Turkey, there has been heightened interest in travel to the region to locate its remains. Separating the clean from the unclean animals and birds was not an easy task in Noah's ark. Cooped up so long in the ark without a bath left most of the animals pretty unclean, except for the few that might have been allowed a quick swim if they promised to return to the ark without getting lost in the dark waters. Even Noah and his family, after 150 days plus 40 days and nights without a shower, could have qualified as unclean if blameless.

Exactly one year after the rains began, and obviously with food and provisions running low, Noah instructed everyone to clear out and to release all the animals. The land was now dry. But the oceans must have been higher. The animals were happy to be out of the ark, and probably grateful that Noah had had the resourcefulness and courage to capture them and save them from extinction. But now they had to find a route back to their homelands and see what was left of the old grazing lands. Cunningly, the serpents propagated themselves on every continent so that this severe reduction in the species would not happen so easily again, because they of all animals knew that the relationship between the Lord and men was very precarious and full of threats for them regardless of their intentions, actions or geography.

In the Noah saga, God regrets even creating mankind. This about-face and lack of resolution even about the creation of humans does not appear to be a trait laudable to the heavenly majesty, but it is similar to the fickleness and volatility of Greek gods. We discover in later texts (*Numbers* 23:19 and *Samuel* 15:29) that God does not repent his actions nor "change his mind." Which biblical text then is more believable, creating humans or repenting only to destroy them? Both are correct if one accepts that later editors allowed earlier sagas to remain without bothering to correct changing views of the deity. The odd choices God made in the earlier epics were reconditioned into promises based on the God's good conduct seal of approval, so that if the people were unfaithful to the pledges all manner of calamities, including human extermination, temple destruction and exile, would ensue. God's actions would in the final scribal descriptions be dependent on the actions of the followers, and man's hubris, his pride in avoiding or ignoring the laws, would bring accompanying wrath, just like the displeased Greek gods who imposed their form of justice on misbehaving subjects.

God's delicate finger extends to Adam's finger in Michelangelo's luminously restored fresco from 1510 on the ceiling of the Sistine Chapel. The artistic representation of the act of creation is a form of covenant, the giving of life. But in Michelangelo's painting, the fully-grown and athletic Adam is already created. Is Adam receiving something besides his existence? Whatever Michelangelo had in mind the limp and extended figure symbolizes a bond, a pledge, a covenant with God.

God sends a nice colorful touch after the flood disaster and Noah lands the ark. The rainbow signifies his peace with mankind and it is the beginning of a long line of covenants that would culminate with the Law of Moses. "I have set my rainbow in the clouds, and it will be the sign of the covenant between me and the earth." (11) Oddly, this covenant is not just with Noah but with the earth "and every living creature with you, a covenant for all generations to come." This was encouragement in advance to people living in Bangladesh who are still victims of periodic floods. If we take the rainbow covenant literally even all the bugs that survived with Noah have a covenant with God.

Later, the covenant is God's contract with land: "To your descendants I give this land, from the river of Egypt to the great river, the Euphrates." (12) And there is a covenant with Abraham's posterity, male circumcision, to make him the father of many nations. And by no means are the people to make a covenant with other gods: "Do not make a covenant with them or with their gods." (13) There are covenants with bread, salt, peace, love, commands (See *Numbers*) and that seem to cheapen the concept of covenant but in fact strengthen the relationship with the God of Israel by increasing the links to him.

It is not until Moses, the Tablets of the Decalogue forming the Ark of the Covenant under Joshua, that God makes a covenant with words, the abstract symbols of thought. "Write down these words, for in accordance with these words I have made a covenant with you and with Israel." (14) With words, the covenant becomes a legal contract, binding and not undone unless both parties agree. The whole Bible with 267 covenant citations is riddled with how the covenant process breaks down when the chosen people violate or ignore covenants, usually when they fail to acknowledge him as the chief god.

The monotheism of the Hebrews, borrowed from Egyptians and modified, defined the Hebrew people as Marduk did the Akkadians, Baal the Canaanites, and Ra and Osiris the Egyptians. Religion in all these ancient societies acted like the social threads holding the fabric of the people together. Covenants are the glue between the people and their god and the people themselves, the instrument and foundation of the social organization binding the allegiance of the people. For all such societies in the Bronze Age, it was the gods that guaranteed the existence of the state. Having established the bond between the people and their god, the covenant then extended to include the land, with promises to Abraham, Moses, Joshua and others.

The word *sacramentum,* from which the Catholics derive the special graces that flow from the seven sacraments (baptism, confirmation, communion, penance, matrimony, holy orders, and extreme unction) originally meant a Roman soldier's vow of loyalty to the emperor. In the Christian faith, sacraments are also expressions of covenants with God, pledges of allegiance through actions.

The sign that the covenant was still maintained is through sacrifice. One of Noah's first acts was to build an altar, although it is uncertain who told him one was needed. (15) This is the first time in scripture that an altar is mentioned. Certainly, Abel didn't need an altar, and his fat sheep portions were readily accepted by the Lord as offerings. Noah built an altar because altars had been built centuries earlier in the land between the two rivers.

I visited one such altar of sacrifice in Jordan in 2002. The ascent of Jebel Attuf in Petra is demanding but affords the curious adventurer stunning views of the Petra valley and the surrounding mountains. The high point is 3,414 feet and is reached after a couple hour hike through flights of steps carved in the rocks, sometimes as ramps carved into the face of the red rock quarry all through narrow valleys ringed by precipitous rock walls. At the top stand two obelisks, one 19 feet and the other 23 feet high, probably representing the Edomite divinities Dushara and Al Uzza. (16) It was at the summit of this mountain and open-air sanctuary where the religious celebrations occurred three thousand years ago and where the Hill or High Place of Sacrifice is located. It was at such locations that the early Edomites performed their sacrificial ceremonies. Tradition has it that Aaron, brother of Moses, sacrificed here.

The faithful gathered at this site in a large rectangular-hewed section of the rock, about 48 feet by 21 feet, surrounded on three sides by stone benches. A rock altar, known as a *mensa sacra*, or sacred table, is a perfect rectangle just six inches high, where, non-blood offerings were placed. I rather believe, because of its smallness, it was a ritual table where large animals like bulls were slain. A small drain for the entire rectangle or courtyard is at the northeast corner where liquids, blood among them, drained steeply down the hillside. I stared down the sculpted edge of the drainage where the blood would have run off in a torrent during ceremonies and wondered how the spectators would have reacted emotionally to this sacrifice atop this hill with the awesome view in all directions.

Facing south at the edge of the mountain are an altar and carved pools for collecting blood and washing. The rock-carved altar is reached by ascending three steps. In the top is a square hole where the non-human representation of the divinity, such as an ovoid rock form known as a baetyl, was likely placed. Standing before the altar you can see a panorama of the wadis and mountains below. The officiating priest or priestess had a commanding view to enhance their rituals. To the immediate left of the altar is a rock basin that drained its contents onto the four steps where clearly other sacrifices, possibly of small animals were made. A three-foot deep rectangular basin carved into the rock might have contained water for purification of the officials or cleansing the animals (or humans) to be sacrificed.

When the Lord smelled the sweet odor from Noah's offerings, however, but apparently not the smell from all the animals, he promised never again to get rid of mankind. Individuals were, as always, another matter. From this time on, men decided to keep up the tradition of sacrificing animals to the Lord because it left such a unique impression on him from Noah's offering and perhaps overwhelmed other, less fragrant aromas.

Then, the Lord (now called God beginning in Chapter 9) tells Noah to "Be fruitful and multiply and fill the earth." This was certainly a big challenge because Noah knew how big the earth was because he and his sons had to travel all over it to get all the animals needed for the ark. He also knew that multiple wives were not an option for this human multiplication process because of what happened to those men who died in the deluge trying to multiply themselves as fast as they could with as many women as possible but without the Lord's blessing. But this multiplication process is still at work today, according to God's plan, even though famine, disease, malnutrition and tribal warfare often are coincidentally found in places where the fruitfulness of human multiplication is most evident. Mankind is indeed testing the limits of that prescription, some even with multiple wives, although a few with multiple husbands whom they would rather not have acknowledged.

After the offerings have been accepted, and the covenants concluded, life returns to a simpler time. There is no need for a long genealogy any more, since now everyone can be ancestrally traced to one of Noah's three sons, Sem, Ham, and Japheth, although nobody wants to acknowledge that he is descended from a Ham. Pork would later be proscribed in the Jewish and Islamic religions adding a further taint to this name, at least in English. Cousins would have to be re-invented as blood relationships.

But at this point in the narrative a very peculiar thing happens. Noah plants a vineyard, drinks some wine after the harvest, gets dead drunk, and lays naked in his tent. Except for the planting of the vineyard many men can identify with this condition. Here we have another example of the nakedness we found in Adam's story. Since everyone who could have remembered it had died, this story must have come down to us from Noah himself who in turn must have told his sons. How else would anyone have known about nakedness as a scriptural theme? Sem and Japheth covered Noah's nakedness so that no one could see. But this is queer because there still isn't really anyone around on the earth yet, except family members, who could see but really wouldn't care. The earth isn't populated that fast, and everyone knows there wasn't that much privacy on the ark either.

When Noah awakes, he is furious, but not at himself for getting drunk, but at his grandson for letting him drink all that wine. There follows a whole set of curses on Chanaan, the grandson, nearly equal to the curses of the Lord on mankind, from whom Noah must have learned how to curse. Noah curses Chanaan who winds up as a slave to the rest of the sons of Noah. (17) This was not a prosperous beginning for the first grandson, who could have easily blamed the Lord, not cuddly grandfathers, for making it tough to survive in those days.

Here is the short history of humanity thus far in the first nine chapters of *Genesis*. The first man and woman were losers in a big way. Then, after a few fits and starts, the first human being murders his brother and gets banished. Mankind starts fooling around and the flood wipes out the whole lot except for Noah's immediate family. Until this time it appears that you can get only banishment for murder, but killed by the Lord for other kinds of un-named wickedness. The justice system hadn't been perfected yet, nor a hierarchy of crimes established, although eating fruit from certain trees would get your attention. Then the very first human grandson, Chanaan, after whom a whole country would later be named (Canaan), plays a prank on his granddad, and he gets cursed and made into a slave. Nobody said it would be easy raising the first dysfunctional human family.

Of course Noah is the biblical substitute of Gilgamesh who sleeps for seven days besides the boat that would eventually transport him home and when awakened is found to be naked and has to be clothed. (18) What a coincidence.

Flood Stories

The Weld-Blundell Prism, a rectangular stone with writings on all sides, is in the Ashmolean Museum in Oxford, England. Dating from the 19th century BCE and written in cuneiform, it is one of the oldest writings in existence. It comes from the ancient city of Larsa in today's southern Iraq, or ancient Sumer. It is a copy of the King-List and lists the rulers who existed prior to "the flood."

Flood stories have since been found throughout Asia, in Australia and the Mediterranean, and even the Pacific islands. When human settlements occur between two rivers, there must have been numerous occasions when floods inundated the settled plains. Utnapishtim, on the advice of the god, is commanded in *The Epic of Gilgamesh*, to build a vessel.

What I had, I loaded thereon, the whole harvest of life
I caused to embark within the vessel; all my family and relations,
the beasts of the field, the cattle of the field, the craftsmen,

> *I made them all embark.*
> *I entered the vessel and closed the door...*
> *When the seventh day dawned the hurricane was abated, the flood*
> *which had waged war like an army;*
> *the sea was stilled, the ill wind was calmed, the flood ceased.*
> *I beheld the sea, its voice was silent*
> *And all mankind was turned into mud!*
> *Unto mount Nitsir came the vessel,*
> *Mount Nitsir held the vessel and let it not budge...*
> *When the seventh day came*
> *I sent forth a dove, I released it;*
> *It went, the dove, it came back...*
> *I sent the swallow, it came back...*
> *I sent the crow, I released it.* (19)

Like Noah, Utnapishtim leaves the vessel on top of a mountain, sacrifices to the gods, and the gods, smelling the sweet odor of the sacrifice, decide never again to risk the destruction of men. Was there a universal deluge, or merely stories that emerged from local floods that destroyed cities? The universality of the flood narrative has remained one of the more compelling stories in world literature. Let's summarize the similarities between the Gilgamesh and *Genesis* narratives.

- In *Gilgamesh* the gods are displeased with the noise of mankind and decide to send a flood. In *Genesis*, God is upset with "the wickedness of man."
- In *Gilgamesh*, the gods think there are too many people. In *Genesis*, the same argument is given.
- In *Gilgamesh*, one man is spared, Utnapishtim, whose name translated means "I have found life." In *Genesis*, the man is Noe or Noah, whose name implies "one who gives comfort."
- In both legends, the man chosen is asked to build a huge boat for his deliverance.
- In both stories, the gods or god talk with the one man chosen
- There is a long description of the boat in both stories.
- Selected animals are to accompany the man on the trip in the boat.
- Both stories contain a description of the flood and the extensiveness of the rains.
- Birds are sent to reconnoiter the possible land after the rains have ended. In Gilgamesh, first a dove, a swallow, and a raven are sent in succession. In *Genesis*, Noah sends a raven first, and a dove on two occasions. On the second try the dove returns with an olive leaf.
- Both boats land on a mountain.

- When the boat finally touches land and all disembark, the hero conducts a sacrifice: Gilgamesh the hero offers a libation, and Noah animal sacrifice on an altar.

The principal elements in the story do not vary that much and the themes are intact. Man has incurred the displeasure of the gods and so all humankind must be punished. A flood is the vehicle of destruction, but someone has to survive otherwise creation would have to begin anew. All living things are annihilated, and one man, and both men's families, survive with new instructions for a covenant and mankind reputedly better for this purging.

Are the gods the same gods in both narratives? Or is the Hebrew scribe using his god imposed on the earlier flood story? The Judaic-Christian tradition has always been that the God of the Hebrews is the true God and that from *Genesis* onwards the revealed God. As earlier in *Genesis*, the author uses the plural form of gods to address himself, as he does in, "Let us go down," as if referring to multiple gods, as indeed the Gilgamesh epic does. (20) The *Genesis* scribe is borrowing, but with slips in editorial carelessness, the plurality of the gods.

Lastly, the themes of the sin of mankind, the disappointment of the gods and their destructive power over mankind and deliverance from annihilation are found in ancient Egyptian mythology in texts found on the walls of Seti I, Rameses II and Rameses III at Thebes dating from the 14th to the 12th centuries BCE although the texts probably come from earlier sources. Here is a portion of the text from the Seti I with the same theme from *Genesis*.

> *Then Re said to Nun" 'O eldest god, in whom I came into being, O*
> *ancestor gods, behold mankind, which came into being from my Eye*
> *they have plotted things against me. Tell me what you would do about it.*
> *Behold I am seeking; I would not slay them until I have heard what you might say*
> *about it...then this goddess (Hathor) came and slew mankind.* (21)

The Naming of Ancestors

In the fourth chapter of *Genesis* we have the beginning of what occurs throughout all of biblical literature: a genealogical list of male family ties. When there is no exact measurement of time, a standardization of the calendar, the passage of time needs expression in another medium. The compression of time finds a form of expression in the listing of ancestors. But the literary precedent for the listing of ancestors occurs in Hesiod's *Theogony* where the poet names the generations of the gods and who is related to whom and how. (22)

We get a huge dose of family lineage in *Genesis* 5 when the whole list of Adam's descendants is described all the way to Noah. Subsequent to the flood story, *Genesis* 10 contains another ancestral lineage that describes the descendants of Noah. Many of these are possibly tribal family groupings because the scribe describes the area around Palestine and Israel where these people live. (23) This genre of writing is also known as King Lists and exists throughout the extant literature of the ancient Near East found on stone stele, temple walls, papyrus scrolls and clay tablets, and among Babylonians, Hittites, Canaanites, and Egyptians.

The heroic tradition is somewhat manifest in the strange phrase found in *Genesis* 6:4, where the scribe tells us, "There were giants on the earth in those days, and also afterwards, when the sons of God had relations with the daughters of men, who bore children to them." This is similar to the marriages and births we find in Greek myths when gods and men and women intermarried and had demi-god children. Giants are described in Sumerian literature, in Hesiod, in Homer and in Herodotus.

It doesn't take long for a people to recognize that they have a history: significant events in their community, a battle won, a scourge defeated, a plague overcome. The Egyptians were certainly conscious of their history and were meticulous in keeping records. For example, in the Turin Museum there is a fragment of what is known as the Turin Canon of Kings, a list of more than 300 kings of Egypt to about the mid-16th century BCE. The Turin papyrus is a copy of what was once an earlier text and begins with the reign of gods who ruled before the kings, all of whom had extraordinarily long reigns. The parallel between this king list, Sumerian lists, and Hesiod is very similar. Thus, it is not surprising to find ancestor lists in biblical literature. The Turin Canon consciously attempts to record the royal line back to its beginning and to separate the history of the gods from that of men and rulers. Similarly *Genesis* is a Hebrew counterpart, a record of the beginnings of humankind to show how the present inhabitants derive from that tradition of greatness in earlier centuries, to link Hebrews with a great past, to heroic legends, with stories borrowed from Sumerian and Mesopotamian culture. *Genesis* is the use of the past as propaganda and instruction, a way to influence the people to accept the current institutions of kingship and the status quo, with Sumeria, Babylonia, Egypt and Greece as unacknowledged cultural sources.

The Tower of Babel

After describing the many dispersed families of the descendants of Noah, *Genesis* 11 begins with the statement that "The whole earth used the same language and the same speech." These people built a tower, which the Lord came down to see and was very pleased with initially. "And the Lord said, 'Truly, they are one people and they all have the same language. This is the beginning of what they will do. Hereafter they will not be restrained from anything which they determine to do." When even the language of adolescents differs considerably from that of parents, it is hard to accept that all people had an identical language, nobody had a lisp or a wheeze, and that everyone used the same tense and the subjunctive case correctly.

If people didn't have free will before or during the time of any of the ancients, then surely they got free will here. Actually, this statement of the Lord's doesn't exclude even wickedness. But the next phrase reveals a lot about the mischief even gods can conspire to. *Genesis* 11: 7 begins: "Let us go down, and there confuse their language so that they will not understand one another's speech."

Who is "us"? Suddenly, plural gods appear on the scene after we were led to believe that there was only one Lord of creation who can bring about calamity. Men have had a tough time with these playful gods who refuse to define what wickedness is, destroy everyone when they think too much wickedness is occurring, and then, to be spiteful, confound their hard-earned language skills just when they had mastered a nice vocabulary and grammar that everyone in Babylon understood. "For this reason it was called Babel, because there the Lord (he is suddenly singular again) confused the speech of all the earth. From there the Lord scattered them all over the earth." (24) It would be hard to find a simpler explanation of how different languages developed. We must assume that this multiplicity of languages was good for mankind (it certainly would not have been good for commerce), and not the simplicity of one language the Babylonians had developed.

Whether the biblical tower was real or mythical is irrelevant because at that time of the biblical writings the religious areas at Babylon, Nippur, Ur, and Sippar, enclosed by greater and lesser walls, were so extensive that they constituted sacred cities with massive temple buildings built with glazed kiln-dried bricks for durability. The oldest known temple was E-Kur at Nippur about 4,000 BCE, and the first ziggurat within the temple compound dates from 2,700 BCE. The English word "babble" may refer to meaningless and unintelligible sounds, but archaeology, not the biblical scribes, has demonstrated the sophistication of Babylonian architectural splendor.

Then, out of the blue at the conclusion of the Tower of Babel incident, the scribe starts describing the descendants of Sem, one of Noah's boys, as if he had forgotten him. But something is amiss here. The Lord even before the flood had limited human life to 120 years. But for reasons unknown to us, almost all of the descendants of Sem, including Sem himself who died when he was 600 years old, lived far beyond that time frame according to the scribe who obviously forgot his arithmetic as well as his plot.

Here is a breakdown of the ages of Sem's descendants: Arphachsad, 438; Sale, 433; Eber 464; Phaleg, 239; Reu, 239; Sarug, 230; Nahor, 148: Thare, 205. This is an average age of 299.5 years for these elders. Either the Lord had forgotten his injunction about living so long that he gave in *Genesis* 6:3, or wise men who never purchased life insurance simply ignored it, a feat of longevity they cannot seem to duplicate today no matter how many pills they take.

Genesis out-does itself in literary mischief and playful story-telling, its legends re-read, re-told and re-enacted on the stages of elementary schools and in church basements for hundreds of years. But *Genesis* itself is a retelling, the continuation of a tradition of rephrasing older literature. *Genesis* contains all the elements of mythic literature that repeats itself in adventures like *The Lord of the Rings* with warrior heroes, semi-divine beings with superhuman powers, mythical birds, long journeys, rings, staffs, or amulets with special powers to depose evil, fellowship, the presence of evil that seeks to destroy humankind, and a resolution inevitably suitable to both humans and gods.

CHAPTER SEVEN
ABRAHAM, FIRST OF THE PATRIARCHS

When the late author Tad Szulc retraced the steps of the patriarch Abraham he was shown a book containing reproductions of a fresco painted in Mari in northern Syria dating from the early second millennium BCE, a fresco reputedly of Abraham. What Szulc observed in that fresco was an un-mythic, ordinary man with brown skin, semitic-looking, sporting a small black beard. He was wearing a black cap with a white headband. But in his lap was the two-horned head of a sacrificial bull. (1) Was Abraham originally a follower of the bull cult as were the Mesopotamian and Canaanite cultures?

If there is any historical basis for him as an individual, and there is no known external biblical evidence, he was a wealthy Sumerian trader who went frequently to Egypt and retired in a fertile and relatively unsettled region. The patriarchal cycle and fable of Abraham is the story of the birth of the Hebrew family, as later *Exodus* would be the story of the founding of the Israelite nation. Both stories represent Hebrew contributions to epic literary traditions.

Journeys of heroes abound in classical mythology: Gilgamesh in search of the key to immortality, Jason in quest of the golden fleece, Demeter in search of her daughter Persephone, Perseus looking for the head of the Gorgon Medusa, Hercules fulfilling his labors to win his freedom, Odysseus finding his way home after the Trojan War, and Aeneas journeying to find a new Roman republic. Abraham is such a hero on the move, leaving his homeland to found a new country, a story written to justify the possession of the land and the origins of Hebrew ethnic and familial identity.

This story is in a heroic tradition, about a man who can do extraordinary things because of parentage or relationship with the gods, and in which the hero appears much larger than normal humans. Abraham falls in this mythic category. He comes from a distant country to become its father, lives longer than most people can count, has God on his side, so knows in advance that his missions will be successful. His wife is barren, yet he will be the father of many generations. God tests his obedience though the command appears to be perverse. He justifies the possession of the land and the origin of a religious uniqueness. Abraham is a condensation of several important tribal individuals, as in the exploits of Ulysses, for the sake of one heroic story, a concocted myth about a warrior chieftain, the leader of a roving tribe group that conquered villages through military invasion to establish quit claims to the land. The fact that he converses with Yahweh on a regular basis is emblematic of ancient epics when heroes always spoke to patron deities.

Chapters 12 through 50 of *Genesis,* recounts two main stories. Abraham is of a patriarchal family, and is likely based on one man's conquest of the land of Canaan. The second story is about Joseph who, having been abandoned by brothers, rises to power in Egypt and saves his family from destruction. Both Abraham and Joseph are tales of the founding of the Hebrew people to justify the occupation of the land.

Deuteronomy notes: "Then you shall declare before the Lord, your God, 'My father was a wandering Aramean who went down to Egypt with a small household and lived there as an alien.'" (2) Abraham would not have been an Aramean if he came from Ur in the Chaldees but a Chaldean and the slip betrays the scribe's ethnic negligence. Arameans were unknown prior to the 12th century BCE whereas the Chaldeans were a thousand years earlier. (3) Scholars claim that the site is not Ur in the southern Mesopotamia but Urfa in the north where Amorites, Arameans and Hurrians mingled. Some scholars conclude that Abraham, Isaac and Jacob were not directly related but neighboring chieftains because sanctuaries, Hebron for Abraham, Beersheba for Isaac and Bethel and Shechem for Jacob, were geographical spheres of influence. (4)

Abraham receives a promise: "To your descendants, I will give this land." Although this promise was made successively in several passages, we find in *Gen.* 23 that Abraham had to purchase, for 400 shekels or pieces of silver, a burial plot for his wife Sara and his family. If the land was his, why was it necessary to purchase a cemetery?

Abraham is blessed because his ancestors will participate in the land, and because he gets to talk extensively with the Lord. He says, "I have ventured to speak to the Lord though I am but dust and ashes." (5) All epic heroes were favored by the gods and a few like Gilgamesh, Hercules and Ulysses, were greatly favored and part divine. (6)

Name Calling

Abraham's name, clearly representative of a patriarchal hero, comes from the linguistic roots of AV or AB, meaning father, and RAM, meaning exalted. But God changes ordinary men's names. Abram is re-named Abraham, and his wife Sarah is re-named Sara. What is the reason for changing names? Does it suggest a break with their past, a disassociation of personal identity with a new location in a new country? Jacob has his name changed to Israel which becomes the name of the country. Today many religious ceremonies, confirmation for Catholics, marriage for Mormon women, are thought to be transforming religious events that require new names.

In the *Koran*, Abraham is Ibrahim, and his existence for Muslims is the basis for all Arab tribes and Islam itself. The Great Mosque of the Dome of the Rock rests atop the rock of the old Temple Mount in Jerusalem where the mighty temple of Solomon once stood and where it is believed Abraham intended to sacrifice his son Isaac. It is also the place where Muslims believe Mohammed ascended into heaven. This one place is associated with more significant traditions for more religions than any one site in religious history.

One key to the name change is suggested in the Joseph narrative, where the Pharaoh (whose name, oddly, is not given) re-names Joseph "Saphaneth-phanee," the meaning of which is unknown. It is possible that the *Genesis* scribe is borrowing the prerogative of the pharaohs to change the name of a person who had acquired royal honors and ascribing that royal tradition to the Hebrew god. Thus, the Hebrew god, as a king, according to the scribe, could re-name a tribal chief and such a person would then achieve a kind of royal, semi-divine status. Following this same reasoning, is it possible that Yahweh is a name change of the Egyptian monotheistic god Amun?

Abraham travels to Egypt. Since God had spoken to him about his new lands where his ancestors would prosper, why would he suddenly decide to go to Egypt? Why should he be afraid for his wife's beauty and the desire she might arise in Egyptian royalty? (We discover that Sarah is really Abraham's half-sister or possibly niece. "She is indeed my sister, my father's daughter but not my mother's." (*Gen.* 20:12). If this was such a danger to travel to Egypt, why go at all? What was to be gained? As it turns out, Abraham returns from Egypt a rich man with "cattle, silver and gold." (7) How this wealth is acquired is not recorded, because Abraham is previously described as a man with domesticated animals. Gold, silver, cattle and slaves, all of which Abraham has, were often cited by Herodotus as the mark of a famous chief, king or leader of a city.

This land claim for the hill country of Judea, sanctioned by God, is justification for descendants to remain there. Even in recent times, Prime Ministers of Israel used the biblical land argument for not yielding in negotiations on the lands, Judea and Samaria, taken in the West Bank in the 1967 war with Jordan. The right to the land was supposedly given by God, therefore who could dispute it, and in what court could it be adjudicated?

Covenants and Sacrifice

Although the first sacrifices are performed by Cain, Abel and Noah, it is Abraham who perfects these ritual acts and thus earns glorification and prescribes the ideal form for future religious acts. We speak colloquially of "cutting a deal," an idea that occurs in the story of Abraham who cuts a heifer, a she-goat and a ram in half. That night, after Abraham had fallen into a deep sleep, God appeared as a smoking furnace and a flaming torch, and this was a sign of the acceptance of the sacrifices and the binding of a covenant. Similarly, Agamemnon had his men place their swords between the boar that had been sliced in two smearing it with its blood as a bond of allegiance between him and the men and as a symbol of enmity against King Priam of Troy.

The scribe tells us more about Abraham's marriages. "Abraham married another wife whose name was Cetura" (25:3), and the children born to him, deeds performed, etc., before he finally succumbs at the ripe old age of 175 years, to which the scribe adds, as if we don't the idea already, "He died at a good old age, an old man, after a full life." (25:8). What about the ripe old ages of Abraham's eight or ten previous generations who averaged nearly 300 years of life? Abraham was a piker in age compared to those biological progenies. A patriarch could never die a young man, except in a tragedy, and so had to live out an extraordinary number of years to be believable, or, had to be given an extraordinary number of years to create the impression that he was extraordinary and heroic. Although it is easier to think that Hebrews had not yet learned to calculate the calendar as Babylonians had, the age of patriarchs is a literary device made to project the protagonist as superhuman.

Why didn't Abraham sacrifice his son Isaac? The sacrifice of a child under the guidance of the gods is not unusual in ancient literature. Euripedes used human sacrifice as a theme throughout his plays. Perhaps the most illustrious or ignoble example is Agamemnon's sacrifice of his daughter Iphigeneia to obtain a favorable wind for his troops to cross the Hellespont and attack Troy, a dubious procurement of a divine favor at face value but not when a chieftain is faced with mutiny among conscripted soldiers whose pay was pillage from a captured city. Abraham's presumed sacrifice was a literary way, as was Euripedes or Aeschylus, of showing how sacrifice is pleasing and of how powerful and exacting the gods were in preventing further calamities. Agamemnon's action comes back to haunt him literally when Clytemnestra, Agamennon's wife, kills him for murdering their daughter, and she in his turn is killed by her son Orestes for killing his father. God holding back the striking hand of Abraham to slay Isaac may have implied the end of human sacrifice to appease deities.

But the most important, and oft repeated theme throughout this part of *Genesis*, is land. It was necessary that nomadic peoples who had usurped part of a country through a military campaign, of which only a small note is made of Abraham's military prowess, which ends in victory, to justify their continued and extended stay in occupied territory. As a people led by Abraham, they had come from Mesopotamia and did not immediately settle in one place, even though throughout the *Genesis* narrative, God promises them "this" land. "Go from your home...to the land that I will show you."

Abraham journeys from the Fertile Crescent and lives with the Egyptians and then the Philistines. He makes a covenant with the Philistine chieftain Abimelech, as later does Isaac. Justification for the land, commissioned by god and extended to all the descendants, is the dominant theme and is repeated in the narratives of Isaac and Jacob. The metaphor of the journey is the symbol for breaking the pattern of former living and parting from polytheistic beliefs.

The archives of Nuzi a few miles southwest of Kirkuk in northern Iraq have yielded documents from c.1,500 BCE that reveal comparisons with the legal practices of the biblical patriarchs. Abraham laments that he will die without a son. In Nuzi it was customary for a childless couple to adopt a son. If a marriage in Nuzi society was childless, the wife could provide a substitute wife, exactly what Sarah did when she gave Hagar to Abraham, and Rachel gave her maid Bilhah to Jacob. When Rachel stole the household gods (teraphim) of her father Laban, he pursued her relentlessly because in Nuzi society the person who was in possession of them also had rights to the inheritance. (8)

Abraham's misdeeds are never condemned and he receives no reproach for them. The conventional wisdom is to excuse Abraham his actions because he has been chosen by God. Let's put his deeds in proper perspective. God's decision to make him a prophet excuses him, and this is certainly common in the heroic epic tradition, Hercules comes to mind, from the faults and behavior of ordinary men. Here are Abraham's actions.

1) He marries his half-sister Sarah. It was not unusual for great men, including the Pharaohs of Egypt to take sisters as wives. (9)

2) He lies to the Egyptian king about who Sarah is (God, by the way, threatens the Egyptian with death if he has relations with Sarah, but says nothing about Abraham's deceit), and lies to a tribal king Abimelech about his marital relationship with Sarah.

3) Suddenly, upon his return from Egypt, he is rich, although no explanation is given for this great change in financial status. The only way to have gotten "cattle, silver, gold, and jewelry" as a shepherd and pastoral farmer, unless he was a king is to have raided a city that had such luxuries.

4) He accepts his wife Sarah's offer to sleep with his Egyptian maid, Agar, in order to conceive a son. The result is Ismael.

5) Later, he dismisses Agar, because of Sarah's nagging and jealousy about her son, Isaac, and Agar's son, Ismael. He sends Agar and the young child out into the desert. When the child is about to die, God has to rescue Ismael and Agar from certain destruction in the desert.

6) He knows about the destruction of Sodom in advance, but fails to warn his nephew Lot. Lot's wife, who disobeys, becomes a pillar of salt. The daughters of Lot, get their father drunk, lie with him, and their offspring become the origin of two tribes: the Moabites and the Ammonites.

7) He is prepared to sacrifice his son Isaac for an unspecified covenant.

8) He sends his bastard children by his concubines away to the East so that his son Isaac won't be near them or know about them.

The deceit of Abraham follows epic tradition, as in Homer deceit and cunning wisdom are equated, especially in *The Odyssey* (Chap. 13: 294-99) where Ulysses if said to be "he of many wiles," and thus wins the approval of Athene his protective goddess.

At this point in the *Genesis* narrative, we are still uncertain what wickedness is, but it clearly is not lying, marrying half-sisters, sleeping with servants, getting rich by unrecorded means, dismissing children and servants to die in the desert, having concubines, or trying to kill a son. Indeed, those actions will get you the status of a patriarch if you play your cards right. However, we do know that God killed all humans in a flood because of unspecified wickedness. But look at what Abraham did and look what happened to him: he got glorified by God, had special blessings, wifely dispensations, all the land he wanted, and as many descendants as there were stars.

Abraham is not called "blameless" like Noah was. But he is given all the land he can see and made to be the father of all nations. God makes several covenants with him as if he were the best man on the earth. He is blessed by the priest, Melchisedec given numerous visions, walks and talks with God, and even persuades God to save Sodom if he can find ten good men, maybe men like himself. God was originally going to destroy Sodom if there were 50 good men in it. (10)

This curious story about lying to the king about one's marital relationship is oddly repeated again on King Abimelech by Isaac later in the narrative, who lies about his wife, Rebecca, and calls her sister. The King sees Isaac fondling Rebecca and scolds Isaac for deceiving him, and Isaac tells him how he also was afraid for his life. For a family that had been in a military campaign against entire cities, the story of this mild cowardice in both Abraham and Isaac, who commanded many troops, seems farfetched. The Philistine kings must have been a little suspicious about this family of Abraham's, even though the king protects Isaac and Rebecca: "Whoever touches this man or his wife shall be put to death." (11) Here is the mark of Cain with a vengeance.

The scribes and editors of *Genesis* assimilated and repeated tales from the Babylonians, who had in turn imbibed the culture of the Sumerians. Hence, the special relationship of men with divinities, a sort of a covenant between deities and the community, is not a uniquely Hebrew concept. The king was the representative of the people's commune with the god, the agent of the deity who was in a special place of significance. The result of wars, the causes of floods, the outcome of the harvest, the whole governance of man's relation with nature and other men was subject to the decision of the gods. The order of dominion and subordination was settled: men were ruled by gods, but had their king, who might be part god, as their intermediary. As late as the time of Jesus, the king and the Jewish high priest were the same person.

Rebecca and Jacob

We encounter Jacob in more detail in the following chapter, but a few preliminary comments appropriate to the Abraham story are appropriate here too.

The deceit of Abraham continues with Rebecca and Jacob when both lie to Isaac about Jacob's identity so Jacob can receive Esau 's birthright illegally. Unbelievably, Isaac does not undo his blessing when he discovers he has been deceived and does not punish either Jacob or Rebecca. Is this a form of retribution to Isaac for his previous lies? Is it an illustration of how the deceit of a woman, even for her son, can undo the blessing of a father? Jacob is said to have "earned" the birthright earlier when Esau, the hairy one, sold it to him to obtain some food. Is the insertion of this good news meant to assuage the deception of a father to get a blessing Jacob does not deserve?

Jacob takes his mother's advice and flees to Phaddam-Aram, a place said to be in northern Mesopotamia, but could be in Utah. There, because he feels cheated by Laban, his uncle (although Jacob had established the conditions for his work and his marriage to Rachel) he cheats his uncle, as does Rachel. Laban and Jacob reach an agreement, and then, by cunning mating practices, Jacob in effect steals a large part of Laban's herd of sheep and goats, an action which Jacob wrongfully attributes to God's planning: "So God took away your father's stock and gave it to me," Jacob says to his wives Lia and Rachel.

Jacob decides that discretion through flight is the better part of honest valor and trust, so he talks his wives into leaving with him, without so much as a goodbye to the host relatives, and takes a goodly share of his newly acquired herd. Before they leave, Rachel decides to steal the household idols. Once Laban catches up to the escaping party, Rachel then lies about having taken the household gods, by hiding them in the camel's saddle. When Laban inquires why Jacob has left without the common courtesies, Jacob says: "I was afraid, for I thought that you would take away your daughters from me by force."

After settling in the land of the Canaanites, one of Jacob's daughters, now called Israel's, is raped by the son of a local chieftain. This is the stuff tribal warfare thrives on, and it is no different with the sons of Jacob, who, through the deceit of feigning a city's participation in the new covenant of Israel, request that all males become circumcised. In good faith they do, and willingly accept fraternity with Jacob's tribe. But when they do, Jacob's sons kill all the males because of the violation of their sister. The destruction of other cities by Jacob and his family and followers could have been one way of fulfilling the prophecy.

Prophecy is fulfilled through deceit, treachery, and revenge. The standard theological response would be that God allows this to happen, that he permits good to come from evil. But here is an example of the lack of good faith between family relationships, not between God and mankind. Rebecca deceives her husband, and her eldest son. Jacob deceives his father, and his older brother. Where is God's response or reproach against Jacob for stealing, an action that would later become a commandment? Is Jacob better than those who lived in Sodom, and for whom Abraham in discussion with God is said to have wrung the concession that he would have spared the city for 10 good people?

The more human (or less heroic) side of these founding fathers is their relationship with women. All have multiple marriages and concubines and have children with slave girls reportedly given to them by their wives, who may even be their half-sisters. However, there is an important prohibition: one must not marry a Canaanite woman. Abraham would not marry one after Sarah died, and Rebecca warns Jacob not to marry such a woman. The narrative even goes so far as to state that Esau learned that Isaac had forbidden Jacob not to marry a Canaanite woman, when in fact it was Rebecca. So what is so wrong with Canaanite women? Is there a lingering animosity between peoples caused when the nomad Abraham settled among them and waged war? Did the Canaanites also prohibit their men to marry Abraham's descendents? The link with the principal civilizations is contained in the marriages of both Esau and Jacob. Jacob returns to the lands of his ancestors, Mesopotamia, and settles on his uncle's daughters, Lia and Rachel. Esau marries Maheleth, who is a daughter of Agar, Abraham's slave girl, who is part Egyptian. Esau already has Hethite wives.

If anyone were to write a justification for their existence in a region of the world in which they were not the original inhabitants, they would find the main elements for such a rationalization in the story of Abraham. God has promised us the land; our father is ordained by God to populate this territory; our people are the only ones chosen to live here; we have roots from great civilizations. Even though we deceive local kings, like the Philistines, we have a covenant with them and they protect us. And by the way, we don't associate with Canaanites who actually do live in this part of the country. Clearly, no one had yet had a course in multi-cultural understanding and tolerance. The moral justification of this story is on shaky ground. What court of civil or ecclesiastical law would condone the actions of the principal individuals as proper on behalf of some divine purpose? What possible purpose could it be to use the name and authority of God to justify the lying, cheating, capturing of towns and killing people for the sake of laying claim to rocky hillsides? It's as if God had to hold off giving the Ten Commandments until after this moral charade so as not to embarrass the patriarchs who violated several of them in his name. (12)

The famous *Code of Hammurabi* discovered at Susa in modern Iraq and residing today in the Louvre in Paris is mankind's first codified legal text. It was written about 1,900 BCE by a Semitic ruler after the downfall of the Sumerian civilization. (15) It derives its legal foundation directly from the Sumerian culture based at Ur, Abraham's original city. If we compare the Sumerian legal code with that of Hammurabi's, as we do in Chapter Nine, we find strict penalties for certain offenses, particularly those that involve kinship and family ties.

All men were not equal according to the law in these days. Social class had very defined privileges, and we can assume that since Abraham was a member of a patrician order he was not subject to the same rules. Slaves, for example, as in Abraham's treatment of Agar and their son, Ismael, held the lowest social status, and were usually of a different racial stock. Agar was an Egyptian, and Ismael eventually married an Egyptian. The treatment of slaves is particularly topical. (13) Abraham's callous treatment of Agar, in this context, is in conformity with Mesopotamian legal codes.

Monogamy was the standard practice in Sumerian society, although concubinage was tolerated. The rights of the legitimate wife, however, were protected. Barrenness, although it did not dissolve the marriage bonds, did deprive the wife of the exclusive rights of intercourse. Thus, though we may find today Sarah's request for Abraham to take his slave girl in order to get a son unconscionable, this practice was permissible under Sumerian custom. (14)

Sumerians and Semites

The drainage of the Tigris and Euphrates is acknowledged as the geographic site of one of mankind's most extensive civilizations and the origin of western thought, certainly of western literature. Humans have inhabited the area for at least 40,000 years. The irrigation system of the area dates from 4,000 BCE and was one of the great accomplishments of the Sumerians. From this region come most of the elements of civilization and an advanced culture. Archaeologists have found the oldest appearances of the wagon wheel and the potter's wheel.

At the northern tip of the Persian Gulf Arab tribes inhabit the Abu Fuseima marshes practicing a way of life that has existed for at least 3,000 years. This watery zone extends for over 6,000 miles where the rivers converge, a labyrinth of high, reed-covered lagoons filled with cranes and marsh waterfowl, much of it destroyed by Saddam Hussein in an obliteration meant to crush a Shiite revolt in 1991.

Burial excavations from Ur from 5,500 years ago have revealed a high level of urban life. The ziggurat or staged tower of Nannat at Ur, built about 2,200 BCE, still stands in the surrounding barren desert of southern Iraq. The fabled Tower of Babylon was also such a ziggurat, but was destroyed. As the chief city of the Sumerian empire of lower Mesopotamia, Ur was a theocratic state. The king was also its god, responsible for both civil and clerical functions. The teraphim, the little household gods stolen by Rachel in the story of Jacob, and recurring again in David's household but said to be his wife's, are an indication that not all worship took place in the temples in the cities but also in homes as they did well into Roman times.

And where did the Semites, a people who inhabited the broad regions of the northern Arabian peninsula, come in contact with the Sumerian way of life? We know Sargon about 2,200 BCE, who was Akkadian, was Semitic in origin. Hammurabi (c.2,100 BCE) conquered the city states of Elam and Amor, and thus the Semites ruled Babylon for centuries until the rise of the Persians under Cyrus. The Semitic peoples had wide access to the writings and civilized conditions of the Sumerians. A Sumerian tablet has yielded this interesting saying: "The lamb is the substitute for humanity; he has given up the lamb for his life."(15) The phrase "the lamb of god" and similar symbols from Hebrew, Jewish and Christian traditions are Sumerian in origin.

Two Sumerian legends in particular appear in *Genesis*. One story tells of Adapa, a sage of the city of Eridu, he who had been initiated into the priestly craft by Ea, the goddess of wisdom, and the patron of Gilgamesh. But Ea had kept one secret from Eridu: the secret knowledge of immortality. Another legend recounts how the gods had made men happy but how one had sinned and been punished with a flood. One man, Tagtug, a weaver had survived but even he had forfeited long life and good health for eating the fruit of a forbidden tree. (16)

Similar descriptive phrases from a popular Egyptian story, *The Tale of Sinuhe*, (see Chapter 9) of an immigrant wanderer journeying from Egypt into Canaan, appear in *Genesis*. The story of Sinuhe dates from 1,971–1,928 BCE and was written under Pharaoh Sesostris I and describes life in a tent among the Amorites and his descriptions of the flocks and herds, the figs, vines, barley and wheat, olive and honey, all parallel biblical descriptions. (17)

A bill of lading from a ship commissioned by the temple at Ur in 2,048 BCE. (canals had then been dug to permit ships direct access to the Persian Gulf) unloaded at the quay in Ur. The ship contained a cargo of gold, ivory, copper ore, precious wood and fine stone for making statues and vases. (18) Abraham was said to have had jewelry, gold, silver, and other valuables, not the articles normally found in the possession of a shepherd or pastoral farmer. (19) These are articles associated with a commercial trader who must buy and sell goods along the traditional trade routes. Abraham also had cattle, flocks, and herds, both to feed his extended family and to trade. It can be argued that Abraham, if originally his myth was based on a real person, was a trade representative, perhaps for the temple at Ur, and was abroad in other lands for commercial purposes. Excavations of the burial chambers at Ur have revealed how rich were the city's treasures, and burial items included gold, silver, marble and precious stones like lapis lazuli.

Under this hypothesis, Abraham had dealings with Pharaohs and kings like Abimilech because he was trading with them. The reason he lived in a tent city and not a stone house was because he had to travel frequently, as the scribe of *Genesis* notes: Haran, Sichem, the Negeb, Bethel, Egypt, and Hebron, among other places. This would also account for the large size of his household, including slaves, and the reason why his nephew Lot did not live with him. Lot could have been his commercial representative in the city of Sodom. The temple god of Ur, assuming Abraham is a commercial dealer for the temple, has given Abraham his trading territory. He is therefore the chief Sumerian trader among the Semites based in Canaan. His son Isaac must not marry a Canaanite woman because Abraham himself is Sumerian, and he must therefore send his messenger to find a wife for Isaac from among his own people to maintain the purity of his culture.

When Ur, and in fact all of Sumer, was utterly destroyed by the Elamites a carving from a stone stele recounts the savagery of the destruction. (20) The omen of disaster must always have hung over cities that had riches that could be plundered, especially if it was a neighboring city tired of subjugation. The lamentation from that Sumerian text reads like the destruction of Sodom.

Sodom and Early Bronze Age Cities

Cities have existed in the high plains in the Judean hills since the Early Bronze Age, about 3,300 BCE, though river towns like Jericho existed from the Neolithic Age, or about 10,000 years ago. A French archaeological team began excavating the Tel Yarmut site near Bet Shemesh about 12 miles west of Jerusalem in 1992. This could even have been the site of ancient and biblical Sodom, although the probability is that it is near the southern end of the Dead Sea. Structures were built there between 2,900 to 2,400 BCE, several hundred years before Knossos, the great Minoan city on Crete, and about 1,500 years before the arrival of the Israelites. But it is about the same era as the beginning of Sumerian urban civilization.

A place known as Rujm el-Hiri, and Arabic word for "stone heap of the wild cat," has been reconstructed on the Golan Heights. It is over 5,000 years old, a site with a series of five concentric stone circles, the outer ring over a third of a mile long. The walls, some over 12 feet in height, are composed of large and small stone emplacements, a ceremonial site and not a living urban complex. Like Stonehenge, it served as an astronomical observatory because one gate lines up with the summer solstice at sunrise. The central cairn, possibly Beth-El where Jacob prayed, contained a burial chamber looted over 3,500 years ago.

The city at Tel Yarmut was deserted about 2,300 BCE, and the Canaanites in the region became semi-nomadic pastoral peoples who abandoned their fortified cities, perhaps because they had been raided too often. The city had a high degree of urban planning and a well-developed hierarchy as the discovery of the palace compound illustrates. This particular site, however, could very well coincide with the collapse of Sumerian civilization, and the end of the network of trading centers. Messengers describing the fall of the capitol at Ur would have reached their head trader in Sodom, conceivably Lot, before anyone else. Hypothetically, Lot, knowing the raiders would be coming for the cities along the trade route next, would have left town quickly and hid in the mountains with whatever treasures he could manage to take with him. There would be no need to notify Abraham because he didn't live in a city that could be raided.

The destruction of Sodom is a symbol of the destruction of Ur and the whole of Sumerian civilization over 4,000 years ago. So complete was this destruction that as late as the turn of the 20th century no one knew of the Sumerians. In fact, the argument is somewhat conclusive among archaeologists that Sumerian civilization is the forerunner to Egyptian culture that pre-dates Menes, the first pharaoh of the First Dynasty in Egypt at about 3,300 BCE.

But other real cities, celebrated in epic literature, were also destroyed, and made the gods angry. Neptune, in Euripedes' play *The Trojan Women* (415 BCE) notes: "For when once wide through city desolation spreads, the hallowed rites, the worship of the gods, must be neglected." (21) The example of Troy as a devastated city, the anger of the gods over the consequences and the recriminations they inflict, are literary precursors of Yahweh's anger over Sodom and Gomorrah. "Angry Jove" finds a parallel in the wrath of Yahweh, a recognized literary trait of deities.

Lot was Abraham's nephew and accompanied Abraham and Sara from the region of Haran to Canaan. Lot decided to settle in Sodom, not a wise decision considering that God was going to destroy it because there were several wicked people in it, a situation not unlike some of our cities today. Since God promised not to destroy people and cities with floods or rain water, he chose fire this time, although he didn't tell the people in advance what means of destruction he was going to use. Abraham knew about this in advance, of course, because he was always walking and talking with God. But curiously, he forgot to tell his nephew. Instead, a couple of angels, who aren't always recognizable as angels and are often just mistaken for traveling salesmen, came to Sodom to tell Lot that it was time to leave.

The men of Sodom saw the strangers come into town, and heard that they have gone into Lot's house, and they want to know what was up. They created a ruckus outside Lot's house and Lot went out to try and calm their agitation. They wanted the strangers to come out and state their business. This is similar to a city council or school board request for recognition to speak.

Then a very strange thing happens. Lot wants to protect the mob from getting at his strangers to whom he is showing hospitality. To keep the crowd from breaking down his doors, he offers the men his virgin daughters so they won't abuse his strangers. We don't know the daughters' reaction to this paternal decision but the strangers must have been pleased at Lot's generosity. At last, the strangers themselves pull Lot inside and close the door behind him, thereby rescuing Lot, and keeping his daughters virgins for the time being. At that, all the men at the door were struck blind. They were already deaf and dumb as to what was in store for them. But the theme of being struck blind will occur again with Paul on the road to Damascus.

Then the strangers set the record straight. They tell Lot and all his extended family to clear out of Sodom because they have been sent to destroy it. The sons-in-law, being young men, thought Lot was kidding, so they didn't take the advice seriously. They had not heard about the Great Flood. Lot took off with his wife and two daughters. No one was supposed to look back and see what was going on. Thus, it was hard luck for Lot's wife, and for Lot too, that she did look at the sulfur and fire pouring out of the heavens and instantly turned into a pillar of salt. This is a trick not even chemists can perform today.

Lot was still afraid to live in even a small village like Segor, so he lived in a cave in the mountains. His daughters, being young and foolish, just wanted to start a family. But since Sodom and all the surrounding villages had been destroyed, young men in the region were at a premium. In fact, there weren't any men around at all. So the daughters did a bold thing. Their father had offered them to most of the men of Sodom, who were obviously wicked or they wouldn't have been killed by God, so they decided to get their father drunk and get a child from him, as he was the only male in the vicinity. They got Lot so drunk the first night that he slept with his oldest daughter and she conceived. Then, probably still nursing a heavy hangover, he got drunk the second night and slept with his youngest daughter and she conceived.

Now understandably, since this story is reported to have happened to an illustrious patriarch, incest is not considered wickedness yet. Nor is getting drunk a couple nights in a row called wickedness either, and many men who still live and drink in caves will be pleased to know this. Daughters seeking conception by their father is permitted as long as the father is someone whom God has chosen and there are no other men for miles around. We are told that the progeny of these conceptions actually started two major tribal groups, the Moabites and the Amorites. (22) Such is the good fortune of those inhabitants and their descendants that they can claim ancestry from their mother and father's side of the family, an uncomplicated family history much easier for children to remember.

Land and Foreskin

God makes two special covenants with Abraham. Land is the principal bond. No one speaks about purchasing the land. It is simply a gift. But did God take it from the Canaanites, the original squatters? The issue of prior ownership does not arise. This would never happen with tax assessors available. (23)

Neither God nor the scribe talk about where Abraham gets all his silver and gold or jewelry he sends with his servant to Mesopotamia to fetch a wife for his son Isaac. These are just things he has, and God is not reported to have given this wealth to him. But land...well, real estate is another story, and the better part of wealth. God doesn't just tell Abraham once about the land he wants to give him; he has to mention the property giveaway several times. God had not said why he was going to take the land away from the Canaanites and Philistines who had been living in the region for hundreds of years and give it to a wandering immigrant who had come from another country who did not even conquer it by military force. Abraham was already wealthy, so why would he need a whole country as inheritance from God? Is it possible that later people who claimed to be descendants, and who wished that Abraham had owned the land and given it to them in his will simply claimed that God had given it to Abraham? After all, if Abraham had gotten away with lying without God saying anything. So what's wrong with a scribe who was commissioned to write all this down also injecting a little white lie for the sake of the whole people claiming ancestry from the immigrant hero?

People usually go to war fighting to defend their homeland. So for the Israelites to claim that God gave their father, Abraham, the land because he liked Abraham, then the land must already have been in Israelite hands. We are not told what the Canaanite reaction was to God giving these immigrants their land. There might have been some stone throwing if they had been told God's wishes. Perhaps there is some undiscovered manuscript of the Canaanites revealing their side of the story.

Gen. 17 is devoted to God's special covenant with Abraham, a "perpetual covenant," which involves flesh in exchange for land. The blood covenant has universally been the strongest form of agreement, and several forms of this binding accord are in evidence throughout the world. It is as solemn an agreement as it is possible to obtain, short of negotiations for dowries. God promises to make Abraham "exceedingly fruitful." Abraham was allowed to have, or at least not prohibited from having, two principal wives, a servant girl, and several concubines. Who wouldn't be fruitful under such circumstances, especially if he lived to "a good old age," and "after a full life?" One can quickly understand the productivity of these first prophets and patriarchs since they are granted such multiple female privileges.

The circumcision, cutting that little bit of male foreskin, remains today as a sign of the covenant of God with his people, still conducted, among infant Jewish males in the synagogue. It's a kind of sacrifice in a way, although if done at an early enough age relatively painless. One must be sure to engage a doctor with a steady hand. (24) Friedman contends from linguistic evidence that the priestly editor P, writing in the 5th to 6th century BCE, added the material about circumcision, specifically Chapter 17, to the text. (25)

So Abraham gets rich, has a long life, gets the son he wants (Isaac), gets rid of the son he doesn't want (Ismael) by sending him into the desert to die together with his mother, sends all his bastard children off somewhere to the east, has a whole country given to him gratis and all his descendants as many as there are stars, and for all this he only gets to give God a little foreskin. Who said bargaining in the Middle East couldn't pay off? Not bad for a man from upper and lower Mesopotamia who taught the Israelites all they needed to know about striking a deal.

Journey to the West, a classic Chinese mythological novel, grand in style like the biblical mythologies, was written in the 15th century BCE and can be compared to Abraham's journey to his west to locate his destiny, land and home for future progeny. The main character, Sanzang, like Abraham, travels with three companions and a deity for protection and comfort. The deity is able to subdue demons, brute forces, and monsters along the way. The Tang era monk in the 100-chapter novel is based on an historical person, but with mythological and imaginary experiences, able to transform himself into various shapes, who journeyed to India to bring Buddhist scriptures to China. Over a period of 17 years, he traveled tens of thousands of miles, encountering numerous hardships and dangers before he finally brought 600+ scriptures to Chang'an, the capital of the Tang Empire (618–907), now Xian.

The 20 year adventure of Ulysses in Homer's *Odyssey* also serves as a literary example of the archetype of an extended, purposeful journey, ordained by the gods, but revealing the heroic proportions of the hero and protagonist, whether Ulysses, Sanzang, or Abraham.

If I have repeatedly emphasized deception in the description of Abraham and his kin it is not to moralize his behavior. The art of deception is a literary device practiced throughout ancient literature as a method of getting even with the gods for playing tricks on humankind. Zeus disguises himself in order to win the favor of mortal women like Europa he coveted. Ulysses disguises himself to confuse the men who have taken over his household. Prometheus deceived Zeus to capture fire for humans. Theseus deceives King Minos to win the heart of his daughter Ariadne. Odd as it may seem, it would have been unusual for biblical scribes not to have portrayed Abraham as devious, scheming and deceitful, the very survivor qualities found in the literature of all heroic figures and divinities. Patriarch stories are not lessons in moral imperatives but attempts by biblical scribes to imitate a literary tradition.

CHAPTER EIGHT
ESAU, JACOB, AND JOSEPH

Esau, Jacob and Joseph began a progeny that linked the mythical past of the Hebrews with ancestors, a literary convention that conforms with a tribal identity, and an understanding of blood ties, loyalties, commitments, inheritances and birthrights that transcend adversity. The Hebrew ideas of portentous dreams and inheritance, like Rachel's theft of Laban's household gods, were abducted from Mesopotamian literature and law.

Here's how the genealogy is portrayed.

When Sarah was thought to be barren she asked Abraham to get a child with the Egyptian servant girl, Agar. Isaac prayed to the Lord because his wife Rebecca was barren and she conceived twins. A barren wife could be divorced in Babylonian law. So Rebecca bore Esau first, and the scribe notes that "his whole body was like a hairy garment," a peculiar phenomenon for a newly born baby, and a description that might raises eyebrows about paternity. This not only a bias against body hair, but against Esau as inferior. Esau would be the youngest known to shave in scripture. Then Jacob, the fraternal twin, emerged from her womb with his hand gripping Esau's heel, which is why, we are told, he was called Jacob. In the modern idiom, the two would be called "Hairy," and "Heel-gripper."

But Esau is not the first hairy one. "The whole of his body was covered with hair, he was clothed in long hair like a woman. His hair was luxuriant like that of the corn god." Thus does the *Epic of Gilgamesh* describe Eabani, the hero god made out of clay by Aruru to be a champion against Gilgamesh. (1) The Sumerian Eabani becomes the biblical prototype for Esau, and perhaps the hairy model for Shakespeare's Caliban in *The Tempest*. Because Eabani is like a brother of Gilgamesh, this presumes that the analogous person, Jacob, is like Gilgamesh, the brother hero of the Sumerian epic. We know that Endiku was raised by wild animals and was without the benefits of a barber. He too was hairy. The entire episode is imitated from Sumerian texts.

At this point in the narrative it is mindful to recall another mythical hero whose heel was his downfall, as it was for Esau. Achilles, foremost hero of the Trojan War, was a fierce warrior possessed of a vicious rage. Thetis, his mother, daughter of Neptune, in order to make Achilles invulnerable, dipped him in the river Styx by his heels, which thereafter was the one vulnerable part of his anatomy, the Achilles tendon. Paris, after whom the fabled city of lights is named, was the son of Priam King of Troy and Hecuba. Paris killed Achilles by shooting him with an arrow in the heel. Jacob is the Hebrew Achilles, warrior shepherd of his era, and Gilgamesh, as Esau is the

Mesopotamian Eabani, another example of mythical mixing from different cultures and an indication that both Jacob and Esau represents heroic figures.

The next description we learn of these two twins is that Jacob asks for his brother's birthright in exchange for food. Gilgamesh asks Eabani for a drink. We learn that Esau doesn't know how to cook or this incident of who inherits what would not have occurred. So Esau swears to Jacob, after Jacob insists on a swearing, that he will give him his birthright. The scribe notes that Esau valued his birthright lightly. He might have added, "Thus cunningly and with greed did Jacob take Esau's presumed birthright when it wasn't necessary for his standard of living, by first denying his brother's legitimate request for something to eat, insisting on a swearing, and pretending, contrary to law, that this un-recorded and un-witnessed event was legally binding." Gilgamesh has a dream, as does Jacob, consults his goddess mother, Rimat-belit, as Jacob's mother intervenes before Isaac on behalf of Jacob. Jacob is the biblical version of Gilgamesh, another example of the deceit necessary for heroes to survive.

When Esau was 40 years old, he married two women, Judith and Basemath, but the daughters-in-law did not find favor with Isaac and Rebecca. Perhaps this angered Rebecca enough to have her son disenfranchised. Birthrights and inheritances had legal precedents in Babylonia. *The Code of Hammurabi* adopted from Sumerian law required that everything legal be recorded. Indeed, most of the writings excavated are contracts and legal writs accompanied by the seals of witnesses. (2)

According to Sumerian law, incorporated into the Babylonian legal codes and adopted by the Hebrews, children were absolutely under the authority of their parents and could be disinherited or disowned, banished from the city or sold into slavery. (3) There was no primogeniture, a principle by which all the father possessed after death is inherited by his first son. But in the normal course of events, the division of property among the children after the death of the father was divided according to law. (4) There was a "Law of Nisaba and Hani" in the Sumerian tradition that provided for the claim of inheritance by a son during the father's life. The parable of the Prodigal Son–who wants his share of his father's inheritance, gets it and then spends it all–is an example of this ancient legal provision in the gospels. According to Sumerian law, the portion of the estate claimed and given to one or more of the children would be recorded legally, and then no other claim could be made on the father's estate during his lifetime or after his death. (5)

The story of Jacob and Esau is an adapted legend demonstrating that the transfer of ancient Mesopotamian law is relevant to Hebrew law and forming the basis for a tribal identity preparatory to a national and religious identity under Moses and the establishment of the kingdom under David. Jacob and

Esau are the Bible's literary recording of yet another set of brothers imitated from older texts.

Isaac and the Blessing

After the birth of the twins, Isaac sees Abimelech, King of the Philistines, probably to conduct some business left him by Abraham who also had dealings with him. The Lord appears to Isaac and tells him not to go to Egypt, which is odd because Isaac wasn't intending to go to Egypt. Going to Egypt must have been like an annual pilgrimage, something like going to Paris in the spring, or San Francisco or New York anytime for shopping.

Like his father Abraham, Isaac receives a promise from the Lord that "I will give all these lands to you and your descendants," which confirms that this whole area was to be Isaac's sales territory. The Lord also said that he was doing this because Abraham heeded all his commandments, which is greatly exaggerating the meaning of the word, knowing what we do about Abraham's behavior when commandments had not even been documented.

Then, while residing in the land of Gerara, Isaac practices his father's deceits and lies about Rebecca, calling her his sister instead of his wife. But when Abimelech saw Isaac fondling Rebecca (they must not have brought the kids Esau and Jacob with them on this trip), Abimelech realized that Isaac had lied. Since Isaac was 60 years old when the twins were born, by this time he was already an elderly fondler. Why Abimelech should wonder at this deceit is mysterious, because Jacob's father Abraham had also lied to him about his wife Sarah. It was already a family tradition to lie about who was one's wife.

But deceit was not only a paternal trait. Rebecca has her share of conniving as well. She overhears Isaac asking Esau to get him something to eat, so she sends Jacob to get some lamb and convinces him that he should pretend to be Esau. So Jacob, picking up the family tradition of deceiving others, lies to his father about who he is, taking Esau's place in order to receive the blessing of Isaac, who at this time was also hard of hearing, not being able to distinguish his son's voices. "Isaac said, 'Are you really my son Esau?' Jacob answered, 'Yes, I am.'" If this had been Cain instead of Esau, he would now have had a good excuse to kill his brother, or for impersonating a patriarch. When Rebecca and Isaac hear that Esau might actually kill Jacob for his deception they decide to send him away to Rebecca's homeland in northern Mesopotamia. Like Abraham, Jacob is charged not to marry a Canaanite woman.

You may recall that Esau, the firstborn son of Isaac, had actually married two women, both Hethites. Suddenly, Jacob is admonished not to marry Hethite women. He is advised to marry one of his uncle Laban's daughters. This would mean, of course, that he would be marrying first cousins, or possibly younger aunts, since Laban was his mother Rebecca's brother. If one is going to be fruitful in progeny and the father of many nations, you have to go for good genes, and those can sometimes be found right in one's own family as the member of any royalty knows. To spite the whole family on hearing this news, Esau married his third wife, Maheleth, the daughter of Abraham's son Ismael, and therefore his first cousin. Thus the family, in order to become fruitful, was also inbreeding. Perhaps women were scarce. We know men were scarce in the time of Lot. Farmers know too much inbreeding is not good. But this is the Bible.

Dream On: Jacob and Herodotus

Authors used dreams as a literary device to advance the story line and to help describe some traits among the characters. Religious cults like that of Asclepius advocated that a particular god sent messages through dreams and the Bible and gospels imitated this characteristic. Magicians in Egypt used dream predictions regularly.

Herodotus was more sensible when he wrote: "Dreams in general originate from those incidents which have most occupied the thoughts during the day." (6) On the other hand, most epics include dreams that foretell future events, as Aeschylus reveals in *Prometheus Chained:* "I taught the various modes of prophecy, what truth the dream portends." (7) Thus, it is not surprising that Yahweh and angels appear in dreams to instruct the elect in what to do. Yahweh and his messengers appear to biblical heroes more in dreams that when they are awake, which appears to indicate that it is preferable to be unconscious to receive divine instructions and then hope you can remember the dream afterwards.

On the road to Haran in northern Mesopotamia, Jacob dreams one night that he sees angels climbing up and down a ladder to the heavens. This is not the same social ladder he is climbing by marrying one of his cousins. The Lord makes the promise about giving him the land, the same promise he has made to Abraham a zillion times, and to Isaac slightly less. Esau doesn't get this promise. Only Jacob, single, without a wife, and on a dangerous journey to find one, gets the promise of land and abundant descendants. The Lord may appear to work in mysterious ways, but biblical scribes are predictable in following precedents set by previous authors because a similar story occurs with Cambyses, son of Cyrus of Persia.

Herodotus reports that Cambyses had a dream. "While I was in Egypt I beheld in my sleep a vision, which I could wish had never appeared to me. A messenger seemed to arrive from home, informing me that Smerdis, sitting on the royal throne, touched the heavens with his head. It is not in my power of men to counteract destiny; but fearing that my brother would deprive me of my kingdom, I yielded to passion rather than to prudence." (8) The similarities are remarkable: a ladder reaching to the heavens (Jacob), and a head touching the heavens (Smerdis). Cambyses has a brother he is jealous of, and so does Jacob. Equally significant is that dreams connote legitimacy of a truth of some kind. Herodotus is simply recording a legend about the effect of dreams on great leaders.

Jacob's dream is not unique to Jacob but to all heroes of literature 3,000 years ago. We can read also in Herodotus where Croesus, "saw in his sleep a vision, menacing the calamity which afterwards deprived him of his son...Roused and terrified by this dream, he revolved the matter seriously in his mind." It turns out that everyone believed that "the offended deity, who warned me of the evil, has accomplished it [killed his son]." (9) Herodotus also reports that Cyrus has a dream and who then says: "The gods, whose favor I enjoy, disclose to me all those events which menace my security. In the night just passed I beheld your eldest son having wings on his shoulders, one of which overshadowed Asia, the other Europe, from which I draw certain conclusions that he is engaged in acts of treachery against me." (10) How many times in biblical scripture will we find that God warns the patriarch/hero of impending disaster, or the treachery of another, so that that person has to flee? (11)

There is even an Egyptian ladder first used by Osiris from the *Papyrus of Ani* by which the Egyptian deceased ascended from earth to heaven. "Gift of Thoth, mistress of the two sides of the Ladder, open thou the way for the deceased, set him on his way...Come thou therefore to heaven, enter thou therein in its name 'Ladder.'" (12) Jacob's dream and ladder have literary precedents from Mesopotamia, Persia and Egypt.

Once Jacob finds Haran, all the action takes place around a well, a meeting place for itinerant wanderers like an airport bar today. Abraham's servant met his first travel friends around this same well when he went searching for Rebecca, or at least a wife for Isaac. Jesus in later days would meet a woman around a well in Samaria. You could always meet a woman around a well if you waited long enough, though you might have to carry full buckets afterwards for the privilege.

Jacob didn't have to wait long before Rachel came along. Laban, Rebecca's brother and Jacob's uncle, was glad to meet Jacob. Family reunions were not a common happening in those days. Laban really wanted Jacob to have a better look at Lia, his eldest daughter. But the scribe tells us that "Lia's eyes were weak." (13) Maybe Jacob wasn't such a catch either. Anyway, the scribe notes that Rachel "was shapely and beautiful," and these have ever since been two major qualifications for men. So the two men worked out an agreement whereby Jacob would work for Laban for seven years in order to keep an eye on Rachel's qualifications, since Lia wouldn't be able to see him watching her younger sister anyway. Jacob worked for seven years for Rachel and was ready to claim her as wife, and probably plenty of dowry too.

But that night after the seven years are up, Laban pulls a little trick on Jacob, and this trick is the sort of thing men laugh about the next morning when they meet for coffee. Laban throws a big feast for Jacob, his nephew who has journeyed so far to find his relatives and has worked for seven years to lay claim to his youngest daughter as a wife. After the feast and after they have all gone to bed, Laban sends Lia in to Jacob who obliges her by having relations thinking it is Rachel. Is he in for a surprise the next morning when he finds out he had slept with Lia. Lia thought she was with someone else too, but that is another story. Jacob pretends he is upset with Laban's deceit (we told you it was a family trait), but he really can't be that mad. Lia can't see much, but Jacob doesn't need to see in the dark either.

Laban strikes a hard bargain, as patriarchs always do with younger men, and negotiates a deal Jacob can't refuse: to work another seven years for Rachel. He did it for love. But the Lord had pity on Lia and made her fruitful as well, and she gave birth to Ruben, to Simeon, to Levi, and to Juda. Her eyesight may have been weak, but her organs were productive. Then Rachel became impatient and this made her barren, just like Sarah, Rebecca, and half the women in the Bible. Rachel was so very jealous of Lia, her older sister, for having those four cute boys that she wanted to die.

Now just like Sarah had done to Abraham (some family traditions never die, or die harder than others) Rachel gave Jacob Bala, her slave girl, so she could bear him children in her stead. Jacob gratefully complied, just like grandpa had done, and gave Bala two sons, Dan and Nephthali. About this time, names in the Near East started to become unpronounceable. Not to be outdone, Lia, now past her prime, gives Jacob her servant maid, Zelpha to Jacob so he can raise even more sons to the Lord. They name this son Gad (as in Ye Gads, what have I gotten myself into?) and another son, Aser. After an incidental quarrel between the two legitimate wives, Lia and Rachel, Lia wins the argument and gets Jacob for the night. Lia, who was thought to be beyond her change of life, bears two more sons, Issachar and Zabulon, and the first daughter, Dina. Finally, Rachel conceives and bears a son, Joseph.

If you are still attentive after reading this narrative of human production, the tally so far is something like this:

1) Lia has had six sons and one daughter, and she wasn't even supposed to be a wife at all.

2) Rachel was thought to be barren, but she was just too young, and has one son, but only after the whole tribe has been impregnated by Jacob.

3) Two servants girls, who must have had chores to do sometime, one, Bala, Rachel's maid, and Zelpha, Lia's maid, each bears a couple of boys to Jacob.

4) Jacob's total number of children is twelve, a nice round figure, and he hasn't even left for home yet.

Jacob's activities have so far been pretty much confined to reproductive behavior, in cooperation with his two wives and two servant girls given him by his wives. Before he had even completed the return part of his journey, Jacob now had enough children for a complete basketball team, or a jury in case he had legal difficulties.

Jacob's Return
Preparing for his return to Zion, Jacob pulls a little trick on Uncle Laban, probably still smarting from the little trick Laban had pulled on him by switching Lia for Rachel one dark night after the bachelor party. Laban graciously decides that Jacob needs to have some wages, and in the days before coins were plentiful that usually meant you got paid in sheep. Jacob asks Laban to separate the speckled and spotted goats and all the black lambs. The biblical text is a little fuzzy in describing this trick, but essentially Jacob tricked the animals into mating all the speckled and spotted goats and lambs in front of his watering trough and gave the weaker ones to Uncle Laban. *Gen.* 30 concludes: "Thus the man became exceedingly rich and had large flocks, male and female servants, camels and asses." Now after Jacob had basically stolen the animals he had from Uncle Laban by getting Laban's animals to mate with his animals and giving Laban the weaker animals, Jacob decided it was time to leave that country discreetly. So, appropriately, "The Lord said to Jacob, 'Return to the land of your fathers and to your kin, and I will be with you.'" (14) Even Jacob noticed that Laban's "attitude toward me was not what it was previously."

It was time for Jacob to go to Isaac in Canaan. This condition today is very similar to knowing that the IRS is about to conduct an audit on your last five years of tax returns. But even Rachel and Lia wondered about their share of Laban's inheritance. But in the end they agreed that they should do whatever God told Jacob to do. As soon as the party was ready to leave, Rachel steals her father's household idols. So Jacob slips away, and it takes Laban several days to overtake him and ask him why he has left without so much as a fair-thee-well. Now Jacob's response to Laban's legitimate questions about why he has left with his daughters, stealing the household idols and the like, is pretty weak. "Jacob replied to Laban, 'I was afraid, for I thought you would take away your daughters from me by force.'" (15) Jacob doesn't know that Rachel had stolen the idols, which are hidden in Rachel's camel saddlebags while Laban searches in all the tents for them. She refuses to get off her camel lying to Laban that she is having her period, a natural act that men ever since have been afraid to admit confuses them. "Wisdom and an inheritance are good, and an advantage to those that see the sun." (*Ecclesiastes* 7:11).

There follows a couple of long soliloquies from both Jacob and Laban. In the end, they part after making a kind of pact, and each goes to their original land, a parting not unlike those among visiting relatives today, although not the kind of relative, like Jacob, who stay around for 20 years.

As soon as Jacob gets close to his land of Sichem, he thinks that his older brother Esau might do him harm. For all Jacob knows, the Lord has been appearing to Esau and telling him what to do and where to go. So Jacob wants to make a peace offering, gifts of hundreds of sheep, so Esau, who eventually does arrive with 400 men, won't attack him. Why so many men are needed to welcome a younger brother home is not disclosed. But we must assume that that old trick about stealing the older brother's intended blessing from dad and then skipping the country might have something to do with it.

There is a reconciliation of sorts, although the scribe takes pains to note that it is a little strained, and the whole reunited family heads for the homestead. Then an incident occurs which has consequences for a whole village. Dina, Jacob's only daughter, gets raped by a young man named Sichem who is the son of a local chief, Hemor. Sichem wants Dina for his wife, and asks his father, Hemor, to intercede for him to Jacob. However, when Jacob's boys (remember there are 11 of them) find out what Sichem has done to Dina, they take their own action. While Hemor and Jacob are working out the marriage details, like who is going to pay for the orchestra, the sons of Jacob, attacked the city and killed all the males, including Hemor and Sichem, but not before they had first been circumcised, a delicate touch.

They rescued Dina from Sichem, and also took all the other women, "flocks, herds, and asses...all its wealth...and looted whatever was in the houses." (16) This was not behavior Jacob's boys learned in Sunday school. Everyone was still waiting for the Lord to tell them what to do, and hope that he didn't get too mad at them for whatever it was they did. Moreover, this revenge of the boys was not kindly received by Jacob who probably figured correctly that retribution from the other towns would be coming quickly.

At this point in the narrative God asks Jacob to go to Bethel and build an altar and to do away with strange gods. Then God changed Jacob's name to Israel. Jacob, now Israel, build a memorial pillar of stone and called that place *Bethel*, or place of God. Shortly thereafter, Rachel dies in childbirth while giving birth to Benjamin. Soon, someone would have to go to Egypt again and the story picks up there.

Egypt: The Legacy of Civilization

Egypt...the very name rings with the vibrant hum of civilization. Art, architecture, colored illustration, religion, law, schooling, agriculture, astronomy, the calendar and clock, medicine, geometry and arithmetic, monotheism, the notion of an afterlife and embalming, pen and ink, primary and secondary education...there is hardly an aspect of civilized life that the Egyptians either did not invent or improve upon. They passed this legacy to the Hebrews, Greeks, Romans, and thence to Western civilization. Egypt conjures elegance, civilized living, the beginnings of culture, and highly specialized ways of achieving immortality through elaborate burial techniques. Its long-lasting legacy left huge and unacknowledged footprints in the Bible.

Many of the patriarchs had already been to Egypt: Abraham, Joseph, Jacob (asking only to be buried back in his "homeland") and Moses and Jesus. Like a magnet, like Romans sending their sons to Rhodes, Indians sending their children to England, or foreigners coming to university education in the U.S., Egypt with its compelling civilization and lifestyle drew neighbors willing to learn its cultured and literate ways.

However far back we go in a study of Egyptian religion or culture there is never a time when there was not a belief in everlasting life. It was accepted by the masses of people throughout Egypt from the earliest accounts. Eternity and immortality are Egyptian concepts that turned palpable when the ideas were literally buried with embalmed believers. The pyramids are the world's largest monuments to this belief, sarcophagi for the royal dead awaiting the return of the soul, tombs existing only for holding the soul in the body for its resurrection.

One spirit or soul of the deceased is represented in burial tombs as a small bird with a human head. This is the BA, the spirit or soul of the deceased which gives the dead the power of movement, leading the person to the underworld, which is why earthly goods and objects needed for the afterlife were entombed with the person. The second soul or spirit is the KA, literally the spiritual double that provides the person with the means of surviving eternally.

The concept of soul was central to all religious beliefs. The soul transmigrated for Hindus who believe that it moves between different levels of organic life depending on its activities during this life. Most American Indian tribal groups also believed in a dual soul or spirit resident in each individual, one of which died at the body's death and another which floated freely after death, but neither of which was immortal. Buddhists, who do not necessarily believe in immortality at all, do believe that a heavenly state, nirvana or enlightenment, can be attained through heightened meditation in this life. Christianity and Muslims believe in the immortality of the single soul, and among Jews some believe in a soul's immortality and some do not.

If we discuss a man who was both man and god, who suffered a cruel death, but who triumphed over death and attained life everlasting in the next world, and who had the power to confer everlasting life on mortals, to grant the resurrection of the physical body, we may think immediately of Christian beliefs. But this is essentially Egyptian belief, and Osiris was the god (and man) of everlasting life. Osiris was the dominant figure of Egyptian religion for thousands of years. He was believed in because he was man and god, and commanded absolute control over men's destinies, bodies and souls. One could only attain immortality if the life was righteous through Osiris. Souls of unbelievers could not enter Osiris' kingdom of heaven.

The high cultural and religious life and the massive volume of literature was maintained through a formalized education for scribes. When students graduated from the elementary temple school, and if judged acceptable, they also graduated to writing on papyrus rolls. The writing on papyrus, one of Egypt's permanent contributions to the world and a word from which we get our word for paper, was a significant advancement. Written papyrus is intact and legible after 5,000 years. (17)

We have an example of the kind of education at least a high priest had about 3,500 years ago from an autobiographical inscription on a limestone block statute. Bekenhons, a high priest of the temple of Amun at Karnak, attended primary school for four years, then apprenticed for eleven years in the royal stables where he learned basic administrative duties. After 15 years of education he entered priestly service in the temple. At 39 years he achieved the height of the career ladder and served for another 27 years as high priest. (18) Thus, he lived to be about 90 years of age. Whether his longevity was due to his excellent education is not recorded.

In secondary school these future scribes studied government and public administration. After graduation they were apprenticed to government officials where they practiced more writing and learned the transcription of documents. The Egyptian schools (and similar ones operating in Babylonia) were some of the first formalized schools and they provided the machinery of government with a pool of trained youth who could manage and record the business of the state and the expanding empire and satisfy the clerical needs of the religious institutions. We can assume that Hebrew scribes learned their trade from training with, from, or similar to Egyptian scribes.

Reports on daily life in an Egyptian village in the period of the New Kingdom (1,539–1,075 BCE), and on documents found there that shed light on the education system. Deir El-Medina is near the Valley of the Kings where pharaohs are entombed. The villagers were skilled artisans who cut and laid the stone, did the drafting, painted and etched texts on tomb walls. They did not write on papyrus but on smooth, white flakes of limestone known as ostraca. Writings indicate that these working villagers knew the classic Egyptian literature from the Middle Kingdom (2,000–1,640 BC), and held writing in high esteem. These were the highly paid information laborers of 3,500 years ago.

Students learned a complicated script. The Egyptians never had an alphabet. Instead, they mixed pictographs (picture words) with ideographs (ideas represented by symbols) and other signs with letters, consonants without vowels, a language known as hieroglyphs from an Egyptian word meaning "priestly writing." It was a complex form of longhand and shorthand and a scribe needed to learn all of it. Over time, the formal writing was exclusively reserved for carvings on the sacred monuments. Thoth was the ibis-headed god of both wisdom and writing. (19)

Egyptian libraries are among the world's oldest with papyri rolled together and stored in jars dating from 2,000 BCE. Parallelism and repetition found in the Bible's psalms pre-exist in Egyptian poetry. The finest example of Egyptian poetry was composed from the reed pen of Akhenaten, the so-called heretical Pharaoh who proposed the radical idea at the time of one God. About 800 years thereafter, it is reasonably duplicated in *Psalm* 104.

Remarkable discoveries at el-Amarna in 1887, and of continuing linguistic scholarship, have revealed a collection of clay tablets, unusual in Egypt, and written in cuneiform script from Babylon, which is even more unusual. The tablets form part of the pharaoh's archives and are diplomatic records, many from Canaanite kings who were then under Egyptian control. Some of the Amarna letters, like No. 49, are of especial interest: "Letter from Yapahi, ruler of Gezer, acknowledging the receipt of a message from the king and asking for assistance against the Habiru." (20) Some scholars have equated the Habiru with the Hebrews but there is no confirmation. Other letters speak of loyalty from city kings in the area of Palestine, and some speak of the capture of towns, or that a king needs additional forces to rescue him. Overall, the period is one of unrest in Palestine. (21)

But more important than the discovery of these clay tablets is the man whose archives they were found in. Akhenaten ascended the throne in 1,380 BCE. His major accomplishment was the reform of the Egyptian religion and the creation and state establishment of monotheism. He dethroned all the pantheon of gods and established the worship of one deity: the Aten of Ra. We explore Akhenaten and the relationship to Moses in the following chapter.

When Gaza was an Egyptian province, one uniquely Egyptian temple existed during the Iron Age during the reign of Rameses III: the Temple of the Egyptian god Amun. Scores of scarabs written in Egyptian hieratic script have been unearthed at the site testifying to a system of tribute for the temple. Scholars assume that the Philistines took this cult of Amun from this temple site and propagated the veneration throughout the region by using seal amulets.

By the late Iron Age the cultural power of Egypt had declined significantly and that of Assyria had risen. By the 7th century BCE Assyria had driven Egypt from Syria and Palestine and had become a new cultural and religious force in the region. A new era begins in 598 and 587 when Jerusalem is conquered by Nebuchadnezzar and lasts until the age of Nehemiah, c.450 BCE, spelling the loss of independence for Judah. This period is formative for the writings of the Bible and the development of Israelite nationalism and Judaism.

Juda: An Interruption in Genesis

The story is inexplicably interrupted in *Genesis* 38 to describe a story about Juda, one of the other sons of Jacob and brother of Joseph, about killings, not committed this time by any of Jacob's sons, but by the Lord himself. The Lord kills Her, a male person's proper name and not just a pronoun, because he was wicked, although we are not told what this wickedness was which merited death at the hands of the Lord himself. But then whole towns had been wiped out, indeed the whole populated earth in Noah's day, for being wicked in the eyes of the Lord and not knowing it. We may think in today's moral codes that God is acting unjustly but we must remove our moral glasses and put on our allegorical eyes to remember that gods in literature often killed mortals, as Enlil did Endiku.

The second death the Lord did was against Onan who was supposed to have relations with his brother's widow, Thamar, but didn't want relations because the "descendants would not be his own." (*Gen.* 38: 9). So Onan "wasted his seed on the ground" every time he had relations with Thamar, his brother's widow. We do not know what wickedness Her did, but Onan couldn't have been too smart, because for this waste of brotherly semen, Onan was also killed by the Lord. Onan is often associated with masturbation, but his acts with Thamar were really *coitus interruptus*. Of course the other boys, including Sera, decided Thamar was bad luck and avoided her.

But Thamar was tricky like other members of the clan in this narrative. She knew where Sera was tending his flocks, so she put on a veil and pretended to be a temple prostitute, a legitimate occupation in those days known among the Sumerians, but certainly not the Hebrews. Sera didn't recognize his sister-in-law, and told her, Thamar, he would give her a kid (the goat kind, but the other will soon come as well) in exchange for her services. Thamar, carrying out this little deceit so common in the family, decided she wanted something more personal, like Sera's staff, his signet seal from around his neck, and probably some other baubles. Sera, young man that he was, was probably pretty passionate by this time, since veils only hide so much, and gave away much of what he had except the rest of the flock. But when he went to look for the temple prostitute, by this time he had forgotten her name, if he had even asked, and was told there were no temple prostitutes working the fields.

Three months later Thamar, Sera's sister-in-law, the Lord already having killed her first husband and one of her brother-in-laws, is visibly pregnant by a second brother-in-law. But she is the only one who knows this yet. When she is discovered with child, Juda wants to kill her for adultery. This is allowed because the Lord has already killed Onan for ejaculation when he was supposed to have intercourse. However, when Sera is revealed as the father, once Thamar produces the signet seal and Sera's staff, everyone is happy, and thankful that the Lord didn't kill either Thamar or Sera before this nice little entrapment was revealed. Thamar has twins, but the rest of the story is unresolved and we suddenly return to Joseph in Egypt.

Why these events in the life of Juda, one of Joseph's brothers, are included here is a mystery. However, once again, a woman's deceit turns out to be a blessing for the future generations, because the chosen people are called Jews, named after Juda, and not after Ruben or Levi or other sons. Despite the obscurity of the episode, literary theft is still the main biblical practice.

Joseph in Egypt
It is in this time frame, from the late Bronze to early Iron Age that the story of Joseph in Egypt reputedly occurs. (22) It is a touching narrative about the love of brothers, or the lack of it, a success story built on abandonment and the attainment of worldly power and riches. It is also a tale about how Egyptian culture fashioned the culture of Canaan and later of Israel. Joseph is the literary creation of a Hebrew hero who represents chaste principles, wisdom and excellence in administrative skills, shrewdness in acquiring and keeping power and wealth, cleverness in outwitting rivals, and is dedicated to fraternal and family piety. In essence, Joseph is the consummate model of a life story originating less from a warrior hero of other cultures than from the ideal of a Jewish man, a personality profile that has come to dominate perceptions ever since.

Jacob's brothers didn't like Joseph because Jacob favored him, and they hated him even more when Jacob, now called Israel, gave Joseph his favorite son a long tunic. As if this envy wasn't enough, Joseph told them about dreams he had that seemed to make him symbolically like a prophet or a king. This kind of talk never sits well with older brothers, especially if one considers birthrights, inheritances, and similar potentially envious things. So one day, the older brothers threw Joseph in a dry well, leaving him for dead, then decided to rescue him and sell him into slavery to a passing band of caravan travelers. You'll recall that a few of these playful lads, older brothers of Joseph, had already murdered a whole village (*Gen.* 34), so selling their brother into slavery was not so wicked.

Joseph's sojourn in Egypt begins auspiciously. He finds favor with his master and becomes the chief domestic servant. The master's wife takes a fancy to him, and attempts to seduce him, but Joseph resists. Finally, there is a brief struggle in her bedroom, and Joseph flees leaving his garment behind. The abandoned garment becomes the presumed evidence the wife uses to finger Joseph for alleged relations. It's the old case of being framed by the scorned woman, perhaps even more dangerous than actually seducing the master's wife.

The Tale of Two Brothers was found on papyrus in Egypt and dates from c.1,225 BC. The text includes a false accusation of proposed adultery by the wife of the elder brother and therefore has thematic similarities to the story of Joseph and Potiphar's wife.

Joseph finds himself in prison where he again is put "in charge of all the prisoners." (*Gen.* 39: 22). The Pharaoh's chief baker and butler are out of favor and wind up in prison too. It is not known what sin the chief baker committed, and it is doubtful he was able to bring his recipes with him. Joseph consents to interpret dreams as a way of passing time. However, in a great majority of dreams there is a prediction about the future that only the godly and just can interpret. Joseph himself had such dreams and reported them to his brothers, although at no time did he interpret them. But he correctly interprets the dreams of both the butler and the baker. As a result, Pharaoh reinstates the butler, but hangs the baker. Joseph had asked the butler to remember him when he got out of prison but the butler forgot. Finally, he remembered Joseph two years later when the Pharaoh himself had a couple of dreams no one could interpret. Joseph correctly identified the Pharaoh's dreams of seven poor, scrawny cows eating seven fat cows as symbolizing seven years of fat harvests, followed by seven years of famine. Pharaoh is so impressed he placed Joseph in charge of managing the years of storage from the fat years so everyone will have enough during the lean years. Pharaoh gave Joseph a new name, Saphaneth-phanee. Perhaps he found it too difficult to pronounce the Hebrew name. Pharaoh also gives Joseph Aseneth as a wife, and we learn she is the daughter of Phutiphare a priest of On. The biblical scribe never tells us Pharaoh's name.

Genesis 42-45 relate one of the Bible's most enchanting stories of how Joseph's brothers came to Egypt to buy grain, how Joseph recognized them but not them him, and teased them into thinking they are guilty of some great misdeed. The scribe told of how Joseph manipulates Benjamin, the youngest brother, in an attempt to get the brothers to violate the command Jacob had admonished the brothers about letting no harm come to Benjamin. But eventually Joseph relented, told them who he was, and instructed them to return for Jacob and all the family to come and live with him in Egypt where he is master of the food stamp program. God appeared to Jacob in a dream one night before Jacob left for Egypt and says: "I am God, the God of your father. Do not fear to go down to Egypt, for there I will make you a great people." (*Gen.* 46: 3). There are three points worth noting here.

1) Why does God keep appearing only in dreams, and how does everyone who encounters God only in dreams know what is an ordinary dream from a God-encounter dream? How can they tell whether or not they are deluded?

2) Why should Jacob (Israel) be afraid to go to Egypt at all? Abraham had gone to Egypt on more than one occasion, and he was the one who started all this progeny. After all, Israel was going to be re-united with Joseph, his favorite son whom he thought was dead. Why should he be afraid of anything in Egypt, especially if the famine was still in Canaan as well as Egypt, and Joseph had access to food?

3) Because of the situation of the Hebrews in Egypt one cannot realistically say that God was going to "make you a great people" in Egypt. The scribe must have got something wrong here.

Leaving all these speculative considerations aside, Jacob departs with all his 70 descendants and camp followers for Egypt. When he arrives there is rejoicing, celebrations, and a personal meeting with Pharaoh arranged by Joseph who wanted everyone to know how successful he had become without even going to college.

The last couple of chapters of *Genesis*, Chapters 48 and 49, are concerned with domestic affairs. Jacob formally adopts Joseph's sons who were of course half-Egyptian, and thus could be considered suspect minorities. The dying Jacob formally prophesies concerning all his twelve sons, at times waxing quite poetic about Joseph and Juda. It was clear from Jacob's final remarks about the boys that they were not to remain in Egypt but return to the land of the ancestors God had given to them.

Conclusions to Genesis

It does not make sense easily to us, living as we do in an era when historical exactitude is a way of culture, to conclude that people living over 3,000–5,000 years ago had the same concept of human continuity. Isolated events of the day or time and detailed descriptions of real happenings were not perceived as relevant in a clan history. What were important were allegories about the mythological forces, frequently invoked, often alluded to, and sometimes worshipped, that control the universe. Even inscriptions from the Old Kingdom in Egypt after the time of Menes (c.2,700–2,200 BCE) there are few inscriptions with detailed descriptions of actual events. (23)

Genesis is a recording of myths to bolster a nation in need of recognition. The strict recording of events was not important. *Genesis* is a copied collection of circulating legends, myths, allegories, literary symbols and devices that, strung together, produce stories that cannot be fully understood without the literature preceding it. When *Genesis* is read with an understanding of the legends of the era and the myths of the ancient Middle East, all the absurdities and inconsistencies appear to have an already defined literary context.

The first books of *Genesis* represent the first developments of a Hebrew literature complete with cosmology and myths impregnated with Hebrew theology. The first editor of *Genesis* was likely from the tenth century BCE, a J scribe who emphasizes Yahweh, who combined into one story many diverse accounts orally circulating among the various tribal groups. The collection later was ably assisted by the scribes and editors known as E, D and DH during the time of Deuteronomy, and P, the priestly scribe of the prophets and hymns who also edited all the earlier collections.

The literary artifice that unites the stories in *Genesis* is a family tree, a genealogy of parentage that pulls one story into another by linking the actors to a common parent. We observe this when Cain's descendants are described in *Gen.* 4, and the rest of Adam's descendants in *Gen.* 5. In fact, the whole of Chapter 5 is a description of the names of sons and fathers (never the mothers) until Noah, and the re-telling of the Deluge story. There are ten generations between Adam and Noah, where the flood story is told for the first time in biblical prose, a repetition from the Babylonian story of a much early date. (24) It was common in early Greek prose and in Herodotus to use royal genealogies and chronologies as a way of telling a story, and this tradition becomes paramount and standard in the Bible and gospels.

The genealogies are a condensation of time, a pressing of historical events into a generation, or the passing of a generation. The time span of the scribe of *Genesis*, from the time of Adam through to Noah is 7,015 years, subtracting the age of the father of a son from his excessive longevity. None of the progenitors who gives birth to such a recorded son is under 65, and Noah is 500 years old when he becomes the father of Sem, Ham and Japheth. The scribe is not only granting unusual longevity, but supernatural potency to such ancestors. Heroic men need heroic stature and heroic longevity.

In *Gen.* 6 we have an abrupt reversal of this. God states: "My spirit shall not remain in man forever, since he is flesh. His lifetime shall be one hundred and twenty years." God's displeasure is felt again, and another curse for his wickedness is the reduction of human life on earth from the longevity of forefathers. But notice that man is cursed because "he is flesh," and God withdraws his spirit, which at no time after Adam's fall has it been noted that his spirit was available to man. This is a perplexing phrase because earlier Adam "became the father of a son in his own likeness, after his image." (25) Was Adam, that heroic person a man of flesh, a mere mortal, or was he still part God, with God's spirit in him and all his successors? Men of heroic stature in literature are often semi-divine and Gilgamesh was two-thirds divine and only one-third human. Biblical scribes never use percentages of humanity but they certainly intend that the patriarchs are unusual because they are in God's favor.

The statement that precedes this second loss of innocence is men's involvement with women. "When men began to multiply on the earth, and had daughters born to them, the sons of God saw that the daughters of men were fair, and they took wives for themselves, as many as they wished." (26) Through Noah they were "the sons of God," although the women were the "daughters of men." Why weren't women also daughters of God?

Lamech, the fifth generation son of Cain, who was supposedly a "son of God," although perhaps not because of Cain's additional malfeasance, also had multiple wives. Nothing wrong was said about that at the time. What is obvious is a subtle discrimination against women, since they apparently succumb more easily, are never used in the succession of generations, and then, because of their plural status with men, have man's lifetime shortened, and God's spirit withdrawn. It is not a very comfortable plight.

The Abraham story had its origin in upper Babylonia and the Jacob clan stories conform to myths in Gilgamesh and Greek legends. These could then have been separate and un-related family stories of differing tribal groups who migrated into the land called Israel after it was united. It would have been natural for a scribe assigned to the king to combine these stories for a political identity as the beginnings of a nation-state were formed and ethnic unity sought, an assumption strengthened by the recurrent references to the land, which is obviously now under the control of a single leader.

Consider the young man in Egypt who is in a position of power. He frequently digresses on the theme of his birth, his youth, his dream of appointment to a position of power, and then of completing his father's work as a dutiful son. Now this is Joseph, but it is also Rameses II (1,290–1,224 BCE). Although Rameses' life-span would be nearly the same as Joseph, this description fits Rameses in his explanation of his plans for restoring the ruined temple of Abydos. The Hebrew scribe has used the historical heroic figure of Rameses and events in his life to create a similar mythical figure for the Hebrew people. (27)

Before any great biblical event, dreams, visions and discussions with God or commands from God frequently begin the narrative, a common occurrence in Sumerian, Babylonian and Egyptian literature when divine appearances, most often confirmed in dreams, tell of victory in battle and intervention with the gods. This occurs when Rameses does battle with the Hittites in the Battle of Kadesh, and in the Sphinx Stele of Thutmose IV in which Thutmose has a dream-vision from a god which provides the incentive for the subsequent actions. Such divine discussions lend credibility to the authority of the person, whether Rameses, Abraham, Jacob or Joseph. The heroic individual has already been selected. The scribe or editor must re-confirm the individual's power. It is clear that the literary devices of Egypt, as well as earlier literary traditions, had a profound impression on Hebrew scribes.

There are several minor inconsistencies in the patriarchal stories, such as the complicated numbers and chronologies, the two wives of Esau who are mentioned three times but each time with different names, the notation of the 12 tribes of Israel whose numbers actually add to 13. Let's yield a measure of good faith to biblical scribes, and certainly the final redactor P, but fault them for lack of critical control and sound editing, and too much interpolation and extrapolation to make sense of story complexity.

CHAPTER NINE
EXODUS AND EGYPTIAN BIBLICAL THEMES

Route 8 stretches across the southwestern United States from San Diego to Casa Grande, Arizona and then turns south towards Yuma stretching towards the California border along one of the most forbidding deserts in the world. Directly south from the small towns of Sentinel and Mohawk is the Luke Air Force Base bombing range extending about 70 miles to the Mexican border where illegal immigrants frequently attempt to enter the U.S. which, because of the torrid heat searing the xeric sand often reaching 115 degrees Fahrenheit in the late spring and summer months, proves fatal to pedestrian traffic.

The parched Sonoran desert in southern Arizona is similar to the desert topography of the Sinai desert, a lunar landscape fit for tarantulas and scorpions not for human residents or casual travelers who would only attempt to cross it if truly lost, mentally challenged, or preferring a location for the metaphorical description of a heroic and mythical adventure. The Sinai is the land bridge between Africa and Asia, a trade caravan negotiated better by camels than convoys of women and children, a parched land better suited to fugitives and vagabonds than seekers of well-watered pastures. The north Sinai is a series of shifting sand dunes while the south has parched mountains with only a few passes that can be crossed without difficulty.

A leader with a royal upbringing, a preferred education and an Egyptian name like Moses would be familiar with the geography of the region to the west of the Nile, especially since it was for an extended period a part of the Egyptian hegemony, and would definitely not be lost if he entered it with a band of fellow expatriates and would certainly follow the known caravan routes to ensure the availability of food and water if traveling east, particularly since those pursuing were literally in hot water.

Wouldn't it make sense to travel along the 200 miles of coastline from what is now Port Said to Gaza, where water was at least available for filtering and boiling than to trek through endless sand dunes where the horizon is obscured by heat waves and dust? It was a route known as the Way of Horus guarded by Egyptian soldiers who maintained a series of stations for supply and customs. Another miracle, like a parting of the sand, would have sufficed to stop or subdue them. The town that such a traveler would first encounter coming from Gaza to enter Egypt or leaving it is today known as Tell El-Daba which was inhabited in 1,500 BCE but is now covered with agricultural fields, plots of which archaeologists can only partially excavate.

Hebrew life in Egypt is a made-for movie of epic proportions, packed with the kind of action suitable for adults only, a gigantic bloodbath of divinely-inspired carnage and revenge, a battle without remorse. Themes of oppression, the fight for liberation, the collusion of the gods in exacting revenge, and the making of a nation is the narrative of, well, biblical proportions. All that is needed is a hero of mythical status to lead tormented people to a place they can call home, God's kind of person who can condone this spiteful massacre of the first born, the kind of infants who would not be spared under Herod at Bethlehem either. Then, let us show the power that he has, liberally given by the one true God, full of signs and wonders, turning staffs into serpents, getting water to flow from rocks, having bushes burn while a voice speaks, all to prove that this man has authentic credentials and should be followed wherever.

As it is, it is a story of the first recorded genocide, of God killing Egyptians and their children. If it weren't measured against other legends like the *Iliad* it would be a story unfit for children and not celebrated for its brutality and cruelty. God seems to say: "Let's give it to the Egyptians where they live. Let us turn rivers into blood, rain frogs, send locusts and lice, flies and insects, and then let's kill their children."

Neither *Genesis* nor *Exodus* makes an attempt to link its peculiar form of history with extra-biblical history. *Exodus* is at pains to discuss proper Hebrew names, but never gives the name of any ruling pharaoh, although it names captains of the guard. Let's reluctantly assume the account is descriptive of an actual event. The closest time period one can hypothesize the exodus occurs is the reign of Rameses II (1,304–1,237 BC), as we are told that the Israelites were building a royal residence in the Delta region. Most of the exodus chronology is conflicting and inconsistent. We are told, for example, that the 4th generation took part in the *Exodus*, and that there was a period of 400 years to the sojourn. Clearly, we are not dealing here with the arithmetic of accuracy but the science of politics, the establishment of Hebrew religion and nationalism, and the creation of an epic, but fictionalized, journey. *Exodus* narrates the story of leave-taking, led by a heroic figure from a foreign country to a divinely promised homeland, just like *Jason and the Argonauts* and Ulysses in Homer's *Odyssey*. A comparable story of a journey is in *Genesis* when Abraham leaves his country to arrive in a new homeland for reasons unknown, except that God has promised him the land. But the Israelites upon exiting Egypt actually left the land of milk and honey.

The 9th to the 12th dynasties in Egypt, from approximately 2,150–1,950 BCE, witnessed a great profusion of secular literature creating a classical literary archive and model compositions for future scribes and authors. The most famous folk tales from ancient Egypt include: *The Doomed Prince, The Peasant and the Workman, Setna and the Magic Book, The Shipwrecked*

Sailor, The Tale of Sinuhe, The Taking of Joppa, The Tale of Two Brothers, the comic tale of *The Treasure of Rhampsinitus,* and *Tales of the Magicians.* Of these *The Tale of Sinuhe,* which describes a man's love for his country that he must flee, *The Tale of Two Brothers,* in which a youth is seduced by an older woman, and Bau-F-Ra's tale from *The Tales of the Magicians* in which the chief reciter Zazamankh parts the waters, placing "one part of the waters of the lake upon another," and RA also parts the waters in the Tale of "Two Brothers, are all literary motifs that occur in the *Exodus.* A shipwrecked sailor, in the tale of the same name that dates from 2,134–1,785 BCE, speaks extensively with a talking serpent, a motif in *Genesis.* With everyone of importance in Hebrew history journeying to Egypt, scribes had to have known of all this literature.

Sinai
It is no coincidence that religions which developed three or two thousand years ago all had sacred mountains at the center of their mythologies: Mount Meru for the Indians, Mount Olympus for the Greeks, Mount Sinai for the Hebrews, the Mount of Transfiguration and the Mount of Olives for Christians, all served as the abode of the gods. Fire is also a similarity for the presence of the god on a mountain top: with Elias on Mount Carmel (I *Kings* 18), in the burning bush at Sinai. For stealing fire from the gods to give to men, Prometheus was chained by Zeus to a mountain in the Caucasus. And Jesus, according to *Matthew, Mark* and *Luke,* "led them up a high mountain apart and was transfigured before them and his face shone like the sun and his garments became white as light."

Mount Sinai, according to the most recent archaeological evidence, had been a sacred mountain long before Moses led his people to it. Emmanuel Anati, Professor of Paleontology at the University of Lecce in Italy, has uncovered artifacts from the Har Karkom dating from the Upper Paleolithic period, about 30,000 years ago. He believes that this mountain in Israel's southern Negev desert is the site of the biblical Mt. Sinai. (1) There have been over 35,000 examples of rock art discovered in the region, standing stones with cravings, altars and a small temple. One of the most remarkable rock carvings illustrates a lizard with five snakes and two scorpions. If Har Karkom had been a sacred site almost since the beginning of modern humans, it is easy to see why Moses, if he existed. would lead a group of people back to this ancient site of religious rituals and art.

In a land as parched as the Sinai desert where evidence of former human existence would remain on the surface and not decompose there should certainly be artifacts left behind from a huge number of people wandering for 40 years. Yet there is no archaeological record, no pottery shards, no broken pieces of equipment, no campsite embankments, no evidence at all that so many people over so long a period of time ever existed in the region. The conclusion of archaeologists is that no such lengthy sojourn ever occurred. Even noted rabbis like Rabbi Wolpe of the Sinai Temple in the Westwood district of Los Angeles preached that the historical record of scripture is distinct from the meaning of liberation from enslavement. (2)

Further evidence about the exodus is confusing. *Numbers 33*, a long listing of the sites along the exodus route, notes that the invading Israelites encamped in a place called Dibon, east of the Jordan River. The precision of specific sites creates the impression of historical fact. But excavations at Tell Dhiban, ancient Dibon, revealed no settlement there in Late Bronze Age II, the time when exodus was supposed to have occurred. No human habitation occurred until the 9th century BCE. (3) Moreover, according to *Numbers* 13:22 Moses reputedly "went up to Negeb and came to Hebron" in preparation for the invasion, and this city was supposedly a principal target according to *Joshua* 10:36-37 and *Judges* 1:10. But settlements in Transjordan were under the control of the Egyptians who maintained transportation access from Egypt to the rich agricultural plains of Moab, as Egyptian maps of the time describe. Either exodus and so-called conquest did not occur at the time described, the Late Bronze Age, the authors were historically inaccurate, the story is a metaphor of freedom from enslavement, or the journey is a mimicking of a similar literary adventure like those in *Genesis* but now lost. Not only is there no archaeological record, no written reference or artifact, but there is virtual silence about this event from Egyptian records, from a people who recorded everything. The one text, from the Victory Stele of Merneptah about 1,207 BCE speaks of a people of "Israel," but in Canaan, not in Egypt. The Hebrew scribes state simply that "pharaoh" was involved without naming which pharaoh. (4)

Throughout the eastern Mediterranean during the second millennium BCE, the Egyptian empire ruled successfully, put down rebellions, countered the Hittites whenever they got uppity, posted resident governors in Canaanite cities, exacted tributes and taxes for the subjugated populations, and extended its rich culture to intellectually impoverished locales. Yet there is no word of any exodus in the Bible. Nor do the Egyptian records say anything about the patriarchs, the Israelites in Egypt, or Joshua. When Egypt is mentioned in scripture, the inaccuracies are noticeable. The Egyptian king who helps Hosea (2 *Kings* 17:4) has his name confused for his city. Pharaoh Shabtaka winds up in the Table of Nations as a Nubian tribe (*Gen.* 10:7). Taharqa (2 *Kings* 19:9) is incorrectly identified. (5) The arithmetic in the chronologies is even more discrepant.

Egypt has one of the most faithful and comprehensive historical records of any country in the ancient world. Although Egyptian king lists were written as late as the 3rd c. BCE, we are provided the successions in the Old, Middle and New Kingdoms as scribes meticulously recorded all rulers, kept thousands of documents of major events, activities, projects, campaigns, temple buildings and literature. Hebrews did not copy this detailed writing method, perhaps because they didn't have the army of scribes Egypt did, the methods for educating them, or because when constructing their legends, historical details were presumed un-necessary.

Several of the key religious and political ideas said to be unique to the Hebrews during the time of this journey, and later incorporated into Jewish religious practice, originate with the Egyptians. The single most important idea coming from the Egyptians and adopted by the Hebrews, in addition to circumcision, is monotheism. The worship of one single god, to the exclusion of multiple gods, was rare in the ancient world, and was unique to the Near East during the appearance of Zoroaster, about 600 BCE. But the first instance of professed monotheism in history occurs during the reign of Akhenaten of Egypt beginning in 1,358 BCE, or about 100 years prior to the assumed departure of the Hebrews for the land flowing with milk and honey led by the man with an Egyptian name, Moses. "It is I who am God, and there is no one that exists apart from me," notes one Nag Hammadi text. (6)

The exodus story is an epic tale whereby the Hebrews borrowed Aten (just like they borrowed the Mesopotamian EL and Canaanite BAAL) from the monotheism scribes learned while residing in Egypt. The Hebrews did not escape the culture of the Babylonians, Canaanites or Egyptians, having assimilated every religion in the region over the course of centuries. Monotheism, the kingship cult, bodily resurrection, the afterlife, the soul, circumcision, all were known and practiced in Egypt prior to the 13th century BCE, centuries before the Bible took its present form.

Law and Order: Hammurabi and Solon

The *Lipit-Ishtar Lawcode* consists of 38 extant laws and predates Hammurabi's code by about 150 years. Among the Hittite Laws, with its 200 prohibitions and restrictions, are that if a man does evil with a sheep it is a capital crime and he shall be killed, but that there is no punishment for doing evil with a horse or mule. The judicial thinking must have been that the larger animals were consenting.

Torah is a Hebrew word meaning direction or guidance and it is the Law according to Moses found in the first five books of the Bible known as the Pentateuch, a law still in effect among Jews and preserved marvelously as a commitment, adherence to faith and symbol of national and ethnic unity. The scribe D wrote this Mosaic Law and it was likely in effect by the time of the learned priest Ezra about 444 BCE. Hammurabi's Babylonian law code is the most organized and comprehensive from the ancient world but is not the earliest as that honor goes to Urnammu (c.2,028–2011 BCE) in the Dynasty of Ur in Sumer, and the first Babylonian code comes from the kingdom of Eshnunna c.2,100 BCE. These earliest known laws dealt with land ownership, marriage and inheritance in seeking to balance the economic and social needs of the first civilized societies. Subsequently, Hammurabi (1,795–1,750 BCE) established Babylon, the world's first metropolis, a city cursed by Jews and John in *Revelations* because of Jewish enslavement. However, Hammurabi's historical position as the first ruler to institute a systematic code of laws is unquestioned.

The first comprehensive legal code, visible in the Louvre in Paris, was carved upon an eight foot black basalt stele discovered only in 1902, a monument with 3,600 lines of cuneiform intended for public reading. At the top of the basalt column is Hammurabi receiving the scrolled laws from the god Shamash, just as Minos received the law from the supreme god on the sacred mountain, and Moses from Yahweh on Mt. Sinai. *The Hammurabi Code*, based on Sumerian prototypes over 6,000 years old, opens with addresses to the gods, as if it were a prayer and ends by cursing those who would neglect or destroy its proclamations.

When Anu the Sublime, King of the Anunaki, and Bel, the lord of
Heaven and earth, who decreed the fate of the land, assigned to
Marduk, the over-ruling son of Ea, God of righteousness, dominion
over earthly man and made him great among the Igigi, they
called Babylon by his illustrious name, made it great on earth,
and founded an everlasting kingdom in it, whose foundations are
laid so solidly as those of heaven and earth; then Anu and Bel
called by name me, Hammurabi, the exalted prince, who feared God,
to bring about the rule of righteousness in the land, to destroy the
wicked and the evil-doers; so that the strong should not harm the
weak; so that I should rule over the black-headed people like
Shamash, and enlighten the land, to further the well-being of mankind. (7)

Though cloaked in divine reassurances, subsequent courts in Babylon were secular as government administrators assumed the functions of the clergy in dispensing justice. The 282 laws in *The Code of Hammurabi* were based on equivalent retribution, literally, "an eye for an eye," only later and gradually to be replaced with awards of damages. (8) There were no individual rights. Human rights was an invention of the Enlightenment in Europe and carried into American constitutional law and jurisprudence. There were laws for builders and barbers, sailors and shepherds, rules for debt, witnesses, agriculture and gardening, merchants and granaries, fathers and sexual and property relations with wives, sons, daughters, prostitutes and slaves. The multiple laws deal with theft, false accusations, the status and treatment of slaves and personal property. The Mosaic code clearly borrows from a common original of *The Code of Hammurabi*.

In *Exodus* 19, Moses ascends Mount Sinai and receives God's words speaking to Moses through a thick cloud. We are thus prepared for the delivery of laws from divinity to mankind as Hammurabi was, except that in *Exodus* the delivery is accompanied by thunder, lightning and smoke. God instructs Moses to get the people prepared for the message and specifically tells him to have them wash their clothes, not a bad idea for a tribe wandering around in the desert for 40 years. But where did they get the water to wash so many clothes? In *Exodus* 20 God gives the people the list, the 17 injunctions which include the proverbial Ten Commandments.

What is unique, and seemingly contradictory for the God later described by Christians as being of one substance, is that He enters history, giving laws, speaking to Moses, traveling with the lost and immigrant party through space and time. He is a personal God who departs eternity by entering the world of space and time. In heroic literature this is acceptable; in Greek philosophy it is not because it presumes changeableness, not a divine attribute. A God acting in the physical world means a God subject to physical laws.

The first five Hebrew injunctions concern the preservation of one God, including the injunction against graven images, an act that elevates belief above art and condemns the Hebrews to aesthetic impoverishment. Injunctions 7 through 11 speak somewhat redundantly about the Sabbath. But the clear rules are against murder, of which there is more in the Bible than all of Shakespeare's tragedies, and there is adultery, stealing, bearing false witness and coveting property. The real redundancy is that the so-called Decalogue is repeated in *Deuteronomy* with minor variations, and even with a contradiction where in *Exodus* the people watched the fiery deliverance but in *Deuteronomy* they specifically did not. The Mosaic Code recognized the family as the basis for society and marriage the basis of the family.

The Law of Moses, reputedly written about 1,500 years after *The Code of Hammarubi*, offers religion, the family and property as the fundamentals of Hebrew society but makes no advance in criminal jurisprudence or legal philosophy over the more ancient set of laws. (9) The commandments are a combination of allegiance to one God and a rejection of the plurality of gods and legal articles that if followed would stabilize civil order in society: Don't kill, cheat on your wife, steal or even think about stealing anyone else's property, or lie about your neighbor. In both *The Code of Hammurai* and God's edicts in *Exodus* and *Deuteronomy*, the divine nature of the laws is acknowledged: Gods are the lawgivers and kings, or prophets in the Hebrew case, are chosen to deliver, instruct, administer and judge the laws and violators. *The Code of Hammurabi* is more comprehensive about the rules governing common social behavior, though *Deuteronomy* 14 makes all manner of personal habit and behavior, including venereal disease, matters of divine ordinance. Adherence to the Law was the indispensable condition for ethnic and national unity among the Hebrews, as it never was among the Babylonians.

The Ten Commandments still cause controversy. Alabama State Supreme Court Justice Roy Moore added to the unusual August heat of 2003 when he installed a granite sculpture of the Ten Commandments weighing 5,300 pounds, about two and a half tons of granite morality, in the lobby of the Montgomery Alabama supreme court building (on the steps of which Jefferson Davis took the oath of office as President of the Confederacy in 1861), and then defied a federal judge's order to remove it. The federal decision was based on multiple legal precedents citing the 1st Amendment statement about the separation of church and state. The advocate community defended Judge's Moore's defiance of the federal ruling but experts bemoaned his legal indiscretion. (10) A judicial inquiry commission suspended him from office for violating a federal court order.

America perennially wrestles with its religious conscience and its reliance on law as the basis for social harmony and fairness. Those who feel compelled to show the Ten Commandments in public places, despite prohibited court decisions, should also display *The Code of Hammurabi* and the *Papyrus of Ani* to show how similar these antecedent literary traditions are with most of the commandments in *Exodus* and then answer whether or not, because of the similarities, Persian and Egyptian texts should receive the imprimatur of divine inspiration.

About the time of the writing of the injunctions in *Exodus*, similar laws were developed in Greece. Though tyrants still managed to come to power in ancient Greece, Pheidon at Argos (650–630), Pisastratus in Athens (561–527), Polycrates at Samos (546–522), aristocracies usually exercised control as monarchies were abolished and oligarchies established. A constitution for Athens and Sparta was first proposed in 754–753 BCE. A century later in 624–620 Draco introduced a law code for Athens, prescribing death for the most trivial offenses. Our connotation of draconian as a synonym for extreme judgment derives from his name. Solon's law code modified Draco's severe penalties in 594–591 and these inspired the Romans and set the standard for the rule of law directing civil order until Justinian's codification in the 4th century CE. (11) Later, when the church developed a canon law comparable in complexity to the American tax code to guide ecclesiastics, and had courts to judge miscreants, the church proclaimed that the canons did not contain falsehoods, although certain passages in the writings of theologians needed correction.

But the formal commandments given by God to the Hebrews are not the only set of guidelines for living. "He who hates the law is without wisdom," says *Sirach* (33:2), a book of 51 chapters of how to manage the wisdom of understanding the law and duties towards God, the afflicted, children, how to use wealth, how to avoid sin, and even rules for table etiquette.

Since God in *Exodus* reminds the Hebrew population that he rescued them from Egyptian bondage, it serves us well to return to what Egypt was like about that time and ask whether or not the Hebrews were better off in Egypt or wandering in the desert. (12) The Egyptians had laws and codes for behavior, many found in the *Papyrus of Ani* where 38 negative confessions like "I have not," or "Thou shalt not," occur. For example, Ani says he has not done iniquity, has not stolen, committed murder, lied, cursed God, defiled another man's wife, or transgressed. (13)

The Ten Commandments, the precise determination of how many precepts there are is uncertain, define a strict code of relationships within a community, similar to social rules for communal behavior, of relationships to God, the Sabbath, and family and neighbors. The Ten Commandments say nothing about faith or belief, except for the prohibition against plural gods. They do not provide for a government; they are only personal, behavioral commands. There is no citizen input, no provision for due process, no appeal, no trial by jury, no legislative assembly and no judicial review. For a governmental design we turn to Solon and the Greeks who were positive not negative in their codes, emphasizing virtues instead of behavioral prohibitions.

Besides Hammurabi and the Ten Commandments, the more comprehensive legal code that accelerated Numa's legal practices in Rome and propelled law as the crown jewel and authentic basis for civil governance was the code originating with Solon in Athens in the 7th century BCE. As societies evolved from tribal fiefdoms and petty kingdoms, political theories like Solon's accommodated the changes by creating more orderly institutions that preserved state order over private controls, and used state power both to protect private economic interests and the state's power to regulate using Greek ideals of virtue as guiding principles.

When called upon to rectify squabbling legal disputes over property and inheritances, Solon (c.639–c.559 BCE) was selected as the statesman to impose legal changes. His method was radical and rupturing, not merely cosmetic. He abolished Bronze Age tyrannical justice and instituted such dramatic changes that they exist still as the foundation of democracy and law in the western world. Solon made written law and the idea of constitutionality permanent and had his legislative package inscribed on wooden rotating cylinders so the public could read them.

First, he cancelled all mortgages and then established protections against foreclosures. He set maximum interest rates on payments, established new inheritances laws to prevent the breakup of smaller land units among surviving brothers. Fathers were ordered to teach non-inheriting sons trade skills. Widows and some women were granted greater independence in managing business affairs. Solon offered less restrictive conditions for foreign artisans to receive Athenian citizenship. His economic reforms prevented the export of essential agricultural produce, mainly the olive industry.

He gave the popular assembly (*ecclesia*) new powers that extended political representation to all citizens, established a new higher council (*boule*) which set the legislative agenda and passed laws, and inaugurated a court system with jurors drawn from all social classes. The centerpiece of Solon's bold and imaginative governmental system, sounding so contemporary because its principles underpin modern democracies, was to permit citizens to file suit on their own behalf or anyone else. His argument was that democracy is best safeguarded when each person can bring justice for self or anyone.

Unlike *The Code of Hammurabi* and Moses's commandments, Solon's approach is not a laundry list of individual prohibitions but a total program for the ordering of a civil society including citizen participation in governance and redress of grievances, the construction of bodies to pass laws and courts to adjudicate suits. It is highly probable that the code originally attributed to him is the result of systematic legal modifications over at least two centuries. But Solon goes beyond political theory and *oikonomia*, household management, to the establishment of democratic governance as exemplified by the Greek virtues of *eunomia,* good government, and justice. Those who honor justice (*dike*) will reap the blessings of peace (*eirene*), as both are sisters and daughters of Zeus. Solon would incorporate these virtues into his vision of a well-regulated city-state. And, to illustrate how these same virtues became assimilated into western thought, Rome proclaimed *ordo* (order) *pax* (peace) and *justitia* (justice) as Roman state virtues. Augustine in his writings made them Christian virtues. (14)

Solon wrote in extant Fragment #5: "I gave the common folk such privilege as is sufficient for them, neither adding nor taking away...I provided that they should not suffer undue wrong...the people best follow their leaders...for excess engenders *hubris* (pride) when great prosperity follows those whose minds are not fit." (15)

Akhenaten, Founder of Monotheism

Ammianus Marcellinus was the last of the Roman historians writing several books on only a quarter century period, from 354-378. He wrote of Egypt:

> *Anyone who cares to engage in a brisk review of the multifarious books on knowledge of the divine and the origin of prognostics will find that the source from which learning of this kind has spread throughout the world is Egypt. It was there that men, long*

before others, discovered various religions in what may be called their cradle, and now carefully preserve the origins of worship in their esoteric scriptures. (16)

Akhenaten (1,378–1,340 BCE) ascended to the throne of Egypt upon the death at an early age of his elder brother, Prince Tuthmosis, in c.1,358 BCE. It was an era during the late Bronze Age when the Hittites were consolidating their power in central Turkey and the empire of Mycenae was at its height in Greece. The latter part of the name Thutmosis, *mosis*, is similar to Moses, and connotes an Egyptian royal name. Akhenaten was known by the translation of his name as the "the god is satisfied" for the remainder of his days.

The most noteworthy aspect of his life was his complete and total transformation of the ritualistic practices of polytheism to the monotheistic worship of one god: Aten. Akhenaten dismissed all other gods and banished all images of other gods from official precincts thereby offending the prevailing clerics in Thebes, the royal capitol. Temples were closed, other divine services suspended, temple property was confiscated and priests serving only Aten were installed. (17) In order to emphasize the new religion of monotheism and renounce polytheism, Akhenaten not only changed his name but moved his capitol and erected a new temple at Amarna, about halfway along the Nile between Thebes and Cairo. A collection of 337 cuneiform tablets were found there in 1887, mostly diplomatic messages written in Akkadian. (18) After his death, the capitol was left in ruins and subsequent pharaohs resided in Thebes.

From the time of the first pharaoh the gods had always existed in stone carvings and images, whose descriptions were kept in the royal archives. Akhenaten's reign lasted seventeen years (1,358–1,340 BCE), but the religious revolution he created continued in the Hebrew, Christian and Muslim beliefs: that there is only one God. The sole god Aten became the sun, and Akhenaten was the son of the one god, a connotation that would later be used by Roman emperors and gospel narrators. What is more important, although the sun was palpably visible, was that the godhead was an abstraction, a symbol of power and life-giving forces that did not have an image except the visible sun's rays beaming down daily proclaiming the presence of the god among men. The true god had no visible form. This concept is a major religious departure from past religious practices, a god whose power is not localized to an engraved image, a supreme god knowing no rivals for power as all other religious deities had.

Akhenaten defaced all monuments showing rival gods in his lifetime, a fanaticism that eventually led to the destruction of all remnants of his monuments after his death by jealous priests and caretakers of polytheism. Temple priests had had both property and power taken away in the abrupt royal adjustment to monotheism, just as Moses had had to cope with the return of polytheism among his followers.

Akhenaten's exclusive devotion to his religious cause also led him to neglect his military and supervisory responsibilities for the empire, and as a result Egypt lost its military grip on some provinces. This loss of provincial control in parts of Asia and particularly Palestine left the land a vacuum for migrating tribes to settle in. Evidence of warring bands raiding the land of Canaan is in the Amarna letters, royal transactions in cuneiform script found in the scriptorium. We have a fragment of the prayer used by Akhenaten to the sole deity.

> *The great and living Aten...ordaining life, vigorously alive, my*
> *Father, my reminder of eternity, my witness of what is eternal,*
> *who fashions Himself with His own two hands, whom no craftsmen*
> *has devised. Whether He is in heaven or on earth, every eye beholds*
> *him while he fills the land with his rays and makes everyone to live.*
> *With seeing whom my eyes are satisfied daily when He rises*
> *in the temple...and fills it with His own self...beauteous with love,*
> *and embraces me with them in life and power for ever and ever.* (19)

A part of what has come to be called *The Great Hymn*, and surviving on the walls of entombed officials, like Ay's hymn one of Akhenaten's private secretaries, speaks to the authentic monotheistic voice, pre-dating Mosaic monotheism, unique in the world for the Late Bronze Age. (20)

> *How manifold are thy works! They are hidden from the sight of*
> *men, O Sole God, like unto whom there is no other! Thou did fashion*
> *the earth according to thy desire when thou were alone--all men,*
> *all cattle great and small, all that are upon the earth...thou appoint*
> *every man to his place and satisfy his needs. Everyone receives*
> *his sustenance and his days are numbered.* (21)

The similarities of the Great Hymn to *Psalm* 104 reveal a likely derivation from the Egyptian precursor. (22)

There are no separate gods in the passage above, only the "Sole God," and, just as importantly, there is no female counterpart. The monotheism of Akhenaten needs no stone carving and no image to represent the godhead except the ethereal domain of heaven. This god has created the world and everything in it, and his presence is manifested daily. In *Deuteronomy* we find the phrase: "Hear, O Israel,the Lord our God is one God." (*Deut.* 6:4) No other literature in all the Near or Middle East, until this time in history, has ever written of one God. A textual comparison of *Psalm* 104 (c.700 BCE) with a centuries-old hymn to the one god Aten (c.1,250 BCE) reveals similarities. (23)

From the difficult vantage of two and a half millennia, we can only conjecture about what belief in the first monotheistic deity, Aten, meant to Egyptians and the pharaoh/monotheist Akhenaten. Unlike Yahweh, Jesus or Allah, Aten revealing himself to humankind is an improbable event, despite the fact that the pharaoh himself was an extension of the deity.

Writing was so highly esteemed that the Egyptians created a separate god, the voice of the sun god RA, to epitomize their art and craft. Thoth was no only the creator of speech, science, hieroglyphics and wisdom but also the patron of all the arts. The Greeks identified him with Hermes. Thoth appears in Egyptian art in human form with the head of an ibis often holding a scepter and an ankh, the symbol of life.

By the time of the establishment of the Hebrew nation under a strong king like Josiah in the 7th century BCE, about the time the Torah was written, the Hebrew religious culture was entrenched, tribally totalitarian, zealous in its pursuit of one god who demanded universal acknowledgement and submission. This God would send prophets to remind believers of obligations to him but they would not expect further revelations or truths. (24)

Moses

The Egyptian name of Moses means birth and his story in *Exodus* is the story of the birth of a people and a new God. Moses is often associated with the second half of a hyphenated word such as "Ptah-mose," or "Amon-mose," in the list of kings in Egypt names such as Ahmose, Thoth-mose and Ra-mose, where *mose* means child. The translation of Moses would thus be roughly equivalent to "child of God." (25) All this presumes he was a real person.

Was Moses Egyptian or a Hebrew? In a sense, it might be an irrelevant question because in Egypt in 1,350 BCE there were no racially distinct ethnic differences. Slaves imported from military adventures had children who intermarried with Egyptians. If the Hebrews had lived for a few generations in Egypt, then they cannot have exclusively married only among their own ethnic group. Before Moses there was no Hebrew religious distinction. (26) If Moses was an Egyptian a further question arises as to why he should have decided to leave his homeland and become the leader of a band of excluded foreigners to journey to a new land, unless he was the leader of a monotheistic religious faction which wanted to maintain its orthodoxy when such views became forbidden in Egypt after the death of Akhenaten.

In this historical supposition Moses was the leader, perhaps even a priest, of the forbidden monotheistic sect of Akhenaten, forbidden by his successors like his grandson Tutankhamun. Those who practiced or followed the devotion and worship of only one god were ostracized from the regular devotions of the community of believers and all the religious rituals and festivals. It certainly would have been sensible and convenient for monotheists to leave Egypt and to live in more hospitable surroundings, akin to Puritans fleeing England to come to America.

But having asked all the hypothetical questions, we now come to the literary precedent. A popular story from Middle Kingdom Egypt known as *The Tale of Sinuhe*, a narrative copied by scribes learning to write, describes how Sinuhe, an Egyptian courtier, flees from Egypt at a time of social and political instability during the reign of Senwosret I (1,971–1,928 BCE). Sinuhe flees Egypt to land somewhere in Syrian Palestine where he learns to adapt to pastoral and nomadic life and becomes a tribal chieftain. "I was an attendant who attended his lord, a servant of the royal harem, waiting on the Princess, the highly praised Royal Wife of King Sesostris in Khenemsut, the daughter of King Amenemhet in Kanefru, Nefru, the revered." (27)

Was this Egyptian narrative the inspiration for the biblical scribes who wrote *Exodus*? Were other narratives, now lost, the literary sources of parts of the exodus story? Archaeology may provide an answer in the future, but for now we know that there was an Egyptian official, not Moses, who left the service of the pharaoh and settled in Palestine, became a local leader, and that a Theban pharaoh did drive out a band of illegal immigrants, the Hyksos who were Canaanites, who had settled in delta Egypt by the 16th century BCE. These two historical events and written narratives likely served as literary sources for *Exodus*. Thus, high Egyptian officials fleeing Egypt and becoming leaders in a neighboring country while retaining their Egyptian names, indeed fleeing into Canaanite territory that would later become Israel, is already a significant literary event in Egypt four thousand years ago.

Every nation begins early in its recorded history to give legend to its heroes, to glorify kings and princes, to give them heroic names of stature and to make them larger than life in the founding of a nation, religion, city, or in the conquest of other peoples. This is certainly true of the entire history of the Near and Middle East. Moses fits into the pattern of a heroic figure following a literary tradition beginning with Sargon I, King of Akkad (c.2,340–2,305 BCE) who was born of aristocratic parents, abandoned in the Euphrates river in a reed basket, raised by loving parents and returned as leader of his people. Sargon ruled the Akkadian Empire (c.2,360–2,180) that subdued Sumer and added its language and literature to ancient culture that later decorated biblical narratives. Royal parentage, abandonment, independent nurturance and return to kingship is also true of Cyrus the Great and Oedipus in Greek mythology.

Sargon, Osiris, Romulus and Moses were all placed in a reed casket and set adrift on the waters. The birth of Horus by Isis occurred in the papyrus reeds and numerous pictorial representations show Horus suckled by his mother surrounded by anxious attendants. (28) The fact that Moses has a similar beginning in Egypt by a woman of high estate is meant by the Hebrew scribes to elevate his status approximating royalty and divinely chosen.

Romulus, the founder of the city of Rome, together with his brother Remus, were sons of Rhea Silvia, who was supposed to be a vestal virgin by the order of Amulius who usurped the throne of the king his brother, Numitor. But the god Mars intervened and she bore twins, angering Amulius who imprisoned her and set the boys down the Tiber River in a basket. They floated ashore where they were suckled and tended for by a she-wolf until, at maturity they learned their true identity, killed Amulius and restored Numitor to the throne, then established the city of Rome in the year 753 BCE, about the time the Bible was being written and edited by the E and D scribes.

Additionally, in the literary tradition of the hero there is usually a prophecy associated with the birth, life, and possibly death of the hero thus exalted by future predictions. Heroes in religion had already been established in the heroes of legend certainly by the time of Homer and perhaps earlier than the 9th century BCE. Hero legends follow a similar pattern, as one can read in the accounts of Gilgamesh, Perseus, Oedipus, Paris, Heracles, Osiris, Moses and others. The hero's infancy is spent in humble origins and is rescued by poor working people, such as slaves, gardeners or shepherds. The literary themes hold true for Sargon, Cyrus, Moses, Romulus, and Jesus. The child is born of aristocratic parents or lineage and then abandoned. But the nurturing father is of humble origin, like a carpenter.

In Moses there is a role reversal. Moses is the abandoned son of Hebrew Levites, but is reared by the princess of a royal house. (29) According to Josephus, Pharaoh had been warned in a dream that a son of his daughter would be dangerous for him and the kingdom of Egypt and thus had the child abandoned in the Nile's waters where it was rescued by Hebrews but reared by royalty.

Neither Amos, Hosea, nor Isaiah, who supposedly preached prior to the writing of the Pentateuch, mentions Moses. Jeremiah, Micah and Daniel refer to him sparingly. (30) There is no independent verification that Moses lived at all, that Hebrews were enslaved in Egypt, or that an un-named pharaoh died with his army in the Red Sea. (31) In fact, the Egyptian story known as *The Tale of Two Brothers* has a scene similar to the parting of the Red Sea except that the God, in this instance, *RE*, makes a current of water between two brothers so that one will not kill they other: "Thus Anup followed him in a rage, but Re caused a stream of water to come between them, and thus placed the poor Bata in a safe place from his pursuer. Throughout the night they stood on either side of the water." Even the epical parting of the Red Sea has a literary parallel in earlier Egyptian literature, and this short Egyptian tale serves as the source for episodes in the Joseph story and the *Exodus*. (32)

Nor is there any independent verification of the *Exodus*, though commentators treat it as if it were history instead of literature. Trying to reconcile the time of the Hebrews in Egypt, from four generations (*Exodus* 6:16-20) to 430 years (*Exodus* 12:40), is only one of the exaggerated entanglements facing one hoping to harmonize manipulative facts and storied myth. (33) The stele of Merneptah describes his conquests in the area of Palestine against a people then known as Israel. But if the reality of Moses himself is uncertain, the supposed route the Hebrews took on their journey, trying to confirm geographic place names, stopping at which watering holes, walking along which established route, is even more nebulous.

According to Josephus, an historian named Menetho who lived in the 3rd century BCE reports that the exodus occurred because the Egyptians wanted to protect themselves from a plague that had broken out among the Jews and that Moses was an Egyptian priest who was sent as a missionary to the quarantined Jews with instructions on cleanliness modeled after the Egyptian clergy. (34) Indeed, a passage in *Exodus* hints at un-named diseases visited upon the Egyptians: "And said, If you will diligently consider with obedience, the voice of the Lord your God, and will do that which is upright before his vision, and will give ear to his commandments, and observe all his statutes, I will impute none of these diseases to you, which I have imputed to the Egyptians: for I, the Lord, am your Healer." (35)

Moses carries a staff that has power and is fertile, like Hermes and the pharaohs, a clear giveaway to mythological status. Hermes receives a beautiful staff of wealth and prosperity from his brother Apollo, a golden staff with three branches. Chryses, the priest of Apollo, is the bearer of a golden staff. In the *Odyssey* Hermes leads the spirits of Penelope's wooers into Hades with a golden wand. The blind seer Teiresias in Homer's Hades also holds a golden staff. While in Hades, Minos retains his golden scepter. (36) Virgil, who largely drew from Greek sources and was unlikely to have known about the Moses myth, has multiple references to a staff. All the pharaohs held staff as symbols of their authority. Scholars believe the Egyptian god Thoth and Hermes to be inter-changeable gods in their respective cultures. Thoth also carries a staff and an ankh, the symbol of life. Indeed, one of the most ubiquitous artifacts found in Egyptian graves are staff figures of the dead. (37)

Deuteronomy 34:4 enumerates a list of character traits of Moses that may conform to those of a real individual. Moses is irascible. He killed an overseer who was ill-treating a Hebrew woman. In a fit of anger he broke the Tables of the Law that he brought down from Mount Sinai, conveniently destroying them for posterity. Indeed, God punished him for disbelief when he supposedly struck the rock impatiently with his rod twice to bring forth water, instead of as God has commanded, merely speaking to it. (38) For this he was not permitted to enter the Promised Land. The myth of striking the mountain and water pouring forth first appears in ancient Greek lore when Rhea gives birth to Zeus and needs water to wash away the stains of childbirth. But since rivers are not in existence yet, she strikes the mountain and water gushes out. Rhea washes the baby, gives it to the river nymph Neda who carries it off to Crete. Biblical scribes took their stories from all cultures.

But besides land and monotheism, many of the more notable customs adopted by the Hebrews, like the prohibition from eating pork, circumcision, and attitudes towards cleanliness, are borrowed from Egyptian customs. Here are selected examples according to Herodotus, "Male children, except in those places which have borrowed the custom from hence, are left in other nations as nature formed them: in Egypt they are circumcised...They wash themselves in cold water twice in the course of the day, and as often in the night...The Egyptians regard the hog as an unclean animal, and if they casually touch one they immediately plunge themselves, clothes and all, into the water." (39)

The Egyptians occasionally ate the meat of the pig; the Jews never did. What was the motive why these people had such an aversion to this one animal? One deduction is that pigs are not suitable to the nomadic lifestyle. It has been surmised also that the milk of the pig occasioned leprosies and hence the Egyptians entertained a great aversion to it. The Egyptian god Seth in the form of black pig is said to have wounded Horus. Because of the goddess Hathor's respected cow's horns, Egyptians would thus never think to eat cow flesh. The parallels of Egyptian religious traditions with Jewish traditions in circumcision, and the taboos regarding pork and cows are conspicuous.

Immortality was the chief belief passed on by the Egyptians to all subsequent religions, Judaism, Christianity, Islam and Sikhism, and has been the main feature of monotheism. Egyptians buried their dead as if they would some day rise again in the afterlife. Neither Mesopotamians, Persians, or Greeks had the afterlife as a centerpiece of belief. (40)

The Book of the Dead is a title given to an enormous and diverse collection of prayers, incantations and hymns found in funerary texts comprising some of the oldest religious writings in the world. They probably originated in pre-dynastic times, the earliest dating from c.2,000 BCE, and were current into the first millennium CE until supplanted by Christian themes. The most famous and complete of these texts is *The Papyrus of Ani*. Ani was a high ecclesiastical and public official in the 18th dynasty c.1,500-1,400 BCE and his extensive funerary text, together with proclaiming the resurrection of the spirit and the immortality of the soul, yields extensive insights into the culture and religion of ancient Egyptians. (41)

So did Moses who lived (if we even know he existed and could date his years correctly, would have lived about 150 years after Akhenaten) carry the concept of monotheism from Egypt to Judea? (42) It's true that the typology is not the same: Hebrews did not worship a sun god. Nevertheless, the idea of monotheism was so unique, and Hebrews are not known to have invented anything but always to have taken cultural ideas from others, that adopting monotheism is not out of the question. In fact what is in contention is that the normally undisputed belief that the Hebrews were chosen to proclaim the new message of one god may be as mistaken as the belief that a deity like Shamash to Hammurabi actually delivered commandments to them.

The Golden Calf

Although the story of *Exodus* describes the problems the Israelites encountered on their journey, it also shows how thoroughly imbued they were with the flourishing Middle Eastern cultures. Mesopotamians, Hittites, Canaanites and Egyptians all worshipped the bull or cow in one way or another, and in worshipping a golden calf the Israelites were simply following tradition. (43) Egyptians worshipped Apis the bull and Hathor the cow. So the fact that the people erected an altar and made a semblance of a cow god they had known in Egypt should not be surprising. Here is the story.

> *When the people became aware of Moses' delay in coming down from the mountain, they gathered around Aaron and said to him, 'Come, make us a god who will be our leader; as for the man Moses who brought us out of the land of Egypt, we do not know what has happened to him.' Aaron replied, 'Have your wives and sons and daughters take off the golden earrings they are wearing, and bring them to me.' So all the people took off their earrings and brought them to Aaron, who accepted their offering, and fashioning this gold with an engraving tool, made a golden calf. Then they cried out, 'This is your god O Israel, who brought you out of the land of Egypt.' On seeing this, Aaron built an altar before the calf and exclaimed, 'Tomorrow is a feast of the Lord.' Early the next day the people offered holocausts and brought peace offerings. Then they sat down to eat and drink, and rose up to revel.* (44)

> *With that, the Lord said to Moses, "Go down at once to your people, whom you have brought out of the land of Egypt, for they have become depraved. They have soon turned away from the way I pointed out to them, making for themselves a molten calf and worshipping it, sacrificing to it and crying out, 'This is your god, O Israel, who brought you out of the land of Egypt!' I see how stiff-necked this people is, continued the Lord to Moses. "Let me alone, then, that my wrath may blaze up against them to consume them. Then I will make of you a great nation.* (45)

Having talked God out of being wrathful to his people he had just led out of Egypt, Moses then returns to find the Israelites reveling and adoring the golden calf. He then asks who will be on the side of the Lord, and all the Levites rally to him. He then commands them to put on their swords and "slay your own kinsmen, your friends and neighbors," a decidedly capital punishment, cruel and unusual. *Exodus* tells us, "The Levites carried out the command of Moses and that day there fell about three thousand of the people." Here is the second biblical genocide carried out by the just Moses. Apparently, the commandment of "Thou shalt not kill" is restricted to others, not the Chosen Ones. If Moses had been brought before an International tribunal or court of justice, what would be his defense and what legal statute would be cite for his murderous crimes? Here is the first indication that God and his chief ministers can sanction killing thousands for the sake of religious political correctness. The death of heretics has biblical permission. And what was the proximate cause of this human disaster? The image of a calf, hand-sized examples of which have been found by archaeologists in 1990 in ancient Ashkelon dating from 1,550 BCE.

In *Exodus* we find a curious and over-looked allusion to cattle. Just as every firstborn son in Pharaoh's Egypt is to die so is every firstborn cattle in the realm to die. (46) In *Nehemiah*: 10 we find that this is not an incidental phrase but part of the law: "As it is also written in the law, we will bring the firstborn of our sons and of our cattle, of our herds and of our flocks to the house of our God to the priest ministering there."

But the scribe *Exodus* is also steeped in the tradition of cattle and bull sacrifice and describes accurately how this ceremony is to be conducted. "Take some of the bull's blood and put it on the horns of the altar with your finger, and pour out the rest of it at the base of the altar." (47) This same ceremony is described again in *Leviticus*: "The priest shall then put some of the blood on the horns of the altar of fragrant incense that is before the LORD in the Tent of Meeting. The rest of the bull's blood he shall pour out at the base of the altar of burnt offering at the entrance to the Tent of Meeting." (48)

At this time in Hebrew history bull sacrifice is clearly a part of the culture and even Moses takes part as the following passage in *Leviticus* makes clear. "Moses slaughtered the bull and took some of the blood, and with his finger he put it on all the horns of the altar to purify the altar. He poured out the rest of the blood at the base of the altar. So he consecrated it to make atonement for it." (49) Why would Moses, who killed his friends and relatives for worshipping a golden calf participate in a ceremony of slaughtering a bull for sacrifice? To whose god was he thus making propitiation and for what purpose? The *Exodus* scribe is unconcerned that the Hebrews at various times in their history worshipped Baal like the Canaanites and then later repudiated the practice. The condensation of layers of history and myth has resulted in religious and biblical confusion but not literary imagination.

Later in the history of the Hebrews sacrificing a bull is not such a righteous act. According to Isaiah, "whoever sacrifices a bull is like one who kills a man, and whoever offers a lamb, like one who breaks a dog's neck; whoever makes a grain offering is like one who presents pig's blood, and whoever burns memorial incense, like one who worships an idol. They have chosen their own ways, and their souls delight in their abominations." (50) This is indeed degrading since the days when it was not only expedient but essential that bulls be sacrificed, as the example of Moses demonstrates. When Solomon dedicated the temple, he sacrificed 22,000 cattle and 120,000 sheep and goats. (51)

In the gospels, Jesus finds the money-changers in the temple precincts. But there are also men there selling cattle and he drives them and the cattle away with a whip made of cords. (52) Even after the death of Jesus the disciples found bull sacrifice popular among the Greeks living in the region. "The priest of Zeus, whose temple was just outside the city, brought bulls and wreaths to the city gates because he and the crowd wanted to offer sacrifices to them." (53) But for Paul the blood of animals can no longer be expiation for sins. "The blood of goats and bulls and the ashes of a heifer sprinkled on those who are ceremonially unclean sanctify them so that they are outwardly clean...because it is impossible for the blood of bulls and goats to take away sins."(54) After so many centuries when God sanctioned and even commissioned the sacrifice of bulls how and why did it become religiously unacceptable? Did God change his mind (is he thus mutable?), or did men misinterpret the message? According to Paul, the blood of bulls can still "sanctify" those who are "unclean," though it is unclear whether this is because it has been a longstanding Jewish tradition or a new Christian theological conviction. As we have seen from the conflicting biblical references, one could argue that sacrificing bulls is good, evil, or unnecessary.

The domestication of the cow in the Middle East brought meat, milk, bone, leather, traction for planting and reaping and dung for fertilization, all essential elements in a civilization's survival. The cow's presence among its owners signified wealth, as it did for Abraham. *Genesis* 13 describes the conflict between large herd owners, Abraham and Lot, and Jacob's family in Goshen. During David's reign, overseers were appointed to supervise these herds. Young calves were considered a special delicacy for festive occasions. The bull, on the other hand, was the mythical, religious symbol of fertility and power. The golden calf in *Exodus* 32 is just one extended narrative of this ubiquitous religious influence.

Abundant bovine artifacts, emerging archaeological evidence and extensive written references confirm a long cultural heritage of the cow and bull in pre-biblical and biblical scripture. Deities are often portrayed as standing on top of lions or bulls, or as represented as the animals themselves, as with a head of a man and body of a lion, like the Sphinx in Giza, or the entire animal, like Baal as a bull. Bronze bull figurines have been unearthed from early Israelite cult sites and bronze statuettes of EL, the Canaanite deity, dating from c.1,225–1,100 BCE provide supplemental evidence of the existence of the Canaanite bull cult among the early Hebrews. (55)

Despite these misgivings about cattle, it is clear from further biblical entries that bull sacrifices continued. And yet in *Numbers* we find the analogy: "It is God who brought him out of Egypt, a wild bull of towering height." (56) Again in *Numbers* the following scene occurs: "Then Balaam said to Balac, 'Build me seven altars, and prepare seven bullocks and seven rams for me here.' So he did as Balaam had ordered, offering a bullock and a ram on each altar." (57) Clearly, the sacrificing of bulls and the prohibition against cows did not cease among the Hebrews as did the adoration of cattle as a divine image from the Canaanites. Countless bull figurines have been found in Israeli sites in the hill country. There are other written examples including the following:

And finding out a device he made two golden calves and said to them:
Go ye up no more to Jerusalem: Behold thy gods, O Israel, who brought
thee out of the land of Egypt...for the people went to adore the calf as far
as Dan. (58)

And going up to the altar, he did in like manner in Bethel, to sacrifice
to the calves which he had made. (59)

These examples illustrate the prevalence of cattle in the sustenance of the Hebrew people during biblical times and the rebelling against the divine status of the cow and bull inherited from neighboring civilizations in order to establish their separate monotheistic society. Cattle were slain not just for food but were clearly used for sacrifices.

The country of Eritrea, which won its independence from Ethiopia in 1993, was once the heartland of a powerful kingdom known as Aksum that converted to Christianity. Over 3,000 years ago, this region according to legend was ruled by the Queen of Sheba who traveled to Jerusalem to meet with King Solomon. When she returned she was said to be pregnant with Solomon's child, whom she called Menelik, who, after growing to manhood went to Jerusalem to meet his father, King Solomon and stayed for three years. Menelik was escorted home to his African country by the firstborn sons of Solomon's noblemen and assigned the Ark of the Covenant to protect them. (60) Why a boat in the desert? The Ark of the Covenant is the borrowed symbol of an Egyptian barge bearing the soul to eternity. Eritreans believe that the original and fabled Ark of the Covenant came to their country over

3,000 years ago and held the stone tablets containing the Ten Commandments God gave to Moses. Christian Eritreans believe that the Ark resides with them. During the reign of the 4th century king, Ezana, converted to Christianity and today about half of Eritrea and Ethiopia is Christian. They believe that the Ark is more than a holy relic: it is God incarnate.

The Hebrews never invented any economic, cultural and military strategies that enriched their civilization. Cultural transformation occurs because of new methods and techniques that allow superior power to be demonstrated. Unless innovative techniques are constantly renewed, reinvented and developed, systems and institutions, like armies and navies, will be overcome by superior technology, followed by economic, political and cultural dominance. The principal Hebrew endeavor was the copying of the literature and mythic and religious practices of neighbors. (61) So the question is not, when can we pinpoint the date of *Exodus*, because, based on the river-basket myth, the *Tale of Sinuhe* and the *Tale of Two Brothers*, it is not history but literature. Thus, efforts like Gordon and Rendsburg to find an exact date based on internal dates in the Bible are presumptive because they assume the historical accuracy of a mythical narrative. (62)

One such cultural transformation was the creation of houses of worship. Sacrifices among ancient worshippers took place understandably outdoors and on altars because sacrifices were bloody, smelly and the cries of the slain animals needed dispersal on the prevailing winds. Once symbols and commemorations replaced sacrifice, the representations of gods in statuary, the Ark of the Covenant, articles on display, the ejaculations of the divine pharaoh, then prayers, clerical obligations and special ceremonies moved indoors. Temples did not replace animal sacrifice, since bulls, lambs and doves were still slaughtered to appease the gods, but temple hierarchies were established to maintain the instituted and anointed legitimacy of beliefs and practices.

Altars existed throughout Palestine in the pre-exilic period as animal sacrifices occurred throughout this part of the world on altars constructed for the purpose. The size of the altars for the Hebrews is described in *Exodus* 27:1-2 "five cubits long and five cubits wide." A cubit is a non-uniform measurement, the measurement from the elbow to the tip of the middle finger, about a foot and a half. It was not until the reforms of Hezekiah and Josiah in the late 8th century BCE that sacrifices were centralized in Jerusalem. (63)

Soon Gods' houses rose in architectural profusion: the squat Doric order without a base but a massive shaft with twenty flutes terminating in a capital; the slender Doric with its scroll-shaped capital and firm base; ornate Corinthian columns, found everywhere decorating Greek temples in the Mediterranean. The Romans made Greek architecture the imperial style for all government buildings thereby transforming a religious style into a public one.

The Temple of Amon at Karnak in Luxor covers a thousand feet with 134 columns arranged in 16 rows, a complex of shrines and halls. The Temple of Solomon did not survive its multiple demolitions but its beauty was said to be comparable to the stars. Gothic cathedrals pointed to the sky to emphasize the direction of prayers. Today's churches are more functional blending with the environment and made with simple earth colors and can look like shells, fishes, breadbaskets, A-frame homes, corporate headquarters and blockhouses. It isn't clear sometimes when entering if you are in a lecture hall, symphony or concert hall or auditorium. But does God actually enter and reside because of the architect's ingenuity, the cleric's sanction, the blessing of the bishop, or the sanctity of the membership?

Like the Egyptians the Hebrews absconded with the idea of monotheism, and built a single temple where the ceremonies surrounding the sacrifices to Yahweh could be administered. When the temple was repeatedly destroyed by invading marauders and its people dispersed with finality in 70 CE, Judaism was compelled to create another center where the spirit of God resided. It was during this period that a formidable new religious rival proposed that God's presence dwelled within believers and not in stone buildings. This novel idea made the movement mobile and not localized. Christianity was born and assimilated Hellenic ideas with Judaism creating a new religion with literature obtained from heroic ideals from older cultures.

THE STELE OF HAMMURABI IN THE LOUVRE
Hammurabi Receiving the Laws from Shamash, The Babylonian God
c. 1780 BCE

PART II: CHRISTIAN LITERARY ORIGINS

THE HILL OF SACRIFICE
Petra, Jordan

CHAPTER TEN
THE MANUFACTURED JESUS: EVIDENCE AND MYSTERY

There are enough fragments, imperial decrees, Tacitus and Josephus's brief notations and Paul's testimony with Peter, John and James who actually knew Jesus to suggest that he was a real person, crucified under orders from Pontius Pilate, and that he had a brother James who was stoned to death. (1) Everything else in the life of Jesus, his preaching, confrontation with Jewish authorities, miracles, degree of his spiritual nature, relationships with God, angels and dead prophets, and parables, is subject to allegorical interpretation. Nearly a century after his death gospel narrators drew from a variety of literary sources for composition including stoicism, Judaic aspirations for a Messiah, episodes and parables from Homer, sayings from Seneca and Epictetus, designations given to Jesus used by Kings and emperors, from myths of the virgin birth, other-worldly appearances, and death and resurrection motifs. I examine each of these topics to sketch how the gospels relied on literary precedents to reconstruct hagiographic narratives of Jesus.

Let's take two examples to show similarities between existing literature and the gospels. First, he was born the Son of God and of a mortal woman, symbolized as the man who renewed life, was worshipped and reborn as a dead man and a living god. Though not a warrior, he performs legendary feats and always conquers, suffering for humanity, called the Best of Men. Such is Hercules who Euripedes and Sophocles made the hero of tragedies. (2)

Second, a man who was a carpenter, a man of many sorrows, who was said to be born of God, who possessed an exemplary moral life, became accustomed to pain and privation, had uncomprehending followers, and who returned from the dead alive and sought to return to his fatherland is true of Odysseus as well as Jesus. The synoptic evangelists and particularly Mark drew on the characterization and themes of Homeric heroes, principally Odysseus and Hector, to create a short prose narrative around Jesus. Borrowing from Jewish eschatology, Greek literary and Gnostic traditions, gospel narratives make Jesus appear to be both an epic hero and a divine, transcendent savior. (3) The use of supernatural beings as a part of an interaction in the narrative with the main character, whether Gilgamesh, Hector, Perseus, Odysseus or Jesus, is a common feature of epic literature.

Stoicism constitutes the second ingredient in the formation of the gospels. This philosophy helps frame the cultural context of the age and yields a peek into the mindset of writers in the 1st century CE.

Stoicism

Philosophies, like trade goods or ideas discussed in the marketplaces, barbershops, in temples and on street corners, spread as rapidly and widely as rumors. Besides the attraction to religious ideals, there were ethical philosophies from the fertility of the Greek imagination in the first century CE that captivated popular taste. Epicurus is known to have written epistles to his scattered congregations to maintain philosophical unity, a practical method of guidance and instruction Paul used. (4) The Roman tribunes conquered Greece in the 3rd century BCE, but the wine of Greek intellectual vigor conquered the Roman people and all whom they subdued. Rome then distributed this culture to the world.

Through self-control and abnegation, stoicism embraced virtue as the highest objective. It would become one of the main ideologies influencing Christian ethics and dogma. Stoicism, the search for ethical principles, was first proclaimed by Zeno (334–262 BCE) from Cyprus. A stoic phrase was "to live consistently with nature." People can only attain true freedom, stoics said, by putting aside unjust thoughts, indulgence and excesses, and to exercise duty with a correct disposition. The stoic ideal can best be described as a state of human activity that comes closest to representing a divine state, or of behaving with those characteristics that could best be ascribed to a deity. The evangelists borrowed stoicism as the Jews did Roman architecture and subordinated it to Jewish eschatology.

Educated Jews grasped at stoicism as a helpmate in a revived Jewish morality which had not saved them from Roman domination, and as an attractive alternative to an ethical code congenial to Mosaic traditions. Stoicism found an ideological home among the Essenes by the beginning of the 2nd century BCE. The stoical theme of poverty found a ready home in advocates like Seneca and Epictetus as it did for the scribes of *Deuteronomy* (15:11) and *Mark* (14:7): "You have the poor with you always." Several passages in *Proverbs* and in *Mark* and Paul extol poverty. "They all gave out of their wealth; but she, out of her poverty, put in everything, all she had to live on." (*Mark* 12:43-45) "For you know the grace of our Lord Jesus Christ, that though he was rich, yet for your sakes he became poor, so that you through his poverty might become rich." (*2 Corinthians* 8:8-10) Because of stoicism's influence, virtue in poverty and wickedness in the rich was a common rhetorical posture of the era. The funeral oration of Pericles, the founder of the Greek republic and democracy as recorded by Thucydides, shows how poverty was esteemed even among the Greeks who lived 500 years before Jesus. (5) "It is easier for a camel to pass through the eye of a needle than for a rich man to enter the Kingdom of God." (*Mark* 10:25). It appears to signal that entrance to the Kingdom of God is restricted to the amount of money possessed.

Gospel narrators sought to impugn the rich and seek justice for the poor, a common stoic ideal and a theme which resonates throughout the narratives in scenes like the cleansing of the temple of merchants and money changers which has scriptural predecessors in *Jeremiah* 7:11, *Zechariah* 14:21 and collected sayings in *The Book of Amos*. If the account is true, Jesus could have modeled his actions on scriptural prediction, but it's more likely that gospel narrators invented the story to conform to prophetic scripture (*Psalm* 69:9) and culturally accepted stoicism.

There are a few examples of personal ethics without religious standards, like Cato the Elder (234–149 BCE), a Roman ethical ideal because of his conservative, thrifty private principles and public campaigns for a national ethic. Cato, who exemplified the time-honored virtues of simplicity, honesty and courage, rose to the rank of Censor before the fall of republicanism and the rise of dictatorial and tyrannical emperors beginning with Caesar. Like Hesiod, Virgil and Horace, Cato wrote on farming, wore simple clothing though he was wealthy, condemned extravagant practices, mourned the loss of national morality and used his influence to seek senatorial legislation for a moral code. He lived to be 85 and was a farmer-statesman and international diplomat in the mold of Thomas Jefferson. He symbolized the stern role of a public servant who modeled the maxims of his private ethics. Rome casually adopted popular philosophies like Epicureanism and stoicism but few men matched Cato's personal commitment. Like Socrates and Jesus, Cato is a rare example of a man dedicated to a high ethical living standard.

Parallel Stoic and Gospel Sayings

Whether or not the evangelists took passages liberally from stoic philosophers is not as relevant as that they were clearly influenced by stoic ideas. The virtues of detachment from wealth, prestige, power and suffering tribulations willingly even to death are common to both ideologies. Except for later theological commentators, no writer in this era, in prose, poetry, drama or philosophy quotes Jesus. But other authors do quote the stoics, though it is unclear whether or not stoic sayings come from even earlier sources.

An analysis of the similarity of stoical sayings from philosophers like Seneca, (4 BCE–65 CE) a contemporary of Jesus, Musonius Rufus and Epictetus (c.50–138 CE), clarify this literary symbiosis with the gospels. None of these comparative sayings either individually or collectively allows us to conclude with conviction that Paul, for example, borrowed from Seneca, or had even read him. But the analysis does serve as a basis for elucidating the cultural climate of the era.

SENECA	PAUL
God is near you, is with you, is inside you. Yes, Lucilius, there resides within us a divine spirit, which guards us and watches over us in the evil and good that we do. (6)	Do you not know that you are the temple of God and that the Spirit of God dwells in you? (*I Cor.* 3:16)
Start cultivating a relationship with poverty. 'Dear guest (quoting Virgil), be bold to pay no heed to riches, and so make yourself, like him, worthy of a god.'(7)	For we brought nothing into the world, and certainly we can take nothing out...but those who seek to become rich fall into temptation... For covetousness is the root of all evils." (*Timothy* 6:8-10)
"For what is to be gained if something is concealed from man when nothing is barred from God? He is present in our minds, in attendance in the midst of our thoughts." (8)	And there is no creature hidden from his sight; but all things are naked and open to the eyes of him to whom we have to give an account." (*Hebrews* 4:13)

Gaius Musonius Rufus (c.30–100 CE), teacher of Epictetus, the most famous and esteemed of stoic preachers, was born a knight of Etruscan heritage and dedicated his life to preaching moral virtues everywhere in the Roman Empire. (9) Only fragments of his discourses remain. His message was that people were essentially good, that God wants everyone to exercise virtue and that this can be attained through training and practice. He wore plain clothing, kept his beard, praised work on the land, had a strict sexual morality, practiced good citizenship and generosity in giving whatever was necessary to those in need. These stoic ideals are also characteristic of communal standards among early Essenes and Christians whose lives paralleled stoic ethical beliefs and behaviors.

Musonius' parable about the birds who neither sow nor reap is paralleled in *Matthew* 6:27. Here is Musonius: "Whence do the little birds, which are much poorer than you, feed their young, the swallows and nightingales and larks and blackbirds? Homer too speaks of birds in these words, 'Even as a bird carries to her unfledged young whatever morsels she happens to come upon, though she fares badly herself." (10) Musonius and gospel parables are strikingly similar both in substance and tone. Jesus' parables were largely agricultural and about relationships between landowners, slaves and workers, the kind of poetry favored by Hesiod and pastoral poets like Virgil, Horace and Martial. Like Musonius' strict sexual code, Jesus gave stern warnings about divorce, sterner than even the Talmud prescribed, and called those who think of adultery to cut out their eyes. (11) Musonius, like a good Roman citizen like Jesus, yielded to Roman taxation ("Give to Caesar what is Caesar's"), and the parable of the Good Samaritan would assuredly win stoic endorsement.

The most important concept for the stoic was inner freedom, to be the captain of one's soul, and to find enlightenment and truth within. If we substitute the gospel phrase "Kingdom of God" for "inner freedom" we find a thematic match that parallels stoic philosophy, very appealing to any audience of the 1st century and embodied in the classic *Meditations of Marcus Aurelius* (121–180 CE). Jesus is portrayed as a stoic ideal eating in the homes of the rich but living and preaching on behalf of the poor just like a stoic who shunned wealth and scorned luxuries. The early Christians of the *Acts* shared everything in common, interpreting the kingdom as a communal society. (12)

Jesus does not attack existing economic and social institutions of the day, preaching several parables about the slave, and what to do with money. (13) Like a good stoic, Jesus outlines a reformation in radical, personal moral issues, and does not advocate militant revolution against the state. The absence of criticism of the Romans and the presence of stoicism as a guide to ethical living pervades the gospels and these two motifs alone indicate that the gospels were written after the destruction of Jerusalem. If the message Jesus preached was to be successful it had to reach gentiles and not offend Rome as direct criticism would have been suicidal. So the gospels are indirect and even flattering in treating Romans. Moreover, in order to reach foreign ears and minds, the gospel narratives had to be written in the language of the day, Greek, and had to employ concepts understood by educated readers. Exercising poetic license, gospel narrators copied stoic parables as one way to make Jesus' appeal contemporary.

Poverty and the poor are common themes in both stoic and gospel literature. There are multiple examples, but let me select just one from the epigrams of Martial (c.40–104):

If you are poor, you'll always be that way;
Only the rich get richer every day. (14)

And in Matthew Jesus says: *"The poor you will always have with you, but you will not always have me." (Matthew 26:10-12)*

The expression, though perhaps not exactly copied, is nevertheless imitated as an epigram. Martial compares the poor to the rich; Matthew compares the presence of Jesus to the poor. Both are neat epigrammatic examples, and Martial, patronized by the emperors Titus and Domitian, would have been a contemporary of the gospel narrators. Readers would have been drawn to Martial if only because of his wit.

Bill Quick's a barber, but he has the slows:
While he shaves off one beard, another grows. (15)

Eusebius (c.263–339 CE), author of the first *History of the Church* writes: "Matthew compiled the 'sayings' in the Aramaic language and everyone translated them as well as he could." (16) The idea of turning the other cheek, for example, noteworthy as specifically Christian, is a discussion of a virtue found in Plato's *Republic* where Socrates says "the injuring of another can in no case be just," and in the *Crito* where Socrates indicates that no one should do harm to another, especially not in requital. (17) "But I tell you, do not resist an evil person. If someone strikes you on the right cheek, turn to him the other also." (*Matthew* 5:38-40).

Jesus said, "It is easier for heaven and earth to pass away than for one stroke of the Law to fail." (18) But having established the strength of the Law, he himself then violated the laws of the Sabbath according to the Pharisees, and, in apparent contradiction, justified his actions by asserting that the Sabbath was made for man, then relaxed the code for cleanliness and diet, even omitting some fasts. (19)

Like Plato writing about his teacher Socrates, and the evangelists writing about Jesus, the transcriber of the sayings of Epictetus was done by Arrian, a prolific author and historian who first learned from the feet of his illustrious master. He wrote the *Discourses of Epictetus*, a volume assuredly known and used by Marcus Aurelius. Epictetus lived in the generation after Jesus, born about a dozen years after his death, but all the gospels were written in his lifetime when he was famous as a teacher and his maxims widely circulated. (20)

Jesus' message, "Because the kingdom of God is within you" (*Luke* 17:22), is found in Epictetus. "Why do you tumble up and down, wretches, like blind men? You are going a wrong way and have forsaken the right. You seek prosperity and happiness in a wrong place, where it is not; nor do you give credit to another who shows you where it is. Why do you seek it without? It is not in the body." (21) Xenophon has a passage that conveys a similar message. "For the gods have not hidden you in the darkness, but your deeds will be manifest in the eyes of all mankind, and if they be righteous deeds and pure from iniquity, they will blazon forth your power." (22) Stoics sought the good within themselves, just as Jesus urged his disciples to seek the Kingdom of God within. "For if you were willing, you would find it (your goodness) in yourselves." (23)

Forgiving enemies is also a stoical belief and recommended by Socrates. "For there is this very fine circumstance connected with the character of a Cynic, that he must be beat like an ass, and when he is beat must love those who beat him." Or Seneca's prescription: "Treat your inferiors in the way in which you would like to be treated by your superiors." (24)

The lesson of figs is found in the gospels and in Epictetus as an analogy for those who don't bear fruit when they should and "in the appointed season." "Now learn this lesson from the fig tree: As soon as its twigs get tender and its leaves come out, you know that summer is near." (25) "Early in the morning, as he was on his way back to the city, he was hungry. Seeing a fig tree by the road, he went up to it but found nothing on it except leaves. Then he said to it, "May you never bear fruit again!" Immediately the tree withered." (26). Didn't Jesus know that figs don't grow in winter? Didn't he, like Epictetus, "wish for figs in winter?" (27) "For as winter is to a fig, so is every accident in the universe to those things which are taken away from it." Later in the passage Epictetus writes: "Hence a wise and good man, mindful who he is and whence he came, and by whom he was produced, is attentive only how he may fill his post regularly and dutifully to God." (28) The stoic and gospel messages, using the metaphor of a fig tree, are thematically similar.

Homer described a scene in the 7th book of the *Odyssey* that included figs that have no season. "Outside the gate of the outer court there is a large garden of about four acres with a wall all round it. It is full of beautiful trees, pears, pomegranates, and the most delicious apples. There are luscious figs also…The fruits never rot nor fail all the year round, neither winter nor summer, for the air is so soft that a new crop ripens before the old has dropped. Pear grows on pear, apple on apple, and fig on fig." (29) There is a literary precursor for figs available when "out of season."

Here are other parables compared to stoic sayings from Epictetus.

JESUS	EPICTETUS
Anyone who loves his father or mother more than me is not worthy of me; anyone who loves his son or daughter more than me is not worthy of me." (30)	Do not attach yourself to them from thence to your self body, parts of the body, children, wife, brother. Look everywhere around you and throw them off from yourself see that nothing cleave to you

	nothing grow to you that may give you pain when it is torn away. (31)
They brought the coin, and he them, "Whose portrait is this? And whose inscription?" "Caesar's," they replied Render therefore to Caesar the things that are Caesar's and to God's the things that are God's. (32)	What impression has this piece asked for money? Trajan's. Give it to me. Nero's. Throw it away. (33)
Do not judge, and you will not be judged. Do not condemn, and you will not be condemned. Forgive, and you will be forgiven. (34)	Never condemn or censure anyone or common actions, and thus you will be free both of rashness and ill-nature." (35)
Where is your faith, he asked his disciples. In fear and amazement they asked one another, 'Who is this? He commands even the winds and the weather and they obey him?" (36)	Indeed, what is the storm itself but appearance? For, do but take away the fear of death, and let there be as many thunders and lightning as you please, you will find that in the ruling faculty all is serenity and calm. (37)

Episodes of Jesus walking on the water and calming the storm on the Sea of Galilee are illustrative of the analogy Epictetus uses for the tranquility of the soul, as Jesus uses the storm to set the Apostles' mind at ease about him. (38)

There are similar literary sayings from Egyptian writings that evangelists possibly drew upon for Jesus' parables. For example in the precepts of Ptahhetep we find: "Pray thou with a loving heart all the petitions which are in secret. He will perform thy business, he will hear that which you say and will accept your offerings." (39) And Matthew's parallel: "But when you pray, go into your room, close the door and pray to your Father, who is unseen. Then your Father, who sees what is done in secret, will reward you." (40)

For example, there is this in *John*: "In my Father's house are many rooms; if it were not so, I would have told you. I am going there to prepare a place for you." (*John* 14:1-3) Compare this with Plato's observation in the *Phaedo*: "And of these, such as have purified themselves with philosophy live henceforth altogether without the body, in mansions fairer still which may not be described, and of which the time would fail me to tell." (41) There are many mansions in the afterlife for the true followers of Plato's philosophy. For John, borrowing a rich insight into immortality from Plato, there are many mansions for the true followers of Jesus.

Then there are the parables.

Textually, the 33 total gospel parables have agricultural analogies, seeds, weeds, sowers of seeds, vineyard workers, fig trees, sheep and goats and lost sheep, and treasures, pearls, lost coins, gold talents, and personal relationships, servants, porters, prodigal sons, tenant farmers, householders, masters and servants, friends in need, widows, judges and tax collectors. But the collection is curious for what is absent, no parables about domestic relations between husbands and wives, parents and children, friends, father and mothers, lovers. The women are few and atypical. Mary, the widow, the woman taken in adultery who washes the feet of Jesus, and the enigmatic Mary Magdalene are the primary gospel female notables. (42) Jesus recommends that those serious about entering the Kingdom abandon their wives, a singular monastic and ascetic action and again atypical, but not from a stoic perspective. Are women similarly to abandon their husbands and children? This patriarchal and male-oriented saying is not typical of Musonius Rufus who is tolerant and liberal towards women and whose egalitarian views were rare even for a stoic sage, but it was common for Essene monks.

Even family members are not immune from criticism. The 4th Commandment was to honor one's father and mother. Jesus repudiates that declaring: "If anyone comes to me and does not hate his father and mother, wife and children, brothers and sisters...(he) cannot be a disciple of mine." (43) Indeed for a man who wanted to transmit his message for everyone's salvation Jesus managed to alienate his brothers James, Joses, Judas and Simon, his sisters (44), the townspeople of Nazareth, Galileans, Herod Antipas ruler of Galilee, the Pharisees, overseers of the synagogues and teachers of the Talmud, the Sadducees, priests of the temple, and the Roman Procurator, in fact everyone with whom he came in contact except his disciples who rarely understood his parables or the meaning of the miracles.

The relations in the parables are between what seem like prosperous Romans who could afford servants and relations with them (*Luke* 12:42-48, 17:7-10, 19:11-27), stewards (*Luke* 16:1-10), porters (*Mark* 13:34-37), tenant farmers (*Mark* 12:1-12, *Luke* 20:9-18), debtors (*Luke* 7:41-43) and workers. Thirteen of the parables relate to the rich and subordinates. Such domestic and socio-economic conditions, although known, would not be typical among Jesus' audience in the Galilean countryside. Jesus drew his apostles from fishermen in Galilee yet there are no fishing parables, only fishing miracles. But parables about the growing of corn, wheat, grapes, fig trees would be applauded as much by Hesiod, Homer, Virgil and Horace as anyone in Galilee or Judea. The agricultural and human relationship parables, if not extracted from stoic writings, would certainly appeal to a Greek and Roman clientele.

The Essenes

If the stoics were paragons of virtue then the Essenes, numbering about 4,000 during the life of Jesus according to Josephus, and therefore significant enough to be a notable cultural force, were homespun models of faultless behavior and exemplars of asceticism. The Essenes were a religious fellowship, a society of Jewish ascetics and fundamentalists of the Law, heavily influenced by the success of the revolt of the Maccabees, which began the re-dedication of the temple and inaugurated the seven-day festival of the lights known as Hanukkah. The Essenes combined an ascetic and stoic lifestyle with a prophetic vision of a messiah and a fundamental Judaic purity of practice.

They followed strict dietary practices and sexual codes and sought sanctity in specialized behavior, like bathing in cold water. They lived throughout the province of Judea and were not just confined to the scriptoria of the Qumran monastery near the Dead Sea. Both John the Baptist and Jesus are said to have lived for a time in the desert and must have known about them if they were not members. It is therefore probable that they imbibed many of their beliefs and practices, certainly in asceticism, simplicity in diet and apparel, and appeals to the virtues of following the Law and the prophets. Josephus notes that the Essenes "devote themselves solely to husbandry." (45) The majority of the parables of Jesus, as we saw, are agricultural.

Prior to the Jewish revolt in 66 CE, members of the Essenes and Jewish zealots of Qumran, living in a period variously defined as 100 BCE to 70 CE, wrote the *Dead Sea Scrolls*, documents filled with righteous indignation about the unjust, evil and venomous people, and contain curses, vitriol for transgressors of the law and violators of temple purity. This is exactly the kind of language the gospels say Jesus used against the Pharisees. (46) Moreover, the Qumran writing style of the Essenes, forms of address, phrases, idiomatic expressions, xenophobic exclusion of gentiles and violence towards them, apocalyptic visions and eschatological sentiments, even beatitudes, can also be found in the *Acts,* the *Epistle of James,* and the gospels indicating that gospel scribes were familiar with this literature and used its righteous themes. (47)

The Essenes were the ancient Jewish equivalent of the Mennonites and Amish who share common religious principles and communal practices, who farm almost exclusively, stay in each others' homes when traveling, wear uniform and identifiable clothing like simple tunics of the kind, incidentally, Jesus supposedly wore the day he was crucified. They were a conspicuous presence in Judea, but unlike Pharisees and Sadducees, are unrecorded in the gospels even though their communal practices were adopted by the first Christian community in Jerusalem. (48)

The pre-Christian Qumran community had in *The Dead Sea Scrolls* eschatological documents known as *testimonia* collected in apocalyptic, messianic and legal categories with introductory phrases or sentences such as, "Now this is come to pass so that it can be fulfilled which has been spoken by the prophet." Such phrases and formula quotations became embedded in Matthew's gospel and may have been a tradition of Greek translators. These documents lost for 2,000 years reveal much about Hebrew religious literature in the age of Jewish zealots prior to the destruction of Jerusalem. Without the *Dead Sea Scrolls* we would not have been able to notice common idioms and writing styles that creep into the gospels and that defined this extreme form of Judaism, a manner of thinking and acting that approximates what the gospel scribes wrote except in Hebrew instead of Greek.

There is a strong messianic theme running throughout the *Dead Sea Scrolls* and there is little doubt among scholars that Christianity's principal appeal to Jews is linked to this prophetic vision. (49) In the Dead Sea document 4Q246 we find: "Until the people of God arise and causes everyone to rest from the sword," (50) for which we can compare a militant Jesus in *Matt.* 10:34: "I came not to send peace but a sword." Placing the *Dead Sea Scrolls* in the literary context of Jesus gives a background for understanding Jewish eschatological and prophetic vision of the age with its nationalistic, xenophobic, militant and apocalyptic moods, all of which appear in the gospels and some in the epistles.

Names and Designations

Paul and the gospel narrators gave Jesus several names and designations common to kings, emperors and other deities. John calls him the "only begotten son of God," (*John* 1:18) and Paul "the first-born of all creation." (*Colossians* 1:15). The designation "Son of God" was typically reserved for emperors, where the concepts of kingship and divinity were linked. Caesar and Augustus had annihilated the Republic and senatorial governance and usurped the titles of deities. The tyranny of the emperor, whose will was law, would in time pronounce the state attached to a new deity resulting in a parallel administration, the eventual Holy Roman Empire with a Pope as equally powerful as any emperor, and European kings who exercised corresponding "divine rights."

Octavian, Julius Caesar's adopted son, exploited his personal relationship with Caesar, the first divine emperor, by naming himself *divi filius*, "son of god" on his coins. Belief in the existence of a soul and the afterlife was pervasive throughout the Roman world and it was therefore not unusual to have emperors associate themselves with divinity.

Similarly, the cult of a ruler or leader of a religious movement might also be accorded this distinction, as the rulers of Greece were after Alexander, and Egyptian pharaohs as a matter of course. Mark opens his gospel with: "The beginning of the gospel about Jesus Christ, the Son of God." (*Mark* 1:1-2) Jesus is addressed in the gospels as "Son of God" by Gabriel to Mary, by a temple elder, assorted demons, un-named disciples, Simon Peter, the High Priest, a centurion, various unclean spirits, and Nathaniel. He never acknowledges the title himself. Still, the gospel narrators give him this designation repeatedly through the mouths of demons, who appear to recognize him as divine when no one else can.

Deification of the emperors permits us to wonder whether the upper classes who approved these titles thought too much of their rulers or too little of their gods. An inscription found on the Parthenon in Athens in the late 19th century goes like this: "The Areopagos and Senate and assembly of the Athenians honored with (a crowning) the emperor, Caesar Claudius Augustus Germanicus Nero, Son of God." (51) Caligula, the Roman emperor who ruled from 37–41 CE, exaggerated the idea of divine kingship. (52) The Decree of the City Council of Ephesus regarding Caligula (38 CE) reads: "The Council and the people (of the Ephesians and other Greek) cities which dwell in Asia and the nations acknowledge Gaius Julius, the son of Gaius Caesar as High Priest and Absolute Ruler the God Visible who is born of Ares and Aphrodite, the shared Savior of human life." (53) Octavian Augustus, Julius Caesar's successor and heir, minted coins describing himself on one side as "Caesar, Son of God," and on the reverse, "the God Julius." (54)

These designations, in part because of the widespread circulation of Roman coins, would have been known throughout the world of educated Hebrews and Greeks, including the gospel evangelists. The imperial divinity cult began with Augustus in 14 CE during the lifetime of Jesus and prior to gospel composition, and was still flourishing during the reign of Trajan in 117 CE when the gospels were already likely written.

The consent of emperors to accept deification was a departure from constitutional governance and even the insanity of Caligula and Domitian did not diminish the practice nor lessen the despotism. But enlightened citizens knew that the policy was political and not religious, commonly accepted where polytheism prevailed, and they thought the practice not as profaning as any other profligacy, and would not in any circumstance have placed the emperor's image among their household gods.

Jesus' most common designation is Messiah, but this is also a title conferred on a non-Jew, as it was on Cyrus in *Isaiah* 45:1. The Greek "Lord" (*kyrios*) Paul used for Jesus was occurs throughout scripture as a designation for God, and by Syrian-Greek mystery cults the name for the death and redemption of Dionysius. "Lord" was not a common designation among Greek mystery cults as a term for deities with whom devotees could become united in a mystical way. Paul's use of Lord for a human recently executed by the Romans would be considered blasphemous by Jews. Homer used Lord as a prefix for Ulysses and his son Telemachus in *The Odyssey* and commonly for anyone of high rank. But neither Paul, Mark, Matthew, or Luke called Jesus God, only John. Had John's gospel not been admitted into the canon, the divine designation might never have occurred since there would have been no other scriptural confirmation.

The name Jesus is an adaptation of the Hebrew name Joshua which means savior. Christ is a Greek word meaning the christened or anointed. The elders of Israel anointed David as King, but in the name of Yahweh, and this ceremony indicates that the king is God's son. (1 *Samuel* 10:1) So the actual name of Jesus may not have been the name we know him as now. Jesus Christ is a combination of Hebrew and Greek names indicating that he is a person illustrative of the convergence of two cultural contexts. Paul thus described Jesus as appealing to both Jews and Gentiles.

Towards the end of his life, as described by gospel narrators, Jesus unambiguously accepted terms addressed to him like Christ, the Son of the living God, or King of Israel, and, though he had earlier prohibited it, proclaiming himself unequivocally, and allowing others to proclaim him, as the Messiah. But these are gospel terms without precedent that a Jew would not have used on himself. They are terms used among Hellenes to describe relations with divine beings. In the garden of Gethsemane Jesus was reluctant to accept the obligation of his death: "Father if it be possible let this cup pass from me." (55) The hesitancy to accept an onerous duty was also true of a few Roman emperors including Tiberius, Galba, Vespasian and Marcus Aurelius.

In 9 BCE the Roman governor of Asia wrote the following to all the cities in his province:

*The divine providence that guides our life has displayed its zeal
and benevolence by ordaining for our life the most perfect good,
bringing to us Augustus, whom it has filled with virtue for the
benefit of mankind, employing him as a savior for us and
for our descendants, him who has put an end to wars and adorned
peace; and he being manifest to us has exceeded the hopes of
all who brought good tidings, not only outstripping all benefactors
before him, but leaving no hope to those who shall come to surpass
him; and the birthday of the god is the beginning of all good
tidings brought by him to the world.* (56)

Savior. Prince of Peace. Unsurpassed benefactor of Mankind. The One hoped for. He who brings glad tidings. No one greater can appear. Him whose birthday would be the beginning of remembrances about him. We have so long associated these phrases and concepts with Jesus that it is surprising to find them spoken of a Roman emperor just a few years before Jesus' birth. We must countenance the possibility that evangelists simply applied widespread Roman imperial designations to Jesus in a mystical sense. Signs and portents were universally thought to presage auspicious events. The star said to have appeared in Bethlehem is a common literary tool for auspicious good fortune. A comet appeared on the days of the games ordered by Augustus in honor of Julius Caesar and it was believed to signify his soul joining the immortals. As a result, a star was attached to the head of the statue of Caesar in the Forum. (57) Even earlier, the kings in the dynasty of the Akkadian Sargon (c.2,251–2,071 BCE) sometimes placed a star before their names indicting their divine kingship.

The term King of Kings applied to Jesus is found in Assyrian cuneiform texts applied to both to Darius (521–486 BCE) and his son and successor Xerxes (d. 465 BCE), known as Ahasuerus in the Bible: "Great king, king of kings." (58) King of Kings is also used extensively in the *Papyrus of Ani*. (59) For example, "Hail, O my lord, who does traverse eternity, and whose existence endures forever. Hail, Lord of Lords, King of Kings, Prince, the God of gods who live with you, I have come unto you." (60) Such titles occur elsewhere in the *Book of the Dead*: "Homage to thee, King of Kings, Lord of lords, Prince of princes, who from the womb of Nut has possessed the world and ruled all lands." (61)

In addition to titles, symbolic relationships are everywhere in ancient literature. Cyrus is compared to the good shepherd, as was the Babylonian god Tammuz, the Greek god Adonis and Jesus, sacrificed as the lamb in order to redeem. "Indeed, a saying of his (Cyrus) is handed down comparing a good king to a good shepherd, the shepherd must manage his flock by giving them all they need." (62) All are commanded to eat and drink the body and blood of Jesus. An ancient Canaanite text from Ugarit notes: "She ate his flesh without a knife, she drank his blood without a cup."(63) The purloining of older literary symbols and the characteristics of divinities, pharaohs and kings is recurrent throughout the gospels, consistent with the eulogistic writings of the age.

Roman culture during the time of Jesus was intellectually Hellenic, though Galilee was thoroughly Jewish in belief. (64) Evangelists writing in Greek placed Jesus in the orbit of legendary heroes, where he is likened to a Persian mystic, a Mithras who comes as a savior, a Zoroaster, a Greek philosopher and mystic like Pythagoras, who spouts sagacious sayings and performs wonderful miraculous cures, a stoic philosopher like Gaius Musonius Rufus with moral sayings, a god like Osiris who, risen from the dead, judges the dead who plan to enter into an afterlife, a peripatetic Jewish rabbi and sage like Hanina ben Dosa, a near contemporary of Jesus who wanders the Galilean countryside healing and preaching, and a man named Jesus who shouted epithets about the destruction of Jerusalem in 66 BE, who was captured by Jews, was scourged, did not defend himself or rebuke his accusers, who appeared before the Roman procurator and who was killed by Romans.

The Book of Revelations, almost certainly not written by John the Apostle but ascribed to him and placed in the canon, is an enigmatic and supposedly revelatory essay on the return of Jesus. It is apocalyptic, full of gripping images and poetic insights, whose prophecies went unfulfilled as succeeding generations attempted to find new interpretations to its mysticism. One of its more famous symbols is the four horsemen of the Apocalypse which the scribe likely borrowed from the *Enuma Elish*: "He harnessed and yoked unto it four horses, destructive, ferocious, overwhelming, and swift of pace." (65)

It is clear from the miraculous embellishments of Jesus' early life that it was a common technique of the gospel narrators to borrow mythic legends and allegories. We find named and un-named celestial beings, actions attributed to superhuman causes, the prediction of future occurrences, the presence of wise men, testimonials to greatness, personalized temptations with the devil, all the quintessential stuff of ancient myths. The tempting devil in the desert baiting Jesus with land is like Homer's Calypso tempting Ulysses to stay on her island and be forever young.

Birth, Ministry and Mission
Before the composition of the gospels, literate readers of Greek knew that Perseus (son of Jupiter and Danae), Amphion (son of Jupiter and Antiope, queen of Thebes), Aeacus (son of Zeus and Aegina, who became judge of the dead in the underworld), Hercules (son of Zeus and Alcmeme) and Minos (son of Zeus and Europa) all had divine births, and among the Romans that Aeneas, hero of Virgil's *Aeneid* was the son of Venus. Thus, the association of divinity and mortality, if tinged with literary license, was plausible and believable. Painted scenes of many of these myths are visible still on the walls of private residences in Pompei.

The birth of Jesus begins with the confusion of his conception. Mark omits the story, but Joseph, presuming adultery after finding Mary pregnant, receives the announcement in a dream from an unnamed angel in *Matthew*, whereas Mary receives the news from the archangel Gabriel in *Luke*. In both accounts the actual inseminator is the Holy Spirit, the key to understanding this episode. (66) Few see the conception of Jesus, not as a commentary from haggadic midrashim and Hebrew scriptures, but as a literary scheme whereby a god gives his seed to a mortal woman. The Greek world of two thousand years ago would not be troubled by this biological anomaly. The idea of virgins giving birth, of spontaneous generation, though abhorrent in nature, is abundant in myth. Danae gave birth to Perseus after impregnation by Zeus. Leda and the swan, where Zeus takes the form of a swan who impregnates Leda; Persephone and the serpent; Aphrodite emerging from the sea after the testicles of Uranus fell from the sky; and Cupid and Psyche are a few Greek examples.

According to *Luke*, Jesus was born in Bethlehem then spent some early years in Egypt before returning to Nazareth. (67) "An angel of the Lord appeared to Joseph in a dream. 'Get up,' he said, take the child and his mother and escape to Egypt. Stay there until I tell you, for Herod is going to search for the child to kill him...where he stayed until the death of Herod." (68) Virgil (70–19 BCE), chosen by Dante to be his epic guide, writes in his *Fourth Eclogue* about the birth of a savior and the dawn of a golden age. (69) This appears to be the Roman poetic equivalent of the Hebrew vision of an eschatological future foretold in *Micah* and *Isaiah* and promulgated in Paul's epistles and the gospels about Jesus coming again "in power and glory" to install an apocalyptic kingdom. However, Virgil was celebrating the consulship of his friend Pollio. So literary content, like the compositions of the gospels, is determined by context.

The Star of Bethlehem was a Babylonian literary artifice designed to show regal significance. The Magi were supposedly Zoroastrian priests whose arrival at the crib was meant to show subservience to the new leader, prophet and king. The shepherd story is pulled from Herodotus about Cyrus and Mithras. December 25 is the birthday of Mithras and was a Roman festival known as *Dies Natalis Invicti*, the "birthday of the unconquered," and the celebration of the winter solstice and the last day of the Saturnalia. December 25th was not celebrated as the Christian birth of Jesus until 533 CE.

The portrayal of a chosen child in peril is a common literary mechanism to win sympathy for the elect and to defame despots. Famous figures said to have been exposed to death as infants were Sargon of Akkad, Moses, Romulus and Remus, Cyrus the Great, and Augustus among mythical figures like Oedipus whose father Laius had him maimed and rejected. (70) The Getty museum displays a bronze statute of Saturn eating one of his infant boys because, according to myth, he was told one of his sons would replace him as ruler of the earth. Myths about succession to the throne were common and the narrators have rolled this particular myth into Christ's birth and used it as an aspersion against Herod.

Jesus is said to have had brothers ("James, Joseph, Simon and Judas" and unnamed "sisters" *Matt.* 13:55, *Mark* 6:3). *Luke* and *Matthew* are quick to justify him as descending from David but Jesus himself later repudiates the claim. (71) None of these relatives are instrumental in writing his history and only James has any part in the gospel narrative after Jesus' death. Why were brothers not his constant companions during his mission? Why were they not in Jerusalem during the high holy days, at his trial, at his crucifixion, at the resurrection or ascension, or on the missionary road with Paul? (72) They are named and then inexplicably disappear from the narrative.

Jesus is said to have been a carpenter and the "son of a carpenter." But it is difficult to know how the trade prospered such a large family since the homes of all Galilean villages were constructed with basalt from eastern Galilee and the southern Golan and of mud and straw, or wattle and daub, and occasional wooden beams. The homes of Nazareth and Capernaum of the period show no visible signs of workmanship, and are without masonry, tiles, frescoes, or marble as would later be found in Tiberias or Sepphoris, or as still can be seen in the restored villas in Herculaneum and Pompei. The only carpentry required for a few extended families would have been wooden chairs or cabinets, insufficient in a small community to sustain a living wage. Building boats for the fishermen of Capernaum would make sense, but then Jesus would have been a shipwright and not a carpenter and would not have lived in Nazareth. Odysseus, however, was a carpenter.

Unlike the synoptic gospels, the divinity of Jesus is the message of John's gospel in which he is described symbolically as the water, the way, the light, the truth, the vine, the lamb, all metaphors representing divine sources since Mesopotamian times. This divinity runs counter to the so-called apocryphal writings and even *Matthew, Mark* and *Luke*, who sought to portray Jesus as a superhuman, semi-divine messenger pointing the way to God, a man God raised to divine status, and to urge people to seek the divine within: "The Kingdom of God is within you." (73)

In the beginning of his ministry, Jesus, according to *John* 2:1-12 visited Cana a small village a short walk from Nazareth and attended a wedding where he is said to have performed his first sign by turning water into wine. But there is another, older tradition associated with banquets and symposia where *kraters*, Greek bowls with wide mouths, were used for mixing water and wine at special meals and stood on the floor where guests could dip goblets for drinking. (74) The earliest examples of *kraters*, decorated elegantly with scenes of couples relaxing and dining or colored from ancient Greek mythic scenes like those of Zeus and Europa, come from Attic and Corinthian Greece about the 8th century BCE.

The Greek word in *John* for water pot or jar is *hudria*, like a waist-high amphora. But the drinking cup for diners and celebrators is *krater*, a bowl in which water and wine would be mixed, usually in ratios of three, or less often two, parts water to one of wine. Wine would not have been imbibed separately. (75) Hence, the wedding party at Cana would be drinking from *kraters* in which water and wine were already mixed, a miracle only if one is ignorant of how drinks were prepared. John explicitly mentions that only the attendants knew what Jesus had done. But attendants actually mixed the wine and water together as neither was drunk separately and that guests knew what they were drinking such a mixture.

The symbolism of the Cana scene is also relevant because it points to a traditional Greek celebration based on Orphic mysteries. The *krater* image is in Plato's *Timaeus* as a cosmic symbol of God mixing different kinds of souls. According to Orphic legend, the initiate not only is expected to drink from the liquid but to immerse himself in it to become purified. The mixing of water and wine, a 2,600 year old tradition symbolically prefigured in the Cana story, survives in the Catholic mass as the drinking of the body and blood of Christ.

Telemachus, the son of Ulysses, also attends a wedding feast in the palace of Menelaos, the Lord of Atreus, as he begins his journey in Homer's *Odyssey* to find his father. At that feast the wine is altered by Helen who administers a drug so the men will forget their troubles. Hence, a similar scene where wine is altered at a wedding feast occurs in Book 4 of *The Odyssey*. What the scribe of the 4th gospel intends is that Jesus, a Lord like Menelaos, Ulysses and Telemachus and favored by the chief God, can also perform miraculous feats.

Jesus walks on water on the Sea of Galilee to show his powers to his disciples. Hermes walks on water to visit Priam in the *Iliad* 24. Poseidon and his sons walk on water. Empedocles (c.495–435 BCE), statesman, political philosopher, teacher, physician and magician, one who thought of himself as a god and so told his followers, is said in his *Fragments* (345) to be able to teach his disciples to calm the waters, and even to raise the dead to life. (76) According to Diogenes Laertius, Empedocles cured a woman named Panthea who had been given up by physicians. Comparing Jesus with a man who said he was a god, calmed the waters and made people rise from the dead, but who lived c.450 years earlier, is yet another example of the gospel scribal use of earlier literary sources.

After John the Baptist was beheaded Jesus took up his mission and began preaching repentance and drawing John's followers to himself, many of his listeners believing he was John risen from the dead. His message was repentance, that the "Kingdom of God" was at hand, though many followers interpreted it as the end of Roman rule. John had to say of Jesus that "My Kingdom is not of this world." (77) Yet his followers, as is clear from the disciples he met on the road to Emmaus who said in *Luke* 24:21 "that it was he who should redeem Israel," identifying an earthly kingdom.

A further message of Jesus is that he had come to complete the Law and the prophets. Going beyond Judaic Law and the Torah is a tactic of gospel narrators so that the Romans will not confuse Christianity with any form of resurrected Judaism. This is exemplified by the scorn heaped on the scribes and Pharisees in the gospels, referred to as "snakes and vipers' brood," "hypocrites," "tombs covered in whitewash." To placate the Romans, *Luke* in

23:47 even has a Roman centurion have an epiphany about Jesus who began glorifying God and calling him a just man, though in *Matthew* in 27:54 and in *Mark* 15:38 the centurion proclaims that Jesus is the Son of God.

While excoriating the political and religious leaders of Judaism, Jesus also condemns Gentiles as "dogs," an unflattering designation, (78) and tells his missionaries to avoid Samaria between Galilee and Judea, a non-Jewish area, revealing an intolerance and chauvinism against non-Jews not even found in the Talmud. Commentators typically give these statements liberal interpretations. But such passages reveal the original intention: that Jesus' message was to be a reform of Judaism and not a separate religion. But after the destruction of Jerusalem Gentiles became the source of converts.

The Gnostic gospels of *The Apocalypse of Peter*, *Second Treatise of the Great Seth* and *Acts of John* offer a quite different interpretation of Jesus' crucifixion from the evangelists noting that only his body substitute was crucified, not the living Jesus, and describing his appearance after his death more precisely than the four evangelists. (79) But at the time of these writings what was orthodox and canonical had not yet been determined.

Consider Jesus' trial before the Sanhedrin. Josephus reminds us that according to the law only the Sanhedrin can condemn a man to death, and thus when Herod the Great killed a revolutionary, Hezekiah, and his followers without Sanhedrin approval he was called to account for his actions punishable by death. (80) Herod appeared in royal purple with a large security guard causing the leadership pause in their deliberations and it refused to act. When Herod became king he slew all the members of the Sanhedrin. This historical episode would have been well known among the gospel scribes. A king, or one who said he would be a king, or who others said would be king like Jesus, thus had a link with the recently past Sanhedrin trial.

A trial at night for Jesus would have been illegal. The charge of blasphemy is *prima facie* trumped up. Witnesses who could not agree on testimony would have lawyers called for a mistrial. The Sanhedrin did not have the right to charge anyone with death. The fact that the crucifixion occurred during Passover would have been sacrilegious. The Romans executing Jesus as "The King of the Jews" would have been preposterous. And by the time of Mark all witnesses or critics of the real story, if there was one, would have been dead.

The trial of Jesus also has a parallel in the trial and execution of Socrates and is meant to portray the accusers as culpable of envy and malice using suspicious charges against the accused, perverting justice to execute a scapegoat. Socrates had done no wrong; Jesus was a good man dealt with unjustly. The comparison is intended to appeal to the literate audience, familiar with the trial of Socrates, and to portray Jesus as comparable to the wisdom and goodness of Socrates and the injustice of his unfair trail and death sentence. Both Socrates, in his prison reply to Crito, and Jesus, in prayer in the garden, placed their fates with God.

The trial of Jesus is further paralleled in *Acts* with the trial of Stephen. Both trials are meant to be unfavorable to the Jews and non-critical of the Romans, who alone had the power to crucify, and to show the viciousness of official Judaism, its judgment based on capriciousness, false charges and intimidation. In both trials the original charge is forgotten or ignored and new charges brought during the trial itself, a highly improbable judicial occurrence. In both trials the Jews are said to have condemned the defendants to death when in reality the Sanhedrin had no such power.

Why would the Pharisees, with their political base in Galilee, the hotbed of religious activism and reform movements, be opposed to someone who claimed to want to deliver them from oppression, a liberator who sought to release them from foreign domination? Pharisees were portrayed by the gospel narrators as evildoers when in reality they likely would have been favorably disposed to Jesus and his mission. Evangelists framed the Jews, not the oppressive Romans, and made the story of Jesus and Stephen's trial an example of Jewish religious hostility towards Jews, a characteristic carried on by Paul in his epistles. Despite the fact that the Romans, by the time of the gospels' composition, had destroyed Jerusalem and the temple and killed over one million Jews, the gospels are sympathetic to them.

Then take the issue of eyewitnesses. Jesus and Pontius Pilate have a private conversation about the nature of truth, among other things. Who is the source for this? Pilate did not know Aramaic and Jesus did not speak Greek or Latin. Pilate would certainly not speak to one of Jesus' collaborators or followers, as anyway Pilate was soon banished from Palestine and by the writing of the narrative Jesus was said to have risen and ascended into heaven. Was another bystander, perhaps a converted Roman soldier, in attendance taking notes? Absent a witness to the conversation, even in a court of law, the result is hearsay.

The Halo Effect

The glow we observe in early western paintings of the saints showing a shining radiance around their heads associated with a holy identity is just like Hathor's representations in her temple with the glow of the sun revealing her solar and divine status. The sun disk survives in western art of religious figures as a halo comes from Sumerian, Babylonian and Egyptian symbols of sanctity.

Melammu means "mask" in ancient Akkadian and is a kind of halo used in royal art to describe the king's radiance, terrible splendor and supernatural awe-inspiring sheen. *Melammu* can also represent the supernatural nature of garments, cloaks, even headgear, and we find this technique often in Homer.

This nimbus or aureole indicates divinity associated with a person or thing, like any endowment of a king, the Hittite shield goddess, the shield of Achilles or the helmet of Hermes, to show divine legitimization or divine or kingly royalty. (81) In *The Iliad*: "Achilles favorite of Zeus leapt up. Athene cast her tasseled aegis round his sturdy shoulders; and the great goddess also shed a golden mist around his head and caused his body to emit a blaze of light." (82) The Trojans and the charioteers were thrown into chaos when they saw such intense light and were overcome. Biblical scribes would employ similar metaphors like columns of smoke and pillars of fire to describe the actions of Yahweh or to people or things associated with Yahweh's presence against enemies. In *The Frogs* by Aristophanes (c.448–388 BCE) the chorus chants about the luminosity, a transfiguring experience around Bacchus, god of wine and fertility. (83)

The literary device of a bright light to highlight a divine presence is evident from the 5th BCE. "And during the morning watch, Yahweh looked down upon the camp of the Egyptians from the column of fire and cloud." Assur the Assyrian god attacked the enemy in the pose of a winged disk, as did Horus in Egyptian mythology. (84)

Ezekiel writes about: "an immense cloud with flashing lightning and surrounded by brilliant light." (85) Daniel has a similar experience: "His clothing was as white as snow; the hair of his head was white like wool. His throne was flaming with fire, and its wheels were all ablaze. A river of fire was flowing, coming out from before him." (86) These are the biblical equivalents of a *melammu*, what would become in Hebrew and Christian theology, an aura, burning bushes, tongues of fire, a transfiguration, an epiphany, a cloud, a halo over sainted individuals. The divine presence speaks to Moses from a bush that appears to be on fire, and in a cloud in his tent, and Jesus appears with Moses and Elijah covered with this luminous aura. (87) Likewise, the aegis of Zeus protected Achilles and made him invisible with a "golden cloud above his head."

These divine epiphanies, the apparitions of god among men, such as when Yahweh and two angels appear at Abraham's tent, when God appears to Moses in a volcanic eruption or in a cloud, or to Jacob and speaks face to face, conform to the Greek epic experience when gods converse with men all the time. Homer's *Iliad* is full of such appearances and encounters, and the biblical narrative is closer to the Greek epics than to a subsequent, more transcendent and distant Hebrew idea of a deity. A sanctuary has the same purpose today as a *melammu*, and the lighted candle in a Catholic church indicates the divine presence in the tabernacle on the altar. (88)

Under Christianity, the emanation, the epiphany, like the appearance of the dove at Jesus' baptism and the tongues of fire at Pentecost, would devolve into a single God, the Holy Ghost. (89) God's actions in *Exodus* were preceded by thunder and lightning, and the Pentecostal appearance of tongues of fire by the rush of a mighty wind. Angels appearing at the tomb of Jesus are irradiated with a brilliant light.

The resurrection of Jesus is pre-figured during the Transfiguration when Moses and Elijah appeared talking to Jesus. (90) How did the Apostles recognize them since they did not identify themselves? And what was the appearance of Jesus? "His face shone like the sun, and his clothes became as white as the light." It is the aegis of the gods, the nimbus of divinity. "The god breathed daring into his heart, and leaning against an oak he stood by him in person, though hidden by a thick mist," writes Homer of Apollo in *The Iliad* (91)

The transfiguration is also prefigured in the histories of Xenophon about Cyrus. "As night closed in on their march, the legend runs that a strange light shone out, far off in the sky, upon Cyrus and his host, filling them with awe of the heavenly powers." (92) Like Apollo who hid Agenor "in a thick mist," Jesus suddenly disappears from the crowd at Nazareth. "And they rose up and put him forth out of the town and led him to the brow of the hill...that they might throw him down headlong. But he, passing through their midst, went his way." (93) The transcendence of Jesus reinforces the notion of divine rule and a divinely imposed ethic existing without a temple, ark, king or an occupying power. Mosaic tradition provided the Law, but Christian interpretation provided a spiritual overlay adopted from earlier myths, religions and histories. (94)

Death and Resurrection

Mark did not describe any risen apparitions of Jesus, though subsequent editors added three distinct endings. There are several widely differing descriptions of the resurrection in *Matthew, Luke, John* and *Acts* that climatically adds a bodily ascension. Paul's 1st *Letter to the Corinthians* argues the case for resurrection from the dead and cites apparitions not found in the gospels. Everything else varies, the number of apparitions, the location (Galilee, in a room, on a road), the time (same day, over 40 days), the substance of the message and what was said to whom.

Homer describes Hector as god's beloved son, and predicts that someone will strike him down and pierce him. His mother stands nearby weeping. A debate and trial among the divinities occurs whether to permit him to live or die, and the gods finally relent to let someone else convict and permit his death though they do not approve. Hector accepts his fate and succumbs to the will of the gods and predicts disaster for the city. All around him were moved to lamentation by his words. Crowds gather round, reviling him. He is buried without delay. Someone came with a ransom to take away the body. The women washed and anointed the body, put on a tunic and wrapped it with a sheet. They laid him in a hollow space and put large stones over it.

Hector and Jesus have predicted heroic deaths, are abandoned by the gods, taunted by adversaries, expire in soliloquies of pathos, stabbed by onlookers, and Homer and Mark both link the deaths of their heroes to the destruction of a city. Jesus' crucifixion for a relatively minor offense would not be unusual as Horace notes that slaves were crucified for stealing bits of food and scourged with pieces of metal attached to lashes. Mary Magdalene, Mary the mother of James, and Salome who play subordinate roles in watching at the death of the hero, wailing, anointing and washing the body, and checking on the remains later, are a likely imitation of Homer's three Trojan women, Helen, Andromache, and Hecuba who perform the same rituals at the death of Hector.

Who or what died when Jesus did and who or what rose from the dead? (95) Origen, writing in *Contra Celsum* in the 2nd century CE, gives God two existences. "Therefore we worship the Father of truth and the Son who is truth; they are two distinct existences, but one in mental unity, in agreement, and in identity of will." (96)

A *Dead Sea Scroll* fragment (4Q285), in amazing conformity with the gospel sequence about Jesus' death, speaks about the death of a leader. "They will enter into Judgment with...and they will put to death the Leader of the Community, the Branch of David...will put him to death...and with wounding, and the high priest will command." (97)

After the resurrection of Jesus, the most famous resurrection story in the gospels, but appearing only in *John* (11:1-44), is the raising from the dead of Lazarus. Why would the synoptic gospel narrators who wrote prior to John omit such an important miracle, especially since John notes that Martha and Mary, sisters of Lazarus, are such good friends?

The most important religious site in Larnaca, Cyprus is the Church of St. Lazarus. (98) Lazarus reputedly came to this city, then known as Kition, probably fleeing persecution, certainly political upheaval, and possibly to escape his unusual notoriety. According to legend, he settled there, was made Bishop and lived another 30 years. Why didn't Lazarus, a predilection of the resurrected Jesus, become an evangelist, apostle or at least missionary? Why did he choose to live in a modest Roman backwater, away from major trading cities and not become a religious spokesperson for the cause of Christianity, particularly since he had been given a real second chance at life? (99)

Jesus' raising of the dead son of the widow of Naim to life parallels Elijah's raising of the widow's son in *I Kings* 17:10-24. His raising of the centurion's son (*Matt.* 8:5-13) is similar to the description of the Talmudic report of the raisings by Hanina ben Dosa. (100) Unnamed others in the gospels appear to have been resurrected but no explanation is offered.

Matthew has this odd scene in 27:52-53 where he describes: "The tombs were opened, and many bodies of the saints who had fallen asleep arose; and coming forth out of the tombs after his resurrection, they came into the holy city and appeared to many." The special privilege of getting out of one's tomb in order to walk the streets again and enjoy the company of friends is something to celebrate. Presumably they had plenty of deodorant to mask their odor as even Lazarus stunk after three days. And they must have had some cosmetic repairs done on worn or disfigured parts in order that the many who saw them could recognize who they were.

Did this saints' sighting imply that their souls had gone but the bodies only were resurrected, or that the souls were still in the bodies waiting for the final decision about their destination? Did they return voluntarily to their tombs or continue patronizing the city's restaurants to astound and amaze other customers? Or did they stay and die another death to rise again as a further sign and wonder? Apparently no one sought to interview these saints, first to know how they got their designations, or to solve the weighty questions about their status. *Matthew* imitated Book 11 of *The Odyssey* when spirits or both genders and all ages appeared to Ulysses as he was making votive offerings. He had to keep the surging phantoms from crowding around him as, ironically, he guarded from them the sacrificial blood of the slain lamb.

Plato in his dialogue on the soul in the *Phaedo* says that "shadowy apparitions" of men already dead have appeared to some people around tombs. The belief in the soul acting in a luminous body after death was a common belief even by the time of Origen in the 2nd century. Thus, the occurrence of such an episode as the appearance of ghosts in the gospels would not seem fantastical to readers, like Clytemnestra's ghostly appearance before the Temple of Apollo at Delphi in Aeschylus' play *Eumenides* and asking no one in particular "to look at these scars." (101)

Mythical characters said to have risen from the dead and seen as resurrected by witnesses in many in parts of the world and accounted as gods abounded in ancient literature. The Dioscuri (Castor and Pollux) or the sons of Zeus. Herakles. Asclepius. Dionysius. Aristeas. Osiris. Empedocles. Zamolxis. Herodotus writes that the Getae "believe themselves to be immortal: and whenever any one dies they are of the opinion that he is removed to the presence of their god Zamolxis...was himself a man and formerly lived at Samos in the service of Pythagoras." (102)

Asclepius was the son of Apollo and Coronis, a mortal woman, and was worshipped throughout the Greek world as the god of medicine and healing. He is said to have raised from the dead Lycurgus, Capaneus and Tyndareus. His visible symbol is the caduceus. Coronis his mother was unfaithful to Apollo and was burned upon a funeral pyre. As her body began to burn,

Apollo felt sorry and snatched the unborn child Asclepius from his mother's corpse and gave him to Chiron who taught him healing and medicine, surgery, the use of drugs, love potions and incantations. Athena is said to have given him magic potion made from the blood of the Gorgon who can return the dead to life. Asclepius, like Prometheus, offended Zeus by accepting money in exchange for raising the dead, upsetting the natural order of the universe by helping men to escape death. Zeus sent down a thunderbolt killing him. But because Asclepius had brought good to mankind, Zeus made him into a god. The cult of Asclepius became popular during the 3rd century BCE and the Asclepieion cult centers, like Christians shrines, were used by priests to cure the sick.

According to the Canaanite *Legend of Aqhat*, Baal withheld the rains until Aqhat rose from the dead. "And so Baal went before El, and El caused Aqhat's flesh to grow once again upon his bones. Aqhat rose from the grave, living once again, and he embraced his sister and father. The fields became green with plants, and rain fell from the sky and blessed the land. Thus the land was saved by the bravery of Pagat, and Aqhat the hero lived once again." (103)

Euripedes has Hercules, after surviving all his multiple trials, descend to Hades where he dwells for a long time letting others believe that he is dead before he rises and returns. His wife Megara sees him return from Hades and says: "Yes, it is he who we heard was beneath the earth, unless it is a dream in broad daylight that we are watching. But what am I saying? What sort of dreams am I seeing in my confused mind?" (104) It is the same kind of astonishment the disciples display when they see Jesus appear to them after the resurrection.

As for those not accepted into the abode of the blessed in Egyptian myth, as in Christian theology, they will burn as the *Papyrus of Ani* describes. "As concerning (the words) 'that night of the reckoning of destruction,' it is the night of the burning of the damned, and of the overthrow of the wicked at (the sacred) block, and of the slaughter of souls." (105) A man who is both man and god, who has risen from the dead, who acts as judge of the living and the dead based on the actions of their life, and who admits individuals into everlasting life or condemns them to hell fire, this is Osiris, whose origin as Judge of the Dead dates from the Middle Kingdom (c.2,100–1,750 BCE), but whose conception was much earlier. (106) The Egyptians believed that gods became incarnate in man as early as 3,500 BCE. (107) In Osiris Christian Egyptians in the first centuries found the prototype of Christ and the images and statues of Isis sucking her son Horus fitting examples for the Virgin Mary and her son. (108) As Osiris held the highest place in the Egyptian pantheon, one who was both human and divine and the symbol of a resurrected life, he was the perfect symbol for evangelists. After his death, Jesus was wrapped in a linen shroud. For five thousand years men were mummified in imitation of the form of Osiris who had risen from the dead and attained life everlasting, was the cause of the dead rising, and the judge of those who would enter eternal life. (109) *The Pyramid Texts* note that Osiris had a righteous rule and kept a written account of the words and deeds or all men. (110)

Docetism, an early form of Christian thought condemned by the Council of Chalcedon in 451, believed that Jesus really did not have a body and therefore did not actually die on the cross because God could not suffer nor be associated with matter which was evil, an extreme view also central to Manichean belief. Against such heresies John wrote: "For many deceivers have gone out into the world, those who do not acknowledge Jesus Christ as coming in the flesh. This is the deceiver and the antichrist." (111) Yet the evangelists never mention the soul of Jesus, only his resurrected body. Greeks and Romans alike believed in soul. Lucretius, who wrote his poetical masterpiece, *On the Nature of Things* in 55 BCE, a man of scientific, moral and poetic conscience, an Epicurean believer, articulated the essence of common belief in the 1st century before Christ. (112) Lucretius believed that everything was composed of atoms, an extremely prescient insight for 2,000 + years ago, and that consequently it was not possible to see dead ghosts separate from real bodies.

According to *I Peter* (3:18-19), Jesus also descended to preach to those who were in a sort of limbo or purgatory. "Put to death indeed in the flesh, he was brought to life in the spirit, in which also he went and preached to those spirits that were in prison," an allusion to the Greek Hades but unrecorded in the gospels.

According the Council of Nicaea held in 325 CE, the resulting doctrine, known as the Nicene Creed proclaims:

> *Lord Jesus Christ, the only begotten of the Father, that is, of the substance of the Father, God of God, light of light, true God of true God, begotten not made, of the same substance with the Father, through whom all things were made both in heaven and on earth; who for us men and our salvation descended, was incarnate, and was made man, suffered and rose again the third day, ascended into heaven and comes to judge the living and the dead.* (113)

Council fathers decreed that Jesus was of one nature with the Father and had two persons, one human, but left unanswered whether or not Jesus had a soul, a topic that includes whole treatises by Plato, Aristotle, Lucretius, Plotinus, and Porphyry among others. Porphyry spent three successive days questioning his mentor, Plotinus, about the connection between the body and the soul. For example, how does one account for the presence of a soul in a body while preserving its essential unity as an incorporeal substance? Does soul transform itself from a lower to a higher state when it leaves the body? How are souls generated? Yet 3rd century bishops meeting in council could not seem to come to grips with the soul of Jesus, whether it exists, or how it connects with the body.

"Do not touch me, for I have not yet ascended to my Father." (114) This is an odd admonition Jesus says to Mary Magdalene because it implies that something is wrong about touching a dead body but not one that is resurrected. Yet it makes sense if we consider the scene in *The Odyssey* where three times Odysseus tries to embrace his mother in the Underworld but cannot because she is dead and he is still mortal.

The confusing account of the day of resurrection in the gospels is like a novel with no plot, worse than eyewitness accounts of what happened at a road accident. *Mark* describes only an empty grave as a sign of resurrection and has an angel appear to the women for validation of the incident. The other evangelists add new material that in effect has Jesus appearing to the disciples as evidence of his resurrection.

Herodotus tells the story of Aristeus, a poet, born of an influential family, who died accidentally in the workshop of a fuller. His family and friends came to the shop to arrange for the funeral but could not find him. A man from another city said that he had met him while journeying into town and had spoken to him. Seven years afterwards he was seen in his hometown, writing more poetry, but then vanished again. Here, centuries prior to the gospels, is the tale of a man who died, whose body could not be found, who re-appeared talking to friends while walking to a nearby town, the earlier literary traces of the empty tomb of Jesus and the story of his appearance to two disciples on the road to Emmaus. (115)

There is a series of post-resurrection appearances not described in the gospels but appearing in *Corinthians* 15:5 in which Jesus appears separately to Peter, then afterwards to the other eleven, then 500 un-named individuals, and then by James, "and then by all the apostles," including finally Paul himself. Were the evangelists too excited or forgetful to record these other appearances? In the *Acts* (1:6-7) Jesus speaks for another 40 days after his death, another unrecorded event in the gospel narratives, then ascends into heaven.

Though the gospels do not mention a descent into the Underworld, essential for a Greek's view of the dead, other texts do elaborate on this necessary part of dying, notably *Peter* in chapters 3 and 4 and *Ephesians* 4 where Paul notes that Jesus descended "into the lower parts of the earth." This implies that the underworld is literally a known geographic place and that it is material. In the Nag Hammadi text *Testimony of Truth* Jesus "went down to Hades and performed many mighty works. He raised the dead therein; and the world-rulers of darkness became envious of him, for they did not find sin in him. But he also destroyed their works." (116) If you wish to go home, like Ulysses, you must first enter the underworld.

The resurrection of Jesus with the promise of eternal life is the cornerstone of Christianity, gaining credibility from the theology of Paul, the death of martyrs and the support of the Roman Empire once it adopted Christianity. However, the people of Tarsus where Paul was born believed that the god they worshipped had died for them, had risen from the dead like Orpheus, Osiris and Mithras and would, if they only believed fervently enough, be saved from Hades and share in an eternal life. This was the belief of the Orphic mysteries. The central theology of Christianity is neither specifically Christian nor Jewish, but partly Greek and Egyptian in origin and substance. Death, resurrection, judgment and eternal life are the eschatological crusts laid upon the gospel narratives, borrowed from Greek and Egyptian lore, tinged with Gnosticism, as the bedrock of a divine persona in Jesus.

According to the Ebionites, a group labeled as heretical by the early church, Jesus was a religious Jew whose teachings conformed to reform Judaism attempting to recapture the spirit of a messiah, in doubt about his own role, but not divine. He appealed to the unlettered and the poor and like the stoics railed against the rich, the powerless, the elite, and hypocritical clerics. After his death his followers made him into the foretold Messiah. Converted non-Jews, scattered by the destruction of Jerusalem and the Jewish revolt, deified him like a dead Roman emperor and attributed to him the divine characteristics of Orpheus, Mithras and Osiris, while Paul and others covered the accompanying theology with a mixture of Gnosticism and Judaic messianic prophecies.

In conclusion, Jesus was raised in the hills of Galilee, was possibly literate but not educated, was inspired by the asceticism and teaching of his cousin John the Baptist and the Essenes, and after John's death collected John's followers to carry on his preaching mission of religious reform. Sayings he reportedly made were repeated as if he were an oracle. He was made to appear like an Essene, some in his own day also named Jesus, who had preached righteousness and worked cures. Though politically cautious at the beginning of his ministry, he became emboldened by the acceptance of his message and the devotion of disciples and took his mission into Jerusalem where he antagonized Jews and Romans whose goal was political stability and not religious fervor or reform. (117)

Two generations after his death four canonical evangelists and several unaccepted authors created hagiographies characterized by borrowed myths, presumed prophecies, and collected sayings circulating through stoic sources, and purported events of Jesus' life recalled from secondary sources or the diminished memories of elderly participants, and several manufactured stories to bolster the claim of divine authenticity. (118) Three of the writers, Mark, Luke, and Paul did not know him in his lifetime, and it is questionable whether or not the gospels attributed to Matthew and John were actually written by them. Mark likely relied on oral tradition to craft his text. But subsequent gospels and the *Acts* among Hellenized communities added new meanings to the extant tradition and reworked narratives to conform to varying beliefs. Matthew, Luke and John essentially used Mark as a template, and possibly the Q source, but certainly Herodotus and Homer as literary precursors.

The Q source is not a document or even a set of documents but a hypothesis of a probable source of Jesus sayings the synoptic gospel narrators drew upon. The inferences indicate a strong oral tradition among very early Christian communities, but even the existence of such a tradition does not prove authenticity. The amalgam of sayings could be merely collected sayings from a variety of sources and then attributed to Jesus by believers partial to his cause. What is lacking is a Q source of ancient writings, not other canonical or apocryphal texts that have similar passages in scripture. (119)

Paul, in his epistles to cities he had visited gave to Jesus and the new religion a theology he never preached, a blend of Judaic culture, pagan rituals, Greek philosophy and stoic sayings forming the core of Christian theological beliefs not found in the gospels. (120) The healer and preacher who lived and worked in Galilee was transformed by gospel narratives and missionary epistles using borrowed literary and eschatological writings into a transcendent Messiah.

The intermingling of Persian, Hellenic and Roman philosophic and literary influences defined the cultural context of the Mediterranean world two thousand years ago and consequently could not have escaped the mindset of the gospel narrators who wrote using symbols, archetypes, themes, stories, allegories and sayings from several cultural sources. Jesus is the Jewish Messiah, the savior of mankind. He is Perseus, the conqueror of evil who is tempted but overcomes the blandishments and wins divine support. He is Mithras the savior whose followers must eat his body and drink his blood to be redeemed, and Osiris, the conqueror of mortality who rose from the dead and judges everyone according to their actions for qualification into the heavenly kingdom. Jesus is the Hebrew Son of God and the Asiatic son of gods, an example of the combination of cultural derivatives cunningly exploited by the narrators to appeal both to Jews and Gentiles. (121)

Was Jesus simply a good and holy man (Ebionites), the Messiah (Jews), the Son of God (Greeks and Egyptians), the Son of God as the Roman emperors designated themselves, the Logos of God (John and the Gnostics), the resurrected god like Osiris, the appearance of God in a human body (Docetism), or the equal of the Judaic God (Christians by the 4th century)? Or was he, as Arius suggested, simply a holy man who God granted special favors made into a God that those who believed he qualified for that designation? Gospel narrators made Jesus into a latter-day Socrates who also never wrote anything but whose wise annunciations were preserved by his followers, a Hermes who walks on water, a Hector who dies a noble death, an Osiris who rises again to judge the living and the dead. Ideas from the Hellenized Roman world over the first 250 years of the first millennium folded into Christian beliefs and doctrine, coloring Christianity but obscuring cultic and mythic origins. The gospels are replete with little flags, like post-it notes, of literary episodes from Homeric epics, Gnostic understandings and stoic expressions. The scribes treat the Bible as a source of documentation about a new mythical figure, except that Jesus is elevated to a divine status in the Greek epic tradition and beyond the limited role of Hebrew prophets whose voices God uses to proclaim new decrees.

Gospel narrators created a Jesus who is a combination of a leader like Moses, a warrior, lawgiver and protector of his people, and Homeric heroes like Hector, Achilles and Ulysses exercising the Greek virtues of goodness and justice with a touch of the divine. Like Moses, Jesus seeks to become a leader of the people. Like Ulysses who condemns the parasitic and selfish behavior of Penelope's suitors, Jesus condemns the narrow-mindedness of the Pharisees. Like Achilles who sacrifices to obtain the divine gift and then retreats to its security when given the opportunity, Jesus reveals his divinity only when necessary, as it is a revelation of God's will in the gospels and a recognized trait in a hero and Zeus' will in Homer. Mary the mother of Jesus has a counterpart in the enigmatic Penelope, Ulysses' wife, a woman of obvious virtue, a paradigm of patience but whose real qualities are unknown. Descriptions of her, where they occur at all, are flat and uninteresting. The disciples, too, are stick figures, often just used to pose a question, and are usually described as a group, without much individuality, trailing along with Jesus as necessary accompanying baggage but without purposeful usefulness, except perhaps as symbols of the twelve tribes of Israel. The gospels are flights of literary imagination grounded in mythic, divine intervention like Homeric epics, and the thematic, linguistic and allegorical parallels are so similar that textual imitation is the only justifiable conclusion.

CHAPTER ELEVEN
THE GREEK INFLUENCE ON SCRIPTURE

Greek epic literature differed from Hebrew literature because of the contexts of the respective cultures. Hebrew literature, highlighting the worship of Yahweh, the peoples' chosen status, faithfulness to the Torah, and interspersed with mythical heroes revealing Yahweh's beneficence, was not intended for the illiterate masses but for the priestly caste. Greek literature, on the other hand, was an integral part of social life intended for religious ritual, dance, social bonding, moral instruction and only incidentally as entertainment. Greek literature was celebratory; Hebrew literature religious and legalistic. We examine in this and the following chapters how Christian commentators imitated topical, philosophical ideas not included in the gospel narratives to create dogma.

Greek language and culture entered Palestine after Alexander's troops marched triumphantly into Egypt and founded the city named after him at the mouth of the Nile that would become the foremost intellectual capitol of the eastern Mediterranean drawing immigrants to its heady intellectual atmosphere. Within a few years, with the leadership of Ptolemy I who created the great library at Alexandria literate Jews moved there in large numbers.

Within this eminent Alexandrian circle moved Callimachus (c.310–240 BCE), a lyrical poet of exceptional talent admired for his varied meters, hymns, epigrams and vivid imagery. He would not have been imitated by a biblical scribe because of his choice of erotic poetic inspiration, but he is illustrative here for two reasons. First, his salutations to deities are examples of the deep piety and consciousness of Greek poets. Secondly, he was a librarian at Alexandria and hence had immediate access to all the known literature, an awesome collection which included 42,800 books in the library of the Temple of Serapis, 90,000 "simple and unmixed books," and 400,000 books within the court and palace. Callimachus was born in Cyrene, the same small city of Simon of Cyrene who helped Jesus bear his cross. One of Callimachus' students was the illustrious mathematic and scientific thinker Eratosthenes who, among other achievements, calculated the approximate circumference of the earth. Catullus translated Callimachus's poem *Aetia* ("Explanations") into Latin and Virgil borrowed some of its lines to incorporate into the *Aeneid*. (1) Callimachus exhibited a special devotion to gods and the style, spirit and poetic brilliance he brings to religion is unique. It is that spirit, rather than just imitation, that could have influenced gospel narrators.

Egeria, a Spanish nun who journeyed to Jerusalem in 384 recorded her liturgical experiences in Jerusalem for her convent companions. "Now, forasmuch as in that province some of the people know both Greek and Syriac, while some know Greek alone and others only Syriac; and because the bishop, although he knows Syriac, yet always speaks Greek, and never Syriac, there is always a priest standing by who, when the bishop speaks Greek, interprets into Syriac, that all may understand what is being taught." (2) Note that the vernacular language of the region was Syriac (Syrian Aramaic) not Greek and that the Greek of Palestine even in the 4th century had to be translated in sermons. Hence, gospel narrators were not writing for the population of Palestine.

Moreover, Hebrew scribes are curiously silent about this Hellenic cultural inebriation. There is not a word in scripture about Alexander or the Greeks, though Greek cities, the Decapolis, the "ten cities" in the Gospels, would spring up like cultural flowerings all around Jerusalem. Where are the Jewish historians, the scribes and recorders of this most vital period in Jewish life two thousand years ago? The world of Zeno, Heraclitus, Euripedes, Aeschylus, Sophocles, Plato and Aristotle seems not to have penetrated into Jewish consciousness. Culture enters unannounced and seeps into the thinking habits and behavioral patterns of every civilization. (3) But Jews did digest this culture and the gospels reflect its profound penetration.

By the 4th century BCE after Cyrus conquered Babylon he allowed the Jews in captivity to return to their homeland and even permitted the high priest the right to mint silver coins. Coins excavated from this period bear the imprint "Yehud," "Judah," and on one side are decorated with the portrait of Zeus, and on the reverse the owl of Athens, just like the Attic drachma, evidence of the Greek influence in Jerusalem even prior to the conquest by Alexander. We can begin to see Hellenic influences in *Ecclesiastes* when there is a distinct break from apocalyptic visions and a turning towards wisdom and knowledge, decidedly Greek intellectual concerns. "I turned my thoughts toward knowledge; I sought and pursued wisdom and reason." (*Ecclesiastes* 7:25). Seeking knowledge and wisdom had never been a Hebrew or patriarchal objective but was central to Greek thinking.

The spread of Hellenism widened during the reign of Antiochus IV (175–163 BCE), a Syrian Seleucid ruler. According to the *First Book of Maccabees* "customs of the Gentiles" were introduced, like gymnasiums in Jerusalem. (4) The Maccabeean revolt was less a rebellion against Hellenic existence than a reassertion of Jewish religious usages that had been curtailed or in some cases eliminated.

But the use of prophecy did not wane as Jewish authors celebrated Hellenic oracles. For example, the third Sibylline oracle, written by Jewish scribes and composed between 163–145 BCE in Egypt, contain prophecies about Alexander the Great. A large fragment (lines 350-488) was later inserted noting a conflict between Egypt and Rome, written before the naval battle of Actium in 31 BCE where Octavian defeated Mark Anthony and Cleopatra. The original Sibylline oracles, prophetic priestesses, flourished in the Etruscan and early Roman era, beginning in the 6th century BCE and their scrolls were preserved as sacred documents until burned in an accidental fire in 83 BCE and the remainder in the 4th century CE by Christians. They were Jewish and Christian forgeries. *Revelations*, with its similar apocalyptic themes, was accepted into the Christian canon; the Sibylline oracles were not.

The Greeks were the first to begin thinking about the nature of the external world as scientists, mathematicians and philosophers, like Thales (c. 636–546 BCE) who proposed that there was an underlying reality (water) that explained the cosmos. Thales' insight is not so profound because of his conclusion about water as it is that the universe could be explained at all without reference to divine intervention. Thales was a student of astronomy, fixed the solstices and eclipses of the sun, and was the first to favor the soul's immortality, and who thought that no good or evil thought could be withheld from the gods. (5) Anaxagoras (c. 500–428 BCE) believed that mind was superior to matter, that the sun was a hot stone and the moon made of material like earth, ideas that earned him a charge of atheism and blasphemy. He proposed that material was composed of an infinite number of particles or atoms. He suggested, as Plato notes, that if everything were combined and nothing split into separate entities the result would be Chaos, a condition that just happens to have been proposed in *Genesis*. (6)

Greeks were the first to propose a non-religious view of the structure of the universe, its causes and effects on humans, that life should be enjoyed, and that the life of the mind was eminently worth pursuing. Painted vases dating from the 5th century BCE reveal not just geometric shapes, but people at games, at work, dancing, at athletic events. As far as we know, the Greeks invented national games and athletic competition (the Olympics began in 776 BCE), enjoyed plays and theatrical competitions, festivals, enthusiasm in creating new aesthetic forms of beauty, and the power of reasoning and persuasion rather than coercion. By applying reason to the solution of the problems of life, and by creating a place where people began to think freely for the first time in history, the Greeks invented our present way of life.

Greeks also had their Dionysian, emotional and passionate side, as portrayed in Greek tragedies. Dionysius is the dynamic power of the force of inexhaustible nature and its power, through wine, to change human consciousness. The working religions of the ancient world revolved around the food supply: corn (Demeter), grapes (Bacchus), cattle (Baal), the hunt (Diana), and the seasons. Dionysius is one of the many forms of the Vegetative God, whose annual death and resurrection symbolize the yearly cycle of decay and rebirth, like the gods Tammuz, Attis, Adonis and Osiris. The dead gods, Mithras, Osiris, Asclepius, Adonis, Serapis, Jesus, rise again, celebrate their triumph over death, and in them one finds the fulfillment of life. The mystery of life is symbolized in the life of vegetation. And like wheat for the Middle East, the great civilizations of Mesoamerica could not have survived without corn (*maiz*), the major food staple in Mayan culture. The Mayan corn god was *Yum K'aax*, shown in limestone carvings as a young man with a corn-stalk head with long tresses, illustrative of the long tresses on the cob, with its headdress made of a corn stalk surrounded by leaves.

The most venerated of the Greek mystery rites was that of Adonis and the blending of the themes of love, death and resurrection. Greeks borrowed this theme from the Phrygian god Attis and the Babylonian god Tammuz. The exclamations of "Adonis is dead" and "Cease from your mourning" in the poem *Epitaph on Adonis* by Bion of Smyrna, poetically recreates this ancient death and resurrection theme and shows how easy it is to transition this ancient festival celebration into a Christian context. (7)

Christian participation in the sacred Christian mysteries were reserved for those accepted into membership, just like Greek mystery initiates. Even catechumens in instruction were excluded, as the diary of Egeria in 384 makes clear. "In that hour no catechumen approaches the Anastasis, but only the neophytes and the faithful, who wish to hear concerning the mysteries, enter there, and the doors are shut lest any catechumen should draw near...the mysteries are so unfolded that there is no one unmoved at the things that he hears to be so explained." (8)

Greek gods extolled nature. Judaism and Christianity believed in justice and truth but not beauty or the divine in nature, nor in the glories of nature's bounty, nor in the singular attraction of the human form, nor in goddesses and the powers that regulate the created cosmos. This absence of the femininity of the divine leaves a spiritual void in believers. Thus when Christianity began its lengthy rule over the European landscape the beauteous side of what the Greeks had possessed was lost and the veneration of the Mary, Mother of God arose as an essential replacement of Isis, Spider Woman, Demeter, Persephone, Hera, Europa and all the subtle, generative female forces that once balanced aggressive male patriarchies.

The relationship between Hellenic culture and Christianity is not tenuous and obscure but a part of the intellectual milieu at the time of gospel composition. There are conspicuous textual correlations in Homer's *Iliad* and *Odyssey* with Mark's gospel and the *Acts of the Apostles*. (9) But additionally, there are seminal ideas, mystery rites, secrecy, acting in common, sharing a divine meal, asceticism, purity of body, God as transcendent, the son of God as the Logos, that Christianity has in common with Hellenistic ideas and practices. Augustine's triumph in the 4th century was to unite Platonism so thoroughly into Christian dogma that the union of Hellenism and philosophical speculation was complete and seemed so natural an alliance. Borrowed myths passed through Hebrew hands into the Bible, and the philosophies of the Greeks through theological commentators to become Christian dogma.

Miracle stories are an example of how gospel narrative duplicated Hellenic literature. Over the centuries, oral stories circulated about the feats of Hercules, for example, some perhaps written in notes, letters or documents that were eventually assembled to become a unified story when all tasks, the twelve labors in Hercules' case, were completed. Miracle workers like Hercules or Jesus have superhuman births from a deity, then undergo various trials, are opposed by adversaries, and in the end are justified for all actions and found agreeable to the gods. Gathering such stories, interspersed with sayings and conversations, then formed a quasi-biography of the chosen hero.

Pythagoras, Orpheus, & the Eleusian Mysteries

Pentheus: What ceremonious rites have these among you?
Bacchus: These to the unhallowed may not be revealed.
Pentheus: What profit to their votaries do they bring?
Bacchus: You may not hear, though worthy to be known.
(Euripedes, The Bacchae, 1832, p. 19)

The philosophy of Pythagoras was as much religious as mathematical and his group is the beginning of the flourishing of mystery cults throughout the Greek world. Pythagoras founded a highly secretive school, a monastic life and form of socialism without any known formal religious beliefs. As a result of this secrecy we have no written accounts of this belief system, although one belief is in a soul that survives and becomes ennobled. (11) Pythagoras had chosen members who were to hold property in common, observe certain food rituals, and be governed by a code of conduct supported by proverbs. This is also a similar description of early Christians in *The Acts*. The ideas of Pythagoras, like the fate of the soul and its immortality and its transmigration into other bodily forms after death, were later absorbed by Plato, then by Christianity as baptism became the initiation of the elect into the mysteries, and ritual meals became the central celebration of its mysteries. (12)

The sacred site of Eleusis just west of Athens originated about 2,000 BCE, over a thousand years before Homer, and was not formally abandoned until after the edict of Theodosius in 390 CE ostracizing all pagan religions and shrines. Here began the mysteries surrounding the cult of Demeter, goddess of grains and cereals, and of her daughter by Zeus, Persephone, the goddess of the harvest and fertility. The cult highlighted Dionysius, god of wine, of the unconscious and uninhibited, of the non-rational, as Apollo was of the rational mind, a representation of the power of a life force. The other deity of the life force is Orpheus, the fisher, who pulls people from the abyss, out of the water. Jesus says to his Apostles, "I will make you fishers of men," the orphic ideal. The Pope's ring is the ring of the fisherman.

Apuleius describes his own initiation experiences into these mysteries in *The Golden Ass* that included a ritual bath, the learning of secrets in stages, culminating in ten days of fasting prior to a concluding ceremony. The deprivation of food can lead to hallucinations that permit the initiate to "see" visions and hence enter into the realm of gods. (13)

The god of the underworld, Pluto, abducted Persephone as a beautiful young maiden and Demeter was so disconsolate and inconsolable that the earth became barren and unproductive without her ministrations. Demeter sat by a well at Eleusis (as does Isis seeking her brother, as does the woman of Samaria at the well seeking the waters of life from Jesus) while searching for her daughter. Demeter persuades Pluto to return her, but the compromise is that she is to remain with Pluto in the underworld for four months every year. Ancient agricultural societies planted in the fall and harvested in the spring. During the excessive heat of the summer months, all grains were stored in the earth, the underworld, for safekeeping.

The symbols of seeds growing, flowering, dying and becoming reborn again, are also the chief symbols of religion, of birth, transformation, death and resurrection, of physical realities transposed into spiritual forces. Wheat is the nourishment of the body. Like deities, wheat was cut, buried, eaten and then kept rising again as if the stocks had never died. We eat divine substances and our lives are supported by transcendent powers. Eating a meal, like the Eucharist at the Mass, is the ritual of eating deities of the Eleusian mysteries. The Christian ritual of the Eucharist is built upon both the Eleusian and Mithraic divine mysteries of bread and wine cloaked with Christian reinterpretation. But the message of both the Eleusian and Christian mysteries is the same: for initiates to enter into a relationship with the divine.

Paul's knowledge of these mysteries became incorporated into his theology in the *Ephesians* (1:9-12, and 3:2-9). He juxtaposes Greek mysteries with the mysteries of Christ, contrasting the Greek initiate of the ancient mysteries with the inductee of the new "saint" into Christian thinking, "the mystery which has been hidden from ages and generations, but now is manifested to his saints." (*Col.* 1:26). Christian mysteries will be reassembled as sacraments and the believer inducted into each of their secrets through grace, a mystery itself.

Vases in the Naples museum show the artistic representation of parts of Eleusian initiation ceremonies. First, a laurel tree, the symbol of Daphne and Apollo's unrequited love, protects the sanctuary from evil powers. In the next panel, a candidate carries a torch. From another sculpture, a kneeling candidate's head is covered and Bacchus and Dionysius stand near an altar with offerings of fruit. Nearby Demeter is seated on a sacred basket of food with a serpent lying near her feet and Persephone, the resurrected one, stands next to her, while Dionysius carries a chalice of wine. Demeter holds her torch skywards purifying the upper regions, while Persephone holds hers downward purifying the lower. In several vase paintings Demeter carries a cornucopia of harvested fruits and vegetables. Christianity celebrates the continuation of the ancient rites associated with the mysteries of food and agriculture. (14)

It has been surmised that hallucinates like wine were used for reaching the divine or at least for inducing ecstatic states. Another possible choice is the mushroom *amanita muscaria* that induces the imbiber to engage in ecstatic activities with remarkable fits of energy. References to ambrosia and nectar in the literature may be symbols for the intoxicating influences of these mushrooms. Seeing visions by ingesting these intoxicants may be one reason why members were induced to silence.

The mysteries are also based on the myth of Dionysus Zagreus, son of Zeus, whom Zeus proposed to make the ruler of the universe. The Titans were so enraged at this proposal that they ate him. But Athena saved Zagreus' heart and gave it to Zeus, who swallowed it begetting another Dionysius, the mythical equivalent of cloning. Zeus then destroyed the Titans with lightning and from their ashes sprang the human race, part divine (Dionysus) and part evil (Titan). This dual side of human nature, the Dionysian and the Titanic, is essential to the understanding of Orphic mysteries, as members believed in the divine origin of the soul. Through the process of transmigration the soul can be liberated from its Titanic (read demonic) inheritance and achieve eternal life. The cult emphasized a rigid ethical conduct for its members who purified themselves and abstained from eating animal flesh in order to overcome evil and promote the positive, Dionysian side.

The most enduring religious belief in western civilization is the concept of soul, an idea derived from extremely ancient ideas. As late as the 4th century CE, Symmachus, the Roman prefect who recommended Augustine for a teaching post in Milan, believed that: "As souls are separately given to infants as they are born, so to peoples the genius of their destiny." (15) Roman mosaics and wall paintings, visible in the museum in the Roman amphitheatre in Amman, Jordan, represent the soul as a bird in a cage and the body as a bird outside the cage looking in. The duality of human nature has been accepted since the 6th century BCE even though the existence of a soul is completely hypothetical. A list of beliefs about soul reveals the diversity.

Interpretations of Soul

Egyptians	Two souls: BA, the moveable shadow of the body; KA, the spiritual double of the body surviving death
Plato	Three souls independent from the body (rational, passionate & appetitive)
Aristotle	Soul = the Form of the body
Stoic soul	Divine breath with 8 parts: rational soul, five senses & procreative powers, all material
Sadducees	Denied spiritual existence
Pharisees	Preexistent soul & transmigration
Gnostics	The body corrupt, the soul perfect
Philo	Divine origin of soul
Origen	Soul preexistent to the body
Manichees	Body the prison of the soul
Apollinarius	(310–390, Bishop of Laodicea) Jesus had a human body but a divine soul (condemned by Council in 381)
Augustine	Soul the highest good of the body
Aquinas	Rational soul is the form of the body (same as Aristotle)

Eternity and immortality are originally Egyptian concepts that turned palpable when the ideas were literally buried with the embalmed believers. The pyramids are the world's largest monuments to this belief, sarcophagi for the royal dead awaiting the return of the *KA*. One spirit of the deceased is represented in burial tombs as a small bird with a human head symbolizing the *BA*, the soul of the deceased which gives the dead power of movement leading the person to the underworld, which is why earthly goods and objects needed for the afterlife were entombed with the deceased. The second soul is the *KA*, literally the spirit double that provides the person with the means of surviving eternally.

The Greeks were not so immodest as to claim that their ideas came from gods. Having absorbed much from Greek philosophy and myth, Jews and Christians did not adopt the Socratic rule to question everything in order to learn. (16) But Christians did adopt the Platonic concept of the soul that Plato enunciated in the *Phaedo*: "That while we are in the body, and while our soul is infected with the evils of the body, our desire will not be satisfied, and our desire is of the truth. For the body is the source of endless trouble." Manichees adopted the idea about the evilness of the body from Plato. The Gnostics and Christian mystics and ascetics would also claim Plato: "For if while in the company with the body, the soul cannot have pure knowledge, one of two things follows, either knowledge is not to be attained at all, or if at all, after death...In this present life, I reckon that we make the nearest approach to knowledge when we have the least possible intercourse or communion with the body." (17) Christianity, with a boost from Augustine, adopted Plato's non-Christian but philosophical definition of soul.

But the Jews too were influenced by the ideology of the Greeks, by Plato's immortality of the soul, by the heroic ideals of the intervention of the gods in the life of men, by rewards and punishments in an afterlife, by the transcendence of spirits, by the mysteries and secret ceremonies of elite groups. The Romans had totally assimilated the mythology and speculative philosophy of ancient Greece and preserved it in poetry, prose, drama and histories and made it the core of their educational curriculum. The suggestion among many Greek and Roman writers like Virgil, who exemplifies the religious feeling of the value of suffering, is that there is a supernatural presence in the world and that the anthropomorphism of the gods, nymphs, fauns, domestic deities like the Lares, the household gods, are simply expressions of that belief. (18)

Ulysses and Jesus

Hector, Achilles, and Ulysses (the Latin form of Odysseus), and the semi-gods of mythology, like Hercules, Perseus and Hermes, are not only celebrated in *The Iliad* and *Odyssey* but were used as models in student writing compositions. In real life these epic heroes would not be invited to a dinner party (Socrates might be the exception) because their personalities and actions were not always amenable to normal human intercourse. Jesus as portrayed in the gospels is more approachable than such divinities and epic heroes, but still appears distant and constrained. Jesus appeals, at the places where he dines, in much the way Socrates might have at one of his evening symposia. Socrates discusses with dinner companions the nature of truth and justice. Jesus uses parables and moral pronouncements to tell his message.

But the parallels between Ulysses and Jesus imply a literary association so strong that gospel narrators, as they borrowed from each other, borrowed from Homer as well. The events, the sequences, the comparative episodes have a compelling similarity. (19)

ULYSSES	JESUS
Carpenter	carpenter (son of carpenter)
Foolish companions	non-comprehending companions
Twins the Sons of Thunder (designating sons of Zeus)	Twin disciples, the Sons of Thunder

fought usurpers who attempted to steal authority and to murder him	fought Pharisees who sought to kill him
upset with sleeping companions during a time of trial	upset with sleeping disciples at a time of great stress in Gethsemane
disguises identity in beggar's clothes	disguises real identity on multiple occasions and tells disciples not to reveal his identity
The power of Athena calms the stormy sea for favored Ulysses	Jesus calms the storm on Galilee with divine power because Jesus is in Father's favor
escapes death in a cave from the Cyclops using superhuman strength in rolling back a stone	escapes death in a cave tomb when angel superhumanly rolls back stone humans cannot
descends to the Underworld to find Tereisias	descends to the underworld to comfort the prophets

GOSPEL IMITATIONS FROM HOMER'S ODYSSEY

ODYSSEY	GOSPELS
The deity takes the form of a bird (Book 1, pp. 11, 285, 417)	The Spirit of God descending like a dove and lighting on him. (*Matt.* 3:15)
God's brilliance shone upon him (pp. 19, 111, 125, 235)	Transfiguration (*Matt.* 17: 1-3)
Zeus sends a sign (p. 23)	"Teacher, we want to see a sign from you."(Matt. 12 & 16)
The men mix water in a wine bowl with sweet 11 year-old wine	Jesus changes water into wine at wedding feast at Cana (*John* 2

Telemachus attends a wedding feast of the son & daughter of Menelaos; Helen alters the wine	Jesus changes the water into wine at the wedding feast of Cana
Ulysses passes through town "with folds of sacred mist." (p. 112)	Jesus escapes unseen from the clutches of Nazarenes who seek to harm him. (*Luke 4*)
Luscious figs bearing fruit "winter and summer they bore" (p. 114)	Jesus cursed the fig tree for not bearing figs out of season (*Mark 11*)
Spirits and ghosts appear from their tombs and speak to Ulysses (p. 186)	"Many bodies of the saints who had fallen asleep arose & coming forth out of tombs appeared to many." (*Matt 27*)
"Ulysses wept." (p. 236)	"Jesus wept." (*John* 11)
O Father Zeus, if over land, and water, after adversity, you willed me home, let someone in the waking house give me good augury, and a sign be shown too in the outer world." (p. 378)	"My Father, if this cup cannot pass away unless I drink it, thy will be done." (*Matt.* 26: 42)
"Now you too go to sleep. This all night vigil wearies the flesh. You'll come soon enough on the other side of trouble." (p. 376)	"Then he returned to his disciples and found them sleeping. 'Could you men not keep watch with me for one hour.'" (*Matt.* 26)
Suitors for Penelope plan to kill Ulysses' son for the inheritance	"But when the tenants saw the son, they said to each other, 'Come let's kill him and take his inheritance.'" (*Matt.* 21:37-39)

"Going forward, he kissed the young man's head, his shining eyes and both hands, while his own tears brimmed and fell. Think of a man whose dear and only son...has lived ten years abroad and now returns."
(pp. 289-90)

"His father ran and fell upon his neck and kissed him. This my son was dead and has come to life again; he was lost and is found." (*Luke* 15)

Ulysses goes as a beggar to his home and people.

Foxes have holes and birds of the air have nests, but the Son of Man has no place to lay his head." (*Matt.* 8: 19)

Ulysses is kicked in his hip by a Goat-tender and gets hits in the shoulder with a footstool but does nothing to his persecutors
(p. 236)

"But I tell you, Do not resist an evil person. If someone strikes you on the right cheek
turn to him the other also." (*Matt* 5)

"Well, let the company plan his high destruction and leave him no way out this time
I see our business here

that it is unfinished while he lives...
I say act now before he brings the whole body of Akhaians to assembly."
(p. 302)

"But one of them, Caiphas, being

priest that year, said to them, 'You nothing at all; nor do you reflect that it is expedient for one man to die for the people instead of the whole nation perishing." (*John* 11:50)

Eurykleia recognizes Ulysses by

placing her hand on the scar on his thigh.
Here let me show you something else, a sign that I am he, that you may trust me, look: the old scar..." (p. 398)

Then he said to Thomas, Put your finger here; see my hands.

reach out your hand and put it in my side. Stop doubting
and believe." (*John* 20:26)

The suitors revile Ulysses and taunt him.

The Jews revile Jesus and taunt him.

When juxtaposed with selected narrative passages, we can see the intended imitation between Ulysses and Jesus. Gospel narrators copied the themes, episodes and certain passages to show Greek readers that Jesus was like the hero Ulysses, and the readers who were familiar with *The Odyssey* as their school textbook would have understood the comparative message.

Socrates and Plato

Socrates (469–399 BCE), who exhibited high intelligence and personal courage, an example of a man willing to die for his principles, influenced succeeding philosophers and served as an ideal character model. Socrates was interested in people defining themselves through a quest for moral knowledge. He was an extraordinary man who not only defined his age, but with Confucius and Buddha, was an exemplar of moral integrity and intellectual honesty. Jesus resembles the sagacity and lifestyle of Socrates, even to the neglect of family.

Socrates follows in the tradition of free intellectual inquiry by debating virtues and challenging superstitious beliefs and social conventions. (20) He used logic to confound myth and dialogue to expunge mental error. He formulated the method of dialogue or dialectic, a questioning process, to follow as discussants sought the enhancement of moral character. Socrates' main inquiry, can there be a natural ethnic without a supernatural belief, challenged the conventional belief of his day in the gods, and hence the religiously orthodox considered him dangerous. He was brought to trial on charges of corrupting the youth of Athens and of religious heresies against the gods, found guilty and put to death. His method of talking about behaviors for proper human conduct, his ideas about knowledge, and his death at the hands of his enemies are similar characteristics of Jesus.

Does there exist true, immutable, timeless and universal values, valid for all people everywhere and for all time? Are such values realizable on earth? Do these values form a harmonious and coherent system that lead to a perfect society? These are questions posed and answered by Plato, the first great speculative thinker to construct a comprehensive philosophical system to which all subsequent philosophies appear to be just endnotes. Soul, mind, reason, ideas, thinking are concepts from Plato who may have received them from Indian philosophy. (21) Homer lifted the archetype of the human struggle for existence to a contest between humans and gods. Plato lifted philosophy and its application to the status of the divine.

Plato's friends purchased a small grove of trees, dedicated to the local god Academus, from which we get the word Academy, and it lasted over 900 hundred years until closed in 529 CE by Emperor Justinian. (22) It was in the shadow of the Acropolis in Athens that Plato founded after the death of Socrates the equivalent of one of the world's first universities where he taught learning for its own sake, with a curriculum consisting of math, music, astronomy, and geometry, and the principles of the good life.

Plato's concept of an *Idea*, which defines his whole philosophy, was slightly different from what we understand popularly today. Plato's concept of an idea is not that of a mental reality but a separate, independent existence in a transcendent world. Ideas are the absolute forms of eternal, unchangeable things, and what we perceive are only appearances, illusions of the real thing. Plato believed that each object, including people, had a mirror representation, its Form, existing in another dimension that the senses cannot experience. There is an independent reality to Ideas and Forms and they are the archetypes of all temporal reality. The purpose of education and knowledge through dialectic and reasoning was to lead to a vision of the Ideal Forms.

Plato's *Republic* contains an allegory symbolizing his theory of Idealism. A group is seated chained inside a cave, facing a wall on one side of the cave and can only see in only one direction. Behind them is a large fire that casts shadows of people moving along a raised platform. These shadows of people walking are the only visible reality they see. If they were to spend their entire lives in this position, they would assume that the shadows are the real thing, "truth would be literally nothing but the shadows of the images." (23) However, if they could be unchained and allowed to turn around and see the actual people walking, they would have to revise their understanding of reality. Imagine further what would be their understanding if they were to be led outside into the full glare of the sun and experience a world they could not have imagined.

Plato says that is the way we view the world now. Our five senses grasp only shadowy appearances. (24) To seek truth and arrive at true knowledge one must be able to distinguish between appearances and reach towards unseen reality. The way to achieve knowledge of the higher good is through dialectic, a constant questioning of assumptions, to discover truth from error, and by examining particular ideas to reach more general ones.

We can draw a modern analogy from nuclear physics. Plato's universal forms are like sub-atomic particles, which indeed comprise (as far as we know) the essence of all matter. Their various combinations constitute the nature of whatever it is we experience. In Plato's day the archetype symbol for this was mathematics, wherein numbers, as Pythagoras maintained, underlay the reality of all existence, because everything can be quantified. Math was a demonstration of the existence of Pure Forms for Plato and verification for his philosophy of Idealism.

Consider another example from the world of particle physics. Experiments in physics in the past 50 years have revealed the existence of sub-atomic particles of anti-matter. Ordinary atoms are composed of electrons orbiting a nucleus. Physicists hypothesize that when a particle of matter meets a particle of anti-matter the collision results in the annihilation of both particles and the release of a burst of energy. Anti-matter particles do not appear to exist naturally but have been created artificially. Anti-matter particles remain in existence for just 40 billionths of a second before annihilation. Do other words for anti-matter exist that are similar to Plato's ideal states of all perceived appearances? (25) Plato's ideas of the immortal soul, transcendence, an ethereal God, and the physical world as a place of appearances, contributed to Christianity's intellectual substance and which commentators eagerly folded into doctrine.

Ancient Greek mystery cults also became absorbed into Plato's philosophy. (26) Discussants in Plato's *Phaedo* agree that the soul is infected with the evils of the body during life, that true knowledge can only be attained by the soul, that true philosophers are only concerned about the things of the soul, and that death is the separation of the soul from the body. These concepts sound Christian but are Orphic and Pythagorean in origin, at least three centuries prior to Plato. Releasing the soul from the chains of the body has become the foundation for Christian salvation, though its ideological origin predates Christianity by over six centuries. Platonists were not altogether pleased when Christians adopted Plato's transcendence and then added the incarnation, a Greek mythical concept, into the philosophical mix, an idea they believed was incompatible with divine immutability.

Plato's genius was in conceptualizing the nature of God and man. Like his proposal of three parts to the soul (vegetative, sensate and rational), Plato proposed three divine natures in God: the first cause, reason (logos), and spirit (soul). (27) This divine partitioning and its Trinitarian expression would surface 600 years in the future when Christianity was in the ascendancy and clarification of theological ambiguities were essential for unity of belief.

Epictetus (c. 50–138 CE)

Epictetus was another seeker of moral truth who taught that the chief good was inside a person, that there was a brotherhood of man. He preached detachment from this world and indifference to worldly goods, typical stoic ethical ideals. He believed that man was part animal with a body, and part divine with reason and a soul. (28)

Epictetus, whose name means "acquired" (he was a slave), was born in today's northern Iran and lived during the reigns of Nero and Hadrian. About the year 89 CE he was given his freedom and became a teacher of philosophy in Rome, but was soon exiled and resided in northern Greece where he remained as a teacher the rest of his life. Like Jesus, he left no writings of his own, but his *Discourses* are the faithful transcriptions of his lectures by students. He said in his *Handbook*: "Do not seek to have events happen as you want them to, but instead want them to happen to you as they do happen, and your life will go well." (29) There is an element of fatalism and determinism in this and similar stoic sayings. "So detach your aversion from everything not up to us, and transfer it to what is against nature. And for the time being eliminate desire completely, since if you desire something that is not up to you, you are bound to be unfortunate." (30) This notion of the elimination of desire is Buddhist in belief but becomes asceticism in Christian monasticism.

The stoic ideal was character development. "Set up right now a certain character and pattern for yourself which you will preserve when you are by yourself and when you are with people." (31) One of the means of achieving this goal was detachment from this life. "Take what has to do with the body to the point of bare need, such as food, clothing, house, and cut out everything that is for reputation or luxury." (32) Sounds quite ascetic.

In words similar to Jesus' response on what to do with a coin of Caesar, "give to Caesar what is Caesar's and to God what is God's" (*Mark* 12: 16-18) Epictetus writes: "For as a money-changer or a gardener is not at liberty to reject Caesar's coin, but when once it is shown is obliged, whether he will or not, to deliver what is sold for it, so it is in the soul…Nor will the soul any more reject an evident appearance of good than they will Caesar's coin." (33)

Epictetus says: "For if you lay a rotten and crazy foundation, you must not build; and the greater and more weighty the superstructure is, the sooner will it fall." (34) And in *Luke*, the parable is: "He is like a man building a house, who dug down deep and laid the foundation on rock. When a flood came, the torrent struck that house but could not shake it, because it was well built." (*Luke* 6:47-49).

Epictetus had a profound influence on the Roman world with a useable philosophy of life, pithy colloquialisms on how to live, and appealing principles of behavior. Whatever sources evangelists used, many of the parables and saying of Jesus modified and attributed to him, were already known, radiating throughout the Mediterranean world in Greek, the language of their writings. And such sayings were collected in *The Gospel of Thomas*. Educated apologists were familiar with these scholar philosophers of the day, and used their methods and ideas to convert pagans in cities like Antioch where Paul made his headquarters, and in trading and market centers like Ephesus, Philippi, Thessalonica, Athens, Corinth and Rome where he preached.

Philo of Alexandria (c. 20 BCE-50 CE)

Philo (a.k.a. Philo Judaeus) was a Jewish philosopher and theologian, an aristocrat living in Alexandria, the most intellectually stimulating city in the ancient world. He was a man who combined Platonic Greek philosophy with biblical interpretation, who could read and write Hebrew and Greek, who lived during the lifetime of Jesus. He is a link between the Torah legacy and the beginnings of Christianity. He linked Jewish reform with Hellenism to explain theological mysteries. (35)

Philo brought Greek philosophy to traditional Jewish process of commenting on scripture. Many Jewish scholars opposed Greek philosophy on religious grounds, believing it to be a form of impiety. Philo wanted to use philosophy as a method for interpreting the allegories of scripture to satisfy inquiring minds and to defend Judaism from attacks of heathen writers. Palestinian rabbis had no acquaintance with Greek philosophy, science or ethics, nor did they want to. Judaism had no response to the questions of Greek philosophy, how do we know, what do we know, what is virtue, how does man relate to nature and the state? Philo did have such knowledge and assumed that all Hebrew scripture had a literal and allegorical meaning. (36) As he commented on scriptural chapters he answered each selected passage both literally and allegorically, commentaries that were likely used as sermons in the synagogue. (37)

Allegory is the use of symbolic language and generalizes about the truths of existence. Allegory was an attempt to discover the truths of transcendent reality for Plato. (38) St. Paul writes in his letter to the *Galatians*: "This is said by way of allegory. For these are the two covenants, one indeed from Mount Sinai which corresponds to the present Jerusalem, and is in slavery with her children. But that Jerusalem which is above is free, which is our mother." (*Gal*: 24-26). Jerusalem has an allegorical double meaning: the current bondage with Rome and the true Jerusalem in covenant with God, an idea Augustine would turn into his major work, *The City of God*.

Greeks used allegory in interpreting the popular beliefs of Homer and Hesiod, and Mark and Luke imitated episodes from Homer to recreate mythical adventures in the life of Jesus. (39) Philo applies an allegory to scriptural exegesis. Several Greek philosophers, like Thales, Heraclitus, Anaxagoras and Democritus, saw inspiration in the poets and sought to interpret meaning through allegory never believing they were interpreting divine revelations. But for Philo reason and philosophy are subordinate to faith, a theme that echoes in subsequent centuries throughout Jewish, Christian and Islamic thought. What Philo doesn't do is compare the Bible with any previous mythical writings except ideas from the Greek philosophers with whom he was familiar. He quotes 54 classical authors accurately and in depth. (40) Philo's distinction between myth and scripture is instructive because he contrasts mythology, which he says is man-made, with scripture that holds the truths of God, which contains no mythical inventions. (41) "Philo," says Goodenough, "knew nothing of the oral traditions on which Talmudic law was ultimately based." (42)

Judaism two thousand years ago was Pharisaic, crafted by scribes imbued with learned commentaries on scripture, a religion untouched by Greek rationalism and philosophy as Greek speculation was unconcerned with Jewish religious belief. Nevertheless, by the 1st century CE Philo, and in the following century Clement and Origen, attempted to reconcile the two extremes of Jewish scriptural exegesis and Greek rational and mythical traditions. Greek culture created a tension among Hebrews between fulfillment of the Law and the ubiquitous Hellenic urbanized, sophisticated culture everywhere in the Jewish Diaspora. (43)

One form of the assimilation of Hellenism into Judaism is the absorption of the Greek language into meanings of deities. Editors of the Bible who translated the Torah from Hebrew into Alexandrian Greek known as the Septuagint used Greek terms for Hebrew words for God which slightly altered the meaning, giving to Hebrew theology identification with divine figures from Greek mythology. The Greek word for God was *theos*, a word often referring to Zeus. The expression "most high god" in Greek refers exclusively to Zeus. The word for Jehovah, which Jews were told they could not pronounce, was translated as *Adonai*, Lord, a Greek term that often referred to multiple gods. The Greek term for "Almighty" referred to Hermes (Roman Mercury), the messenger of the gods and the son of Zeus. Philo often refers to God as "peace," knowing that the Greek term referred to Irene, the Greek goddess. Jewish translators borrowed heavily from the terms used to describe ritualistic forms of worship, such as altar, sanctuary, sacrifice, votive offering, etc. (44) The word for the Jewish place of worship, synagogue, is Greek for a meeting place.

The Corpus Hermeticum is a collection of Gnostic Greek texts composed in Egypt during the 1st century CE purported written by Hermes Trismegistus, an amalgam of a mythical person representing Thoth, the Egyptian god of wisdom and patron of scribes. The book is a series of twelve dialogues written to an imaginary companion about the interpretation of meaning for God, man, demons, the soul, intellect and immortality, indeed the kind of explanations that philosophers discuss among themselves. The text is an interpretation of the composition of the world, of man's nature and relationship to God, of death and how the mind becomes eternal and celestial. It is a rewarding text in this sense: it does not refer to ancient Greek gods, earlier literary texts, or to Jesus but is a Gnostic interpretation of the universe and reveals much about the intellectual wordplay of the 1st century CE without moralizing or sentimentality. It is very readable and hence was likely consumed by large swaths of the literate population. It had a profound influence on Christianity.

The word Logos, translated into the Latin *verbum* or "word," is laden with ancient Hindu and Greek meanings, one of those ambiguous words that when applied to deities provides a glaze that coats its essential meaning. In its most immediate sense, it is the articulation of speech produced by thought. A further meaning is the thought itself, a principle, like a formula in chemistry.

Logos represents reason or mind, the science of making thoughts. The sacred Logos was the secret revelation given to initiates in Greek mystery religions, and Heraclitus (who lived in Ephesus like John) proposed an eternal Logos. Coupled with the idea of beams of light coming from the sun, the Logos, in Philo's biblical interpretation, becomes the creative power of God, the Idea of God in the Platonic sense, irradiating everyone and everything. The true Logos, like a seal that God uses to imprint upon matter to give it form, is the real world and the material world a defective copy.

When John's gospel declared that Jesus was the Logos of God, theological apologists had to scramble to describe how this was possible without re-defining themselves as polytheists. Allusions to Jesus as the Son of God became the personal reason of God, the Logos, a kind of clone of God, in which all men can partake, except that the whole of the Logos resides in Jesus. If Jesus were a separate being, and not simply a facet or emanation of the Father, the explanation became more difficult to accept. The Nicene creed is unhelpful when it solemnly declares that belief is to be "in one God" but also in "one Lord, Jesus Christ," then compounds this by proclaiming they are of one substance, and then as an afterthought adds "and in the Holy Ghost," an enigma complicating the puzzle neither an oracle or a philosopher could easily resolve.

Even after borrowing Platonic ideas, for example that there was really only one God but several emanations, theological expositors still found it difficult even with tortuous exegesis to get around the charge of polytheism without complicated equivocation producing more questions than answers. Philo and Justin Martyr both used the Bible as a starting reference and blended its passages with exegetical explanations from stoicism and Platonism to form descriptions of how the Logos applied to God and Jesus. The stoic primal principle was fire and these ancients viewed what they called the *logos spermatikos* as a kind of pantheistic air in which conception occurred. Christian apologists like Justin elevated this stoic material substance to a cosmic, spiritual kind of air, the "seeds of truth," a kind of intuition of God implanted in mankind. (45) Nevertheless, with John's gospel, the Logos became incarnated dogma: "And the Word was made flesh." Origen saw scripture as a form of Logos, midway between the Word as spirit and the Word as flesh, or Jesus, elevating the language of the scribes to unintended rarified heights. For this Gnostic interpretation Origen was branded a pariah and exiled. (46)

The biblical God almost always used a host of intermediaries to communicate ideas or events to humanity, from the voice from a bush, to the messages of angels like Michael and Gabriel. As the Hebrews and Jews had angels, so the Greeks had *daimones*. For Philo such entities were not persons in the literal sense, but the thoughts, energies and powers of God or spirits.

For Philo the Logos was "the first begotten of God," and for John the incarnation of the Logos was Jesus. This understanding was common among the scholars of the day as the Nag Hammadi texts note: "Now the Logos that is superior to all beings was sent for this purpose alone: that he might proclaim the unknown." (47) Because he lived in an enriched intellectual environment, John gave to Jewish mystical theology a Hellenistic twist and in thus made Greek ideas integral to emergent Christianity. (48)

Philo was influenced by the idea of the Logos but as a Jew saw its application to God not Jesus. He conceived Ideas as Logos, or the Reason of God, into a divine principle by means of which God communicated to the world. Philo does not search for any philosophical theory in his commentaries on *Genesis* nor for this or that truth, but rather for a description of the attitudes of the soul towards God. Nor does he envisage a conflict between scriptural exegesis and philosophical discussion, but rather a difference in method and purpose. His treatises reveal his considerable knowledge and erudition of both Hellenistic philosophy and the Bible. (49)

Philo is the first to open the door to scriptural interpretation by not relying exclusively upon the exact interpretation of the words of scripture. He often rejects the literal meaning altogether, as he does the six days of creation, by using allegory to interpret scripture. Although thoroughly Jewish and a defender of the contemplative life, he is the first rationalist of biblical exegesis and became a model for later Christian theologians. But Philo is also among the first to propose that Moses was the author of the Pentateuch. And that myth, even though discredited, has persisted. Though Philo was encased in the Jewish and Hellenic traditions, he inaugurated a Jewish reform movement that catapulted a new religion with embedded Jewish, Hellenic and Egyptian themes.

Justin Martyr (c. 100–165 CE)

Beginning with Christian apologists like Justin and Clement we encounter a Greek tradition of Platonism, already merged with its mystical twin Gnosticism, into a metaphysics of salvation. While budding Christian theologians in the first centuries espoused ideas almost exclusively in defense of the new religion, they are also recreating ancient ideas in a new religious context, borrowing from the past to reinvent a new faith. Moreover, the claim of these first theological commentators is that after Christ humanity received a form of deification, a participation in the divine through the Incarnation.

The 2nd century witnessed a literary outpouring of Christian apologetic works designed to counter the calumnies against the struggling new religion and to add robustness to the intellectual climate. Early Christian writings like those of Justin Martyr were meant to appeal to Christians who might waver in their faith by the attraction of philosophy, to Jews influenced by Hellenism, and to non-Christians to demonstrate that Christianity held popular appeal.

Justin Martyr is one of those inquisitive minds yearning to study philosophy, and having satisfied his thirst for knowledge decided that Christianity had the foremost appeal. He became a Christian convert, then advocate, and foremost apologist, a profoundly Christian mind before theological definitions had become orthodox, the first Christian philosopher who did not appreciate he was writing the first theological tracts. Justin was born a gentile in Samaria and did not become a convert until adulthood and only after he had studied Pythagoras, Platonism and stoicism. He was converted about 135 CE, came to Rome about 150 where he founded a school of philosophy, and was martyred in the reign of Marcus Aurelius in 165.

The account of his study, journey, encounter with a sage and conversion has been linked to a similar story told by Lucian, illustrating that non-biblical fables also borrowed from pagan literature to enliven the lives of Christian apologists. (50) Justin compared the death of Socrates to that of Jesus, and often quotes Plato, Xenophon and even Euripedes. (51) Curiously, he does not quote John's gospel, and it is surmised that John's gospel had not been written, or that he may have been familiar with its contents but did not regard it as canonical. (52) Because of his erudition in Greek legends and philosophies, he appealed to an educated non-Christian audience. His few extant writings show his familiarity with Plato and his argument justifying Christianity as the one, true philosophy is similar to the gospel narrators borrowing Greek legends. (53)

Clement of Alexandria (c.150–215 CE)

Clement is the second generation of Christian commentators defending Christianity as superior to all other studies by incorporating the powerful appeal of Gnosticism. Probably born in Athens where he studied philosophy, Clement converted to Christianity and traveled widely before eventually settling in Alexandria where, according to Eusebius, he headed a catechetical school. He left Alexandria about 202 when the persecution under the emperor Severus drove Christians from the city and went to Jerusalem and then Caesarea before settling in Antioch where he died.

His principal work known as *Stromateis* (miscellanies) is the largest and most complete Christian writing from this period. It reads like a series of sermons or programs for initiates to the faith. (54) These writings are not only miscellaneous in name but in content. The one coherent theme is his interpretation of Gnosticism to indicate that the true knowledge is knowledge of Christ and that the philosophy of the Greeks is preparatory to faith.

Clement was the most notable theologian to systematize Christian and Greek Platonic thought. Not distinguishing myth from faith, he thought Greek mythical and religious ideas inferior and, like an early Christian Puritan, condemned the stories, mysteries, amorous gods, idolatry, licentiousness and festivals marking Greek life. He quotes over 300 Greek authors whose works are otherwise unknown. He castigates the Greeks for copying each other's works, calls them thieves, and reveals their propensity for plagiarism. (55) He brazenly asserts that the best of Greek wisdom and its virtues were taken from the Hebrews, and claims that the gospel was preached to Jews and Gentiles alike in Hades. He writes: "And the gnosis itself is that which has descended by transmission to a few, having been imparted unwritten to the Apostles. Hence, then, knowledge or wisdom ought to be exercised up to the eternal and unchangeable habit of contemplation." (56) In *Exhortation to the Greeks*, he writes: "How in the world is it that you have given credence to worthless legends...while the bright face of truth seems alone to strike you as deceptive, and is regarded with unbelieving eyes." (57)

Clement suggests that philosophy is the work of divine providence, one of the first Christians writers after Paul to link Greek with Christian thought. The Greeks, he maintains, provided "preparatory exercises" in philosophy for the true philosophy found only in Christ. Clement is one of the first in a litany of Christian theologians to argue that philosophy is the handmaiden of theology and a useful tool for finding God's truth, but not a helpful intellectual exercise in itself, a conclusion even students of philosophy might find agonizing and counter-intuitive. His arguments do not begin with philosophical premises or even with particular points about the five major schools of philosophy but with biblical quotations. His sole purpose in eulogizing philosophy is to emphasize that studies should be pursued solely to understand divine scripture better, "approving only the sort of investigation that strengthens our faith." (58) But this is a hasty and false appraisal since ancient Greek philosophers were the first to turn away from the use of gods as a premise in all intellectual pursuits and towards an analysis of the material and ethical world. Clement missed the point about the original purpose of Greek philosophers.

Clement does not describe the rituals of the mysteries, perhaps realizing that his readers were familiar with them, and has no sympathy for their followers. Paul preached to audiences who were well acquainted with Greek mystery rites and used symbolic terms easily incorporating them into his explanations of Christian teaching. (59) Clement had no difficulty in keeping the truths secret like the advocates of the mysteries. "It follows that we have to keep secret (quoting Paul in *I Cor.* 2:7) the wisdom which is imparted in the context of a mystery." (60) Clement would embolden fundamentalists and diminish intellectual activity. "We destroy arguments, and all the exalted attitudes raised against the knowledge of God. We take every thought prisoner, bringing it into subjection to Christ." (61)

With Clement, Christians became the first anti-intellectuals. As early as the 5th century BCE Euripedes was calling those who engaged in inquiry blessed because this activity harmed no one and helped us understand the structure of nature. Nearly a thousand years later, Augustine took a directly opposite view that he characterized as the "disease of curiosity," the temptation to try to discover the secrets of nature which he thought beyond human understanding. Paul too had similarly declaimed against the rational Greek tradition, except for the mystical side, and "the empty logic of philosophers." The spirit of investigation under institutional Christianity avoided inquiry and began an anti-intellectualism caused by the absolutism of Christian dogma as the only knowledge necessary. What the Greeks had unleashed as the search for knowledge was squelched by Christian faith that saw no need for inquiry except that which fostered devotion.

Clement was once admitted into the company of saints but was later purged when his Gnostic views, clearly contravening doctrinal belief, were perceived as heresy. He held an elitist view, that the gnosis was superior to material entities and that this was true of Jesus' body. (62)

In the space of about 150 years since the death of Jesus, Christianity as a religious movement in reform Judaism fused with the spirituality of Gnosticism and turned Jesus' parables and his ethical behavior into spiritual ideals. "It is our purpose to prove that the Gnostic alone is holy and pious and worships the true God in a manner worthy of him." (63) Clement raised the consciousness of incarnation of Christ to a new level of divine revelation and demonstrated how this deified humankind. (64) Moses would not have recognized, and not been able to understand, these radical changes to Yahweh's dispensation.

The Greek and Roman ideal of an ethical life and the examples of Pythagorean and stoic methods for leading lives in accordance with nature yielded in Clement's theological perspective to a life embodied in Greek Gnostic, transcendent ideas, a misapplication of the meaning of Logos and Judaic eschatological thought. Plato had been combined with Philo to produce a new synthesis and worldview based on metaphysical interpretations of who Jesus was and humanity's relationship with him. (65) Theology was born out of misguided philosophy that lost, neglected or forgot its origins in myth. By the 3rd century faith had supplanted allegory, Gnosticism replaced belief in the power of the material world, and natural ethics jettisoned for faith in the unknown. For succeeding centuries, the ascent of the soul curtailed the ascent of mind, caused sclerosis in art and literature and gave way to the dullness of theological speculation.

Science would henceforth bow before scripture and faith triumph over reason. The dogmatism that blinkered Christians for centuries, that pagan literature is irrelevant to God's message, closeted the intellectual exploration that can be both pleasurable and illustrative of the dynamism that possessed the inspired writings even of scriptural scribes.

Plotinus (205-270 CE)

Perhaps the most influential but abstruse of the ancient philosophers in the 2nd century, Plotinus expounded so systematically on the concept of soul that his theory became ingrained permanently into Christian doctrine although he was himself opposed to Christian belief.

He was a native of Egypt, studied at Alexandria, made his way to Rome where he opened a school of philosophy in 244 CE that attracted students and favorable notoriety. His principal work, *The Enneads*, a Greek word meaning a group of nines (Pythagoreans believed that nine, three times three, was a magical number) is a treatise explaining the attributes of the soul, the spiritual forces emanating from the Creator, and the release of sense experiences to attain a mystical vision of the Godhead. His writings are the most arcane of philosophies, an unwelcome but representative trait of this era when commentators substituted abstractions for art, literature, poetry and plays.

Plunging unaided into reading the works of Plotinus can leave you a little like those confused dwellers in Plato's cave before they saw the light. Plotinus is a follower of Plato, but having said as much, one must not indelicately or incautiously read modern terms into the ancient Greek philosophy of idealism he espoused. It takes enormous efforts of mental deconstruction to comprehend "The One," "The All Soul," "The Intellectual Principle" (which exists in God and man), "The Person of the Godhead," "The Supreme Wisdom," "The Superior of the Universe," each of which emanates from one or the other, and to distinguish these philosophical terms from adopted mystical understandings in Christianity. It isn't clear if these philosophical metaphors are essences, acts, thoughts, existences, or some combination. For Plotinus, The One, The Intelligence and the Soul, like the Father, Son and Holy Spirit, are the three principal existences from which all other existences emanate.

Plotinus assumes there is a soul. But unlike others who thought the body was evil, he thought the soul was evil because it was aligned with the evil body. "As the soul is evil by being interfused with the body and by coming to share the body's states and to think the body's thoughts, so it would be good, it would be possessed of virtue, if it threw off the body's moods and devoted itself to its own Act, the state of Intellection and Wisdom, never allowed the passions of the body to affect it, knew no fear at the parting of the body." (66)

His theory is unconvincing because it is so ethereal, subject to linguistic scrutiny but not observation or validation. Christianity followed philosophy's decline when it abandoned the senses and the rough beginnings of empirical science in Aristotle to pursue the ascetic ideal of a mystical soul degraded by the body. Plotinus exemplified this trend of the soul's imprisonment. He constructed a sublime theory, an intellectual *tour de force*, a mystical vision admirable in scope that was extremely influential among early Christians. Writers of monastic mysticism, like the medieval ascetics John of the Cross, Teresa of Avila, Bernard of Clairvaux, and the 20th century Thomas Merton wrote in terms which Plotinus would find acceptable.

By the time of gospel composition the Mediterranean world was thoroughly Hellenized and everyone literate schooled in its language and culture. Soon, however, the majority of Greek literature was irretrievable lost or destroyed in the fire of the library at Alexandria or the periodic purges of early Christian zealots and iconoclasts. We may never know the full extent of possible adoption of biblical scribes or gospel narrators from lost Greek sources. Mark writes not in a classical style but in the common or demotic language (*koine*) and idioms of the marketplace though he would have been educated and memorized portions of *The Iliad* and *Odyssey* and knowledgeable about the plays of Sophocles, Euripedes and Aristophanes, and the poetry of Pindar and Theocritus just like all students. (67) Ordinary language use made gospel narratives accessible to a literate audience, if not appealing to classical readers more accustomed to the prose style of someone like Thucydides. The great appeal of the gospels and epistles of Paul was in the acceptance of Roman authority and their incorporation into their writings of allegory, symbolism and known themes from classical literature.

Also by the time of the gospel compositions, Homer was still the poet to emulate. However, by as late as the 4th century BCE the pantheon of the gods Homer described had no motivating powers and the quest was to seek new meanings for the cosmos and humanity. Zeno tried to find a purpose in nature and persuaded followers to obey nature's harsh realities whatever they might entail. Diogenes rejected the world's values altogether. Plato sought refuge in higher realities one could only imagine but not perceive. Epicurus exhorted men to free themselves from superstition and that by locating virtue and a right balance with nature they could be happy. Aristotle carried on scientific experiments while positing a Final Cause, an unsatisfactory explanation to those who had always lived with anthropomorphic deities, even though Christian theology linked it with the rationality for God's existence. All of these intellectual adventures were in fact a rejection of the older Greek religious beliefs.

Into this whirlpool of energetic inquiry, the gospel narrators created the legends of Jesus based on heroic traits and Jewish prophetic ideals. To understand the religious flux generated in these first centuries imagine if the other apocryphal documents, not the canonical gospels, had been selected as authentic representations of the Christian message. Attempting to understand what Christianity was based on from all these writings conveys the same sense of ambiguity the first Christians experienced with variants in chronology, miracles, sayings, questionable philosophies and not just philosophies with questions, and events in the life of Jesus to reveal the nature of legendary narratives. Thus, in constructing the life of Jesus was born Christian hagiography ever after believed as biography.

CHAPTER TWELVE
CYRUS, MITHRAS AND JESUS

Persian mythic influences have been as influential in forming Christian theology and practices as has Greek philosophies. After overcoming the Babylonians, the Persian king Cyrus freed captive Hebrews to return to Palestine. We know of his conquests from the *Nabonidus Chronicle* dating from the middle of the 6th century BCE and parts of his life from Herodotus and Xenophon. Because Cyrus allowed the Jews to manage their customs and religious affairs throughout Palestine, hoping to create a buffer state between Persia and Egypt, he figures repeatedly and gratifyingly throughout the Bible. Cyrus is mentioned in 2 *Kings*, *Ezra*, *Isaiah* (40-48) who viewed him as God's appointed agent, and *Daniel*. (*Dan*. 6:28) (1) Moreover, the ancient Persian demi-god Mithras, who constitutes the second section of this chapter, provided architectural, organizational and ritual contributions to Christian modalities.

Parallels Between Cyrus and Jesus

Herodotus gave rise to generations of historians, including his near contemporary Thucydides. Both set precedents in writing history for Roman historians like Seneca, Pliny, and Plutarch and the Jewish historian Josephus (37-95 CE). Herodotus selected portions of actual events to capture the interests of his readers and reflect his biases. He wrote extensively on the life of Cyrus, whose descriptions of birth and childhood had a potent and direct influence on the gospels, such as the account of the slaughter of the innocents under King Herod.

According to Herodotus, the story of Cyrus' birth goes like this. Astyages, father of Cyrus, feared that his daughter, Mandane, whom he refused to marry off, would conceive a son who would rise up and overthrow him. Instead, he gave her in marriage to Cambyses, a Persian. Astyages concluded after a dream vision that his grandson Cambyses would replace him on the throne, so he contrived to have the child put to death as soon as it was born. "The purport of this vision, when explained in each particular by the Magi, the usual interpreters, terrified him exceedingly. The Magi, official royal interpreters of dreams and visions, had declared the vision to intimate that the child of his daughter should supplant him on the throne. They told the king to take the boy, remove him to his own house, and put him to death. Astyages then commanded a confederate named Harpargus to kill the child."(2)

Harpargus and his wife, simple shepherds, could not bring themselves to put the child to death. Unwilling to refuse the command of their king, they therefore gave the child to a herdsman saying that the king had commanded the herdsman, called Mithridates, to expose the child in the most unfrequented part of the mountains. Oddly, the herdsman's wife had also been in labor with a child the previous day, but it had died during birth. The wife of the herdsman persuaded her husband to expose instead the dead child she had delivered, and to raise the child given to them and no one would be the wiser. The herdsman agreed, and witnesses later verified that a dead child lay in the mountains and was properly buried. That child was Cyrus who was thus spared an arranged death. This legend is similar to the exposed infancy of Oedipus and Moses, and of course to the episode about Herod who reputedly killed all the infants of Bethlehem fearing a successor king foretold by the Magi.

The oracles at Delphi (for the Greeks) and at Cumae (for the Romans) stand in their respective cultures as decipherers of dreams and visions and fortune-tellers and soothsayers. Since there were no Magi resident in Palestine, Matthew has them fictionally journey to Bethlehem and then granted them their personal dreams and visions. "Being warned in a dream not to return to Herod, they went back to their own country by another way." (*Matt* 2:12)

Dreams and visions dictate prodigies and future events. The king fears that a newly born child will overthrow him. He commands the Magi to tell him the meaning of this dream and vision. He is horrified at the thought of a child supplanting him as king. He contrives to kill the child so there can be no possibility of the child coming of age and taking over his realm. The child is saved because of a warning delivered in a dream and because of the saving graces of a couple wanting a child. The child is delivered to a foreign place for safety. *Matthew* and *Luke* mimicked this legend of Cyrus in Herodotus.

A tyrant king has a vision that a child will succeed him as king and contrives to have the child put to death is a legend in Sophocles' *Oedipus*, the story of an abandoned child who does replace his king as father and marries his mother unwittingly. Confirming the prophecy, the child (Cyrus, Oedipus, Jesus) does grow up to be king. In Book II of Xenophon's history, Cyrus and his adopted father Cambyses meet a good omen when an eagle swept into view and went before them to lead the way. And they then crossed a threshold into a new country where Cyrus meets a relative, his uncle Cyaxares. The appearance of a bird is a regular portentous sign in all of ancient literature, especially in Homer.

A good omen. A father who is present. Meeting a relative. An emblematic bird that signals the way to go and leads the way. It's all in Herodotus and in the gospel episode of the baptism of Jesus. Jesus' father is pleased with him and sends the good omen: the flight of a dove. Jesus is baptized by his relative, his cousin John the Baptist. The symbolism of preparing for a battle in the legend of Cyrus is extended in the gospels to preparation for a religious mission. Both Cyrus and Jesus have their fathers present for this significant transition event, both have the symbol of a bird presenting divine presence and guidance, and both go to meet a relative.

Herodotus relates how Cyrus, when he was "at the age of ten years," was playing with boys his age and they chose him as their king even though he apparently was the son of a herdsman. He played the role and gave managerial positions to the other youths so they could administer his kingdom. The boys beat one of their playmates, the son of a nobleman, when he refused to do as the young Cyrus commanded. The boy's father sought out the son of the herdsman and requested that the king himself intervene, and Herodotus is quick to remind us that no one knew him as Cyrus then.

When called into the king's presence the young son of the herdsman, the future Cyrus, astounded the king with his willingness to accept the consequences of the actions of his playmates and youthful but regal subordinates. Astyages, the king, noticed the resemblance of the young boy to himself, his countenance and his royal manners, and the approximate age of his own son whose death he had arranged. The king agreed to let the boy live when the Magi concluded that in acting out the part of a king in a youthful drama, the future Cyrus had already fulfilled the prophecy.

The parallel of this legend concerning Cyrus is in Luke's account of Jesus remaining in the temple and astounding the elders by his wisdom. Jesus' reply to his parents, "Did you not know that I must be about my father's business," is indicative of a future kingly role. His mother is said to "ponder these words in her heart," as indeed those of us who read analogous passages likewise ponder the literary sources. According to Herodotus, "As Cyrus grew up, he excelled all the young men in strength and gracefulness of person." (3) And for Luke (2:40), "And the child grew and he was full of wisdom and the grace of God was upon him." Not only the legend is repeated but some of the Herodotus' phraseology.

But if Cyrus served as a literary exemplar, Mithras, a Persian semi-deity, was the template for the usurpation of divine attributes granted to Jesus.

Mithras, The Bull-Slayer

The Aventine Hill, one of Rome's famous seven hills surrounding the eternal city, has a sweeping view of the west along the Tiber River towards Ostia on the coast. During the Roman imperial period this was the luxury quarter of Rome and the Emperor Trajan (53–117 CE) built himself a private villa here. (4) On the site today stands the church of St. Prisca, named after a 2nd century Christian woman who used her home to entertain Christians. In the 1950s archaeologists uncovered a Mithraeum, or sanctuary devoted to the bull-slayer deity, Mithras, directly under the present church. According to inscriptions found on bricks from the site, the sanctuary was dedicated on November 20, 202 CE. The cult of Mithras had been a favorite among Roman soldiers and practiced everywhere throughout the empire until suppressed after Christianity was declared the state religion by Constantine in 325 CE. Another Mithraeum lies under the church of San Clemente in Rome. But who was Mithras, what was the cult and secret mysteries surrounding him, and why is he represented as killing a bull?

Mithras' religious cult originated in Persia and quickly became associated with the domination and worship of the bull. The first reference to him occurs in a treaty in the 14th century BCE between the Mitanni, an Aryan peoples living in upper Mesopotamia, and the Hittites, the dominant people in what is today south central Turkey. The great king of Pontus, Mithridates (132–163 BCE), took his name from this cult figure.

According to legend, Mithras had a miraculous birth, appeared from the face of a rock on December 25th while nearby shepherds heralded his birth. Immediately, he was hailed as a god who would bring about the people's salvation, a god of justice, truth and light. He performed many miracles while on earth. He ate sacred meals with his followers, chiefly bread and wine, symbolizing flesh and blood. After his death he ascended into heaven and is scheduled to return on the final day to judge the living and the dead. If this legendary story sounds familiar, it is because the heroic legends of ancient literature, many only recently discovered, have been repeated in the gospels. Moreover, when Jesus reputedly rises from the dead he emerges, born again, from a rock sepulcher, where, in fact, a rock too heavy to be moved by men is rolled away from the entrance by angels. It is the same kind of immoveable rock that the Cyclops in *The Odyssey* had to move from the entrance to his cave in order for Ulysses and his men to escape certain death. Supernatural or superhuman beings emerge in literature to assist protagonists escape death.

Mithras is always shown as a handsome youth with a divine-like countenance, often with a halo of light around his head as a symbol of his affinity with the deified sun. From sculptures from Gaul showing him in various poses, he wears a loose, knee-length tunic, girded at the waist, and his footwear is leather laced to the ankle. He is sometimes shown with a cape and his hat, purportedly Phrygian (today's Kurds in northern Iraq and Iran) in origin, is about 6 inches tall, with a round-pointed top, usually protruding or flapped forwards. His hair is a series of luxuriantly curly locks.

In the most famous legend, and in what is construed as a symbol of human suffering, Mithras one day saw an enormous white bull grazing. He wanted to capture the bull without killing it, and so mounted the bull and rode it until the bull collapsed then dragged it into his cave where he slit its throat with his dagger. He is shown in stucco and stone carvings with his left knee embedded in the upper torso of the kneeling bull's back thrusting his dagger upwards, or sometimes downwards, into the bull's neck while he tugs on the bull's nose or mouth. The blood of the bull is precious and has to be ritualistically drunk among devotees. The killing supposedly represents the act of creation and renewal, but also the ultimate domination of the bull, a high point in human civilization, whether or not associated with religious purposes.

A bull-slaying scene is represented in the equatorial summer constellations as perceived by the ancient world, and that he whom the Greeks called Orion is really Mithras. The figures in the Mithraeum sanctuaries conform to the astral constellations: Taurus (bull), Canis Minor (dog), Hydra (snake), Crater (cup), Corvus (raven), Scorpius (scorpion), and Leo (lion). (5) Here we place ourselves in the perspective of the ancient world, seeing the heavens as filled with minor deities revolving around the night sky. We know these constellations still by their ancient Babylonian designations.

One theory holds that Mithras' slaying of the bull represents the movement of Taurus, the bull in the night sky towards Aries the ram, viewed as a shift in equinoxes. The ancient world perceived the planets and stars revolving around the earth. The slaying of the bull by Mithras thus symbolizes that his power, coming from outside the visible sphere of the heavens, is so strong that it can causes shifts in the visible sky. Slaying the bull means that Mithras has caused the heavens to shift to the ram, the next astrological sign, and hence the bull is no longer in the ascendant. The season when Taurus descends below the level of the horizon in the night sky signals the end of winter and the beginning of spring. The cult of Mithras is a secret society based on astrological beliefs and not simply animal worship. Others make the case for the adoption of Mithras into the pantheon of Greek divinities and perhaps even of Greek origin, turning him into Apollo or Perseus, the slayer of Medusa.

This astral analogy is evident in Paul whose home town was Tarsus (Taurus?) and who writes in a *Letter to the Philippians*: "Our homeland is in the heavens, from where we also expect a savior...who will transform our humble bodies so as to resemble his glorious body, by means of the power which he has to subdue the entire universe." (6) The control of the cosmic forces is ascribed both to Mithras and Jesus. This longing for a celestial power capable of determining one's fate and control of human destiny persists in the belief in astrology and in astrological signs representing personality characteristics influencing human behavior.

The Mithras cult spread quickly throughout the ancient world, to India, Turkey and thence to Rome where it was enthusiastically adopted by Roman soldiers for the virility of its hero. According to the Roman historian and biographer Plutarch, the religion of Mithras came to Rome in 67 BCE culminating in widespread adoption when it was later suppressed after

Theodosius and Justinian. Religious shrines of Mithras have been found wherever Roman legions were stationed: in Romania, Yugoslavia, Italy, Germany, France and England. But prior to its suppression, the cult of Mithras, whose devotees were enlisted in the fight against good and evil, light and darkness, spread rapidly among the Roman soldiers serving on the borders of the empire, including outposts next to Hadrian's wall on the border with Scotland. Soldiers quickly identified with the cult's manly and military virtues.

Although several legends associated with Mithras, his birth from a rock, his command of water flowing from a rock (7), his ability to perform miraculous deeds, are extraordinary, it is his slaying of the bull in a cave that is the essence of the mystery cult of him and his veneration. This act of slaying a white bull was repeated annually in special ceremonies in sanctuaries that resemble the design of early basilicas, including a narthex where the shrine of Mithras was venerated. (8) The bull's death in this theology reputedly gave birth to the earth, the sky, the planets, all animals and plants.

Zoroaster was the first to dedicate a natural cave in honor of Mithras and others quickly adopted the custom of performing rites of initiation in caves and grottoes. (9) Subsequent sanctuaries of Mithras, true to the purpose of representing a cave, never developed into large and luxurious temples but remained simple locations where the faithful gathered to perform ceremonies as befits a religious cult that practiced austerity and simplicity as its chief characteristics. The form of early Christian churches adopted the same elongated building design throughout the Roman Empire until they too were supplanted by the towering elegance of Gothic churches in the Middle Ages pointing their spires heavenward, reversing the symbolism of the cave.

But in a similar fashion, Christian churches kept an altar at the far end of the shrine or sanctuary where the celebration of the ceremonies occurred. A font for holy water stood at the entrance of the Mithraeum, as it does today in Catholic churches. A perpetual fire was kept burning upon the Mithraic altars, as today the lighted candle in Catholic churches symbolizes the presence of the consecrated host. Both priests were clothed in sacerdotal robes, and each liturgy was accompanied by hymns and chants. Sunday was an especially holy day. The highest clerical rank of the Mithras sectaries is *pater patrum*, father, a designation used still for Catholic priests who alone are able to perform the functions of the sacraments.

The cult involved a pact, probably with blood, between the sun god Sol and Mithras showing how they were linked in the battle to do good and conquer evil. Mithras ascends in a chariot into the heavens at the end of his worldly deeds as, we are told, did Elijah. We may never know for certain the rites and ceremonies attached to this belief because the votaries were all sworn to silence about the mysteries and died with the secrecies intact. Over 500 representations of the bull-slaying scene exist, but no primary literature source.

Mithraism is a synthesis of previously cherished gods and middle eastern myths, having absorbed Zoroastrian beliefs, Syrian and Canaanite gods, prevailing philosophies of the separation of good and evil, idolatry, deification of nature, cosmological beliefs, popular religious sentiments, and ritual ceremonies which only the chosen few can perform. Christianity simply continued that religious tradition in its practices.

Before his ascension, Mithras finishes his sojourn on earth with a banquet in which he and Sol partake of the flesh of the bull. This bloodless sacrifice ritual was accompanied by offerings of incense, prayers and hymns. Archaeological artifacts portray the divine meal almost as often as the bull slaying. Initiates into the sacred mysteries partook of a similar meal, sitting along the raised platforms in the Mithraeum. In one painting from 220 CE from the Aventine Mithraeum, Sol and Mithras recline on a couch joining earthly followers in a meal. The divine presence is manifested while the followers and initiates into the mysteries perform the ceremonies in commemoration of the god's command to eat bull's flesh and drink its blood. When bull's blood was unavailable, bread and water and wine were also used. Initiates believed that by eating and drinking the bull's flesh and blood they would be born again. The Eucharistic ceremonies of Christianity, and similar quotes from John's gospel of sayings of Jesus, have unacknowledged similarities to Mithraic and Zoroastrian religious mysteries.

The initiate had to be a novice in training for the reception of the mysteries and to take a solemn oath never to reveal what he learned. A part of the initiation included blindfolding and a member walking behind and pushing the novice, or, in one scene, standing on his calves while the novice is kneeling. The ceremony of induction was performed by two dignitaries, one known as the father and the other as herald. Upon completion, the initiate was known as brother and the son of the father. There are a number of trials, including branding or tattooing for which the initiate had to demonstrate his courage, after which he becomes a regular member of the fraternity.

There were seven grades of initiation in the Mithraic code: raven, bride, soldier, lion, Persian, sun courier, father or high priest. Coincidentally, these conform to the then known seven planets. Not surprisingly, there are seven gradations, seven sacraments, of a person intent on assuming clerical office in the Roman Catholic Church, from initiate to the mysteries of faith with baptism, confirmation, clerical novice, lector, sub-deacon, deacon, to priest (father), at which stage one can perform the mysteries of bread and wine which turn into flesh and blood of the sacrificial lamb of God. The high priest, father, of the Mithras cult had as his symbols the Phrygian high hat, a dagger, a ring, and a staff, all closely resembling that of a Catholic bishop or abbot with his miter or liturgical headdress, crosier or staff, and bishop's ring for the faithful to kiss.

The London museum contains a marble carving of Mithras and a bull-slaying scene from the late 2nd to early 3rd century CE, surrounded by the 12 signs of the zodiac. An inscription reads (in Latin) "Ulpius Silvanius initiated into a Mithraic grade at Orange, France, paid his vow to Mithras." Nearby, another delicate carved head of Mithras rests. It dates from about 1,800 years ago and reveals the head and torso of a handsome youth, adorned with a Phrygian cap, averting his eyes from the bull slaying as, reputedly, eternal life flows from the bull. (You can take a virtual tour of a Roman shrine of Mithras at the website of the Newcastle Museum of Antiquities in England at http://museums.ncl.ac.uk/archive/.

At its height, the Roman emperor Diocletian in 307–308 CE dedicated an altar to Mithras as "benefactor of the empire" at a shrine east of Vienna. But after the reign of Commodus in 192 CE the triumph of the Mithraic mysteries was secure and emperors began affixing various titles to their name and became associated with the imperial protocol.

Pius, felix and *invictus* were terms associated with the cult of Mithras. The monarch was *pius*, or pious, because his devotion secured the continuance of special heavenly favors. He was *felix* or happy or fortunate because he was illuminated by the divine graces. He was *invicta*, or unconquerable because his legitimate authority did not allow him to suffer defeat at the hands of his enemies. Both *pius* and *felix* became imperial names taken by popes who later adopted the Roman terminology for their status that had been borrowed from this ancient Persian mystical belief. It was then only a slight step to assume that this divine prerogative extended from emperors to popes. The divine right of kings became the governing concept until overthrown by the Protestant Reformation and, later, the democratic concept of popular sovereignty.

Parallels Between Mithras and Jesus

If we begin with the birth of Jesus we encounter amazing parallels with Mithras. In a bas-relief found in the crypt of St. Clements in Rome, Mithras emerges from a rock under the shade of a sacred tree, on a birthday celebrated on December 25th, and in such humble beginnings only shepherds witnessed and heralded his miraculous entrance into the world. Mithras embodied the sidereal powers of the empyrean, the highest heaven beyond the planets, the true paradise symbolized by fire and light. In the Christmas story about Jesus, a star appears symbolizing fire and light. Magi, the Persian magicians, appear at Bethlehem to offer homage.

After a last supper shared with chosen companions, Mithras ascended into the heavens where he constantly protects his faithful devotees who piously serve him. The services included ritualistic washing with ablutions in a catharsis of purification (as Jesus washes the feet of the Apostles), abstinence from certain foods, to choose good over evil, and to resist the prince of darkness. The prince of darkness comes to Jesus in the desert and offers him, well, a devil's bargain in the form of a huge land grant that he refuses.

Followers of Mithras believed in the immortality of the soul and the resurrection of the body after death. Mithras will descend to earth and banish evil once and for all, separate the good from the bad, and offer them the divine beverage, bull fat with consecrated wine, and all souls will enter life everlasting. Since the most ancient times, blood is the embodiment of vital energy, a source of strength, and those who place it on their tongue are supposed to receive the courage of the slaughtered animal. "I tell you the truth, unless you eat the flesh of the son of man and drink his blood, you have no life in you." (10)

These parallels between the life, stories, rituals and doctrines of Cyrus, Mithras and Jesus are literary adaptations. Biblical scribes and evangelists were consciously attempting to link mythical religious figures to biblical figures and Jesus. Mithras discharging his arrows to draw water becomes Moses tapping the rock at Horeb to let water flow. One scholar has concluded that the Mithras cult heavily influenced Plato and his school. (11) The sun arising out of the ocean is Elijah ascending in a chariot of fire. Mithras holding the nostrils of the bull becomes Samson rending the lion. (Yet another exemplar for the Samson and Delilah myth is Antaeus, the giant son of Gaia and Poseidon. He wrestled with all strangers who came to his country, Libya, and either defeated or killed them. He was invincible for as long as he remained in contact with the earth, his mother who gave him his strength. Hercules discovered his secret and lifted Antaeus from the ground, from the power of his mother, and then crushed his ribs, just as the Hebrews sought to crush the Philistines).

Who is it that purifies themselves through a baptism, who receives a power to combat the forces of evil or the devil, who expects, by eating the Lord's supper, to be granted access to eternal life, who holds Sunday sacred, who celebrates December 25th (*natalis invicta*), who has a firm code of ethics embedded in forms of asceticism, abstinence, continence, and self-control, who will be judged on the last day by their actions, who believes in the existence of heaven and hell peopled by demons, who sees their god as savior and intermediary?

Mithraism reached its apex about the middle of the third century, just about the time Christianity was declared the official state religion by Constantine whose successors, with the exception of Julian (331–363 CE) were openly hostile to the Mithraic worshippers and indeed to all other beliefs then and now universally known as pagan, a word of odious religious disapproval originating from a harmless Latin word that means country dweller.

Do these resemblances imply imitation or caricature, as the religious similarities could have passed effortlessly from one cult to the next as religious doctrines and rituals passed from generation to generation? Legends of Mithras were borrowed by gospel evangelists to enhance the stature of the life of Jesus. They adopted the Mithraic stories of the shepherds at the birth, the appearance of a star, the setting of the nativity as December 25th, the winter solstice, the waters of life, the rock of the church, the fire of the divine spirit or holy ghost, the communion service and sacrifice, ascension into heaven, immortal life, divine judgment in the formation of gospel narratives. Sacraments, vestments, priestly orders, church structure, as well as the doctrinal issues were folded into ecclesiastical ritual, liturgy and doctrine.

CHAPTER THIRTEEN
GNOSTICISM

I am Poimandres, the Mind of the Sovereignty... I know what you wish, for I am with you everywhere; keep in mind all that you desire to learn and I will teach you. (1)

In 1945 a camel driver with his brother went to a cliff near Nag Hammadi, a village in Northern Egypt to dig for nitrate-rich fertilizer. They came across a large clay jar buried in the ground and, suspecting that it might contain gold or something of value. They also feared that it might contain an evil spirit. In fact, the jar contained a library of Gnostic documents of 51 different works on 1,153 pages over 1,700 years old. Of these, the *Gospel of Thomas*, a collection of the sayings of Jesus recorded early in the Christian era and translated into English during the late 1960's, is the most notable. Written in Greek during the second and third centuries CE, these documents were translated into Coptic during the early 4th century, and apparently buried about 365. (2) The discovery of the scope and variety of these documents illustrates the pervasiveness of Gnostic elements in literature in the first three centuries and the mysticism that appealed to early Christian communities.

Gnosticism was a pre-Christian movement that infiltrated Christian thinking. In time, when dogma was clarified and the movement became too closely associated with orthodox Christianity, it became subject to the treatment accorded other heresies. (3) Gnosticism was a threat to ecclesiastical authorities because its power came from personal visions and not from bishops. The active intellectual climate that produced Gnosticism cloaked the interpretation of early Christianity and compelled apologists to see Jesus and his message with Christian eyes but through a Gnostic prism.

No key individual epitomized the Gnostic movement and no single philosopher represented the source of its popularization. Rather, Gnosticism is a literary dialogue, an intellectual conversation thriving on an esoteric and transcendent understanding of the world. John's gospel and *Revelations* are testaments to its influence. Original Gnostic works were freely circulating in the first two centuries of the common millennium. But partly because of the calumny heaped about authors like Menander, Saturninus, and the Ophites, Gnostic documents and books have been lost or destroyed by Christians eager to preserve doctrinal purity by eliminating competing heretical texts.

Gnostics believed that spirit is good and of divine origin, that the self is alienated from God, and that the body is inherently earthly and under the power of the demiurge promoting evil. They believed that trapped within people's bodies were the sparks of divinity or seeds of light that were supplied to humanity by Sophia, the goddess of wisdom. A person attains salvation by learning secret knowledge of spiritual essence with the opportunity to escape from the prison of their bodies at death. Their soul can ascend to be reunited with the Supreme God at death. They did not look upon the world as having been created perfectly and then having degenerated as a result of the sin of Adam and Eve. The world was seen as being evil at the time of its origin, having been created by an inferior God. Historians believe that Gnostics were solitary practitioners. Christian monks, borrowing from Gnostic ideals and the communal and ascetic life of the Essenes, would popularize the contemplative search for mystical union, intuitive knowledge and enlightenment about divine mysteries.

The Cistercian or Trappist Order, a part of the Rule of St. Benedict, sponsors a monastic life whose agenda is contemplative. Its most illustrious 20th century spokesman was Thomas Merton (1915–1968) who wrote: "Contemplation is always beyond our own knowledge, beyond our own light, beyond systems, beyond explanations, beyond discourse, beyond dialogue, beyond our own self. To enter into the realm of contemplation one must in a certain sense die: but this death is in fact the entrance into a higher life." (4)

Gnosticism slowly merged with Judaic and Christian ideas to form beliefs in the Sophia myth, asceticism, an ascendant soul, the search for knowledge leading to a higher wisdom limited to a select few or the elect (Coptic in Greek, still the term used to identify Egyptian Christians), and the return of the "healer." Gnostic Christians saw the inner life of wisdom, the spiritual vision of the church, as the most relevant aspect of Christianity. On the other hand, orthodox Christians without a Gnostic persuasion placed their faith in an ecclesiastical hierarchy. With the backing of its military, Christian Rome imposed the accepted ecclesiastical view until Martin Luther initiated the return of multiple forms of Christian beliefs based on personal faith.

For Christians, moral evil was the result of individual choice in relation to the laws of God, not the cosmic universe. Whereas Christians believed that sin was transgression against the law of God and evil was perpetrated by mankind, Gnostics saw evil as inherent in nature and in demons, in human bodies originating in the creation of the universe. In Gnostic systems, human beings are a combination the forces of light and darkness, spirit and matter, good and evil, as cosmic forces (expressed as good and bad angels) hostile to God and responsible for the plight of humanity. Salvation is accomplished when individuals find and hold the uncontaminated divine in them. (5)

Gnostic beliefs, like that of a savior, divine grace, devils in competition for souls, have become so assimilated into Christianity that it is difficult to disentangle the original from the adopted. The rejection of bodily pleasures, the practice of asceticism, the aspiration to a perfect knowledge, and the desire for direct knowledge of the divine are a part of Gnostic belief prior to the advent of Christianity that, like the stern gaze from a Byzantine icon, now thoroughly resonates with these themes. (6) The Gnostic way in various guises permeated the ideology of the Mediterranean world in the first two centuries as Christian defenders like Iraeneus, Clement, Tertullian, Hippolytus and Jewish rabbis branded it as blasphemous and perilous to faith.

Literary motifs like a journey, a stranger, visitor or messenger, a hidden treasure like a pearl, are symbols and metaphors for Gnostic experiences. The medieval John of the Cross used the metaphor of *The Dark Night of the Soul*, his book describing his adventures in mysticism and descent into depression. The parable of the Prodigal Son relates how a young man receives an inheritance, leaves home on a mission, falls prey to worldly pleasures, wastes his fortune, returns to his father who receives him joyously, clothes him richly and spoils him. Likewise, embedded in *The Acts of Thomas* we find the *Hymn of the Pearl*, the story of a prince sent to Egypt (the evil place, symbolic of the house of pleasure) by his father to recover a pearl. (7) He succumbs to worldly pleasures, forgets his assignment and has to be reminded by a messenger, recovers the pearl, puts on a royal cloak and returns to his country. The *Hymn* is a parable open to Gnostic interpretation, just as is the Prodigal Son, a parable probably adopted from the *Hymn*, of the soul is lost in its wanderings, losing sight of its bearing, and needs a divine messenger, symbol of the divine utterances, to awaken the memory of one's origin and life's meaning.

Gnosticism is modified from Hindu and Platonic thought, an inner awakening of true knowledge that had a wide appeal to those interested in getting in touch with the divine more immediately. For Plato this meant getting in touch with one's soul. (8) One can see the embryonic origins of Gnosticism and Christian asceticism, each viewing the body as an encumbrance, imprisoned, a hindrance to be punished to free the divine.

The Gospel of Truth, dating from before 180 CE, was one of those short Gnostic documents found at Nag Hammadi that failed to get included in the canon. It was possibly composed by Valentinus (c.135–c.160), a brilliant Gnostic expositor. Valentinus believed that Christ appeared in the world to reveal the knowledge that would restore mankind to a divine order. *The Gospel of Truth* in its opening sentence expresses an inner knowledge that represents this belief. "The gospel of truth is joy for those who have received from the Father of truth the grace of knowing him, through the power of the Word that came forth from the *pleroma*, the one who is the thought and the mind of the Father, that is, the one who is addressed as the savior." (9)

Here are some comparative examples of Gnostic and Orthodox Christianity.

ORTHODOX CHRISTIANTY	GNOSTIC CHRISTIANITY
God made the world good and sin corrupted it	the material world originated because of conflict in heaven
Christ died for the sins of all for salvation	Christ brought salvation bringing truth to set the soul free
faith in Jesus brings salvation; God redeems the sinful world	salvation comes from knowledge; saving knowledge comes to souls entrapped in the world
bodily resurrection	resurrection of the spirit (10)

The mysticism of Gnostics, those literally "in the know," the spiritual elite, perplexed the advocates of gospel purity and their interpretation of the message of Jesus. The argument over what constituted orthodox belief prevailed until the third century when bishops ruled dioceses like Roman officials and an ecclesiastical hierarchy controlled doctrine by condemning heresies. Christianity inherited monastic asceticism from the Essenes, Greek mystery cults and Gnostic influences to attain some measure of the divine. Select Christian mystics have described their experiences, like John of the Cross, Teresa of Avila, the medieval mystic Hildegard of Bingham, or 20th century contemplatives like Thomas Merton.

For humans to become divine without acquiring *hubris*, in classic epics like the *Iliad* or *Aeneid*, was the privilege of one who either had copulated with a god or goddess or was born of such a union. One could somehow mentally shuck off the burden of the body and let the divine principle seek human unity, or permit the godhead to mystically enter the person, preserving individuality while condensing the distance between human and divine by providing the human with a new religious identity. Doesn't it make sense that having once been separated from the divine by a fall from grace, and having experienced life without a divine consciousness, that it should be a part of human existence to seek to return to a life once lost? This was both the Gnostic Christian and Orthodox Christian quest. (11) "The Lord possessed me in the beginning of his way, before his works of old. I was set up from everlasting." (*Proverbs* 8:22).

The pseudo- Denis, the so-called Areopagite, a 6th century Syrian monk, wrote a series of books proposing a mystical and Neo-Platonic vision to the Christian message. Denis surrounded the gospel meaning with a cloak of mystical fabric in which words were incapable of exposing the real truths and symbols behind them. The liturgical rites were "sacred veils" that hid ineffable meanings and divine powers only able to be apprehended through prayer and meditation. Plato had called such an experience *theoria*, contemplation.

But in order to achieve some forms of divine intimation, Gnostic intermediaries were needed, like demiurges, demons, former gods and sons of god, called upon to assist in the divine achievement. The expression of God, the *Nous* or Mind for the Platonists and Gnostics, and the *Logos* or Word for the Christians, became those divine intermediaries who would liberate humans from the disputatious universe of life's shadows. Philosophical abstractions, just like natural forces and animal representations for ancient people, had assumed the powers of divinity. Transcendence is beyond human apprehension, yet the human intellect and psyche searches for the unquenchable, like Tantalus relentlessly reaching for the unobtainable fruit.

In the *Corpus Hermeticum* dating from the end of the 1st century CE, Hermes, the messenger of the gods, has a vision of the divine when the shepherd god, Poimandres, appears to him, then changes his appearance. "Even with these words His aspect changed, and straightway, in the twinkling of an eye, all things were opened to me, and I see a Vision limitless, all things turned into Light, sweet, joyous Light. And I became transported as I gazed." Poimandres then lets Hermes know his secret. "That Light, He said, am I, thy God, Mind, prior to Moist Nature which appeared from Darkness; the Light-Word (Logos) that appeared from Mind is Son of God. What then, say I? Know that what sees in thee and hears is the Lord's Word (Logos); but Mind is Father-God. Not separate are they the one from other; just in their union rather is it Life consists." (12)

Similar quotes reveal the Gnostic view of the world, part of which has been derived from Persian dualism:

> *The word of the lord is the mind of God the Father; one cannot be separated from the other for their union is life.* (CH, pp. 8-9).

> *The intellect is the source of knowledge of God's goodness. Goodness does not exist in the world; the world is the totality of evil.* (*Ibid.*, p. 74)

> *Terrestrial man is a mortal god; celestial god is an immortal man. Through the intermediary of the world and man, all things exist, but all other things are produced by the One.* (Ibid., p. 126)

> *The human intellect is a part of God's substance.* (Ibid., p. 173)

Calypso, daughter of Atlas whose name means the concealer, who entertained Ulysses in Homer's *Odyssey* for seven years on the island of Ogygia, is an immortal Greek goddess who represents the light and dark duality in nature and people. Like Atlas, she is a mediator between heaven and earth, and between the world of the living and dead. She promised Ulysses immortality if he would remain with her but he refused. Instead, he built a boat and sailed home to Ithaca.

Whether demi-gods in Greek myths, angels, devils or prophets in the Bible or Jesus in the gospels, mythical revealers, messengers, or witnesses, are invariably accompanied by cosmic signs, storms at sea, polymorphous shapes, luminosities, epiphanies, dark skies, birds, even earthquakes. For Gnostics, John the Baptist is the messenger. The risen Jesus is the revealer. Gnostics looked upon Christ as a revealer or liberator, rather than a savior or judge. His purpose was to spread knowledge that would free individuals from demiurge control and allow people to return to their spiritual home. The real challenge to evolving Christian doctrine came from consolidated communities of thought, like the Docetism advocates who claimed that the Christ figure was a spiritual phantom who only appeared to be mortal, or the Ebionites who claimed that Christ was a distinct person from Jesus.

But some Christian writers whose works have survived condemn Gnostic writers using transcendent words and concepts to denounce them. Irenaeus (c. 125–202), one of the first to systematize Christian doctrine in Greek, and saw philosophy as the source of all errors. By 180 CE, Irenaeus denounced all gospel works except *Matthew, Mark, Luke* and *John*. Thereafter, all Gnostic writings were considered heretical.

Tertullian (c.160–230), a Christian convert and Roman theologian was the most vigorous apologist in Latin and formidable defender of Christianity of his era who saw philosophy as a corruption and devoid of truth. Tertullian did not view the Gnostics as much of a threat to orthodoxy Christianity, devoting only 29 pages to refuting them, as he did the Marcionites to which he penned five books covering 311 pages, calling Marcion every pejorative name short of obscenity. (13) He repeatedly called Gnostics the "sting of the scorpion," and in refuting them added little logic but much invective and polemic. You would not be able to learn much about the tenets of Gnosticism from reading his diatribe, only that he didn't like them.

Clement of Alexandria, as we saw, attempted to synthesize Christian and Platonic thinking, an endeavor Augustine accomplished more successfully. Often classified as a Christian Gnostic, he attacked Gnosticism while trying to reconcile Christianity with contemporary thought. Clement wrote that the Logos, the divine teacher, led the initiate through a moral purification to a higher wisdom, or *gnosis*. Knowledgeable in Greek thought, Clement's intent is similar to Aristotle's ideal of a perfectly good man in the *Ethics* and the wise man in the stoic code. (14)

John's gospel contains the most relevant symbolism between Christianity and Gnosticism: "And the Word was made flesh." (*John* 1:14) The Word is John's interpretation of the Gnostic divine messenger assuming human form.

The Greek Logos is the Thought of God, a Gnostic interpretation of the conception of Jesus. The idea of a god impregnating a woman, especially a virgin, was a common myth among Hellenes. A transformed god who assumes human shape, who comes as a messenger, redeemer and savior, who is the Logos generated by the eternal *Nous*, the only begotten son who rises again to divine status, that is the thoroughly Gnostic perspective assimilated into Christian dogma. There is a hint of Gnostic understanding in *1 Corinthians* where Paul comments: "We know that we all have knowledge. Knowledge puffs up, but character edifies. If anyone thinks that he knows anything, he has not yet known as he ought to know." (15)

Another notable of this period was Nestorius (c.385-451), Patriarch of Constantinople, who, in believing that Jesus was two persons with two natures, one divine and one human, dutifully received all the vitriol orthodoxy could produce: condemnation by Pope Celestine I and Cyril, Patriarch of Alexandria, the alienation of friends and supporters, anathema and exile. The Council of Ephesus (431) and the Council of Chalcedon (451) pronounced Jesus true God and true man, or one person with two natures, a distinction of mythic heroes Greeks could applaud but Christians would ever after have to ascribe to under pain of excommunication. Prior to the ascent of political power of Christianity under Roman rule, the church of necessity had to concede dissent. Later, it proscribed all unorthodoxies and destroyed incriminating writings. Christian fanatics left nothing but the shelves in the great library of Alexandria when they stormed it in 387, though the city remained the greatest center of intellectual activity where Syrian and Arabian, Greek and Roman, Egyptian and African met, conversed, wrote, mingling cultures, ideas and writings.

These doctrines played havoc with Paul's belief in the resurrection of the body (*Rom.* 6:4), an idea culled from Egyptian beliefs in bodily immortality. Still, as a counter to the perpetual tug between the body and soul, Peter writes that baptism is "the putting off of the filth of the flesh," an odd description of an organism to become ennobled through resurrection, but a very Persian and Gnostic interpretation. (16) Gnostic texts reveal that there was a broad range of beliefs among the various independent Gnostic systems or schools. This group believed that they alone understood Christ's message and that other streams of thought within Christianity had misinterpreted Jesus' mission and sayings.

As an intellectual and religious movement, Gnosticism attempted to synthesize Christian and a few less offensive Jewish beliefs into its cosmology. Some believed the Demiurge was separate from the Supreme God of the Jews and Christians. Others thought of Jesus was the Demiurge personified. Some thought of Judaism as a preparation for Christianity. Others were hostile to that idea and believed Christianity was merely a branch of

Judaism. Gnostics could find deeper and more esoteric meanings in the parables of Jesus. Paul would implicitly reject the Gnostic interpretation that philosophy could substitute its knowledge for the simple truths contained in the gospels (*Col*, 2: 8-9 and I *Tim*. 1:4). From the 3rd century Gnosticism and philosophy capitulated to theology as proponents like Irenaeus and the intolerant Tertullian vigorously defended Christian truths while vitiating adversaries. In their writing zeal, early Christian patristic apologists obscured and distorted the meanings of Gnostics the better to vilify and lampoon them.

Hindu Roots

The sacred Hindu script, the *Bhagavad Gita*, was composed about 800–600 BCE, about the same time as the initial books of the Bible, and contains several passages eluding to secret wisdom, meditation and enlightenment, the keys to Gnostic beliefs. Two quotes illustrate the themes. "When the mind, that may be wavering in the contradictions of many scriptures, shall rest unshaken in divine contemplation, then the goal of Yoga is yours. Seers in union with wisdom forsake the rewards of their work, and free from the bonds of birth they go to the abode of salvation." (17) For Hindus, this wisdom of spiritual understanding also exists in the divine One, Krishna, who says: "For my glory is not seen by all: I am hidden by my veil of mystery: and in its delusion the world knows me not, who was never born and forever I am." (18)

Likewise, the *Upanishads* composed between 800–400 BCE, contain passages eerily similar to those found in Gnostic and Gnostic Christian writings. "He who sees, knows, and understands this, who finds in Atman, the Spirit, his love and his pleasure and his union and his joy, becomes a Master of himself. His freedom then is infinite." (19) "But if, with the three sounds of the eternal *OM*, he places his mind in meditation upon the Supreme Spirit, he comes to the regions of light of the sun. There he becomes free from all evil, even as a snake sheds its old skin...he goes to the heaven of Brahma wherefrom he can behold the Spirit that dwells in the city of the human body and which is above the highest life." (20) *The Upanishads* declare meditation, the search for the spirit world, for immortal life, the avoidance of sense experiences as the highest of all life's goals. It is easy to see how these ideas and writings could have influenced subsequent writers and seekers of spiritual and mystical life.

All religions have believers who seek a natural form of consciousness, not a formal, intellectual philosophy that enlightens them about God and the secrets of the universe. Mystical searches for understanding arise from time to time often as a spiritual response to a personal and national traumatic experience, like the Ghost Dance among the Sioux Indians in the 1890s, or as a reaction to a strict interpretation of religion.

Modern Gnostic Movements
Similar mystic strains exist in the Kabbala that traced its origins to oral traditions from Abraham. This mystical cult group contains the secret teachings of the Jews, where traces of Gnosticism are in the Zohar, the *Book of Light*, a mystical commentary on the Torah, which taught believers how to seek the inner meanings of the Torah just as the Gnostics sought the inner meanings of spiritual existence. (21) Kabbala is grounded on Neoplatonic assumptions about other-worldly existences, that life could be simpler if one understood the secrets of how God operates in the world. Like Pythagoras, adherents sought these secrets in numerology and obscure meanings hidden in alphabetic letters and wore amulets to ward off evil, often symbolized as the evil eye.

The difference is that adherents of the Kabbala still believe in the obligations of *mitzvoth*, the traditional forms of Judaism and that one has to engage in a commitment to the Torah and the *halacha*, the Jewish law before committing to mystical beliefs. Many believe each commandment has a mystical meaning. The sect has typically been open only to married, observant Jewish men schooled in the core texts of Judaism, although rock stars have popularized one of its symbols, the red string bracelet. Kabbalah is a spiritual quest like Gnosticism that tempts believers to explore life's purposes through physical and spiritual realities in the universe. Once in touch with the principles of the universe one can obtain peace and understanding. The Kabbalah arose during a period when Christian mysticism received great impetus from Bonaventure (1221-1274). (22)

The Gnostics are the ancient precursors of medieval and modern occultism, like the Templars, the Masons, Rosicrucians, and scientologists and visionaries like William Blake. Scientology, founded by L. Ron Hubbard (1911-1986) a science fiction writer in his early career, proclaims to be a religion whereby modern technology is applied to learning about the spirit that governs everyone. Scientology reputedly investigates the higher states of spiritual being. This "dianetics" technique has been reputedly borrowed from all the great religious movements, as noted in its literature and web sites, except that it neglects to mention Gnosticism, a movement it clearly resembles and derives is objectives from. Scientology operates The Delphi Schools Network, with locations in several states in the U.S. Like ancient Greek mystery rites, it maintains secrecy about its teaching until a member is recruited. Its members have been found guilty of fraud in courts in the U.S., England, Australia, Canada, Greece, France, Ireland, Spain of masquerading as mental health workers but without qualifications, of siphoning funds from the guileless, of violence against opponents and violating the civil rights of members.

A 20th century new age, space age kind of Gnosticism is the Urantia Foundation, a group which believes that the earth, known as urantia, is just one of many similar inhabited planets making up a super-universe, a central Gnostic tenet. This religion has no priesthood, no missionaries. The 2,093 page tome, *Urantia Book* (1955), whose authors are said to be extra-terrestrial beings, seeks to explain various religious movements, who add new material to existing religions and debunk Christian beliefs. Its appeal is primarily intellectual and offers mystical hope to people who await a benevolent future. (23)

The Catholic Apostolic church of Antioch, Malabar rite, is a mystically-oriented religion with about 3.5 million members worldwide. Churches are often referred to as Chaldean and use the Syriac language. Some groups use a liturgy resembling the Catholic Mass but with an emphasis on a direct approach to seeking God. Members of the approximately 25 congregations in the United States, walk in procession with icons representing enlightened beings. The origin of this rite dates to the Apostle St. Thomas who reputedly Christianized parts of Kerala province in southern India. Its combination of the cosmic dimensions of Christ and its meditative format blends Indian mysticism with Gnostic roots. Alternative congregations omit the Eucharistic celebration completely and hold no creedal beliefs. Its web site is: (www.churchofantioch.org).

Extreme forms of Gnosticism exist. The bodies of 39 men and women in sport shoes took their own lives in a mass suicide in San Diego on March 26, 1997. This cult group known as Heaven's Gate was led by Marshall Applewhite who believed that a flying saucer with heavenly spirits was traveling behind the Hale-Bopp comet and that members had to leave their physical bodies behind to find redemption in an extraterrestrial "Kingdom of Heaven" by joining them spiritually.

Gnosticism was a major intellectual challenge to Christianity. The Gnostic mind readily incorporated young but ill-formed Christian beliefs, while Christianity only adopted Gnosticism with hesitation. John's gospel and *Revelations* were a response to, and acceptance of, Gnostic knowledge in Christianity. Although parts of its roots are traceable in later Christian belief, like the higher wisdom attainable in mystic contemplation or in heaven, the Gnostic reputation relies less on its persuasive vigor than its successful suppression by state and clerical authorities. The view that eventually prevailed was that Judaism and Christianity maintained separate religious identities and all other religions were branded unorthodox. Heterodoxy, the great flowering of the world before Christianity, when deities had no theology and multicultural religions were practiced in conjunction with state obligations, fell from grace and everyone not a Christian became a heathen.

By the 4th century CE the church, borrowing its hierarchical nature from the Roman organizational structure and military apparatus, including the sacerdotal dress of priests and bishops and other Mithraic practices, prevailed over Gnostic beliefs by using its imperial power to silence dissenters. Within a hundred years of defining its dogma, the established church, having borrowed philosophical terms like substance, being, nature, person and used them to form a theology that stretched the boundaries of ordinary thought, admitted into communion only those who accepted its doctrines without equivocation, ordered all apocryphal books burned and heretical tendencies purged. It maintained a rigid grip on all western society's beliefs and behaviors by displacing diversity in religious experiences and stifling intellectual discourse and aesthetic expression until the Renaissance a thousand years later.

THE SOUL AS A DOVE IMPRISONED IN THE BODY

CHAPTER FOURTEEN
CHRISTIANITY AND FIRST CENTURY IDEOLOGIES

Christianity assimilated all the religious and mythical sagas, legends and epics of Egypt and Western Asia, molded their curious peculiarities into a dynamic synthesis and used the full weight of imperial authority to invest the western mind. Christianity would not have emerged if pagan polytheism had been intolerant and unreceptive to a multitude of beliefs that incorporated all persuasions into its expansive pantheon. There is no reference in any Jewish writings prior to 70 CE of Christians or of a Christian movement. Despite painstaking scholarship there is no text suggesting the *Dead Sea Scrolls* contain specific Christian allusions or messages. Apparently the history of Christianity begins with the first writings of Paul and the canonical and non-canonical gospels about the Jesus movement. These writings alone, either for want of undiscovered texts or their extermination to preserve religious orthodoxy, constitute the only testimony of this embryonic religious group in the 1st century. As we've seen thus far, it's a fabled literary history.

Christianity evolved from a parochial Judaic reform movement into a missionary movement primarily because of the proselytizing of Paul and the transforming document of the *Acts of the Apostles* that supported Gentile conversion. As widely differing opinions and communities generated doctrinal discord and varying beliefs about who Jesus was, the imperial court tried to mitigate growing discord and convened councils to settle differences, always unsatisfactorily. Then under Constantine and Theodosius, after granting the clergy state privileges, the emperor imposed imperial rule to silence dissenters fomenting civil unrest because of theological differences.

Christianity in the 1st century was a separate religious movement from its origins among the Jerusalem disciples known as Nazarenes. Documents existing prior to the imperial establishment of Christianity provide a broad understanding of the religious context of the era ideologically removed from the political, social and literary life of the Augustan age. Christianity percolated throughout the Roman world primarily because it broadened its borrowings both from Judaic scripture and extra-biblical narratives and myths to create a heroic figure and a visionary message woven with apocalyptic content suited to contemporary readers. Gospel scribes created devotional biographies of Jesus from epic episodes to interpret his life and mission as an epic hero. In a time of confusion and intense persecution, each gospel is a response to convince followers of the legendary view of Christ's meaning and a response to a growing number of theological adversaries.

If you were to write even a short epic you would include an extraordinary birth and/or parentage of the hero, an incipient and then prolonged struggle against real or perceived adversaries, the gathering of colleagues who would journey with you, close encounters with enemies who seek your death, separations, miraculous escapes, reunions and all under the umbrella of God's favor. Such themes are the stories of Cyrus, Ulysses, Aeneas, Moses and Jesus. All are heroes and the stories written about them are epic adventures.

If the gospel writers had chosen to write history, there were scores of historians from which to derive precedents. Plutarch (c.45–90), whose *Parallel Lives of Famous Greeks and Romans* contains the biographies of 46 eminent individuals, set an unrivaled standard for historical biographies. Herodotus wove a pattern of legends, rituals, heroic figures and anecdotes into his histories. Livy used portents just like the gospel narrators used miracles to show how history can be predictable and fate unbending. Tacitus is loose with the facts but his moralizing tone could have been a credible example for gospel themes. Josephus records the war of the Romans against the Jewish revolt with evidence unknown without his eyewitness accounts. There are no external sources to validate the claims of the gospels and little confirmatory evidence of the Christian movement in the Roman world in the 1st century. The exceptions are correspondence between Pliny and Vespasian about Christian incitements in Asia Minor, a pessimistic note by Tacitus in his histories, and some writings by Origen and other commentators. (1) *The Dead Sea Scrolls* are one example of extra-biblical set of documents from the era when Jesus lived and provide understanding of the eschatological and legalistic context of Jewish zealotry leading to the Jewish revolt in 66 CE, about the time when Mark's gospel was written. (2)

Though separated monastically from temple practices in Jerusalem, the Essenes, as we saw, sought a religious reform and revolutionary change in their writings and lifestyle, their outlook and temperament likely shaped by the Maccabean revolt (167–135 BCE) and zealots who opposed Roman rule. For example, the term "Way" as a form of life appears frequently in the scrolls and becomes an alternate designation of Christianity. Like other Asian mystical writings, the scrolls also reveal how initiates will seek and obtain mystical insights. (3) "The Way" or *Tao* is also a term in the *Tao Te Ching* of Lao-Tzu and denotes a practice of following the balance found in nature.

The main events of the life of Jesus as described by the narrators occurred roughly in the years 28–30 CE. An oral tradition of his life, notoriously inaccurate and subject to legends, likely followed from those who knew him. But there are no written records about his life for the next 40+ years after his death, beyond the lifetime of most eyewitnesses. Peter's epistles written from Rome do not mention episodes in the life of Jesus but only the glory of the transcendent Christ. Peter urges communities to live blameless lives and await the coming of the last days, and he castigates those who deny the Second Coming and the end of the world, a minor rebuke of the Jerusalem congregation that did have such an apocalyptic vision. Then, after 70 CE when Romans destroyed the Temple of Jerusalem and the cult of temple worship, the writings of the evangelists began to emerge. (4)

Most scholars agree that the gospels are not authentic representations of the life of Jesus. The narrators used existing literary sources, symbols and allegories, phrases and episodes, to interpret the life of Jesus for their congregations. (5) By the end of the 1st century when the gospels were completed, most citizens of Rome had never heard of Christians and no Roman or Greek writer of significance mentions them. (6)

The gospel narrators wrote in Greek, the international language of the time, not in Aramaic their vernacular language of belief, nor in Latin the language of their occupiers. (7) The gospels were not biographies but rather portrayals of Jesus' integration into a Jewish vision of a savior, the perception of him as a stoic ideal, and judge of the living and dead. The key to Christian theology lies partly in Paul whose epistles were the first writings to expostulate the meaning of Jesus' life before written biographies of him existed.

Paul and the Invention of Christianity

Paul imposed Greeks ideas of a pre-existing Son of God, divine death as salvation of everyone's sins, bodily resurrection, re-birth and immortality on a Jewish idea of a messiah. For Paul the coming of Christ meant the abolition of Jewish Law, and his Hellenic interpretation of the life and meaning of Jesus dominated the theology of Christianity and forced the first disciples then living in Jerusalem to radically alter their apocalyptic vision and Jewish practices and accept his gentile explanations. Paul redefined what faith was and was presumptuous enough to claim what God would do to those whom he thought unworthy. He created the theology of Christianity without ever having read the gospels as they were unwritten.

Paul neglects the life and events in the life of Jesus because his message is the cosmic importance of who he was and what he means for all humanity. There was nothing in rabbinical literature suggesting that God would become man and save the world through a sacrificial death. But Paul insists that Jesus existed prior to his life on earth and that his death and resurrection are the most significant saving events in history. Such ideas would baffle Jews but appeal to the Hellenes whose mythical gods and semi-gods acted similarly.

The first Christian doctrinal dispute, whether new converts would have to be circumcised, arose during Paul's early missionary efforts and he journeyed to Jerusalem for the church's first council about 50 to resolve it. Was faith in Jesus to be a new religion or an offshoot of Judaism? Peter and James thought all who were to be baptized should also be circumcised. Paul did not think so and a decision was purportedly reached whereby new converts would not have to undergo circumcision. The Jerusalem community led by James and Peter clearly favored Judaic interpretations. But Paul would introduce elements of Gnosticism in his epistles, originating the transcendent Christ thereby inventing Christian theology. (8)

Paul would transform the religious landscape more than anyone, despite the questionable truth of his conversion on the road to Damascus, by claiming an authority beyond any of the Apostles: that he had a revelation directly from Christ. (9) Paul claimed the prerogative of a divinely appointed messenger, just like a Gnostic believer, and said he was "caught up in the third heaven," (how did he know how many there were?) and heard secret words no human can repeat. (10) We are expected to believe him, not because he learned these lessons from Jesus, nor because he witnessed the events of Jesus' life, nor because he studied everything from the Apostles and other witnesses, but because he had a private revelation. Everything Paul writes, the whole structure of Christian theology, rests on accepting the premise that the risen Christ spoke personally to Paul. We are forced to conclude that the ministry of Jesus, his choosing of disciples, making witnesses and missionaries is suddenly abandoned because Christ decides to choose another, one who once persecuted him to deliver Christianity's main message out of compulsion and not inclination.

Paul's alleged epiphany and conversion in *Acts* 9, 22-26 is beset with inconsistencies between his account and that of *Acts*. Paul falls to the ground, sees a great light, hears the voice of Jesus giving him instructions and becomes temporarily blind. Ananias, the Damascus resident he is sent to see (*Acts* 9) is a Christian who baptizes him and tells him to instruct the Gentiles. But in *Acts* 22 Ananias is a pious Jew, presumably one of those in the community who sought to murder Paul. Paul's account of his mission in Damascus in the employ of the High Priest in *II Corinthians* 11:32-33 is that King Aretas wanted to arrest him and so Paul's companions found a means for him to escape. But the same episode in *Acts* 9:22-25 describes the Jews of Damascus as seeking to murder Paul. The *Acts'* version was written at least 40 years after the alleged event. This description in *Acts* is another illustration of how the gospel narrators twisted history to make the Jews the perpetrators of Christian problems, biasing all activities of the new movement. (11)

Paul's transformation is solely attributable to his personal revelation, not his baptism, nor his instruction in the fundamentals of the faith, nor communion with fellow believers. Yet Paul's visions lie at the cornerstone of Christian belief. According to Paul, God revealed "his son in me," a bold and audacious assertion not even accorded the original Apostles. (12) The entire theology of Paul's interpretation of the status, mission and purpose of the life of Jesus rests on whether or not one accepts that Paul had a personal revelation at all, and that his explanation is the correct one for all Christian believers for all time.

Paul's epistles set the tone for the establishment of the new religion against the Torah and the Law. His perspective of good against evil, light against darkness, Jesus against the Jews, smacks of Greek mystery rites, Persian dualism between the God of Light and the God of Darkness, and Gnostic beliefs about the sacrifice of death and resurrection. Was God's covenant with Abraham and Moses eternally binding or merely temporary awaiting a higher covenant dictated by God's son later? "Do not think I have come to destroy the Law and the prophets. I did not come to destroy but to fulfill?" (*Matt.* 5:17) Matthew derides the Pharisees for not keeping the Law. So why is Paul proclaiming that the Law is un-necessary as long as one has faith in Christ? Or did Paul actually make such assertions (some scholars suggest he did not) because *Romans* and *Galatians* where these claims are made may not have been written by him. (13)

Paul is the first to reveal that the Eucharistic communion, the sacred meal of the mystery religions and the Mithraic members, is the basis of Christianity and a separate religious rite from the Passover. (14) He thus anticipates what the gospels write about the Last Supper, a ceremony like the Seder meal, and John's prescription on Jesus' words, without a ceremony, that only those who eat the body and blood will be saved. (15) Eating a god is very much a pagan ritual, certainly a part of Mithraic and Zoroastrian rites and acceptable to Gnostics, but would have been abhorrent to Jews. Indeed, the Jerusalem contingent of Apostles and followers, who "kept up their daily attendance at the Temple," (16) that is, acted as observant Jews keeping the Torah in force. There is no account of them following the commandment to partake of Christ's body and blood. In other words, Luke, who presumably wrote both his gospel and the *Acts* and was a Greek friend of Paul, does not describe the Jerusalem disciples as participating in any ceremony except the common Jewish rite of taking a communal meal and breaking bread together. There is no mention of wine, or of performing any ceremony akin to that described by Paul. It's conceivable that Paul's account of the Eucharist, written decades before the gospels, is actually the source of the gospel record and not the other way around. At the time Paul wrote *Corinthians* the movement was not in agreement about even eating with Gentiles, either for not following the Jewish dietary laws or eating the meat sacrificed to idols, unless they converted to Judaism before becoming Christians. (17)

Paul and the disciples at Jerusalem had contentious differences in all their encounters. (18) The purpose of *Acts* was to minimize differences between Paul and Peter and the Jerusalem elders. Peter's rejection of fellowship with Paul's Gentile converts revealed Peter's adherence to Jewish law and Paul's complete break with it, as one who made himself "outside the Law" but "under the law of Christ." (19) In his summons to Jerusalem Paul was compelled to capitulate and undergo ritual purification in the Temple in what appears to be a recantation. But there are major discrepancies between what Paul says and what *Acts* says about him.

Here are a few scriptural differences showing how the author of *Acts* has an agenda that appears to rebuff historical accuracy.

PAUL	ACTS
Did not consult with Apostles Before going on mission (*Gal.* 1:17)	did consult with Apostles (*Acts* 9: 26 ff)
pagans who worship idols guilty of violating what they know about him (*Romans* 1:18-32)	innocent before God because they are ignorant of the truth about him (*Acts* 17:22-31)
missionary who abandons Jewish Law in favor of Gentiles	A good Jew who never acts contrary to Jewish law
Paul in disagreement with Apostles over mission (*Gal.* 2:11-14)	All is harmony among the fledgling community (*Acts* 15:1-24)

If the original believers, men who had walked with Jesus, heard his speeches, assimilated his messages, could not agree on the fundamentals of belief apart from adherence to the Torah, why would they need a Gentile like Paul, who had not known Jesus in his lifetime, nor witnessed any of his signs and wonders, nor heard him speak, to elucidate them on the chief ingredients of Christian belief? Why would Jesus, who had not chosen Paul as a disciple, admit him as an Apostle after his death and resurrection and grant him alone inspiration as to his message more than his original followers?

Paul's unique theological contribution integrates Gnosticism into the concept of a Jewish messiah. The essence of Gnosticism, derived from ancient Persian dualism, is that the earth is in the throes of an evil power, that messengers are sent by the powers of Light to a select few initiates who are privileged to be informed with knowledge about the secrets for escaping from the clutches of evil demiurges. There is a world above which is all light, and a world below which is filled with darkness and evil. Paul would take this basic myth, popular among Hellenic literati during his time, and impose the person of Jesus as the messenger, the Anointed One of the Father, who will instruct his novices in the faith of what they must do to gain salvation and escape damnation and the forces of darkness.

Paul, not Peter or James, was the inventor of Christianity. Like Simon Magus and Apollonius of Tyana, colorful characters of his time, Paul was a charismatic figure full of sincerity, obviously some charisma, and loaded with Hellenic ideas, fusing concepts like the atonement of a divine being for mankind's benefit with the Judaic idea of a messiah while minimizing if not abolishing the Law of the Torah. (20) We can only conclude that the pre-Christian movement in Jerusalem prior to the writing of the gospels, gave no intellectual, organizational or ritual impetus to Christian theology, and in fact supported in all important discussions and practices the Torah and Jewish rituals. The doctrine of the mystical Jesus, his divinity, his sacrificial death and resurrection, the break from Jewish restrictions, and Eucharistic celebration, all core elements in Christian doctrine, came exclusively from Paul who blended mystery rites, Gnosticism with a touch of messianic Judaism into a new unity of faith. Paul made Jesus into a god with whom the Greeks could identify by stoically denouncing the body as evil and transforming a pious Jew into an eschatological deliverer. In the same era emperors like Claudius were inscribing monumental tablets designating themselves as Deliverers.

Paul created the myth of Jesus in *2 Corinthians* by using allegory. He convinces the congregation, and all subsequent believers in his interpretation, that Jesus is the new Adam, the new Moses, and the creator of the new covenant written not in the law but in the spirit, a simultaneous renunciation of the Judaic code and acceptance of the mysticism of the Greeks. It was audacious. By reinventing what the Law was for Jews Paul in fact ruled out all Jewish believers and written covenants, invented the distinction Christians have between the Old and New Testaments, and on his own declared through allegory what the meaning of Christ's life was for all time.

The era when Paul was composing his epistles to adherents in various churches and condemning those who opposed his doctrines was one of political agitation in Judea and it is against this background that we can comprehend the historical context of gospel compositions.

The First Century: Political Turmoil

The heirs of Alexander's dominions were centered in Antioch. About 200 BCE Greek armies overwhelmed the region and promoted an aggressive program of Hellenization. This prompted the guerilla warfare of the Maccabees whose subsequent dynasty became was known after the family name, Hasmonean. The Maccabean revolt that seized Jerusalem in 165 BCE from the Seleucids and cleansed the temple of impurities was a defining moment in the history of Judaism and in the Hebrew mindset. The victory strengthened the belief that the preservation of national destiny could be solidified with military force. It revived the actions of God through messengers, prophets and action agents who, finding their guidance in the *Book of Daniel* that foretells the falling of empires, could keep their religion and nation pure from foreign occupation and secular influences. Hence, two centuries after the Maccabees, the belief was still strong, especially among the followers of Jesus, that a messiah could do for the Romans what the Maccabees had accomplished with the Seleucids. The idea that God would come himself, or that God would send his son (since for Jews he was not known to have a son) was not a part of that conviction.

With the history of the Maccabees as backdrop, fast forward to the time of Jesus and the perception of his followers and Galileans in general about the mission of a messiah during Roman occupation. The Roman destruction of Jerusalem and the temple in 70 CE not only ruined the architecture and construction of the city but devastated Jewish ideals, dreams and political ambitions for an independent nation. Worse followed when in 135 the Bar Kochba revolt was crushed and infuriated Romans made Jerusalem into a Roman provincial capitol called *Aelia Capitolina* which Jews were not permitted to enter, humiliating them even further, dispersing them throughout the Roman imperial rule, and eviscerating all claims to cultural normalcy, political authenticity or independence. After this, the Mishnah, documents of rabbinic Judaism for Diaspora Jews, replaced temple sacrifice and partially restored some social fabric and the law for synagogue congregations.

During the lifetime of Jesus the Roman Empire was a union of prosperity and religious toleration. As the empire absorbed new peoples it automatically assimilated diverse religious beliefs. The Roman indulgence for religious plurality enlarged the number of divine protectors without creating complicating accompanying dogmas. Hadrian's Pantheon, the greatest free-standing hemispheric structure ever built at the time (c.130 CE) and the model for all domed buildings thereafter, was dedicated to twelve Greek deities. The Romans permitted various altars of belief to preserve civil concord. The freedom of the city of Rome became a common temple for all gods and religious worshippers.

As Roman tribunes pushed the boundaries of the empire eastward, oriental religions engaged the curiosity of the population while threatening the goals of national unity, patriotism and established Roman deities. From southern Italy emerged the mystery cult of Pythagoras; from Asia Minor came Astarte and Baal; from Persia Mithras followed by Manicheeism; from Egypt Isis and Osiris and their brood; from Palestine Yahweh and the new deity said to be his son. The religious tolerance of the Romans was surpassed by their priority of maintaining civic order in an empire hemmed in by barbarians. Rome would not accept any religious cult that professed to undermine its authority or promote separatism or a religious identity that withdrew from traditional values.

Roman patience was strained and its tolerance expired only at the first visible signs of the use of religion to initiate insurrection. It was not always the case. During the time of Cato (234-149 BCE) unearthed parchments thought to be Pythagorean were burned because they were considered subversive to the Latin religion. But Rome was suspicious of Christians precisely because they were intolerant of the worship and devotion shown to other gods. Periodic persecutions were intended to maintain Rome's plurality of divinities and not to target specific minority religions for reprisals, especially a religious group willing to suffer death for its beliefs.

Galilee at the time of Herod, or about the time of the birth of Jesus, was a hotbed of Jewish zealotry. Quarreling factions could not agree among themselves on what Jewish law was with its collection of questionable prescriptions, though clarification was kindly offered with Pharisee casuistry. Everyone would have preferred a theocratic state and would have welcomed anyone, like a messiah, who preached and worked to overthrow the Romans. Of course Romans were on guard for just such a messenger prefiguring insurrection. Indeed, the Essenes possessed a real war plan.

About the time of the birth of Jesus, c.4 BCE, a certain Judas Galileus led an assault on the royal arsenal at Sepphoris, only four miles from Nazareth. This same Judas returned a decade later to urge the people not to pay Roman taxes. (Gospel narrators naming the betraying apostle Judas, closely aligned with the history of Judas Galileus' treachery against the Romans, perhaps is meant to evoke blame for the Jews in Jesus' demise and to pacify the Romans). Simon the Zealot was among one of Jesus' disciples, so he was aware of the prevailing political dissension and rebellious spirit in the neighborhood of Nazareth. (21) Mark is predictably evasive about this delicate political situation. But the beheading of John the Baptist is alarm enough of the dangers of zealotry, strident reform and calls for penitence. Strangely, Jewish leaders in Jerusalem had to seek Roman concurrence to put Jesus to death but Herod Antipas (banished by Caligula in 39 CE) did not have to ask any Roman to put John the Baptist to death. (22)

The spiritual and temporal home of all Jews was the Temple in Jerusalem. The background of the life and times of Jesus and the period immediately following his death and the composition of the gospels includes insurrection, religious fanaticism, sedition and rebellion against Roman authority. The series of tumults, massacres and assassinations colors the cultural context of the gospel narratives by omission because the narrators nowhere discuss the intense political and military activity, and describe the life of Jesus as if it was devoid of the convulsions of the age. The gospel narrators scrupulously avoid any criticism of Roman authorities, cautiously side-stepping the issue for fear of retaliation, and especially of portraying Jesus as a political king. But Peter in his second epistle describes Rome as Babylon, thereby judging it as a city of unacceptable moral behavior and enslavement and not as it was: the greatest political, economic and cultural capitol in the civilized world. The epistles of James and Peter are filled with admonitions of moral rectitude and for maintaining faith, a mixture of Essene asceticism and stoic idealism, helpful for understanding the sources of early Christian thinking but not useful for piecing together episodes from the life of Jesus from those who actually knew him, and not helpful for understanding the feelings about the disciples towards Rome.

From the year of Jesus' death in c.33 until the completion of the canonical gospels, several Roman emperors reigned. This is not just incidental to the purposes here because other events and figures place the composition of the gospels in a wider cultural context, such as Christians' relationship to civil society and how their aberrant behavior led to persecution. Paul exercised pragmatic caution when faced with the real life situation of a slave and his master, and in his *Epistle to Philemon* he walks a delicate balance between his mystical interpretation of Christ's mission and the realities of living under the Roman code that included slavery.

The prevailing Roman virtue was *civitas*, the right of the individual to be secure in property and rights combined with the obligation to maintain the peace of the realm and social order. Romans saw their chief duty as dedication to the Roman sense of stability. Christians saw their chief duty to a higher master, a very individual commitment that did not include obeisance to Roman gods for civil order. All emperors were entitled to the status of *pontifex maximus*, the supreme priest responsible for religious ceremonies. The Roman emperor of the West, Gratian (359–383), with Ambrose as his Christian advisor, was the last emperor to refuse the title of *pontifex maximus*. But later popes unabashedly and readily adopted it even though its duties originally were meant to serve pagan gods.

For the Jews in Jesus' lifetime, the occupation of the Romans was grating and humiliating. But this changed after 70 CE when everyone realized that keeping social peace was more essential than relying on revolution that could incur the total devastation of the Jewish state and nationality. The tension between a Roman sense of duty and a Christian sense of personal religious belief would ultimately lead to persecution.

Jesus was born during the reign of Caesar Augustus (Octavian) who ruled from 31 BCE to 14 CE, and lived during the reign of Tiberius (14-37 CE). The approximate years of gospel composition were between the rule of Vespasian (69–79), and his sons Titus (79–81) and Domitian (81–96). It is probable that the civil disorder in the empire from the death of Nero through the turbulence of spontaneous insurrections and the imperial civil wars from 67–69 precipitated the revolt in Judea that led to the destruction of Jerusalem. It was Nero's accusation of the Christians for the great fire in Rome that likely led to the deaths of Peter and Paul. A combination of disruptive force, guerilla bands, economic depression, warring factions, the theft of treasury funds, led first to confusion in Jerusalem and then the complete breakdown of social order in the decades following the death of Jesus. The period of 66–70 determined the fate of Judaism, the scattering of Jews, the decimation of the countryside and the economy, the destruction of the temple and prepared the social context for the rise of Christianity.

Just before Nero's suicide in 66, the empire began to experience insurrection among the Asiatics, Celts and Gauls. Revolutionary Jews whose fortunes and zeal had reached a zenith sensed a military weakness and launched a preemptory revolt. Vespasian, as governor of Judea, succeeded in suppressing it until 68 when news of Nero's death placed the Roman succession in jeopardy and Vespasian ceased his campaign. He eventually entered Rome in 70 and was proclaimed emperor. In the same year to sent his son Titus to complete the unmerciful suppression of the Jewish revolt.

When Titus was 28 years old he fell in love with the Jewish Queen Julia Berenice, then 38, daughter of King Agrippa I of Judea, mentioned in the *Acts*, and sister of Agrippa II the Palestinian and Syrian monarch dependent on Rome. Berenice had tried unsuccessfully to prevent the Jewish revolt as she presciently foresaw the consequences of challenging Roman power in its apparent moments of weakness. Results proved her predictions accurate. Berenice lived openly with Titus in Rome for many years beginning in 71, and her brother Agrippa joined her there. Both were royally feted for their collaboration in helping suppress the Jewish rebellion. Soiled as was the Roman upper class by Anthony's association with Cleopatra during Octavian's reign, the intimacy of Titus as emperor with an oriental queen, and the antipathy created by the Jewish revolt, presented a senatorial hostility Titus could not ignore and, realizing he could not marry her or produce heirs by her, sent her away. (23)

Tiberius is noted in all gospels and Claudius is noted in *Acts* 25:10 when Paul appeals to the Roman emperor. No other emperors are noted in any other scriptures. The murders of Domitian, the persecution of Christians and suicide of Nero, the destruction of Jerusalem by Titus and the consequent dispersal of the Jews nevertheless had an influence on the gospel writers by shaping tolerance towards Romans and avoidance of the appearance of any criticism of imperial rule. Peter in his first epistle even cautions Christian slaves to endure their suffering under severe masters. (24)

Here is a brief synopsis of that turbulent period of about 100+ years from just prior to Jesus' birth and the writing of the gospels between 70–90 CE.

Pompey had put down Judean independence in 63 BCE and entered the sacred temple precincts killing over 12,000. (25) Herod (73–4 BCE), crowned king in Rome by Anthony and the Senate, laid siege to Jerusalem and with the help of Roman centurions, entered the city and killed all the men, women and children in 37 BCE, ending the 126 year rule of the Hasmoneans. (26)

Riots occurred in the reign of Archelaus (4 BCE–6 CE), Herod's son and successor. Sabinus, an administrator, plundered the temple. The Governor of Syria, Varus, intervened and burned the city of Sepphoris, about four miles from Nazareth and crucified 4,000 men, at a time when Jesus would have been a grade school student. Emperor Augustus abolished the rule of Archelaus in 6 CE and placed Judea under Roman Procurators whose presence and actions were designed to curtail religious extremism and prevent civil discord while allowing Judaic religious practices. Yet as soon as one Jewish fanatical group was unmasked and decimated another sprang up to upset the *Pax Romana*. Often claiming divine inspiration, but with motives tinged with inflamed nationalism and Roman hatred, insurgents were continuously slaughtered by the Roman legions. Yet the gospel narrators do not have Jesus bearing hatred to the Romans, but to the Pharisees and Jewish hypocrites who don't respond to his message. The absence of Roman criticism and the censuring of Jews in all the gospels is a conscious appeasement aligned with criticism of Judaic interpretations of Jesus against the Hellenic one Paul espoused.

Several examples confirm this conclusion. Caligula ordered his legate Petronius from Damascus to Jerusalem in 40 to place statues of him in the sanctuary of the temple, an insensitive action meant less to inflame Judaic sensibilities than to promote his own perceived divine status. While journeying to Jerusalem, Petronius was met by a delegation of Jews in Galilee who implored him to spare this sacrilege telling him they would all fight to the death. Placing his own life in jeopardy he agreed with the Jews and withdrew to Damascus to write his disobedient reasoning to Caligula. Fortunately, the news of Caligula's assassination arrived weeks prior to the dispatch from Caligula ordering Petronius' death. (27)

About 55 CE, an Egyptian who professed to be a prophet gathered a force of 30,000 and began marching towards the Mount of Olives to force entry into Jerusalem. Felix the procurator learned of this plot, intercepted the group of militants and slaughtered most of them. (28) After continual uprisings and massive heavy-fisted Roman slaughters, is it any wonder that the Apostles hid in upstairs rooms, decided on missionary activity away from their homeland, and eventually left Jerusalem for safer locations in the empire?

Jewish insurrectionists in 66 captured the temple and insulted the Romans and others by refusing to accept foreign sacrifices. Moderates were appalled and appealed to Florus the procurator who, using civil discord as a pretext, was actually keen to augment discord among the Jews to hide his avarice and mask his atrocities from Roman officials. Some citizens tried unsuccessfully to dislodge the rebels with force from the temple sanctuary. The rebels soon overran the city, killed the high priest and other officials then massacred the Roman garrison. When news of this reached Caesarea, Gentile residents killed over 20,000 Jewish residents. (29) A Roman army left Antioch with a few thousand infantry and cavalry, picked up recruits as it marched south and besieged Jerusalem but abandoned the effort before capturing it. Emboldened by this military tentativeness, the Jewish forces attacked the retreating Romans killing over 5,300 infantry and 380 cavalry. This defeat elated the rebels, as inevitable to zealots as it was catastrophic for the Jewish state, but gave no solace to thoughtful Jews, were any still left in Judea.

The *coup de grace* came in 67 when Nero commissioned Vespasian a man whose life had been spent in the military, who had tamed the Germans, acquired Britain, and quelled revolts throughout the West, to deal with the Jewish insurrection. Vespasian immediately concentrated a large army in Syria while his son Titus gathered one in Alexandria, and the total that assembled in Acco on the coast exceeded 60,000 troops. Camping first at the outskirts of Jotapata, after a 47–day siege, he captured it and killed 40,000 defenders excepting 1,200 women and children and its leader, Josephus. This news made the seditious zealot defenders of Jerusalem bolder in unreasonable ardor, while the chief priests and 12,000 other moderates, eventually all killed by the zealots, were uneasy for impending hostilities and the threat of inexorable ruin. As rival factions competed for supremacy in the city, incensed Jews were everywhere killing each other prior to the arrival of the Roman legions.

Titus entered Jerusalem in 70 with an army of 60,000 killing over 1.1 million while Flavius Silva attacked Masada in 73 where the last 900+ zealots held out. All committed suicide rather than be taken captive. (The Arch of Titus, still intact along the Forum in Rome within sight of the Coliseum, commemorating the victory in Jerusalem was ordered constructed in 80 CE by the Senate). These traumatic political and military events occurring in rapid succession in little over a half century were close in memory to influence the mindset of any writer, but apparently not gospel narrators.

These sobering events frame the turmoil during and shortly after the life of Jesus and during the years of gospel narrators who are silent on all these momentous events. Instead, the gospels carry biblical and epic allusions. Luke's allusion in 1:32-35: "He will be great, and will be called the son of the most high, and the Lord God will give him the Throne of his father David

...For that reason his offspring will be called the Son of God" is redolent with biblical imagery, particularly from *Daniel* 7:13. This idea also occurs in the War Scroll of the *Dead Sea Scrolls* where the heavenly host is described as coming on the clouds of heaven to rain on mankind. (30) But it is also reminiscent of an oral tradition about Herod the Great. According to Josephus, a man named Menachem, an Essene, lived an exemplary life and when Herod was only a schoolboy saluted him as King of the Jews, predicting that he would excel men in good fortune and fame. (31) Similarly, Josephus said he predicted that Vespasian would be emperor, which is why his life was spared.

By blending mythical and biblical streams, the gospel narrators masterfully constructed a tale about divine intervention that appealed to Jews and secular Greeks and Romans. (32) Paul's epistles and the gospels transform Jesus the carpenter into the transcendent Christ whose divine origins can battle Satan in the desert or in the cosmic and apocalyptic hereafter, who is the Promised One come to redeem mankind. Like Zoroaster, who preaches that love is greater than animal sacrifice, who insists that salvation depends on eating his body and blood like Mithras, and who will return to judge everyone according to thoughts and actions like Osiris.

But because of the Roman domination of the whole of Judaism, a radical change occurred in early Christianity. The Nazarene movement, the Jesus movement in Jerusalem from roughly 33 to 70, was essentially Jewish and the disciples scrupulously followed the Torah and Jewish rituals awaiting a second coming of the Messiah. The destruction of the city and temple and the massacre of revolutionaries and devotees of an earthly kingdom ruptured those aspirations and brought about a religious sea change. Driven by Pauline doctrine, the pre-Christian ideology switched conveniently from Jewish to apocalyptic hopes and visions where gentiles were welcomed and selective pagan rituals revived to broaden the appeal. The key success of this adaptation was to maintain some religious persuasion, a modified Judaism under the guise of Christianity, and at all costs to avoid Roman antagonism. This tactic succeeded triumphantly but only because of the obliteration of Jerusalem and both Jews and the early Nazarenes in 70, the widespread appeal of Paul's Hellenic vision and the Constantine's designation of Christianity as the only permissible Roman religion.

By the middle of the second century, defeats of the Roman army east and west, economic recessions, internal discords, the decline of the Senate's political significance, the fear of barbarian invasions and the concentration of power in the hands of Diocletian and, by Constantine's time, the move of the imperial city away from Rome, all contributed to uncertainty, anxiety and the rise of salvation religions like Christianity. Into this dilemma Christian scribes produced gospel documents, incorrectly placing blame for the death of a Jewish reformer on Jews while exonerating the Romans.

The Gospels: Origins and Themes

The gospels and non-canonical documents from c.70–150 CE were narratives intended for specific congregations each of which had varied interpretations of who Jesus was and what his mission implied. The gospels were written for these communities, not to tell a chronological story of the events of Jesus' life but to recount traditions about him. Hence, the gospels are not memoirs but folk literature, a collage taken from a variety of histories, heroic epics, and quasi-biographies. Because they were willingly accepted even though they contain no topographical references, no chronological sequencing, no personality portraitures, no lively descriptions of people or places, no compositional literary techniques, no overall narrative structure, makes their worth as even meritorious literature debatable. Unlike Ammianus Macellinus the Roman historian of the later Roman Empire who interviewed contemporaries, the gospel narrators do not give us even the benefit of multiple eyewitness reports.

There were an abundance of available texts at the time of gospel compositions. The Nag Hammadi cache of documents, the most illuminating discovery of ancient Christian writings, contains 41 separate texts dating from 348 but whose contents date from approximately the time of the gospel compositions. The most famous is *The Gospel of Thomas* which contains almost no narrative but 114 sayings attributed to Jesus about half of which appear in the canonical gospels. These documents are a combination of forgeries and fictions, expositions of episodes, concocted conversations, supposed gospel quotations, secret sayings of Jesus, and gospels presumably written by Peter, Mary, Thomas, Philip and James. Their discovery reveals the variety of fiction written in the first two centuries and the multiplicity of interpretations accorded to legends of Jesus. The fact that early Christianity possessed so many documents with varying interpretations indicates that, though subsequent ecclesiastical hierarchy craved doctrinal confirmation for unity of belief and therefore had to choose from among competing texts, their ultimate decision compromised the integrity of diversity which today actually exists, though more mildly, in Protestantism.

A Spanish priest and poet named Juvencus living in the time of Constantine actually rewrote the gospels in Latin dactylic hexameters, in imitation of Virgil and claiming to produce more easily readable verse. He re-arranged gospel segments to suit his own chronological story line, using *Matthew* as a guide but eliminating *Mark*. He clearly did not think it unusual to re-set the gospels into literary verse, perhaps even unaware that much of gospel content was already derived from Greek mythic literature. Under *Mark*, Jesus brings the Kingdom of Heaven to earth. *Matthew* initiates a new law of the spirit. *Luke* invites Gentiles to join the members' club. *John* (and in

Paul's *Letter to the Hebrews*), the vision becomes an imaginative leap into cosmic reality in which Greek enlightenment is merged with Judaic wisdom thought.

The gospels were interpretations of how the mission of Jesus was supposed to fulfill Judaic prophecy and reconcile the movement as a part of the Law of Moses. *Mark* did not answer why Jesus as Messiah was even necessary to the legitimate cause of Jews. *John* interjected the Logos as a new intellectual concept to reveal the Hellenic truth about Jesus. But none of the gospels writers welded together the multiple contradictions in the individual gospel themes of how Judaism was enriched by Jesus. The next two centuries would engage theologians in vainly trying to interpret the various messages and themes to supply adherents with some unified doctrine that differentiated Christianity from its parent Judaism.

The next step was to create a bureaucratic structure that would codify what the faithful believed. Christianity as a church was only born after this amalgam of interpretive narratives based on literary sources jelled and emperors joined the movement. The literary glue that held the movement together was *The Acts of the Apostles* which appeared to demonstrate unity among the Apostles and a centrality to Christian purpose and mission when in fact there had been angry debates, hostility and entrenched views making it appear as if there were more factions than there were Protestant denominations.

The Jewish intellectual milieu during and after the life of Jesus was rife with religious messages about redemption, salvation, the lifting of oppression, and miracles to convince the doubtful and wavering. Needless to say, these same concepts were also abundant in religious literature outside of Judaism at the same time. The delay in the writing of the gospels so long after the death of Jesus was occasioned by the switch in ideological orientation of the disciples who were initially awaiting the Second Coming and the fulfilling of messianic prophecies, and especially the overthrow of Roman domination. That hope was irrevocably dashed in 70 and then a whole new scheme was required to maintain faith. The change was revolutionary. The new thinking involved a partial rejection of the earthly messiah movement and an acceptance of a heavenly kingdom, an afterlife in accordance with Pharisee belief, a Gnostic interpretation of the mission of Jesus in accordance with Paul's doctrine, and the censorship of the Jews, not the Romans, for the cause of all problems.

Depending of who is counting, the New Testament consists of 27 books, four gospels, *Acts of the Apostles*, letters by Paul, John, Jude, James, Peter and *Revelations*. These accepted texts were arrived at by common consensus and not church decree, and there is lingering doubt about the authenticity of some, the literalness of others and the inspiration for all. Each of the evangelists, Mark, Matthew, Luke and John wrote from scattered sections of the Roman Empire and it is not clear that these are the names of the actual authors or only attributions to known individuals. (33) Luke writes "Many have undertaken to draw up a narrative." (34) The variety of narratives detail the multiplicity of convictions about Christianity in the first three centuries. The views are as diverse as that Jesus was a man only but divinely appointed (Ebionites); that Jesus was a man with divine prerogatives (Arians); that there was an Old Testament God and a New Testament God (Valentinians); that Jesus was not real but a manifestation of the Father (Marcionites); that the material world was evil and Jesus was the deliverer of secret knowledge that would liberate the soul (Gnostics); that a new prophet had arisen where ecstatic visions announced the second coming of Christ imposing a strict asceticism and penance on its members (Montanism). The writings of these so-called heresies were subsequently obliterated in periodic purges.

According to some scholars, Paul did not write the letters to the *Colossians, Ephesians, Hebrews, Timothy* or *Titus*. (35) The anonymous authors of the gospels, some of Paul's epistles and other Jesus movement documents were trying to give a particular spin to their belief by using exhortations that are part rhetoric, part philosophy and part the symbol of Christ as the Gnostic messenger, Jewish Messiah or sacrificial high priest.

Mark is accepted as the first gospel, written perhaps as early as 70 CE, and probably in Asia Minor as the author shows ignorance of Palestinian geography. Mark creates fictional accounts, influenced by events from Homer's epics of the *Iliad* and *Odyssey*, to compare Jesus favorably to the literary antecedents of Achilles, Hector and Ulysses, as performing similar feats, except that neither Mark nor the other gospel narrators wrote in hexameters like Homer did and imitated only thematic episodes not poetic formulae.

Matthew's gospel may have been written from Alexandria. Luke wrote his gospel toward the end of the 1st century probably in Antioch. John, heavily influenced by Gnostic and Hellenistic philosophy, who died in Ephesus about 100 CE, has had the fourth gospel attributed to him. He is readily conceded as the author of *Revelations*, or the *Apocalypse*, though some evidence, like his advanced age, points to another John, or a scribe who attributed the book to him written on the island of Patmos. All gospels, with the exception of Matthew's written in Hebrew, were composed in Greek. The commercial and ethnic language of Palestine and of Jesus at the time was Syric/Aramaic, the Semitic language Jesus spoke and adopted by the Jews while in Babylonia and still spoken in villages in southern Syria and northern Iraq.

There are no original gospel documents. The earliest manuscripts of biblical scriptures date from the 8th century. Assuming that there were multiple copies circulating throughout the world and that normal human errors crept into the transmissions, it's conceivable that the version relied upon for all future translations may not conform to originals in every sense. Mark's gospel has 661 verses and 430 are substantially duplicated in *Matthew* and *Luke*. Another 167 verses occur just in *Matthew*. Only 30 verses of *Mark* do not appear in either *Matthew* or *Luke*. (36)

Mark's gospel argues for Jesus as the resurrected Lord but not even his followers formulated this view until well after his death. The gospels attempted to reconstruct his life according to the theology of a promised Messiah, the eschatology of the final days, the judgment and to show how he is the one foretold by previous prophets. Mark distances Jesus from the Jews, places him at odds with Jewish leaders like the Pharisees, questions the rigid interpretation of the laws, and exonerates and pacifies the Romans. Jesus' speeches in John's gospel are anti-semitic, vituperative in condemnation of the Jews and consequently are likely attributed to him rather than spoken by him.

If he wanted to get his message out correctly, why didn't Jesus write his own book? Why wasn't one member of the disciples appointed to take notes during the ministry, as Judas was appointed to keep the purse, so the accuracy of the story could be verified? Why leave his message to correspondents, two of whom were not eyewitnesses, who waited decades to write down anything about his life and then who produced multiple inconsistencies, like the time of the Last Supper, the confusing story of the Resurrection, and ambiguous stories about who Jesus really was necessitating council definitions centuries later about the nature of his person? And then why, after his death, appear to a Gentile foreigner and give him, Paul, a special revelation as if the message had not been properly given in the first place? Why did narrators wait so long to record the most momentous experiences of their lives?

The dominant theme in the gospels is the Kingdom of God or Kingdom of Heaven, a phrase found 37 times in *Matthew* and 32 in *Luke*, a repetitive idea central to the commentary. The Kingdom predicted by the prophets had arrived, but it was a spiritual not an earthy kingdom and therefore apparently not in conflict with Roman stability. Gospel proclamations of the Kingdom of God, the wish fulfillment of a rival political order based on Jewish virtues and governed by the newly appointed ruler, the divine Christ embodied in the person of Jesus, can best be understood from the perspective of the Kingdom of Rome in the first century.

The kingdom theme appears to be a rival deity to the Emperor. It was also a theme that would have been acceptable to the Pharisees, victimized and pilloried by Jesus in the gospels. Corollary themes in the Bible prior to Jesus are the struggle against idols (or foreign powers), the championing of those oppressed, of performing miracles, of curing lepers, of ascending into heaven.

Elijah fought against heathen gods and for the poor, performed miracles and rose to heaven in a chariot like Mithras. His disciple Elisha also worked miracles and cured lepers. The monks at Qumran anticipated another prophet. Gospel narratives present Jesus as a new beginning, the fulfillment of all prophecies. They compared him to Elias, announce that he is the Messiah predicted by Elijah, and will come again in the days of final judgment.

The 1st century also bred individuals who resemble miracle workers and messianic prophets. In 62 a man named Jesus, son of Ananus a farmer, stood in the temple precinct and like a doomsday prophet began shouting the woes that were to befall Jerusalem. Alarmed, ordinary citizens seized and scourged him while he continued to shout his admonitions without reproaching his attackers. He was brought before the Roman procurator who quickly concluded he was mad and released him. During the siege of Jerusalem in 66 he woefully wandered the walls prophesizing destruction, was struck by a missile launched by the Romans and instantly died. Thus, even as an historical comparison, a few years before the gospels was there a story about a man named Jesus alerting the Jewish population to impending lamentations and destruction, was scourged, did not defend himself and willingly accepted the blows, brought before the Roman procurator, released, but then killed by the Romans.

Hanina ben Dosa, a near contemporary of Jesus born about 20 CE just north of Nazareth, a first-century rabbinic teacher quoted in the Mishna, was also said to have performed miracles and to have cured people at a distance. He lived in the lower Galilee and was distinguished for his extreme piety and zealous observance of religious precepts, acknowledged as an example of a completely righteous man who was frequently requested to pray for the sick and those in trouble. More is known about his pious deeds and his wonders than about his religious rulings and dicta. He heard a voice that proclaimed him a Son of God. (38)

Another holy man in the first century, Onias (*Honi* in Hebrew) described by Josephus, was widely believed by people of his day to have performed at least one amazing miracle and to have the ability to perform more. Thereafter known as Honi the Circle Drawer, he was a man of peace and was killed in Jerusalem at Passover. (39) Jesus was not the only holy man said to be working miracles in Galilee and Judea in the early first century.

Mary's eloquent *Magnificat* (*Luke* 1:46-55) is based on the song of Hannah in *Samuel* 2:1-10, a continuation of a long literary tradition of hymns of praise sung to gods. Luke tells us that the births of Jesus and John the Baptist took place in the reign of Herod in 4 BCE but writes that Caesar Augustus orders a decree for a census and everyone has to go to his hometown to register. However, the census did not have occur until 6 CE, or ten years later, the first year Judea came under direct Roman rule, as Josephus relates. A new census was always taken when a province came under Roman purview. Luke is inventing his own chronology.

And what about those shepherds in Luke at the birth near Bethlehem? What were their names? Herodotus would have found out who their names were because they witnessed such extraordinary sights. Would not Mary and Joseph have wanted to know them, talk to them more, perhaps keep in touch over the years, send them Christmas cards? Why were not some of them disciples since they supposedly knew who Jesus was? If the details of Jesus' birth are inconsistent and confusing, the year and details of his death are equally perplexing, and the synoptic gospels say that the Last Supper was a Passover meal while John says that it was "Passover Preparation Day." (40)

Besides the historical mistakes, there are other discrepancies. Mark writes (Chapter 7) that Jesus went through Sidon on his way to Tyre to the Sea of Galilee. But Sidon is in the opposite direction and in the 1st century there was no road from the Sea of Galilee to Sidon, only a road to Tyre. Mark's 5th chapter refers to the land of the Gerasenes as on the east shore of Galilee, yet Gerasa (today's ancient city of Jerash, about 35 miles north of Amman, Jordan) is more than 30 miles to the southeast of Galilee, far from the land for the story requiring a steep cliff down to the water. Mark writes (10:12) that "If a woman divorces her husband and marries another she is guilty of adultery," whereas Judaic grounds for divorce in Jesus' lifetime were surprisingly relaxed, liberal and without censure, and a woman could sue for divorce and retain her property rights. (41)

Mark portrays the disciples are dim-witted, imperceptive and unenlightened about who Jesus is and what his message is. But suddenly, in *Mark* 8:29 Peter blurts out that Jesus is the Christ, an alarming and abrupt role reversal of inspired intuition as the disciples were dense moments before. *Mark* describes the message of Jesus as suffering and death, a concept the disciples even when they understand it refused to accept. This conflict, a drama without a denouement, is never resolved and is only concluded centuries later by an assembly of bishops, a bewildering sequence of dissonant misunderstanding by chosen disciples, non-acceptance and failure to communicate such an important mission. We have to raise the question of why a son of God would choose such dolts who are faithless, non-comprehending and in the final days escapists who run from association with him during his trial and death. *Mark* is unsympathetic and critical of the disciples and his gospel ends abruptly with them dispirited, disorganized, unbelieving and un-rehabilitated. His bias reveals his mythical, Greek superhuman interpretation of Jesus and not the Jewish messianic one. Reading the *Odyssey* helps us understand a similar relationship between the leader and his doltish companions.

The gospels are primarily instructional aides and preaching tools used by the scattered communities that had no central place of sacrifice or worship. Without such centers and sanctuaries, these communities sought unity in a central figure. The differences between the gospels are indicative of the diversity of beliefs about the new prophet with the reformist message. The gospels evolved into a blend of epic hyperbole and religious enthusiasm, espousing a variety of elements for reforming Judaism that mimicked episodes from Hellenic heroes centered around a prophetic figure who was never intended to be canonized as a god upholding a radical new dogma by a breakaway church.

A SACELLUM FOR THE HOUSEHOLD GODS
From Herculaneum

CHAPTER FIFTEEN
CHRISTIANITY IN THE SECOND AND THIRD CENTURIES

The first generation of Christian zealots had died by the end of the first century, there had been no second coming, and the faithful were in doctrinal disarray and engaging in bizarre rites, as Paul's ceaseless admonitions and reproaches in his epistles testify. The Diaspora of Jews brought an end to the Galilean ministry, the oral traditions about Jesus, and the pusillanimous fumbling of Peter and James who could not agree on the content of the message or the manner of advocating it. The Nazarene Christians in Jerusalem were scattered and their Jewish observances dissipated. *The Acts of the Apostles* was composed to rally the believers and offer a background for their belief. To perform this service they had to enlist the Greek educated physician Luke who had to take time from his surgeries and bloodlettings to write a greatly modified history of apostolic activities.

Acts of the Apostles
The Acts offers confused history with legends and apocryphal accounts. *Acts* has been attributed to Paul's trusted Greek friend Luke but the document was likely a composition expanded by the hand of a later editor to mollify Roman hostility and to support Paul's teaching against that of Peter and James. *Acts* is a legendary epic in which the author and editors modified Homeric episodes to demonstrate that the gospel was meant to extend to gentiles and not just Jews.

Paul is treated by all Romans in *Acts* with every courtesy, a sure sign that the author is manipulating the facts. Paul appears before tribunes, governors, Kings of Palestine where he distances himself from Jews, a disposition that gives him credibility as a Roman citizen. He is portrayed as a solid, righteous citizen who is not a threat to Roman civility. A tribune rescues him from an angry crowd and gives him a guard on the route to his trial before Felix the Governor. Felix's wife, a Jew, wants to hear more from Paul about faith in Christ Jesus. Neither Felix nor his successor seek to harm Paul, and instead protect him from murderous Jews, and agree to his request to be tried in Rome.

The Jews were stung by the Roman occupation as they had been by Egyptian and Assyrian conquests and linked their religious aspirations with political realities by seeking a political liberator sent by God. But after the destruction of Jerusalem and temple, the slaying of zealots and insurrectionists, the dispersal of Jews and the elimination of a political messiah, a spiritual messiah loomed as the only viable alternative. The gospel narrators feared the wrath of Roman authorities by declaring that Jesus was King of the Jews or any other title that would have imperiled Christians and their activities. The borrowed notion of dead emperors as gods was not an idea that would have been favorably tolerated in a Jewish religious preacher from Galilee. The gospels are quite insistent in denying that Jesus aspired to any worldly kingdom such as that most desired by those who awaited a Jewish messiah. Jesus had emphatically rejected a Davidic or terrestrial concept of the Messiah as that idea would have been too subversive for the Roman authorities. Indeed, the concept of messiah was used by the Jews of the Sanhedrin as a violation of Jewish law to help convict Jesus before Pilate.

The evangelists writing after Paul's epistles amplified their original texts to include a wider use of sayings, parables and allegories and, like Luke, to expand the context of Jesus' time to appeal to urban members, and like Paul and John to frame Jesus' life to appeal to Gnostics. *The Acts* created fictions like the trial and execution of Stephen, a narrative concocted to portray Stephen's death as religious persecution like the trial of Jesus. Stephen is accused of speaking against the Temple, but was summarily executed by a mob for blasphemy. That the sedate and formal Sanhedrin would allow a mob to execute a defendant for an offence during a trial, and what Stephen said during his speech would not under Jewish law be considered blasphemy, and to forget the original charge is absurd. The key phrases of "Messiah," "Son of Man," "Son of God," for which Stephen was accused of blasphemy, were unknown in Judaism and only existed in later doctrines of the Christian church where the terms under Pauline doctrine refer to the divinity of Jesus. (1) The author of *Acts* altered the reason for Stephen's martyrdom from anti-Roman to anti-Jewish and inserted Saul's presence at Stephen's stoning to highlight his later dramatic conversion.

In *Acts 8* Luke notes that the followers were scattered throughout the country districts but the Apostles remained in Jerusalem, reversing the normal order of persecution whereby the leaders are the first ones ejected. Contrast the trial of Peter in *Acts* where the claims of Jesus' messianic claims were treated with tolerance to capture the inconsistency and disparity of the presumed judicial methods and results.

Within a few decades the population of Christians had shifted from poor and semi-literate fishermen in Galilee to a literate Greek-speaking, gentile world. But those faithful to the teachings of Jesus, who regarded him as a man with divine powers, a prophet in the tradition of Israel, and who believed Paul had misled the people with Gnostic beliefs and attributes Jesus did not give himself were the Ebionites, the first rural Christian followers of the Jerusalem church. They followed the Mosaic Law closely but were repressed, persecuted and driven underground and eventually to extinction by subsequent ecclesiastical powers. The Ebionites (from the Hebrew *ebionin* meaning poor) were ideological followers of the Qumran sect of Judaism who held James in the highest favor. (2) They were Jews who faithfully observed the Sabbath and saw Jesus as a natural man whose justification was that he was righteous, a term constantly referenced in the *Dead Sea Scrolls*. Paul considered the Ebionites apostates. The fact that they were condemned shows the supremacy of the lobbying for a Pauline theology over the Jewish reform movement of the Jerusalem community in the 1st century.

Acts adds the ascension into heaven into the history of Jesus not found anywhere in the gospels, and notes that the chosen Apostles convey a unified message. The reality is that it was not a unified message for the first three centuries. The message is that every missionary will suffer at the hands of non-believers and scoffers and perhaps endure death, and that the Holy Spirit will prevail and Jesus will come again. Paul's message was slanted toward Hellenistic beliefs by repudiating the Judaic prophetic message, adherence to Mosaic laws and Pharisaic beliefs, and adding the Holy Spirit as a new God, by giving unusual powers to the Apostles and their successors, and pacifying the Romans by placing them among the new converts. It was an audacious literary accomplishment, the perpetration of a particular Christian ideology and even the introduction of a new god designed to appeal to polytheists.

Acts creates the Apostolic church, that the chosen Apostles not only carry the message of Jesus but can deliver the new, non-biblical God, the Holy Spirit, in his name. This account, complete with the historians' use of speeches, the rhetorical use of argument and persuasion, and the epic poet's use of miracles, signs and wonders, angels and messengers who free Peter and Paul from danger, were meant to show that this message was not for the Jews but for Gentiles, a contradictory meaning from that found in the gospels. "On hearing this the Gentiles were delighted and glorified the word of the Lord, and all who were destined for eternal life believed." (*Acts* 13:48) Jesus himself would have been astonished that his message, at least as written in the gospels, was so strangely interpreted.

Peter's conversion and appearance to Cornelius, the Roman centurion, is an episode meant to show that the Apostles could eat unclean foods with Gentiles, thus further divorcing themselves from Jewish laws, and that hated Romans, like Sergius Paulus, could also be upstanding Christians. The visions of Cornelius and Peter are comparable to the dream of Agamemnon in *Iliad* 2. The use of the descent of the Holy Spirit in tongues of fire is reminiscent of Persian and Greek mystery rites. Foreign tongues are signs of the necessity for missionary activity. Curing the sick and raising the dead is a sign that God is with the messengers. The comparison of the casting of lots to replace Judas and the casting of lots to fight Hector is in *Iliad* 7. Paul's farewell address to the Ephesian elders compares with Hector's farewell speech to Andromache in *Iliad* 6. And finally Peter's escape for Agrippa's prison is like Priam's escape from Achilles' bivouac in *Iliad* 24.

In *Acts* we see the merger of epic myths and literary methodology forged to create a document that evokes history while glorifying fiction, filled with journeys, heroic speeches, hardships, whippings, stoning, arrests and detentions in prison, and the intervention of angels and earthquakes. If we substitute Achilles or Ulysses for Paul, the literary methods to create the story and glorify the hero have similar themes.

Irenaeus (c. 140–200 CE)

In the hundred or so years after the composition of the gospels a transformation occurs that is almost as momentous as the production of the gospels themselves. Like the Pentateuch documents before them, certain gospel documents become a part of sacred canon while others are vigorously excluded. This expansion of belief in approved documents was brought about by the writings of a select few, industrious and learned men whose ecclesiastical position elevated their pronouncements to the status of imperial decrees for fledgling Christian communities.

During the 2nd century while building a hierarchy based on the bishopric, Christians were on the defensive from Jewish scoffers, Roman imperialists and philosophical critics and skeptics like Celsus. The gospels, prior to their promulgation as canonical, were political missionary propaganda, a response to critics and a testimonial to the faithful of the new sect, a continuation of the narrative traditions of the Jewish chronicles. Christians were initially ignored by the Romans, then in successive centuries viewed as just a nuisance religion, but soon seen as a secretive menace to social order and were persecuted under Nero and Diocletian.

A convergence of philosophies, like stoicism and Neo-Platonism, and emerging religious beliefs, Mithras, Manicheeism, the cult of Isis and Christianity, washed over the Roman Empire in the 3rd century and brought about deep societal changes toward mystery religions focusing chiefly on the question of immortality. Numerous sarcophagi of non-Christians tastefully presented the soul of the deceased as entering the Isles of the Blessed, the Elysian Fields, the life beyond. "The Greeks," said Clement of Alexandria, "assume their gods to be human in passions as they are human in shape." (3) But as Christianity gained new recruits and imperial edicts imposed Christian beliefs, the ecclesiastical establishment set about systematically demonizing the opposition, presenting all non-Christian thought and practices in the most sinister and perfidious manner. (4)

The major Christian apologist in the 2nd century is Irenaeus (c.140–200), Bishop of Lyons. Born in Asia Minor, he was consecrated Bishop of Lyons and is the first theologian to systematize Christian teaching in his major work,

Proof of the Apostolic Teaching, written in the form of an epistle, a manual for understanding early Christianity. He asserted that Christians who have faith endorse the spirit that supersedes the Mosaic Law. (5) Because of his systemization of Christian teachings, borrowing liberally from the Bible, and his purported refutation of Gnostic teachings which sought to find God through dreams, revelations and personal illuminations, he is the acknowledged first Episcopal Christian apologist. (6) Irenaeus argues that Gnostics seek the divine reality through personal experiences and not through Christ and that such views are heretical. What he fails to appreciate is that his acknowledgement of the divine spirit is itself a Gnostic belief. He is the first to literally shape the institution of the church and its major doctrines by insisting that only four gospels are authentic and that all other writings claiming divine authority should be destroyed. His views prevailed and, once the episcopate established the unifying principle of the church, shaped Christian doctrine for all time. (7)

Literary Fragments from Canaan and Egypt

Just as the gospel evangelists borrowed with impunity from the Greeks, they also extracted myths and legends from Canaanite and Egyptian literature. One textual reference for early Canaanite and Hebrew mythical sources is Philo of Byblos (20 BCE–40 CE), a contemporary of Jesus and of his Jewish counterpart, Philo of Alexandria described in Chapter 11. (8) Philo is a valuable source of Canaanite mythology and of the ways religious traditions have been preserved.

Philo's contribution is that he summarized his ethnographic findings and concluded that ancient Phoenician civilization had elevated famous men to a divine status. These men then had cosmic elements assigned them, temples were built to them and finally they were worshipped as gods. Many like Kronos, Uranus, Hercules, Persephone and the Canaanite Astarte (Aphrodite), were assumed into Greek mythology. Philo claims that the Greeks, and Hesiod in particular, appropriated the tales of previous historical religious or mythological individuals, dramatized them with ornamental embellishments, and passed them on as literary history. The idea of a god bodily resurrecting himself, as Baal did, and the symbolism of the Good Shepherd leading his flock are but two of these thematic legends appearing in the Canaanite canon. (9)

After having been slain, Baal, to whom the epithet "Shepherd" is applied, emerges triumphantly by rising on the third day in the Canaanite *Legend of Aqhat* as described in the Ugarit texts, an event which means he has been deified. (10) Texts about Baal were essentially a description of the religious liturgy of the Canaanite harvest festival, Baal's symbolic descent into the earth and his triumphant return. (11) The rising of the god who is a savior, similar to the rising of crops, is symbolic of a harvest ritual among the Canaanites as it would later among the Greeks in the myths of Demeter and Persephone. Resurrection becomes an embodiment of two cultural streams: one Canaanite from the cult of Baal, and a second Egyptian. Jesus embodies these two streams about the resurrection that attains a slightly different, but no less significant, theological importance: the realization of hope in an afterlife based on deeds done in this life. (12)

The documents from Egypt tell a similar story. Oxyrhynchus, (modern Behnesa) is an ancient Egyptian provincial capital 125 miles south of Cairo where at the turn of the 20th century one of the largest collections of ancient manuscripts was discovered dating from the 1st–9th century CE, among them the *Gospel of Thomas*. (13) In 367 Athanasius (297–373), Patriarch of Alexandria and champion of the Nicene Creed, banned all unapproved scripture. Local monks near Nag Hammadi took their books, bound them into leather volumes, and buried them in an urn where they remained untouched for 1,600 years. These texts are among the most important historical source for knowledge of Jesus that exists outside of the scriptures and significant for the history of earliest Christianity.

Seventeen previously unknown papyrus manuscripts of portions of the gospels were published in 2000 of *The Oxyrhynchus Papyri*. Mostly small fragments, they comprise seven early manuscripts of *Matthew*, four of John's Gospel, and one each of *Luke, Acts, Romans, Hebrews, James* and *Revelations*. The absence of any manuscripts of Mark and the relative lack of manuscripts of Luke, suggests that, whatever function the gospel canon had it did not translate into four-gospel manuscripts in general, nor into equal numbers of copies of manuscripts of each of the four gospels.

One fragment of a gospel narrative, fragment 840, describes a conversation Jesus has with a Pharisee in the Temple. This description is not found in any other of the canonical gospels and some believe that it is descriptive of a controversy among early Christians about the symbolism of baptismal purity as opposed to purity and cleansing of the heart. (14) Does the author mean to suggest that Christian monks were so perverse as to fabricate stories about Jesus that weren't true? Is the text a recounting of an actual occurrence?

These Greek texts were translated in the 2nd or 3rd century into Coptic. About 200 both Orthodox and Gnostic Christians had opposing interpretations of Jesus, his nature and message, and accused each other of every kind of hypocrisy and heresy. (15) The Nag Hammadi texts contain hundreds of cross-references to sayings of Jesus in *Matthew, Mark, Luke* and *John*. Among them are apocalypses, gospels, collections of sayings of the resurrected Jesus to his disciples, homilies, prayers, and theological treatises. Some sayings criticize common Christian beliefs, such as the virgin birth or the bodily resurrection, as misunderstandings. For example, one curious text in *The Acts of Peter and the Twelve Apostles* seems to infer that mingling with the rich is undesirable for Jesus followers.

> *The rich men of the city, however, those who did not see fit even to acknowledge me, but who reveled in their wealth and pride, with such as these, therefore, do not dine in their houses nor be friends with them, lest their partiality influence you. For many in the churches have shown partiality to the rich, because they are also sinful, and they give occasion for others to sin. But judge them with uprightness, so that your ministry may be glorified, and that my name also may be glorified in the churches.* (16)

One of Jesus' parables does speak unkindly about the rich: "Indeed, it is easier for a camel to go through the eye of a needle than for a rich man to enter the kingdom of God." (17) And whether or not the text is authentic is probably less important than that the community of scribes expressed a belief that the rich were unwelcome in Christianity, an extreme side of stoicism. This was not the accepted view in following centuries when Christianity became less reliant on the asceticism of Judaism and more urbanized and Hellenic as the religion began to capture converts in Rome and major Greek-speaking cities primarily among slaves and lower class citizens.

Scholars assume that *The Gospel of Thomas* was written prior to 140 CE. Most of the sayings show no signs of having any knowledge of the gospels implying that these sayings derive from possibly several oral traditions and/or a common source or sources, the so-called Q document. The Q source is a hypothesis that, like dark matter, everyone assumes exists but no one has ever seen. It's possible the sayings of Jesus in *The Gospel of Thomas* are more authentic that those in the writings of the evangelists. Here are two similarities between sayings in one or more of the four canonical gospels and *The Gospel of Thomas*.

1) *Matthew* 18:20: "For where two or three are gathered together in my name, there am I in the midst of them." The *Gospel of Thomas* notes: "Jesus said, "Where there are two, they are not without God; and where there is one alone, I say, I am with him. Raise the stone, and there you will find me; split the wood, and there I am."

2) In the *Gospel of Thomas*: "Jesus said, let him who seeks continue seeking until he finds. When he finds, he will become troubled. When he becomes troubled, he will be astonished, and he will rule over the All." In *Matthew* 7:7-8, the wording is: "Ask, and it shall be given you; seek, and you shall find; knock, and it shall be opened unto you: For every one that asks receives; and he that seeks finds; and to him that knocks it shall be

opened." Luke copies this saying and shortens it in 11:10: "For every one that asks receives; and he that seeks finds; and to him that knocks it shall be opened."

Can anyone recall with certitude after a half century what someone said?

The 2nd Century CE: Celsus and Origen (c.185– 254 CE)

Christians in the first centuries had to preserve themselves from idolatry without the special protection and license of Jews who were excused with a special dispensation by the Romans from public ceremonies of obeisance to multiple gods. The innumerable deities were an integral part of Roman life and observances to them were expected at public functions and ceremonies where solemn sacrifices were common. While permitting devotions to personal deities, the Romans viewed participation in public religious spectacles as a national obligation and an exercise in civic duty. Those who resisted were viewed as enemies of the state. Polytheistic practices sanctioned by the state that demanded participation were one part of the agony of Christians in exercising their devotion to just one god.

Celsus is one of those who became a serious critic and wrote the most informed early polemic against Christians, castigating their beliefs and practices, often in the form of caricature. (18) Although his major works have been lost because they were destroyed once Christianity became the only authorized Roman religion, Celsus was less an aggressor against Christians than a defender of Roman morality. His principal work, *On the True Doctrine* written about 180 are found with many of his arguments intact in the eloquent Origen, a contemporary Christian apologist. Celsus, in the manner of Plato who uses hypothetical speakers to construct a dialogue, uses a hypothetical Jew to voice his derision of Christianity.

Although Romans were tolerant of the uniqueness of native religions, Christians in the 2nd century were increasingly despising towards the rituals and conventions of Roman morality. Christians, in short, became intolerant towards the rulers and self-righteous towards other religions, asserting their moral superiority, and eventually were seen as enemies of the state. Greeks and Romans had permitted the worship of gods by anyone and had specific gods designated as official state gods like Jupiter. When Christians insisted on only the worship of their god, then their faith became a matter of public apprehension.

If the Christians saw non-Christians as atheists because they worshipped the wrong god or too many gods, non-Christians said that Christians were impious atheists for not recognizing the gods of the empire and worshipping an insignificant person as a god. Celsus defends the existing Roman civil order and viewed Christians as a seditionist cult, reviving or instigating outlandish religious claims that would undermine Roman stability, in effect cutting the bonds between religious persuasion and sound social order and national allegiance. Celsus saw Christians as dangerous because they placed their religious beliefs above the laws of the commonwealth. At the time there was no distinction between church and state, civil or religious laws. (19)

Celsus had a strong appeal to intellectuals who viewed Christians as a cultic group only causing mischief. He saw its members unwilling to serve in the army, to support the Emperor in his struggle to maintain peace, or to hold public office or share in civic responsibilities. He wanted to convert Christians by showing them the futility of their beliefs and recalling them to the ancient and illustrious Roman virtues.

In 529 the emperor Justinian closed the school of philosophy in Athens, the last intellectual stronghold of Greek inquiry and the bastion of learning. Thereafter, philosophy, and in practice all of higher education, defeated more by imperial degree than logical persuasion and intellectual vigor, and in one of history's ironies, went underground to escape persecution from the dominant religion as had the first Christians. Christians perpetrated malicious diatribes and actions once directed against them towards less fortunate philosophers who dared question doctrinal integrity. Philosophy suffered from verbal disputes with Christians, from endless quibbles over metaphysical word meanings given divine weight, seeking to explore hidden meanings in an invisible world, and from the usurpation of the theory of universal Forms into a suspect doctrine. The immortality of the soul had never been admitted in the Law of Moses. By believing it had hit upon the remedy for freeing the soul from its corporeal prison and claiming to have discourses with spirits, Christianity reduced the study of philosophy to theology for nearly two thousand years. It heightened its own intellectual experiments to the level of occultism by admitting to the presence of demons and other extravagant fictions of ancient mythologies. Genius retreated, art and discovery stagnated, and magic, demons, dead spirits and ecclesiastical zealots reigned in European civilization until the Enlightenment in the 17th and 18th centuries.

Origen was the most prolific apologist for Christianity in the first centuries, the most influential theologian until Augustine and the most imitated by later commentators. His father Leonides, who had urged Origen to toil incessantly at his religious studies, was beheaded as a Christian martyr and his property confiscated leaving Origen, his mother, and six younger brothers destitute. (20)

Learned in Greek humanities and philosophy, he taught himself Hebrew and mastered the scriptures. Sternly ascetic, and out of zeal for purity following the advice of Jesus, he castrated himself at a young age. He was ordained a presbyter by the Bishop of Jerusalem but his own Bishop of

Alexandria banished him. He fled to Caesarea where he founded an equally famous school and drew students who studied with him for years. He must not have slept much since his writings, illustrating the rule of faith and approximating over 2,000 works that Jerome describes, appear to be inexhaustible. His patron Ambrose furnished him with seven shorthand writers, an equal number of copyists and several girls trained in penmanship to help him compose his commentaries of scripture which included 22 books from the Hebrew canon. Origen accepted only the traditional four gospels, and his acceptance and Irenaeus' endorsement led to their selection as the acknowledged canon.

His knowledge of Greek made him a formidable adversary against anti-Christian advocates like Celsus. Together with others of an elite but growing intellectual aristocracy, he was adept at blending Greek logic, philosophy and allegory with scripture to project Christianity as the most reasonable religious choice. He used Greek methods and imitated the arguments of stoic philosophers who were opposed to the Greek gods in his defense of Christianity. (21) While most Christians shunned philosophy as a pagan pursuit, Origen showed that philosophical methods can be useful in theological persuasion and that Christianity was an intellectual equal with the best of philosophies.

According to Eusebius, Origen wrote his most illustrious treatise *Contra Celsum* when he was about 60 years old. He concluded that belief was essential in deciding what to believe and what not to believe about Greek fables. But his comment is equally applicable to scripture. (22)

His knowledge of Greek lore is evident when, in refuting the charge of Celsus that the disciples of Jesus were ill-educated and infamous men, Origen uses the example of how Socrates chose Phaedo from a house of ill-fame to study philosophy. (23) But almost unanimously, his argument relies on the wisdom of scripture to counter the arguments and attacks of Celsus. In fact both Celsus and Origen miss the point. Celsus ridicules the belief in Jesus because he compares the incredulity of the Christians with those who believe in fabled stories. Neither writer even argumentatively considered that biblical scribes might have elaborated on biographies by imitating themes and passages from more ancient fables.

This documented controversy between one of the first caricaturists and satirists of Christianity, Celsus, and one of its most noble defenders, Origen, highlights the intellectual challenge of the age. Christians did not defend the acquisition of knowledge, the liberal freedom of reasoning, or the free flow of ideas. Fathers of the early church defended only that knowledge that was useful for salvation, despised the activities of the body and corporeal delights, seeing chastity as nearer to divine perfection, and exalted every interest in the soul and its immortal destiny. By contrast, Islamic believers in subsequent centuries simply conquered lands and peoples by the sword and dispensed with the niceties of theological discourse.

The 3rd Century: Constantine and Christianity

By the 3rd century CE Greek culture and academic refinement began to fade and ultimately disappear as Christianity usurped control over literacy by destroying unacceptable texts and by granting imperial blessings to those who adhered to official orthodoxy and practices. Greek mysticism and Gnosticism had taken deep root in the Christian psyche, but faith was rapidly replacing reason and the healthy and robust skepticism and aesthetic sensibilities the Greeks had bred and instilled.

By institutionalizing Christianity to preserve social harmony, Constantine created a weapon of social conformity against divergent ideas that might further fracture the empire. His enormous power, concentrated in his imperial hands because of the slow deterioration of the economy and the clamoring of barbarians at the gates, allowed him to choose a state religion, an act that would not have occurred under the Republic when the Senate controlled power. Just like the gospels made Jesus equivalent to Homeric epic heroes, Eusebius made Constantine a Christian hero, equating him with Moses. But scholars are dubious about the extent to which Constantine was knowledgeable about Jesus or any aspect of Christianity other than that the Christian population should support his rule and that the new religion should be integrated into imperial designs. Within 150 years after Constantine, the Gothic rule of Theodoric was less cultural than Romans desired and the seat of western rule abandoned Rome for the gutters of Milan and the marshes of Ravenna, choosing s ites for military defensiveness over cultural hegemony.

Jesus became God, and the political fate of the Roman Empire according to Eusebius changed forever, on a particular date in history: October 28, 312. The previous night Constantine, then only ten miles north of Rome, preparing to enter the city and to depose the existing emperor Maxentius, and assume the imperial throne had a dream in which he saw the Greek letters *Chi Rho*, which form the beginning of the monogram word for Christ, accompanied by the words, *In hoc signo vincis*, "In this sign you will conquer." Why he believed that the sign represented Christ and not himself as the soon to be newly anointed or christened one (*Christos*) of Rome is a mystery only the propagators of the legend can answer. Superstitious military men carried many ornamental fetishes on their shields for divine protection.

As Constantine knew well, there were sizeable numbers of Christians then living in Rome and perhaps he thought their presence was an omen. In the early morning of October 28th, he gave a command that each soldier should paint the monogram of *Chi Rho* on his shield. Through clever military strategy and some misfortune on the part of the troops of Maxentius,

Constantine won the battle of Milvan Bridge, entered the city, became emperor of the Roman Empire, and thirteen years later endorsed Christianity as the official state religion. The episode was allowed to become legend so as to endorse success in war with religious belief and re-emphasized his shrewd, decisive and ambitious nature. However, just two years earlier, in 310, he had claimed that Hercules and then Apollo had appeared to him in dreams. But the association of religious acceptance with military victories is essential to understanding his purpose. The Christian legend took historical precedence.

His arch, hurriedly built in 315 and still standing near the Roman Colosseum, has a sculptured relief of Mars, Jupiter, Hercules and the sun god, all associated with war. He is portrayed with son god images, with rays emanating from his head, and nothing of the famous Christian sign, hence rendering Eusebius's account disputable. Constantine was politically astute enough to know that his appeal to all segments of the population was to preserve and combine religious allegiances and to use symbols like the *Sol Invictus*, the unconquerable sun, *Hagia Sophia*, or Holy Wisdom, and the good shepherd, all of which appealed to both pagans and Christians. His brought the same policy for consensus to bear on the disputes among Christians when his convened the Council of Nicaea in 325.

A further event revealed how the imperial will favored toleration. Constantine and Licinius were each regional emperors and met in 313 CE to conclude one of the most tolerant treaties in history, the *Edict of Milan*, a great charter by which individuals would have the privilege of choosing their own religion. But its real object was to secure for Christianity the privileges of an acceptable cult. Within twelve years this charter would be violated by Constantine himself when he declared Christianity the religion of choice for everyone. Having once abandoned attempts to control individual freedom of religion by the Edict, Constantine reversed himself and made conformity to one religion state law. Freedom of religion would not be achieved again in law until the First Amendment of the U.S. Constitution in 1791. (24)

Despite the eulogizing and sycophancy of Eusebius and subsequent Christian apologists, Constantine was a malignant and murderous emperor who, in addition to executing his multiple enemies and at one time compatriots like Licinius, had his son, Crispus, and first wife, Fausta, his maternal grandfather, his uncle, stepbrother and 11 year old son of a rival, all killed. This is the same Constantine, we are expected to believe, who vowed under oath that he would never murder his brother-in-law, but did, and who retained all the old gods on coins struck during this reign. (25) Though he built Christian churches, he also continued to construct pagan temples. Although forever remembered as the patron of early Christianity, Constantine had no moral scruples and used religion for political expediency.

When he chose the proposal of Eusebius of Caesarea at the Council of Nicaea in 325 and compelled the 318 delegates to endorse it, banishing those who disagreed, he helped define an orthodox theology that made Jesus divine for all time. The two delegates who refused to sign the document, Theonas of Marmarica and Secundus of Ptolemais, worth noting for their courage, were rewarded with excommunication and deposed for their principled stand. Many who did sign later regretted their coerced decision even writing to Constantine of their hesitancy and fear. But it was too late. The Nicene Creed is the result and the decision made Jesus consubstantial in essence with God, although some theologians like Origen saw him as consubstantial in existence only. Here are the key words in the three languages revealing the metaphysical and etymological complexity and bewilderment.

Greek	**Latin**	**English**
Ousia	Substantia	Being
Hypostasis	Substantia	Personality

Books of those who objected to the royally accepted doctrine were burned, dissenters banished and their property confiscated. This was the climate of intolerance for the official royal and new Christian policy, insuring it greater permanency than the imperial intrigues, machinations, and assassinations of the short reigns of Constantine's disgraceful sons.

Constantine's establishment of Christianity as the only state religion can be attributed to his prescient recognition that the Christians were the only organized group in the Roman world other than the army. His judicious use of its membership did indeed further his consolidation of power, until slowly and perceptibly the organization of the church and its ecclesiastics became an arm of the imperial bureaucracy under the orthodox Christian emperor Valentinian (321–375). By moving the Roman capitol to the East, Constantine repudiated Rome as the eternal city. By accepting Christianity as the sole imperial religion, he also repudiated the polytheistic traditions of Roman ancestors and the forbearance Rome had extended to all religions thereby instituting religious discrimination that would remain intact for 1,100 years until the Protestant Reformation.

In the first 300 years of its existence, Christianity was a movement with multiple names because of an emerging identity, built on an ethos of an heroic figure, Jesus, around simmering intellectual debates like Gnostic views about resurrection, immortality, the final days (*perousia*), the nature and powers of gods, demi-gods and mysticism. Some Jewish reformers saw Jesus as another prophet. Jewish ascetics adopted him into their purification beliefs. Gnostic mystics saw Jesus as a Son of God, but not the creator God. Some Romans added him to their pantheon of idols.

Try your Greek pronunciation, knowledge of early Christian histories and heresies by wrapping your tongue and mind around: Arianism, Eunomians, Arminianism, Homoians, Manichees, Macedonians or Pneumatomachians, Socianism, Nestorians, Apollinarianism, Sabellianists, Monophysicists. All these groups and its members, claiming to be Christians, would be vilified, harassed, excommunicated, their teachings banned and writings purged from history because they differed from official doctrine and by the political and ecclesiastical figures who said they alone were in possession of true belief. A few hundred years later, when Islam ruled the Middle East, had they simply announced they were Muslim, the whole Muslim world, unused to doctrinal neatness, would have been compelled to admit them as brothers. Christians uniformly agree on the canonical gospels, the Apostles' Creed, and, for some like Catholics, the institutional nature of the church. But none of these conditions existed prior to 325 CE and thus for the first three centuries there was no accepted group of texts, no defined doctrine, and, except for scattered deacons, priests and a bishops, no hierarchical church structure. Some Christians now think it necessary to return to the early era of the church to find there a purity of understanding lost today in the welter of denominations. But this representation of simple purity of faith is unfounded. For example, followers of the Ebionites accepted only the gospel of *Matthew* and followers of Marcion accepted only *Luke*. (26)

Constantine tried to remain indifferent to Christianity's verbal disputes, uneasy about how to solve the quarrels of theologians, seeing their disputations as incomprehensible quibbles. Moreover, he knew that Christian recruits had come largely from disenfranchised populations, those vulnerable to financial and sexual exploitation like freedmen, slaves and non-Roman citizens (27), and that from such a disaffected group could come civil war. (28)

His call for delegate bishops to assemble in Ancyra, which he cancelled, and then Nicaea where 318 bishops assembled (coincidentally, the same number of men Abraham raised to rescue Lot in *Gen.* 14:14) was to quell the Arian controversy and ratify a consensus so the empire might have some religious peace. Constantine could not understand how such inconsequential technicalities could be the cause of so much controversy. He addressed the delegates in Latin though nearly all the delegates were Greek-speaking. The majority of Christians then were in the eastern empire, the location of all the disputatious groups. Rome sent only observers. The Council of Nicaea was convened, not so much to define a belief in the minds of the assembled Christians as to condemn the opinion of Arius who believed that Jesus was a man with divine status and not God, and in the mind of Constantine, to end religious speculation and dissension leading to political instability. Here is what the delegates agreed upon:

> *We believe in one God the Father Almighty, Maker of all things visible and invisible; and in one Lord Jesus Christ, the only begotten (gennthenta, from genus + birth) of the Father, that is, of the substance [ek tes ousias] of the Father, God of God, light of light, true God of true God, begotten not made, of the same substance [homoousion] with the Father, through whom all things were made both in heaven and on earth; who for us men and our salvation descended, was incarnate, and was made man, suffered and rose again the third day, ascended into heaven and comes to judge the living and the dead. And in the Holy Ghost. Those who say: There was a time when He was not, and He was not before He was begotten; and that He was made our of nothing (ex ouk onton); or who maintain that He is of another hypostasis or another substance [than the Father], or that the Son of God is created, or mutable, or subject to change, [them] the Catholic Church anathematizes.* (29)

The Creed proclaims belief in "one God the Father Almighty," but then announces two other gods, all "of the same substance," or in Greek *homoousion*, a term familiar to the Platonists and Aristotelians. Aristotle had written that substance was "eternal and unmovable." *Homoousian* would become the homogenization of belief. But this decision appeared to contradict scripture where Jesus says: "The Father is greater than I," and about the dissonance between the Father's knowledge and the son's: "No one knows, not even the angels in heaven, nor the son, but only the Father." (30) But the argument that only biblical statements should be the basis for creedal beliefs did not receive extended encouragement. And so, reaching beyond so-called sacred texts, council delegates, and later theologians and commentators, borrowed the language of Greek philosophy to perpetuate concepts about rival traditions of divinities, a dreaded pagan belief to promote polytheism under the guise of monotheism.

Reconciling philosophical arguments with mythology of divine attributes was less the pursuit of a goal ignorant of the obstacles than persistence in a goal that was unattainable. No one was able to explain, for example, much less conceptualize, how the father begat the son when both were supposedly equal. Conceding that such a mystery was an obligation of faith rather than an exposition of reason, future commentators in effect professed a declaration of ignorance created by their own ecclesiastical introduction of metaphysical language invented to reveal characteristics of the natural world and not attributes of divinity. A few, like the unoriginal Ambrose only produced polemical attacks condemning opponents, even denouncing them as enemies of the state and suggesting that barbarian hordes had been dispatched by God as vengeance for heretical beliefs in opposition to the creed.

A century earlier a Christian priest and theologian named Sabellius (fl.215) argued that God was indivisible in substance but had as many as three modes or activities, a doctrine which became known after his name, Sabellianism or monarchianism, which in effect denied the existence of separate persons in God's divinity. (31) Sabellius was excommunicated by Pope Calixtus I in 220. Somehow, we are led to believe, a spirit extends into a triad without any loss in essential unity. Indeed, Augustine wrote 15 books of a treatise *On the Trinity*, the first part of which deals with the scriptural basis and the second part where he urges that the human mind be purged of reason so that faith might enter. Here is a sample of his reasoning: "Therefore, they are not three Gods but one God; although the Father has generated the Son, and so He, Who is the Father, is not the Son. And the Son is generated by the Father, and so He, Who is the Son, is not the Father. And the Holy Spirit is neither the Father nor the Son, but the Spirit of the Father and the Son, yet Himself co-equal with the Father and the Son and belonging to the unity of the Trinity." (32) Such tortuous prose was advanced as reasoning so that faith could be secured. Thomas Aquinas more sensibly, but equally unconvincingly, argued that the Trinity cannot be demonstrated and had to be believed. (33) No one suggested that the church got it wrong to begin with.

The Trinity accepts monotheism while denying polytheism. Yet its doctrine is so ingrained in Christianity that it is difficult to imagine that its origin was once precarious and hotly debated. Nicene Council delegates simply equated the opposing concepts with arcane yet familial language, and previous existing divine trinities like Osiris, Isis and Horus, thus merging Greek and Egyptian traditions, and through twisted logic confirming this contradictory idea as central to all belief anathematizing those who disagreed. The little known and unacknowledged Council of Ariminium in 359 passed a degree that stood in opposition to Nicene doctrine.

The Nicene Creed departs radically from Jewish exegesis and tradition that had always relied upon scripture for its interpretive findings and relies upon metaphysical concepts like substance to resolve ambiguities about the nature of Jesus yet cites no biblical references for its convictions. Baruch Spinoza (1632–1677), the great Jewish philosopher, excommunicated from Judaism in 1656 for his intellectual independence including criticism of the Bible, theorized that all reality, all of nature, was but one substance: God. Such pantheism was considered blasphemous to Christianity. But because Spinoza died before his major work *Ethics* was published, and because he was Jewish not Christian, he is only classified as a silly moral philosopher and not a heretic.

The First Council of Constantinople, but the second church council, was convened in 381 by Theodosius and established the principle of belief in the Trinity. The Council of Chalcedon in 451 would continue a philosophical imposition on biblical reality and proclaim that Jesus as God has two distinct natures, one divine and one human and, testing the limits of reason, philosophy and the belief of all subsequent Christians, that these natures exist separately in one person, a ruling which does not contradict the laws of nature any more than does the exploits of semi-divine figures like Achilles, Hercules, or even Samson. Even a DNA test, were it possible to obtain, might not solve this riddle. Hence, new religious writings, no matter how contentious, will never be admitted into the accepted canon without jeopardizing the whole belief system based on the Greek philosophical concepts of divinity, nature and person, the one and the many.

Eutyches (c.378–452) insisted that Christ's humanity was absorbed in his divinity and that to accept two natures at all was unacceptable. For such perfidy he was deposed from his ecclesiastical position and exiled. (34) Nestorius (c. 386–451), Patriarch of Constantinople condemned as a heretic by the Council of Ephesus in 431, held that Mary could not be the mother of God because this would compromise the divinity of Jesus. Nestorius defined nature like substance, distinguished between the human and the divine natures, and refused to attribute to the divine nature the human acts and sufferings of Jesus. (35) Theologians in the 4th century did not take these writings figuratively but literally and, applying metaphysics to literary drama where it did not belong, twisted an art form into theology, creating a new academic study with an emerging historical content but devoid of the substance, metaphorically speaking, said to define its central tenet.

Nor did any debate occur in church councils until the Fourth Lateran Council in 1215 that decreed that the bread and wine in the Eucharist is "transubstantiated" into body and blood of Christ, a doctrine and term confirmed by the Council of Trent in 1551. The body and blood were *substances* maintained under the *accidents* of bread and wine. But substance and accidents are metaphysical terms describing the ancient properties of the physical universe, decidedly unhelpful in understanding atomic and particle physics since such "accidents" extend to the microscopic components of all matter. This is yet another illustration of how much Christian theology owed to Greek philosophy, particularly Aristotle, and how the inappropriate use of Hellenic terminology in theology confused rather than elucidated concepts central to faith.

Once this Catholic (i.e., universally accepted) dogma became proprietary to the Roman state, the military handled conformity to doctrinal purity by accelerating severe penalties for heresy. Arius who had declared that Jesus was a chosen person of God but not equal to the Creator God, was condemned, his writings anathematized, his books cast into the fire, and he was exiled. But it became necessary to decide whether there was one God, two gods, or three, whether Jesus was human with divine powers, or if he was

God whether he had two natures in one person, or two persons, one divine and one human. After Jesus, monotheism itself appeared to be on trial, but church authorities avoided the charges of polytheism by cleverly using the word *persona* instead of godhead.

Around these debates evolved all the schisms, heresies, false doctrines, dissensions, apostasies, martyrdoms, excommunications, and beliefs of tormented souls and contentious minds. The Greek words and meaning attached to them, "being," "essence," "spirit," "substance," "nature," and "person" would be instrumental in deciding forever the faith of billions by linking philosophical abstractions with concepts of divinity thereby confounding the laws of physics and biology, laws presumably generated by the Creator. Yet the complicated formula crafted at Chalcedon in 451 only increased antagonisms among opponents. Its popular decree in the East became apparent when Islamic armies rescued schismatic churches from the traumas of misplaced philosophy and theology and militarily imposed the simplicity of belief in Allah.

In the interim, contentious struggles for the hearts and minds of bickering Christians often resorted to political intrigue and false caricatures, such as that between Cyril, Bishop of Alexandria and Nestorius, Bishop of Constantinople who argued over whether or not Mary was the Mother of God. Nestorius argued that Mary was the Mother of Jesus but that God was the Begetter of the Son. Cyril opposed this rational view and won the backing, possibly through bribery and certainly through chicanery, of the imperial court. He used distortion of Nestorius' views to have his books burned in 435, anathematized him twelve times, and connived to have him banished as a heretic. Employing scurrilous invective, Cyril, who kept his own private army, ruined Nestorius' career. Under his envious watch, Hypatia, one of the most learned mathematicians and philosophers living in Alexandria, was stripped, dragged through the streets to a church and there butchered, her flesh scrapped from her with oyster shells, and subsequent investigation and justice permanently postponed. Thus died Greek mathematics until Descartes. And for all this as a reward, using power and questionable methods to promote orthodoxy, Cyril was made a saint in the church.

Early Christian Theological Disputes

Ebionites (c.100–400)	Jesus was the human Jewish Messiah & Jewish Laws had to be kept
Marcion (c.100–165) (Marcionites)	Two gods, one of the Old Testament and Jesus of the New; accepted only 10 of Paul's epistles & an edited version of Luke

Arius (256–336)	Father & Son not equal, Father created Son (condemned by Nicaea, 325)
Athanasius (328–373) (Bishop of Alexandria)	Father & Son equal, same substance, different persons
Eutyches (c.378–452)	Christ = one divine nature (Christ's Humanity absorbed into the divinity; (Monophysitism condemned)
Cyril (d. 444) (Patriarch of Alexandria)	Christ = 1 person, 2 natures
Nestorius (d. 451) (Patriarch of Constantinople)	Christ = 2 persons, 1 human, 1 divine (condemned, Council of Ephesus (451)

Mani and Manichaeism

Manichaeism is a close cousin of Zoroastrianism and competed with Christianity for converts in the first centuries CE. Founded by Mani (c.216–276 CE) the prophet who called himself, "Mani, Apostle of Jesus Christ," his religion extended its influence into the Middle Ages and Thomas Aquinas felt compelled to write at length refuting it. Mani claimed to be the Paraclete promised by Jesus sent to all men though his heroes were Buddha, Zoroaster, Hermes and Plato.

Mani was born near Baghdad likely of Persian parentage and emerged as a Persian mystic and reformer of morals and religion. He had a vision in his youth and, like John the Baptist, wandered for several years as an ascetic. Soon he appeared as the prophet of a new religion, a synthesis of Buddhism, Gnosticism, Zoroastrianism and Christianity. After his death Manichaeism spread rapidly throughout the Roman Empire and Asia. Mani, like Mohammed for Islam and Joseph Smith for Mormons, saw himself as the last of the prophets, beginning with Adam and including Buddha, Zoroaster, and Jesus and the bearer of a universal message replacing all other religions. Roman emperors, after the adoption of Christianity as the state religion, assiduously persecuted Manichees as did all early Christian communities.

The body, Mani believed, was the battlefield where the struggle for good and evil occur, because the body has parts of good and evil in it. This was a doctrine held by stoics like Epictetus and had an echoing Zoroastrianism theme. Therefore for Mani it was necessary to perform certain ascetic practices to cleanse the body of impurities. The good in man was represented by the light and spiritual enlightenment of god, and the evil by the darkness and material things of the devil. The central tenet of Manichaeism, a belief Augustine held for nine years in his youth, is that there is a struggle between God represented by light and enlightenment, and Satan, represented by the material world and darkness. Humans, composed of matter governed by Satan with a touch of immaterial soul, are in the middle of this struggle. Spiritual illumination (*gnosis*) reveals that the soul that shares in the spirituality of God has fallen into dark world of matter and is saved by spirit or intelligence (*nous*). To know one's self is to transcend the world. Sinners after death wander about in torment, surrounded by demons, and condemned by the angels, till the end of the world, when they are cast into hell.

Mani's Ten Commandments forbade idolatry, lying, avarice, killing, fornication, theft, seduction to deceive, magic, hypocrisy, and religious indifference. Prayer and fasting were common duties. Prayer, preceded by a ceremonial purification with water, was obligatory four times a day: at noon, late in the afternoon, after sunset, and three hours later, made facing the sun or, in the night, the moon. When neither sun nor moon was visible, then the petitioner faced North. The spacing and sequencing of prayer times is similar to that used by Muslims who face towards Mecca instead of the sun. Prayers of the Manis, like Buddhist incantations, consist mainly of praiseworthy epithets without supplication and were accompanied by twelve prostrations addressed to the various personalities in the realm of light. Everyone fasted on the first day of the week in honor of the sun. The Perfect or Elect, the elite of the group, fasted on the second day in honor of the moon. A monthly fast was begun on the eighth day of the month.

About the year 1,000 CE a group appeared in southern France that denied miracles, the sacraments, baptism, Christ's presence in the Eucharist and the efficacy of prayers to saints. At the time there flourished as many as 140 different sects and religious interpretations, some which convinced their adherents to live chaste lives, to walk barefoot in sandals, to live in communes, practices at the time not out of keeping with Christian monastic groups like the Benedictines. These movements, which had spread throughout Europe, eventually rejected doctrinal beliefs like the Trinity and Virgin Birth, liturgical rituals, even the priesthood. Medieval troubadours used such groups as satirical cover to lambaste and heckle the clergy, pilgrims and religious practices.

The most influential of these groups were the Cathars (Greek for pure), also known as the Albigenses, who flourished in the 11th and 12th century in southern France. They were religious descendants of Gnosticism and Manichaeism. Cathars believed in a dualistic universe where the earth was governed by the forces of Light, or God, and the forces of Evil, or Satan, and rejected the outward rituals and ceremonies of the Catholic Church. (36) The beginning of the Catholic Church's Inquisition dates from this period.

In *Deuteronomy* we find the admonition: "If there arise among you a prophet, or a dreamer of dreams...saying 'Let us go after other gods'...that prophet or dreamer of dreams shall be put to death," thus lending divine authority to kill those of alternative beliefs. (37) At the height of classical Rome, the worship of Jupiter was closely allied with the Emperor and both heresy and blasphemy were classed as treason. A Roman judge would convene an *inquisitio*, an inquiry, into the case, and this same procedure was adopted by ecclesiastical authorities in the Middle Ages. (38) The inquisition, commonly associated with the Catholic Church's persecution of deviant beliefs, dates from the Romans who also had commissions that sought to extirpate unorthodox religious dissent.

The medieval Inquisition begun by Pope Innocent III, compelled to protect the ecclesiastical organization from doctrinal impurities and disunity, was established to root out what became known as the Albigensian heresy. After 30 years of conflict, hundreds were converted from heresy when extended the opportunity, but thousands succumbed to death rather than renounce their belief. (39)

For Euripedes, the gods are the cause of human tragedy, just as they would be in the early sagas of *Genesis*. By the time of *Deuteronomy*, the Hebrew God would sanction the killing of anyone who worshipped pagan gods. Euripedes wrote in *Hippolytus*: "Men make their choice: one man honors one God, and one another." (40) Euripedes in *Hippolytus* pits one god, Aphrodite, goddess of love, against another god, Artemis goddess of the hunt, which results in the tragic deaths of a queen, Phaedra, and a prince, Hippolytus, step-son of Phaedra and illegitimate son of Theseus. Aphrodite makes Phaedra fall in love with her stepson who is chaste. When a nurse reveals her secret to him, he rebuffs her and she hangs herself leaving a written message that implicates him in her presumed rape. Theseus banishes Hippolytus who dies when Poseidon answers Theseus' prayer to have him killed by chasing his chariot into cliff rocks.

The Bible was written with mythical traditions. The gospels were written with a combination of biblical prophecies, apocalyptic visions, Gnosticism, stoicism and purloined episodes from epic literature. But once the written words were codified, the discussions over meaning and the institutionalization of the church impelled by imperial power and proclamations began in earnest. The plurality of beliefs in the first three hundred years of Christianity created a diverse mixture of religious ferment such as today exists in Syria among Nestorians driven out of Iraq, Armenians forced to leave Turkey, and Palestinian Christians deported from Israel.

Whoever called themselves exclusively Christian in the first couple of centuries lacked doctrinal clarity but not passionate conviction. In the earliest centuries Christians were little more than a sect without a coherent set of doctrinal beliefs but with established rituals. The adoption of the Bible as a part of the Christian canon by Jerome and others by the 4th century softened the criticism that Christianity had no roots but obscured the evidence that its literary derivatives were adaptations from fables.

The evidence for the lack of doctrinal Christian unity resides in period art that reveals symbolic images from adornments common throughout the empire. Early sanctuaries have frescoes and statuary that model decorative features of other religions, and I have seen examples in, among other places, the Cairo museum where crosses are linked together with the Egyptian ankh, the sign of life. (41) Christianity adopted the language, mystery cults, and stoic and Platonic philosophies of the Greeks and folded them all into the liturgy of the Mass. The doctrine of the Trinity, the last judgment and personal immortality came from the Egyptians. Persia lent Christianity the millennium ideology of a final conflagration, a cyclic series of ages of the world, the cult of Mithras, and the dualism of light and darkness and good and bad divinities, God and Satan.

Christianity is a synthesis of swirling ancient ideas, the final and greatest of the mystery religions, the last invention of the pagan world, a template for the aggregate of religions and myths preceding it. Having thoroughly absorbed the past, commentators strong in belief but weak in literary knowledge extolled Christianity's superior doctrine to so-called pagan beliefs, elevated theological invective to an art form and suppressed intellectual inquiry for twelve hundred years by executing dissenters. By believing that God's providence had favored them from the persistence of theological error, the clerical hierarchy, adopting the imperialism of the emperors, created absolutism in religion that eliminated doctrinal confusion and ambiguities that even Yahweh would have envied. Thus, the pope, bishop, abbot or religious superior could command and each had to obey as if it were God's will, and the abdication of the power to think for oneself was installed as the highest Christian virtue. The eschatological visionaries had actually got it right: the world had come to an end. But it was the ancient mythological world of multiple deities.

CHAPTER SIXTEEN
ARIUS, ATHANASIUS AND AUGUSTINE

Christians in the 4th century had more gospels, testaments, and epistles than they could count on an abacus. Yet most of these documents were subsequently lost and only a few were included in the official canon of authorized texts. Many are acknowledged forgeries. (1) There are at least 16 gospels, 6 Acts, 12 epistles and 9 apocalypses classified as disavowed documents. The number of non-canonical documents with varying accounts of the life and sayings of Jesus is only part of the literary confusion.

Mixing metaphysics with theology was even more bewildering. Differentiating terms like essence from existence, substance from accidents, and person and nature was the stuff of cocktail and coffee house conversations as well as theological discourse. Was the essence of Jesus as man and God equivalent to his existence? Was his divine substance revealed or hidden in his appearance? In nuclear physics the quest today is for the nature of matter as it was the nature of God and Jesus in the 4th century. Was Jesus the word (Logos), the Son of God, the equal of God, a man with divine status, consubstantial with God, a divine part of God, a person in God's nature, or some combination? Whichever answer prevailed, the result was theological equivocation.

A short history of the 4th century is a record of inflexible minds in pursuit of a single doctrine that would unify the squabbling communities with a multitude of meanings for what Christianity meant. In this final chapter we look at how metaphysics contributed to the formation of Christian dogma, capping all the precedents that evolved from ancient mythical literature, and that covered scripture with ideological icing. Defining who Jesus was is the key to all subsequent meaning to Christianity.

When Constantine died in 337, his three sons Constans, Constantinus and Constantius, the last a confirmed Arian, divided the empire into three parts. Ecclesiastical authorities were viewed at the time as Roman subordinates answerable to the Emperor. The patriarchs of Constantinople and Alexandria were the principal ecclesiastical seats of power. The Bishop of Rome did not have any more power than did any other bishop and in fact reported to the Emperor of the West, Constans, as the bishops of the East reported to Constantius.

Several significant individuals and church councils defined the nature of Christianity in the first centuries, but three figures in particular illustrate the political and religious controversies generated: Arius, a popular priest with a theological interpretation that Jesus had divine powers but was not God; Athanasius, Bishop of Alexandria who adhered strictly to the Nicene Creed; and Augustine who more than any other theologian solidified Christian belief.

The word "heresy" from the Greek *hairesis*, meaning, among other things, "choice," has evolved to mean a religious opinion contrary to church dogma. Heresiarchs, the cleverest speculative theologians, are originators of a heresy. All discussion was colored by the fact that those in error might be consigned to hell if they did not prevail, or suffer imperial exile if they chose the wrong side of the argument. Arianism was the most popular belief and, except for a few minor political setbacks and intrepid adversaries, could easily have become the principal Christian belief.

Arius (c.256–336 CE) and Arianism

Arius, a Libyan-born ascetic parish priest and theologian living in Alexandria, founded the most controversial alternative view of the identity of Jesus. Though his early education is uncertain, he was a certified public preacher in Alexandria and Master of a Christian School. (2) His heresy elicited imperial and ecclesiastical indignation. Eusebius, Bishop of Palestine and author of the first ecclesiastical history of the church, and another Eusebius, Bishop of Caesarea, together with Athanasius, Bishop in Cilicia (southern Turkey) believed in him and his doctrines and supported him in exile. (3) His pride was bolstered by the additional support of two Egyptian bishops, assorted presbyters and deacons and, if Gibbon is to be believed, over 700 virgins. (4) His popularity was enhanced by his preaching zeal as much as it was by the vitriolic writings of his implacable adversaries.

Arius said that Christ was not one with the Creator God but rather was the Logos. For Arius the Son of God was a creature made "out of nothing" by the Father and thus a super-angelic nature. He argued that if the Son had been begotten by the Father it had to have been in time and that therefore the Son is not coeternal or coequal in substance with the eternal Father. (5) God was not always a Father, since he had not yet created a son. The son is one of the beings created by the Word of God. The created son is by nature subject to change and variation like all creatures. (6) Arius raised questions like: If God became man in the person of Jesus, he entered a world of time and motion. If Jesus was "begotten not made," as the Nicene Creed proclaimed, then he became subservient to natural laws. If we take contemporary speech and ask if a divided cell is begotten or made, the question appears nonsensical since the division and multiplication of cells defines the process of life's regeneration. A "begotten" person without any physical act but by spiritual or creative energies stretches the language boundaries even of metaphysics.

Here are some gospel texts supporting the Arian view that Jesus was not divine.

Why do you call me good? No one is good but God alone. (Mark 10:18)

My father, if it is possible, let this cup pass me by. Nevertheless, let it be as you, not I, would have it. (Matt. 26:39)

And eternal life is this: to know you, the one true God and Jesus Christ whom you have sent. (John 17:3)

My God, why have you forsaken me? (Mark 15:34)

The logic of this argument is persuasive with scriptural texts. But logic and reason do not necessarily win converts or friends in orthodox land. Though Arianism had an impressively large following and widespread influence, Arius' ideas ran into serious conflict with important ecclesiastical authorities like Alexander, Patriarch of Alexandria, and his successor Athanasius, who sedulously pursued him as a heretic. Emperor Constantine, a military man of no reflective study and less education, who abhorred Christian dispute in his realm believing it to be civilly divisive, in 325 called the determinative Council of Nicaea to resolve the theological dilemma as we saw. No such theological purity had clouded Jewish belief that had allowed, for example, the Pharisees to believe in life after death, and equally allowed the Sadducees to reject it. Jesus never condemned the Sadducees.

The Council of Nicaea declared that the Son is "consubstantial," (*homoousion*), or "of one being with the Father." A delegate named Marcellus had proposed a more diplomatic "of a similar nature" (*homoiousion*) which the Arians favored. According to Gibbon, the faith of the church hung on one diphthong. The council, however, choosing the more esoteric of the descriptions, and in order to preserve both the idea of God incarnate and monotheism, anathematized Arius who suffered the rancor of theological wrath through banishment, and his works, the chief of which is *The Banquet* and *Thalia* (only fragments remain) were ordered burned. For his beliefs Arius was first excommunicated locally by a synod in Alexandria 321, but declared orthodox in Asia Minor, where he fled in 323 supported by Eusebius. The Councils of Tyre in 334 and Constantinople in 336 declared him orthodox. But in the disputatious reaction after Nicaea Arius came again into imperial favor under Constantine. The emperor had ordered the Athanasians at Constantinople to receive him at communion, after a synod at Jerusalem, meeting first at Tyre and thereafter known as the Council of Tyre, had approved his reinstatement. After a triumphal procession through the city, he suddenly died at age 80. The Catholic Church today still regards him as a heresiarch. The birth of orthodoxy began a theological tradition of vehement prejudice against early Christians with divergent views.

Un-recognized church councils like Nicomedia (327), Tyre (334), and Constantinople (336) nonetheless did recognize Arius, which is why the Greek Orthodox Church does not accept their validity. Constantius, who may have felt more comfortable in war than listening to the petty battles and theological invectives of his clergy, fell under the influence of Arians and supported them. The un-recognized Council of Antioch in 342 in fact ignored the central issue of *homoousian*, the key sticking point of Nicaea. (7) Isaac Newton, convinced of the logic of Arius, became an Arian by belief, though secretly to avoid similar ecclesiastical condemnation. (8) Arius accomplished something very Hellenic: he used logic and Aristotelian metaphysics to describe nature, person, substance and how such attributes could describe divinity. His logic was compelling but his fortune unlucky.

But the theological dispute did not go away with the death of Arius. When Constantine died in 337, his son, Constans, became emperor in the West and another son, Constantius, who was sympathetic to the Arians, became emperor in the East. At a council held at Antioch in 341, an affirmation of faith was issued that omitted the word *homoousion*, "of the same substance." Arian delegates then declared at Sirmium in 357 that the Son was "unlike" the Father whereas moderates claimed that the Son was "of similar substance" with the Father. These Arian views were approved in 360 at Constantinople, where all previous creeds were rejected, and the term "substance" was repudiated. A statement of faith was issued stating that the Son was "like the Father who begot him."

After Constantius' death in 361 the Christian majority in the West consolidated its power base again. The emperor Valens persecuted Arians, and when Emperors Gratian and Theodosius I took up the defense of orthodoxy, Arianism collapsed. In 381the Second Ecumenical Council met at Constantinople. Arianism was proscribed and the Nicene Creed was re-approved. (9) Thus did imperial power dictate the onus of Christian belief when Christians preferred to be democratic and argue among themselves.

Could the controversy have been resolved in deliberate consultation without the intricate cavils and power plays of emperors and clerics? Could practicing Christians share dissimilar beliefs about the nature, essence and substance of God without prejudice? The answer is No. Once you admit that Jesus is God, and that there is only one God, you must reconcile how the Father relates to the Son as one person, otherwise you must admit a greater and a lesser god, a popular and widespread idea in heroic literature. Or you must admit there is more than one god, or, agreeing with Arius, that Jesus was not God but had divine powers. Once you accept more than one person within an essence or substance, you can always add another, as was done with the Holy Spirit, making a philosophical trinity of persons in one God, but somehow not a trinity of gods. Having its written tenets born in myth, the early Christian church soon swan in the heady sea of metaphysics and used the abstractions of the most obtuse of all philosophies to define who Jesus was. Once doctrine was defined in concrete, dissenters were lucky if only exiled since the unrepentant and skeptical in the following centuries met far worse fates.

In the century that followed the adoption of the Creed, Christian apologists did nothing except write the dogma repeatedly, fight about its words and meaning, inquire about new novelties in thinking which might become heresies, and blunder through theological ambiguities all the while anathematizing each other. Smaller groups of Arian sympathizers like that headed by Aetius of Antioch, called the "atheist" by Christian opponents, believed that "the substance of the Son is unlike the substance of the Father," a view shared by the short-lived Gallus, half brother of the emperor Julian. The fortunes of theologians fluctuated according to the beliefs of emperors. (10) Theology became homogenized so that social chaos would not disrupt the empire. The Roman Empire's collapse came about soon enough by barbarians. Had it not fallen when it did Christians might easily have hastened its disintegration through theological disputes.

Religious zealotry prompted the burning of outlawed books. In Alexandria in 641, General Amru, said to be second in succession of the prophet Muhammad, used the books and parchments of the great library of Alexandria to fuel for six months the 4,000 baths of the city, a story probably more legend than truth. (11) If the documents were not in the Koran, Amru thought, they were pernicious. He might have said heretical but he didn't know Greek and was not Christian.

Ancient religions prior to Christianity had the good sense not to attempt to define the ineffable with imperfect language but to confer sacred significance on images, usually of animals like bulls or birds, or forces in nature like the sun and wind. Hebrews declared that the pronunciation of God's name was an offense. The first Christians, abandoning this useful principle to discourage polytheism, reverted to metaphysics to describe the invisible, unattainable, and mysterious. Had the arcane abstractions of Neo-Platonism not been introduced into the theology of Christianity we might only have the Jewish legacy of allegory and stoic parables.

Arianism was prejudiced by subsequent Christian apologists after the political and doctrinal triumph of the Nicene creed and after the complete ascendancy of this doctrine by the emperor Theodosius by 388 whose anti-heretical legislation effectively ended theological conflicts but not its polemics. (12)

Athanasius (297–373)

The Catholic Church lists him as a saint and doctor of the church for his championing of creedal orthodoxy. But his life had an uncertain beginning, a suspicious election to the patriarchy in 328, and a checkered history of exile and condemnation by various councils and emperors. Though he spent 20 years in exile or as a fugitive and was expelled from his Episcopal see five times, he held his position intermittently as Bishop of Alexandria for 46 years.

Athanasius had opposed Arius and his views at the Council of Nicaea and for the rest of his life fought Arian proponents and the emperor Constantius who supported the Arian cause. The Nicene Creed and the view of Athanasius prevailed because the church and emperor Theodosius destroyed the buildings and persons of those who resisted. Councils conveniently at odds with church doctrine were declared invalid and not listed on the roster of acceptable ecclesiastical assemblies. A short history of unaccepted councils denouncing Athanasius is instructive because it illustrates the progression of the lingering tensions created after Nicaea. (13)

1) The Council of Tyre in 335 (which concluded its business at Jerusalem where Constantine ordered it to dedicate the new church of the Resurrection) found Athanasius guilty of grave counts of misconduct and, believing his election to the bishopric in Alexandria to be illegitimate, appointed a successor to his see.

2) The 1st Council of Constantinople in 336 declared Arius to be orthodox and reinstated him. Arius was returning to Constantinople in triumph when he abruptly died in 336. The same year Athanasius was exiled to Trier, and the following year, 337, Constantine died and his son Constantius, a confirmed Arian, reigned as emperor in the East.

3) The Council of Antioch, an assembly of 90 bishops associated with Eusebius an Arian supporter, met in 338-39 with the Emperor Constantius present, totally ignored the *homoousian* issue, supposedly central to belief, and condemned and deposed Anthanasius who fled to Rome and an eight year exile. A list of 25 canons it passed still regulates the discipline of the Greek Orthodox church. Believing this council had been coerced by his political enemies, Athanasius never accepted this condemnation from the Council of Antioch (or any other convened council) even though it had the Emperor in attendance. However, while he was in exile in Rome in 341, 50 bishops, supported by the Bishop of Rome Julius, pronounced Athanasius innocent.

4) A council was called to meet in 323 in Serdica, Thrace, on the southeastern tip of the Balkan peninsula. Approximately 170 bishops assembled, 66 from the East and about 90 from the West, including Athanasius and Julius, Bishop of Rome. Before the council could formally gather, word came that the Emperor Constantius had won a battle against the Persians and the outnumbered and hence outvoted eastern bishops used the victory as an excuse to return to their sees. But eastern bishops in a synod letter composed after leaving Serdica excommunicated their opponents, abusively denounced Athanasius, including the Bishop of Rome for harboring him, and castigated the usual suspects they deemed dissident if not heretical. In the same letter they raised again the central theological belief about the Oneness of the Trinity, but used the Greek term *hypostasis*, which refers to the substance of an individual but not the same substance, thereby muddying the idea of how each God in the Trinity could in any way be separate entities. This re-definition of the Nicene Creed, designed to elucidate the obscurities of multiple gods in one God, seemed to be replacing the Creed. (14)

The western emperor Constans wrote petitioning his brother Constantius to reverse his decision, to re-instate Athanasius, and implied the use of military force unless his request was granted. Athanasius returned to Alexandria in 346, but his sojourn was brief because in 350 Constans died and Constantius, a pro-Arian, assumed the imperial throne for East and West. He convened a council in Arles in 353, placing two Arian bishops in charge and providing the council, attended by two papal legates, a pre-drafted document to sign that included a condemnation of Athanasius with no opportunity to debate the issue. The charge from Constantius was accompanied by an imperial edict threatening with exile any bishop who did not vote in favor of Athanasius' condemnation. There is evidence extensive bribery was used to obtain the vote. All delegates yielded to the imperial demands except Paulinus of Treves who was summarily banished to Phrygia dying soon thereafter.

5) In 351 the Council of Sirmium (there were eventually three such councils at Sirmium) condemned a certain Photinus and Athanasius but its decision about Athanasius was not accepted in Gaul, Italy or Spain.

6) In 353-54 the Council of Arles, organized by the emperor Constantius, who possibly bribed delegates, denounced Athanasius.

7) The Council of Milan denounced and condemned Athanasius.

8) In 359 the Council of Ariminum (modern Rimini on the Adriatic coast of Italy) was held with over 400 bishops in attendance. As moderates attempted to mediate a code of faith as well as unity that everyone could favor, the agenda was prepared in advance and delegates were urged to subscribe to its contents. In effect, the document the council saw deleted the words "substance" (*ousia*) and "consubstantial" declaring that the fathers at Nicaea were acting "without proper reflection." (15) Western bishops, about 80 in number demurred, wrote to the emperor requesting permission to leave, were denied and told to meet the emperor in Adrianople where they politely acquiesced to obvious Arian views.

From 355 to 381 and until Theodosius convened the Second Council of Constantinople, these various synods or councils, depending on their pro or anti-Arian persuasion, restated or inveigled against creedal positions and praise or denounce key church figures. There were always procedural questions about whether bishops deposed by one council could sit in another, whether their votes could count or not, and whether votes taken in secret enclave were legitimate. Inevitably, excommunication, or at the least denunciation and losing the privilege of a bishopric, were imposed on dissidents.

Emperors feared that the Bishop of Alexandria, the most powerful church official in the eastern Roman world, might support a rival claimant to the throne and bring about a civil war. Emperors knew well that the population had turned largely Christian and that theological intervention was risky but necessary, though any punitive action might bring angry mobs into the streets.

Imperial interference does not necessarily imply ignoble intentions. Constantine preferred theological consensus less than he did civil order. His son Constantius believed that the agreement at Nicaea was not popular, was hastily contrived, too authoritatively administered, and sought to obtain ecclesiastical consent to overturn it. Julian, exasperated by the religious divisiveness, petty squabbling and self-righteous indignation of church leaders, sought to return religious freedom to the population by reinstating paganism. Theodosius, an entrenched conformist imbued with passionate conviction, brought the full power of the empire to restore the Nicene intent. After Theodosius and the 2nd Council of Constantinople in 381, Arianism disappears from the Christian and Roman world, lingering only among some Teutonic tribes. Thereafter religious dissent evaporated.

Athanasius had an unknown form of education and his writings reveal a raw, unpolished intellect that derided all inspiration not biblical. He reduced the complications of ecclesiastical politics to those who were for him or against him, and tried to reach policy stability not through diplomacy but absolutism in belief. He minimized differences using caricature and ridicule to rebut his enemies. When persuasion failed he encouraged his followers to partisan disorder. He offered no new profound insights into the theological discourse and used crude rhetorical flourishes and invented dialogue to disarm his adversaries that demean his writings. Athanasius in the official church history appears as the caped defender of the Nicene creed, although it is not entirely clear that the Holy Spirit guided only this first council and no others, especially those that condemned him. Athanasius distorts the historical record and, overlooking that he was many times condemned by the verdicts of several councils of bishops to make his motives seem reputable, and rails against his enemies.

What began as ecclesiastical diplomacy ended as diatribe and denunciation. It was not just the pettiness of the ecclesiastics that settled the theological disputes but the political intrigues and edicts of emperors. Does the Holy Spirit guide the motives and actions of emperors equally or more so than it does a council of elected bishops? Constantine had called a council and forced it to agree to a unanimous outcome, while condemning Arius' alternative view of part human, part divine view about the divinity of Christ. Constantine's son Constantius sided with the opposition and Arianism was upheld by several councils.

Julian, whose father was stepbrother to Constantine, had been schooled in philosophy and religion and became known to history as the Apostate because he relinquished Christianity. He reverted the empire back to paganism to avoid the fractiousness of the Christian theological disputes. He eliminated the prerequisites of the clergy. Freedom of religion was proclaimed with an edict in 362, in effect over-turning the previous edicts establishing Christianity as the imperial religion. Julian did not outlaw Christianity as Constantine did paganism, and citizens were again allowed to practice freedom of religion. Christian historians have since demonized his efforts to placate those who sought religious freedom.

But with the reign of Theodosius, orthodox Christianity by 381 and the 2nd Council of Constantinople installed as triumphant, freedom of religion was abolished. The loss of books declared heretical has not been accidental. Christian emperors, patriarchs, bishops and clerics all condoned or administered the burning of manuscripts and books judged to be un-orthodox. Historians are faced with gleaning objections, retorts, contentions and arguments from Christian authors like Irenaeus, Clement and Tertullian, who condemned heretical writings.

Tertullian's vituperation extends to the rodent and insect kingdom for adjectives against those he considers heretics. He compares Gnostics, for example, to scorpions. Like other commentators who blithely dismisses alternative beliefs, his vitriol is comparable to yellow journalism where his derogatory, purple Latin prose put-downs enhance his defense of the orthodox. He does not adequately present opposing views. Tertullian assumes the wrathful and menacing posture of a Deuteronomic Yahweh angry at his people for unspecified wickedness and urging death upon non-believers. (16)

Augustine (354-430): The Christian Neo-Platonist

Augustine was the greatest thinker of the early Christian Latin era and the last of the late classical Roman period, a teacher of rhetoric for 11 years who underwent an intellectual conversion to Platonism, a rejection of Manichean persuasion, and then a religious conversion to Catholicism while in his 30s. The joining of Platonism and Pauline Christianity in the literary hands of Christianity's most influential writer began a new theological tradition. His greatest accomplishment besides his autobiography, one of the great, poetic works of literature, is his marriage of religious with classical studies. He had unrivaled influence and an all-encompassing grip on Christian thought. His *Confessions* is composed with a dedication, sincerity and a personalized vision rare in literature. (17) Christian theology crystallizes under Augustine. He appropriated the literature of the *Psalms* for his poetic inspiration, Plato for his transcendent vision, and Paul to transform the person of Jesus as the embodiment of creation and fulfillment of salvation.

He was born in Tagaste (Souk Ahras) in eastern Algeria, then a part of the Roman Empire, and lived to witness the destruction of Rome by the Visigoths in 410. He was a student of classics and as a young man became an ardent Manichean for nine years, taught rhetoric in Carthage and Tagaste and won a prestigious poetry prize. But as a youth, according to his autobiography, he chose concubinage, then acceptable under Roman law, rather than licentiousness, becoming a father when he was 18. (18) His son, Adeodatus, died when he was only18 years old. In 383 he left for Rome to teach rhetoric but quickly became disenchanted with many students who attended his lectures but who quit before paying their fees. Learning of a vacancy in Milan for a teacher of rhetoric, he moved north, won an audition, and was accepted into the salaried teaching post as professor of rhetoric.

Hearing the sermons of Ambrose the famous Bishop of Milan he was converted to Catholicism and baptized by him in 387. (19) After his conversion, Augustine retreated to the hills of northern Italy and lived on a communal farm while still instructing younger pupils, including his own son. He returned to North Africa after five years thoroughly transformed. In 388 he founded a retreat in his native city where his son and a few friends and relatives lived semi-monastically, which evolved into the oldest monastic order in the West, the Augustinians. He was ordained a priest in 391 at the demand of the local congregation and consecrated bishop of Hippo in 395. He devoted the next 35 years to writing his classic *Confessions* and *The City of God* and other commentaries on scriptures. He died in 430 at the age of 76.

His several volumes of writings (and 230 treatises) defining Christianity became the central belief of the Middle Ages, and united and strengthened idealistic philosophy and mysticism in Christianity.

Augustine was an illustrious forerunner who combined classical study with religious practice. His writings would be recognized as a sort of second bible, often quoted and easily understood about the meaning and exercise of spirituality in ordinary life. Medieval education and belief thrived on his ideas because they had more depth and were more original and perceptive than anyone's in the ancient Christian world.

Through Augustine we encounter a compelling new worldview suffused with transcendent reality and an abandonment of inquiry into phenomenal realities. (20) It is a theme echoed in *Psalm* 68:33 where the poet-scribe writes, "See you lowly ones and be glad; you who seek God, may your hearts be merry!" and in *Romans* 12:2 where Paul notes "And be not conformed to this world, but be transformed in the newness of your mind, that you may discern what is the good and acceptable and perfect will of God," and in *I Corinthians* 8:2-3: "If anyone thinks he knows anything, he has not yet known as he ought to know." Because of the repudiation of secular learning Europe did not have centers of higher education for 800 years after Augustine.

Augustine outlines two differing kinds of Christianity: an internal mystical experience, and an institutionalized, church experience. What was best was the mystical, internal experience. Augustine believed that nature was the product of God thinking, an idea reminiscent of Hindu as well as Platonic thought. He believed that God revealed truths intuitively to men's minds and held that man's love must stretch towards the love of God and that this was man's purpose in life. He wed Platonic thought and idealism with the theology of the gospels so successfully that his ideas influenced Western thought for over 800 years, and led some Protestant reformers to think that they were on a mission by returning the Church to Augustinian belief. His ideas of the evil resident in the body and the corrupting influence of bodily desires, resonant of Manichean belief, were revived during the Reformation. In *The City of God* he struggles to describe predestination, whereby God knows in advance who will be saved, an idea resurrected during the Reformation by Martin Luther, paradoxically an Augustinian friar.

But Augustine could not rid himself of the idea of evil, why it existed, how it got into the world where only God provided good and why it plagued humanity. Christian evil assumed the idea of Persian evil, an evil god under Zoroastrianism and Mani, an evil body assumed by the Gnostics, and became a cornerstone for the Christian concept of original sin. This idea was founded on questionable scriptural citations from Paul, whereby disobedience under Adam created sin passed on to the whole human race through sexual intercourse. The idea of punishment for sins committed by ancestors is found in Greek myths. Aphrodite speaks about Artemis in Euripedes' *Hippolytus*: "It must be the sin of some of my ancestors in the dim past (that) God in his vengeance makes me pay now." (21)

Original sin becomes the dominant fact of human existence for Augustine and the necessity of death and eternal damnation an acceptable conclusion. It is unclear how something incorporeal emerges from semen and ova, or how individuals can be sinful without free will and be held responsible for the transgressions of another, an idea alien to all ethics. It is even more contentious to understand how original sin gets in a soul if the soul is implanted at the time of conception, a question universally ignored because it is seemingly not resolvable. If the soul is not individualized, but part of a universal spirit, than individuals cannot be held accountable. Would god give each person a soul already tainted with evil? Augustine would argue that God is loving and good and yet without qualms could condemn innocent, non-baptized babies to hell because of something Adam, a mythical figure, had done. (22)

He became enchanted with Plato about the time of his conversion. Plato's concept of the immaterial Idea is in Augustine's mind transformed into the transcendent God. All other "goods" were derivative of God's goodness. The good life for all men is to obey God's law, because the good life, the ethical life, is the one in which worldly desires are subordinated to God's will, as goodness is an approximation to the likeness of God. The Augustinian expression of Christian ethics is that God has created a model for the highest kind of human conduct and that his command is that men should live according to his laws. (23) Paul, who had assimilated Gnostic and Platonic characteristics and gave a mystical interpretation to the mission and message of Jesus, had converted Augustine whose popular theology was a transcendent creation of spirit over matter, eternal immateriality over objective reality, and the adulteration of knowledge and the body. (24)

But the pursuit of God's goodness of necessity means a debasing of other intellectual inquiries. Augustine held men versed in liberal arts in high esteem but was skeptical of men of science. (25) Augustine ignored Aristotle and converted Plato's Ideal into God, heaven, and an immortal soul, made God the origin and objective of all truth, condemned all other intellectual quests as unworthy, and substituted the habit of piety for the acquisition of knowledge. (26)

All Greeks had a tolerance for diversity of opinions that included sophists who could persuade you of anything, and skeptics who doubted everything. But when faith superceded knowledge as a human quest, all scientific, literary, poetic and mystic literature quickly fell into disrepute in the widening Christian world. Aristotle in the first sentence of *The Metaphysics* wrote: "All men by nature desire to know," a perspicacious observation unheeded by theologians who believed that nature's propensity to gain knowledge should be abandoned and faith extolled. (27) The fact that Aristotle also noted that all knowledge is provisional was not enough for Paul or Augustine. Everything in scripture had to fit into the box of orthodoxy. Scriptural commentaries crowded out shelves of books on all other topics. By the Middle Ages even scholars who ventured to study outside of theology could not find previous works.

As the Christian church became associated with the imperial civil administration and the papacy, just as religion in ancient Roman times had become associated with the rituals of governance, the ideas and ideals of Greek antiquity and Roman bureaucracy became intermixed with religious practices. The church assumed the trappings of imperial Rome and used state power to enforce its decrees and proclamations to the detriment of all opponents. By Augustine's time, often characterized as the Byzantine era (324–640), the birthplace of Jesus and his teaching, northern Palestine, was extensively Christian and became almost universally so in the 5th and 6th centuries but largely because of internal social developments, not inspiration or missionary activity. (28) Pagan practices continued in many parts of Palestine well into the 6th century. Memorial churches were established with imperial encouragement but village churches in rural areas occurred hesitatingly and only over several centuries.

During his lifetime Augustine dealt with controversies among Christian sects which proclaimed differing doctrines, many not fully defined by the early Christian church like Donatism, a schismatic group which held that the worth of the sacraments was only as good as the cleric administering them. But his most important theological conviction, one that has endured through the centuries, is built upon the misplaced notion that the *Genesis* story of human creation is historically true. What follows from this erroneous premise is the idea of original sin proposed by Paul (*Romans* 7:23), that all humans are tainted with the error of the so-called first man and woman and is a pervasive attribute of all human beings, a failure to adhere to God's laws and a perverse desire through will to follow personal desire. The real sin here is that people believe the contamination of innocent children before they are aware of their own deplorable condition. (29)

Augustine's voluminous output and his dogged pursuit of understanding and propagandizing Christianity earned him the endearment and admiration of medieval Europe. He was required reading and his acquisition of Plato as a guide was wholly accepted into belief until Thomas Aquinas introduced Aristotle to Europe and reason, like Plato's transcendence, became the servant of theology. Only then was Apollo, the Greek god of reason, born again into European consciousness "and the god Apollo," according to Homer in *The Iliad*, "would set all things to rights once more."

Augustine's abhorrence and fear of sexual proclivities and the joys of life blended with a deep pessimism about the over-powering influence of sin, led him to place faith and the authority of the church over enlightened reason and intellectual curiosity about the natural world. Despite his stature as a scholar he remains an unapologetic puritan at heart.

After Augustine, faith became concretized and scripture accepted as divinely inspired. Absolutism in dogma combined with fervent anti-intellectualism created an ethos of mental inflexibility that bred centuries of cultural torpor. Irenaeus responded to critics by claiming that the interpretation of scriptures was not open to individuals, but that the Apostles were uniform in thinking and that their message was transmitted successfully to Episcopal successors.

As Judaic and Christian mysticism became integral to religious life, the myths created by the Greeks became absorbed into the ceremonies of the sacraments and the rituals and liturgy of the Catholic Mass. It was easier to receive revelation and the impartation of eternal realities from God, like the bread and wine at mass and through meditation than to talk all night, as Socrates and his companions had done, to gain new insights.

Squelching the Arian controversy solidified Christian orthodox doctrine and Augustine interpreted its message for believers thereafter. Because he lost the argument and his status, Arius is viewed today as one who left the truth of faith for an aberrant interpretation. The antagonism of his rival Athanasius and the political factions aligned against him meant that the defeat of Arius was also the loss of religious diversity. Christianity ever after defined its creedal doctrine with metaphysical ambiguities, imposing Greek terms used to describe the physical world upon Jewish ideas of a savior. It made philosophical abstractions more potent than historical accuracy, stretching reason so that future theological commentators relinquished thoughtful explanations and turned to twisted allegorical interpretations.

After Augustine, the rational intellectual's pursuit of knowledge, speculation and empirical investigation permanently yielded to the individual soul's pursuit of its spiritual destiny. Theological commentators strengthened Christianity with the fuel of biblical exegesis, the decrees of the councils became accepted as definitive, and the authority of the hierarchy, modeled after Roman imperial and military organization, made all dogmatic persuasions absolute. Religions always ruled, but Christianity ruled absolutely and unwittingly lifted myth to the status of faith. After Augustine, the church, like the Roman Empire itself, permanently divided into two parts in which linguistic differences were the least noticeable of the distinctions. The Byzantine Empire continued to flourish until the Ottomans overthrew it in 1453 while the West disintegrated into economic, aesthetic, and intellectual impoverishment and barbaric obscurity.

In time the natural world became the Bible of understanding and the gospel of revelation, and the language used for translation was mathematics. Roman gods were formally acknowledged as a part of civic pride but rarely believed in as real. After the collapse of Roman civilization, Europe migrated from a strict monotheistic belief like the Jews possessed to an unswerving faith in its own elaborate doctrine.

The new faith instituted anti-intellectualism and anti-scientific thinking. By absorbing only parts of Greek mythical, mystical lore and philosophic speculation, it scorned the real Greek renaissance of athletic gamesmanship and competition (Olympic games were discontinued under Theodosius), delight in beauty, architecture, poetry and plays, and scientific investigation. By instituting the absolute authority of the clerical hierarchy to define reality and by using scripture and defined creed as the ultimate criteria of truth, the church renounced independent thought and diminished, where it did not outright ban, the role and value of observation and inquiry into the natural world and humanity.

That sun, which first scalded by breast with love,
Hath now revealed to me, by proving and
disproving, the sweet and lovely face of truth. (Dante, Paradiso, III)

EMPEROR JUSTINIAN AND HIS COURT
On the Left Court Officials, On the Right, the Clergy
5th Century, Basilica of San Vitale, Ravenna

EPILOGUE

For this we must spend time in study and in the writings of wise men, to learn the truths that have emerged from their researches, and to carry on the search ourselves for the answers that have not yet been discovered,
(Seneca, Letters from a Stoic)

The enduring lesson of history is that religions, the cultural products of peoples' combined beliefs, succumb to subsequent movements and persuasions, then evolve and spring forth again with new prophets and doctrines. Sikhism is one example of the merger of the polytheism of Hinduism with the monotheism of Islam. All that is necessary is for followers to believe in the revelation of the person, like Mohammed, Nanak, Joseph Smith, or Mary Baker Eddy, who proclaims the new message. Furthermore, all religions have a sacred book that reveals the message of what the religion is, what is to be believed or accepted and what the core of faith entails. (1)

Indeed, it is common for the beginning of a new religion to begin a new calendar and restart the calculation of time from the origin of the prophet or leader. There are, in addition to the Chinese lunar calendar, years that begin with the lunar cycle for Jewish, Christian and Muslim religions. The time of particular feast days, like the moveable celebrations of Yom Kippur and Easter, are still determined by lunar time associated with sacred events, like Passover, Christ's resurrection or Muhammad's death.

This inquiry has focused on discovering literary myths, rituals, and doctrines that link ancient religious beliefs to relatively modern ones. The hypothesis has been objectively plausible if uncomfortable to the orthodox faithful unaware of previous literary antecedents to scripture or unwilling to accept the contributions of literary legacies. But the truth is that ancient myths graduated to articles of faith. Archaeological discoveries and advances in biology and physics did not fit into adopted mythical literary patterns. Eventually, as in science, the volume of troublesome information becomes unsustainable and doctrine begs either for revision or rejection.

A Babylonian poet laments: "Who knows the will of the gods in heaven? Who understands the plan of the underworld gods? Where have mortals learned the way of a god? He who was alive yesterday is dead today. I am appalled at these things; I do not understand their significance." (2) Paul Tillich, in his personal search to find meaning between the Bible, religion and ontology, noted that "religion is a function of the human mind, the futile attempt of man to reach God." (3) What prevails in religious literature is the inscrutability of the divine. Plaintive hymns record distress at failing to understand what God wants or how people should act in accordance with divine directives.

Humankind is central to the drama of religion. But the natural world existed for billions of years prior to human habitation and it is the apex of folly to believe that the scribe of an ancient document is presumptuous enough to be an eyewitness at its origin. Did the Sky Goddess Nut arch over the Earth God Geb separated by the Air God Shu as the Egyptians believed in 1,000 BCE? To snigger at such beliefs betrays a lack of understanding of how anthropomorphic divinities evolved from the mysteries of nature. Science, the quantitative analysis of nature's interactions, is no different an inquiry than ancient man's attempts to discover invisible powers at work in the universe and the biology of life. Science today is what myth and religion were thousands of years ago, inspiring the same sense of wonder but providing more objectivity and validation for its conclusions, though bickering among scientists approaches the controversial contentions of theologians.

To place revelation as the key to understanding God is to make God dependent on human writing as a tool for communication. "The word of the lord is the mind of God the Father; one cannot be separated from the other for their union is life," presumptuously states the *Corpus Hermeticum*. (4) Were it not for mankind's ability to question, to have a consciousness of identity, to stand in awe and to speak, God would have no categories at all identifiable to humans. As it is, the language of religion based on revelation, decrees, fiats, pronouncements, commandments, where God's voice through scribes is not outright contradictory, punitive or absurd, is the attribution of all known qualities and powers extended to God infinitely. Zealots chanting "God is Great" does not make the assertion either true or false. Whether or not God as an identifiable, personal entity is a living reality is less conjectural than the certainty that billions of people believe it.

The great civilizations of Sumer, Babylon, Canaan, Greece and Egypt preceded the Hebrews in economic, political, religious, artistic, architectural, military and literary accomplishments. Hebrew society was relatively late in developing because of its remoteness to natural resources like abundant water, its precarious agricultural existence in the hill country, its tribal raiding mentality, and because more militaristic and adventuresome societies periodically overran it. This occurred despite the repeated claims in *Deuteronomy* that God would cause all cities to fall before the invading Hebrew believers. Hebrew scribes liberally usurped literary nuggets from all civilizations and consolidated various mythical strands into a nationalistic literature.

Biblical scribes created Yahweh who absorbed all the combined attributes of deities like Enlil, Baal, Zeus and Aten. With the *Code of Hammurabi* as a guide, Hebrews authorized a legal system, the Ten Commandments, to accompany the new belief in one God. Scribes created a litany of heroes, Adam, Abraham, Isaac, Joseph, Moses, Joshua, Samson, to rank with heroes from other epics and help establish Hebrew ethnic and national consciousness. As prophets called for adherence to the prescriptions of the Torah, rebellions against Hellenic secular influences led by the Maccabees and later by Jewish insurgents against the Romans, resulted in the annihilation of the Temple, the site of all religious ritual and observance. (5)

The Bible is a rehash of stories from the literature of other civilizations to boost Hebrew pride, a mélange of authors and editors, Lords of the Scrolls, who retold episodes from epic adventures while perpetuating an ancient heroic mythology in kingly and religious contexts. Except for Islam, the Bible has survived as the principal sacred text of divine authority, containing all the ideas, virtues, figures and ethical precepts presumably needed for salvation. Yet it is filled with inconsistencies, verbal mirages and conflicting views, like God and Satan playing dice over whether or not Job will succumb and curse God. This is the same kind of squabbling among deities occurring in *The Epic of Gilgamesh* and Homer's epics. In *Genesis,* trickery and deceit are the main virtues of the patriarchs and the characteristics of the heroes battling deities in Homer. (6)

The crude living guidelines in *Deuteronomy* where even genocide is a form of piety cannot serve as a paragon for ethical standards. David glories Yahweh when he slaughters neighboring tribes. Biblical scribes never reconciled the inconsistencies between adapting Mesopotamian and Greek gods and goddess fighting over the destinies of humans. When a single god, was transposed into Hebrew scripture, scribes did not plot the narrative so that Yahweh would appear to be decisive as a single god without the conflicts between multiple gods gleaned from older epics.

By the same token, gospel authors and Paul, while keeping intact ancient religious beliefs in good and evil, light and darkness, and an apocalyptic vision of a transcendent life with Mosaic prerogatives embodied in the persona of Jesus, sprinkled their message with Neo-Platonic ideals and Gnostic mystical beliefs to appeal to displaced Jews and educated Greeks. They endowed Jesus with the collective characteristics of a prophet, a Messiah, a semi-divine figure like Ulysses, and finally, in John's last gospel, the Son of God, just like a Roman emperor.

Once a gospel template was written and accepted, the first was probably Mark's, the other testaments were able to copy the essential episodes, using suspect prophetic quotations from scripture skewed with messianic and eschatological perspectives and stoic parables. John's gospel is a variant interpretation, often chronologically inaccurate, and he elevates the status of Jesus to the divine and inserts a Gnostic and more poetic twist to the narrative. (5) What he did not write was biography. Gospel narrators are representatives of a heroic literary tradition with a religious motive that, with the blessings and entitlements of Roman imperial rule, was initially welcomed as scripture then forcibly promulgated as doctrine permitting no criticism or deviation.

If we consider a few of the principal events in the life of Jesus in older texts we find several standard commonalities. That Jesus was born in or near an open field, a natural setting, with shepherds present, on or about December 25th, the winter solstice, are conditions also true of Mithras. That Jesus had miraculous attributions to him at an early age, and that he was thought of as a shepherd of his people was also true of Cyrus and Mithras. That he gathered disciples to him and that they testified to his miraculous powers is also true of Zoroaster, Mithras, Cyrus, Ulysses and Asclepius. That he had a final meal of consecrated bread and wine with his closest followers was also true of the Zoroaster, Canaanites, Dionysius and Mithras. That he died, rose from the dead, ascended into heaven like Mithras, will come again to judge the living and the dead, and that bodies will be resurrected and enter into eternal life is also true of Asclepius, Orpheus, Osiris and Mithras.

Just as the scribes of the Torah had used older literature to tell their tales of national identity, Christian scribes used Greek lore and epic myths to describe a new hero who blended Mosaic prophetic wisdom with Greek mysticism and a divine status. Gospel narrators, writing in an age when magic, mysticism and demons were a part of the popular culture, and shrines and temples were ubiquitous, personalized Jesus as a believable superhuman hero, as Homer had personalized his gods and heroes. Gospel narrators were writing for the benefit of the literate Greek-speaking world who were by and large polytheistic but believing in a supreme principal deity, Zeus, as Jews and Christians believe in God but also in lesser spirits like angels and devils.

The warrior heroes of epics like Gilgamesh, Achilles, Hector or Ulysses, were an aristocratic ideals, mythical persons to be emulated for their exploits, semi-divine personages with superhuman attributes. The tragic hero of the Greek dramatists, on the other hand, is a caution for those who have too much hubris, who descend into unbearable suffering and are faced with choices that lead to death despite their virtue. The Greek tragic hero may believe he is god-like and invincible but his pride makes him a tragic figure, a man who refuses to accept his limitations, an Orestes, Macbeth, Lear or Othello. It is unlikely gospel narrators appreciated these Grecian distinctions. But the result in Jesus is a combination of the epic and tragic hero, a combination of archetypes. Jesus is the religious version of the warrior hero whose actions lead to his tragic death. Additionally, the scribes added the salsa of stoic sayings to season the sagacity of wisdom to Jesus who is unlikely to have uttered any of the passages ascribed to him. Nevertheless, the imitation of the heroic and tragic ideals in the gospels followed literary tradition perfected by the Greeks and added the dimension of Jewish religious personalities, prophecy fulfillment, apocalyptic visions and ascetic mission. (6)

The gospels link Jesus as "Son of God" to divine power; church councils and clergy linked him to ultimate divine power. Homer's Zeus has the last say in men's battles, as Jesus has the last say in the battle with evil and Satan. Human actions alone, according to Paul, are insufficient. Nevertheless, like Homer's gods who are active and supportive in human affairs, punish wrongdoers and even have human feelings, Jesus is with humans "until the end of time." Yet neither Zeus' or God's Will is known until it is manifested. The gods care about humans in Homer but we don't know why. The belief about the gods in Homer's time and about their power and intervention in human affairs is similar to the belief about divine power and intervention in the 1st century CE. The gospels scribes cannot divest themselves of their cultural context.

Jesus is elevated to divine status just like Homeric heroes and the themes of righteousness, kingship, battles with demons, or oddities like Cyclops or pacific spirits like Calypso, wickedness among men, resurrection, salvation, some recurring in the Bible and all in more ancient stories, are revisited and reiterated. If there is a Holy Spirit, as the Greeks believed before Christianity, it is the inspiring muses sitting on the shoulders of all scribes.

After the gospels mimicked epic heroes in their portrayal of Jesus, Christian intellectuals in the first centuries after Christ took Greek philosophical ideas about God, transcendence, logos, spirit, substance, person and nature, and philosophy's tools like logic and reason, and united them with the Bible's prophetic and apocalyptic visions, transforming an obscure religious sect into a philosophy in its own right. Additionally, the Jewish tradition, as the Dead Sea Scrolls remind us, also incorporated significant features of Persian, Babylonian and Canaanite legends. Others would claim that Christian apologists, like Gregory of Nyssa, were only trained in philosophy and used its ideas and methods to promote a theology that passed for philosophy. But none of the Christian commentators, when they weren't actually attacking philosophy, approached the inventive creativity and distinctive thinking of even the middling competent of the Greek philosophers. By later Christian centuries and certainly by the Middle Ages, theology had become so dogmatic that philosophy was only used to confirm existing beliefs rather than welcome new ones. Philosophies of ethics were diluted into moral imperatives and codes of canon law and philosophies of life became regulations for monastic living.

But the absorption of these twin, often opposing, currents of thoughts, Greek philosophy and Hebrew culture, had its difficulties. Only the Pharisees could conceive of a body surviving death, and Paul, likely a Pharisee himself or at least thinking like one, gave impetus to the idea of bodily resurrection. But because of the generally accepted Zoroastrian tradition, lauded by the Manicheans, that the body was the source of evil, and by the Neo-Platonists who scoffed at the body's resurrection as un-necessary to the soul's survival, Christianity never did fully resolve the dilemma of why the body was essential to the afterlife or why it should have to wait until the last day to join with its soul.

The principal argument in the history of the Christian development is that Christianity was the fulfillment of the Hebrew prophecies, and that for some apologists even selected individuals like Plato and Virgil were chosen to be precursors of this recognition of the truth. The presumption is that the Bible and Greek rites, epics and philosophy stand alone as independent realities when in fact both are embodiments of earlier religious beliefs and traditions. The marriage of Hebrew and Greek traditions encapsulates all previous written literary traditions.

As Christianity absorbed Platonism under Augustine, it quickly assimilated Aristotle under Aquinas enlarging Catholicism with the intellectual vigor of rational methodology, though Aristotle himself was diminished for his empiricism if his ideas contravened faith and scripture. After Aquinas, reason, shuttered out of discourse for centuries, entered in quietly through a small intellectual aperture, and independent thought was again reluctantly recognized and accepted as a gift of God to humans.

The combination of state privileges granted the clergy beginning in 325 eventually culminated in the Holy Roman Empire when church interests became state's interests imposing a totalitarian papal rigidity on the Christian populace. Today, a new totalitarian ideology with clerical leaders is in the forefront, inspired by its own mythologizing vision of the past. It seeks to use force to kill or convert infidels and propagandize its religious beliefs. Islam has adopted the power relationships of state control and religious persuasion to challenge the Christian view of the world and advance its own mythologies. Its clerical hierarchy has not repudiated violence as a method of fulfilling this mission of preserving its so-called purity and purging the world of those who choose not to believe in its uncivil ethics.

In sum, this inquiry has investigated ancient and classical literature to discover to what extend biblical and gospel scribes used themes, stories, episodes, passages and sayings in the Bible and gospels. The composite findings reveal extensive copying and imitation of writings from older and contemporary cultures. The evidence is persuasive, an identifiable literary pattern difficult to ignore. If this kind of literary imitation were to happen today, lawsuits for plagiarism would be filed by the original authors.

Faith is an intellectual conviction more daunting than doubt that can breed cynicism. But faith's doctrinaire comfort can also ignite intolerance and close-mindedness, the antithesis of a valued education and humane achievement. The danger of unwavering faith is that the introduction of new knowledge places old knowledge in jeopardy by challenging assumptions.

The choices for the faithful are retreat into denial of the new knowledge and attempts to falsify scientific findings, or to tentatively accept its premises and somehow incorporate them into the belief system, or to accept the new knowledge and question belief.

How the Bible and gospel writings strengthen or diminish faith, however, is another matter. The extent to which a person's faith is based on scripture is ultimately personal and the personal approach to religion will also trump the institutional as William James noted. (7) Unquestionably, deep religious faith offers courage in adversity, insurance against depression, a sound basis for morals, and optimism for a better future life. The transcendental experience of divinity, or what is believed to be divinity, is not necessarily found in written documents. It certainly is not for Sikhs. Symbolic representations etched on clay or stone, and ink left on paper or parchment can still put people on their knees, send armies on the march, and place nations at each other's throats. The greatest of all human achievements, writing, is the real lasting miracle that moves humankind.

NOTES

Introduction
1. Frazier (1918, Gordon (1962), and Gastor (1969) are among the most noteworthy. Gordon's 1962 comparisons between Greek and biblical texts identified multiple texts with common sources found in Sumerian, Mesopotamian and Canaanite writings. Weitzman concluded that songs from ancient cultures, predating the Bible and existing independently, like the Song of Deborah and Barak in *Judges 5*, the Song of David in *2 Samuel*, and the song of Daniel's three friends in *Daniel 3*, were incorporated into biblical narratives for literary effect. MacDonald (2000) claims that Mark left traces of Homeric imitation throughout his gospel.
2. J. Winsten, (1999), p. 25ff. The British Museum has an Assyrian tablet of the original creation story (#BM 930177), and the EG fragment from Nineveh recording the Babylonian story of the flood (#K3375).
3. S. Bar-Efrat, (1989) and M. Sternberg, (1987 are examples of studies of the narrative tradition within the Bible without examining any other literary sources.
4. P. Burke, (1997), p. 44. Brettler (1995) obfuscates the distinctions of history, literature and myth.
5. Clement of Alexandria (See Chap. 16) Clement even presumes that Plato derived his understanding of the Laws from Moses, when there is no evidence Plato had even heard of Moses. (Clement of Alexandria. (1953), p. 144.
6. Hackett, J. A. "There was no King in Israel, The Era of the Judges." In M. Coogan, OHBW. (New York: Oxford University Press, 1998), p. 133ff.
7. C. H. Gordon, *Forgotten scripts*. (New York: Dorset Press, 1987) and M. Dahood, Ebla, Ugarit and the Bible. In Pettinato, G., *The Archives of Ebla, An Empire Inscribed in Clay*. (Garden City, NY: Doubleday and Co., 1981).
8. Aristotle notes in *The Poetics* "Imitation is natural to man from childhood...he is the most imitative creature in the world, and learns at first by imitation." R. McKeon, (1947), p. 627.
9. D. R. MacDonald, *The Homeric Epics and the Gospel of Mark*. New Haven, CT: Yale University Press, 2000) and *Does the New Testament Imitate Homer?* (New Haven, CT: Yale University Press, 2003.
10. Friedman has shown the writing and editorial sources of the Torah over the centuries of its composition by J, E, JE, and RJE, the redactor, P, and D. (R. E. Friedman, (2003).
11. "A cultured Greek speaker would be expected to know Homer well and the plays of the great tragedians, which insured familiarity with the Greek myths. He or she could be expected to have some acquaintance with Herodotus and Thucydides, the historians of the fifth century BCE, and with the greatest of the orators, such as Demosthenes and Aeschines of the fourth century BC. He or she would know something about classical Athens and Sparta but not necessarily much about Greek history since Alexander the Great." M. Goodman, (1997), p. 154. See also A. De Selincourt. (1962).
12. Gordon, C. H. & Rendsburg, G. A. BANE. (New York: W. W. Norton, 1997). I am indebted to the pioneering work of Sir James Frazier, *Foklore in the Old Testament* (3 vols) (London: Macmillan, 1918), augmented by the prodigious scholarship of Theodore Gaster, *Myth, Legend and Custom in the Old Testament* (2 vols). (New York: Harper Torchbooks, 1969) detailing all comparative folklore necessary for the interpretation of the Old Testament.

Chapter 1
1. Karen Armstrong in *A History of God, The 4,000-year quest of Judaism, Christianity and Islam* (New York: Ballantine Books, 1993), A. Momigliano, *Essays on Ancient and Modern Judaism*. (Chicago: University of Chicago Press, 1994), p. 9, and M. Coogan, "In the Beginning, The Earliest History," in Coogan, M. (Ed.). OHBW. (New York: Oxford University Press), p. 21: "The cumulative evidence shows that most biblical genres, motifs, and even institutions have ancient Near Eastern parallels." Cantor (2003) notes: "The first millennium of

Jewish history, as presented in the Bible, has no empirical foundation whatsoever. It was made up later as a work of imagination and shaped by doctrinal and political needs." (p. 99). Even the renown church father Ambrose, Bishop of Milan, mentor to Augustine, stated that he had been a poor man putting his children to auction to pay his debts, a known literary ruse and purely fictitious. (J. Moorhead, 1999, p. 5). Indeed, Ambrose's editors agree that some of his letters are written to fictitious correspondents as vehicles for the exposition of the Bible.

2. There is no word in Hebrew for fiction. The closest approximation is *siporet* translated as narrative prose. Among Semitic languages fantasy, literary invention, confessional literature, documentation, even historical accuracy, are not as conventionally classified as in western literature. The mentality of Hebrew authors may never be known but, like all authors everywhere, they must have been profoundly affected by political turmoil around them. See F. McConnell, (Ed.) (1986).

3. God was prominent even among the so-called pagan religions and celebrated by poets like Virgil. (*The Georgics*, IV, 221).

4. V. Bourke, *The Pocket Aquinas*. (New York: Washington Square Press, 1960), p. 312. The assumption among Christian commentators is that pagans were less devout and faithful. Yet even in Aeschylus we find expressions of pagan piety. (Aeschylus, in Agamemnon, in P. Landis, FFGP. (New York: The Modern Library, 1929), p. 10.

5. *Ibid.*, p. 316. Origen asserts that the stories and myths of the Greeks were written by demons while those of the Jews and Christians were composed by God and the angels. OCC. (New York: Cambridge University Press, 1965), p. 486). Augustine wrote: "They are deceived too by those highly mendacious documents which profess to give the history of many thousand years, though, by reckoning by the sacred writings, we find that not 6,000 years have yet passed (W. J. Oates, BWST. Vol. 2. New York: Random House, 1948, p. 189).

6. "That the Bible is a library of scraps of other documents, of very various dates edited and re-edited; that the older deposits of the Jewish portion draw largely from the mythology of other nations and falsify history to an incredible extent; are in their oldest deposits profuse in unmoral doctrine and patent absurdities and paint the picture of a God that revolts all thinking minds." G. R. S. Mead, FFF. (1960), p. 20. The current lively expression over the current controversy between science and religion is in N. Angier, "My God Problem—and Theirs. *The American Scholar*, (2004, Spring) 73(2), 131-34.

7. H. Bloom, *The Book of J*. New York: (Vintage Books, Random House, 1990) where Bloom claims that J was likely a woman scribe. For one source of Ebla see W. T. Pitard in M. Coogan, OHBW. (1998), p. 32. Origen writes: "Then if anyone has the ability to understand what is expressed in the form of a story which has both something true in its literal meaning and also indicates some secret truth, let him consider those who have preserved the language from the beginning." (OCC, p. 288).

8. Hesiod. *Theogony.* (www.sunsite.berkeley.edu/OMACL/Hesiod/theogony.html)

9. G. Josipovici. (1988), pp. 135-52.

10. *Deut.* 32:7.

11. *Matthew* 16:3-5.

12. D. Schmandt-Besserat. (1992). Once papyrus and parchment became popular, ink, as found at Qumran in the scriptorium, was made of a combination of soot, resin and oil. Crossan, J. D., & Reed, J. L., (2001), pp. 154-55. .

13. H. W. G. Saggs,(1989), pp. 99-100.

14. C. H. Gordon, (1987), p. 41.

15. Aramaic was the common spoken language of the Jews at the time of the Babylonian exile but is distinct, though closely resembling, Hebrew. Returning exiles brought Aramaic back with them to Judea and it was the common language for centuries. The Jewish prayer for the dead is still recited in Aramaic. Cantor (2003), p. 78.

16. According to legend, Cadmus, the founder of Thebes, was responsible for introducing the Phoenician alphabet into Greece.

17. Joseph Campbell's books are enlightening. *The Masks of God: Primitive Mythology.* (New York: Penguin Books, 1987); *The Hero's Journey, Joseph Campbell on his Life and Work.* (San Francisco: HarperSanFrancisco, 1991); *The Power of Myth* (with Bill Moyers). (New York: Doubleday, 1988).
18. C. G. Jung, *The Development of Personality.* (Princeton: Princeton University Press, 1954): *The Undiscovered Self.* (New York: Penguin Books, 1958); *Two Essays on Analaytical Psychology*, Vol. 7, (Princeton: Princeton University Press, 1966); *The Archetypes and the Collective Unconscious*, V. 9, Part 1. (Princeton: Princeton University Press, 1969); *The Portable Jung.* (New York: Penguin Books, 1971); *Word and Image.* (Princeton: Princeton University Press, 1979).
19. G. Dumezil, (1973), p. 37. The Romans would not have allowed tampering of official documents. A certain Quintus Veranius, legate in Greece during the reign of Claudius (41–54) had men lashed for carelessness in the registration of documents or erasures or blemishes of any kind. (R. K. Sherk, 1988), pp. 90-91).
20. T. J. Lomperis, (1984).
21. Trade was extensive between modern day Iraq, Iran and Persian Gulf states as early as Neolithic times. A nearly intact pottery vessel found in the United Arab Emirates near Abu Dhabi dating from 5,000 BCE is similar to pottery designs from southern Iraq and southern Iran from the 5th millennium BCE. "Abu Dhabi Discovery," *Archaeology*, September/October, 2004, pp. 10-11.
22. www.fiu.edu/~northupl/populvuh.html
23. Thomas Murphy (2002) not only has provided genetic evidence that casts doubt on that claim but has rocked the LDS church with a major challenge. Murphy found no genetic evidence that American Indians are linked with ancient Israelites. Murphy has been compared with Galileo, similarly condemned by the Catholic Church in 1633. Even historians like Diodorus in the 1st century BCE knew when tales were far-fetched: "But if many people find what we have said thus far to be incredible and rather like fiction, the wonders yet to be told will seem far more marvelous still." All convictions should be demoted to the status of hypotheses where they can then be subjected to review and analysis. (*Diodorus on Egypt.* (Jefferson, NC: McFarland and Co., 1985), pp. 108-09.
24. R. L. Fox, (1992). pp. 161-74. For more on Greek historians see G. Murray, (1946).
25. Herodotus. HH. (1830), p. 197. Juvenal the satirist was not so kind: "Next I address the writers of history: what about your work? Is it any more fruitful? More time and oil is wasted... you see the mounds of papyrus growing—along with the cost...Who will pay a historian as much as a newsreader earns?" Juvenal, (1991), p. 64.
26. W. Boutcher, JHI, (2003) 64(3), 489-510. The Book of Judith is articulated in the same military sequence as a scene from a section of Herodotus. The thirsty Jews besieged in Bethulia give themselves five days before surrendering which is a counterpart to the five days the thirsty Greeks give themselves before surrendering to the Persians as noted in the *Chronicle of Lindos*, an ancient script compiled in 99 BCE. The author of Judith was acquainted with the documents of Greek historians particularly about the wars with Persia. (A. Momigliano, 1994, pp. 8-9).
27. L. Spence, MLBA. (1916), p. 16.
28. The major prophets are Isaiah, Jeremiah, and Ezekiel. Minor prophets (not less important but shorter in length) are Hosea, Amos, Joel, Obadiah, Jonah, Micah, Nahum, Habakkuk, Zephaniah, Haggai, Zechariah, and Malachi. N. Podhoretz, (2002).
29. *Ibid.*, p. 6.
30. I. Cornelius, (1994).
31. O. Keel, O. & C. Uehlinger, GGIG. (2003), pp. 219 ff.
33. B. L. Mack, WWNT. (San Francisco: HarperSanFrancisco, 1995) and D. R. MacDonald, *Does the New Testament Imitate Homer? op.cit.*, 2003).
34. T. Irvin, 1989, pp. 20-67.
35. Thucydides.V.1. (1831), p. 19.

36. J. Bright, (2000), pp. 3-4.
37. C. Aldred, (1998), p. 203.
38. *Setna and The Magic Book*, c. 1305-1196 BCE, & Saggs, (1989), 74.
39. P. Veyne, (1988). Dever (1990) notes that not only the scribes but the classical prophets were elitist, and that the biblical texts were written for the upper classes, priestly circles and the court. (pp. 7 & 123-24). See also S. Goranson, BAR, (1994), 20(5), 1994, 37-39.
40. H. Bloom, (1990) and R. E. Friedman, op. cit.
41. Bloom, 1990, *op. cit.*
42. R. E. Friedman, (1998). Others like R. L. Fox, (1992), and B. F. Batto, (1992) attempt to separate historical truth from fiction in biblical writings. Nietzsche has a more cynical view of the usurpation of Hebrew scribes of other literary traditions. (F. Nietzsche, 1990, p.148-49).
43. Weber, M. (1952). 194 ff.
44. Akenson, 1998, *op. cit.*, p. 152. Because of the cache of fragmentary documents found in Qumran, not necessarily attributable to the Essenes, we can safely say that there was a trove of scriptures dating roughly from the period of the Second Temple c.515 BCE to the destruction of Jerusalem in 70 CE testifying to a rich intellectual ferment but whose works were not included in the biblical canon and many that have been undoubtedly lost.
45. C. H. Gordon, C. H. & Rendsburg, G. A. BANE (New York: W. W. Norton, 1997), pp. 324-25.
46. C. H. Gordon, (1962), p. 132.

Chapter 2
1. "Nothing in the Biblical record makes it possible to establish a firm link with extra-Biblical history," notes Kathleen Kenyon (1978), p. 31.
2. In *2 Chronicles* 34:15.
3. "And Lot lifted up his eyes and saw that the Jordan valley was well watered everywhere like the garden of the Lord." (*Gen.* 13:10)
4. J. Bronowski, (1973).
5. According to J. R. Bartlett, (1982).
6. Kenyon, 1978, op. cit., p. 36.
7. *Ibid.*, pp. 40-42. Anthony gave Jericho to Cleopatra (34 BCE), but after Octavius's victory over them at Actium, Herod regained it and founded a fortress where the spring and brook of the Kelt (or wadi Qelt) and the Jerusalem road emerge from the mountains, built a royal winter palace, reservoirs, a hippodrome and amphitheater, and where Herod himself died. (4 BCE) Jesus was said to be baptized nearby in the Jordan and was reputedly tempted by Satan on the overlooking hill to the west. Jesus cured two blind men at the gates of the city (*Matt.* 20:29-34), or only one according to *Mark* 10: 46 and *Luke* 19:1-5, converted Zacchaeus after he climbed down from a sycamore tree. The parable of the Good Samaritan occurred on the road between Jericho and Jerusalem.
8. http://wesley.nnu.edu/noncanon/ot/pseudo/jubilee.htm.
9. The oldest existing copy of the Talmud dates from the 7th century CE and was in Baghdad. As of this writing it has not been recovered from the theft of the museum after the invasion of Iraq 2003.
10. J. Drummond, J. (1888). p. 156.
11. C. Freeman, (2003), pp. 275-76.
12. *Lev.* 24:15-16.
13. E. A. W. Budge, EBD. (1967, 1895) and C. O'Brien, (1985).
14. *Gen.* 33:20.
15. Durant, 1954, *op. cit.*, p. 310. Nietzsche has a slightly different view of the emergence of Yahweh. (Nietzsche, 1990, *op. cit.*, p. 147).
16. *Exodus*, 3:1-2. The Koran speaks about other messengers who were not believed. "Then we sent Our messengers, one after another; whenever its messenger came to a community, they

counted him false; so We caused them to follow each other, and made them stories." (R. Bell, (1960, p. 329). But who is "We?" The pronoun is a recurring plural form of divinity in the Koran that, like EL, is gleaned from earlier texts referring to plural gods.
17. The Confraternity text of the Bible in a footnote describes this discrepancy: "An angel of the Lord: the visual form under which God appeared and spoke to men is referred to indifferently in the Old Testament either as God's angel or as God Himself." This is a most apologetic and unhelpful description and a corruption of the linguistic syntax.
18. O. Keel, O. & C. Uehlinger, GGIG. (1998), p. 191.
19. Ugarit text, 1,400-1,220 BCE, in De Moor, 1987, *op. cit.*, p. 25. Did Yammu morph into Yahweh?
20. Keel & Oehlinger, 1998, *op. cit.*, p. 280.
21. *Exodus* 6:23.
22. Dahood, 1981, *op. cit.*, p. 277.
23. *Proverbs* 22:1. And from the BG: "Know that with one single fraction of my Being I pervade and support the universe, and know that I AM." (Mascaro, 1962, *op. cit.*, p. 88). As to what's in a name the Sikh Holy Book, *Guru Granth Sahib* has a response: "Very fortunate are those who meditate on the Lord's Name; they alone are the Lord's devotees. Whoever chants His Name is liberated; whoever listens to it is saved, as is anyone who seeks His Sanctuary. The treasure of the Naam, the Name of the Lord, is everything for me."
24. E. Stern, BAR, 27(3), 2001, pp. 21-29.
25. As even *Acts* proposes: "And God made from one stock every nation of men to live on all the face of the earth, having determined allotted periods and boundaries of their habitation." (*Acts* 17:26). Cf. also G. London, BASOR, 1989, 273, pp. 37-55.
26. C. Myers, in M. Coogan, OHBW. (1998, pp.165 ff.
27. Until Christianity presented another challenge: whether gentiles could be legitimate converts if they did not become Jews first. For the confused account of this see *Acts* 10 and the story of Cornelius the Centurion and Peter for the justification from God that gentiles need not become Jews and thus do not need to follow dietary laws or be circumcised to be admitted into the communion of the faithful. The incident also portrays how ethnocentric Jews were, prohibited from even entering the homes of non-Jews, much less eating with them.
28. I. Finkelstein & N. A. Silberman, (2001). See also a book review, P. Trible, "God's Ghostwriters," in *The New York Times Book Review*, February 4, 2001.
29. E. Gruen, (1998), p.128-135 & 128n.
30. W. T. Pitard, in Coogan, M. OHBW.(1998), pp. 45-46.
31. *Gal.* 3:28. E. Gruen, *op. cit.* argues that Judaism was altered because of the introduction of Hellenism.

Chapter 3
1. What is "light of light" supposed to mean and is it an oblique reference to an earlier god? The Indian and Sanskrit word Guru is derived from the root words Gu, which means darkness or ignorance, and Ru meaning light or knowledge. The Guru is the experience of Truth or God.
2. Of course other pious individuals felt the same way. "No visit delights us more than a visit to the temple; no occasion more than a holy day; no act or spectacle than what we see and do ourselves in matters that involve the gods, whether we celebrate a ritual or take part in a choral dance or attend a sacrifice or ceremony of initiation." (Plutarch, *Moralia.* (1967, p. 113). "Either the gods have no power, or they have power. If they have not, why pray? If they have, why not pray for deliverance from the fear, or the desire, or the pain that the thing causes rather than the withholding or the giving of a particular thing? For certainly, if they can cooperate with men, it is for these purposes they can cooperate." (Marcus Aurelius, *The Meditations*) "If there are gods, the gods will reward your goodness. If there are none, what does anything matter." (Clytemnestra in Euripides' *Iphigenia in Aulis*). Who today worships Thor, the Norse god of thunder after whom Thursday is named? A thousand years ago it was common practice

in Europe to view him as the patron of warriors and peasants. On the hundreds of ostraca found in the past few decades from a period prior to Hellenization in Judah. A. Lemaire, BAR, 30(4), pp. 38 ff.

3. The Babylonians absorbed all the gods of Sumer. Shamash was worshipped at Sippar, Sin, the moon god at Ur, Anu at Erech, Bel (Enlil to the Sumerians) at Nippur (see the *Book of Daniel* for how Daniel showed Cyrus that Bel did not have the power he claimed), Istar at Nineveh, and Marduk at Babylon. Marduk (Merodach and other variants) was a Babylonian usurpation of Ea (sometimes known as Oannes) the Sumerian earth god whose qualities became associated with the sun by the ingenuity of the Babylonian clergy. He was the creator of the world having formed it out of the body of the slain Tiawath. He is the god of irrigation, strength, war and battle and rules as sovereign god. (Spence, 1916, *op. cit.*, p. 94 & p. 199).

4. *Genesis* 35:2-4. The household gods of Laban and Rebecca were called in Hebrew terephim. The word used to describe these gods was also used to describe the household gods David had, he who is claimed to be the greatest upholder of the law.

5. The belief in demons, evil spirits and demiurges continues today among animistic societies. In 1977 I purchased in a rural Malaysian jungle village a 15-inch high wood carving of a distorted figure, looking like a space alien. Partially squatting, it was shown with eyes half the size of its head, bared teeth and over-sized drooping fangs with long extended arms hanging on the ground. These totems were placed in strategic locations around the outside of the village and along nearby paths. Village elders told me that each carving represents a group of bodily ailments and that if a demon planned to enter the village and infect villagers that it would recognize itself as a carrier of one of the infections, become frightened by its own image and quickly exit back into the jungle. Villagers in this vicinity were nominally Muslim but animistic beliefs still held sway.

6. W. Durant, (1963, 1935), pp. 234-35.

7. Istar to the Greeks is Astarte, to the Hebrews Ashtoreth.

8. Spence, 1916, *op. cit.*, pp. 123-144, and Durant, 1963, *op. cit.*, pp. 235-36.

9. Ulysses is gored by a wild boar in *The Odyssey*, Hector is pierced with a sword, and Jesus is pierced in the side by a Roman spear. Most mythical heroes suffer wounds in their sides.

10. Durant, *ibid.*, p. 241n.

11. *Mark* 8, 27-29.

12. M. Dahood, (1981), p. 299.

13. *Ibid.*, p. 304.

14. *Psalm* 81:1 or 82:1.

15. See J. Gelb (1961).

16. U. Oldenburg, (1969), p. 15.

17. *Ibid.*, p. 64. I have journeyed to Palmyra in Syria, a thriving metropolis even before the Roman occupation and seen the magnificent remains of Baal's great temple.

18. The association of the cultic ruler and the divine is not just a clever association from the past. In Nepal today, the king is revered as the embodiment of the Hindu god Shiva, as the Dalai Lama is of the spirit of enlightenment for Nepalese Buddhists.

19. Such household shrines, with a corniche, jamb and base to support the stele are in the ruins of Pompei and Herculaneum dating from 79 CE. Earlier examples come from Deir-el-Medina, the middle Bronze Age necropolis worker and artist city near the Valley of the Kings in Egypt.

20. *Genesis* 35:2-4. See also Note #4 above.

21. Oldenburg, 1969, op. cit., p. 170. "Your judgment, Ilu, is wise. May your wisdom last forever! Long live the sharpness of your judgment. Ba'lu the Almighty is our king, our judge—nobody is over him." (Ugarit Texts, 1400-1200 BCE, in J. C. De Moor, ART. (Leiden: E. J. Brill, 1987).

22. *Ibid.*, pp. 143-44.

23. Euripedes (1832). V. 3., p. 178 line 431.

24. Euripedes, 1955, p.163.

25. Dahood, 1981, op. cit., p. 309.
26. *Book of Psalms*, Jewish Publication Society of America, Philadelphia, 1972.
27. *The Holy Bible with the Confraternity Text.* (Chicago: Good Counsel Publishing Company, 1963), p. 467.
28. Like Aristophanes writing in *The Frogs* we may be compelled to ask: "Well, after all my pains, I'm quite at a loss to discover which is the true, real deity." (P. Landis, FFGP. New York: The Modern Library, 1929, p. 248).
29. The 1832 edition, p. 50.
30. John Wesley Powell, exploring the Grand Canyon by rafting along the Colorado River in 1879, named one of the imposing peaks rising from the first tier on the north side of the river east of Bright Angel gorge "Zoroaster's Temple."
31. J. B. Noss, (1956), p. 437, and M. Seymour-Smith (1996), and G. Avesta, HZ. Tr. J. Duchesne-Guillemin. (1963). Nietzsche wrote *Thus Spake Zarathustra* which has nothing to do with Zoroaster and instead justifies his moral theme of choosing good and evil. P. Kriwaczek has a sort of travelogue about finding the roots of Zoroastrianism. (2003).
32. Noss, 1956, *op. cit.*, p. 447. The Zoroastrian scripture is the *Avesta*, fragmentary texts written in old Iranian resembling Vedic, an old version of Sanskrit.
33. *Ibid.*, p. 448.
34. L. Browne, (1946), pp. 364-65.
35. William Safire's intriguing book, (1992).
36. The US Capitol building is not an edifice where coronations occur. But in a bizarre ceremony, the Rev. Sun Myung Moon, eccentric Korean religious leader of the Unification Church, who happens to own (at this writing) *The Washington Times* and the wire service United Press International, was crowned by Rep. Danny Davis (D. Illinois) as King and Messiah on March 23rd, 2004 in a Senate office building. In a statement Moon declared that he was "declared to all heaven and earth that Rev. Moon is none other than humanity's Savior, Messiah, Returning Lord and True Parent." (S. G. Stolberg, "A Crowning at the Capitol Creates Stir," *The New York Times*, June 24th, 2004, A17).
37. *Acts*: 2. There is a hidden miraculous fire described in *II Maccabees* 1:18-36.
38. Zoroaster, HZ. Tr. J. Duchesne-Guillemin, (1963), p. 55.
39. *Ibid.*, p. 57.
40. *Ibid.*, p. 39.
41. *Ibid.*, p. 65.
42. R. C. Zaehner, TM. (1956).
43. A modern equivalent of Zoroastrianism is belief in the prophet Bahaullah, an Arabic word which means "light or glory of God," the founder of the Bahai faith. Bahais believe it is this light, symbolic of knowledge, that is the final destination of human progress towards the Absolute through spiritual realms. The Bahai faith was founded by Abdul Baha, who was born in Tehran in 1817 and died in Palestine in 1892. Bahaullah according to his followers is considered to be the latest of the great teachers. There are no formal methods, rituals, priestly hierarchy, oratories and initiations. Prayer and meditation are their only practices.

Chapter 4
1. *Gen.* 45:1-4.
2. classics.mit.edu/Plato/timaeus.html. In Benjamin Jowett's exemplary translation: "Now when the Creator had framed the soul according to his will, he formed within her the corporeal universe, and brought the two together, and united them center to center. The soul, interfused everywhere from the center to the circumference of heaven, of which also she is the external envelopment, herself turning in herself, began a divine beginning of never ceasing and rational life enduring throughout all time."
3. G. Pettinato, (1981)
4. *Ibid.*, p. 252.

5. In Hesiod's *Theogony* chaos came first, as it did in *Genesis*, and then were born Gaea (earth) and Eros (love). The offspring are Erebus (a vast realm of unfulfilled emptiness) and Night, also empty and devoid of substance. Together, Night and Erebus produce day. (F. Solmen, 1995, p. 27). Plato (1961) describes creation: "For which reason, when he was framing the universe, he put intelligence in soul, and soul in body, that he might be the creator of a work which was by nature fairest and best. Wherefore, using the language of probability, we may say that the world became a living creature truly endowed with soul and intelligence by the providence of God." Virgil (70–19 BCE) has a more poetic and realistic conception of creation in Eclogue VI, *The Eclogues of Virgil*. (1963), p. 31).

6. Available in full at: http://www.sacred-texts.com/ane/enuma.htm. A copy exists in the British Museum. For a photo see T. C. Mitchell, BADB. (1988), p. 69. Cf. Durant, 1954, *op. cit.*, p. 237. In Egyptian folklore, Sobek on the day of creation emerged from the "Dark Waters" in order to arrange the world. The concept of creation, of making something out of nothing, is still a difficult idea as knowledge of microscopic chemical, physical and causal changes does not answer how life originated. "Then Pistis Sophia stretched out her finger and poured upon him some light from her light." Evans, C. A. *et al.*, NH. (1993). Cf. M. Heun, *Science*, 278, (1997), 1312-14.

7. *Gen.* 1:3-5. Astronomers agree that the first stars did not appear in the universe until about 100 million years after the Big Bang, and that another billion years elapsed before galaxies began to expand and proliferate. The cosmos evolved into stars from dense, fluctuating matter, then grouped themselves into supernova and galaxies. Light was not a spontaneous combustion but a slow, intermittent process after stars formed and began to burn their hydrogen and helium and thus emit energy. Ultraviolet radiation ionized the environment of surrounding gases, mostly hydrogen, and the fire of these chain explosions became visible light coming from billions of galaxies in the universe. Energy gives light. R. B. Larson, & V. Bromm, *Scientific American*, 285(6), 2001, pp. 64-71.

8. Anaxagoras writing in the 6th century BCE noted: "By rainbow we mean the light in the clouds that shines opposite the sun." D. Sider, (1981), p. 123, a philosopher's commonsense observation and not the strategy whereby God places the rainbow as a sign he will not to send another flood. Even the renowned and learned Origen saw the tale of the creation of the days and light as fiction. "What man of sense will suppose that the first and the second and the third day, and the evening and the morning, existed without a sun or moon or stars? Who is so foolish as to believe that God, like a husbandman, planted a garden in Eden, and placed in it a tree of life...so that the one who tasted of the fruit obtained life?" (Origen, *De Principiis*). "Some attribute every event to the play of fortune, holding that the sky revolves without a guiding spirit, and that nature itself brings round the phases of day and year." Juvenal, (1991), p. 114.

9. "And God said, let us make man in our image." (*Genesis* 1, 26). Cf. P Kahn & A. Gibbons, *Science*, 277, (1997), 176-78. The creation of Pandora in Hesiod weaves an equally fantastic tale as does a Native American Zuni creation myth. (J. R. Farella, 1984). Unlike other creation myths, the Zuni God does not have a goddess creator. And unlike other creation myths where gods have many sons, the Hebrew tradition is repulsed by the idea of a son of God, a concept that would become central to Christianity. Juvenal is more poetic: "People, of course, lived differently then, when the world was young and the sky was new, people born from the riven oak or freshly fashioned from mud, who had no proper parents." (Juvenal, *op. cit.*, p. 36) The jesting question is Did Adam have a navel? If not, how did we get them?

10. "Besides, you do not seem to have shown any great regard to this two-legged creature, seeing you have left him with so few means of defense, subjected him to so many disorders, and provided him with so few remedies; and formed him with such a multitude of passions, and a small portion of wisdom and prudence to resist them." (Plato to Demogorgon in *Plato's Dream* by Voltaire, 1940, p. 275). For the contemporary evidence see my colleague Don Johanson & L. Johanson (1994), and the earlier D. Johanson & M. Edey, (1981). Clement of

Alexandria, (1953), p. 17. Augustine writes that the only way God could have spoken to man is if he appeared to Adam in the guise of a man. (W. J. Oates, 1948, p. 711). On June 21, 2001 leaders of an offshoot of the Presbyterian Church meeting in Dallas voted to allow varying interpretations of the Bible's account of creation. Members debated whether the creation of the world in six days meant real clock days or figurative days. Even though Presbyterians technically believe in a literal interpretation of biblical writings, in this case a more liberal interpretation was voted in by a two to one margin.

11. See Lenski, *et al., Nature*, 423, 2003, pp. 139-144. Rebecca Martinez, a Dominican Republic girl, was born with two heads in 2004, a rare occurrence known as *craniopagus parasiticus* happening once in every 2.5 million births. Rebecca was only the eighth documented case in the world. She died in surgery that attempted to remove her underdeveloped second head. Had she lived, she would have had two brains, but would she had had two minds? Two souls?

12. H. Skaletsky, *et al. Nature* 423, (June 19, 2003), pp. 825 – 837. God tells the man and woman "to increase and multiply," and most theologians and linguists believe this implies procreation and not obesity from eating too many fruits in the garden. Nevertheless, the UN Food and Agricultural Organization reported in 2000 that one billion persons in the world were over-weight and 300 million obese. By the time of Abraham, multiplication is a secondary rule and selective choice of peoples, of a Chosen People, and becomes Rule Number One. Leakey, R. & Lewin, R., (1992).

13. J. W. Townsend, *American Psychologist*, 58(3), 2003, pp. 197-204. Cf. Brown, J. L. & Pollitt, E.. *Scientific American*, (1996, February), 38-43, where the results of over-population leads to conditions specified in the title.

14. E. M. Murphy, *American Psychologist*, 58(3), 2003, pp. 205-210.

15. "Do you mean I shouldn't have created men at all, that leaving them lie as so much clay would have been preferable? Or do you mean it was all right to have created them but I should have used some other form?" (*Prometheus*, Lucian, c.125–180, in L. Casson, (1962), 129-30.

16. Aeschylus, *op. cit.*, p. 15. Prometheus remains the subject of numerous literary works: Aescylus' *Prometheus Bound*, Shelley's *Prometheus Unbound*, and Elizabeth Barrett Browning's *Prometheus Unbound*.

17. M. Pollan, (2001). Almaty, the former Alma-Ata in Kazakhstan where I journeyed in 1991 and 1994, is a city whose name means "father of the apple," a region where the apple first propagated and began its global dispersion.

18. G. E. Mendenhall, TG. (1973), p. 40. "And this tree is to the south of Paradise, so that it might arouse the souls from the torpor of the demons, in order that they might approach the tree of life and eat of its fruit." (NH, Evans, 1993, *op. cit.*, p. 193). It was a garden yet "No plant of the field was yet in the earth and no herb of the field had sprung up." (*Gen.* 2:5) The world's most valuable coin dating from the 5th century BCE, minted near Mt. Etna in Sicily, shows Zeus seated on a throne on one side and on the other Silenos, a mythical bird perched atop a tree of life. (BAR, 30(4), p. 11).

19. N. K. Sanders, EG. (1972), p. 107. For a photo of Tablet XI of this epic on baked clay consult T. C. Mitchell, BADB. (1988). P. 70.

20. When Nana ate the fruit of the almond tree, generated by the blood of Cybele, she conceived Attis. (Spence, MLBA, p. 138).

21. F. Durando. (1997). Serpents have been mythical creatures for thousands of years. "But deep in the pool there was lying a serpent, and the serpent sensed the sweetness of the flower. It rose out of the water and snatched it away." (EG, in Sanders, 1972, *op. cit.*, p. 117). The *Enuma Elish* notes: "Fierce monster-vipers she clothed with terror." And Phil of Byblos writes: "They built temples and consecrated, in the temples' innermost shrines, the first letters, those created by serpents, and for them they celebrated feasts and sacrifices and rites. They considered them the greatest gods and the founders of the universe. So much, then, for serpents." (Philo of Byblos, *The Phoenician History*, 1st century CE).

22. Herodotus, 1830, Vol. 2, *op. cit.*, p. 133.
23. Zoroaster, HZ. (1963), 105. "The Destructive Spirit first created the Lying Word," the very embodiment of the serpent in the biblical garden. (Zaehner, TM. (1956). Absent the concepts of the devil and original sin, some ancients, like the Roman historian Sallust, saw humans as naturally defective. "The first quarrels arose among us through a defect in human nature which, restless and unbridled, is always immersed in struggles for liberty or for glory or for power." (Sallust, 1992, 24).
24. *Ibid.*, p. 46-47.
25. Roberts, 1995, *op. cit.*
26. De Moor, 1987, *op. cit.*, p. 147.
27. J. Campbell, 1987, p. 385.
28. N. W. Ross, (1966), pp. 89-90.
29. Guzzo, P. G. & A. d'Ambrosio, (1998), p.121.
30. Ross, *op. cit.*, p. 37.
31. N. K. Sandars, EG, p. 119.
32. *Ibid.*, p. 67.
33. *Gen.* 3:21.
34. *Gen.* 3: 6.
35. *Esdras* 7:18.
36. *Psalm* 18. "Man, proud man, dressed in a little brief authority, most ignorant of what he's most assured, (whose) glassy essence, like an angry ape, plays such fantastic tricks before high heaven as make the angels weep." (Shakespeare, *Measure for Measure*, II, 2).
37. Mendenhall, 1973, *op. cit.*, p. 51.
38. Sandars, EG, *op. cit.*, p. 61.
39. *Ibid.*, p. 62.
40. *Job* 33:6.
41. *Gen.* I: 26.
42. *Gen.* 3:14.
43. *Gen.* 2:12.
44. Sandars, *op. cit.*, p. 91, & p. 100 ff.
45. *Gen.* 2: 9.
46. Sandars, *op. cit.*, p. 107.
47. *Ibid.*, p. 84.
48. *Gen.* 3:17.
49. Sandars, *op. cit.*, p. 100.
50. *Ibid.*, p. 102.
51. A Scandinavian creation story offers a parallel with the Middle Eastern narrations, but with even more unpronounceable names.
52. http://www.personal.psu.edu/faculty/o/x/oxf3/atrahasis.html
53. T. C. Mitchell, BADB, p. 24.
54. Poetic but not scientific. "Thus we can understand how it has come to pass that man and all other vertebrate animals have been constructed on the same general model, why they pass through the same early stages of development, and why they retain certain rudiments in common. Consequently, we ought frankly to admit their community of descent; to take any other view, is to admit that our own structure, and that of animals around us, is a mere snare laid to entrap our judgment...It is only our natural prejudice, and that arrogance which made our forefathers declare that they were descended from demigods, which leads us to demur to this conclusion. But the time will before long come, when it will be thought wonderful that naturalists, who were well acquainted with the comparative structure and development of man, and other mammals, should have believed that each was the work of a separate act of creation."(Darwin, 1888, p. 25).

Chapter 5
1. The beginning of Chapter 4 in *Genesis* notes that "the man knew his wife," the biblical euphemism for sexual intercourse. Nakedness becomes the most prominent feature of the post-fruit eating incident, and we had been forewarned that this was coming. She was a "wife" at this time, not just "the woman," or "helper," and therefore the name change indicates a sexual relationship prior to the temptation. The scribe wants us to think that sexual proclivities, which must have been noticeable throughout the animal kingdom, have suddenly been discovered by the human race. Elsewhere, brothers are not to be trusted at all. "Let every man take heed of his neighbor, and let him not trust in any brother of his: for every brother will utterly supplant and every friend will walk deceitfully." (*Jeremiah* 9:4). Gilgamesh weeped for the loss of his brother. "Hear me, great ones of Uruk, I weep for Endiku, my friend, Bitterly moaning like a woman mourning I weep for my brother, O Endiku my brother." (N. K. Sandars, EG, *op. cit.*, pp. 94 & 97).
2. *Gen. 3:17.* "Now Abel was a keeper of flocks and Cain a tiller of the soil." *Gen.* 4:2
3. Sandars, *op.cit.*
4. In a later myth described by Hesiod, Kronos would swallow a stone thinking it was one of the children he is said to have devoured.
5. The mythical lesson for the conception of Isis is that from death comes resurrection and new life, and this is true of all gods, Attis, Adonis, Osiris, Gilgamesh and Jesus. In the Egyptian *Papyrus of Ani*, a description of passing through death to life illustrates how Ani as a glorified soul not only conquered death but avenged Osiris' murder by Seth. "I have passed through the underworld, I have seen (my) father Osiris, I have scattered the gloom of night...I have come...I have stabbed Seth to the heart." (E. A. W. Budge, 1967, p. 321).
6. http://catal.arch.cam.ac.uk/catal/catal.html.
7. T. Szulc, *National Geographic*, 200(6), 2001, pp. 90-129.
8. *Gen.* 4:5.
9. *Gen.* 4:6-7.
10. *Gen.* 4:25. Friedman notes that Adam's line is traced through Cain only and does not mention other children. The editor, probably J, adds the line that Seth was born to Adam and Eve as a replacement for Abel which may reconcile two differing sources. (R. E. Friedman, *op. cit.*, p. 40n).
11. Herodotus, *op. cit.*, p. 30.
12. *Ibid.*, p. 56.
13. "The combined evidence of a break in urban development spreading all over Syria and Palestine, and affecting the major powers in Mesopotamia and Egypt...shows the great importance of the nomadic peoples in Western Asia at this time." (Kenyon, 1978, *op. cit.*, p. 16). "After the major upset of these Amurru incursions into the settled lands, the city states pushed back the nomads towards the desert fringes and re-established the groups of minor kingdoms." (*Ibid.*, p. 19) Those who stayed on to become sedentary, perhaps even farmers themselves, joined the socio-political structure and combined the nomadic traditions with the urbanized elite.
14. *Gen.* 4:15. There is a tradition that Cain was not only a farmer but a nomadic smithy. The Hebrew word for "smith" is *qayin*. Such a person with a technical skill, presuming a much greater population than the scribe describes, would not have been killed because of his usefulness. The mark of Cain could have been the sign of his smithy status in the itinerant community. Thus, even though someone killed another, if he had a valued skill, he was not himself to be killed. The phrase, "a marked man," has come to mean an outcast, a pariah among all communities. (Bloom, 1990, *op. cit.*, p. 67).
15. *Gen.* 4: 23-4.
16. There follows in Genesis a chronology of the names of those first descendants and their ages. Seth lived 912 years; Enos, 905; Cainan, 910; Malaleel, 895; Jared, 962. By a simple calculation using 70 years as the realistic extent of a man's life, and taking 900 as the

approximate number from the scribe, using months instead of years (900 divided by 70 = 12.85) we can conclude that the scribe may be figuratively using a lunar month as a year and not the excessive hyperbole of a twelve month year. But since everything else is equally unbelievable, 900 years fits into the unreasonable pattern. Herodotus writing in the 5th century BCE, notes with some realism that "I will suppose the term of human life to extend to seventy years." (Herodotus, *op. cit.*, p. 27). Actuaries already have this knowledge.
17. *4 Kings*, 2:11.

Chapter 6
1. From EG in Sandars, *op. cit.*, p. 108. Berossus, a Babylonian priest and author living at the time of Alexander the Great, is said to have written three volumes of Babylonian history c.250 BCE including the story of the flood.
2. *Ibid.*, p. 109. A petroglyph etched into a stonewall at Largo Canyon in New Mexico describes pictorially the story of the Monster Slayer, one of the twins born to Changing Woman and the sun, part of the creation story of the Navajos. Monster Slayer and his twin brother, Child-Born-for-Water, were given weapons by their father the sun to kill the monsters, the wicked animals, and make the world safe again for humans. The similarity between the gods, with help from humans or demigods killing the wicked things appears to be universal in creation myths.
3. Exploits of the hero might correspond to the movement of heavenly bodies and the placing of the flood story on the 11th tablet might be linked to the 11th sign of the zodiac, Aquarius, the waterbearer. (L. Spence, MLBA, p. 183).
4. http://www.personal.psu.edu/faculty/o/x/oxf3/atrahasis.html.
5. Noah is listed as the 10th patriarch just as Sisuthrus is listed as the 10th Babylonian king in the Gilgamesh epic. *Ibid.*, p. 45.
6. *Gen.* 6:2.
7. *Gen.* 6: 6-7 and Sanders, 1972, *op. cit.*, p. 108.
8. *Gen.* 1:9. There was also some "mist": "But a mist rose from the earth and watered all the surface of the ground." (*Gen.* 2:6).
9. *Gen.* 8:7.
10. D. Balsinger & C. E. Sellier (1976). There are many historical quests for antique artifacts but none seems as unproductive as this search.
11. *Gen.* 9:12-14.
12. *Gen.* 15:17-19.
13. *Exodus* 23:31-33.
14. *Exodus* 34:26-28. The first covenants were with individuals: Noah, Abraham, Jacob, Isaac and Moses "But I will establish my covenant with you, and you will enter the ark, you and your sons and your wife and your sons' wives with you." (*Gen.* 6:17-19)
15. "Then Noah built an altar; he took of every clean animal and every clean bird, and offered holocausts on the altar." (*Gen.* 8:20).
16. C. Auge & J-M Dentzer, (2000). Cf. F. Bourbon, (1999).
17. *Gen.* 9:25.
18. Sandars, p. 114 ff.
19. C. L. Woolley, (1965), pp. 123-4. Sandars, pp. 108-113.
20. *Gen.* 11:7.
21. Erman, A. (1969), pp. 47-49.
22. Descriptions of ancestors are literary devices in the heroic tradition, reaching a literary climax in the *Iliad* and *Odyssey*. We find this device in *Matthew* when Jesus is linked to the ancestry of David. Gilgamesh is the hero and unifying theme. Noah falls into this heroic category because of his choice by the Lord involving all of mankind and a new lineage for the human race.
23. *Gen.* 11:9.

24. Spence, 1916, *op. cit.*, pp. 48-49. Recent scholarship points to the invention of agriculture as a causal explanation for the diffusion of languages. With the development of crops, population increased and dispersed and over time language became as differentiated as hybrid vegetables. Today, there exist 1,436 languages of the Niger-Congo Bantu family alone, the largest language group. The second largest family of languages is the Austronesian, a group of 1,236, originally spoken by rice growers in southern China who colonized Taiwan, Polynesia and New Zealand. There were three major language groups in the Fertile Crescent: the Dravidian, now found in southern India, the Indo-European, including English, French, German, Iranian and Hindi, and Afro-Asiatic which includes ancient Egyptian, Hebrew and Arabic. (N. Wade, *The New York Times*, May 6, 2003, D3).

Chapter 7
1. T. Szulc, *op. cit.*, pp. 90-129.
2. *Deut.*, 26:5.
3. J. Winsten. (1999), p. 45. On Urfa as Abraham's birthplace instead of Ur see Gordon, C. H. & Rendsburg, G. A. *op. cit.*, 1997), p. 113. Zoroaster too writes of wandering: "To what land shall I flee? Where bend my steps? I am thrust out from family and tribe; I have no favor from the village to which I would belong, not from the wicked rulers of the country: How then, O Lord, shall I obtain thy favor?" (Zoroaster, *op. cit.*, p. 75).
4. Winsten, *op cit.*, p. 49. Citizens of the city of Urfa in southeastern Turkey revere a cave where they say Abraham was born. A spring flows from the cave and waters nearby have canals where abundant fish swim. The water and the fish are sacred even to the Muslims living there. For an analysis of the trade from Ur to other cities cf. G. Algaze, 1989, V. 30(5), pp. 571-608.
5. *Gen.* 18:27.
6. The multiplicity of gods for the Hebrews means that different names for God are used until such time as God's real name is revealed as YHWH, Yahweh. This does not occur until the time of Moses and subsequent editors like P added material. (*Exodus* 6:3). R. E. Friedman, *op. cit.*, p. 56n.
7. *Gen.* 13:2.
8. Gordon, C. H. & Rendsburg, G. A. BANE, pp.110 ff. and W. Keller, BH, p. 68.
9. See Herodotus and his report of the adventures of Cambyses: "The next victim of his fury was his sister, who had accompanied him into Egypt. She was also his wife." Herodotus, HH, pp.1 ff.
10. *Gen.* 18: 23-33.
11. *Gen.* 26:11.
12. The Greeks had a sensible if somewhat cynical approach to prophets. Agamemnon says: "The tribe of prophets wants only to be important, the whole rotten crowd of them." And Menelaos says: "When they don't prophesy they're useless, and when they do it does no good." (From Euripdes, *Iphigeneia*)
13. "A man and wife might legally sell their own child as a slave, and in payment of debt a man might hand over his wife, his son, his daughter to his creditor to be his slave for the space of three years." Woolley, 1965, *op. cit.*, p. 91.
14. *Ibid.*, p. 99.
15. *Ibid.*, p.126.
16. Durant, 1935, *op. cit.*, pp. 128-29.
17. Keller, 1995, *op. cit.*, pp. 74-78.
18. Woolley, 1965, *op. cit.*, p. 116.
19. *Gen.* 13: 2; 24:22; 24:53. "For their possessions were so great." (*Gen.* 13:6).
20. Woolley, 1965, *op. cit.*, p. 168.
21. Euripedes (1832). Euripedes, V. 2., p. 250, lines 28-31.
22. *Gen.* 19: 37-8. Also see K. Politis, BAR, 30(1), 2003, pp. 21-31.

23. "The Lord appeared to Abraham and said, To your descendants I will give this land." (*Gen.* 12:7). "All the land which you see I will give to you and your posterity forever." (*Gen.* 13:14). "I am the Lord, who brought you from Ur in Chaldea, to give you this land to possess." (*Gen.* 15:7). "To your posterity I will give this land, from the river of Egypt to the Great River [Euphrates]." (*Gen.* 15:18, & 17:6-8).
24. "Every male among you shall be circumcised." (*Gen.* 17:10) "Male children, except in those places which have borrowed the custom from hence, are left in other nations as nature formed them: in Egypt they are circumcised." HH, p. 187. Herodotus says nothing about the practice in Palestine.
25. Friedman, 2003, *op. cit.*, pp. 4-5, and 56-57.

Chapter 8
1. Spence, 1916, *op. cit.*, p. 162.
2. Woolley, 1965, *op. cit.*, p. 93 ff. Woolley reports that the wife had equal property rights with her husband, "and could even disinherit an undutiful son and even have him branded and expelled from the city."
3. *Ibid.*, p. 102.
4. *Ibid.*, p. 104.
5. *Ibid.*, p. 105.
6. HH, V.3, p. 105. See also W. V. Harris, JRS, (2003), 83, 18-34.
7. Prometheus in Aeschylus' *The Tragedies*, p. 18.
8. HH., II, p. 56.
9. *Ibid.*, p. 29-34. There are plenty of dream stories in Herodotus. Camyses, the son of Cyrus, has a warning dream about his brother Smerdis, whom he has murdered. (II, p. 56) Hipparchus receives a vision in a dream about his own impending death. (II, pp. 284-85)
10. HH, p. 155.
11. The "wings on the shoulders" image refers to the Akkadian symbol of the sundisk with wings flying across the sky daily. Bullae (seals) have been excavated showing emblems of Hezekiah (727–697 BCE) with Egyptian iconographic images: on one, a four-winged scarab and on another a six-winged sundisk. Hezekiah supposedly eliminated foreign influences from Judah's religious practices. (R. Deutsch, BAR, 28(4), 2002, pp. 43-51). So why are these foreign seals paramount in his reign?
12. Budge, 1973, *op. cit.*, p. 124-25.
13. *Gen.* 29:17.
14. *Gen.* 31:3.
15. *Gen.* 31: 31.
16. *Gen.* 34: 29.
17. Durant, 1954, *op. cit.*, p. 171.
18. Janssen, R. M. & J. J. (1990), p. 72 ff.
19. On commercial and official documents, a less rigid form of writing was called hieratic, and an even looser form of common writing became known as demotic, a script appearing on the Rosetta stone. Herodotus writes: "The Egyptians have certainly discovered more things that are wonderful than all the rest of mankind. Whenever any unusual circumstance occurs, they commit the particulars to writing." HH, II, p. 82.
20. No. 49 in R. D. Barnett, (1977).
21. *Ibid.*, Letters no, 57, 61, and 68.
22. O. Keel, O. & C. Uehlinger, GGIG. (1998).
23. J. Van Seters. (1983), p. 139.
24. G. E. Mendenhall, TG. (1973).
25. *Gen.* 5:3.
26. *Gen.* 6: 1-2.
27. Van Seters, *op. cit.*, p. 143.

Chapter 9
1. BAR, 30,000-Year-Old Sanctuary Found at Har Karkom, 19(1), 1993, p. 38. The Koran has a strange verse: "And a tree which cometh out of Mt. Sinai which bears oil and a sauce for the eaters." (R. Bell, 1960, p. 328). Did Mohammed mistake Sinai for the Mount of Olives, since no trees grace Sinai?
2. G. Niebuhr, *The New York Times*, 2001, June 2, p. A10.
3. C. R. Krahmalkov, BAR, 20(5), 1994, pp. 55-62.
4. Merenptah (1225–1215 BCE), according to an extant stele, boasts of conquering Isiraal (Israel). "Plundered is Canaan, with every evil...Israel is desolated, her seed is not; Palestine has become a widow for Egypt By King Merneptah." (Egyptian stele c.1229 BCE. In W. Keller, BH, pp.163-64). An historical exodus, which is questionable, must have occurred earlier than c.1,225 BCE since the stele assumes that the tribes of Israel were already organized enough to be defeated. See also T. C. Mitchell, BADB, p. 41. And cf. F. J. Yurco, BAR, (1990, September/October), pp. 21-38.
5. D. B. Redford, (1993), p. 258.
6. C. A. Evans, *et. al.*, (1993), p. 188. The latest of new monotheistic beliefs is Sikhism, in 2005 claiming 22 million followers, a religious community founded in the Punjab of northwest India by a Hindu ascetic named Nanak (c.1469–1539), roughly a contemporary of Henry VIII in England. Nanak attempted to reconcile Hinduism and Islam by promoting a realization of God through meditation and meditative religious exercises. He opposed the caste system, prescribed rituals, and preached a universal equality. Sikhs accept only one god. In many ways Sikhs imitate the soft, meditative side of Islam, the Sufis. Like Hindus, Sikhs believe in samsara, the repetitive cycle of birth, life and death, and in karma, sum of one's deeds, and in reincarnation, or a rebirth following death. The stricter men not only wear their hair long, they never cut it. They carry a comb, wear short pants, a metal bracelet and carry a ceremonial dagger. The holy book is the *Guru Granth Sahib*, a collection of prayers, devotional hymns, sayings and poetry that proclaim God, provide prescriptions for exercises on meditation on the True God, and moral and ethical rules for development of the soul, spiritual salvation and unity with God.
7. Translated by L. W. King at: http://eawc.evansville.edu/anthology/hammurabi.htm. Cf. Durant, 1954, *op. cit.*, pp. 219-220. In the *Enuma Elish* we find a surprisingly similar passage about tablets of law: "She gave him the Tablets of Destiny, on his breast she laid them, saying: Thy command shall not be without avail, and the word of thy mouth shall be established."
8. Durant, Ibid., p. 231.
9. Clement of Alexandria claims, erroneously, that "The philosopher Plato gained from the teaching of Moses material on his legislation." (*Stromateis*. 1991, p. 144). "All the doctrines I have been discussing seem to have been handed down to the Greeks by the towering figure of Moses." (*Ibid.*, p. 170).
10. "Center Wins Battle for Religious Tolerance." (2003, September). *SPLC Report*, (Birmingham, AL: Southern Poverty Law Center, p. 1). Protestors confused the physical display in a public building with the moral code it represents. Christian advocates believe that in certain circumstances it is necessary to defy civil law when God's law, displaying God's commandments, abortion, sodomy, which they claim is the foundation of all law is at stake. Legal advocates say that the state cannot acknowledge God based on the 1st Amendment's constitutional separation of church and state.
11. *The Ten Commandments of Solon* (in Diogenes Laertius, LEP 1.60), goes as follows: 1. Trust good character more than promises. 2. Do not speak falsely. 3. Do good things. 4. Do not be hasty in making friends, but do not abandon them once made. 5. Learn to obey before you command. 6. When giving advice, do not recommend what is most pleasing, but what is most useful. 7. Make reason your supreme commander. 8. Do not associate with people who do bad things. 9. Honor the gods. 10. Have regard for your parents.

The Athenian orator Antiphon (c.479–411 BCE) made the most perspicacious legal distinction in the 5th century BCE. "The commands of law (*nomos*) are artificial, those of nature (*physis*) necessary. The commands of law are the result of agreement, not of growth; the commands of nature are the result of growth, not of agreement...the majority of rights laid down by law are at enmity with nature." (Antiphon in W. H. Auden, 1948, pp. 476-77).

12. M. Bietak, BAR, 29 (5), 2003, p. 41 ff. argues that *Exodus* is the journey of the Israelites back to their homeland in Canaan.

13. Budge, 1967, op. cit., pp. 347-49. By contrast, the ten commandments of a Hindu believer include: fortitude, patience, self-control, no stealing, purity, control of senses, insight, wisdom, truth and avoidance of anger, all virtues relating to the development of personal character, and irrespective of belief in a god.

14. F. Solmsen, (1995), p. 118. The classic text that shows the influence of Hesiod on other Greek poets and playwrights. For more on Solon see I. M. Linforth. Vol. 6. (1919), where the same quote from fragments of his poems translated into 19th century English, appears on p. 135.

15. http://theosophy.org/tlodocs/teachers/Solon.htm The classic study of Solon is I. M. Linforth (1919). Solon is also featured in Diogenes Laertius, LEP. Vol. 1. (1959), pp. 47-69.

16. Ammianus Marcellinus, LRE. (1986), p. 254.

17. J. Winsten, *op. cit.*, p. 119.

18. C. Aldred, AKE, p. 261-2. The Amarna archives describe conditions in Palestine in the 15th and 14th centuries BCE. See W. Keller, BH, p. 145.

19. *Ibid.*, p. 49. This is in great contrast to the multiple gods the Egyptians did worship, as Juvenal notes: "Who does not know the kind of monsters that that mad country Egypt worships?" (Juvenal, 1887, p. 118).

20. Winsten, 1999, *op. cit.*, pp. 124-26.

21. Aldred, *op. cit.*, p. 242. "Jewish inventiveness expropriated Egyptian myth in order to insert it into their own heroes, their religious superiority, and even their military triumphs." (E. Gruen, 1998, p. 71).

22. Devotees of Aten during the time of Akhenaten believed in eternal life and immortality. Nowhere in biblical scripture is immortality expressly proclaimed. It was, however, a major subject of debate during the time of Jesus among the Pharisees who did believe in life after death. Sadducees, the temple keepers, did not believe in immortality, resurrection, the existence of devils or angels, or the coming of a Messiah.

23. A. Roberts, *op. cit.*, p. 150.

24. Freud wrote: "I should now like to venture on this conclusion: if Moses was an Egyptian and if he communicated his own religion to the Jews, it must have been Akhenaten's, the Aten religion." (Freud, v.23, 1964, p. 24). According to this view, Moses and his followers were forced to flee Egypt, not because they were Hebrews and wanted to escape slavery, but because they were a persecuted religious minority, disciples of the monotheism of the dead king Akhenaten whose monotheistic beliefs had been declared heretical. "It remains possible that the religion which Moses gave to his Jewish people was nevertheless his own—that it was an Egyptian religion, though not the Egyptian religion." (*Ibid.*, p. 20).

25. The final "s" to the name comes from the Greek translation of the Bible.

26. Freud concludes that Moses was an Egyptian whom the literary scribes turned into a Jew. (Freud, 1964, *op. cit.*, p. 15).

27. A. Roberts, *op. cit.*, p. 48.

28. Budge, 1973, *op. cit.*, p. 301.

29. Clement, 1991, *op. cit.*, pp. 135-44. Sargon, the founder of the dynasty of Akkad in 2,360 BCE, did not know his father, was born of a priestess mother who put him in a reed box made and then in the river where he was found by Akki who adopted him and reared him as her son. (W. Keller, BH, p. 123). Compare with *Exodus* 2: 3 ff.

30. Winsten, 1999, *op. cit.*, p. 239.

31. I have stood atop Mount Nebo where Moses is said to have expired and only a small modern stone memorializes Moses near the Franciscan basilica dating from the 6th century CE. Why is there no sign of Moses' gravesite or any Hebrew remembrance of this most significant figure? Jesus spoke about "the tombs of the prophets" and "the monuments of the saints." (*Matthew* 23:29-31) But no tomb or monument exists for Moses.
32. http://www.hope.edu/academic/religion/bandstra/RTOT/CH2/CH2_TWO.HTM Cf. also A. Erman, (1894).
33. Winsten, 1999, *op. cit.*, pp. 136-37.
34. Durant, 1954, *op. cit.*, 301-02 n.
35. *Exodus*, 15:26.
36. For this and similar allusions see J. Stetkevych, (1996)
37. The crozier staff Catholic bishops carry in liturgical ceremonies is a continuation of this ancient symbol of authority.
38. *Numbers* 20, 11-12. The fable is immortalized in Callimachus' Hymn to Apollo: "Poised in her speech with great arm held high, the goddess (Rheia) struck staff to the mountains and water asunder poured from the rift." *Callimachus, Hymns, Epigrams, Select Fragments.* (Baltimore, MD: The Johns Hopkins University Press, 1988, p. 4).
39. HH, pp. 187-195.
40. See Virgil's description of the famous descent into the underworld in *Georgics* 4. 467 ff. Satirists like Juvenal scoffed: "That there are such things as spirits of the dead and infernal regions, the river Cocytus, and the Styx with inky frogs in its waters, that so many thousands cross the stream in single skiff, not even children believe, unless they're still in the nursery." (Juvenal, 1991, p.14).
41. This papyrus was first published with hieroglyphics and an English translation by E. A. Wallis Budge for the British Museum in 1895.
42. Gordon doesn't think so: "Accordingly, it is out of the question to assume Moses…could have shaped Hebrew monotheism directly on the inspiration of Akhenaten's reform."
43. Gordon, C. H. & Rendsburg, G. A., BANE, p. 85.
44. *Exodus*, 32: 1-6. The reveling would be a hardy Egyptian trait, but we don't find much reveling afterwards among the Hebrews unless it's unsanctioned.
45. *Exodus*, 32. 7-10. Of course they had just come from a great nation.
46. *Exodus* 11: 5.
47. *Exodus* 29:11-13.
48. *Leviticus* 4:6-8.
49. *Leviticus* 8:14-16.
50. *Isaiah* 66:2-4.
51. *1 Kings*: 8, *2 Chronicles*: 7. Sacrificial biblical cattle had to have certain requirements and these are spelled out, among other places, in *Exodus* 29, *Deuteronomy* 18 and 21, *Leviticus* 7, *Isaiah* 1 and *Ezekiel* 39. These sacrificial restrictions may have changed over time and place, but a universal prescription is that the yearling calf, or fattened bull for festive celebrations, cannot have been used as a draught animal. (*Deut.* 21). Sometimes, several kinds of animals, heifers, she-goats, rams, turtledoves and pigeons, as God told Abraham, were all sacrificed together. (*Gen.* 15:9) By the time of the establishment of the monarchy under David and Solomon whole herds were sacrificed. (*1 Kings*, 1:9) The ritual of bull sacrifice had been firmly established by the Hebrews in the first millennium BCE, but like much of the rest of the culture the ritual was borrowed in whole or part from the Sumerians, Canaanites, Babylonians and Egyptians.
52. *John* 2.
53. *Acts* 14:12-14.
54. *Hebrews* 9:12-14.
55. W. G. Dever, *op. cit.*, pp. 128-136.
56. *Numbers*, 23, 22.

57. *Numbers*, 23:1-2.
58. *I Kings* 12:28-30.
59. *I Kings* 12:32. "They exchanged their glory for the image of a grass-eating bullock." (*Psalm* 106:19-20).
60. A. Millard, "How Reliable is Exodus?" BAR, 26(4), 2000, pp. 51-57.
61. What served as a cultural continuation was the concept of seven heavens where Angels, Archangels and Powers were said to reside. The top heaven represents wisdom, followed by understanding, counsel, fortitude, knowledge, godliness, and fear of the Spirit. The seven-branched candlestick, the Menorah Moses received, symbolizes these seven heavens. (*Exodus* 25:40; (Irenaeus, 1952, p. 53).
62. Gordon & Rendsburg, *op. cit.*, p. 151.
63. See the description of exactly these dimensions in a recent discovery of such a site in Israel. (Elitzur, Y., & Nir-Zevi, D. 2004, May/June. BAR, 30(3), 35-39).

Chapter 10
1. Josephus' citation is quite possibly a later Christian addition. M. Hadas-Lebel. (1993), p. 224ff. In 1962 archaeologists uncovered in a ruined theater in Caesarea Maritima an inscription with the name of Pontius Pilate but naming him "prefect" and not the more inferior "procurator" noted in the gospels. (Crossan, J. D., & Reed, J. L., *op. cit.*, p. 2). The 40+ years of study of Jesus by Geza Vermes of Oxford is compelling. Together with his Jewish Hungarian parents, Vermes converted to Catholicism, then, disillusioned with Christianity, he married, and has since written persuasively about Jesus from a Jewish perspective at Oxford.
2. Constructing speeches and conversations is a device Herodotus and Thucydides used. Sallust relied on Thucydides as his primary influence. (Sallust, 1992, p. 13-14). Justin Martyr claimed that exegesis of varied cultural texts was a part of the recovery of the truth about the Logos. (R. Lyman, JECS, 2003, 11(2), p. 219). Belief in the gods was a chief characteristic of Greek and Roman life two thousand years ago among all classes. Rabbis, priests, soothsayers, oracles, and astrologers spread the idea of divine intervention in people's lives and affairs. Belief in auguries, omens, or natural disasters as representative of God's favor or displeasure: "Angry Jove to lay down thunderbolts of his wrath," according to Horace, blunted rational inquiry. Lucretius (c.99–55 BCE) in *On the Nature of Things*, and Aristotle's scientific insights were unusual. Most works promoted the likelihood of God's arbitrary interference in human affairs, an idea promulgated from the Sumerians and an integral element in the Greek heroic tradition.
3. M. Grant, (1977). (Michael Grant died as I was completing this work). For the Homeric legends serving as a foundation for New Testament writings see D. R. MacDonald (2000) and (2003). O. Tsagarakis, (1977). Gainsford speaks of "recognition" scenes that can be dissected into motifs, like testing, deceptions, foretelling and recognitions, (P. Gainsford, JHS, 2003, 123, 41-59), found extensively in Homer and in the gospels in scenes such as the transfiguration and Peter's denial. Jesus tests his disciples' loyalty on numerous occasions and even disguises his identity, like Odysseus, says his real persona will emerge later, like Odysseus, and then reveals his true identity, again like Odysseus.
4. Weeks, 1983, *op. cit.*, pp. 83-84. Living a generation prior to Jesus, even the charming, elegant Horace (65–8 BCE), full of patriotic odes, friendship, light love poems and gentle humor, composing poetic feelings from ordinary events, the gathering of friends, the hospitality of his house, his simple life, plenty of wine and song, a lively wit, is concerned with the poor and friendless. The epicurean philosophy of the enjoyment of life is certainly evident in his delightful poetry but a touch of the stoic, of self-control and the shunning of wealth and ostentation, is also present.
5. "Even being poor is no impediment; as long as he can be of value to the state, no man is barred from public life simply because poverty has made him obscure. We cultivate refinement without extravagance and knowledge without effeminacy; wealth we employ more for use than for show and as for poverty—there's no disgrace in admitting it, the greater shame is in not

taking steps to escape from it" (Funeral oration of Pericles in Thucydides, II; 40-41). But Pericles also sought a commonwealth ideal. Epicureanism and Christianity saw "the kingdom" as appropriate only in an afterlife. (C. N. Cochrane, 2003, 1940, p. 42).
6. Seneca, LFS, p. 86.
7. *Ibid.*, p. 69; and in Virgil IV, 653.
8. *Ibid.*, p. 140.
9. A. Birley, (1993), p. 101. The Emperor Julian, educated in rhetoric and philosophy, was an admirer of the stoics (cynics): "Now the end and aim of the Cynic philosophy, as indeed of every philosophy, is happiness, but happiness that consists in living according to nature and not according to the opinions of the multitudes." (*The Works of Emperor Julian.* v. 2. London: William Heinemann, 1913, p. 39). Centuries earlier Pythagoras used homey expressions to make moral points. "Don't stir the fire with a knife: don't stir the passions. Don't step over the beam of a balance: don't overstep the bounds of equity and justice. Don't sit on your bushel: have the same care today and the future, a bushel being the day's ration." (Diogenes Laertius, LEP, p. 337.
10. *Iliad* 9.323 and Musonius quote at: http://www.infidels.org/library/modern/richard_carrier/musonius.html. *The Iliad* was written by Homer in the 8th century BCE about a war story of Troy centuries before. The site known as Hislarik today was first excavated by Schiemann in the 19th century. Archaeological evidence suggests Troy was destroyed in 1,180 BCE. (M. Korfmann, *Archaeology*, 2004, 57(3), 36-41). The question is, Did Homer use poetry to enhance an historical event? The scholarly response is yes, very likely. (G. S. Kirk. 1965, and M. Wood, 1985, also a six-part video and DVD series.
11. *Matthew* 5:27-30, *Mark* 9:43-9.
12. According to Josephus about the Essenes, "Each man's possession went into a pool and, as with brothers, their entire property belongs to them all." Plutarch has similar expositions about the value of poverty over wealth. (Plutarch. *Moralia.* 1969, p. 111 and 277-79).
13. *Luke* 19:26.
14. Martial, (1963), p. 64.
15. *Ibid.*, p. 76.
16. Eusebius, HCCC, p. 152. Jesus wrote nothing.
17. *The Republic.* (1944), p. 43, and this: "Well, then, is it just or unjust to repay injury with injury? Unjust, I would think. Because dong harm to men is no different from doing wrong? Exactly so. So we should never take revenge and never hurt anyone even if we have been hurt." (Socrates in Plato's *Crito* in WP, p. 99. Origen has a lengthy defense of Celsus' assertion that Plato had first announced the virtue of not harming others (OCC, *op. cit.*, pp. 444-46), but argues, not about the precedent of the literary and ethical concept, but instead for its usefulness in living a virtuous life.
18. *Luke* 16:17.
19. *Mark* 2:25.
20. See A. A. Long, (2002). Even death was a stoic ideal. "Set death before me, set pain, set a prison, set ignominy, set condemnation before me, and you will know me." (*Ibid.*, p. 69). Other Epictetus works consulted include: *The Discourses of Epictetus.* In R. M. Hutchins (Ed.), *Great Books of the Western World.* (Chicago: Encyclopedia Britannica, 1952). *Epictetus, Moral Discourses.* (New York: E. P. Dutton & Co., 1942). Aristotle has a similar description of the ethical man: "He does not run into trifling dangers, nor is he fond of danger, because he honors few things; but he will face great dangers, and when he is in danger he is unsparing of his life, knowing there are conditions on which life is not worth having." (W. H. Auden, 1948, p. 377), and in *The Nicomachean Ethics*, Book 4, Chapter 3.
21. Epictetus, *Moral Discourses*, 1942, *op. cit.*, p. 170.
22. Xenophon, *op. cit.,*, p..294.
23. Epictetus, 1942, *op. cit.*, pp. 171-72.

24. Socrates, p. 173. Seneca, LFS, p. 93.
25. *Mark* 13:27-29.
26. *Matthew* 21:17.
27. Epictetus, 1942, *op. cit.*, p. 191. Even the biting, poetic satires of Juvenal, who used indignation as inspiration, have references to barren fig trees. "Often states have been ruined by a few men's greed for fame, by their passion for praise and for titles inscribed in the stones protecting their ashes, stones which the boorish strength of the barren fig tree succeeds in splitting apart." (Juvenal, 1991, *op. cit.*, p. 91). In this context, barren fig trees are allegorically good in breaking down men's ambitions.
28. *Ibid.*, p. 191.
29. http://classics.mit.edu/Homer/odyssey.7.vii.html. The quotations from *The Odyssey* are taken from R. Fitzgerald's translation (New York: Anchor Books, 1963). See also MacDonald, 2000, *op. cit.*, pp. 107-09 who describes this incident. Xenophon has a passage in his histories about Cyrus that is similar: "Such men seem to me like those who desire to be thrifty husbandmen, and who sow well and plant wisely, but when the time of harvest comes let the fruit drop back ungarnered (sic) into the soil whence it sprang." (Xenophon, *op. cit.*, p. 31.
30. *Matthew* 10:36-38.
31. Epictetus, 1942, *op. cit.*, p. 210.
32. *Mark* 12:15-17.
33. Epictetus, 1942, *op. cit.*, p. 225.
34. *Luke* 6:36-38.
35. Epictetus, p. 236.
36. *Luke* 8:24-26.
37. Epcitetus, p. 109.
38. Likewise, in *Adapa*, a Babylonian myth, Adapa, son of Ea one of the first gods, was fishing and a South Wind blew with malevolent violence and cast him into the sea. When he arrived on shore, Adapa vowed revenge on the South Wind god, Shutu, the demon shaped like a large bird. Adapa leapt at her and broke her wings so she could never fly again. (L. Spence, MLBA, pp.117 ff).
39. E. A. W. Budge, (1899, 1980), p. 12.
40. *Matthew* 6:5-7.
41. I. Edman, WP, 184-85.
42. M. Grant, *op. cit.*, p. 84.
43. *Luke* 14:26, *Matt.* 10:37, though Matthew omits "wife." Such unwavering loyalty is not only contrary to nature but contrary Yahweh's biblical injunctions. Was he, who was said in the Nicene Creed to be of the same substance with the father, contradicting himself?
44. *Mark* 6:3-6.
45. Josephus, (1960), p. 51.
46. J. Allegro (1957) where two of the first books to appear on the scrolls. Thiede argues that from Cave 7 of the Dead Sea Scrolls, which contains only Greek papyrus texts, is material from Essenes who converted to Christianity and stored some of the first gospels documents in it for safekeeping. C. P. Thiede, (1992).
47. R. H. Eisenman, & M. Wise (1994), p. 181. Also M. Broshi, BAR, 30(1), 2003, p. 32 ff.
48. *Acts* 2:44.
49. Eisenman & Wise, 1994, *op. cit.*, p. 18. The idea is not uncommon even in Greek mythology. Teiresias the blind prophet of Thebes says about Hercules: "I swear that many a Greek woman as she cards the wool at eventide shall sing of this your son and you who bore him. He shall be the hero of all mankind."
50. *Ibid.*, p. 70.
51. K. Carroll, (2003), and G. Wills, "Looking for the Lost Greeks, *New York Review of Books*, 2003 (October 9), L15, p. 19. See also "The people (dedicate this temple) to the goddess Roma and to Imperator Caesar, son of a god, god Augustus." And: "The agoranomos (a Greek

public official) shall celebrate the first day for god Caesar, son of a god, Augustus the Savior and Deliverer." (R. K. Sherk, 1989, p. 14 and 58). Vermes notes that "son of God" to a Jew was always metaphorical and not that the person was of a divine nature. (G. Vermes, 1983, p. 72).

52. A. Birley, *op. cit*, p. 15.
53. http://www.uncc.edu/jdtabor/divine.html The Roman Senate conferred divine status on Claudius after his death and on his nephew successor Nero using the Greek term *daimon* (Latin, *genius*) for the semi-divine spirit resting in his authority. *Daimon* is the same Greek word used to describe the bad spirits cast out by Jesus. (Schowalter, "Churches in Context, The Jesus Movement in the Roman Word." OHBW, p. 401).
54. Grant, 1975, *op. cit.*, p. 55.
55. Homer wrote in *The Iliad*, in Alexander Pope's translation: "The bitter dregs of Fortune's cup to drain."
56. W. H. Auden, *op. cit.*, p. 204. There are other non-gospel texts that use similar designations and titles, and these are in addition to the Greeks said to be sons of Zeus. From the *Gospel of the Egyptians*, the Nag Hammadi texts we find: "Then a voice came from on high saying 'The Man exists, and the Son of Man." Because of the descent of the image above, which is like its voice in the height of the image which has looked out, through the looking out of the image above, the first creature was formed." And in Epictetus: "For none more his friend than God, for which reason he was believed to be the son of God, and was so." (Epictetus, 1942, p.103). Descriptions in imperial documents furnished some of the theological arguments necessary to transfer obsequious phrases expressed in politics about emperors to Jesus. For example, *An Introduction to the Julian Calendar* by the emperor Augustus in 9 BCE reads: "The providence which rules over all has filled this man with such gifts for the salvation of the world as designate him as savior for us and for the coming generation...By his appearing are the hopes of our forefathers fulfilled; not only has he surpassed the good deeds of earlier time, but it is impossible that one greater than he can ever appear. The birth-day of God has brought to the world glad tidings that are bound up in him." (Mead, G. R. S., FFF).
57. Dittenberger, *Orientis Graecae Inscriptiones Selectae*, in M. Grant, *op. cit.*, p. 65.
58. Grant, 1975, p. 55.
59. Spence, 1916, *op. cit.*, p. 65.
60. Budge, 1967, *op. cit.*, p. cxlv.
61. *Ibid.*, p. 367 & p. 254.
62. Xenophon, *op. cit.*, p. 263.
63. J. C. Moor, J. C. (1987). ART, p. 109.
64. E. P. Sanders, "In Quest of the Historical Jesus." *The New York Review of Books*, 48(18), 2001, pp. 33-36. Also G. Vermes, (1983).
65. Quoted from: http://www.sacredtexts.com/ane/enuma.htm.
66. Many commentators like Crossan and Reed (2001) attempt to reconcile these differences by examining marriage contracts, adultery cases, and Jewish legal codes in the Mishnah.
67. It is probable Jesus was born in Nazareth, his hometown, and only described as being born in Bethlehem to satisfy a prophecy from Micah about a redeemer with ancestral kingship. Nazareth was a cult center 10,000 years ago. (D. Keys, "Pre-Christian Rituals at Nazareth." *Archaeology*, 56(6) 2003, p. 10). For the Roman version of the equestrian officer who was actually responsible for taking the census in 6 CE see R. K. Sherk, *op. cit.*, p. 38-39. For archaeological notices about Nazareth during Jesus' life, see Crossan & Reed, 2001, *op. cit.*, pp. 31-32.
68. *Matthew* 2:12-14. Perry (2003) has a travelogue through Coptic Egypt where spurious legends persist of places Jesus visited. Why the angel would not appear to the mothers and fathers of the other children is unrecorded. God's message through angelic intermediaries is apparently not reserved for public use, even if it means the death of infants. We are not told when the angel re-appeared to Joseph to tell him to return, but if the death of Herod, which

occurred in 4 BCE, is assumed accurate then the infancy of Jesus until he was about a first-grader was spent in the valley of the Nile. More likely the whole story is concocted.
69. Virgil, *The Eclogues of Virgil.* (1963), p. 23. Cf. W. Durant, (1944), p. 237. "God will raise up for you a prophet like myself from among yourselves, from your own brothers; to him you must listen." *(Deuteronomy* 18:15-18) Augustine thought that Virgil's *Fourth Eclogue* was indeed a prophecy of Christ and that Virgil was inspired but unaware that he was. A papyrus fragment No. 721 from Masada has been dated to 73 or 74, or shortly after the conquest of the mountain fortress by the Romans under Silva. The text is in Latin likely written by a Roman officer. One damaged line is identified as coming from the beginning of Dido's speech in Virgil's *Aeneid* (4:9), the oldest surviving text of Virgil written less than a hundred years after his death and found near the Dead Sea. (C. P. Thiede, 1992, pp. 43-44).
70. Parallels between the infancy of Cyrus, whom the Hebrews admired because he released them from Babylonian bondage and the early life of Jesus are delineated more explicitly in Chapter 12 showing Persian influence.
71. *Mark* 12:35-37.
72. In 2002 a discovery was made of a stone ossuary indicating that its contents were of "James, son of Joseph, brother of Jesus." (Lemaire, BAR, 29(5), 2003, p. 27). Few pieces of corroborating evidence exist which lend credibility to figures in the gospels. The only biblical individuals who have inscriptions or tablets otherwise identifying them as historical figures are: Herod, Pontius Pilate and Sergius Paulus, a proconsul in Cyprus, reputedly one of Paul's first converts. This ossuary was discovered to be a forgery. Whether there are lost texts that are at variance with existing Hebrew Old Testament texts, or Matthew was careless in his quotations, his quotes about the prophecies concerning Jesus are at odds with existing texts. There are variations in Matthew's quotes about where the Messiah was supposed to be born (2:6), where Matthew changes the whole sentence structure from Micah, in Jesus' use of parables where Matthew in 13:35 erroneously quotes *Psalms*, and the entrance into Jerusalem where he misquotes *Zechariah* 9:9.
73. *Luke* 17:21. Regarding semi-divine status, Apuleius wrote: "A marriage between a god and a mortal, celebrated in the depth of the country without witnesses and lacking even the consent of the bride's father, won't possibly be recognized at Law." (R. Graves, 1951, p. 132).
74. P. Kingsley. (1995). "cups of wine—which the Greeks mixed with water, the better to swill it." (T. Cahill, 2003, p. 96).
75. "The diluting of the wine with water was an established custom in Greece. This dietetic measure, made necessary by the universal custom even amongst the lower classes...was so common in Greece that the contrary was considered as a characteristic of barbarous nations." (Guhl & Koner, 1994, p. 267). In Rome it was not unusual to mix sea water with the wine to give the mixture an extra tang. (Hamilton, 1993, p. 112).
76. G. S. Kirk, J.E. Raven, & M. Schofield, (1983, 1957). *The Presocratic Philosophers* (2nd Ed.). (Cambridge: Cambridge University Press, 1983), p. 286. More about Empedocles is in Diogenes Laertius, LEP. Vol. 2, pp. 367-91.
77. *John* 18:36. The theme of the Kingdom was unclear even to his closest disciples like those walking to Emmaus. Pliny the Elder (23–79 CE), lover of study extraordinaire, confidante of Vespasian, former Procurator of Spain, complier of ten volumes of comprehensive but questionable natural history, who in his curiosity went to see the damage done by the eruption of Vesuvius in 79 and died of asphyxiation in the neighborhood, wrote his thoughts on death, cases of the dead coming to life again, burial, ghosts and the soul. He raises questions that trouble humanity still: whether the body returns to the same state it was in before it was born, whether the soul is not more sensible after death than it was before birth, and questions of what the substance of the soul is, how is it able to have thoughts, what state will it be in after death. "Quod autem corpus animae per se? Quae materia? Ubi cogitatio ill? Quo modo usius, auditus aut qui tangit?" (Pliny, *Pline l'Ancien, Histoire Naturelle*, Livre VI. Paris: Societe D'Edition, 1977, pp. 110 ff.)

78. *Mark* 7:27, *Matt.* 5:26.
79. E. Pagels, (1979), pp. 72-73.
80. Josephus, *op. cit.*, pp. 83-85. For Mark's account of Jesus' trial see Mack, 1995, *op. cit.*, pp. 158 ff.
81. In the British Museum's splendid bas-relief of the Black Obelisk of Shalmaneser III, a melammu of the Assyrian god Assur floats over the head of a bowing vassal near a winged sun disk. Nearby stands King Jehu of Israel submitting to the Assyrian king.
82. *The Iliad.* (1966), p. 342.
83. P. Landis, FFGP, p. 231.
84. *Exodus* 14:24, and G. E. Mendenhall, TG, p. 58.
85. *Ezekiel* 1:4-8.
86. *Daniel* 7:9-10.
87. *Exodus* 33: 5-10.
88. In the Vedic religion in India the holy transcendental power people experienced was known as Brahman, and the priestly Brahman caste was thought to possess it all the time.
89. When a Roman emperor was cremated an eagle was released as the flames burned to symbolize the flight of the spirit to the abode of the gods.
90. *Matt.* 17:3; *Mark* 9:4; *Luke* 9:30-31."I saw myself on the central mountain of the world, the highest place, and I had a vision because I was seeing in the sacred manner of the world." (J. G. Neihardt, *Black Elk Speaks,* 1961).
91. Homer, *op. cit.*, p. 394.
92. Xenophon, *op. cit.*, p. 118. Compare Jesus' entry into Jerusalem with Xenophon's description: "With that he rode away, the king and all his people escorting him, like a guard of honor, calling him their savior, their benefactor, and their hero, and heaping praises on him." *Ibid.*, p. 98.
93. *Luke* 4:28-30. The energetic Hindu god Shiva, like Jesus also transcended, is represented in stone and bronze carvings at the center of a whirling circle of cosmic activity showing five symbolic aspects of eternal energy: creation, preservation, destruction, favor and concealment. A luminous bronze carving of him stands in the center of a hall of Indian artifacts in the Victoria and Albert museum in London where he is shown as the thin-waisted Lord of the Dance. He balances on his right leg while hooking his left across his body revealing a sense of motion, a characteristic of all Indian sculpture. A cobra curls from one arm and in one upturned palm he holds fire. His dreadlocks fan out from his head like flames or scattered musical scores. He dances inside a ring of fire that is also the circle of life. A nearby drum represents the sound of creation: flames, the sign of destruction and release. In other representations, he is shown with his consort Parvati, also known as Uma, and they are the primordial couple. In these depictions Vishnu holds a trident in one hand, the symbol of his active life, and in the other hand a rosary, sign of his contemplative nature. According to the Chinese sage Mencius (c.371–288 BCE), transcendence is a literary device used to highlight the ethical ideal. The Chinese concept of *Ching* refers to the deep characteristics that lie behind a person's appearance and reveal character, one's essence. (K-L Shun, 1997).
94. During the Transfiguration, the divine form of Jesus was revealed. Origen notes that "The doctrine has an even more mysterious meaning since it proclaims that the different forms of Jesus are applied to the nature of the divine Logos. For he did not appear in the same way both to the multitude and to those able to follow him up the high mountain." Unanswered is whether the "form" of Jesus, as opposed to his "matter," is distinct from his soul and body and divinity, or if each has its own form. OCC, p. 390.
95. "My flesh shall rest in hope; and thou wilt not leave my soul in Hades, and wilt not suffer thy holy one to see corruption." (*Psalm* 15:9-10). The only other unambiguous statement about immortality appears in *The Book of Daniel* written c.160 BCE. The idea of immortality is evident in other cultures. From India: "For this is my word of promise, that he who loves me shall not perish." (J. Mascaro, BG, p. 83). And from Egypt: "May he behold his body, may he

rest in his glorified frame, may he never perish, and may his body never see corruption." (*The Papyrus of Ani*, from EBD, p. 318).

96. Origen, *op. cit.*, pp. 460-461.

97. Eisenman, & Wise, 1994, *op. cit.*, p. 29.

98. The church dedicated to him now is over the crypt of his tomb. By 384 a Spanish nun named Egeria wrote in her diary of the ceremonies conducted at the site known then as the Lazarium outside Jerusalem. "And on arriving at the Lazarium, so great a multitude assembles that not only the place itself, but also the fields around, are full of people. Hymns and antiphons suitable to the day and to the place are said, and likewise all the lessons are read. Then, before the dismissal, notice is given of Easter, that is, the priest ascends to a higher place and reads the passage that is written in the Gospel: When Jesus six days before the Passover had come to Bethany, and the rest." (http://users.ox.ac.uk/~mikef/durham/egetra.html).

99. "A man should take stock of himself, and bear that balance in mind, in matters great and small." (Juvenal, *op. cit.*, p. 100).

100. G. Vermes, (2003), pp. 7-10

101. Aeschylus. (1965), p. 103.

102. HH, V. 2, pp. 183-84. Those oracles said to have risen from the dead, apart from the Greeks and the Egyptians, who had temples and statues erected to their worship in the ancient world are: Zamolxis, Mopsus, Amphilochus, and Trophonius. (Origen, *op. cit.*, p. 151).

103. http://www.courses.psu.edu/cams/cams400w_aek11/wenem.html

104. Euripedes, Heracles. (Warminster, UK: Aris & Phillips, 1996, p. 59). Another quote echoes with symbolism when the chorus chimes: "O Zeus, why hate your son with such exceeding anger? Why have you brought him to this sea of suffering?" *Ibid.*, p. 99.

105. Budge, 1967, *op. cit.*, p. 288. "We are such stuff as dreams are made on, and our little life is rounded with a sleep." (Shakespeare, *The Tempest*)

106. Budge, 1973, *op. cit.*, pp. 305-47.

107. *Ibid.*, p. xxv.

108. Budge, (1980), p. 81.

109. *Ibid.*, p. 61.

110. Budge, 1973, *op. cit.*, pp. 96-97. "Do not think the resurrection is an illusion," notes *The Treatise on the Resurrection* in NH. "It is no illusion, but it is truth. Indeed, it is more fitting to say that the world is an illusion rather than the resurrection," a theme Paul would echo in Chapter 15 of the *I Corinthians*. For Plato the soul had an existence before the body. "So, Simmias, our souls existed long ago, before they were in human shape, apart from bodies, and then had wisdom," a theme later echoed by the Gnostics. Plato in the *Phaedo* (1956, p. 480). Exactly what is the difference between the bodily Jesus, the resurrected Jesus with a body not yet risen, and the risen-to-the-Father resurrected Jesus, since all three are biblically recorded and said to be seen by various followers at differing times? We are left with a mystery of astounding perplexity about an issue so central to belief.

111. *2 John* 7. A learned Syraic teacher named Bardaisan (154–222 CE), a Christian convert, founder of a Christian school later branded as heretical, was said to have converted princes and the city of Edessa to Christianity. He was author of many books lost in history, an extraordinary poet who composed over 15 hymns in imitation of the psalms of David. Eusebius pays acknowledgement to his teaching and literary talents but vilifies him for his refusal to accept the resurrection of the body.

112. "This nature, then, of soul is kept within the body's wholeness, and itself does stand as guardian of the body and cause of life within us." (Lucretius, 1946, p.128). Origen has a strange interpretation of the soul's origin: "When it (the soul) came to be born in the world, it put off the afterbirth, which was useful for its formation in the womb of the mother so long as it was within it; and underneath that it put on what was necessary for one that was about to live on earth." (OCC, p. 420).

113. http://www.mit.edu/~tb/anglican/intro/lr-nicene-creed.html.

114. *John* 20:17. But is Jesus here resurrected or not? He lets doubting Thomas touch him to prove that he is real, and eats bread and fish with the disciples in Jerusalem and Galilee. If he is not resurrected until he ascends into heaven, what state is he in? Did the bread and fish get resurrected too?

115. HH, pp. 136-37. This story is also found in Origen who uses it as an argument against Celsus. Regarding other incidences of men blessed by the gods of leaving their bodies and wandering about in a bodiless state, Origen asserts that "probably certain demons arranged for this story to be written," an untested and certainly improbable hypothesis. (Origen, p. 148-49).

116. NH, p. 363. A group known as the Helkesaites living in Arabia believed in a doctrine that the human soul perishes with the body and then, on the day of resurrection, returns to life with the body. The church convened a synod and condemned this understanding.

117. HCCC, p. 272. Even Origen, writing before the orthodox definitions of who Jesus was, wrote: "For after the incarnation the soul and body of Jesus became very closely united with the Logos of God," an idea that makes the concepts of body, soul, person, nature and Logos even more torturous than what councils decided. (Origen, p. 74). Paul of Samosata who flourished between 260–72 CE, was a Syrian Christian theologian and Bishop of Antioch, who denied the Trinity. He taught that the Logos, a Divine Attribute, came to dwell in Jesus at baptism, but that Jesus possessed no extraordinary nature above other men, a concept in accordance with Arius who may have been his student.

118. J. M. Robinson, "The Gospels as Narrative," in F. McConnell, (Ed.) *The Bible and the Narrative Tradition*. (New York: Oxford University Press, 1986, p. 105). Roman historians like Sallust and Tacitus pessimistically bemoaned the degradation of moral standards. The emperor Julian, in *Against the Galileans* dismisses the more laudatory claims altogether: "Jesus...has been known by name for but little more than three hundred years and during his lifetime he accomplished nothing worth hearing of, unless anyone thinks that to heal crooked and blind men and to exorcise those who were possessed of evil demons in the villages of Bethsaida and Bethany can be classed as a mighty achievement." (*The Works of Emperor Julian, op. cit.*, p. 377). Stories of others who performed similar deeds were rife at the time.

119. J. M. Robinson, P. Hoffman, J. S. Kloppenborg, (2001).

120. Plato in Phaedo in Rouse, *op. cit.*, p. 516. For all her knowledge of Greek and ancient Greek writings, Edith Hamilton never makes the connection between the Greek themes, episodes, figures and events that echo in the Gospels. Her *Witness to the Truth* (1948) reads like devotional literature, very unlike her studies *The Greek Way* and *The Roman Way*.

120. In J. Mascaro, *The Bhagavad Gita*. (1962, p. 96.

121. Krishna, like Osiris and Christ, offer the same message. Krishna says about himself in the BG. "But they for whom I am the End Supreme, who surrender all their works to me, and who with pure love meditate on me and adore me, these I very soon deliver from the ocean of death and life-in-death, because they have set their heart on me." (T. Irvin, 1989, pp. 14-15).

Chapter 11

1. *Callimachus, Hymns, Epigrams, Select Fragments.* (1988, p. 10). And cf. J. Ferguson, *Callimachus*. (1980). The library and museum was a university with lecture halls, botanical and zoological gardens, and an observatory. The complex nurtured such geniuses as Euclid, Archimedes, Apollonius, and Erastosthenes. The most complete source of Greek culture is Gilbert Murray (1866-1957), Regius Professor of Greek at Oxford, whose books are eminently readable and whose scholarship is extensive and impressive.

2. http://users.ox.ac.uk/~mikef/durham/egetra.html.

3. E. Gruen, *op. cit.*, 1998 argues that Judaism changed because of the Hellenic influence. The so-called insidious influence of Hellenism on the Jews can be found in *II Maccabees* (4:7-17) where the scribe describes how Jason bribed the king to obtain the high priesthood and then defiled his office by introducing young men to Greek practices, like throwing the discus. (Gruen, *op. cit.*, pp. 30. ff.).

4. H. A. Fischel, (1948).
5. For Thales see Diogenes Laertius, LEP (1959), pp. 23-47.
6. In Plato's *Phaedo* in Rouse, *op. cit.*, p. 475. And D. Sider, *The Fragments of Anaxagoras*. (Meisenheim am Glan: Verlag, 1981).
7. Bion of Smyrna, *The Fragments and the Adonis*. (1997), pp. 123-31.
8. http://users.ox.ac.uk/~mikef/durham/egetra.html.
9. D. R. MacDonald, 2000 and 2003.
10. http://www.mayadiscovery.com/ing/history/default.htm.
11. Pythagoras is best known to math students for the Pythagorean theorem, arguably the most important geometric discovery from Greek mathematics. Even though the Babylonians and Egyptians had used the triangle to erect architectural marvels like the Hanging Gardens, Pythagoras had jumped from the world of triangular use to the theory of mathematical abstraction, from simple math for practical use to contemplation about the universe. He was also the first to call himself a philosopher, or a seeker after the truth, although he was closer to a sage or religious leader, and probably the first to coin the term philosophy. Pythagoras' mathematical disciple, Euclid, whose book, *The Elements of Geometry* was, after the Bible, the most translated book of all time right up until the modern era, would elaborate on the mathematical laws of shape in the 3rd century BCE. (Diogenes Laertius, LEP. V.2, pp. 321-67).
12. The need for celebration, for ritual and communion with others is powerful and instinctive. Each summer, with painted faces, bizarre clothing and luminescent wires in their hair, over 30,000 come to Black Rock desert in northern Nevada to celebrate the Burning Man festival. The counter-culture and hedonistic gathering pound drums with tribal rhythms and chant and cry out seeking primitive forms of ecstasy and excitement in drugs and alcohol. Towering over the desert is a 77-foot high skeleton of wood and neon lights. About 9:30 the Burning Man, the created and destroyed symbol of nothing in particular, without religious significance, disappears in a cloud of fire and smoke.
13. J. Gollnick, (1999).
14. "The founders of the mysteries would appear to have had a real meaning, and were not talking nonsense when they intimated in a figure long ago that he who passes unsanctified and uninitiated into the world below will lie in a slough, but that he who arrives there after initiation and purification will dwell with the gods." (Rouse, *op. cit.*, p. 472).
15. http://www.fordham.edu/halsall/source/ambrose-sym.html
16. Lucretius (c.99 BCE–55 BCE) proposed that men need not fear the gods because they don't control destiny and there is no immortality of the soul. Virgil had poetry that throbbed with man's grandeur. But the Hebrew scribes and rabbis were either un-interested in Roman writings because they could not or refused to read Latin or were lacking in literary scholarship to imbibe some of the greatest history, prose, poetry and drama of the glorious Augustan age.
17. "The soul is in the very likeness of the divine, and immortal, and intellectual, and uniform, and indissoluble, and unchangeable; and that the body is in the very likeness of the human, and mortal, and un-intellectual, and multiform, and indissoluble, and changeable."(WP, p. 140).
18. C. Bailey, (1969, 1935).
19. *Odyssey* quotations taken from Robert Fitzgerald's 1963 translation. Homer describes Ulysses as *polymetis* (versatile), *polytropos* (many-sided), *polytlas* (enduring), and *polymechanos* (talented tactician), all resourceful traits that could be applied to Jesus. (T. Cahill, *op. cit.*, p. 65).
20. "I tell you that to let no day pass without discussing goodness and all other subjects about which you hear me talking and examining both myself and others is really the very best thing that a man can do, and that life without this sort of examination is not worth living" (Socrates, in Plato's *Apology*).
21. T. J. Lomperis, (1984). "The realm of the visible world should be compared to the prison dwelling...If you interpret the upward journey and the contemplation of things above as the

upward journey of the soul to the intelligible realm, you will grasp what I surmise, since you are keen to hear it. Whether it is true or not only the god knows." (Grube, *Plato's Republic*, 1974, p. 170).
22. B. Russell, (1955), p. 80.
23. Plato, (1944), p. 364. "For it is impossible in company with the body to know anything purely, one thing or two follows: either knowledge is possible nowhere, or only after death; for then alone the soul will be quite by itself apart from the body but not before." (Rouse, *op. cit*, p. 469.
24. Ibid., p. 366. The ultimate purification for Plato is the separation of the soul from the body in order to see the truth.
25. "For everything which is visible is a copy of that which is hidden." *The Teachings of Silvanus* in NH.
26. I. Edman, 1956, *op. cit.*, p. 117.
27. P. Kingsley, (1995). Pythagoras is the first credited with partitioning the soul into three parts: intelligence, reason and passion, a tripartite division Freud would later create into Superego, Ego and Id.
28. OCC, p. 317.
29. N. White, (1983), p. 12.
30. *Ibid.*, p. 12.
31. *Ibid.*, p. 22.
32. *Ibid.*, p. 23.
33. Epictetus, (1942), p. 139.
34. *Ibid.*, p. 98.
35. Philo was appointed by influential Jews of Alexandria to lead a delegation to Rome to seek redress from the notorious, tyrannical and probably insane emperor Caligula who sought to place an image of himself in the synagogue in Alexandria. Caligula was murdered in 41 shortly after this preposterous proposal and the idea succumbed with his death.
36. H. A. Wolfson, (1982, 1947).
37. R. Marcus, (1953).
38. Plato writes of the allegorical method in Timaeus. "And in speaking of the copy and the original we may assume that words are akin to the matter which they describe."
39. MacDonald, 2000, 2003.
40. S. Sandmel, (1979).
41. "Moses...refrained from inventing myths himself or acquiring those composed by others," he writes in *On the Creation of the World, ibid.*, 1-3.
42. E. R. Goodenough, (1940), p. 11.
43. M. Dimont (1994) describes the history of the Jews as the house of western civilization with the furniture of the Greeks. But the history of Judaism is not so much a separate history as an amalgamation of the histories of neighboring nations. Dimont argues that Jews conquered the world with their ideas. On the contrary, Jewish ideas are a composite of the ideas of older civilizations not unique to Judaism. A distinct Jewish history may be gratifying to Jews but is unsettling to historians.
44. Wolfson, 1947, *op. cit.*
45a. http://www.wsu.edu/~dee/GREECE/HERAC.HTM.
45b. L. W. Barnard, (1967), pp. 91-100.
46. H. U. Von Balthasar, (1984), pp. 86-89.
47. Evans, (1993), *op. cit.*, p. 207. And in the *Upanishads* we find: "The source of all names is the word, for it is by the word that all names are spoken. The word is behind all names, even as Brahman is behind the word." (*op. cit.*, p. 127). Brahman and Jesus enjoy the same privilege of being known as the Word. The Egyptian word that signified right order, truth and justice was *maat*, any decision the divine pharaoh handed down to the courts, a word and concept expressive of the moral authority of the state. (N. Cantor, 2003, p. 60).

48. C. M. Carmichael, (1996), and then compare *John* 1:3, *Heb.* 1:2, *Col.* 1:16, *Rev.* 3:14. Even Heraclitus writing in the 6th century BCE speaks of the Word: "It is wise to hearken, not to me but to my word, and to confess that all things are one. Though the Word is true evermore, yet men are as unable to understand it when they hear it for the first time as before they have heard it al all." (W. H. Auden, *op. cit.*, pp. 69-70). Some scholars propose that John's gospel postulates Jesus as Logos as present at the creation, as one who bears witness to the light, and the day on which light was separated from darkness. John joins Hellenistic philosophy with the idea of God communicating with humanity, of creating the world, and makes Jesus the ultimate Logos of God. Christ, says Paul, "is the wisdom of God. He is before all things, in him all things exist...through him all things have been created." (*Cor.* 1:15-17).
49. D. T. Rania, (1990), pp. 1-18.
50. http://www.thedyinggod.com/lucian.htm. Cf. Barnard, (1967), pp. 7-8.
51. *Ibid.*, pp. 56-58.
52. *Ibid.*, pp. 660 ff.
53. *Ibid.*, p. 37.
54. J. Potter, CE. (Oxford Georgii Mortlock, 1715). John Potter was the Bishop of Oxford and has the most complete edition of all Clement's work. Cf. *Clement of Alexandria.* (Cambridge, MA: Harvard University Press, 1953, 1972), p.5. *Clement of Alexandria, Stromateis.* (Washington, DC: Catholic University of America Press, 1991). For an analysis of procreation and kinship imagery in Clement see D. K. Buell, *Making Christians, Clement of Alexandria and the Rhetoric of Legitimacy.* (Princeton, NJ: Princeton University Press, 1999).
55. Book VI, Chapter 2 at:
http://www.earlychristianwritings.com/text/clement-stromata-book1.html
56. *Ibid.*, Book 6, Chapter 6, and Chap. 7. For insights into the development of Clement's assimilation of Greek philosophic ideas of infinity, transcendence and participation in the divine see A. Choufrine, (2002), pp. 180-85.
57. Clement, 1991, *op. cit.*, p. 23, and 41 ff.
58. *Ibid.*, p. 59-60. He equates Greek philosophers like Leucippus and Democritus "who hypothesize the atoms as first principles, wearing covertly the name of philosophy, but really being godless, all too human and pleasure-loving." (*Ibid.*, p. 61).
59. See *1 Cor.* 2:6-7 and 15:51.
60. Clement, *ibid.*, p. 63.
61. *Ibid.*, p. 229.
62. "But in the case of the Savior, it were ludicrous (to suppose) that the body, as a body, demanded the necessary aids in order to its duration. For He ate, not for the sake of the body, which was kept together by a holy energy, but in order that it might not enter into the minds of those who were with Him to entertain a different opinion of Him." (*Ibid.*, Book 6, Chap. 9).
63. *Ibid.*, Book 7, Chap. 1. "Thus also it appears to me that there are three effects of Gnostic power: the knowledge of things; second, the performance of whatever the Word suggests; and the third, the capability of delivering, in a way suitable to God, the secrets veiled in the truth." (Book 7, Chap. 1)
64. A. Choufrine, *op. cit.*, pp. 199-200.
65. For Clement's use of Philo see A. Van Den Hoek, (1988).
66. Plotinus, *The Enneads*. (London: Faber & Faber, 1962), p. 32.
67. H. Chatwick, "Envoi: On Taking Leave of Antiquity," in Boardman, J. & J. Griffin, O. Murray (Eds.) *The Oxford History of the Roman World.* (Oxford: Oxford University Press, 1991, p. 465).

Chapter 12
1. HH. Xenophon, *The Education of Cyrus*. (London: J. M. Dent, no date).

2. HH, pp. 87 ff. (Book I, Clio, No. 107). According to Diogenes Laertius, "The Magi spent their time in the worship of the gods, in sacrifices and in prayers, implying that none but themselves have the ear of the gods." Diogenes Laertius, LEP, p. 9.
3. HH, p. 98.
4. V. J. Walters, (1974). M. J. Vermaseren, (1963). M. P. Speidel, (1980). D. Ulansey, BAR, 1994, 20(5), pp.40-53. R. Turcan, *Mithras Platonicus, Recherches sur L'Hellenisation Philosophique de Mithra.* (Leiden: E. J. Brill, 1975). F. Cumont, *The Mysteries of Mithra.* (New York: Dover Publications, 1956).
5. The Holy Communion of Zoroastrians is the Hom or Haoma, a liquid derived from the fat of the bull, Hadhayans, who has been slain by Soshyans, the hero and Savior of his people, who is not a god. This consecrated liquid is the elixir of eternal life and insures bodily immortality and is performed during the raising of the dead. "While the resurrection of the dead proceeds, Soshyans and his helpers will perform the sacrifice of the raising of the dead, and in that sacrifice the bull Hadhayans will be slain, and from the fat of the bull they will prepare the white Hom (Haoma) (the drink of) immortality, and give it to all men. And all men will become immortal for ever and ever." (R. C. Zaehner, TM, pp. 148-49). Partaking of a holy sacrament was always a part of the ceremonies of Greek and Roman rituals. "Then why, when about to partake of my holy sacrament, do you hesitate to resign yourself to a poverty of which you will never need repent?" (Apuleius, *The Golden Ass*, 1951, p. 285).
6. *Phil.* 3:20-21.
7. *Exodus* 17, 5-6.
8. "On the rear wall of every Mithraeum there was a representation of the bull-slaying, which was regarded within the cult as the most outstanding of Mithras's deeds, performed as it were for the benefit of mankind." (Vermaseren, 1963, *op.cit.*, p. 104). The building of the Mithraeum had a vaulted, rounded ceiling and an exterior brick covering. The interior hall measured about 25 yards long by 10 yards wide. From a large anteroom, the central hall led to the altar and shrine at the rear of the hall. Two parallel, elevated walkways on either side flanked the main hall. Along either side of the central aisle were arched openings at the entrance often decorated with statues on pedestals. Climbing three or four stairs, members could walk or sit along twin, low but elevated walkways or platforms running the length of the building, both of which faced the central aisle. The building resembles a grotto to simulate the cave in which Mithras killed the bull. A flame was kept burning before the crypt where Mithras was portrayed killing the bull. The sanctuary was decorated with inscriptions, which may have been hymns, painting, inlaid mosaics and marble sculptures and statues.
9. Macmullen, R. & E. N. Lane, (1992), p. 73.
10. *John* 6:52-54.
11. R.Turcan, *Mithras Platonicus.* (Leiden: E. J. Brill, 1975). "De toutes les religions orientales, celle de Mithra etait la plus foncierement optimiste et peut-etre la plus logique, optimiste et rigoriste a la fois, mystique et rationaelle. On concoit que le monde ne soit pas devenu mithriaste. Mais on comprend que le mithriasciisme ait seduit les platoniciens." (p. 133).

Chapter 13
1. *Corpus Hermeticum* at: http://www.gnosis.org/library/hermes1.html.
2. B. D. Ehrman, LS. The standard virtue of knowledge can be found in *The Gospel of Philip*: "Faith is our earth in which we take root; hope is the water through which we are nourished; love is the air through which we grow; Gnosis is the light through which we become fully grown." (*Gospel of Philip* 79: 25-31 and in E. Pagels, (2003), p. 131.
3. K. L. King, (2003). In *The Frogs* by Aristophanes these mystic undertakings were, accorded chants of the chorus: "Mystic orgies, that are known to the votaries alone, secret, unrevealed, and holy." (P. Landis, 1929, *op. cit.*, p. 231). For Orthodox Christian apologists this was all so much "heathen philosophy," or a "perverted interpretation of Plato." J. Pelikan, (1971).

4. T. Merton, (1961), pp. 2-4. And (1948). Merton became a Catholic convert, joined a Trappist monastery in 1941, and became the author of over 70 books. *The Seven Story Mountain* is still in print after more than half a century. The inculcation of Gnostic contemplative ideas folded into Christianity in Pascal's *Pensees*, the *Cautelas and Avisos* of the Spanish mystic St. John of the Cross, and Thomas a Kempis' *Imitation of Christ*.
5. A. H. B. Logan, (1996). Cf. B. Lazier, JHI, (2003), 64(4), 619-37.
6. G. Filoramo, *A History of Gnosticism*. (Cambridge: MA: Basil Blackwell, 1990).
7. R. M. Grant, (1961).
8. Plato's *Phaedo* in Rouse, *op. cit.*, p. 584.
9. B. D. Ehrman, LS, p. 45.
10. *Ibid.*, p.128.
11. "I have wisdom above all those who were in Jerusalem before me, and my heart has had great experience of wisdom and revealed knowledge. This is the choice of the spirit, since in copious wisdom there is copious true knowledge." (*Ecclesiastes* 1:16-18) John Milton's *Paradise Lost* has battlegrounds of angels and demons roaring with poetic siege cannons and explosive devices to determine winners and losers in a celestial struggle for future status and influence over uncreated mankind. Milton's poetic license is an expression of Gnostic persuasion in which a layered hierarchy of angels as guardians, archangels, seraphim and cherubim compete with a similar bureaucracy of the malevolent armies of the sons of darkness.
12. G. Filoramo, (1990), p. 45 and R. M. Grant, (1961), p. 212.
13. Tertullian, Q. Septimii Florentis, *Tertulliani Opera Omnia*. Tomus I. (Wirceburgi: In Officina Libraria Staheliana, 1780, pp. 265-294.
14. CE. (Oxford: Georgii Mortlock, 1715) (Vols. 1 & 2).
15. *1 Cor.* 8:1-2.
16. *1 Peter*, 3:21.
17. J. Mascaro, BG, 1962, p. 53, and J.Mascaro, *The Upanishads*, 1965.
18. *Ibid.*, 1962, p. 76. "And when a man sees the God in himself is the same God in all that is...then he goes indeed to the highest Path."(p. 101-120).
19. Ibid., 1965, p. 73. "While with an eye made quiet by the power of harmony, and the deep power of joy. We see into the life of things" (Wordsworth, *Tintern Abbey*). "The Kingdom of God is within you." (*Luke*, 17:21). Traces of Gnosticism abound in Dante, Milton and in the 20th century in Carl Jung.
20. T. Churton, (1987), p. 5.
21. Halevi, Z. B. S., (1979).
22. Bonaventure. (1993).
23. *Urantia Book.* (no author). (1955).

Chapter 14
1. The Roman historian Lucian, writing a generation after the evangelists, wrote in *How to Write History*: "This then is my sort of historian. He must be fearless, incorruptible, free, a friend of frankness and truth...influenced neither by hatred nor by friendship, showing no compunction, pity, shame or embarrassment, an impartial judge...independent, subject to no king, unconcerned by what this or that man will think, but stating the actual facts." (M. D. MacLeod, 1991). The letter from Pliny the Younger, then Governor of Bithynia, can be found as the first document in M. Viorst, (1994).
2. R. Eisenman, & M. Wise, *op. cit.*, p. 140. A second bloody Jewish revolt occurred in the reign of Trajan in 115-117 CE in Egypt, Cyrene, Cyprus and Mesopotamia when thousands were killed, and then a third revolt in 132-35 when tens of thousands died. (Sherk, 1988, *op. cit.*, pp. 169-70, pp. 191-92).
3. *Acts* 16:16,18:24 and 24:22.
4. Eisenman & Wise, 1994, *op. cit.*, p. 36. Women could not write anything under their own name. (R. S. Kraemer, 2004, pp. 93-4).

5. See Mack, B. L. WWNT. When Pompey invaded Judea in 64 BCE, he took with him to Rome the Hasmonean ruler Aristobulus and several hundred Jewish prisoners. This large and formative Roman Jewish community would later be partially receptive to the importunities of Christian missionaries like Peter and Paul. (A-J. Levine, "Visions of Kingdoms, From Pompey to the First Jewish Revolt." OHBW, p. 353).
6. T. D. Barnes, (1994), I-232.
7. Greek not only became the language of 3 of the 4 gospels but of Jewish institutions as well. Synagogue comes from a Greek word meaning "bringing together," and Sanhedrin owes its origin to the Greek *synedrion*, meaning "sitting together or assembly."
8. H. Maccoby, (1986).
9. *Galatians 1*.
10. *II Cor.* 12.
11. Maccoby, 1986, *op. cit.*, p. 87.
12. *Gal.* 1:16 and in the New Testament Greek in F. Brandscheid, *Novum Testamentum Graece*. (Friborg: Sumptibus Herder, 1901, p. 494).
13. Crossan, J. D., & Reed, J. L., 2001, *op. cit.*.
14. *I Cor.* 11:23-30.
15. *John* 6:53-58 and Maccoby, 1986, *op. cit.*, pp. 110 ff.
16. *Acts* 2:46.
17. Peter's account of a dream (*Acts* 10) to help reconcile his religious differences and Paul's account of a face-to-face confrontation over the issue of eating and associating with uncircumcised gentile Christians (*Gal.* 2:11-14) differ in several important aspects: "But when Peter came to Antioch, I opposed him to his face, because he was clearly in the wrong." (*Gal.* 2:11). So whose authority is pre-eminent: he who has been given the keys to the Kingdom of Heaven, or the self-proclaimed Apostle to the Gentiles?
18. *Acts* 22-24.
19. *I Cor.* 9:20-22.
20. Maccoby, *op. cit.*, pp. 16-17.
21. *Luke* 6:15.
22. The shrine where the head of John the Baptist, revered among Muslims as a prophet, presumably lies in an inner tabernacle inside the great mosque in Damascus. His hands, gilded with silver, are on display in the Topkai palace in Istanbul.
23. M. Grant, 1975, *op. cit.*, pp. 231-33.
24. *I Peter* 2:18. A Letter to the Alexandrians by Claudius in 41 CE is particular in urging the city to tolerate Jews. "Therefore, even now I earnestly ask of you that the Alexandrians conduct themselves more gently and kindly towards the Jews...and that they do not inflict indignities upon any of their customs in the worship of their god, but that they allow them to keep their own practices..." (R. K. Sherk, 1988, *op. cit.*, p. 85).
25. Josephus, *op. cit.*, pp. 72-75. M. Goodman, (1997).
26. Josephus, pp. 93-95.
27. *Ibid.*, pp.148-50.
28. *Ibid.*, p. 160.
29. *Ibid.*, pp. 184-85. Josephus remains the principal source of these last gasp Jewish revolts, but other sources are equally descriptive. BH, 364-73.
30. Eisenman & Wise, 1994, *op. cit.*, p. 68.
31. Josephus, *op. cit.*, pp. 117-18.
32. Especially the suffering servant role in *Isaiah*, Chapters 49, 52 and 53, is used extensively in gospel narratives.
33. I. Wilson, (1984), and D. H. Akenson, (1998), p. 538 ff. According to Mack, "the writings selected for inclusion in the New Testament were not written by those whose names are attached to them." (WWNT, p. 6). Mack also says that Mark's gospel is a fiction. (*Ibid.*, p. 154). Origen, according to Eusebius, had written: "I accept the traditional view of the four

gospels which alone are undeniably authentic." (Eusebius, *op. cit.*, p. 265). Zimmermann argues that the gospels were first written in Aramaic and then only later translated into Greek. (F. Zimmermann, 1979). Though it is generally but not universally accepted that the gospels were written 70–100, there is no reason to believe that the gospels were composed in any particular order or produced in one year over another. (T. Irvin, 1989, p. 204).

34. *Luke*, 1:1-2. Of course the "many narratives" may not refer to the gospels but to other epics. MacDonald (2000, 2003) has suggested that Mark imitated Homer for Jesus' comparable miraculous feats, and has located four episodes in the Acts that parallel Homeric tales. Thiede (1992) has concluded that a papyrus fragment from the *Dead Sea Scrolls* is likely from *Mark* 6:52-53. I visited the gravesite of Matthew in what is now Northern Cyprus. According to Greek Orthodox tradition, when Matthew was exhumed in the 4th century a manuscript of his gospel was found buried with him. The site today is distinguished only by a large hole in the ground just outside an abandoned monastery.

35. B. L. Mack, 1995, *op. cit.*
36. Akenson, 1998, *op. cit.*, p. 566.
37. "Zion shall be ploughed as a field and Jerusalem shall be a heap of stone." (*Micah* 3:12).
38. M. Grant, 1977, *op. cit.*, p. 75.
39. http://members.aol.com/FLJOSEPHUS/HoniTheCircleDrawer.htm.
40. *John* 19:14.
41. Maccoby, 1986, *op. cit.*, p. 199. Mark has a distinct bias against the Apostles and this theme runs throughout his narrative. It seems clear that Mark favors a Pauline interpretation of how the message of Jesus is to be interpreted and not that favored by the Jerusalem church. (T. J. Weeden, 1971).

Chapter 15
1. T. J. Weeden (1971), p 77.
2. Eisenman & Wise, 1994, *op. cit.*, p. 233, 254 for quotes. LS, pp. 99-103.
3. J. E. L. Oulton & Chadwick, (1954), p. 106.
4. "And for this reason we should here make most use of the reasons from philosophy, which introduce us into the knowledge of things sacred, that so we may think piously of whatever is said or acted in religion." *Plutarch's Miscellanies and Essays*. (Boston: Little Brown & Co., 1888, p. 125).
5. "Therefore we have no need of the law as pedagogue." Irenaeus, (1952), p. 106.
6. E. Pagels, 1988, *op. cit*,, p. 73.
7. E. Pagels, 2003, *op. cit.*, pp. 145-60.
8. H. W. Attridge & Oden, R. A. (1981). This Philo is distinct from Philo of Alexandria, a 1st, century CE Jewish philosopher and theologian. Philo is skeptical of the literary artifices some writers use. For example, Philo writes: "But the more recent writers on religious matters have from the first rejected what really happened. By devising allegories and myths and by inventing a kinship with cosmic phenomena, they established mysteries and introduced into them tremendous delusion, so that it is not easy for anyone to perceive that in truth happened." (*Fragments*, in Attridge and Oden)
9. *The Ugarit Texts*, in J. C. De Moor, ART, p. 266. See also A. R. Petersen, (1998).
10. De Moor, op. cit., p. 267.
11. *Ibid.*, p. 272.
12. As Cyrus said: "He who works the hardest and does the most for the common good deserves the highest recompense." (Xenophon, p. 62). Compare with Jesus' saying: "By your works you shall know them."
13. Head, P. M. "Some Recently Published NT Papyri from Oxyrhynchus: An Overview and Preliminary Assessment." (*Tyndale Bulletin*, 51, 2000, pp. 1-16). Among papyri unearthed were lost poems of Pindar and Sappho as well as the plays of Sophocles and Euripides. In

Egyptian Hellenic schools, texts, written on papyrus, on ostraca and on waxed tablets that could be reused, were copied in various scripts. Homer was the main textbook.
14. F. Bovon, "Fragment of Oxyrhynchus 840, Fragment of a Lost Gospel, Witness of an early Christian Controversy over Purity." JBL, 119(4), 2000, pp. 705-728.
15. Pagels, 1979, *op. cit.*, 104.
16. C. A. Evans, & Webb, R. L., Wiebe, R. A. NH, p. 267.
17. *Luke* 18:24-26.
18. "One ought first to follow reason as a guide before accepting any belief, since anyone who believes without testing a doctrine is certain to be deceived." (Celsus, *On the True Doctrine, A Discourse against the Christians*, (New York: Oxford University Press, 1987).
19. A few of the most edifying characters of the early days of Christianity—Seneca, the elder and younger Pliny, Tacitus, Plutarch, Galen, Epictetus, Marcus Antoninus, to name a few—filled their days with study, purified their minds with philosophy, and spent their days in pursuit of active virtue and contemplation, yet could find no inducement that would engage them in Christianity. Cato the Elder lived a puritan life of principles and sought to legislate ethical standards long before stoicism became popular. (See N. W. Forde, 1975).
20. HCCC, pp. 239-72, OCC, and H. U. Von Balthasar, Origen, 1984).
21. Origen, *op. cit.*, p. x-xiii. Paul writes: "Take heed lest there be anyone that makes spoil of you through his philosophy and vain deceit, after the tradition of men, after the elements of the world, and not after Christ." (*Col.* 2:8).
22. "Anyone who reads these stories with a fair mind, who wants to keep himself from being deceived by them, will decide what he will accept and what he will interpret allegorically, searching out the meaning of the authors who wrote such fictitious stories, and what he will disbelieve."(*Ibid.*, p. 39).
23. *Ibid.*, p. 59.
24. "When I, Constantine Augustus, as well as I, Licinius Augustus, fortunately met near Mediolanum (Milan), and were considering everything that pertained to the public welfare and security, we thought, among other things which we saw would be for the good of many, those regulations pertaining to the reverence of the Divinity ought certainly to be made first, so that we might grant to the Christians and others full authority to observe that religion which each preferred; whence any Divinity whatsoever in the seat of the heavens may be propitious and kindly disposed to us and all who are placed under our rule. And thus by this wholesome counsel and most upright provision we thought to arrange that no one whatsoever should be denied the opportunity to give his heart to the observance of the Christian religion, of that religion which he should think best for himself, so that the Supreme Deity, to whose worship we freely yield our hearts) may show in all things His usual favor and benevolence." http://gbgm-umc.org/umw/bible/milan.stm. The first known *Edict of Toleration*, however, belongs to Galerius' Edict in 311 inviting the Christians to find themselves back in the Roman fold and offering clemency by adhering to the old code of the state religion. (Viorst, 1994, pp. 12-13).
25. The classic biography of J. Burckhardt, (1949, 1880).
26. Pagels, 2003, *op. cit.*, p. 134.
27. Pagels, 1988, *op. cit.*, p. 59.
28. "I determined," Constantine writes in a letter to Chrestus, Bishop of Syracuse, "to cut short such quarrels among them." (Eusebius, 1965, *op. cit.*, p. 405.
29. The Nicene Creed was first adopted in 325 at the First Council of Nicaea but went through subsequent modifications. At first, the text ended after the words "We believe in the Holy Spirit." The second Council in 381 added the remainder except for the words "and the son," the version used by Eastern Orthodox and Greek Catholic churches today. The 381council stated that no further changes could be made to it, nor could other creeds be adopted. http://en.wikipedia.org/wiki/Nicene_Creed

30. *John* 17:3 & *Mark*, 13:32 and *Matt.* 24:36. Irvin writes: "It is difficult to see, then, how Christ can be both 'one with the Father' to the degree that he claims and till fully human. To be fully human he must be really distinct from the Father (not just the Father under another name). Moreover, he would not be one person at all if he were really an alliance of two persons, one human and one divine; and so his divine and his human characteristics must not constitute two persons." (T. Irvin, 1989, *op. cit.*, p. 212). Church doctrine clashed with the gospels and the gospels lost.

31. J. H. Newman, (1890), pp. 116-132.

32. V. J. Bourke, (1993) pp. 203-04.

33. V. Bourke, (1960), p. 291. For a more radical, philosophical viewpoint see L. Feuerbach (1989). The success of the Trinitarian view is attributed to vigorous proponents like Hilary of Poitiers and Eusebius of Vercelli in the late 4th century and the untimely death of emperors like Constantius (361) who were opposed to the Nicene doctrine and the rise of Theodosius who favored it. (D. H. Williams, 1995, pp. 38-68). Nevertheless, by 384, the creed was used as a criterion for acceptance into church membership in Jerusalem according to a diary of Egeria, a Spanish nun. "And when they have recited the Creed to the bishop, he addresses them all, and says: "During these seven weeks you have been taught all the law of the Scriptures, you have also heard concerning the Faith, and concerning the resurrection of the flesh, and the whole meaning of the Creed, as far as you were able, being yet catechumens. But the teachings of the deeper mystery, that is, of Baptism itself, you cannot hear, being as yet catechumens. But, lest you should think that anything is done without good reason, these, when you have been baptised in the Name of God, you shall hear in the Anastasis, during the eight Paschal days, after the dismissal from the church has been made. You, being as yet catechumens, cannot be told the more secret mysteries of God. "This "secrecy of the mysteries" recalls the Eleusian mystery rites. (http://users.ox.ac.uk/~mikef/durham/egetra.html)

34. He was an archimandrite, a rank below a bishop, like an abbot, usually as a superior of a monastery or group of monasteries.

35. A column commemorating the Nestorian belief stands tall today in the courtyard of the old imperial palace in Xian, ancient Chang An, the capitol of China in the 8th century CE, placed there when Nestorian missionaries arrived from along the Silk Road to bring their message to Asia. My Chinese guide didn't know what it was.

36. M. Roquebert, (1988).

37. *Deuteronomy* 13:2-5. But much of *Deuteronomy* is filled with these wrathful denunciations against anyone one or any city opposed the Jews.

38. W. Durant, *The Age of Faith*, p. 776.

39. I have wandered inside the Cathar citadel fortress of Montsegur near the French town of Albi. The adherents surrendered after an expended siege, and over 200 were burned on a large funeral pyre on March 16, 1244.

40. Euripedes, (1955), p. 167.

41. J. Elsner, JRS, (2003), 83, 114-128.

Chapter 16

1. B. D. Ehrman, LS.

2. J. H. Newman, 1890, *op. cit.* Newman began as an Oxford scholar and an Anglican who converted to Catholicism and became England's Roman Catholic Cardinal. This early scholarly treatise lacks objectivity.

3. *Ibid.*, p. 239.

4. E. Gibbon, DF, p. 393. Gibbon was indebted to Ammianus Marcellinus, the last of the Roman historians and the best since Tacitus 250 years earlier. Ammianus Marcellinus, LRE. Cf. Timothy Barnes, (1998).

5. "If the Father begat the Son, certain conclusions would follow." Newman, 1890, *op. cit.*, p. 28.

6. In a letter to Alexander, Bishop of Alexandria, Arius wrote: 'We believe that this God gave birth to the Only-Begotten Son before age-long times, through whom he has made those ages themselves, and all things else; that He generated Him, not in semblance, but in truth, giving Him a real subsistence (*hypostasis*) at His own will, so as to be unchangeable and unalterable." (*Ibid.*, pp. 213-14).

7. T. D. Barnes, (1993). The issue of orthodoxy is complicated among even Catholics. Although the Roman Catholic, Greek and Slavic Orthodox communions have the largest memberships. Maronite, Coptic, Armenian and Chaldean groups also define themselves as Christians. Chaldean Christians, for example, typically follow Nestorius and do not believe Mary is the Mother of God but only the mother of Jesus the man. They only acknowledge the validity of the first two councils. Maronite Christians fell out of doctrinal favor with the church in the 7th century but returned in the 12th century.

8. R. Westfall, (1993) and M. Wiles, (1996).

9. R. Williams, (2001, 1987).

10. Julian, 1923, *op. cit.*, v3, & pp. xxx ff.

11. G. R. S. Mead, FFF, p. 106.

12. D. H. Williams, (1995), pp. 7-10.

13. Much of the history of this controversy I obtained in Barnes, *op. cit.* It is relevant to describe this in more detail because the church does not include it in its histories. Yet it reveals the disputatious theological wrangling that engaged everyone's energies and shows how unrelenting some were in the pursuit of Athanasius whom more councils condemned than condemned Arius.

14. Barnes, 1993, *op. cit.*, p. 77.

15. *Ibid.*, p. 144.

16. Tertullian, 1790, *op. cit.*, pp. 265-94 and pp. 295-606.

17. N. F. Cantor, (1993), p. 79. (Norman Cantor died as this chapter was being re-written and I am very grateful for his life of scholarship and fluid prose). Cf. V. J. Bourke, (1993), and W. Durant, 1950, pp. 64-79.

18. G. Wills, (2003), pp. 4 ff. See also H. A. Deane, (1963), pp. 13-38.

19. Ambrose, Augustine's mentor, was the son of a Roman prefect and became a judge. He had to be baptized quickly so he could be consecrated Bishop of Milan by appointment of the Emperor Valentinian. (J. Moorhead, 1999).

20. "By avoiding this world, the soul lives;" Augustine writes in *The Confessions*, "by seeking it the soul dies." (1998, p. 291). He declaims against academic philosophers in *On the Trinity* in W. J. Oates, BWSA. Vol.1 & 2. (1948), pp. 849-51. See also R. W. Dyson, (1998).

21. Euripedes, *op. cit.*, p. 198.

22. *Ibid.*, pp. 55-56, 177 ff., and 152-53.

23. W. J. Oates, BWSA, pp. 620-654.

24. Augustine's descriptions opened wide the debate on issues that had been never satisfactorily answered. If God is good and all-powerful, why is there evil in the world? If there is a Satan with certain powers, then God is not all powerful because he cannot control Satan's will and purposes.

25. He writes: "Lord, God of truth, surely the person with a scientific knowledge of nature is not pleasing to you...The person who knows all these matters but is ignorant of you is unhappy." (*The Confessions*, p. 75). By the time of the Enlightenment that argument had been turned on its head and science was said ready to rescue the spirit, like Robert Boyle, the father of modern chemistry. (R. Porter, 2004, pp. 80 ff.) C. Freeman devotes his entire text to the rise of faith and the decline of reason in *The Closing of the Western Mind, The Rise of Faith and the Fall of Reason* (2003).

26. It was a time, as Gibbon remarked, when "The name of the Poet was almost forgotten, that of Orator was usurped by the sophists. A cloud of critics, of compilers, of commentators,

darkened the face of learning, and the decline of genius was followed by the corruption of taste." (Gibbon, DF, 83).
27. R. McKeon, (1947), p. 243.
28. C. Bar, C. (2003, July, JEH, 54(3), 401-21.
29. "So there is in nature...in essence not power to make an evil intent. An evil intent arises in any spiritual being capable of change when it twists or diminishes the good nature in which it resides, and nothing can make this evil intent but some unmaking of beings by a departure from God's being." (Augustine in Wills, 2003, *op. cit.*, p. 85).

Epilogue
1. *The Upanishads*, the BG, the *Avesta*, the *Bible*, the gospels, the *Koran*, *Sri Guru Granth Sahib* and *The Book of Mormon*, among others. *A Dream of Red Mansions*, written by Cao Xueqin (Ts'ao Hsueh-ch'in) (c.1715–1763) is the undisputed Chinese classic, an acknowledged masterpiece of encyclopedic scope, depicting the rise and fall of dynasties, describing the emergence of feudal societies in interlocking families, with over 700 characters in 120 chapters, filled with nobility, concubines, peddlers, and people from all walks of life.
2. N. Cohn, (1993), p. 50.
3. Paul Tillich, (1955), p. 2-4.
4. Nock, A.D. (1945) *Corpus Hermeticum*. Tome 1, Traites I-XII. Paris: Societe d'edition, Les Belles Lettres. pp. 8-9.
5. The collapse of the religious center and the death of over a million Jews also led to a religious power vacuum quickly filled by the construction of a temple to Jupiter built over the destroyed Jewish temple compound and Hadrian's new Roman city of Aelia Capitolina in 130–31. This sacrilege to the Jews was the cause of the Bar-Kochba revolt in the years 132–135 CE.
6. Greek epic poets and tragedians were content with granting partial divinity to their heroes or heroines, like Perseus, Hercules, Apollo, and Ulysses, mortals who were born of combined divine and mortal parentage, a tradition Luke follows in making Mary Jesus' mother and the Holy Spirit the progenitor, a biological impossibility but mythically acceptable.
7. William James, (1997). *The Varieties of Relgious Experience*. New York: Simon & Schuster, pp. 41-42.

GLOSSARY OF SELECTED TERMS

Academus	A local Athenian god from which Academy
Amen	meaning "so be it;" derives from Amun, Egyptian god,
Apatheia	freedom from passion; self-control
Apocrypha	non-canonical early Christian books
Apocalypse	revelation
Apostasy	standing apart, deserter
Apostle	representative
Aramaic	semitic language related to Hebrew
Archimandrite	superior of one or more monasteries
Arête	virtue, a combination of goodness, excellence
Askesis	disciplined training
Atheist	not a god-believer
Basileus	originally, King
Basileia	kingdom
Basilica	palace, a large building, later a large Christian church
Byblos	in Lebanon where scriptures were found
Blasphemy	evil speech
Canon	guideline; also the proclamations of a council
Catholic	universal
Chaos	the void; in some scriptures water
Charisma	special gift
Christ	Anointed one (with oil) (see Messiah)
Decapolis	(ten cities) Greek-speaking cities related by trade with its capitol in Damascus
Democracy	demos (people) and kratos (rule or power)
Devas	Hindu word for divinities; devils in English
Dike	justice, law
Dynamis	power
Christos	The Anointed One (see Messiah)
Ecclesia	assembly (see synagogue)
Ecstasy	literally, out of oneself
Eirene	peace
Epinoia	creative consciousness
Episcopus	overseer; bishop
Eros	passionate joy
Eschatology	the study of a vision of a divine utopia
Eucharist	gratitude; to show favor
Eudaemonia	literally, good demons; a state of well-being
Eunomia	good government

Evangel	good news or gospel, same root as angel = messenger
Exegesis	to explain; text interpretation
Gnosis	knowledge
Hairesis	heresy, choice
Heterodoxy	different opinion
Historia	inquiry
Homousian	consubstantial = of one substance with
Homoeusian	similar in substance
Horkos	an oath (literally, a fence)
Hubris	pride, insolence
Hypostasis	to stand under; a foundation or support
Infidel	non-believer
Kabbalah	tradition (mystical Judaism)
Kurios	Lord
Laos	the people, from which the English word, laity
Logos	thought, reason
Martyr	witness
Messiah	Anointed One (Hebrew)
Mishnah	to repeat and study; interpretations of the Torah
Moira	fate; a man's due
Nomos	a law, convention or moral norm
Nous	for Plato, the highest form of the soul; more generally, mind
Oikonomia	household management
Orthodox	right way
Pagan	peasant (Latin pagus = country)
Pantheon	all gods
Pantheism	god everywhere
Paradosis	tradition
Physis:	instincts, appetites, impulses
Pistis	trust, pledge
Pleroma	the Gnostic fullness of the Godhead
Pneuma	spirit, breath (E.g., pneumatic)
Pseudepigraphia	false or non-accepted writings
Psyche	soul
Rhema	one word
Scripture	writings
Synoptic	taken together
Sophia	wisdom
Sophosyne:	moderation, discretion, temperance
Synagogue	gathering (see ecclesia)
Techne	art, craft
Telos	end, purpose (teleology = study of design in nature

REFERENCES

Adams, R. E. W. (1977). *Prehistoric Mesoamerica*. Boston: Little Brown.
Adkins, L. & R. (1991). *Introduction to the Romans*. Secaucus, NJ: Chartwell Books.
Aeschylus. (1833). *The Tragedies* (tr. R. Potter). London: A. J. Valpy.
Aeschylus. (1965). *Aeschylus*. (Ed. R. W. Corrigan). New York: Dell.
Afnan, R. M. (1965). *Zoroaster's influence on Greek thought*. New York: Philosophical Library.
Algaze, G. (1989). "The Uruk Expansion: Cross Cultural Exchange in Early Mesopotamian Civilization." *Current Anthropology*, V. 30(5), pp. 571-608.
Ajami, F. (1998). *The Dream Palace of the Arabs, a Generation's Odyssey*. New York: Vintage.
Akenson, D. H. (1998). *Surpassing wonder, The Invention of the Bible and the Talmuds*. New York: Harcourt Brace.
Albright, W. F. (1966). *Archaeology, Historical Analogy and Early Biblical Tradition*. Baton Rouge: Louisiana State University Press.
Aldred, C. (1998). *The Egyptians*. (3rd ed.) London: Thames and Hudson.
Aldred, C. (1988). *Akhenaten, King of Egypt*. London: Thames & Hudson.
Allegro, J. (1956). *The Dead Sea Scrolls, A Reappraisal*. Baltimore, MD: Penguin Books.
Altman, L. K. (2003, May 6). Lessons of AIDS, applied to SARS. *The NewYork Times*, D1.
Ammianus Marcellinus. (1986). *The Later Roman Empire (A.D. 354-378)* New York: Penguin.
Andrews, C. (1984). *Egyptian Mummies*. London: British Museum Publications.
Angier, N. (2004, Spring). My God Problem—and Theirs. *The American Scholar*, 73(2), 131-34.
Aquinas, T. (1920). *The Summa Theologica*. Part I, London: Burns Oates & Washbourne.
Aries, P. & Duby, G. (1987). *A History of Private Life, from Pagan Rome to Byzantium*. Cambridge: Harvard University Press.
Aristophanes (1955) *Five Comedies of Aristophanes*. (Trans. B. B.Rogers). Garden City, NY: Doubleday Anchor Books.
Aristotle (1975). *The Nicomochean Ethics*. (tr. David Ross). London: Oxford University Press.
Aristotle (1984). *The Complete Works of Aristotle, The Revised Oxford Translation*. Princeton: Princeton University Press.
Armstrong, K. (2001). *The Battle for God*. New York: Ballantine Books.
Armstrong, K. (2000). *Islam, A Short History*. New York: Modern Library.
Armstrong, K. (1993). *A History of God, The 4,000-year quest of Judaism, Christianity and Islam*. New York: Ballantine Books.
Arndt, W. F. & Gingrich, F. W. (1979) *A Greek-English Lexicon of the New Testament and Other Early Christian Literature*. Chicago: University of Chicago Press.
Atrahasis at: http://home.apu.edu/~geraldwilson/atrahasis.html.
Attridge, H. W. & Oden, R. A. (1981). *Philo of Byblos, The Phoenician History*. Washington, DC: The Catholic Biblical Association of America.
Aubarbier, J-L, & Binet, M. (1987). *Prehistoric Sites in Perigord*. Bretagne:Quest-France.
Auden, W. H. (1948). *The Portable Greek Reader*. New York: Viking Press.
Auge, C. & Dentzer, J-M. (2000). *Petra, the Rose-Red City*. London: Thames and Hudson.
Augustine, (1960). *The Confessions*. Garden City, NJ: Doubleday.
Augustine. (1998). *The Confessions*. (Trans. H. Chadwick). Oxford: Oxford University Press.
Augustine, (1950). *The City of God*. New York: Modern Library.
Aurelius, M. (1952). *Meditations*. In R. M. Hutchins (Ed.), *Great Books of the Western world*. (Chicago: Encyclopaedia Britannica, 1952).
Avesta, Gathas. (1963). The Hymns of Zarathustra. (Tr. J. Duchesne- Guillemin).Boston: Beacon Press.
Backhouse, J. (1981). *The Lindisfarne Gospels*. Oxford: Phaidon.
Bacon, F. (1955). *Selected Writings of Francis Bacon*. New York: The Modern Library.

Bacon, F. (1944). *The Advancement of Learning and New Atlantis.* London: Oxford University Press.
Bacon, F. (1853). *The Essays, or Counsels Civil and Moral.* London: John Parker and Son.
Bacon, R. (1683). *Speculum Alchymiae, The True Glass of Alchemy.* London: William Cooper.
Bacon, R. (1928). *Opus Majus.* (Trans. B. Burke). Philadelphia: University of Pennsylvania Press.
Bailey, C. (1969, 1935). *Religion in Virgil.* New York: Barnes & Noble.
Bahn, P. G. (1997). *Lost Cities.* New York: Barnes & Noble.
Bain, D. H. (2003, September 7). The great Utah mystery. *The New York Times Book Review,* 14-15.
Balsinger, D. & Sellier, C. E. (1976). *In Search of Noah's Ark.* Los Angeles: Sun Classic Books.
Balter, M. (1998). Why settle down? The mystery of communities. *Science* 282, No. 5393, pp 1442-1445.
Bar, C. (2003, July). The Christianization of Rural Palestine during Late Antiquity. *The Journal of Ecclesiastical History,* 54(3) 401-21.
Bar-Efrat, S. (1989). *Narrative Art in the Bible.* Sheffield, UK: The Almond Press.
Barnes, J. (1995). *The Cambridge Companion to Aristotle.* Cambridge: Cambridge University Press.
Barnard, L. W. (1967). *Justin Martyr, His Life and Thought.* Cambridge, UK: Cambridge University Press.
Bartlett, J. R. (ed.) (1997). *Archaeology and Biblical Interpretation.* London: Routledge.
Barnes, T. D. (1998). *Ammianus Marcellinus and the Representation of Historical Reality.* Ithaca, NY: Cornell University Press.
Barnes, T. D. (1993). *Athanasius and Constantius, Theology and Politics in the Constantinian Empire.* Cambridge, MA: Harvard University Press.
Barnes, T. D. (1994). *From Eusebius to Augustine, Selected Papers 1982-1993.* Brookfield, VT: Variorum.
Barnett, R. D. (1977). *Illustrations of Old Testament History.* London: British Museum.
Barzun, J. (1989). *The Culture We Deserve.* Middletown, CT: Wesleyan University Press.
Benario, H. W. (1991). *Tacitus' Agricola, Germany, and Dialogue on Orators.* Norman, OK: University of Oklahoma Press.
Bartlett, J. R. (1982*). Jericho.* Guildford, Surrey: Lutterworth Press.
Bayral, M. (1985). *Secret Ephesus.* Izmir, Turkey: Ticaret Matbaacilik.
Bell, R. (1960, 1937). *The Qur'an.* Edinburgh: T & T Clark.
Benario, H. W. (1991). *Tacitus's Agricola, Germany and Dialogue on Orators.* Norman, OK: University of Oklahoma Press.
Bergman, C. (1996). *Orion's Legacy, A Cultural History of Man as Hunter.* New York: Dutton.
Bhattacharjee, Y. (2003, February 18). With an evolutionary milestone, the race for survival began. *The New York Times,* D3.
Biblical Archaeology Review,(1993). 30,000-Year-Old Sanctuary Found at HarKarkom. 19(1), 38.
Bietak, M. (2003). Israelites Found in Egypt. *Biblical Archaeological Review,* 29(5), p. 41 ff.
Bion of Smyrna. (1997). *Bion of Smyrna, The Fragments and the Adonis.* (J. D. Reed Ed.) Cambridge: Cambridge University Press.
Birley, A. (1993). *Marcus Aurelius, A Biography.* London: Batsford.
Bleeker, C. J. (1973). *Hathor and Thoth, Two key figures of the ancient Egyptian religion.* Leiden: E. J. Brill.
Bloom, A. (1987). *The Closing of the American Mind.* New York: Simon & Schuster.
Bloom, H. (1990). *The Book of J.* New York: Vintage Books, Random House.
Bock, K. (1994). *Human Nature Mythology.* Urbana, IL: University of Illinois Press.
Boardman, J. & J. Griffin, O. Murray (1991). *The Oxford History of the Roman World.* Oxford: Oxford University Press.
Boisselier, J. (1993). *The Wisdom of the Buddha.* London: Thames & Hudson.

Bonaventure (1993). *The Journey of the Mind to God.* Indianapolis: Hackett Publishing.
Borowski, O. (1998). *Every Living Thing, Daily use of animals in ancient Israel.* Walnut Creek, CA: AltaMira Press.
Bourbon, F. (1999). *Petra, Jordan's extraordinary city.* New York: Barnes & Noble.
Bourke, V. J. (1993). *Augustine's Quest for Wisdom.* Albany, NY: Magi Books.
Bourke, V. (1960). *The Pocket Aquinas.* New York: Washington Square Press.
Boutcher, W. (2003, October). The Analysis of Culture Revisited: Pure Texts, Applied Texts, Literary Historicisms, cultural Histories. *Journal of theHistory of Ideas,* 64(3), 489-510.
Bovon, F. (2003, Summer). Canonical and Apocryphal Acts of Apostles. *Journal of Early Christian Studies,* 11(2), 165-194.
Bovon, F. (2000). Fragment of Oxyrhynchus 840, fragment of a lost gospel, witness of an early Christian controversy over purity. *Journal of Biblical Literature,* 119(4), 705-728.
Bowen, J. (1972). *A History of Western Education, Vol 1, The Ancient World.* London:Metheun.
Bowerstock, G. W. (2003, April 6). Seeing the voice of the Lord. *The NewYork Review of Books,* 22.
Bowman, A. K. (1986). *Egypt after the Pharaohs.* Berkeley: University of California Press.
Brandscheid, F. (ed.). (1901). *Novum Testamentum Graece.* Friborg: Sumptibus Herder.
Brettler, M. Z. (1995). *The Creation of History in Ancient Israel.* London:Routledge.
Bright, J. (2000, 1946). *A History of Israel.* (4th Ed.) Louisville: Westminster: John Knox Press.
Brisson, L. (1998). *Plato the Myth Maker.* Chicago: University of ChicagoPress.
Broshi, M. (2003). What Jesus Learned from the Essenes, The Blessing of Poverty, the Bane of Divorce. *Biblical Archaeology Review,* 30(1), pp. 32 ff.
Brothwell, D. (1986). *The Bog Man and the Archaeology of Peoples.* London: British Museum.
Bronowski, J. & Mazlish, B. (1960). *The Western Intellectual Tradition.* NewYork: Harper & Brothers.
Bronowski, J. (1973). *The Ascent of Man.* Boston: Little Brown.
Brown, J. L. & Pollitt, E. (1996, February). Malnutrition, poverty and intellectual development. *Scientific American,* 38-43.
Brown, M. P. (1998). *The British Library Guide to Writing and Scripts, History and Techniques.* London: The British Library.
Brown, R. (1995). *Managing the Learning of History.* London: David Fulton Publishers.
Browne, L. (1946). *The World's Great Scriptures.* New York: Macmillan.
Browning, E. B. (1896). *Prometheus Bound and other poems.* London: Ward,Lock & Bowden.
Buber, M. (1965). *Between Man and Man.* New York: Collier Macmillan.
Buell, D. K. (1999). *Making Christians, Clement of Alexandria and the Rhetoric of Legitimacy.* Princeton, NJ: Princeton University Press.
Budge, E. A. W. (1983, 1910). *Egyptian language, Easy lessons in Egyptian Hieroglyphics.* New York: Dover Publications.
Budge, E. A. W. (1973,1911). *Osiris and the Egyptian Resurrection.* (Vol. 1). NewYork: Dover.
Budge, E. A. W. (1980, 1899). *Egyptian Religion, Egyptian Ideas of the Future Life.* London: Routledge & Kegan Paul.
Budge, E. A. W. (1967, 1895). *The Egyptian Book of the Dead, The Papyrus of Ani.* New York: Dover Publications.
Bulfinch, T. (1962). *The Age of Fable.* New York: New American Library.
Bullock, A. (1985). *The Humanist Tradition in the West.* New York: W. W. Norton.
Bulyer, E. (1872). *The Odes and Epodes of Horace.* London: George Routledge & Sons.
Burckhardt, J. (1979, 1943). *Reflections on History.* Indianapolis: Liberty Fund.
Burckhardt, J. (1949, 1880). *The Age of Constantine the Great.* Berkeley: University of California Press.
Burke, P. (1997). *Varieties of Cultural History.* Ithaca, NY: Cornell University Press.
Burkitt, F. C. (1925). *The Religion of the Manichees.* New York: AMS Press.

Burn, L. (1990). *Greek myths*. London: The British Museum.
Cahill, T. (1998). *The Gifts of the Jews, How a tribe of desert nomads changed the way everyone thinks and feels*. New York: Nan A. Talese/Anchor Books.
Cahill, T. (2003). *Sailing the Wine-Dark Sea, Why the Greeks Matter*. New York: Nan A. Talese/Doubleday.
Callimachus (1960). *Callimachus, Hymns and Epigrams*. (Trans. G. R. Mair). Cambridge, MA: Harvard university Press.
Callimachus. (1988). *Callimachus, Hymns, Epigrams, Select Fragments*. Baltimore, MD: The Johns Hopkins University Press.
Cantor, N. F. (2003). *Antiquity, The Civilization of the Ancient World*. NewYork: HarperCollins.
Cantor, N. F. (1993). *The Civilization of the Middle Ages*. New York: HarperPerennial.
Campbell, J. (1955). *The Mysteries, Papers from the Eranos Yearbooks*.Princeton: Princeton University Press, Bollingen Series. V.2.
Campbell, J. (1987). *The Masks of God: Primitive Mythology*. New York: Penguin Books.
Campbell, J. (1991). *The Hero's Journey, Joseph Campbell on his life and work*. San Francisco: HarperSanFrancisco.
Campbell, J. (1988). *Joseph Campbell, the Power of Myth* (with Bill Moyers). New York: Doubleday.
Carmichael, J. (1989). *The Birth of Christianity, Reality and Myth*. New York: Dorset Press.
Carmichael, C. M. (1996). *The Story of Creation, Its origin and its interpretation in Philo and the Fourth Gospel*. Ithaca: Cornell University Press.
Carter, J. (1986). *The Blood of Abraham*. Boston: Houghton Mifflin.
Casson, L. (1962). *Selected Satires of Lucian*. Chicago: Aldine Publishing.
Catullus, G. V. (1966). *The Poems of Catullus* (Trans. P. Whigham). London: Penguin.
Celsus (1987). *On the True Doctrine, A discourse against the Christians*. (Tr. R. J. Hoffmann). New York: Oxford University Press.
Center Wins Battle for Religious Tolerance. (2003, September). *SPLC Report*,Birmingham, AL: Southern Poverty Law Center.
Ceram, C. W. (Ed.) (1966). *Hands on the Past, Pioneer archaeologists tell their own story*. New York: Alfred Knopf.
Chesterton, G. K. (1933). *St. Thomas Aquinas*. London: Hodder & Stoughton.
Choufrine, A. (2002). *Gnosis, Theophany, Theosis, Studies in Clement of Alexandria's Appropriation of His Background*. New York: Peter Lang.
Churton, T. (1987). *The Gnostics*. New York: Barnes & Noble.
Chrisomalis, S. (2003, September). The Egyptian Origin of the Greek Alphabetic Numerals. *The Classical Journal*, 77(297), 485-96.
Cibelli, J. B., Lanza, R. P., West, M. D., & Ezzell, C. (2002). The first human cloned embryo. *Scientific American*, 286(1), 44-51.
Cicero, (1951). *The Basic Works of Cicero*. Hadas, M. (ed.) New York: The Modern Library.
Cicero, (1892). *Life and letters*. Edinburgh: W. P. Nimmo, Hay, & Mitchell.
Clement of Alexandria (1715). *Opera Quae Extant*. Oxford: Georgii Mortlock.
Clement of Alexandria (1953, 1972). *Clement of Alexandria*. (Tr. G. W. Butterworth). Cambridge, MA: Harvard University Press.
Clement of Alexandria (1991). *Clement of Alexandria, Stromateis*. (Tr. John Ferguson). Washington, DC: Catholic University of America Press.
Clottes, J. (1991). *The Cave at Niaux*. Boulogne: Castelet.
Cochrane, C. N. (2003, 1940). *Christianity and Classical Culture, A Study of Thought and Action from Augustus to Augustine*. Indianapolis: Liberty Fund.
Cohn, N. (1993). *Cosmos, Chaos and the World to come*. New Haven: YaleUniversity Press.
Colson, F. H., & Whitaker, G. H. (trans). (1929). *Philo*. Cambridge: Harvard University Press.
Conniff, R. (2003). Rethinking primate aggression. *Smithsonian*, 14(5), 60-67.

Coogan, M. (1998). *The Oxford History of the Biblical World*. New York: Oxford University Press.
Copeston, F. (1959). *A History of Philosophy*. Westminster, Md: Newman Press.
Cornelius, I. (1994). *The Iconography of the Canaanite Gods Reshef and Ba'al*. Fribourg, Switzerland: University Press.
Covington, R. (2003). Mesopotamian Masterpieces. *Smithsonian*, 14(5), 68-71.
Cumont, F. (1956). *The Mysteries of Mithra*. New York: Dover Publications.
Cupit, D. (1984). *The Sea of Faith, Christianity in change*. London: The British Broadcasting Corporation.
Cresson, A. (1962). *The Essence of Ancient Philosophy*. New York: Walker and Company.
Crews, F. (2001a, October 4). Saving us from Darwin, Part I. *The New York Review of Books*, 24-27.
Crews, F. (2001b, October 11). Saving us from Darwin, Part II. *The NewYorkReview of Books*, 51-55.
Crick, F. (1994). *The Astonishing Hypothesis: The Scientific Search for Soul*. New York: Charles Scribner.
Chrisomalis, S. (2003, September). The Egyptian Origin of the Greek Alphabetic Numerals. *The Classical Journal*, 77(297), 485-96.
Crossan, J. D., & Reed, J. L. (2001). *Excavating Jesus, Beneath the Stones, Behind the Texts*. San Francisco: Harper San Francisco.
Cruz-Uribe, E. (1989, September/October). Oasis of the Spirit. *Archaeology*, 48.
Dahood, M. (1981). Ebla, Ugarit and the Bible. In Pettinato, G., *The Archives of Ebla, An empire inscribed in clay*. Garden City, NY: Doubleday.
Dalley, S. (1989). *Myths from Mesopotamia, Creation, The Flood, Gilgamesh and Others*. Oxford: Oxford University Press.
Dante (1966). *The Divine Comedy*. (Tr. L. Biancolli). New York: Washington Square Press.
Daraul, A. (1989). *Secret societies*. New York: MJF Books.
Darwin, C. (1888). *The Descent of man and selection in relation to sex*. (2nd Ed.). London: John Murray.
Darwin, C. (1998). *The Expression of the emotions in man and animals*. London: HarperCollins.
Davies, P. (2003). E.T. and God. *The Atlantic Monthly*, 292(2), 112-118.
Davis, T. W. (2004). *Shifting Sands, The Rise and Fall of Biblical Archaeology*. Oxford: Oxford University Press.
Dawkins, R. (1989, 1976). *The selfish gene*. New York: Oxford University Press.
Dawson, C. (1958). *Religion and the Rise of Western Culture*. New York: Image Books.
Deane, H. A. (1963). *The Political and Social Ideas of St. Augustine*. New York: Columbia University Press.
De Chardin, P. T. (1959). *The Phenomenon of man*. New York: Harper & Row.
De Chardin, P. T. (1961). *Hymn of the universe*. New York: Harper & Row.
De Selincourt, A. (1962). *The World of Herodotus*. London: Phoenix Press.
Dehan, E. (1984). *And the walls came tumbling down*. Tel Aviv: Emmanuel Dehan.
Delluc, B. & G. (1990). *Discovering Lascaux*. Bordeaux: Sud-Quest.
De Moor, J. C. (1987). *An Anthology of Religious texts from Ugarit*. Leiden: E. J. Brill.
De Sandoli, S. (1984). *Calvary and the holy Sepulcher* Jerusalem: Franciscan Printing Press.
Descartes, R. (1941). *A Discourse on Method*. London: J. M. Dent.
Dever, W. G.(1990). *Recent Archaeological Discoveries and Biblical Research*. Seattle: University of Washington press.
DeWitt, N. W. (1954). *St. Paul and Epicurus*. Minneapolis: University of Minnesota Press.
Deutsch, R. (2002). Lasting impressions, New bullae reveal Egyptian-style Emblems on Judah's royal seals. *Biblical Archaeology Review*, 28(4), 43-51.
Diamond, J. (2002). The religious success story. *The New York Review of Books*, 49(17), 30-32.

Digeser, E. D. (2004). An Oracle of Apollo at Daphne and the Great Persecution. *Classical Philology*, 99(1), 57-77.
Dimont, M. (1994). *Jews, God and history.* (2nd edition.) New York: New American Library.
Diodorus (1985). *Diodorus on Egypt.* (Trans. E. Murphy). Jefferson, NC: McFarland and Co.
Diogenes Laertius (1959). *Lives of Eminent Philosophers* (Trans. R. D. Hicks) Vol. 1 & 2. Cambridge, MA: Harvard University Press.
Drummond, J. (1888). *Philo Judaeus, or the Jewish-Alexandrian philosophy in its development and completion.* Edinburgh: Williams and Norgate.
Dumezil, G. (1973). *From myth to fiction, The Saga of Hadingus.* Chicago: University of Chicago Press.
Dundes, A. (1984). *Sacred Narrative, Readings in the Theory of Myth.* Berkeley: University of California Press.
Durando, F. (1997). *Ancient Greece, The dawn of the western world.* New York: Barnes and Noble.
Durant, W. (1927). *The story of philosophy.* Garden City, NJ: Garden City Publishing Co.
Durant, W. (1963, 1935). *Our Oriental Heritage.* New York: Simon &Schuster.
Durant, W. (1966). *The Life of Greece.* New York: Simon & Schuster.
Durant, W. (1944). *Caesar and Christ.* New York: Simon & Schuster.
Durant W. (1950). *The Age of Faith.* New York: Simon & Schuster.
Durant, W. & A. (1963). *The Age of Louis XIV.* New York: Simon & Schuster.
Durant, W. & A. (1967). *Rousseau and revolution.* New York: MJF Books.
Durant, W. & A. (1975). *The Age of Napoleon.* New York: MJF Books.
Durant, W. & Durant, A. (1963). *The Age of Louis XIV,* New York: Simon & Schuster.
Durant, W. (1953). *The Renaissance.* New York: Simon & Schuster.
Durant, W. & Durant, A. (1961). *The Age of Reason Begins.* New York: Simon & Schuster.
Drosnin, M. (1997). *The Bible Code.* New York: Touchstone.
Dyson, R. W. (1998). *Augustine, The City of God Against the Pagans.* Cambridge: Cambridge University Press.
Edman, I. (1956). *The works of Plato.* New York: The Modern Library.
Edwards, I. E. S., (1971). *The Cambridge Ancient History.* (3rd ed.) V. 1 & V. II, (1975) Part 2, Cambridge: Cambridge University Press.
Ehrman, B. D. (2003a). *Lost Christianities, The Battle for Scripture and the Faiths We Never Knew.* New York: Oxford University Press.
Ehrman, B. D. (2003b). *Lost Scriptures, Books that did not Make it into the New Testament.* New York: Oxford University Press.
Eisenman, R. & Wise, M. (1994). *The Dead Sea Scrolls Uncovered.* New York: Barnes and Noble.
Eliade, M. (1978). *A History ofRreligious Ideas, from the Stone Age to the Eleusinian mysteries.* (Trans. W. R. Trask) V.1. Chicago: University of Chicago Press.
Elitzur, Y., & Nir-Zevi, D. (2004, May/June). Four-Horned Altar Discovered in Judean Hills. *Biblical Archaeology*, 30(3), 35-39.
Elsner, J. (2003). Archaeologies and Agendas: Reflections on Late Ancient Jewish and Early Christian Art. *Journal of Roman Studies*, 83, 114-128.
Epictetus (1942). *Moral Discourses.* New York: E. P. Dutton & Co.
Epictetus (1952). *The Discourses of Epictetus.* In R. M. Hutchins (Ed.), *Great Books of the Western World.* Chicago: Encyclopaedia Britannica.
Epicurus (1995). *A Guide to Happiness.* London: Phoenix.
Easterling, P. E. & Knox, B. M. W.(1985). *The Cambridge History of Classical Literature.* V.1. Cambridge: Cambridge University Press.
Euripedes (1996). *Heracles.* (Ed. S. A. Barlow). Warminster, UK: Aris & Phillips.
Euripedes (1832). *Euripedes*, V. 1, 2, & 3. (trans. R. Potter). London: A. J. Valpy.

Euripedes (1955). *The Complete Greek Tragedies*. (Tr. R. Lattimore). Chicago: University of Chicago Press.
Eusebius (1965). *The history of the church from Christ to Constantine*. (Tr. G. A. Williamson). New York: Dorset Press.
Erman, A. (1969). *Life in Ancient Egypt*. (Trans. by H. Tirard). (New York, B.Blom), pp. 47-49.
Evans, J. A. S. (1982). *Herodotus*. Boston: Twayne Publishers.
Evans, C. A., Webb, R. L., Wiebe, R. A. (1993). *Nag Hammadi texts and the Bible*. Leiden: E. J. Brill.
Farella, J. R. (1984). *The Main Stalk, A synthesis of Navajo philosophy*. Tucson, AZ: University of Arizona Press.
Feuerbach, L. (1989). *The Essence of Christianity*. (Tr. G. Eliot). Amherst, NY: Prometheus Books.
Ferguson, J. (1980). *Callimachus*. Boston: Twayne Publishers.
Filoramo, G. (1990). *A history of Gnosticism*. (Tr. A. Alcock). Cambridge: MA: Basil Blackwell.
Finkelstein, I. & Silberman, N. A. (2001). The Bible Unearthed, Archaeology's new vision of ancient Israel and the origin of sacred texts. New York: The Free Press.
Fischel, H. A. (1948). *The First book of Maccabees*. New York: Schocken Books.
Flussas, F. (1574). *Mercurij Trismegisti Pimandras Utraque Lingua Restitutus Burdigale*: Apud Simonem Millangium Burdigallensium Tprograhum via Jacobea.
France, P. (1993). *Greek as a Treat, An Introduction to the Classics*. London: BBC Books.
Freeman, C. (2003). *The Closing of the Western Mind, The Rise of Faith and the Fall of Reason*. New York: Knopf.
Freedman, D. N. (1998). *The Leningrad Codex*. Grand Rapids, MI: William B.Eerdmans.
Freeman, K. (1952). *God, Man and State, Greek Concepts*. Boston: The Beacon Press.
Freud, S. (1964). *Moses and Monotheism*. In *The Complete Psychological Works of Sigmund Freud*. v. 23. London: The Hogarth Press.
Friberg, J. (1997). Numbers and measures in the earliest written records. In Rennie, J. (Ed.). *Origins of Technology*. New York: Scientific American.
Friedman, R. (2003). City of the Hawk, Deciphering the Narmer Palette. *Archaeology*, 56(6), 52-53.
Friedman, R. E. (2003). *The Bible with Sources Revealed, A New View into the Five Books of Moses*. San Francisco: HarperSanFrancisco.
Frymer-Kensky, T. (1977, December). Judicial Ordeal in the Ancient Near East. *Biblical Archaeologist*, pp. 147-55.
Fouts, R. (1997). *Next of Kin, What chimpanzees have taught me about who we are*. New York: William Morrow & Co.
Forde, N. W. (1975). *Cato the Censor*. Boston: Twayne Publishers.
Frankfurter, D. (1998). *Religion in Roman Egypt*. Princeton, NJ: Princeton University Press.
Friedman, R. E. (2003). *The Bible with Sources Revealed*. San Francisco:HarperSanFrancisco.
Friedman, R. E. (1998). *The hidden book of the bible*. San Francisco: HarperSanFrancisco.
Frazer, J. G. (1923). *Fork-Lore in the Old Testament*. New York: Tudor Publishing Co.
Fuller, T. (2003, February 5). Europe debates whether to admit God to union. *The New York Times*, A3.
Gainsford, P. (2003). Formal Analysis of Recognition Scenes in the Odyssey. *The Journal of Hellenic Studies*, 123, 41-59.
Gaster, T. H. (1969). *Myth, Legend, and Custom in the Old Testament*. V. 2. New York: Harper Torchbooks.
Gaugh, S. (2004, March 4). At a Mountain Monastery, Old Texts Gain Digital Life. *The New York Times*, E5.
Gaur, A. (1984). *A History of Writing*. New York: Charles Scribner's Sons.
Gelb, J. (1961). *Old Akkadian writing and grammar*. Chicago: The University of Chicago Press.

Gibbon, E. (1952). *The Decline and Fall of the Roman Empire*. New York: Penguin Books.
Gilbert, K. S., Holt, J. K., & Hudson, S. (1976). *The Treasures of Tutankhamen*. New York: Metropolitan Museum of Art.
Gilgamesh (1960). *The Epic of Gilgamesh* (Trans. N. K. Sandars), Hammondsworth, UK: Penguin Books.
Gollnick, J. (1999). The Religious Dreamworld of Apuleius' Metamorphoses: Recovering a Forgotten Hermeneutic. Waterloo, Ontario: WilfridLaurier University Press.
Glover, T. R. (1920). *The Conflict of Religions in the Early Roman Empire*. (9th ed.). London: Metheun & Co.
Goode, E. (2002, May 3). Experts see mind's voices in a new light. *The New York Times*, D1.
Goodenough, A. (2004, May 1). Darwin-Free Fun for Creationists. *The NewYork Times*, A15.
Goodenough, E. R. (1940). *An Introduction to Philo*. (2nd Ed.). New York: Barnes & Noble.
Goodman, M. (1997). *The Roman World, 44 BC-AD 180*. New York: Routledge.
Goodstein, L. (2002, September 18). Conservative churches grew fastest in 1990s, report says. *The New York Times*, A16.
Gould, S. J. (2002). *The Structure of Evolutionary Theory*. Cambridge: Harvard University Press.
Gould, S. J. (1989). *Wonderful life*. New York: W. W. Norton.
Gould, S. J. (1999). Rocks of Ages: Science and religion in the fullness of life. New York: Ballantine Books.
Goranson, S. (1994). Qumran, A Hub of Scribal Activity? *Biblical Archaeology Review*, 20(5), 37-39.
Gordon, C. H. (1962). *Before the Bible, The Common Background of Greek and Hebrew Civilization*. New York: Harper & Row.
Gordon, C. H. (1987, 1968). *Forgotten scripts*. New York: Dorset Press.
Gordon, C. H. & Rendsburg, G. A. (1997). (4th ed.) *The Bible and the Ancient Near East*. New York: W. W. Norton.
Gore, R. (2001, April). Pharaohs of the sun. *The National Geographic*, 199(4), 34-57.
Gore, R. (2003). The Rise of Mammals, Adapting, evolving, surviving. *National Geographic*, 203(4), 2-37.
Gore, R. (2002, August). The first pioneer, A new find shakes the human tree. *National Geographic*, special edition.
Gotoff, H. G. (1993). *Cicero's Caesarian Speeches*. Chapel Hill: University of North Carolina Press.
Grant, R. M. (1961). Gnosticism, A source book of heretical writings from the early Christian period. New York: Harper & Bros.
Grant, M. (1975). *The Twelve Caesars*. New York: Barnes and Noble.
Grant, M. (1977). *Jesus, An Historian's review of the gospels*. New York: Charles Scribner's Sons.
Grant, M. (1992). *Readings in the classical historians*. New York: Charles Scribner's Sons.
Graves, R. (1992, 1955). *The Greek Myths*. London: Penguin Books.
Graves, R. (1951). *The Transformations of Lucius Otherwise Known as the Golden Ass*. New York: Farrar, Straus & Young.
Gray, J. (1985, 1969). *Near Eastern Mythology*. New York: Peter Bedrick Books.
Grube, G. M. A. (1974). *Plato's Republic*. Indianapolis: Hacket Publishing.
Gruen, E. (1998). *Heritage and Hellenism, The Reinvention of Jewish Tradition*. Berkeley: University of California Press.
Gribben, J. & J. Cherfas, J. (1982). *The Monkey Puzzle*. London: The Bodley Head.
Guhl, E., Koner, W. (1994). *The Greeks, Their life and customs*. London: Senate.
Guthrie, W. K. C. (1975,1950). *The Greek Philosophers, From Thales to Aristotle*. New York: Harper Torchbooks.
Guzzo, P. G. & d'Ambrosio, A. (1998). *Pompeii*. Napoli: L'erma d' Bretschneider.

Hackett, J. A. (1998). There was no King in Israel, The Era of the Judges. In M.Coogan, *The Oxford History of the Biblical World*. New York: OxfordUniversity Press, pp. 133 ff.
Hadas, M. (1951). *The Basic Works of Cicero*. New York: The Modern Library.
Hadas, M. (1962). *Greek drama*. Toronto: Bantam Books.
Hadas-Lebel, M. (1993). *Flavius Josephus, Eyewitness to Rome's First Century Conquest of Judea*. New York: Macmillan.
Halevi, Z. B. S. (1979). *Kabbalah, the tradition of hidden knowledge*. London: Thames & Hudson.
Hamilton, E. (1993, 1930). *The Greek Way*. New York: W. W. Norton.
Hamilton, E. (1964, 1932). *The Roman Way*. New York: W. W. Norton.
Hamilton, E. (1948). *Witness to the Truth, Christ and His Interpreters*. NewYork: W. W. Norton.
Hargis, J. W. (1999). *Against the Christians, The rise of early anti-Christian Polemic*. New York: Peter Lang.
Harris, W. V. (2003). Roman Opinions About the Truthfulness of Dreams. *Journal of Roman Studies*, 83, 18-34.
Hart, G. (1990). *Egyptian Myths*. Austin, TX: University of Texas Press.
Hartog, F. (2001). *Memories of Odysseus, Frontier Tales from Ancient Greece*. Chicago: University of Chicago Press.
Hawkes, J. (1968). *Dawn of the Gods*. New York: Random House.
Hawking, S. (2001). *The Universe in a Nutshell*. New York: Bantam Books.
Hawking, S.W. (1988). *A Brief History of Time*. New York: Bantam Books.
Head, P. M. (2000. Some Recently Published NT Papyri from Oxyrhynchus: An Overview and Preliminary Assessment. *Tyndale Bulletin*, 51, 1-16.
Hegel, G. W. F. (1888). *Lectures on the Philosophy of History*. London: George Bell & Sons.
Heidel, A. (1949). *The Gilgamesh Epic and Old Testament Parallels*. Chicago: University of Chicago Press.
Herenschmidt, C. (2003). Zarathustra's Ritual: Conserving a Charismatic Domination. *History of Religions*, 43(1), 1-17.
Herodotus (1830). *The Histories*. (Trans. by William Beloe). London: Henry Colburn & Richard Bentley.
Heschel, A. (1962). *The Prophets*. New York: Harper Torchbooks.
Hesiod. *Theogony*. At: sunsite.berkeley.edu/OMACL/Hesiod/theogony.html
Heibert, T. (1996). *The Yahwist's Landscape, Nature and religion in early Israel*. New York: Oxford University Press.
Holt, J. (2002, April 14). Intelligent design creationism and its critics:supernatural selection. *The New York Times* books.
Hodder, I. (1986). *Reading the Past, current approaches to interpretation in archaeology*. Cambridge: Cambridge University Press.
Holy Bible. (1963). Chicago: Good Counsel Publishing Company.
Homer. (1966). *The Iliad*. (Tr. E. V. Rieu). Baltimore, MD: Penguin Books.
Homer. (1963). *The Odyssey*. (Trans. R. Fitzgerald). New York: Anchor Books.
Hume, D. (1990, 1799). *Dialogues Concerning Natural Religion*. New York: Penguin Books.
Hume, D. (1967, 1739). *A Treatise of Human Nature*. (Ed. L. A. Selby-Bigge). Oxford: The Clarendon Press.
Hunt, D. (1982). *Footprints in Cyprus*. London: Trigraph.
Horace (1961). The Odes of Horace. (Tr. H. R. Henze). Norman: University of Oklahoma Press.
http://catal.arch.cam.ac.uk/catal/catal.html
http://users.ox.ac.uk/~mikef/durham/egetra.html
Irenaeus, (1952). *Proof of the Apostolic Teaching*. (Tr. J. P. Smith).New York: Newman Press.
Irvin, T. (1989). *A History of Western Philosophy 1, Classical Thought*. New York: Oxford University Press.

Isaacs, H. (1972). *Idols of the Tribe, Group Identity and Political Change*. Cambridge: Harvard University Press.
Iyer. R. (1983). *The Gospel according to Thomas*. New York: Concord Grove Press.
Jacobs, A. (2004, January 30) Georgia Takes on Darwin. *The New York Times*, A10.
James, W. (1997). *The Varieties of Religious Experience*. New York: Simon & Schuster.
Janssen, R. M. & J. J. (1990). *Growing up in ancient Egypt*. London: The Rubicon Press.
Johanson, D. & Johanson, L. (1994). *Ancestors, In Search of Human Origins*. New York: Villard Books.
Johanson, D. & Edey, M. (1981). *Lucy, The Beginnings of Humankind*. New York: Simon & Schuster.
Johnson, P. (1976). *A History of Christianity*. New York: Atheneum.
Josephus (1960). *Jerusalem and Rome*. (Selected N. N. Glatzer). New York: Meridian Books.
Josipovici, G. (1988). *The Book of God, A Response to the Bible*. New Haven: Yale University Press.
Julian (emperor). (1913). *The Works of Emperor Julian*. (v. 1) (trans. W. C. Wright) London: William Heinemann.
Jung, C. G. (1954). *The Development of Personality*. Princeton: Princeton University Press.
Jung, C. S. (1958, 1957). *The Undiscovered Self*. New York: Penguin Books.
Jung, C. S. (1966). *Two Essays on Analytical Psychology*, Vol. 7. Princeton, NJ: Princeton University Press.
Jung, C. S. (1969, 1959). *The Archetypes and the Collective Unconscious*, V. 9 Part 1. Princeton, NJ: Princeton University Press
Jung, C. S. (1971). *The Portable Jung*. New York: Penguin Books.
Jung, C. S. (1979). *Word and Image*. Princeton, NJ: Princeton University Press.
Justinian (Tr. C. F. Kolbert). (1979). *The Digest of Roman Law*. London: Penguin Books.
Juvenal. (1887). *Thirteen Satires of Juvenal*. (Trans. A. Leeper). London: Macmillan and Co.
Juvenal. (1991). *The Satires*. (Tr. Niall Rudd). Oxford: The Clarendon press.
Keel, O. & Uehlinger, C. (1998). *Gods, Goddesses, and Images of God in Ancient Israel*. Minneapolis: Fortress Press.
Keller, W. (1981, 1955). *The Bible as History*. (2nd revised Ed.). New York: William Morrow.
Kenyon, K. (1978). *The Bible and Recent Archaeology*. London: British Museum Publications.
Kermode, F. (2003, June 15). Another gospel truth. *The New York Times Book Review*, 10.
Kerenyi, C. (1992, 1951). *The Gods of the Greeks*. London: Thames & Hudson.
Keys, D. (2003). Pre-Christian Rituals at Nazareth. *Archaeology*, 56(6), 10.
King, C. W. (1889). *Plutarch's Morals*. London: George Bell and Sons.
King, K. L. (2003). *What is Gnosticism?* Cambridge, MA: The Belknap Press.
Kingsley, P. (1995). *Ancient philosophy, mystery and magic, Empedocles and the Pythagorean tradition*. Oxford: The Clarendon Press.
Kirk, G. S. (1965). *Homer and the Epic*. Cambridge: The University Press.
Kirk, G. S., Raven, J. E., Schofield, M. (1983, 1957). *The Presocratic Philosophers* (2nd Ed.). Cambridge: Cambridge University Press.
Kirsch, J. (1998). *Moses, a life*. New York: Ballantine Books.
Kitto, H. D. F. (1951). *The Greeks*. Baltimore, MD: Penguin Books.
Klosko, G. (1986). *The Development of Plato's political theory*. London: Metheun.
Koestler, A. (1959). *The Sleepwalkers, A History of Man's Changing Vision of the Universe*. London: Arkana.
Korfmann, M. (2004). Was There a Trojan War? *Archaeology*, 57(3), 36-41.
Kraemer, R. S. (2004). *Women's Religions in the Graeco-Roman World, A Sourcebook*. New York: Oxford University Press.
Kuhn, T. S. (1985, 1957). *The Copernican Revolution, Planetary Astronomy in The Development of Western Thought*. Cambridge: Harvard University Press.

Kuhn, T. S. (1970, 1962). *The Structure of Scientific Revolutions*. Chicago: University of Chicago Press.
Kung, H. (1976). *On Being a Christian*. Garden City, NY: Doubleday & Co.
Kurth, D. (2004). *The Temple of Edfu, A Guide by an Ancient Egyptian Priest*. Cairo: The American University in Cairo Press.
Krahmalkov, C. R. (1994). Exodus itinerary confirmed by Egyptian evidence. *Biblical Archaeology Review*, 20(5), 55-62.
Kriwaczek, P. (2003). *In Search of Zarathustra, The First Prophet and the Ideas that Changed the World*. New York: Knopf.
Krystal, A. (2001). Why smart people believe in God. *The American Scholar*, 70(4), 69-78.
Landis, P. (1929). *Four famous Greek plays*. New York: The Modern Library.
Lane Fox, R. (1992). *The Unauthorized Version, Truth and Fiction in the Bible*. New York: Alfred A. Knopf.
Lane Fox, R. (1986). *Pagans and Christians*. New York: Viking.
Lange, K. (2002). Wolf to woof, The evolution of dogs. *National Geographic*, 201(1), 2-31.
Lange, K. (2005). Unearthing Syria's Cult of the Dead. *National Geographic*, 207(2), 108-123.
Larson, R. B. & Bromm, V. (2001). The first stars in the universe. *Scientific American*, 285(6), 64-71.
Lawler, A. (2003). Saving Iraq's treasures. *Smithsonian*, 14(3), 42-55.
Lawrence, T. E. (1926,1935). *Seven Pillars of Wisdom*. London: Jonathan Cape.
Lazier, B. (2003, October). Overcoming Gnosticism. *Journal of the History of Ideas*, 64(4), 619-37.
Leakey, R. & Lewin, R. (1992). *Origins Reconsidered, In Search of What Us Makes Human*. New York: Doubleday.
Leeming, D. (2004). *Jealous Gods and Chosen People*. New York: Oxford University Press.
Lemaire, A. (2004). Another Temple to the Israelite God, Aramaic Hoard Documents Life in the Fourth Century B.C., *Biblical Archaeology Review*, 30(4), pp. 38 ff.
Lemaire, A. (2002). Burial Box of James, the brother of Jesus. *Biblical Archaeology Review*, 28(6), 24-33.
Lenski, R. E., Ofria, C., Pennock, R. T., & Adami, C. (2003). The evolutionary origin of complex features. *Nature*, 423, 139-144.
Lewy, H. (1946). *Selections from Philo*. Oxford: East and West Library.
Levine, A-J. (1998). Visions of Kingdoms, From Pompey to the First Jewish Revolt. In M. Coogan, *The Oxford History of the Biblical World*. New York: Oxford University Press, 1998).
Linforth, I. M. (1919). *Solon the Athenian*. University of California Publications in Classical Philology. Vol. 6. Berkeley: University of California Press.
Loffreda, S. (1985). *Capharnaum, The town of Jesus*. Jerusalem: Franciscan Printing Press.
Logan, A. H. B. (1996). *Gnostic Truth and Christian Heresy, A study in the history of gnosticism*. Edinburgh: T & T Clark.
Lomperis, T. J. (1984). *Hindu influence on Greek philosophy, The odyssey of the soul from the Upanishads to Plato*. Calcutta: Minerva Publications.
London, G. & Clark, D. R. (1997). *Ancient Ammonites & Modern Arabs*. Amman, Jordan: American Center of Oriental Research.
London, G. (1989). A Comparison of Two Contemporaneous Lifestyles of the Late Second Millennium B.C. *Bulletin of the American Schools of Oriental Research*, 273, 37-55.
London, G. A. (1987, June). Homage to the Elders. *Biblical Archaeologist*, 70-74.
Long, A. A. (2002). *Epictetus, A Stoic and Socratic guide to life*. Oxford: Clarendon Press.
Lorblanchet, M. (1981). *Pech-Merle*. Cabrerets, France: Musee de Prehistorire.
Lorblanchet, M. (1988). *Art Prehistorique Du Quercy*. Toulouse: Fournie.
Luibheid, C. (1987). *Pseudo-Dionysius, the complete works*. New York: The Paulist Press.
Lucretius (1946). *On the Nature of Things* (Tr. C. E. Bennett). Roslyn, NY: Walter J. Black.

Lyman, R. (2003, Summer). 2002 NAPS Presidential Address: Hellenism and Heresy. *Journal of Early Christian Studies*, 11(2), 209-222.

McConnell, F. (1986). *The Bible and the narrative tradition.* New York: Oxford University Press.

McKechnie, P. (2001). *The First Christian Centuries.* Downers Grove, ILL: InterVarsity Press.

McKeon, R. (1947). *Introduction to Aristotle.* New York: The Modern Library.

Mack, B. L. (1995). *Who Wrote the New Testament? The Making of the Christian Myth.* San Francisco: HarperSanFrancisco.

MacMullen, R. (1984). *Christianizing the Roman Empire.* New Haven: Yale University Press.

Macmullen, R. & E. N. Lane (1992). *Paganism and Christianity 100-425 CE.* Minneapolis: Fortress Press.

Madigan, N. (2003, February 3). Professor's snub of creationists prompts U.S. Inquiry. *The New York Times*, A11.

Magill, F. N. (1990). *Masterpieces of World Philosophy.* New York: HarperCollins.

Malandra, W. W. (1983). *An introduction to ancient Iranian religion.* Minneapolis: University of Minnesota Press.

Mansel, H. L. (1875). The Gnostic heresies of the first and second centuries. London: John Murray.

Margalit, A. (2003, January 16). The suicide bombers. *The New York Review of Books*, 36-39.

Marshall (1989). Consciousness and Bose-Einstein Condensate. *New Ideas in Psychology*, 7, 73-83.

Mascaro, J. (1962). *The Bhagavad Gita.* New York: Penguin Books.

Mascaro, J. (1965). *The Upanishads.* New York: Penguin Books.

Massing, M. (2002, March 9). As rabbis face facts, Bible tales are wilting. *The New York Times*.

Martial. (1963). *Selected Epigrams.* (Trans. R. Humphries). Bloomington: Indiana University Press.

Maccoby, H. (1986). *The Myth-Maker, Paul and the Invention of Christianity.* New York: Harper & Row.

MacDonald, D. R. (2000). *The Homeric Epics and the Gospel of Mark.* New Haven, CT: Yale University Press.

MacDonald, D. R. (2003). *Does the New Testament Imitate Homer?* New Haven, CT: Yale University Press.

MacFarquar, N. (2003, January 3). A sect shuns lettuce and gives the devil his due. *The New York Times*, yne A4.

MacLeod, M. D. (1991). *Lucian, A selection.* Warminster, UK: Aris & Phillips.

McConnell, F. (1986). *The Bible and the narrative tradition.* New York: Oxford University Press.

McDowell, A. (1996). Daily Life in Ancient Egypt. *Scientific American*, 275 (6), 100-105.

McNamara, K. J. (1997). *Shapes of time, The evolution of growth and development.* Baltimore: The Johns Hopkins Press.

Manichaeism. Encyclopædia Britannica Online. http://search.eb.com/bol/topic?eu=51774&sctn=1&pm=1

Marcus, R. (trans). (1953). *Philo, Questions and Answers on Genesis.* Cambridge: Harvard University Press.

Margalit, A. (2003, October 9). After Strange Gods. *New York Review of Books*, L, 15, p. 29-32.

Margalit, A. & Buruma, I. (2002, January 17). Occidentalism. *The New York Review of Books*.

Martial. (1963). *Selected Epigrams.* (Trans. R. Humphries). Bloomington: Indiana University Press.

Maziarz, E. A. & Greenwood, T. (1968). *Greek Mathematical Philosophy.* New York: Barnes & Noble.

Max, D. T. (2003). Two cheers for Darwin. *The American Scholar*, 72(2),63-78.

Mead, G. R. S. (1960). *Fragments of a faith forgotten, The Gnostics, a contribution to the study of the origins of Christianity.* New Hyde Park, NY: University Books.
Meeks, W. A. (1983). *The First Urban Christians, The Social World of the Apostle Paul.* New Haven: Yale University Press.
Meinardus, O. F. A. (1973). *St. Paul in Greece.* Athens: Lycabettus Press.
Mellor, R. (1993). *Tacitus.* New York: Routledge.
Mendenhall, G. E. (1973). *The Tenth generation, The origins of the biblical tradition.* Baltimore: The Johns Hopkins University Press.
Mercatante, A.S. (1995). *Who's Who in Egyptian Mythology.* (2nd ed. by R. S. Bianchi). New York: Barnes & Noble.
Merenlahti, P. (2002). *Poetics for the Gospels? Rethinking Narrative Criticism.* New York: T&T Clark.
Merton, T. (1961). *New Seeds of Contemplation.* New York: New Directions Books.
Merton, T. (1948). *The Seven Story Mountain.* New York: Harcourt Brace.
Millard, A. (2000). How reliable is Exodus? *Biblical Archaeology Review*, 26(4), 51-57.
Miller, J. (1996). *God has Ninety-Nine names.* New York: Touchstone.
Mitchell, T. C. (1988). *Biblical Archaeology, Documents from the British Museum.* Cambridge: Cambridge University Press.
Momifliano, A. (1994). *Essays on Ancient and Modern Judaism.* Chicago: University of Chicago Press.
Moore, A. M. T. (1978). *The Neolithic of the Levant.* Unpublished PhD Dissertation, Oxford University, pp. 479-495.
Moore, R. (2002, July). The sad status of evolution education in American schools. *The Linnean*, 18(3), 26-34.
Moorhead, J. (1999). *Ambrose, Church and Society in the Late Roman World.* London: Longman.
Mullett, G. M. (1979). *Spider Woman Stories, Legends of the Hopi Indians.* Tucson, AZ: University of Arizona Press.
Murphy, C. (2004, March). The Next Testament. *Atlantic Monthly*, 293(2), 139-140.
Murphy, E. M. (2003). Being born female is dangerous to your health. *American Psychologist*, 58(3), 205-210.
Murphy, T. W. (2002). Lamanite Genesis, Genealogy, and Genetics. In Vogel D. and Metcalfe, B. L. (eds.). *American Apocrypha: Essays on the Book of Mormon.* Salt Lake City: Signature Books, 47–77.
Murray, G. (1946). *Greek Studies.* Oxford: The Clarendon Press.
Murray, G. (1934, 1907). *The Rise of the Greek Epic.* Oxford: Oxford University Press.
Murray, G. (1947, 1913). *Euripedes and His Age.* Oxford: Oxford University Press.
Myers, C. (1998). Kinship and Kingship, The Early Monarchy. In M. Coogan, *The Oxford History of the Biblical World.* New York: Oxford University Press, pp. 165 ff.
Neihardt, J. G. (ed). (1961). *Black Elk speaks, Being the life story of a holy man of the Oglala Sioux.* Lincoln: University of Nebraska Press.
Newman, J. H. (1890). *The Arians of the fourth century.* (6th Ed.). London: Longmans, Green and Co.
News scan (2001) Data points: A demon-haunted world. *Scientific American*, 285(3), 26.
Niebuhr, G. (2001, June 2). A rabbi's look at archaeology touches a nerve. *The New York Times*, A10.
Nietzsche, F. (1990). *Twilight of the Idols and The Anti-Christ.* NewYork: Penguin Books.
Nock, A.D. (1945) *Corpus Hermeticum.* Tome 1, Traites I-XII. Paris: Societe d'edition, Les Belles Lettres.
Norwich, J. J. (1988). *A Short History of Byzantium.* London: Penguin Books.
Noss, J. B. (1956). *Man's Religions.* New York: Macmillan.
Oates, J. (1986). *Babylon.* London: Thames and Hudson.

Oates, W. J. (1948). *Basic Writings of Saint Augustine*. Vol. 1 & 2. New York: Random House.
O'Brien, C. (1985). *The genius of the few, The story of those who founded the garden of Eden.* Wellingborough, UK: Turnstone Press.
O'Grady, J. (1985). *Early Christian Heresies*. New York: Barnes & Noble.
Ogg, O. (1983). *The 26 Letters*. New York: Van Nostrand.
Oldenburg, U. (1969). *The conflict between el and ba'al in canaanite religion*. Leiden: E. J. Brill.
Origen. (1965). Origen: *Contra Celsum*. (Tran. H, Chadwick). New York: Cambridge University Press.
Orr, H. A. (2003). What's not in your genes. *The New York Review of Books*, 50(13), 38-40.
Oulton, J. E. L. & Chadwick, H. (1954).*Alexandrian Christianity*. Philadelphia: Westminster Press.
Overbye, D. (2001, December 11). Cracking the cosmic code with a little help from Dr. Harking. *The New York Times*, D5.
Paine, S, W. (1961). *Beginning Greek*. New York: Oxford University Press.
Pagels, E. (1979). *The Gnostic gospels*. New York: Vintage Books.
Pagels, E. (1988). *Adam, Eve, and the Serpent*. New York: Random House.
Pagels, E. (2003). *Beyond Belief, The Secret Gospel of Thomas*. New York: Random House.
Parpola, S. (1997). *State Archives of Assyria*. Helsinki: Helsinki University Press.
Patai, R. (1986). *The Seed of Abraham, Jews and Arabs in contact and conflict.* Salt Lake City: University of Utah Press.
Patti, T. S. (1995). *Manuscripts of the Bible*. London: The British Library.
Pelikan, J. (1971*). The Christian Tradition, A History of the Development of Doctrine. Vol. 1 The Emergence of the Catholic Tradition (100-600).* Chicago: The University of Chicago Press.
Penella, R. J. (1979). *The Letters of Apollonius of Tyana*. Lugduni Batavorum: E. J. Brill.
Perry, P. (2003). *Jesus in Egypt, Discovering the Secrets of Christ's Childhood Years.* New York: Ballantine Books.
Petersen, A. R. (1998). *The royal god, Enthronement festivals in ancient Israel and Ugarit?* Sheffield, UK: Sheffield Academic Press.
Pettinato, G. (1981). *The Archives of Ebla, an empire enscribed in clay*. New York: Doubleday.
Pitard, W. T. (1998). Before Israel, Syria-Palestine in the Bronze Age. In Coogan, M. *The Oxford History of the Biblical World*. New York: Oxford University Press.
Plato. (1956). *The Works of Plato*. (Ed. I. Edman). New York: The Modern Library.
Plato (1944). *The Republic.* (tr. B. Jowett) New York: The Heritage Press.
Plato (1961). *The Collected Dialogues.* Princeton: Princeton University Press.
Plato (1994). *Symposium.* (Tr. R. Waterfield). Oxford: Oxford University Press.
Plotinus (1962). *The Enneads.* (Tr. S. MacKenna). London: Faber & Faber.
Plutarch (1932). *The Lives of the Noble Grecians and Romans.* New York: Modern Library.
Plutarch (1967). *Moralia.* (Trans. B. Einarson & P. H. Delacy). V. 14. Cambridge, MA: Harvard University Press.
Plutarch. (1969). *Moralia.* (Trans. F. H. Sandbach). V. 15. Cambridge: Harvard University Press.
Plutarch (1888). *Plutarch's Miscellanies and Essays.* (tr. & revised, W.W. Goodwin, V. 4). Boston: Little Brown and Co.
Podhoretz, N. (2002). *The Prophets, Who They Were, What They Are*. New York: The Free Press.
Poirier, J.C. (2003). General Reckoning in Hesiod and in the Pentateuch.*Journal of Near Eastern Studies*, 62(3), 193-199.
Pollan, M. (2001). The Botany of Desire, A plant's eye view of the world.New York: Random House.
Polybius (1960). *Polybius, The Histories.* V. 1.Cambridge: Harvard University Press.
Porter, R. (2004). *Flesh in the Age of Reason, The Modern Foundations of Body and Soul.* New York: W. W. Norton.

Powell, B. (1989). Why was the Greek Alphabet Invented? The Epigraphical Evidence. *Classical Antiquity*, 8 (2), 321-50.
Prabhavananda, S. & Manchester, F. (1975). *The Upanishads.* Hollywood, CA: Vedanta Press.
Pritchard, J. B. (1955, 1969). *Ancient Near Eastern Texts Relating to the Old Testament.* (2nd ed.). Princeton: Princeton University Press.
Prose, F. (2003). Genocide without apology, Parsing the Book of Exodus. *The American Scholar*, 72(2), 39-43.
Rania, D. T. (1990). *Philo, Alexandrian and Jew. Exegesis and Philosophy: Studies on Philo of Alexandria.* Variorum, Aldershot, 1-18.
Reade, J. (1991). *Mesopotamia.* London: The British Museum Press.
Redford, D. B. (1993). *Egypt, Canaan and Israel in ancient times.* Cairo: The American University in Cairo Press.
Reiner, E. (1991). First-Millennium Babylonian Literature. In Edwards, I. E. S., *The Cambridge Ancient History.* V. III, Part 2, Cambridge: Cambridge University Press.
Richards, R. J. (2002, October 13). The Evolutionary War. *The New York Times Book Review*, 9.
Ridley, M. (2002, May 8). Research that evolves from fossils to genes. *The Times* (London), 18.
Rilke, R. M. (1996). *Rilke's Book of Hours.* (Tr. Barrows, A. & Macy, J).New York: Riverhead Books.
Roberts, A. (1995). *Hathor Rising, The Serpent Power of Ancient Egypt.* Totnes, UK: Northgate Publishers.
Robinson, J. M., P. Hoffman, J. S. Kloppenborg, *The Sayings Gospel Q in Greek and English, with Parallels from the Gospels of Mark and Thomas.* Leuven: Peeters, 2001.
Robinson, J. M. (1986). The Gospels as Narrative. in F. McConnell, *The Bible and the Narrative Tradition.* New York: Oxford University Press, 1986, pp. 97-112.
Romer, J. (1981). *Valley of the Kings, Exploring the Tombs of the Pharaohs.* New York: Henry Holt.
Roquebert, M. (1988). *Cathar Religion.* Garonne, France: Editions Loubatieres.
Rosenberg, D. & Bloom, H. (1990). *The Book of J.* New York: Vintage Books.
Rosenblatt, J. P. & Sitterson, J. C. (1991). *Not in Heaven, Coherence and complexity in biblical narrative.* Bloomington: Indiana University Press.
Ross, N. W. (1966). *Three Ways of Asian Wisdom.* New York: Simon & Schuster.
Rossini, S. (1989). *Egyptian Hieroglyphics, How to Read and Write Them.* NewYork: Dover.
Rouse, W. H. D. (1956). *Great Dialogues of Plato.* New York: Mentor Book.
Rozen, S., Skaletsky, H., Marszalek, J. D., Minx, P. J., Cordum, H. S., Waterston, R. H., Wilson, R. K., & Page, D. C. (2003, June 19). Abundant gene conversion between arms of palindromes in human and ape Y chromosomes. *Nature* 423, 825–837.
Rudolph, K. (1978). *Mandaeism.* Leiden: E. J. Brill.
Russell, B. (1997, 1935). *Religion and Science.* New York: Oxford University Press.
Russell, B. (1955). *A History of Western Philosophy.* London: George Allen & Unwin.
Russell, B. (1967, 1932). *Education and the social order.* London: Unwin.
Russell, L. (2004). Drinking from the Penholder: Intentionality and Archaeological Theory. *Cambridge Archaeological Journal*, 14(1), 64-67.
Safire, W. (1992). The First Dissident, The book of Job in today's politics. New York: Random House.
Saggs, H. W. G. (1989). *Civilization Before Greece and Rome.* New Haven: Yale University Press.
Salamon, J. (2001, September 24). A stark explanation for mankind from an unlikely rebel. *The New York Times*, E5.
Salmon, E. T. (1968). *A History of the Roman World, 30 BC to AD138.* London: Metheun & Co.
Sallust. (1992). *Sallust, The Histories.* (Tr. P. McGushin) V. 1. Oxford: The Clarendon Press.
Salmon, E. T. (1968). *A History of the Roman World, 30 BC to AD 138.* London: Metheun.
Sandars, N. K. (1972). *The Epic of Gilgamesh.* New York: Penguin Books.

Sandas, N. K. (1971). Poems of Heaven and Hell from Ancient Mesopotamia. London: Penguin.
Sanders, S. (2004) Performance Utterances and Divine Language in Ugaritic. *Journal of Near Eastern Studies*, 63(3), 161-182.
Sanders, E. P. (2003). Who was Jesus? *The New York Review of Books*. 50(6), 49-51.
Sanders, E. P. (2001). In Quest of the Historical Jesus. *The New York Review of Books*, 48(18), 33-36.
Sandmel, S. (1979). *Philo of Alexandria, An introduction.* New York: Oxford University Press.
Sanneh, L. (2001, September 23). Faith and the secular state. *The New York Times*, A17.
Scafa, P. N. (1999). The Scribes of Nuzi. In Owen, D. I. & Wilhelm, G. Studies in the *Civilization and Culture of the Nuzi and the Hurrians.* V. 10. Bethesda, MD: CDL Press.
Schaeffer, C. F. A. (1939). *The Cuneiform Texts of Ras Shamra-Ugarit.* London: The British Academy.
Scheidel, W. (1998). Quantifying the Sources of Slaves in the Early Roman Empire. *The Journal of Roman Studies*, 87, 156-169.
Schmandt-Besserat, D. (1992). From counting to cuneiform. Austin: University of Texas Press.
Schmidt, P. (1955). The Ancient Mysteries in the Society of Their Time, Their Transformation and Most Recent Echoes. In Campbell, J. (ed.). *The Mysteries, Papers from the Eranos Yearbooks.* Princeton: Princeton University Press, Bollingen Series. V.2. pp. 93-118.
Schmidt, K. L. (2002). *The Place of the Gospels in the General History of Literature.* Columbia, SC: University of South Carolina Press.
Schopenhauer, A. (1998). *The World as Will and Idea.* London: J. M. Dent.
Schowalter, D. N. (1998). Churches in Context, The Jesus Movement in the Roman Word. In M. Coogan, *The Oxford History of the Biblical World.* New York: Oxford University Press.
Segal, R. A. (1986). *The Poimandres as Myth, Scholarly Theory and Gnostic Meaning.* Berlin: Mouton de Gruyter.
Seneca (1969). *Letters from a Stoic.* London: Penguin Books.
Seneca (1997). *Dialogues and letters.* London: Penguin Books.
Senner, W. M. (1989). *The Origins of Writing.* Lincoln: University of Nebraska Press.
Seymour-Smith, M. (1996). *Gnosticism, The path of inner knowledge.* San Francisco: HarperSanFrancisco.
Sharpes, D. K. (2002). *Advanced Educational Foundations for Teachers, The History, Philosophy and Culture of Schooling.* New York: Routledge.
Sharpes, D. K. (2000). Book Review: *The Feeling of What Happens*, by Damasio, A. Harcourt Brace, 1999, and The Astonishing Hypothesis, by Francis Crick, Charles Scribner, 1994 in *British Journal of Educational Psychology*, 71, 343-44.
Sheed, F. J. (1957). *Theology for Beginners.* New York: Sheed & Ward.
Sherk, R. K. (1988). *The Roman Empire: Augustus to Hadrian.* Cambridge: Cambridge University Press, 1988.
Shorter, A. W. (1979, 1939). *The Egyptian Gods.* London: Routledge and Kegan Paul.
Shun, K-L. (1997). *Mencius and early Chinese thought.* Stanford: Stanford University Press.
Sider, D. (1981). *The Fragments of Anaxagoras.* Meisenheim: Verlag.
Skaletsky, H. *et al.* (2003, June 19). The male-specific region of the human Y chromosome is a mosaic of discrete sequence classes. *Nature* 423, 825 – 837.
Smith, M. S. (2002). *The Early History of God, Yahweh and the Other Deities in Ancient Israel.* (2nd ed.) Grand Rapids, MI: William B. Eerdmans.
Smith, A. (1974). *Porphyry's place in the Neoplatonic tradition, A study in Post-Plotinian Neoplatonism.* The Hague: Martinus Nijhoff.
Smith, C. (2003, April 9). Former captives recall horror of Hussein's prisons. *The New York Times*, B2.
Smith, D. (2003, June 14). The heresy that saved a skeptic. *The New York Times*, A17.

Soleki, R. S.(1971). *Shanidar, The first flower people.* New York: Alfred Knopf.
Sollberger, E. (1971). *The Babylonian legend of the flood.* London: British Museum Publications.
Solmsen, F. (1995, 1949). *Hesiod and Aeschylus.* Ithaca, NY: CornellUniversity Press.
Solomon, R. C. & Higgins, K. M. (1996). *A Short History of Philosophy.* New York: Oxford University Press.
Solon. http://theosophy.org/tlodocs/teachers/Solon.htm.
Speidel, M. P. (1980). *Mithras-Orion, Greek hero and Roman army god.* Leiden: E. J. Brill.
Spence, L. (1916). *Myths and legends of Babylonia and Assyria.* London: George G. Harrap.
Spencer, R. (2000). *Islam unveiled, Disturbing questions about the world's fastest growing faith.* San Francisco: Encounter Books.
Spindler, K. (1994). *The Man in the Ice.* New York: Harmony Books.
Stack, P. F. (2003, August 16). Exiles in Zion. *The Salt Lake Tribune.* C1.
Starr, C. G. (1973). *Early man, prehistory and the civilizations of the ancient near east.* London: Oxford University Press.
Stead, C. (1994). *Philosophy in Christian Antiquity.* Cambridge: Cambridge University Press.
Stendahl, K. (1984). *Meanings, The Bible as document and guide.* Philadelphia: Fortress Press.
Stern, E. (2001). Pagan Yahwism, The folk religion of ancient Israel. *Biblical Archaeology Review,* 27(3), 21-29.
Sternberg, M. (1987). *The Poetics of Biblical Narrative, Ideological Literature and the Drama of Reading.* Bloomington: Indiana university Press.
Sternberg, M. (1998). *Hebrews Between Cultures, Group Portraits and National Literature.* Bloomington: Indiana university Press.
Stetkevych, J. (1996). *Muhammad and the golden bough, Reconstructing Arabian myth.* Bloomington: Indiana University Press.
Stille, A. (2002, March 2). Radical new views of Islam and the origins of the Koran. *The New York Times,* Arts.
Stolberg, S. G. (2001, December 18). Controversy re-ignites over stem cells and clones. *The New York Times,* D1.
"Storm over the Bone Box." (2003). *Biblical Archaeological Review,* 29(5), 27.
Strauss, D. F. (1972, 1840). *The life of Jesus critically examined.* 4th Ed. (Ed. P. C. Hodgson, Tr. George Eliot). Mifflintown, PA: Sigler Press.
Sullivan, A. (2001, October 7). This is a religious war. *The New York Times Magazine,* 44-53.
Szulc, T. (2001). Abraham, Journey of faith. *National Geographic,* 200(6), 90-129.
Tactitus (tr. K. Wellesley). (1995). *The Histories.* London: Penguin Books.
Talas, L. (1987). *The Late Neolithic of the Tisza Region.* Budapest: Szolnok.
Tarnas, R. (1991). *The Passion of the Western Mind, Understanding the Ideas That Have Shaped our World View.* New York: Ballantine.
Tattersall, I. (1997). Out of Africa Again...and Again. *Scientific American,* 276(4), 60-67.
Tattersall, I. (2001). How we came to be human. *Scientific American,* 285(6), 57-63.
Tattersall, I. (1998). *Becoming Human, Evolution and human uniqueness.* New York: Harcourt Brace.
Tertullian (1790). *Q. Septimii Florentis Tertulliani Opera Omnia.* Wirceburgi: In Officina Libraria Staheliana.
Thiede, C. P. (1992). The Earliest Gospel Manuscript? The Qumran Papyrus 7Q5 and its Significance for New Testament Studies. Carlisle, UK: ThePaternoster Press.
Thousand Years of the Bible, A. (1991). Malibu, CA: J. Paul Getty Museum.
Thucydides (1880). *A History of the Peloponnesian War.* New York: Harper and Brothers.
Thucydides. (1831). *Thucydides.* (Trans. W. Smith). Vol. 1. London: A. J. Valpy.
Tillich, P. (1955). *Biblical Religion and the Search for ultimate Reality.* Chicago: University of Chicago Press.
Tod, M. (1957). Sidelights on Greek philosophers. *Journal of Hellenic Studies,* v. 77, 137.

Tooby, J. (2002, October 6). The greatest Englishman since Newton. The *New York Times Book Review*. 12.
Townsend, J. W. (2003). Reproductive behavior in the context of global population. *American Psychologist*, 58(3), 197-204.
Tsagarakis, O. (1977). *Nature and Background of Major Concepts of Divine Power in Homer*. Amsterdam: B. R. Grunder Publishing Co.
Treasures of Tutankhamen (1976). New York: The Metropolitan Museum of Art.
Trinkaus, E., Moldovan, S., Milota, S., Bîlgar, A., Sarcina, L., Athreya, S., Bailey, S. E., Rodrigo, R., Mircea, G., Higham, T., Ramsey, C. B., & van der Plicht, J. An early modern human from the Petera cu Oase, Romania. *Proceedings of the National Academy of Sciences*, 2003, 100: 11231-11236.
Tropper, A. (2004, May). The Fate of Jewish Historiography After the Bible:A New Interpretation. *History and Theory*, 43, 179-97.
Tubb, J. N. (1998). *Canaanites*. London: British Museum Press.
Tubb, J. N. & Chapman, R. L. (1990). *Archaeology and the Bible*. London: British Museum
Turcan, R. (1975). *Mithras Platonicus, Recherches sur Hellenisation Philosophique de Mithra*. Leiden: E. J. Brill.
Ulansey, D. (1994). Solving the Mithraic mysteries. *Biblical Archaeology Review*, 20(5), 40-53.
Ulansey, D. (1989). *The Origins of the Mithraic mysteries, Cosmology and salvation in the ancient world*. New York: Oxford University Press.
Urantia Book, The. (no author), (1955). Chicago, ILL: Urantia Foundation.
Van Buskirk, W. R. (1929). *The saviors of mankind*. New York: Macmillan.
Van Doren, C. (1991). *A History of Knowledge, The Pivotal Events, People, and Achievements of World History*. New York: Ballantine Books.
Van Seters, J. (1983). *In Search of History, historiography in the ancient world and the origins of biblical history*. New Haven: Yale University Press.
Vermaseren, M. J. (1963). *Mithras, the secret god*. New York: Barnes & Noble.
Vermes, G. (1975). *The Dead Sea scrolls in English*. New York: Penguin Books.
Vermes, G. (1983). *Jesus and the World of Judaism*. London: SCM Press.
Vermes, G. (2003). *Jesus in His Jewish Context*. Minneapolis: Fortress Press.
Vernant, J-P. (1982). *The Origins of Greek Thought*. Ithaca, NY: Cornell University Press.
Veyne, P. (1988). *Did the Greeks believe in their own Myths?* (Trans. P. Wissing). Chicago: University of Chicago Press.
Virgil (1983). *The Aeneid*. New York: Random House.
Viorst, M. (1994). *The Great Documents of Western Civilization*. New York: Barnes & Noble.
Voltaire (1972). *Philosophical dictionary*. New York: Viking Penguin.
Voltaire (1956). *Candide and other writings*. New York: The Modern Library.
Voltaire (1966). *Candide or optimism*. New York: W. W. Norton.
Voltaire (1940). The White Bull. In Voltaire, *The best known works of Voltaire*. New York: The Book League, 96-118.
Voltaire (1940). *The best known works of Voltaire*. New York: The Book League.
Von Balthasar, H. U., *Origen, Spirit and Fire, A Thematic Anthology of His Writings*. Washington DC: The Catholic University Press, 1984.
Wade, N. (2003, May 6). World's farmers sowed languages as well as seeds. *The New York Times*, D3.
Wade, N. (2001, December 18). In tiny cells, glimpses of body's master plan. *The New York Times*, D1.
Wade, N. (2002a, September 17). In nature vs. nurture, A voice for nature. *The New York Times*, D1.
Wade, N. (2002b, November 12b). Geneticists track more of earliest humans' first itineraries. *The New York Times*, D1.
Walker, A. T. (1907). *Caesar's Gallic Wars*. Chicago: Scott, Foresman.

Waley, A. (1971). *The Analects of Confucius* (6th ed.). London: George Allen & Unwin.
Walters, V. J. (1974).The Cult of Mithras in the Roman Provinces of Gaul.Leiden: E.J. Brill.
Waters, F. (1977, 1963). *Book of the Hopi*. New York: Penguin Books USA.
Watkins, C. (2002). Homer and Hittite Revisited II. In Yener, K. A. Hoffner, H. A. *Recent Developments in Hittite Archaeology and History*. Winona Lake, IN: Eisenbrauns. pp. 167-176.
Weeden, T. J. (1971). *Mark, Traditions in Conflict*. Philadelphia: Fortress Press.
Weeks, J. (1971). *The Pyramids*. Cambridge: Cambridge University Press.
Weeks, K. (1998). *The Lost Tomb*. New York: William Morrow and Co.
Wellesley, K. (1995). *Tacitus, the Histories*. London: Penguin Books.
Westfall, R. (1993). *The Life of Isaac Newton*. Cambridge: Cambridge University Press.
White, N. (1983). *Handbook of Epictetus*. Indianapolis: Hackett Publishing.
White, T. Berhane, A., Degusta, D., Gilbert, H., Richards, G. D., Suwa, G.F., & Howell, F. C. (2003, June 12). Pleistocene Homo sapiens from Middle Awash, Ethiopia. *Nature* 423, 742 – 747.
White, J. E. M. (1970). *Ancient Egypt, Its Culture and History*. New York: Dover Publications.
Wiles, M. (1996). *Archetypal Heresy, Arianism Through the Centuries*. Oxford: Clarendon Press.
Wilford, J. N. (2001, December 2). Artifacts in Africa suggest an earlier modern human. *The New York Times*, A1.
Wilford, J. N. (2002a, August 6). Skulls found in Africa and in Europe challenge theories of human origins. *The New York Times Science*.
Wilford, J. N. (2002b, October 23). Jesus' inscription on stone may be earliest ever found. *The New York Times*, A12.
Willard, H. F. (2003, June 19). Genome biology: Tales of the Y chromosome. *Nature* 423, 810 – 813.
Williams, S. & Friell, G. (1994). *Theodosius, The Empire at bay*. New Haven: Yale University Press.
Williams, R. (2001, 1987). *Arius, heresy & tradition*. Grand Rapids, MI: William B. Eerdmans.
Wilson, D. S. (2002). *Darwin's Cathedral, Evolution, Religion and the Nature of   Society*. Chicago: University of Chicago Press.
Wilson, I. (1984). *Jesus, The Evidence*. London: Pan Books.
Wilson, R. M. (1958). *The Gnostic problem, A study of relations between Hellenistic Judaism and the Gnostic heresy*. London: A. R. Mowbray.
Wilson, R. M. (1968). *Gnosis and the New Testament*. Philadelphia: Fortress Press.
Wilson, E. O. (1978). *On Human Nature*. Cambridge, MA: Harvard University Press.
Wilson, E. O. (1998). *Consilience, The Unity of Knowledge*. New York: Knopf.
Winsten, J. (1999). *Moses Meets Israel, The Origins of One God*. Boston, MA: Rumford Press.
Weber, M. (1952). *Ancient Judaism*. Glencoe: ILL: The Free Press.
Weinberg, S. (2001). The future of science and the universe. *The New York Review of Books*, 48(18), 58-63.
Weitzman, S. (1997). *Song and story in biblical narrative, The history of a literary convention in ancient Israel*. Bloomington: Indiana University Press.
Westacott, E. (2004). Americans Don't Really Believe in the Ten Commandments. *The Humanist*, 64(1), 7-9.
Westfall, R. (1993). *The Life of Isaac Newton*. Cambridge: Cambridge University Press.
Williams, D. H. (1995). *Ambrose of Milan and the End of the Nicene-Arian Conflicts*. Oxford: Clarendon Press.
Wills, G. (2003). *Saint Augustine's Sin*. New York: Viking.
Wolfson, H. A. (1947, 1982). *Philo, Foundations of religious philosophy in Judaism, Christianity and Islam*. Vols. I & II. Cambridge, MA: Harvard University Press.
Woolley, C.L. (1965). *The Sumerians*. New York: W. W. Norton.
Wong, K. (2005, February). The Littlest Human. *Scientific American*, 292(2), 56-65.

Wood, M. (1985). *In Search of the Trojan War*. New York: New American Library.
Woods, F. E. (1994). *Water and Storm Polemics against Baalism in the Deuteronomic History*. New York: Peter Lang.
Wooley, C. L. (1965). *The Sumerians*. New York: W. W. Norton.
www.fordham.edu/halsall/ancient/philo-creation.html.
www.webcom.com/~gnosis/library/hermes1.html
Xenophon, (no date). *The Education of Cyrus* (Tr. H.G. Dakyns). London: J. M. Dent.
Yadin, Y. (1957). *The Message of the Scrolls*. New York: Touchstone.
Yartz, F. J. (2004). Myth, Knowledge and Homer. *The Ancient World*, 34(1), 83-89.
Yurco, F. J. (1990, September/October). 3,200-Year-Old Picture of Israelites Found in Egypt. *Biblical Archaeological Review*, 21-38.
Zaehner, R. C. (1956). *The teachings of the magi, A compendium of Zoroastrian beliefs*. New York: Oxford University Press.
Zaehner, R. C. (1962). *Hinduism*. New York: Oxford University Press.
Zernicke, K. (2002, August 23). Georgia school board requires balance of Evolution and Bible. *The New York Times*, A8.
Zielinski, T. (1926, 1975). *The religion of ancient Greece*. (Translation from Polish by George R Noyes). Chicago: Ares Publishers.
Zimmer, C. (2001). How old is it? *National Geographic*, 200(3), 78-101.
Zimmer, C. (2003, March 2). Adam's family. *The New York Times Book Review*, 27.
Zimmermann, F. (1979). *The Aramaic Origin of the Four Gospels*. New York: KTAV Publishing House.
Zoroaster. (1963). *The Hymns of Zarathustra*. (Tr. J. Duchesne-Guillemin). Boston: Beacon Press.

INDEX

Aaron 113
Abel 67, 91, 93 ff.
Abimelech 125, 126, 131, 139
Abraham 2, 4, 14, 17, 24, 27, 32, 47, 58, 112, 121 ff., 139, 174
Abydos 84, 95, 153
Academus 223
Accidents 297
Achilles 4, 6, 24, 27, 49, 58, 88, 137, 210, 219, 284, 297, 322
Acts of the Apostles 29, 30, 35, 68, 214, 215, 259, 262, 274, 281 ff.
Ada 61
Adam 2, 15, 17, 82 ff., 93, 111
Adeodatus 312
Adonai 42
Adonis 18, 56, 57, 82, 214
Aelia Capitolina 266
Aeneas 260
Aeneid 211
Aeschylus 3, 47, 54, 79, 124, 140, 204, 212
Aesop 23
Aetis 306
Agamemnon 24, 124, 283
Agar 125, 129, 137
Agenor 202
Augustus (see Octavian)
Ahriman 65, 84, 85
Ahura Mazda 64-65, 66-69, 88
Akhenaten 35, 60, 147, 158, 164 ff., 171
Akkadian 3, 18, 21, 32, 49, 50, 53, 54, 61, 75, 89, 130, 165, 200
Albigensian 300, 301
Aleppo Codex 38
Alexander 22, 24, 35, 48, 65, 265
Alice in Wonderland 23
Allah 167, 298
Allegory 4, 12, 18, 25, 226, 290, 307, 316
Allusions 6
Amarna 21, 60. 147, 165, 166
Ambrose 290, 295, 312
Amesbury Archer 74
Ammianus Marcellinus 26, 273
Amorites 39, 46, 59, 60, 81, 102, 122, 126
Amos 28, 169
Amphion 195

Amun 44, 123, 146, 147, 177
Amru 307
Analects 5
An 57, 97, 105
Ananias 262
Anata 86
Anaxagoras 16, 50, 51, 213, 227
Anaximander 5, 31
Andromache 203, 283
Andromeda 18, 19
Ankh 167, 170, 302
Anquetil-Duperron, Abraham 64
Antaeus 245
Antioch 30, 231, 265
Antiochus 212
Anu 97, 105
Anubis 94
Aphrodite 18, 49, 61, 196
Apis 172
Apollinarianism 295
Apollonius 265
Aprippa
Apollinarius 218
Apollo 51, 170, 202, 204-05, 215, 291, 315
Apuleius, Lucius 216
Apsu 49, 75
Aquinas, Thomas 218, 295, 299, 315, 324
Aramaic 21. 38, 54, 200, 261
Arameans 5, 122
Archelaus 370
Argonauts 156
Ariadne 136
Arianism 275, 294, 307, 310
Arjuna 25
Aristeus 204, 207
Aristobolus 12
Aristophanes 19, 201, 235
Aristotle 5, 16, 206, 218, 235, 252, 295, 297, 314, 324
Arius 210, 294, 297, 299, 304 ff., 316
Ark of the Covenant 27, 39, 40, 88, 112, 175, 176
Arminianism 295
Arrian 186
Artapanus 12
Artaxerxes 48
Aruru 89, 93, 137
Asceticism 35

Asclepius 140, 204, 214, 322
Asherah 56, 60
Ashkelon 173
Ashur 88
Assurbanipal 21, 50, 56, 75, 89
Ashurasirpal 21, 81
Assyrian 18, 19, 27, 45-47, 54, 56
Astarte (Ishtar) 18, 285
Astyages
Aten 159, 165, 320
Athanasius 286, 299, 308 ff.
Athene (Athena) 126, 201, 205, 220
Athens 5, 23, 49, 51, 162, 192, 212, 215, 223, 289
Atlas 251-52
Atrahasis 1, 50, 73, 92, 105-107
Attis 57, 82, 214
Augustine 214, 218, 219, 233, 252, 296, 300, 312 ff.
Avesta 8, 11, 12, 66
BA 145, 218
Baal 7, 43, 44, 57-61, 112, 159, 173, 175, 205, 213, 285, 320
Baalbek 44
Babel 118 ff.
Babylon 23, 37, 46, 48, 49, 75
Babylonian 5, 18, 21, ff., 43, 46, 50, 54-56, 118, 124
Bacchus 81, 201, 213, 217
Baptism 67
Bar Kochba 266
Bata 77, 169
Batu cave 54
Benjamin 150
Beowulf 14
Bethel 144
Bethlehem 54, 68, 194, 244
Bhagavad Gita 5, 12, 25, 254
Bilhah 125
Bion of Smyna 214
Blake, William 255
Boccachio 14
Bodi tree 82
Bonaventure 255
Book of Amos 183
Book of Daniel 12, 22, 44, 169, 237, 266, 272
Book of the Dead 171, 194
Book of Esther 18, 34
Book of Ezekiel 22
Book of Job 67, 90
Book of Jonah 19

Book of Joshua 39
Book of Jubilees 34
Book of Judith 34
Book of Judges 60
Book of Kings 26, 46, 55, 237
Book of Maccabees 40
Book of Mormon 12, 25
Book of Revelations 22, 70, 160, 195, 213, 247, 256, 274
Book of Solomon (see Songs of Songs)
Book of the Dead 1
Book of Zechariah 22
British Library 41
British Museum 3, 21, 81, 105
Bronze age 16, 20, 22, 28, 38, 39, 47, 53, 57, 112, 131 ff., 149
Buddha 5, 82, 86, 223, 299
Buddhists 8, 11
Buto 84
Bull 61, 70, 121, 174 ff.
Bundahishn 84, 85
Byblos 37
Caduceus 85, 86, 204
Caesar 26, 183, 194, 226
Cain 67, 91, 93 ff.
Caliban 137
Caligula 192, 267, 270
Callimachus 211
Calypso 195, 251, 323
Cambyses 35, 46, 93, 100, 140, 237, 238
Campbell, Joseph 23
Cana 197
Canaanite 3, 17 ff., 43, 45, 47, 54, 58, 59, 63, 74, 118. 128, 132, 134, 172, 285
Capernaum 197
Carpenter 197
Castor 93, 100 ff.
Catal Huyuk 43, 95 ff.
Cathars 300
Cato 183, 267
Catullus 211
Celsus 284, 288 ff.
Ceres 18
Cervantes 14,
Chaldean
Chanaan 115
Chaos 74, 75, 213
China 20
Cherubim 3, 56, 59, 81, 88
Chosen People 46
Christianity 259 ff.
Chronicles 14

Chryses 17
Circumcision 27, 62, 112, 128, 134 ff.
158, 171, 261
City of God 313
Ci Xi 86
Claudius 265, 269
Clement of Alexandria 77, 228, 231 ff.,
249, 252, 311
Clytemnestra 124, 204
Code of Hammurabi 3, 27, 129, 138, 320
Codex Sinaiticus 41
Codex Vaticanus 41
Colosseum 292
Commodus 244
Concubinage 129, 312
Confessions 312
Confucius 5, 223
Constans 303, 306, 309
Constantine 50, 259, 272, 291 ff., 303, 305
Constantinus 303
Constantius 303, 306, 308-10
Corinthians 263
Corpus Hermeticum 228, 251, 320
Council of Arles 309
Countil of Antioch 308
Council of Ariminium 295, 309
Council of Chalcedon 253, 296, 298
Council of Constantinople 296, 305, 306, 308
Council of Ephesus 297
Council of Nicaea 5, 206, 292, 294, 305, 308
Council of Nicomedia 306
Council of Serdica 308
Council of Sirmium 306, 309
Council of Trent 297
Council of Tyre 305, 306, 308
Covenant, 111, 123 ff.
Crito 186, 200
Cumae 19, 54, 238
Cuneiform 20, 75, 89
Cupid 196
Cybele 54, 56
Cyclops 240, 323
Cyril 298, 299
Cyrus 46, 48, 64, 130, 140, 169, 194, 196,
202, 212, 237 ff., 260, 322
Dagan 59, 60
Daimones
Danae 196
Daphne 57
Darius 35, 46, 64, 194

Dark Night of the Soul 249
Damascus 61, 133, 262
Darwin, Charles 31
David 5, 46
Dead Sea 38, 70, 131, 190
Dead Sea Scrolls 11, 21, 41, 70, 190, 191,
203, 259, 260, 271, 283, 323
Deification 192 ff.
Delphi 19, 54, 84, 204, 238
Demeter 57, 121, 213, 216-17
Demiurge 253
Democritus 237
Democracy 164
Descartes, Rene 8, 298
Destiny 57, 58
Deuteronomy 27, 33, 34, 49, 63, 122, 166,
170, 182, 301, 320, 321
Diana 24, 213
Dibon 158
Didymus the Blind 41
Diocletian 272, 284
Diogenes Laertius 197
Dionysius 193, 204, 213, 215, 217
Diopeithes 51
Dioscuri (see Castor & Pollux) 101
Djoser 84
Docetism 252
Domitian 186, 192, 268, 269
Donatism 315
Doomed Prince 156
Dushara 113
Draco 162
Dravidian 80
Dreams 140 ff., 149-50, 196, 238
Ea 105, 106, 108
Eabani 137, 138
Easter
Ebionites 208, 209, 252, 275, 294, 298
Ebla 1, 6, 45, 58, 74, 75, 282-83
Ecclesiastes 212
Echidna 15
Eddy, Mary Baker 319
Eden 14, 59, 75 ff.
Edict of Milan 292
Edomites 113
Egeria 212, 214
Egypt 145 ff.
Egyptian Book of the Dea 42
Ehohim 42, 43, 58, 59
Eleusian 215 ff.
Elohist 34
Einkorn 39

El 42, 50, 59, 60, 159, 175, 205
Elamites
Eleusis 54
Elijah 277
Emmer 39
Empedocles 50, 198, 204
Endiku 49, 89-91, 93, 94, 137, 148
Enlil 57, 61, 75, 91, 94, 105, 148, 320
Enki 57
Enlightenment 289
Enos 98, 99
Enuma Elish 1,3, 49, 55, 75 ff., 195
Ephesians 216, 283
Epic of Gilgamesh 1, 3, 8, 11, 14, 15, 34, 49, 50, 53, 76, 87, 89, 97, 100, 103, 105, 115, 137, 321
Epicurus 182
Epicureanism 183
Epictetus 181-83, 186, 187-88, 225 ff., 299
Eratosthenes 211
Erishkigal 57, 73
Eritrea 175-76
Esau 127, 128, 137 ff.
Esras 88
Eschatology 182, 191, 196, 276, 302
Essence 298, 303
Essenes 70, 182, 184, 189, 190 ff., 208, 248, 267
Eucharist 216, 243, 263, 300
Eunomians 295
Euripedes 3, 37, 47, 51, 61, 63, 91, 124, 132, 181, 205, 212, 231, 233, 235, 301, 313
Europa 136, 197, 214
Eusebius 186, 231, 290-93, 304, 308
Ethnocentrism 45 ff.
Eutyches 297, 299
Eve 83 ff., 93
Excommunication
Existence
Exodus 3, 12, 27, 34, 43, 47, 155 ff.
Ezekiel 22, 47, 58, 201
Ezra 34, 35, 44, 48, 67, 159, 237
Faith 31, 291, 295, 306, 314, 316, 317, 319, 324-25
Felix 270
Figs 187 ff.
Fire 157, 229, 246
Florus 271
Fourth Eclogue 196
Gaea (Gaia) 61, 245

Galba 193
Gallic Wars 26
Gamaliel 30
Garuda 88
Gathas 66, 67
Genesis 1,3,4, 12-15, 18, 21, 25, 34, 37, 42-47, 61, 67, 73-75, 101, 105, 117, 120, 122, 124, 126, 151 ff., 321
Gerada 139
Gethsemane 193, 220
Ghost Dance 254
Gibbon, Edward 26
Gilgamesh 1, 3, 21, 24, 49, 87, 90, 94, 101, 106, 108, 122, 138, 153, 322
Gita Govinda 55
Gnosticism 2, 35, 208, 231, 247 ff., 264, 291
Gnostic 8, 11, 16, 20, 77, 218, 233, 263, 293, 311, 321
Gnostic gospels 189
Golden Ass 14, 216
Golden Calf 172 ff.
Golden Fleece 27, 121
Golan 132, 197
Good Shepherd 69
Gordon, Cyrus 35
Gospel of Thomas 226, 247
Gospels 1,7, 273
Gratian 268
Greek Orthodox Church 41
Guru Granth Sahib 71
Habakkuk 34
Hadad 60
Hades 61, 170, 205, 207, 232
Hadrian 225, 266
Hagar 125
Hammurabi 130, 159 ff.
Hanina ben Dosa 195, 203, 277
Halo 200 ff.
Hanukkah 190
Haoma 70
Haram 132, 140, 141
Har Karkom 157
Harappan 79
Harpargus
Hasmonean
Hathor 171, 172, 200
Hazor 81
Hebron 58
Hecataeus 26
Hector 4,6, 27, 181, 202, 210, 219, 283, 322

Hecuba 137, 203
Helen 203, 221
Henoch 103, 104
Hera 49, 81, 214
Heraclitus 5, 31, 50, 212, 227, 229
Herculaneum 22, 197
Hercules 18, 19, 81, 84, 121, 122, 125, 169, 181, 195, 205, 215, 291, 297
Heresiarchs 304, 305
Hermes 86, 167, 170, 198, 210, 219, 299
Herod 155, 199, 267, 269
Herodotus 1, 26-28, 31, 35, 37, 46, 65, 84, 100, 118, 123, 140-41, 152, 196, 207, 237, 238, 260
Hesiod 15, 54, 61, 74, 76, 92, 117, 183, 185, 190, 285
Hesperides 81
Hethite 139
Hieroglyphics 22, 25
Hildegard 250
Hincks, Edward 22
Hindu 8, 11, 12, 71, 145, 254, 313, 319
Hippocrates 31
Hippolytus 61, 91, 301, 313
Historiography 2,
Hittites 17, 21, 43, 47, 59, 118, 154, 158, 172, 240
Holy Spirit (Ghost) 30, 68, 195, 201, 283, 306
Homer 19, 27, 28, 30, 34, 36, 49, 54, 88, 89, 92, 118, 126, 135, 156, 169, 190, 202, 215, 235, 310
Homoians 294
Homoousian 295, 306, 308
Honi 277
Horace 183, 185, 190, 203
Horus 61, 84, 95, 155, 168, 171, 205, 296
Hosea 158, 169
Hubbard, L. Ron 255
Humbala 94, 97, 98, 102
Hurrian 59, 74, 122
Hypatia 298
Ianna 14, 56, 57
Idea (Platonic) 224, 229, 314
Iliad 3, 6, 14, 35, 49, 88, 155, 197, 201, 214, 219, 283
Immortality 66, 68, 69, 89, 121, 130, 145, 171, 215, 218, 284, 289, 293, 302
India 25, 86
Iphigeneia 124
Iraeneus 249, 252, 254, 284 ff., 311, 316

Iron age 16, 28, 38, 39, 44-46, 57, 147, 149
Isaac 5, 17, 123, 124, 126, 135, 139 ff.
Isaiah 28, 48, 55, 66, 169, 174, 196, 237
Ishtar 14, 18, 49, 56, 81, 89, 97, 98
Isis 17, 54, 56, 61, 94 ff., 214, 296
Islam 60, 71, 319, 321, 324
Ismael 125, 129, 135
Israel 14, 17, 21, 33, 35, 40, 43, 44, 47, 63, 149
Jacob 4, 60, 127 ff., 137 ff., 140 ff., 151
Jainism 5
Jason 27, 100, 121, 156
Jebef Attuf 113
Jehovah 42
Jefferson, Thomas 26, 183
Jericho 38-40
Jeremiah 183
Jerome 41, 302
Jerusalem 4, 18, 23, 37, 38, 40, 48, 81, 148, 175, 185, 208, 263, 264, 266
Jesus 6, 11, 56, 65, 67, 69, 127, 141, 167, 169, 174, 181 ff., 219 ff., 237 ff., 259, 260
Job 4, 17, 59, 67, 79
John 275 ff.
John of the Cross 235, 249, 250
John the Baptist 190, 198, 208, 238, 252, 267, 299
Jonah 18
Joppa 18, 19
Joseph 123, 137 ff, 149 ff.
Josephus 26, 169, 170, 181, 190, 260, 271, 272
Joshua 4, 5, 27, 37, 39, 40, 54, 58, 112, 158
Journey to the West 135
Juda 148 ff.
Judah 18, 33, 35, 39, 44, 48
Judaism 1, 2, 9, 12, 13, 65, 70, 191, 199, 214, 282
Judas Galileus 267
Julia Berenice 269
Julian 245, 310, 311
Jung, Carl 24
Jupiter 100, 288, 301
Justinian 162, 223, 241, 289
Justin Martyr 230 ff.
Juvencus 273
KA 145, 218
Kaaba 24
Kabbala 255
Karma 71

Karnak 24, 146, 177
Kenyon, Kathleen 39, 102
Ketef Hinnon 38
King James version 42
Kingdom of God 276
Kingu 76
Knossos 83, 131
Koran 8, 123, 307
Kot Diji 79-80
Kraters 197
Krishna 55, 254
Kronos 59, 61, 62, 285
Laban 60, 125, 127, 137, 141 ff.
Lakshmi 88
Lamech 102, 103, 153
Land 134 ff., 171
Lao Tzu 5, 260
Lares 219
Lateran Council 297
Law (Mosaic) 17, 69, 97, 159, 202, 274, 285
Laws of Manu 25
Lazarus 203 ff.
Lebanon 44
Leda 196
Legend of Aqhat 58, 205, 285
Legend of Kret 58
Leningrad Codex 38
Leviticus 42, 44, 173
Levites 173
Lia 127, 141 ff.
Linear A 20, 22
Linear B 22
Lipit-Ishtar Lawcode 159
Livy 260
Logic 306, 323
Logos 214, 228 ff., 251-53, 274, 303, 304
Lord of the Rings 14, 24, 120
Lourdes 54
Louvre 129, 160
Lot 126, 131, 140, 294
Lucius 14
Lucretius 206
Luke 29, 35, 65, 263, 281 ff.
Luther, Martin 248, 313
Macbeth 19
Maccabees 34, 190, 212, 265, 321
Magi 19, 65, 67, 68, 196
Mani 58, 299 ff.
Manichees 266, 284, 295, 299 ff.
Marcion 275, 294, 298
Marcus Aurelius 185, 186, 193, 231

Marduk 7, 42, 57, 59, 60, 75, 112
Mari 31, 81
Mark 6, 35, 275 ff.
Martial 28, 185-86
Mary Magdalene 189, 203, 207
Masada 271
Matthew 275 ff.
Mayan 25, 214
Maxentius 291
Mecca 60, 65
Medusa 60, 83, 84, 121
Megara 205
Megiddo 58
Melchisedec 126
Menander 247
Menelaos 198
Menes 132, 152
Menelik 175
Mercury 85
Merenptah 40, 158, 170
Merton, Thomas 248, 250
Metis 15
Michaelangelo 111, 112
Micah 55, 169, 196
Midsummer Night's Dream 14
Milton, John 87
Minoans 22
Minos 136, 160, 170, 195
Mishna(h) 40, 266
Mithraeum 24, 239, 241 ff.
Mithras 54, 194, 196, 209, 214, 237, 239 ff., 266, 272, 284, 322
Mithridates 238, 240
Moabites 46, 126
Mohommad 60, 65, 123, 307, 319
Monophysicists. 295
Monotheism 17, 19, 20, 63-65, 67, 70, 73, 85, 112, 145, 147, 158, 165, 166, 171, 177, 295, 298, 319
Montanism 275
Moore, Judge Roy 162
Moroni 25
Mosaic Law (see Law)
Moses 2,4,5, 14, 17, 24, 27, 43, 63, 69, 112, 167 ff., 210, 260
Mount Ararat 111
Mount Gerizim 96
Mount Nebo 38
Mount of Olives 270
Mount Parnassus 106
Mount Sinai 34, 157, 161, 170, 226
Mount of Transfiguration 157

Mucalinda 86
Muslims 12, 123, 294, 300
Musonius Rufus 183, 184-85, 189, 194
Myth 3, 11, 23, 26, 30, 31, 73, 74, 170, 196, 227, 233, 306, 316
Nabonidus Chronicle 237
Nag Hammadi 85, 158, 207, 230, 247, 273, 286
Names 191
Nanak 71, 319
Naturalism 30
Nebuchadnezzar 18, 35, 48, 148
Nehemiah 26, 34, 48, 67, 148, 173
Neolithic Age 79, 131
Neo-Platonism 284, 307, 321
Nephthys 94
Neptune 132, 137
Nereids 19, 27
Nero 225, 269, 271, 284
Nestorians 301
Nestorius 253, 295, 297, 298, 299
Newton, Isaac 306
Nicene Creed 53, 229, 286, 293 ff., 296, 311
Nineveh 18, 19, 21, 48, 56, 75, 105
Nimrud 21
Ninsun 49, 87, 94
Nippur 119
Noah 46, 106 ff., 114, 153
Numa 163
Numitor 169
Numbers 34, 38, 58, 158, 175
Nut 94
Nuzi 125
Oceanus 49
Octavian (Augustus) 191, 192, 194, 268
Odysseus (Ulysses) 4, 27, 76, 121, 126, 181, 197, 207
Odyssey 6, 19, 35, 49, 135, 156, 170, 204, 207, 214, 278
Oedipus 169, 196
Oedipus Rex 19, 238
Ophites 54, 85, 247
Orestes 124
Origen 14, 41, 203, 204, 218, 228, 229, 260, 288 ff.
Original sin 315
Orpheus 208, 215 ff., 322
Orphic 197, 208, 217
Osiris 24, 54, 57, 61, 82, 93, 94 ff., 112, 141, 146, 168, 169, 194, 204, 205-06, 209, 210, 214, 272, 296, 322

Ostraca 54, 146
Oxyrhynchus Papyri 286
Palestine 32, 33, 35, 47, 89, 147, 166, 170, 200, 212, 315
Pallas Athene 5, 15
Palmyra 43
Pandora 83
Papyrus of Ani 141, 162, 163, 171, 194, 205
Paris 4, 169
Paradise Lost 87
Parsees 65
Paul 30, 41, 48, 62, 133, 174, 181, 182, 184, 193, 196, 200, 207, 208, 216, 232, 259, 261 ff., 312
Parthenon 192
Passover 17, 96, 278
Patroklos 49
Peasant and the Workman 156
Penelope 49, 170, 210, 221
Pentateuch 14, 41, 63, 102, 159, 169
Pericles 182
Persephone 18, 57, 101, 121, 196, 214, 215, 216-17
Perseus 19, 60, 84, 121, 169, 181, 195, 196, 207, 219
Persians 22, 27, 48
Petra 113
Petronius 270
Phaedo 51, 188, 204, 219, 225, 290
Phaistos Disk 20
Pharisees 69, 191, 200, 218, 220, 276, 286, 305, 323
Pheidon 162
Philistines 47, 125, 134, 139, 147
Philo of Alexandria 5, 41, 42, 50, 218, 226 ff., 285
Philo of Byblos 285
Phoenicians 22, 32, 45
Phoroneus 76
Physics 224-25
Pindar 235
Plagiarism 33, 324
Plato 5, 25, 51, 64, 73, 186, 188, 204, 206, 212, 215, 218, 223 ff., 231, 299, 312, 314
Plautus 19
Pliny 237, 260
Plotinus 234 ff.
Plutarch 17, 26, 55, 237, 260
Pluto 216
Pneumatomachians 295
Poimandres 251

Pollux 93, 100 ff.
Polybius 26
Polycrates 162
Polytheism 19, 45, 48, 62, 65, 156, 165, 192, 229, 259, 288, 295, 307, 319, 322
Pompei 86, 195, 197
Pompey 39, 270
Popul Vuh 12, 25
Pontuis Pilate 181, 200
Porphyry 206
Poseidon 19, 54, 62, 197
Purim 18
Priam 124, 137, 197, 284
Primogeniture 138
Prodigal Son 249
Prometheus 50, 76, 105, 136
Prometheus Bound 54
Prometheus Chained 79, 140
Plotinus 206
Proverbs 3, 5, 34
Psalms 4, 5, 8, 11, 58, 62, 63, 166, 312
Pseudepigrapha 40
Psyche 196
Ptah 59
Ptolemy 48
Pythagoras 5, 50, 54, 194, 204, 215 ff., 224, 231, 255, 266
Pythia 84
Pytho 84
Q source 208, 287
Queen of Sheba 175
Quintilian 28
Qumran 34, 190, 277
Ra 112, 167
Rachel 60, 137, 141
Radha 55
Rameses 40, 73, 117, 147, 153, 154
Ras Shamra 43, 81
Rebecca 126, 127 ff., 137, 138
Religion 3, 291, 302, 319-20
Remus 169, 196
Republic (Plato's) 25, 186, 224
Resurrection 202 ff., 253, 276, 285-86, 323-24
Revelation 320
Rhea 171
Rhind Mathematical Papyrus 32
Rig Veda 8, 54, 66, 74, 79
Romulus 168-69, 196
Ruth 5
Sabbath 161, 163, 186
Sabellianists 295, 296

Sabellius 296
Sacrament 70, 113
Saddam Hussein 130
Sadducees 68, 191, 218, 305
Samaria 81, 123, 141, 199, 231
Samaritans 96
Samsara 71
Samson 4, 245, 297
Samuel 277
Sanhedrin 199, 200, 282
Sanzang 135
Saoshyant (Soshyans) 65
Saqqara 84
Sara(h) 125, 137
Sargon 24, 28, 34, 130, 168, 169, 194, 196
Satan 14, 65-68, 73, 272, 300, 302, 321
Scheherazade 14
Scribes 31 ff., 146
Sea Peoples 47
Secundus 293
Sem 119
Seneca 181-84, 187, 237, 319
Seraphim 3, 56, 59
Sergius Paulus 283
Serpent 83 ff.
Sesostris 130
Seth 93, 94 ff., 102, 103, 171
Seti
Setna and the Magic Book 156
Severus 231
Shakespeare 2, 14, 78, 137, 161
Shamash 57, 97, 172
Shem 46
Shiite 130
Shipwrecked Sailor 156-57
Shiva 56
Shulgi 32
Siddhartha (see Buddha)
Sibylline oracle (see Cumae)
Siduri 91
Sikhism 70, 171, 319, 325
Simon Magus 265
Sin 73, 98
Sinai 157 ff.
Sinuhe (see Tale of)
Sirach 162
Sistine Chapel 111
Smerdis 93, 100, 140
Smith, George 105
Smith, Joseph 25, 319
Socianism 295

Socrates 5, 16, 50, 51, 187, 199-200, 233 ff.
Sodom 126, 128, 131 ff.
Solomon 5, 18, 27, 32, 45, 46, 73, 123, 174, 175
Solon 27, 159 ff., 163
Song of Songs 8, 11, 13
Sophia 247
Sophocles 3, 19, 181, 212, 235
Soul 3, 145-46, 206-07, 215, 217-18, 230, 234 ff.. 290, 324
Sphinx 175
Spinoza, Baruch 296
Spirit (see soul)
Stephen 28, 200, 282
Stoicism 2, 35, 181, 183 ff., 284
Stone Age 86
Stonehenge 74, 132
Substance 293, 296, 297, 298, 303, 306, 307, 309
Sufi 71
Sumer 14, 23, 24, 32
Sumerian 20, 27, 32, 43, 54, 59, 61, 74, 75, 97, 105, 129 ff., 137, 138,
Superstitions 56
Styx 137
Syncretism 17, 55
Tabernacle 17
Tacitus 26, 181, 260
Taking of Joppa 157
Tale of Sinuhe 130, 157, 168, 176
Tales of the Magicians 157
Tale of Two Brothers 77, 150, 157, 169, 176
Talmud 40, 199
Tammuz 18, 56, 57, 194, 214
Tantalus 251
Tao Te Ching 4, 260
Telemachus 193, 198, 221
Tell Arad 57
Templars 255
Temple 176-77
Ten Commandments 129, 161, 162, 163, 176, 320
Teraphim 59-60, 125, 130
Tereisias 19, 170, 220
Teresa of Avila 250,
Terra cotta 20
Tertullian 249, 252, 253, 311
Tethys (Thetis) 49, 137
Thales 5, 31, 213, 227
Theonas 293

The Tempest 137
Theaetetus 51
Thamar 148
Thebes 23, 32, 49, 73, 165
Theocritus 235
Theodoric 291
Theodosius 215, 241, 259, 296, 307, 310, 311
Theogeny 54, 74, 76, 117
Theseus 136, 301
Thousand and One Nights 14
Thoth 32, 141, 146, 167, 170, 228
Thucydides 26-28, 31, 46-47, 54, 182, 235
Thutmose 154
Tiamat 49, 60
Tiawah 18, 19, 75
Tiberius 193, 268
Tilath-Pileser 17, 35, 48
Tillich, Paul 319
Timaeus 51, 73
Titans 15, 73, 217
Titus 186, 268, 271
Tolkien, J. R. R. 10
Torah 2,3,5, 17, 33, 38, 40, 41, 69, 159, 198, 211, 228, 263, 265, 321
Trajan 192, 239
Transfiguration 202, 220
Trappist Order
Treasure of the Rhampsinitus 157
Tree of Knowledge 81 ff.
Tree of Life 81 ff.
Trinity 295 ff., 302, 306
Trojan War 137
Trojan Women 132
Troy 124, 132, 137
Turin Canon of Kings 118
Tutankhamun 167
Tuthmosis 165
Ugarit 14, 22, 43, 44, 58, 60, 85, 194
Ulysses (Odysseus) 24, 54, 73, 122, 135, 136, 156, 195, 204, 210, 219 ff., 259, 322
Upanishads 5, 8, 11, 12, 24, 25, 65
Ur 32, 49, 61, 82, 96, 119, 122, 129, 130, 131, 254
Uraeus 84
Uranus (Uranos) 61, 196, 285
Urantia 256
Urnammu 81, 159
Urfa 122
Uruk 20, 81, 89, 91, 94, 96

Urus 57
Utnapishtim 49, 91, 106, 115, 116
Valens 306
Valentinian 275, 293
Valentinus 249
Varuna 62
Venus 195
Vespasian 39, 193, 260, 268, 269, 271, 272
Vesuvius 22
Virgil 28, 170, 183, 185, 190, 196, 211, 273
Viruses 83
Vishnu 86, 88
Vishnu Purana 18, 19
Visigoths 312
Vulgate 41
Zeno 212
Zeus 5,7, 15, 54, 59, 60, 61, 73, 79, 105, 136, 164, 171, 196, 197, 320, 322
Ziggurat 24, 130

Weld-Blundell Prism 115
Wisdom of Amenemope 34
Works and Days 76
Writing 20, 22, 325
Wycliff, John 41
Xenophanes 54
Xenophon 186, 202, 231, 237, 238
Xerxes 46, 64, 194
Ya 44
Yahweh 4, 17, 18, 33, 34, 42-45, 48, 49, 54, 59, 61. 122, 123, 132, 140, 152, 160, 167, 177, 201, 211, 233, 302, 312, 320
Yammu 43
Yom Kippur 319
Zamolxis 204
Zechariah 183
Zend-Avesta (see Avesta)
Zohar 255
Zoroaster 12, 54, 64 ff.158, 194, 241, 272, 299, 322
Zoroastrian 5, 73, 84, 88